The Antiquities Trade in Egypt 1880-1930
The H.O. Lange Papers

CW00919370

Abstract

The vast collections of Egyptian objects on display in Western museums attract millions of visitors every year, and they reinforce a cultural fascination for this ancient civilisation that has been a feature of European intellectual history since Roman times. This book tells the story of how these objects came to be here.

The model of transmission that is most frequently communicated to the general public is that of archaeological excavation, such as the narratives surrounding the discoveries of the tomb of Tutankhamun and the Rosetta Stone. These are good stories, easily told in both entertaining and informative ways, and they are seen to promote our Western ideals of science and enlightenment: they are an integral part of the origin-myth of Egyptology as a science. But they are exceptional. The majority of the Egyptian antiquities on display in the great collections, such as those in Berlin, London, New York and Paris, were bought on the antiquities market. Most museum objects were legally acquired, but much of what appeared on the market had in fact been illicitly excavated before it was sold through established dealers; relatively little was brought to light through carefully planned and supervised scientific fieldwork.

The book presents the first in-depth analysis of this market during its "golden age" in Egypt in the late 19th and early 20th Century. It is primarily based on the archival material of the Danish Egyptologist H. O. Lange (1863-1943) who, during two prolonged stays in Egypt (1899/1900 and 1929/1930), bought objects on behalf of Danish museums. The travel diaries, and the accompanying photographs, are complemented by a wide range of other sources, including contemporary travel guides and various travel memoirs, which together paint an extraordinarily detailed picture of the extensive antiquities trade.

The book looks at the laws governing trade and export, both in theory and practice, and the changes over time – such as the introduction of official licences in 1912 – and the various attempts by the state to curb the illegal trade. The practicalities of the trade are described: its seasons, the networks of supply, the various methods available for acquiring antiquities, and the subsequent routes of transmission of objects, as well as the different types of dealers operating in Egypt. The geographical distribution of dealers is mapped, both in major cities like Cairo and Luxor, but also in smaller centres near the larger archaeological sites. The village of Kafr el-Haram near the great pyramids at Giza, for example, is identified as a major centre for the illegal antiquities trade. The role of the Egyptian state as dealer is investigated, both through the official Sale Rooms at museums in Cairo and Alexandria, and as a seller and exporter of more or less complete tomb-chapels directly to Western museums.

A separate chapter on the trade in papyrus uses the Papyrus Carlsberg Collection and the Papyrus Hauniensis Collection as case-studies to investigate how such material was distributed and sold, touching on the German *Papyruskartell*, the world-wide distribution of the Tebtunis temple library, and some other famous manuscripts like the Copenhagen copy of the wisdom poem *The Teaching for Merikare*.

The final part of the book contains a list, with short biographies, of over 250 dealers active in Egypt from the 1880s until the abolishment of the trade in 1983. Most of them are described here in detail for the first time.

The book will be of interest to archaeologists, Egyptologists, papyrologists, museum curators, and historians of science, and is a useful starting point for anyone wishing to understand how the great Western collections of Egyptian antiquities were formed.

The Antiquities Trade in Egypt 1880-1930

The H.O. Lange Papers

By Fredrik Hagen and Kim Ryholt

Scientia Danica. Series H, Humanistica, 4 · vol. 8

DET KONGELIGE DANSKE VIDENSKABERNES SELSKAB

Submitted to the Academy December 2015
Published November 2016

Contents

This book is dedicated to H.O. Lange in recognition of his services to Danish Egyptology.

Frontispiece: studio photograph of H.O. Lange. Courtesy of the Royal Library.

Preface

The idea for the present book grew out of work that we carried out independently on the travel diaries of H. O. Lange (1863-1943) in connection with other research projects.[1] We were both struck by the comparable richness of Lange's first-hand descriptions of his two visits to Cairo (in 1899-1900, and then again thirty years later in 1929-1930), and in particular his detailed accounts of his activities as an agent for Danish museums vis-a-vis the antiquities market. Our original idea was for this to be an article, but it quickly became apparent that it would be too long for that format. Turning it into a book had several advantages, not least that of an index, but also the opportunity to include a significant number of illustrations. The latter was particularly important because of the extensive photographic material from Lange's trips which complement the diaries.

We are painfully aware of the limitations of the present book. Our presentation and description of the material – and we are primarily descriptive in our approach – is by necessity narrow both in focus and in the range of material utilised. We focus almost exclusively on the acquisition of ancient Egyptian objects by Lange, and on his experiences in connection with these acquisitions as reported by himself and his wife in the travel diaries. However, as we note in the introduction below, the diaries are much broader in scope than is suggested by the selected passages discussed by us, and we offer this contribution partly in order to alert colleagues to the existence of the archive, in the hope that others may be inspired to use the material for other projects. It will be obvious to the reader, as it is to us, that this book is in fact little more than a first step. This is true not only in the way we explore the Lange material, but also in a wider sense: the study of the antiquities trade in Egypt is a potentially vast field which is still in its infancy. The lack of comparative material available in published form meant that we occasionally felt that we were stumbling around in the dark, and some of our conclusions and descriptions will, unavoidably, be revised and reinterpreted in the future as more material comes to light. We have been unable to explore many of the institutional archives that house further relevant material because of other commitments. In particular, the records of the major European and American museums will no doubt play a vital role for future studies of the trade in Egyptian antiquities, as will material in Egypt itself; this is true not only of the Egyptian Museum in Cairo but also foreign archaeological institutes like the Deutsches Archäologisches Institut Abteilung Kairo, the Institut français d'archéologie orientale, the Schweizerisches Institut für Ägyptische Bauforschung und Altertumskunde in Kairo, etc. Private archives and records, like those of Lange, are another important part of the puzzle.[2] Museum curators are in a unique position to explore these resources, but the data are generally accessible to scholars wishing to consult them, and we hope that others will continue the work that we have begun here by doing so.

In order to put the material into context, and also to make it useful to colleagues, we have included additional information from a variety of sources. However, we are not modern historians and have only a passing familiarity with the period in question, so we will undoubtedly have missed much that could have been of relevance.[3] As Egyptologists our primary con-

---

1. See Hagen, in Nyord and Ryholt (eds.), *Fs Frandsen*, 87-102, pls. 3-5; Christiansen and Ryholt, *The Carlsberg Papyri 13*; and Ryholt, *Carbonized Papyri from Tanis and Thmuis*, forthcoming.

2. The papers of William Myers at Eton may be a case in point. Gange, *Dialogues with the Dead*, 171, notes that 'His diaries of military life are punctuated with disputes (occasionally violent, often unpleasant) with local antiquities dealers', but cf. Reeves, *MMJ* 48 (2013), 29, n. 10 ('Myers' diaries … shed disappointingly little light on his collecting activities').

3. Observant readers will note that a number of references are

cern has been to map the antiquities trade as a part of the history of our discipline. Although we have made some effort to highlight the involvement of Egyptians in this business, we do this without engaging with or referring to the ongoing debate about orientalism and post-colonialism; this is because we are primarily descriptive rather than analytical in our approach, and the lack of a more explicit theoretical framework should not be read as an ideological statement. Similarly, we make no attempt to analyse the political aspects of the history of Egyptology and the antiquities trade, although as the work of Donald Malcolm Reid and Elliott Colla has shown, they often go hand in hand.[4] Our reason for doing so is again pragmatic rather than ideological; we simply lack the necessary expertise to evaluate the interconnections between our historiographical work and the modern history of Egypt.

There has been a notable increase in research dealing with archival material in Egyptology over the last ten years, not least on the subject of collecting practices in relation to museums and private individuals. The emergence of a journal dedicated to archival work (*Egyptian & Egyptological Documents Archives Libraries*), of which four volumes have so far appeared, perhaps signals a change in current research agendas, with a renewed impetus towards preserving and making accessible the extensive archives related to the history of our field. Although we are not aware of other books that cover the subject treated here, there is much research being done on the history of museums and their collections, and this overlaps, at least to a degree, with some of our concerns – most Egyptian objects in Western museums have been purchased rather than excavated. Stephanie Moser's book on

the formation of the Egyptian collection at the British Museum, for example, is representative of this development, although her focus is more on the role of the museum and its collections in knowledge production (through its exhibitions) than on acquisition practices *per se*.[5] Along similar lines, Maya Jasanoff's general study of the collecting practices of France and Britain from 1750-1850 also deals with the Egyptian collections of their respective national museums, but explicitly in the context of imperial ambitions and political history.[6] The momentum has been steadily growing, and 2013 saw a veritable explosion of interest in the history of Egyptology as a discipline.[7] This development is also seen in the increasing number of conferences covering such topics: recent examples include the *Forming Material Egypt* conference (organised by UCL in May 2013), or the *Egyptian Archives / Egyptological Archives* (organised by the University of Milan in September 2008).[8] Many similar examples could be cited, and they – along with the digitalisation efforts of institutions like the Griffith Institute in Oxford – suggest that Egyptology as a discipline is becoming more aware of how modern history affects what is available to us to study, but also how an understanding of the modern history of objects can fundamentally change our interpretation of the objects themselves.

Despite the relatively recent interest of Egyptology in the collecting practices associated with our field

to material accessible online, and this is no coincidence. We have made cursory searches through internet search engines, dedicated bibliographical websites, and digital archives, but ours has been neither a systematic nor a particularly thorough approach, and the search parameters as well as the search terms have occasionally been fuzzy (searching for names of Arab dealers, for example, was a challenge in view of the almost endless spelling variations in use).

4. Reid, *Whose Pharaohs?*; Colla, *Conflicted Antiquities*.

5. Moser, *Wondrous Curiosities*. See esp. pp. 93-94, 126-129, 173-177, and 218-219 for the acquisition practices of the museum in relation to British consular agents. For an analysis of the acquisition practices of the museum in an international context, cf. Hoock, *The Historical Journal* 50 (2007), 49-72.

6. Jasanoff, *Edge of Empire*.

7. Gange, *Dialogue with the Dead*; Bickel et al. (eds.), *Ägyptologen und Ägyptologien zwischen Kaiserreich und Gründung der beiden Deutschen Staaten*; Gertzen, *École de Berlin*; Schneider and Raulwing (eds.), *Egyptology from the First World War to the Third Reich*; Fortenberry (ed.), *Souvenirs and New Ideas*.

8. The significant efforts of Milan in collecting material relating to the history of the field is admirable and has already resulted in several publications. More research on this is under way, including work on the history of the antiquities trade; Piacentini, *EDAL* 4 (2013/2014), 116.

of study, the topic has occasionally attracted the attention of writers, albeit primarily from outside the discipline. Brian M. Fagan's *The Rape of the Nile*, and Peter France's *The Rape of Egypt*, from 1975 (revised and reprinted in 2001) and 1991 respectively, are examples of works that cast a critical eye on the early history of collecting, but neither dealt with the buying and selling of antiquities in any depth. We believe that our book fills a gap in the available literature, particularly in that we do not focus on a single museum or collection; rather, we attempt to describe the actions of an individual buyer and the system within which he operated.

As relatively young scholars we do not have any first-hand knowledge of the antiquities trade in Egypt (the antiquities trade was abolished by law in 1983), unlike some of our more senior colleagues who can still remember what it was like in Egypt in the 1950s, 60s and 70s, and whose stories paint a picture of a market not very different from that in which Lange operated some thirty or forty years earlier. Informal conversations with such colleagues over the last few years have revealed a wealth of anecdotes and observations, none of which have been included in this book, but many of which we feel deserve to be recorded nonetheless.[9] We would like to take this opportunity to encourage our colleagues to record such reminiscences for the sake of posterity. Oral history as an academic sub-field of history is rapidly evolving and

expanding, and Egyptology is not unaffected – recent work by Chris Naunton at the Egypt Exploration Society in London has resulted in invaluable testimonies from people who took part in some of the legendary excavations that feature in every undergraduate narrative of Egyptian archaeology. Recorded as video and, at least in some cases, being made available online, these descriptions and discussions have become a valuable complement to the published excavation reports. Similarly, written or oral testimonies from colleagues who have experienced the antiquities trade in Egypt in the first half of the 20th Century may turn out to be central to future historians, and we urge colleagues to at least consider the preservation of the memory of their experiences, however imperfectly remembered and however tangential they may seem today.

There are a number of colleagues who have assisted us in various ways during the writing of this book, and it is a pleasure to be able to note their generous help here. At the Royal Library in Copenhagen Bo Alkjær and his colleagues facilitated access to the archival material kept there, and provided useful background literature on some of Lange's contemporaries. Thomas Christiansen diligently went through much of the Lange material kept at our Institute and provided useful additional information, including some field-notes written by Lange while travelling around Egypt. Amber Jacob patiently standardised our references and bibliography and compiled the indices. She and Dora Petrova further scanned and catalogued a number of photographs at the institute. Anne Haslund Hansen at the National Museum and Mogens Jørgensen and Tine Bagh at the Ny Carlsberg Glyptothek helped us track down many of the objects bought by Lange and allowed us to consult museum records for references to these transactions. We are also very grateful to Stephen Quirke who read through an early draft of our book (then an overly long article) and provided a thought-provoking list of questions, comments and additional references, all of which considerably improved the final book. Another reader of the book was Patricia Usick, whose kind words and comments also did much to improve it.

9. The subject is sensitive, particularly to archaeologists and museum employees, and so any frank discussion, even in private, requires a degree of trust and discretion. We cannot elaborate on these issues here, but – in the interest of providing at least one perspective on the modern history of the antiquities trade – we refer the reader to Tokeley's controversial *Rescuing the Past: The Cultural Heritage Crusade*, especially pp. 185-243. For all its polemical prose and explicit pro-trade agenda, it remains the only published account by someone with extensive first-hand knowledge of the modern market from the inside. We cannot vouch for the accuracy of the information provided there – Tokeley is a convicted criminal who has served a jail sentence for smuggling antiquities, and the book comes across as a defence writ more than anything else – but even the casual reader will find his account eerily similar to what we describe in this book.

Tom Hardwick read through the manuscript and made numerous helpful suggestions – his keen eyes also caught several mistakes. We are also grateful to the anonymous reviewers for their comments and references. Other colleagues whose help we would like to acknowledge are Cornelius von Pilgrim who kindly provided us with information about Ludwig Borchardt; Hratch Papazian and June Dahy who translated various Arabic passages for us, the former also accompanied us on our trip to Egypt in 2013; Ken Cuno who answered questions on the sources and reconstruction of the demography of modern Egypt; Elisabeth David who answered questions about the *Salle de vente* of the Egyptian Museum; Rosario Pintaudi who permitted us to reproduce photos relating to Maurice Nahman; Rita Freed, Arielle Kozloff, Marianne Eaton-Krauss, Christian Loeben who helped identify sculptures offered for sale to Lange; Emily Teeter who provided information about J. H. Breasted; Peter Der Manuelian and Joseph Greene of Harvard Semitic Museum who brought additional archival material to our attention; and Annette Felgenhauer who provided information about dealers mentioned in the records of Übersee-Museum Bremen. Our Assyrological colleague here in Copenhagen, Nicole Brisch, checked our transcriptions of German archival material and quotations and saved us from the odd slip of the pen. Adrienne L. Fricke graciously allowed us to reproduce her translation of the Egyptian Antiquities Law of 1912 (cf. Appendix 1). Bertrand Khawam and Lucien Viola, whose families were prominent dealers in Cairo from the late 19th Century until the 1960s and 70s, have kindly shared photographs and other information with us, including the informative newspaper clipping 'In Relation to the Case of the American Scholar who Stole Egypt's Antiquities: A New Law Prohibits the Sale of Antiquities and Trade in History' (قانون جديد يمنع بيع الآثار وتجارة التاريخ) which we cite on several occasions.[10] Geoffrey Martin carefully

read through the manuscript and caught a number of inconsistencies. Finally, Rob Demarée read through the book and shared his first-hand knowledge of the antiquities market of the 1960s and 70s with us, and made many useful comments, in addition to sharing some of his own archival material with his characteristic generosity.

It is becoming common practice – perhaps spurred on by the current obsession with measuring 'research output' – to indicate which author is responsible for which part of a jointly written book like this. However, this is, at least in our case, not straightforward. Although certain chapters were initially drafted by one or the other, every paragraph has been read and revised numerous times by both of us, and it is difficult now to separate out the different parts of the text in this way. All we can say is that it was a joint undertaking and that neither of us is more responsible than the other for whatever merits or faults the book may be thought to contain.

Finally, we have tried to avoid letting our moral views of the antiquities trade influence our work; this book is meant to be a historical study and not a political statement about the trade in antiquities. This decision has not been taken lightly; while writing this book (2011-2016), Egypt has seen large-scale looting of both museums and archaeological sites – at a frightening pace – and there can be no question that this is partly fuelled by the market's demand for antiquities. Like most colleagues we have watched these developments with horror, and it it is clear that this book is, sadly, more topical now than when we started writing it.

---

10. The source and exact date of the article is unfortunately not known to us. However, Abd el-Fattah Hilmy, who became Director of the Antiquities Service in 1959, is referred to as Deputy Director and the article must therefore predate that

year. The American scholar alluded to in the title of the article is apparently C. A. Musès who excavated the pyramid of the 13th Dynasty King Ameny Qemau. The story of the excavation and the alleged theft is described by Dodson, *KMT* 8.3 (1997), 60-63; cf. also Musès, *Die Königspyramide des Ameny-Qemau*.

Introduction

Egyptian galleries in Western museums are almost invariably the most popular ones in their respective institutions, attracting thousands of visitors every year, and this is no coincidence: such institutions have often invested heavily in these collections over generations by sponsoring archaeological excavations and then displaying the objects brought back from the field. The majority of Egyptian objects currently on display in museums, however, were not excavated by archaeological expeditions; they were bought (or bought and then donated/bequeathed to the museums by collectors). The circumstances of their acquisition are frequently obscure, and until recently were rarely considered relevant in scholarly publications. Yet the acquisition policies of museums and collectors – above all the decision about which types of objects were worth acquiring and exhibiting – have played a decisive role in determining what empirical material is available for study and hence have, if only indirectly, dictated research agendas. Certain object categories and historical periods have traditionally been favoured over others, and as a result of this other groups of source material are under-represented. The bias in acquisition has inevitably affected the market and the efforts that were made to secure the most profitable objects. Moreover, virtually all objects acquired on the market were disassociated from their archaeological contexts, and assemblages found together were frequently split up, sometimes for practical reasons, sometimes to optimize profits. What we attempt in this book is to provide a sketch of the system that encouraged this trade in antiquities, and in so doing shed light upon the practices that underlie the survival of a material culture that has guided the Egyptological research agenda for many years.

Even at the time the trade was often shrouded in secrecy, for many of the dealers operated outside the law, and objects passed through many hands before reaching European and American buyers. Because of the level of secrecy there are few descriptive sources to draw on in a reconstruction such as ours – most of the material available is in the form of letters and receipts relating to various transactions, and the people who took part during the period in question (c. 1880s-1930s) are no longer alive. Many of them no doubt regaled their colleagues and friends with stories of deals cut and objects acquired, but it was seldom recorded in writing – it was simply not a suitable topic for austere academic journals and books. A notable exception to this general lack of description is the account of *Haj Hamid and the Brigand*, as recorded by Herbert E. Winlock of the Metropolitan Museum of Art in 1922. Winlock was one of the big players in the trade, and he wrote down the story for publication in a popular magazine. The narrative concerns *Haj* Hamid (the "I" in the passage below), son of one of the largest dealers in Luxor, who has travelled some 400 km north to the Fayum Oasis to buy a pot of ancient gold coins, and it is a story that hints at the secrecy, the tension and the danger involved:

> "I am not Hadji Hamid. By the life of our Lord..." I began, but the little man raised his hand and said very politely: "Your Excellency does not know me perhaps – Ahmed es Suefi, your servant and a robber of some reputation in these villages here."
>
> "Whatever is, is God's will," I murmured. "Yes, I have heard of you, Sheykh Ahmed."
>
> "That is better" he said, grinning at me. "Now I shall tell you what you are up to. You came to buy a pot of gold coins from So and So, and I am here to get the money you have brought. So hand it over and then you can go back and get some more. If you make no trouble I will let you by the next time and God will increase your prosperity."
>
> What was the use of pretending any more? Here, after all, was the brigand Ahmed es Suefi. He knew me and all of my affairs, and his men had half a dozen thick

clubs to crack our heads if we made any fuss. And with broken heads what chance would we have to save those [money] belts? Perhaps it was the thought of one of those naboots coming down on my pate that made my tongue go slower and my head work faster, searching for an idea…[11]

The story, with all its drama and poetic license, is a powerful reminder of the limitations of our sources, and of our inability to describe the trade in anything like a comprehensive manner: hope, fear and excitement is rarely expressed or even detectable in the archival material at our disposal. Nonetheless there is a story to be told here, and it is one which goes to the heart of all museum galleries with Egyptian objects: how did they get there?

Our work is part of a broader trend relating to the history of collecting (and collections), an area of research that has grown considerably over the last thirty years, albeit only to a limited extent in relation to Egyptian material. The Oxford-based *Journal of the History of Collections*, launched in 1989 (vol. 25 of which was recently published) is symptomatic of this development, and testifies to a thriving and abiding interest in the modern history of antiquities.[12] However, our focus is not on a single collection, nor, strictly speaking, on a single collector (although Lange features prominently throughout), but rather on a system of acquisition; we try to outline the general characteristics of the antiquities trade in Egypt while analysing the activities of one particular individual within it.

The structure of the book is as follows. After a brief introduction we start by outlining the archival material on which the book is based, and the scope of our study (Chapter Two). The material is extraordi-

nary in content, containing as it does the very detailed accounts of a western Egyptologist and his experience of life in Egypt at two points in time, some thirty years apart. Lange's professional training and the diverse reasons for his visits make for an interesting perspective, and he paid attention to aspects that casual tourists might have passed over or not perceived in the same way. At the same time, his travel diaries are unusually comprehensive compared to those of contemporary colleagues, covering a very wide range of activities and experiences, a fact that can be partly explained by the fact that he only visited Egypt twice. Both journeys were undertaken with the understanding that he might never return, and he (and, on the first visit, also his wife) consequently wrote down much that others might have thought inconsequential. This chapter outlines the material itself – primarily the aforementioned travel diaries, as well as an accompanying archive of photographs – not simply as an introduction to the aspects discussed by us, but also to raise awareness of the material as others may find it enlightening for different reasons because of its extraordinarily wide range of descriptions. There is no doubt that publishing the travel diaries separately would be a worthwhile undertaking in its own right, but this will have to be left to others.

Chapter Three deals with the trade in antiquities in Egypt during the years covered by Lange's travel diaries, c. 1899-1930. Here we look at Lange's mission to buy on behalf of Danish museums (primarily the Ny Carlsberg Glyptotek), and the role of his wife, Jonna Lange. We then move on to a general description of the antiquities market, its infrastructure, types of dealers, and the geography of the trade, with sections on the main sites of Cairo, Kafr el-Haram, Medinet el-Fayum, Qena, Luxor and Alexandria. The chapter also includes brief descriptions of the laws in force at the time of Lange's purchases, his and other colleagues' reactions to these - some of which had been introduced between Lange's two visits - as well as a case-study in how objects were purchased and then exported ('A tale of two heads', p. 152). In this instance the objects are in fact fakes (unbeknownst to Lange), and the case is revealing not just for its depic-

11. Winlock, *Scribner's Magazine* 71 (January-June 1922), 287-292; we reproduce the story in full in Appendix 5.

12. The journal, which includes themed volumes on e.g. the Classical collection of the Fitzwilliam Museum, *JHC* 24, no. 3 (2012), has only a handful of articles relating to Egyptian material: Stevenson, *JHC* 26, no. 1 (2014), 89-102; Persson, *JHC* 24, no. 1 (2012), 3-13; Hardwick, *JHC* 23, no. 1 (2011), 179-192; Hill, Meurer, and Raven, *JHC* 22, no. 2 (2010), 289-306; Quirke, *JHC* 9, no. 2 (1997), 254-262; and Whitehouse, *JHC* 1, no. 2 (1989), 187-195.

tion of the processes involved, but also because it adds to our knowledge of the production and transmission of fakes. This particular case-study features the famous 'Berliner Meister', Oxan Aslanian, a master forger who specialised in Old Kingdom and Amarna Period art, and whom Lange describes in some detail. The chapter ends with a summary of the development of the antiquities market up to and including the Egyptian revolution of 1952.

The next chapter deals with Lange's acquisition of papyri, including the formation of the Papyrus Carlsberg Collection and the Papyrus Hauniensis Collection in Copenhagen. We trace his first forays into the field during his initial stay in Egypt, and then look at his subsequent activities while Head Librarian of the Royal Library in Copenhagen; he continued seeking out papyri for many years, and renewed his personal contacts and purchasing ambitions during his second and last stay. The chapter ends with the story of how the famous 18th Dynasty fragment of *The Instruction for Merikare* came to Copenhagen (a good example of how one prominent academic fought back against the politics of the Nazi regime), and a summary of the results of Lange's labours.

The final part of the book is devoted to a list of dealers and sellers of antiquities that were active in Egypt c. 1880-1930. The list is admittedly incomplete in that it is largely based on the Lange material, but it is reasonably exhaustive in relation to those sources, and we have expanded the list with those dealers whose names are mentioned by us in the text itself. In a handful of cases the dealers are already well-known, and here we supply details only where these corroborate, contradict or illuminate already known information. In the other cases, which account for the vast majority of the entries, we have included as much information as could be extracted from Lange's diaries on the assumption that readers are unlikely to have access to this in any other form in the foreseeable future. This means that there is material included here that may not seem of much relevance or value at present, but we know from experience that research agendas change over time and we find it difficult to predict what colleagues may find useful in the future.

We are Egyptologists by training, which is to say that our knowledge is mainly of ancient, rather than modern, Egypt, and no doubt our unfamiliarity with many aspects of its modern history has led to inaccuracies and misunderstandings in the book. We hope that readers will forgive such mistakes as may have crept in. The book was written for an Egyptological audience, and this carries with it the danger of excluding other casual readers by assuming a level of knowledge of the history of our subject, for example in the way we talk about famous figures like Budge, Petrie, Wilbour, etc. This is perhaps regrettable but it should not present an insurmountable obstacle to the non-specialist because all such individuals can be conveniently looked up in M. Bierbrier's *Who was Who in Egyptology* (4th edition, 2012). We have made no attempt to map Lange's wider social network in Egypt, either in terms of colleagues or other persons of interest, although the travel diaries would no doubt be suitable for this kind of undertaking; in addition to meeting many of the most prominent Egyptologists at the time, he also met people like Thomas Mann who, as a recent recipient of the Nobel Prize for Literature (1929, for *Buddenbrooks*), was in Egypt 'to gather experiences and undertake research as preparation for writing a novel set in ancient Egypt'.[13]

Many of the names have been standardised to facilitate reading; this applies to Muslim (e.g. Husein/Hussein) as well as Coptic (e.g. Gubriel/Gubrian) names. Such names were mostly rendered phonetically by foreigners, which means that one and the same individual may be described as Tadros, Todros, Toudrous, etc., often in a single document – naturally this can make it difficult to find supplementary information about any given individual. This standardisa-

---

13. Lange, *Dagbog fra Ægypten, 1929-1930*, 338. The work in question was of course T. Mann's *Joseph and His Brethren*, which he had already begun writing. We do not know if Lange ever read this work (the fourth and final volume appeared in 1943, the year of Lange's death), but he certainly expressed an intention to do so, despite being sceptical of the project: 'It is something of a dangerous undertaking if one wants to avoid distorting history. But of course we have to read the book when it is published.'

tion means that readers should not, when looking for individuals mentioned in our book, consider alternative spellings as obstacles to possible matches (many of the variants are obviously minor, such as el-Megid for al-Meghid, or Mohassib for Mohasseb). Although many of the Coptic names have Western equivalents (e.g. Girgis/George, Bolos/Paul[us], Gubrian/Gabriel, Todros/Theodore), substituting these seemed unnecessary if not not positively misleading. We have also standardised the title *hajji* or *el-hajj*, referring to someone who has made the journey to Mecca, from the numerous variants attested across our sources (e.g. haj, hadj, hagg, etc). We are not Arabists: consequently we have, simply for convenience, attempted to represent the glottal stop only where this was marked by our sources (e.g. Isma'il, var. Ismaïl).

In our discussion of Lange's acquisitions we often refer to 'pounds', rather than 'Egyptian pounds' or 'British pounds'. This is in deference to the original documents where the currency is often not given, but luckily this does not, in practice, create much confusion, because the Egyptian pound was tied directly to the value of the British pound in the period under consideration: 1 GPB was valued at 0.975 Egyptian pounds.[14]

Finally, it might be useful to outline briefly Lange's itinerary during his visits to Egypt. Throughout the first visit in 1899-1900 he was primarily based in Cairo because of his work in the Egyptian Museum, where his work on the great *Catalogue Générale* required the presence of both him and his wife for most of the time (see further below, p. 22). This state of affairs was disrupted on a handful of occasions. The most prolonged was a nine-day trip to Upper Egypt (Aswan, Luxor, Qena, Dendera, Abydos), a trip which he later described as 'the most interesting time during this journey to the land of my dreams' (c. 28 Jan. - 6 Feb. 1900).[15] Other trips included a short two-day visit to the Fayum with his colleague Speyer (10-11 April

1900),[16] and a visit to Mansoura (in the Delta) with his wife, where they stayed at the 'palace' of the Mixed Tribunal as guests of the two Danish judges there (29-30 April 1900).[17] The second trip in 1929-1930 was likewise mostly spent in Cairo, with the exception of a five-week trip to Upper Egypt (Philae, Aswan, Kom Ombo, Edfu, Luxor, Qena and Abydos; 12 Dec. 1929 - 18 Jan. 1930)[18] and a short day-trip to Merimde in the Delta as guests of Junker at his excavations there.[19]

14. Hagen, *JEA* 96 (2010), 76.

15. Lange and Lange, *Dagbog fra Ægyptensrejsen 1899-1900*, 289-379, with quote on p. 379.

16. Lange and Lange, *Dagbog fra Ægyptensrejsen 1899-1900*, 500-528. Sir Edgar Speyer was an English-American businessman who built up a modest collection of Egyptian antiquities during his visit to the country in 1900.

17. Lange and Lange, *Dagbog fra Ægyptensrejsen 1899-1900*, 551-572. The Mixed Tribunal was set up to handle court cases where Europeans were involved; in addition to the one in Mansoura, there was one in Cairo and one in Alexandria. The principle was to have both Egyptian and European judges on the same case; in earlier periods consuls for the various foreign powers had possessed a similar judicial authority. The Danish judges mentioned by Lange were Nyholm and Kraft, who at this point were in charge of the Mansoura Tribunal. On the history of the Mixed Tribunal, see Hoyle, *The Mixed Courts of Egypt*, esp. pp. 6-7 (on consular jurisdiction before the mixed tribunal), 118-150 (on the mixed court during the time of Lange's visit).

18. Lange, *Dagbog fra Ægypten, 1929-1930*, 130-303. Lange and his wife spent eight days in Aswan (13-21 Dec. 1929), but he then left his wife there to recuperate (she was bedridden with an upset stomach) and travelled downstream on his own for a few days; they reunited in Luxor in the beginning of January. He was in Luxor for approximately four weeks, first in the Thebes Hotel (where he first met W. Dreiss), then with Ludwig Borchardt in the Deutsche Haus on the West Bank, and then in the Thebes Hotel again.

19. While at Merimde he picked up a number of minor Predynastic objects (pottery sherds, flints, etc.) which he later bequeathed to the National Museum (NM 11611-12, 11635-75 and 11697-98); Nationalmuseet, *Fortegnelse over Antiksamlingens Forøgelse i aarene 1942-1949* 8, 67, 70-72.

Materials and Scope

The present research is primarily based on the comprehensive archival material relating to H. O. Lange which is preserved in the Royal Library, the National Museum, and the Papyrus Carlsberg Collection in Copenhagen. For the convenience of the reader, it may be useful briefly to outline the contents of this material. It can be divided into the following categories:

(1) Correspondence consisting of several thousand letters in the Manuscript Department of the Royal Library.[20] A substantial number of the letters were sent to Lange by colleagues involved in Egyptological research.[21] Lange generally does not seem to have kept copies of the letters he sent out himself, although a few drafts are preserved.

(2) The travel diaries from Lange's two visits to Egypt in 1899/1900 and 1929/30 (Fig. 1-2).[22] The first diary (819 pages) covers 9 October 1899 through 25 September 1900, and the second (360 pages) covers 24 October 1929 through 30 March 1930. Many of the entries in the first diary were written in the hand of Jonna Lange, who consistently refers to her husband by his Christian name Hans. All the extracts from the diaries here cited have been translated into English by the authors.

There is no doubt that the diaries were written in order to be read. An obvious point, perhaps, but worth keeping in mind when using them as a historical source; naturally this will have had consequences for how they chose to describe colleagues, for example. Precisely who was the intended audience is not entirely clear. Certainly it was meant, at least to an extent, for Lange himself and his wife, as an aid in recalling their trips later in life. This is made clear on several occasions; one refers specifically to 'the pleasure we will have from (reading) these records in the future'.[23] However, numerous references in the first diary to people 'back home' who will be reading the text (and what they might be interested in hearing about) show that it was intended for at least limited dissemination, presumably primarily among the family and close friends.[24] At one point they express a fear of repeating themselves, saying that it is impossible to check the earlier parts of the diary because these pages have already been sent back home,[25] while in the margin of another page Lange has pencilled in a short greeting ('I am well. Can hopefully travel to Luxor on

20. Catalogued as 'NKS 3736 kvart' at the Royal Library. There are also a few letters from Lange's correspondence in the Papyrus Carlsberg Collection, but none of these are relevant to the present book.

21. The list includes G. F. Allen [sic: for G. T.], F. W. Freiherr von Bissing, A. M. Blackman, L. Borchardt, C. Boreux, G. Botti (II), J. H. Breasted, A. de Buck, J. Capart, J. Černý, J. J. Clère, W. E. Crum, W. Diemke, E. Drioton, E. Dévaud, W. F. Edgerton, W. Erichsen, A. Erman, R. Faulkner, A. H. Gardiner, J. Garstang, H. Gauthier, W. Golénischeff, H. Grapow, F. Ll. Griffith, B. Gunn, H. R. Hall, S. Hassan, J. J. Hess, H. Ibscher, E. Iversen, H. Junker, C. Kuentz, P. Lacau, F. Lexa, Gr. Loukianoff, Henry Madsen, E. Meyer, J. de Morgan, H. W. Müller, O. Neugebauer, P. E. Newberry, T. E. Peet, O. Koefoed Petersen, W. M. F. Petrie, A. Piankoff, H. Polotsky, J. E. Quibell, H. Ranke, G. A. Reisner, G. Roeder, M. Sandman, H. Schack Schackenborg, H. Schäfer, A. Scharff, C. Schmidt, V. Schmidt, S. Schott, W. Schubart, K. Sethe, S. Smith, W. Spiegelberg, G. Steindorff, L. Stern, E. Suys, H. Thompson, A. Volten, and W. Wreszinski.

22. Catalogued as 'NKS 3919 kvart' at the Royal Library. The title page of the first journal reads 'Dagbog fra Ægyptensrejsen 1899-1900. H. O. Lange og Jonna Lange.' The second has no title page, but the binding reads 'H. O. Lange. Dagbog i Ægypten.'

23. Lange and Lange, *Dagbog fra Ægyptensrejsen 1899-1900*, 623.

24. A passing mention of letters being written to family and friends back home in 1899-1900 includes the following recipients: 'The two homes [i.e. their respective parents], uncle Karl, Sino Christiansen, the Hansens, Arthur Ravn, Mrs. Grabow [sic], Miss Holst, Miss Obel and Mrs. and Miss Böthcer [?], Mrs. Lange and Miss Bock'; Lange and Lange, *Dagbog fra Ægyptensrejsen 1899-1900*, 204.

25. Lange and Lange, *Dagbog fra Ægyptensrejsen 1899-1900*, 622.

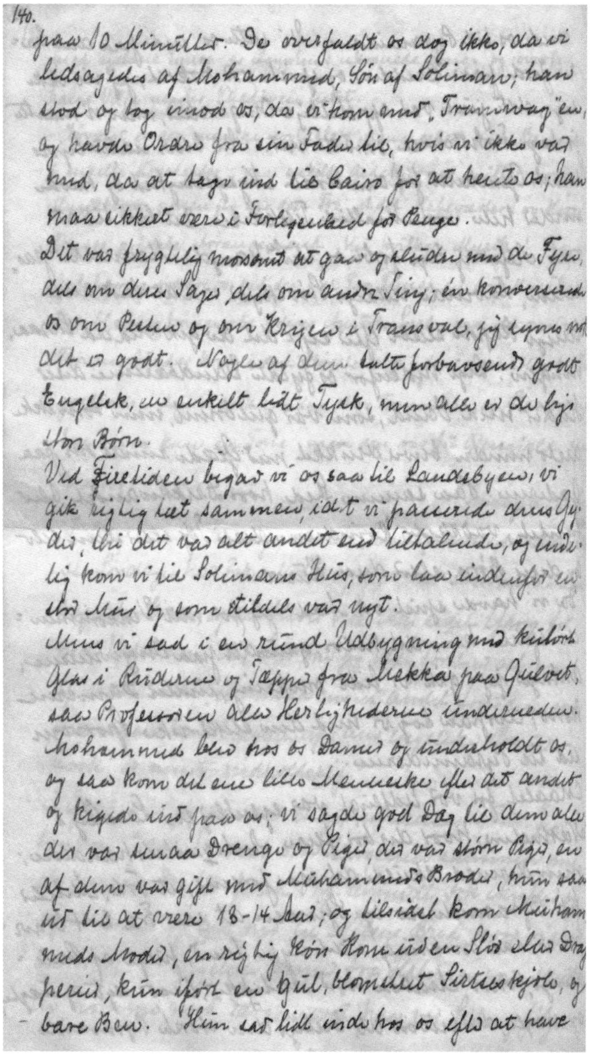

Fig. 1. A page from the Langes' travel diary from their first visit to Egypt in 1899/1900 entitled *Dagbog fra Ægyptensrejsen*. The handwriting is that of Jonna Lange. Courtesy of the Royal Library.

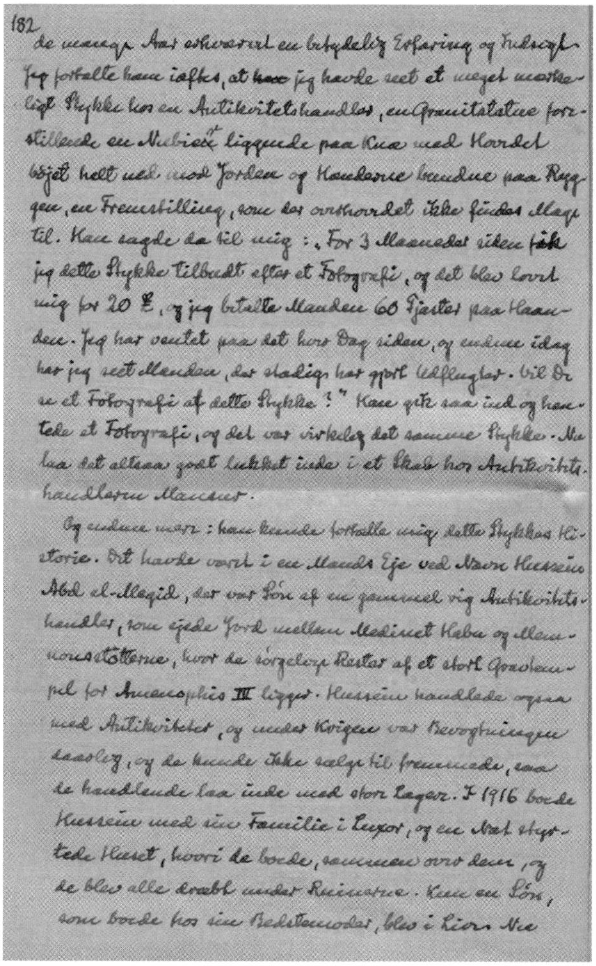

Fig. 2. A page from the Langes' travel diary from their second visit to Egypt in 1929/1930 entitled *Dagbog fra Ægypten*. The handwriting is that of H. O. Lange. Courtesy of the Royal Library.

Monday. All the best!').[26] It seems clear that the pages were sent back to Denmark in batches and circulated in a manner similar to the famous Petrie journals, and the physical form of the diaries still bear witness to this fact: they were all folded once along the middle in order to fit into an envelope, and have been bound together at some later point.

Apart from serving to disseminate news to family and friends back home and preserving an account of their experiences, the diaries served a further purpose which, to Lange, was fundamental.

> The diary trains our ability to observe, it forces us to notice many things which we would otherwise pass by without further ado, and to make us account for circumstances which we would otherwise make no attempt to understand.[27]

---

26. Lange, *Dagbog fra Ægypten, 1929-1930*, 161.

27. Lange and Lange, *Dagbog fra Ægyptensrejsen 1899-1900*, 623.

Fig. 3. The Lange couple at Abu Ghurab visiting the excavations of their close friend, Ludwig Borchardt. Photograph by Borchardt, 1900. Courtesy of the Royal Library.

(3) Photographs taken by H. O. and Jonna Lange during their two visits to Egypt, a number of which are reproduced in this book. The photographs include, above all, two albums that each formed a pair with one of the travel diaries. The first one from 1899/1900 (300 photographs, all but a few made by the Lange couple themselves) includes the sites of Abu Ghurab (Fig. 3), Abu Rawash, Abusir (including Borchard's excavations), Ahnas, Behbit el-Hagar, Biga, Dendera, Giza, Hawara, Heliopolis, Karnak, Medinet el-Fayum, Medinet Habu, Memphis, Philae, the Ramesseum, Saqqara (including Barsanti's and Loret's excavations), Shellal, the Theban necropolis; the Egyptologists von Bissing, Borchardt, Schäfer, Schweinfurth, Steindorff; as well as scenes of daily life.[28] The second one from 1929/30 (241 photographs, about half of which are commercial) includes the sites of Abydos, Aswan, Dendera, Esna, Giza, Heliopolis, Karnak, Kom Ombo, Luxor, Merimde (including the German excavations), Philae, Saqqara, Thebes (including Deir el-Bahri, Medinet Habu, Ramesseum); the Egyptologists Bisson de la Roque, Borchardt and his wife, Selim Hassan, Junker, Scharff's wife, Schott's daughter; the antiquities dealer Grégoire Loukianoff's wife and daughter, Zaki Mahmud Abd es-Samad and his family; as well as scenes of daily life.[29] In addition to the two albums, further photographs are arranged in boxes; there are three with images of Middle Kingdom and New Kingdom stelae in the Cairo Museum (arranged according to museum inventory nos.), and another of various objects in Cairo (arbitrary sequential numbering). We have included a number of photographs from this archive in the book, and several others have been digitised and can be accessed through the website of the Royal Library in Copenhagen. Readers wishing to get a more visual impression of Cairo in the late 19th and early 20th Century might consider

28. 295 photographs were originally inserted in the album, two of which are now missing, and another five have later been added and are lying loose between pages. One of the missing photographs, showing the Lange couple making tea, was used as an illustration in Helweg-Larsen, *H.O. Lange: En Mindebog*, unnumbered plate, and was apparently never returned to the album; the second, which shows their room in Borchardt's apartment, may have been removed on the same occasion.

29. 236 photographs were originally inserted in the album, five of which are now missing, and another nine have been added later and are lying loose between pages.

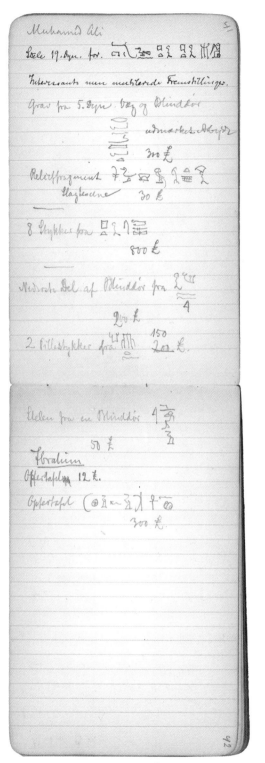

Fig. 4. Pages from one of H. O. Lange's notebooks providing brief descriptions and in many cases also the price of antiquities seen with various dealers in 1899/1900. The five dealers here mentioned were all based at Kafr el-Haram; Mohammed Ali, Ibrahim [Abd es-Samad], his brother Soliman [Abd es-Samad], Mansur [Ismaïn], and an unnamed son of Farag [Ismaïn]. Courtesy of the Egyptological Archives, University of Copenhagen.

the sumptuous *Fous de Caire: Excentriques, architects & amateurs d'art en Égypte 1867-1914* by Mercedes Volait (Paris, 2009), which evokes the atmosphere of the city at the turn of the century in a particularly vivid way.

(4) Notebooks from the two visits to Egypt in 1899/1900 and 1929/30. These are kept in the Papyrus Carlsberg Collection. We refer to two of them as 'Notebook 1899/1900' (Fig. 4) and 'Notebook Thebes, Dec. 1929 - Jan. 1930', respectively.[30]

(5) A personal collection of antiquities. Virtually the entire collection was bequeathed to the National Museum in Lange's last will and testament, and entered the Collection in April 1943.[31] The individual items that passed into the Near Eastern Department were catalogued under 586 inventory numbers, viz.: 11553 to 12138.[32] They comprise a variety of objects, mostly small and portable items; stelae, parts of statues and statuettes, a wide range of vessels (ceramic and stone; full size and miniatures), palettes, arrowheads, ostraca (hieratic, demotic and Coptic), amulets, oil lamps, funerary cones, shabtis, beads, cylinder seals, scarabs, rings, etc. Lange also owned a small group of papyri which passed into the Papyrus Carlsberg Collection; unfortunately they were not individually labeled and their exact number cannot presently be established.[33] It remains unknown whether Lange kept a personal register of his collection of antiquities.

30. University of Copenhagen, Egyptological Archive, A101 and A103.

31. National Museum, Register 1943, 53-112.

32. These objects were recorded as Group A: Egyptian antiquities. Other miscellaneous objects were passed onto the Hama Collection (Group B: mainly ceramics collected at el-Fustat), the Numismatic Department (Group C: coins), the Ethnographic Department (Group D: ethnographica) and the Zoological Museum (Group E: shells).

33. A small undated hand-list of papyri in the Papyrus Carlsberg Collection details some or all of Lange's personal papyri (University of Copenhagen, Egyptological Archive, I100): 'A larger fragment of a beautiful hieratic text of the Book of the Dead spell 17 [= P. Carlsberg 488]; fragment of a Book of the Dead with beautiful drawings [= P. Carlsberg 201]; Coptic letters 7+4+2+3+2+2 = 20 [i.e. twenty frames or folders; unidentified]; fragments of two Arabic papyri [= P. Carlsberg 574-577?]; twenty fragments of a Greek papyrus [= P.

(6) Research material in the form of assorted notebooks, an extensive paper slip dictionary, and numerous photographs. This material is kept at the Papyrus Carlsberg Collection. Regrettably the bulk of his once vast collection of photographs of Egyptian papyri (including much Coptic material) and monuments in various collections, which numbered several thousand, has disappeared over time.

All of the material written by Lange and his wife is written in Danish, and we have translated all cited passages into English for the convenience of the reader. These translations are sometimes loose, aimed at capturing the sense of the Danish rather than a literal translation. The word 'dealer' in these translations generally corresponds to the Danish word 'Handlende' (literally 'those who trade'), and is not a technical term for antiquities dealers as such. The use of the English term 'dealer' in our own text potentially masks different types of roles, and the reader is urged to read the book with this in mind. We discuss types of dealers in some detail later in the book (p. 29), but for now it may be useful to note that the term covers:

(1) 'Finders', that is to say people who find or excavate the actual objects in the field and then sell them on, either to collectors or museums ('end users' in modern parlance) or to other traders who in turn sell them on for profit. These are generally not full-time 'dealers' in the sense of having antiquities dealing as their main source of income, or having a dedicated shop or other trading premises, but more or less opportunistic individuals who in some way come across antiquities in their local environment.

(2) 'Middlemen', those who buy from 'finders' and then sell on to other traders: people with significant networks throughout the country. These are of-

Carlsberg 791-796]; three pieces of mummy linen, two with text, one with drawing [= P. Carlsberg 678-679, 783]; three larger fragments of a hieratic papyrus [= P. Carlsberg 427].' The acquisition of P. Carlsberg 201 and P. Carlsberg 488 is described below. The latter papyrus was acquired in 1929 and hence the hand-list must be later in date.

ten highly mobile individuals who bring objects from peripheral sites to cities like Cairo and Luxor.

(3) 'Top tier dealers' who buy from middlemen (and sometimes directly from finders/excavators) in order to sell on to Westerners; often professional dealers with shops and, after 1912, also formal licenses (like the Abemayor family, Blanchard, Nahman and the Tano family). Many of these had significant funds at their disposal and could orchestrate excavations (legal and illegal) in their own right.

These are not absolute categories – and individuals may move from one to the other at different points in their lives (an example is Zaki Mahmud Abd es-Samad) – but they may serve as a reminder of the complex social networks that form the basis for the antiquities trade in Egypt at this point.

We have also made use of material relating to Lange's teacher, Valdemar Schmidt (1836-1925), including his Danish autobiography *Af et Langt Livs Historie*, published in 1925, as well as what remains of his personal correspondance in the Royal Library and Ny Carlsberg Glyptotek.[34] Once again we have translated all relevant passages into English. Schmidt also published a long account, in Danish, of his first visit to Egypt in the winter of 1860/61, which we have also utilised.[35]

Additionally, we have drawn on the material relating to the acquisition of the items in the Papyrus Hauniensis Collection. The archives kept in that collection, covering the years 1924-1941, have recently been published in transcript by Adam Bülow-Jacobsen.[36] Further records pertaining to the acquisition of these papyri have been found at the Royal Library in connection with the present research; especially those that concern the first acquisition in 1920-21, which represent the bulk of the collection and involve H. O. Lange directly, are important.[37]

We have consulted contemporary guidebooks for contextual information, among which the Baedeker

publications are by far the most significant. The Baedeker guidebooks were often bought by visitors to Egypt, and Lange himself makes explicit reference to them on several occasions.[38] They were sold in large numbers, and Lange remarks in 1899 that in the last two years alone some 6,000 copies had been sold, of which 4,000 were of the English edition, 'and the English even had other guidebooks [at their disposal]'.[39] Several of the guidebooks were written, in part, by Egyptologists with extensive experience of Egypt (e.g. Georg Ebers and Georg Steindorff),[40] and they appear to have been relatively conscientious in their research and reporting. For example, Lange mentions that Steindorff stayed 'in a hotel in the middle of the Arab quarter in order to conduct research for the next edition of Baedeker', which allowed Lange and his wife to move into Borchardt's flat in his stead.[41] On another occasion, Lange and Schäfer made measurements in, and drew a map of, a tomb at Saqqara, so as 'to be able to send Steindorff a plan and a description for the new edition of Baedeker'.[42]

The Baedeker guides were repeatedly updated (in German, French and English) which provides the modern historian with a useful year-by-year snapshot of various aspects of Egyptian tourism. For example, the Baedeker guidebooks contain advice to travellers

---

34. Schmidt, *Af et Langt Livs Historie*.

35. Schmidt, *Reise i Grækenland, Ægypten og det hellige Land*, 154-264.

36. Bülow-Jacobsen, *Aegis* 12 (2012), 1-60.

37. The relevant references will be found in Chapter 4 below.

38. E.g. Lange and Lange, *Dagbog fra Ægyptensrejsen 1899-1900*, 318, 455; Lange, *Dagbog fra Ægypten, 1929-1930*, 173, 254. His personal copy of Baedeker, *Ägypten*, 4th edition, which he acquired in 1899 before going to Egypt for the first time, is in the library of the Egyptology Department. It includes a few annotations made on-site in Egypt.

39. Lange and Lange, *Dagbog fra Ægyptensrejsen 1899-1900*, 262. He does not state where he has the numbers from, but they are likely to be from his friend Steindorff who had been hired to provide information for the next edition.

40. Petrie also sent at least one letter with updates for the Baedeker guides after a stay in Egypt (in 1881); Drower, *Flinders Petrie*, 47.

41. Lange and Lange, *Dagbog fra Ægyptensrejsen 1899-1900*, 288.

42. Lange and Lange, *Dagbog fra Ægyptensrejsen 1899-1900*, 637. The tomb in question is Saqqara mastaba D64 (Akhethotep and Ptahhotep), which was being re-excavated and cleared at the time; see de Garis Davies, *The Mastaba of Ptahhetep and Akhethetep*.

wishing to buy antiquities as souvenirs, and helpfully list the main dealers in Cairo and Luxor at any given point.[43] The Baedeker guides were highly influential and many tourists seem to have followed their advice closely. For dealers of all kinds, including those in the antiquities trade, inclusion in the guide will undoubtedly have had a significant influence on business. An example of this is offered by the wealthy industrialist Carl Jacobsen who visited Egypt in 1909 and who had little independent knowledge of Egypt.[44] He acquired antiquities both from the *Salle de vente* of the Egyptian Museum and from the premises of the well-established dealers Paul Philip, Michel Casira, and Panayotis Kyticas, all three of which were located right next to Shepheard's Hotel. These four venues correspond exactly to the four reliable sources for antiquities indicated by the most recent edition of the Baedeker guide at the time.[45]

We have also consulted such published and accessible letters from the period as seemed relevant, the most important of these being the letters of Charles Edwin Wilbour and James Henry Breasted,[46] but as noted above many archives around the world contain supplementary material. Naturally we anticipate that others will make use of these in due course, but we hope the reader will understand our decision to omit this vast corpus of material here.

Three sources which we became aware of too late to investigate for this book are two address books belonging to Howard Carter, dating to the 1930s, and a diary belonging to Oxan Aslanian, all of which contain information about antiquities dealers. Carter's address books were sold at auction at Bonhams in 2012; one is now in private possession and is currently offered for sale on Abebooks for €10,000.[47] The diary of Aslanian, as well as a number of sale contracts for antiquities, were discovered in an abandoned bank vault in Egypt and were confiscated by the Supreme Council of Antiquities in 2010 after remaining unclaimed for fifteen years.[48] The address books and diary are likely to contain relevant information about which dealers were active at the time and could prove important for future studies.

---

43. It is not clear what the criteria for the inclusion of dealers were. The Baedeker guidebooks were certainly not exhaustive with respect to the dealers listed, and several major dealers who are known to have been active at the time were occasionally excluded. For a list of the dealers mentioned in the various editions, see Appendix 3.

44. Carl 'The Brewer' Jacobsen (1842-1914) was the founder of the Ny Carlsberg Brewery and a great patron of art in Copenhagen, whose personal collection of antiquities formed the basis for the Ny Carlsberg Glyptotek established in 1882.

45. Baedeker, *Ägypten und der Sudân*, 6th edition, 33; idem, *Egypt and the Sudân*, 6th edition, 36; idem, *Egypte et Soudan*, 3rd edition, 37.

46. Capart (ed.), *Letters of Charles Edwin Wilbour*; Larson (ed.), *Letters from James Henry Breasted to His Family, August 1919 – July 1920*. For Breasted's activities as a collector on behalf of the Oriental Institute in Chicago, see Grant, *OLNN* 205 (2010), 3-7.

47. Auction of 12 June 2012 (Auction 20137, lot 39); cf. http://www.bonhams.com (accessed 10 June 2013); http://www.abebooks.com/Carters-Own-address-book-autograph-Entries/4142278294/bd (accessed 10 June 2013). A page from one of the address books, which includes the address of the dealer Abemayor, is reproduced in Reeves, in Goring, Reeves, and Ruffle (eds.), *Fs Aldred*, 248.

48. Al-Ahram Weekly on-line (http://weekly.ahram.org.eg/2010/1024/he1.htm (accessed 10 June 2013).

The Antiquities Trade in Egypt

Fig. 5. The Danish Egyptologist H. O. Lange (1863-1943). He was the Director of the Royal Library from 1901 until 1924 when he founded the Egyptological Institute and became its first professor. Unknown photographer, c. 1930. Courtesy of the Royal Library.

Lange's mission

The travel diaries of Lange contain detailed descriptions of the trade in antiquities in Cairo from the turn of the century to 1929-1930, and in this section we offer an overview of this trade as experienced by a professional Egyptologist at the time.

Lange (Fig. 5), who at the time of his first visit was employed as a librarian, arrived in Cairo in 1899-1900 to work on the catalogue of the Middle Kingdom stelae at the Egyptian national museum of antiquities,

then known as Gizeh Museum (Fig. 6-7, 25-26). He does not appear to have been formally instructed to buy on behalf of the Danish National Museum or the Glyptotek prior to his departure. In fact the Glyptotek was only opened as a public museum some years after his first visit (in 1906), but his old professor, Valdemar Schmidt (Fig. 8), had by then been buying Egyptian antiquities for 'the brewer' Carl Jacobsen – whose collection was the basis of the Glyptotek's holdings – and Lange may well have been told to keep his eyes open for further acquisitions. He first contacted the National Museum in December of 1899 after he had spent some weeks in Cairo and had personally experienced the thriving antiquities trade.[49] Christian Blinkenberg, the curator of the Antiquity Collection (*Antiksamlingen*), sent him a positive reply two weeks later, and the letter gives some insight into what a smaller cultural-historical collection at that time might wish to acquire:

> Many thanks for your kind letter of 14 December, which I hereby take the liberty of answering on the authority of Director Müller. The museum should, in my view, take advantage of the opportunity afforded by a Danish Egyptologist currently residing in Egypt to acquire some nice pieces, and I am very pleased that you have offered your services in this regard.
>
> Our ordinary budget is very limited and all but spent for the current year – in the case of a substantial acquisition one would, in other words, have to apply for an extraordinary grant. I am hopeful that such a grant could be obtained if one presented for purchase specific pieces of extraordinary quality at reasonable prices. Of such outstanding museum pieces your letter ap-

49. Lange and Lange, *Dagbog fra Ægyptensrejsen 1899-1900*, 187; 'I must write home to the Director of the National Museum, Joh. Müller, to ask about how much money I have at my disposal'. Some ten days later he writes that 'I long to know how much I can spend on purchases, and have written to Director Müller about it' (p. 198).

SCI.DAN.H. 4 · 8LANGE'S MISSION

Fig. 6. East facade of the Gizeh Museum where H. O. Lange worked 1899-1900 on the *catalogue générale* of Middle King-dom stelae with Heinrich Schäfer. A former harem palace of the Khedive Ismaïl, the building housed the Egyptian anti-quities from 1890 to 1902. The sarcophagus in which the founder of the Egyptian antiquities service, Auguste Mariette (1821-1881), was buried can be seen in front of the museum (Fig. 7). The museum gardens can be seen in the background on the right (Fig. 26). Commercial photograph by J. Pascal Sébah, inscribed 'Musée de Ghizeh'.

pears to include two examples; however, there is simply not enough information included to allow us to evaluate them thoroughly, much less apply for a grant. I am speaking of 1) The complete tomb wall of the 5th Dynasty, priced at c. 220£, and 2) the exquisite relief at c. 30£. – Could you, if not too inconvenient, produce a fuller description of these two pieces, which according to your letter are also the ones you would primarily recommend. Would it be possible to acquire photographs of them; the museum would be happy to cover any expenses incurred. Your description of these pieces

(and perhaps some others) could be used as attachments for an application for an extraordinary grant, if the appropriate circumstances should present themselves.

Concerning the other pieces mentioned (albeit briefly) in your letter, simply the following remarks. Prof. Vald. Schmidt is currently engaged in trying to secure for us one of the excellent flint knives. As concerns common spears and arrow-heads we already have plenty. We are also reasonably well-stocked, for a collection of our size, with prehistoric stone vessels.

Fig. 7. H. O. Lange (seated) with his colleague, Freiherr von Bissing (standing), by the tomb of Mariette in front of the Gizeh Museum. Lange photograph, 1899/1900. Courtesy of the Royal Library.

If you would like us to send you a smaller sum of money for immediate purchases, I suppose some 3-400 Francs could be made available and sent whenever you wished.

You will not be offended by me repeating in writing what I already spoke to you about in relation to these kind of acquisitions. The Antiquity Collection is a special kind of collection, and we have to use our funds sparingly and according to certain rules. We should only acquire:

1. Whole and complete pieces, no fragments of any kind.

2. Pieces that are of a good quality and representative of their kind, but not pieces which are truly unique.

3. Every type should only be represented by a single example (or, exceptionally, by a couple). We cannot buy duplicates of any kind. In other words we should only buy pieces which are otherwise not represented in the collection.

Please excuse the briefness of my words; I am afraid to bother you with too verbiose rhetoric, and may have erred on the side of caution. You will see from my remarks that the Antiquity Collection could never entertain the acquistion of the collection of stone vessels to the price of c. 5000 Francs that you mention. On the

other hand, if specific and characteristic examples could be singled out, forms and types which would otherwise not be represented in our cabinets, then such objects would be well suited for purchase, and could result in an application for a grant. Similarly, for example, a good prehistoric jar with well-preserved ship drawings, if such a piece could be had for a reasonable price.

I very much hope that you can help us make a fine acquisition.[50]

While the reply from the museum was relatively positive, the demand for detailed descriptions, before it would commit to any acquisition, and the complicated procedure for transferring funds (which must have been discussed in a later letter) apparently frustrated Lange. He made this known to Blinkenberg who, after some delay, on 2 April 1900 writes that he is very sorry to hear that Lange has entirely given up acquiring objects for the National Museum. This settled matters as far as the National Museum and Lange's first visit to Egypt was concerned, but the muse-

---

50. Letter from C. Blinkenberg to H. O. Lange, dated 30 Dec. 1899 (Royal Library, Copenhagen).

um was still well-disposed towards the acquisition of objects for the Egyptian collection, and after Lange's return it acquired a number of objects from him directly, which he had purchased with his own means, and it acquired further objects through Ludwig Borchardt in Cairo in 1901 and 1902 with his aid.

Lange explains in some cases who he is buying for, and the Glyptotek is usually mentioned by name or by reference to its founder, 'the brewer' Jacobsen, and the National Museum is simply referred to as 'the museum'. It is clear that the intended destination for any given object did not necessarily correspond to the final destination. In one case he states that he has bought (on 18 December 1899) 'the first piece for the museum, a long narrow relief from a 5th Dynasty tomb, with harvest scenes and granaries; it is not complete ... a rare find for the cheap price of 7 pounds (130 Danish crowns)'; here Lange had evidently intended to pass the object on to the National Museum, but when he had still not received any funds several weeks later (he had paid for the relief out of his own pocket), it was instead offered to the Glyptotek, where it ended up.[51] Lange had also decided to look for things for himself, primarily – but certainly not exclusively – in the form of papyrus fragments. If he came across particularly promising pieces, and thought the price was reasonable, he would sometimes buy them out of his own pocket and then subsequently write to the Glyptotek or the National Museum and offer it to them if they would refund his expenses.[52]

During his second trip in 1929-1930, at which point he was a professor in Egyptology at the university and

Fig. 8. Valdemar Schmidt (1836-1925). Schmidt introduced Lange to Egyptology and became his first teacher. He was also instrumental in introducing him to the antiquities trade in Egypt. The industrialist and philanthropist Carl Jacobsen regarded Schmidt as the creator of his Egyptian collection in the Ny Carlsberg Glyptotek. Unknown photographer, c. 1915. Courtesy of Ny Carlsberg Glyptotek.

well-connected in Danish academia, he also considered buying objects for a teaching collection to be kept at the department, although it is not clear whether he ever bought anything for this purpose.[53]

---

51. Lange and Lange, *Dagbog fra Ægyptensrejsen 1899-1900*, 198. For Lange's problems in obtaining funding from the National Museum, see p. 24. The relief is Ny Carlsberg Glyptotek, ÆIN 939 and 940 (the museum records list Valdemar Schmidt as the buyer as Lange acted on his behalf), from the mastaba tomb of Sopduhotep at Saqqara (D15); Jørgensen, *Egypt I*, 60-63; Manniche, *Egyptian Art in Denmark*, 64-66, fig. 23. Lange sometimes makes reference to objects intended for 'my museum' (pp. 360, 421, 738), but it is uncertain what this refers to; it could be the National Museum, or even his own private collection.

52. Lange and Lange, *Dagbog fra Ægyptensrejsen 1899-1900*, 428.

53. 'I am considering whether I should spend some £10 of the laboratory's [= 'the laboratory of Egyptology' at Copenhagen University] money to buy some examples of antiquities cheaply, as teaching material for the laboratory. One can get good squeezes of the nice pieces in the museum, but they are too expensive, and originals would be much better. One would not get a lot for £10, but some minor objects should be possible. The budget of the laboratory will be increased as of

Fig. 9. Jonna Lange visiting the ruins of the temple of Ramesses II at Memphis (Mit Rahina). Photograph by Lange, 1899/1900. Courtesy of the Royal Library.

His visits to antiquities dealers were primarily to purchase objects, but he seems often to have copied interesting inscriptions he came across in their shops, even when he had no intention of buying. His interest in stelae in particular is clear both in the first travel diary and in the second; at Luxor in 1930 he noted in passing that 'Today too I have copied some inscriptions at another dealer's', suggesting that it was a common occurrence.[54]

It is worth keeping in mind that Lange, despite his Egyptological training and his self-professed talent at spotting fakes as well as bargains, was at all times rela-

tively inexperienced as a buyer. His activities as a purchaser of antiquities were limited, based on just two – admittedly extended – visits. Many of the dealers he bought from, on the other hand, were professionals with decades of experience of selling to Egyptologists and museums (in addition to tourists), who will have had a keen sense of the financial value of any given object. Lange remarks again and again in his travel diary that the Egyptians have no real sense of the value of an object, but this has to be evaluated against the nature of the sources at our disposal; as the main protagonist in his own narrative we have only Lange's view of these transactions. Dealers may well have felt that they came away from the exchanges with the upper hand (we simply cannot tell), and in any case the fact that a transaction was completed at all indicates

this April, so perhaps the money could be found'; Lange, *Dagbog fra Ægypten, 1929-1930*, 121.

54. Lange, *Dagbog fra Ægypten, 1929-1930*, 192, 243.

that the terms (and monetary values) involved were acceptable to both parties. The question of what constitutes the 'value' of an object is complex, and a high historical – or Egyptological – value does not necessarily correlate with a high financial value; the latter is determined by market forces that are only partly influenced by aspects such as historical importance.

Jonna Lange

In our account Lange's wife Jonna (Fig. 3, 9-10) is a rather peripheral character, primarily because she features only rarely in Lange's descriptions of the transactions in which he takes part. That is not to say that she *was* peripheral in the transactions, however, as Lange makes clear on several occasions; she was in fact 'almost always' present.[55] She built up a collection of her own which consisted mostly of small objects, many of them given to her by dealers when a transaction was completed in her presence (as *baksh-ish*), while others were bought by her directly from the dealers.[56] Most of the objects were subsequently bequeathed to the National Museum upon her death in 1955, although a proportion had already been donated to Antikmuseet in Aarhus; the latter is described as a 'Gift from ... Mrs Head Librarian H.O. Lange (May 1951)', but explicitly said to have been 'bought by her deceased husband in Egypt'.[57] It is not certain to what extent this should be taken literally. The gift was catalogued under some 66 different inventory numbers (nos. 0.381-0.447), all of which consisted of small finds like scarabs, faience sherds, beads (glass and faience, some mounted as necklaces), small figurines or statuettes, amulets and shabtis. This gift is focused in its contents, with variety clearly having been one priority when it was being compiled – this is obvious in the range of deities represented by figurines and amulets, most of which are represented by only one or two ob-

Fig. 10. Jonna Lange (1870-1955), H. O. Lange's wife of 50 years, accompanied him on both visits to Egypt. She was an accomplished photographer, shown here developing photographs in Cairo, 1899/1900. Courtesy of the Royal Library.

jects: Isis, Sekhmet, Amun-Ra, Ptah, Anubis, Thoth, Shu, Sokar-Osiris, Bes, etc.

Jonna sometimes visited dealers without Lange, including those living at Kafr el-Haram – on one such occasion she viewed the collections of Soliman and Ibrahim Abd es-Samad with some friends.[58] Jonna was linguistically gifted, and she studied Arabic more systematically (and more successfully) than Lange himself;[59] her presence frequently facilitated transactions, and Lange remarks when he is in Luxor without her that 'I miss Jonna a lot in my negotiations [with an Arab dealer] ... which are conducted in Arabic. Naturally I pretend to understand his long speeches, and luckily I know the numbers and a few polite phrases ...'.[60] These brief remarks suggest that Jonna played a more central role in Lange's acquisitions than our account might otherwise indicate.

55. Lange, *Dagbog fra Ægypten, 1929-1930*, 286.

56. Lange, *Dagbog fra Ægypten, 1929-1930*, 67 (buys from Oxan Aslanian); 115-116, 286 (objects as *bakshish*).

57. Antikmuseet, *Inventory*, 1951, 94, 117.

58. Lange and Lange, *Dagbog fra Ægyptensrejsen 1899-1900*, 140-141. The party included Professor Valdemar Schmidt and a Mrs. Müller, as well as two unnamed English ladies (p. 138).

59. Lange and Lange, *Dagbog fra Ægyptensrejsen 1899-1900*, 77; cf. Lange, *Dagbog fra Ægypten, 1929-1930*, 360.

60. Lange, *Dagbog fra Ægypten, 1929-1930*, 188.

Jonna was also by far the better photographer of the two, and it was she who took virtually all the photographs during both visits.[61] In fact during the last trip in 1929-1930, when Lange was forced to take some photographs himself (Jonna was in bed with an upset stomach), he remarks while awaiting the results of his efforts that 'I am not optimistic [about the outcome]. I have not the skill to impose on Jonna's domain'.[62] In a much earlier letter from 1901 also Borchardt comments very favourably on her skills; although himself a skilled photographer, he states that a series of 160 photographs, which he had just shot at Karnak, are only 'fast so gut wie sie Ihre Frau macht.'[63]

Language, bargaining skills, and Egyptological knowledge

Lange knew little or no Arabic when he arrived, and this was a source of irritation to him: he realised quickly that it would be a problem when buying antiquities. His first recorded visit to an antiquities dealer was on 29 October 1899, approximately two weeks after his arrival in Cairo, when after lunch he and some colleagues (Steindorff, Borchardt, von Bissing and Schäfer) left the museum:

> [We] drove down to the village of Giza to visit antiquities dealers, one of whom was not at home; at the other's place we were shown a number of pieces. Borchardt bought some things for the Berlin Museum and Bissing a couple of minor pieces. It was a very difficult transaction which took a long time, unfortunately all the negotiations took place in Arabic, so I could not understand a word, but he was both expensive and stubborn.[64]

Lange had been aware of his linguistic limitations for a while, and he had voiced his frustration in an entry written ten days earlier:

> I am at a disadvantage with the Arab language. Yesterday Borchardt wasn't going to the Museum, and I was unable to negotiate with a taxi driver to drive me there and back. I therefore had to walk both ways. Jonna walked with me halfway there.[65]

Some of the dealers spoke European languages with various degrees of fluency, like an unnamed old man and his son from the village at Giza who spoke 'remarkably good English, which they have learned from talking to strangers,'[66] while others spoke no English at all, and necessitated the use of an interpreter.[67] The one who was used most frequently by Lange during his first visit was his guide, a certain Abdallah, who was helpfully also the cousin of one of the main antiquities dealers, Ali at Kafr el-Haram.[68] Lange's language skills seem to have improved gradually during his first visit in 1899-1900, partly because his assistants at the Museum spoke only Arabic, but he never attained any kind of fluency, and often relied on his wife Jonna to interpret during transactions with dealers.[69] Despite his shortcomings on the linguistic side, Lange was asked to accompany colleagues to bargain with antiquities dealers on their behalf shortly after arriving in Cairo for the first time:

61. This includes also the photographs of the nearly 800 Middle Kingdom stelae in the Egyptian Museum published in the *Catalogue Général* which Lange and Schäfer co-edited in 1899/1900; cf. Lange and Lange, *Dagbog fra Ægyptensrejsen 1899-1900*, 615, and Appendix 6.
62. Lange, *Dagbog fra Ægypten, 1929-1930*, 179.
63. Letter from L. Borchardt to H. O. Lange, dated 31 May 1901 (Royal Library, Copenhagen).
64. Lange and Lange, *Dagbog fra Ægyptensrejsen 1899-1900*, 85. This visit is also recorded in the Borchardt diary, Sept. 1899

- Jan. 1900, entry 29 Oct. 1899 (Swiss Institute, Cairo; transcript kindly provided by Cornelius von Pilgrim, 21 Jan. 2015): 'Mit Lange, Bissing, Steindorff u. Schäfer zu Ali. Skizze aus der Zeit Amenophis IV u. Papyrusfragm. gekauft. Zus. 12 £ (ich 5 £, Sch. 6 £, St. 1 £) ...'.
65. Lange and Lange, *Dagbog fra Ægyptensrejsen 1899-1900*, 51.
66. Lange and Lange, *Dagbog fra Ægyptensrejsen 1899-1900*, 131.
67. A dealer called Todros Girgis Gabrial (see the list of dealers at the end of this book) came to Lange in 1930 with a colleague who spoke no English and acted as an interpreter for him; Lange, *Dagbog fra Ægypten, 1929-1930*, 271.
68. Lange and Lange, *Dagbog fra Ægyptensrejsen 1899-1900*, 143, cf. also p. 136.
69. Lange, *Dagbog fra Ægypten, 1929-1930*, 188-189; cf. the section on Jonna Lange above.

These days I am not writing as much in the diary as I should, and the reason for that is that my time is entirely taken up by looking at antiquities with Arab dealers, and trading with them. I have not myself made any purchases, but I am assisting Dr Thiersch from Munich who is buying papyri; he prefers to have me along because he thinks that I am good at pushing the Bedouins' prices down.[70]

Lange did this happily and saw it as good training: 'I learn a lot from this and get some experience in how to deal with the Bedouins which may be of use later when I begin to buy antiquities for the museum back home'.[71] As time passed he and his wife acquired the services of domestic servants, and these sometimes assisted him in the transactions that took place at home, such as the following visit by a dealer called Soliman (sc. Soliman 'the young'), described by Jonna Lange:

> Here, too, a deal was struck; Ḥalîb [the servant] stood beside him and made some good suggestions; it was strange to see him with his one eye stand there and examine the different pieces, and like a faithful servant he certainly looked out for his master.[72]

The diaries include many episodes where Lange bargains with dealers, and it is clear that he relished these occasions ('There is something very exciting about this hunt for antiquities', he remarks at one point),[73] and he goes on at some length about the stages of negotiation, the tricks and techniques of successful bargaining, and the personality traits involved.[74] On one occasion he self-deprecatingly remarks that 'The Armenians are experienced traders, and one has to be careful with them and drive a hard bargain. In other words I must use all of my Jutlandish talent for trade'.[75]

During his second visit in 1929-1930, the price of antiquities had risen dramatically compared to thirty years earlier,[76] but his memory of those early days could apparently be used as a bargaining tool; he says he tended to insist on only paying 1900-prices to drive the price down.[77] His Arabic was still rudimentary, and Jonna's, although better, was far from fluent. This was a source of regret to him, and looking back on that trip he reflected that this lack of understanding had effectively resulted in there being 'a wall between us and the majority of Egyptians'.[78]

Socio-economic aspects

The antiquities market in Egypt was many-faceted, and the individuals involved were diverse to say the least. Before describing Lange's experiences with dealers in more depth, it may be helpful to briefly outline the demography of the market. It is admittedly always risky to attempt to impose simplistic social categories – and it's safe to say that no two dealers were exactly the same – but it can be a convenient way to provide a sketch of a rather complex system: there were a great number of 'dealers' active in the antiquities trade, but they operated in different ways.[79]

One group of individuals consisted of those involved in the actual discovery of ancient artefacts which subsequently ended up on the market. This was almost invariably a local occurrence (A. H. Sayce once observed that 'fellahin and antika-hunters [are] two synonymous terms'),[80] where local inhabitants either by design (looting) or by accident (e.g. through *sebakh*-digging) gained possession of objects that they

70. Lange and Lange, *Dagbog fra Ægyptensrejsen 1899-1900*, 146; Dr Thiersch is said to be buying primarily Greek papyri for the libraries of Munich, Strasbourg, and Basel (p. 147).

71. Lange and Lange, *Dagbog fra Ægyptensrejsen 1899-1900*, 153-154.

72. Lange and Lange, *Dagbog fra Ægyptensrejsen 1899-1900*, 481.

73. Lange, *Dagbog fra Ægypten, 1929-1930*, 86.

74. E.g. Lange and Lange, *Dagbog fra Ægyptensrejsen 1899-1900*, 154-155, 363, 418-420; Lange, *Dagbog fra Ægypten, 1929-1930*, 104, 272-273.

75. Lange, *Dagbog fra Ægypten, 1929-1930*, 62. In Zealand and

Copenhagen, where Lange lived for most of his adult life, people from Jutland had a reputation for being rather frugal and for driving a hard bargain, and Lange's father was himself a merchant.

76. 'The prices these days have increased to a ridiculous degree'; Lange, *Dagbog fra Ægypten, 1929-1930*, 86.

77. Lange, *Dagbog fra Ægypten, 1929-1930*, 322.

78. Lange, *Dagbog fra Ægypten, 1929-1930*, 360.

79. For an early attempt at categorising types of dealers, see Rhind, *Thebes, its Tombs and their Tenants*, 245-248.

80. Sayce, *Reminiscences*, 251.

then sought to sell. A partial exception was the common practice amongst workmen on archaeological excavations of palming small finds – and sometimes not-so-small finds – and then selling these off-site: Lange reports in his travel diary that it was rumoured at the time that at Pierre Montet's excavations at Byblos, 'over half of the objects found were stolen by his own workers who sold them to antiquities dealers and collectors'.[81] This may be an exaggerated figure, and H. W. Fairman claimed, some five years later, that 'the general agreement in Egypt is that anything from 10% to 20% of the total number of finds is stolen'.[82] Workmen, or at least their supervisors, were often not local, precisely because they were thought to be less of a security risk if they came from another area. A mix of local and 'imported' workers was seen as ideal, as the groups would then keep a mutual eye on each other and thus minimize the risk of theft. Petrie, for example, famously employed both workers and supervisors from villages some distance away from the place he was excavating.[83] This practice was adopted by many colleagues, although sometimes ostensibly for different reasons. The Egyptian Egyptologist Labib Habachi, for example, took a group of workers from the Fayum in the north to assist him in his excavations on the island of Elephantine in the south in 1945-1946.[84]

Objects acquired then had to be sold, and there were several possible routes of transmission. Workmen might sell objects found (back) to archaeologists working the site, a form of transaction sometimes formalized by prior agreement between the archaeologist and his workforce,[85] or to local dealers, from which the archaeologists could then buy them back. Bernard Bruyère, for example, who excavated the well-known workmen's village at Deir el-Medina (on the Theban West Bank), started his excavation seasons by visiting local dealers in Luxor, looking for objects from his site that had appeared on the market.[86] Objects could also be sold directly to Western tourists visiting the sites (Lange himself occasionally bought objects this way), or, particularly in the case of larger or more valuable objects, they could be sold to members of another group of dealers who might be best described as semi-professional.[87] This group, like the first, was diverse, comprising a range of different people from different backgrounds. There were local merchants and traders who bought and sold antiquities as a side-business: a butcher in Ismaïla,[88] a herb

81. Lange, *Dagbog fra Ægypten, 1929-1930,* 88 (the entire passage is translated below, p. 132).

82. Memorandum (of Sept. 1935) from Fairman to the Committee of the Egypt Exploration Society, cited by Shaw, in Leahy and Tait (eds.), *Fs Smith,* 279. Fairman made the claim in the context of a complaint about an unusually high number of objects from the Society's Amarna excavations, where he was a field assistant, turning up on the antiquities market.

83. Quirke, *Hidden Hands,* 29-34, 41-43. The most famous example is his use of workers from the Upper Egyptian village of Quft, known as *quftis,* whose experience and training made them popular on many excavations, up to and including in modern times.

84. Kamil, *Labib Habachi,* 111-112. Habachi claims that his motivation was not primarily related to the fear of finds being stolen, but did note that 'It was not that I did not trust them, it was simply a question of removing temptation. To recruit men from various villages to work together does wonders to

hinder double-dealing, you know' (p. 113). The psychological aspects of such 'displacement' is well captured by his description of the train ride south to Aswan when he, unusually in a hierarchical society like Egypt, spent some time with his workers in their third-class carriage, preparing them for their meeting with Nubian culture (p. 116, compare their reactions described on pp. 148-149).

85. On the practice of paying for finds made by workers on excavations, see Quirke, *Hidden Hands,* 97-104. The practice also had the unintended consequence of inciting workmen to plant forgeries, according to Ahmed Fakhry who was Inspector at Luxor in the 1930s; Lilyquist, *The Tomb of Three Foreign Wives of Tuthmosis III,* 270.

86. Cf. excavation diary of Bernard Bruyère, accessible online at http://www.ifao.egnet.net/bases/archives/bruyere (accessed 9 Nov. 2012), entry of 16 Feb. 1926 (objects from Deir el-Medina seen with Todros Girgis Gabrial and Mohammed Mohasseb), entry of 17 Dec. 1929 (objects with Mohammad Mohasseb, Abd el-Megid and Girgis Gabrial).

87. Any entrepreneur could apparently, given the resources, make profitable journeys of 60-80 miles into the countryside to buy smaller finds and then resell them at a profit in Cairo and Thebes; cf. Rhind, *Thebes, It's Tombs and their Tenants,* 249.

88. Clédat, *RT* 36 (1914), 103.

seller in the Fayum,[89] or a 'travelling tobacco and antika dealer' visiting Tanis.[90] These would often in turn
sell objects on to more professional dealers (see below), or, in some cases, directly to European collectors. The latter was probably the most lucrative op-
tion, and Lange records several cases where such
semi-professional traders had travelled to Cairo to sell
directly to him, having heard about his interest in antiquities from colleagues.[91] Anyone who found or
somehow acquired antiquities might turn 'dealer',
and Lange describes the following scene during a
crossing of the Nile on a local ferry at Qena:

Among these [passengers] there were some farmers
from the other side, who tried to sell me antiquities.
One young man offered me a silver ring which he had
on his finger, in which a scarab had been set; he valued
the scarab at 2 shillings and the ring at 1. A distinguished old man in a brown camel hair coat then dragged
forth an apron-like piece of cloth, and from the individually tied corners he pulled out various small objects
that he wanted me to buy, but I conducted no trade on
this occasion.[92]

These individuals appear to have been locals who
dabbled in dealing only as and when the opportunity
arose; along these lines it makes sense to distinguish
between more professional dealers and those who
only rarely took part in the antiquities trade.

Another group of semi-professional dealers consisted of foreigners who worked in Egypt but who
dealt in antiquities on the side. There are numerous
examples of this. A traveller in Egypt in 1817-1818, for
example, remarked on the number of Italian doctors
who also traded in antiquities.[93] One of the most fa-

mous members of this group was the Rev. Chauncey
Murch, director of the American Presbyterian Mission at Luxor (1883-1907), who supplied, amongst
others, the British Museum with significant quantities
of objects.[94] Another example associated with a Christian mission was Mischriky Girgis, of the 'Deutsche
Sûdân-Pionier-Mission' at Aswan.

Perhaps the largest category of such semi-professional dealers, however, consisted of those individuals
who were appointed consular agents for various foreign states.[95] These had been central to the antiquities
market for many years, some as collectors but also as
agents for European museums, and as independent
dealers.[96] Already in the first edition of the Baedeker

disinter statues, and make out very well by the exchange';
cited by Colla, *Conflicted Antiquities*, 285, n. 40.
94. Bierbrier, *Who was Who in Egyptology*, 4th edition, 392; Ismail,
Wallis Budge, 289-302.
95. The scale of the trade conducted by consuls is difficult to
quantify. We know of only one attempt, but this is from 1812
when the trade in antiquities was relatively small-scale; the
export value of mummies is then said to have been comparable to the total export value of Egyptian lentils; see Colla,
Conflicted Antiquities, 290, n. 123. In the middle of the second
decade of the 19th Century the consuls of France and Austria
apparently 'had a near total monopoly in the antiquities
commerce'; Colla, *Conflicted Antiquities*, 27. For a general account
of the collecting activities of European consuls, see Fiechter,
La moisson des dieux.
96. Examples are numerous, but for a selection see e.g.
Bierbrier, *Who was Who in Egyptology*, 4th edition, 19-20 (Giovanni
Anastasi, Consul-General for Sweden and Norway, fl.
1828-1857, Alexandria), 363 (V. Galli Maunier, Consular Agent
for France, fl. 1840-1875, Luxor), 394 (Mustafa Aga Khan,
Consular Agent for Britain, Belgium, and Russia, fl. 1850-1887,
Luxor), 481 (Raymond Sabatier, Consul-General for France, fl.
1852-1879, Alexandria and Cairo), 484 (Henry Salt, Consul-
General for Britain, fl. 1815-1827, Alexandria and Cairo), 507
(Shenuda Makarios, Consular Agent for Austria and Consul
for France, Vice-Consul for Denmark, fl. 1869-1904, Luxor),
542 (Todros Bolos, Consular Agent for Prussia, fl. 1856-1898,
Luxor), 599 (Stephan Zizinia, Consul-General for Belgium, fl.
1840-1868, Alexandria). Another example is Abd en-Nur (fl.
1881-1890 at Girga) who was first Consular Agent for France
and later for the United States. Several of the consuls were
Copts, such as Abd en-Nur, Shenuda Makarios, and Todros
Bolos and his son Mohareb Todros.

89. Lange and Lange, *Dagbog fra Ægyptensrejsen 1899-1900*, 518.
90. Petrie, *Journals*, 1883-1884, 175. Compare Lange, *Dagbog fra
Ægypten, 1929-1930*, 149, where a stall-owner whose primary
products are photographs and postcards had 'some wretched-
looking antiquities'.
91. E.g. Lange and Lange, *Dagbog fra Ægyptensrejsen 1899-1900*,
420-421.
92. Lange and Lange, *Dagbog fra Ægyptensrejsen 1899-1900*, 351.
93. The traveller N. de Forbin claims that he 'saw Italians who
claimed to be doctors in Upper Egypt. They bury Agas, and

guide to Upper Egypt from 1891, the reader was advised concerning Luxor that 'all the consuls sell antiquities',[97] and some years earlier – in 1881 – Wilbour reported that the local consular agents Mustafa Aga and Todros Bolos, both well-attested antiquities dealers, 'get nearly all the antiquities found here of value'.[98] The central role of the consuls is clearly described by the following extract from a guidebook from 1880:

> Antiquities and curiosities should be purchased with great caution. The traveller desirous of obtaining trustworthy specimens should consult the consular agents, who are good judges. Genuine things are to be had: but there is a regular manufacture of antiquities, especially scarabæi and basalt images at Luxor: and some of the imitations are very clever and difficult to detect. Both at Mustafa Agha's and at the house of Todros, the German Consul, examples of spurious 'anticas' are kept for the warning of the traveller. The most tempting objects, as a rule, are papyrus rolls. When genuine they should if possible be bought, but forgeries are very common, and it is seldom possible to tell what the roll contains. Should the roll be a valuable one, injudicious attempts at opening may seriously injure it. Many of the best papyri in existence in European museums want the first lines, owing to want of care in opening them.[99]

Here too consuls, 'who are good judges', are emphasised as the main dealers, and some – again Mustafa Aga and Todros Bolos are mentioned specifically by name – could apparently show travellers examples of forgeries as well as genuine antiquities. This may not have been an altogether altruistic business, and consuls are attested deliberately selling forgeries.[100]

A few words on the offices of consul general, consul (or consular agent) and vice consul might be appropriate here.[101] The consul-general of any given nation in Egypt was a high official, appointed by the nation in question and often a citizen of the same; he possessed certain judicial powers, including the right to detain and take into custody anyone of a corresponding nationality who was involved in or suspected of criminal behaviour while in Egypt.[102] Formally the role of the consul general was to facilitate and oversee trade, and advance the mercantile interests of his nation, in any given location; in some cases they also levied taxes on local trade involving their countrymen. They were also occasionally involved in intelligence gathering but this varied greatly from place to place and period to period. The British consuls general were generally traders themselves, and for this reason had a notoriously complex relationship with the high-born diplomats of the Foreign Office.[103] In

97. Baedeker, *Ober-Ägypten*, 1st edition, 115; idem, *Upper Egypt*, 1st edition, 102.

98. Cf. Capart (ed.), *Letters of Charles Edwin Wilbour*, 60. Erman, *Mein Werden und mein Wirken*, 219, similarly notes that the antiquities trade at Luxor was in the hands of the consular agents during his visit in 1885.

99. Wilkinson, *Handbook for Travellers in Egypt*, 6th edition, 1880, 452.

100. See Drower, *Flinders Petrie*, 47, for an example of a German consul at Luxor selling fake scarabs; this is presumably Todros, cf. p. 110.

101. For the terminology, see Middleton, *The Administration of British Foreign Policy 1782-1846*, 245. The archival material relating to consuls is vast in most countries because much of their official correspondence was filed by their respective governments, and we have made no attempt to evaluate this material. An impression of the scale is given by Ridley, *Napoleon's Proconsul in Egypt*, x-xii, who for his work (which concentrated on the first half of the 19th Century) relied on six volumes of published correspondence relating to the French consuls, and twenty unpublished volumes of records relating to English consuls.

102. This description of the role and function of consuls general and consuls is partly based on the presentation of the American model in Lynch, *Egyptian Sketches*. See particularly pp. 7-10 (on the status of consuls general in Egyptian society), and pp. 136, 148-151, 190 (on their legal authority). Consular jurisdiction, and its relationship to the mixed tribunal, is discussed by Goldberg, *Islamic Law and Society* 6 (1999), 193-223; cf. McCoan, *Consular Jurisdiction in Turkey and Egypt*, 21-29; Manley and Rée, *Henry Salt*, 190, 194.

103. Middleton, *The Administration of British Foreign Policy 1782-1846*, 245-253; Platt, *The Cinderella Service*, London, 1971. Compare also the biography of Henry Salt, Consul-General of Great Britain; Manley and Rée, *Henry Salt*, 309 (index, s.v. 'consular role'). The potential conflict of interest arising from the dual role of a consul general being both a trader himself and an official regulating trade, led to the British Foreign Office prohibiting certain consuls from trading in 1832, including those in

addition to the consul-general, many major powers had a consul or consular agent at significant urban sites along the Nile, at least from the late 19th Century.[104] Those appointed as consuls were generally local businessmen of standing – frequently said to be the richest in the area – but often without any formal ties to the country they represented and sometimes not even able to speak the language: a visitor to Luxor in 1872 met with 'Todros, the Prussian Consul, Ali Murad the American, and Shenudi the Austrian, none of whom spoke English'.[105] Travellers of a certain standing would call on their nation's consular agents during their trip, and Lady Duff-Gordon recorded how in 1862 her boat carried 'the English flag and a small American distinguishing pennant as a signal to my consular agents'.[106] Some visitors remained mystified by the arrangement and could not think why the office of consul should be so attractive to Egyptians[107] –

it was not well paid, if at all[108] – but in practice their special status granted them a certain amount of diplomatic immunity, which could come in handy in the antiquities trade.[109]

Perhaps the best-known example of a consular agent using his diplomatic immunity to protect illegal activities is Mustafa Aga, the British consular agent at Luxor, who was known as the patron of the Abd er-Rasul brothers when they found the famous cache of royal mummies (and various parts of associated burial equipment) around 1871 (Fig. 11).[110] Many of the mummies were sold off over the next decade, before the brothers were arrested; at the time Wilbour thought that Gaston Maspero, the Director of the Antiquities Service, had gone after them because Mus-

---

Alexandria and Cairo; Middleton, *The Administration of British Foreign Policy 1782-1846*, 332.

104. America, for example, had consuls in at least the following locations in the late 19th Century: Beni Sueif (a Copt), Assiut (a Copt), Thebes (Ali Murad, a Muslim), and Akhmim (Khyatt, a Copt); cf. Lynch, *Egyptian Sketches*, 174, 190, 213, 231-235. Of these, all but the last (Khyatt) are said to have kept the office of consul in their family for more than one generation. For comparison, France had some 25-30 consuls and consular agents stationed in various cities and towns in Egypt in 1904; cf. *Annuaire diplomatique et consulaire de la République française pour 1904 & 1906* 25, new ser., 52. There were significantly fewer consuls in earlier periods, and then primarily near important ports: for example, a document of 1828 from the British Foreign Office lists one consul general in Cairo, one consul in Alexandria, as well as two vice-consuls in Rosetta and Damietta; Middleton, *The Administration of British Foreign Policy 1782-1846*, 331.

105. Ferguson, *Moss gathered by a rolling stone*, 50 (he also notes that Todros' son did speak English, and that he 'used to go and have an occasional pipe, and a glass of some curious liqueur' with him). See also Lynch, *Egyptian Sketches*, 174, 190, 235.

106. Duff-Gordon, *Lady Duff-Gordon's Letters from Egypt*, revised edition, 24 (the reason for the American pennant was that she had been asked by the American Consul-General to deliver letters to his consular agents, p. 19).

107. Lynch, *Egyptian Sketches*, 190, 233.

108. The American remuneration system as established in 1874 is outlined in Hale, *The North American Review* 122, no. 251 (1876), 309-337; here the American consul general in Cairo is said to receive some $4000 per annum, and consular agents had to be paid by the consul general from his own salary. Drovetti's annual salary as French consul when appointed in 1802 was 18000 *livres*, and he too seems to have been responsible for paying consular agents from his own salary; Ridley, *Napoleon's Proconsul in Egypt*, 21. The salary for the office of English consul varied a lot depending on location but was invariably too low to live on, and consular agents were in turn paid at the discretion of the consul: Platt, *The Cinderella Service*, 37-48 (19th Century), 81-88 (20th Century). The low level of pay necessitated a sizeable private income, and there were only limited pension provisions so that many consuls saw building up and selling collections of antiquities as a way of providing for old age; Manley and Rée, *Henry Salt*, 74, 125, 202-203, 254; Jasanoff, *Edge of Empire*, 237-238; Middleton, *The Administration of British Foreign Policy 1782-1846*, 246-247. Henry Salt's contemporary Bernardino Drovetti seems also to have collected specifically to provide for retirement; Ridley, *Napoleon's Proconsul in Egypt*, 260.

109. Tagher, *CHE* 3 (1950), 22. The *firman* setting out Henry Salt's privileges and authority as a British consul in Egypt (of 23 Dec. 1815) is preserved in the British Museum (BM EA 74092), but this, as Colla, *Conflicted Antiquities*, 285, n. 37, points out, makes no specific mention of his rights in regard to antiquities.

110. For the story of the discovery, and the relationship between the Abd er-Rasul brothers and Mustafa Aga, see Maspero, *MMAF* 1, 511-788; cf. further the entry on Abd er-Rasul Ahmed Abd er-Rasul (p. 186).

Fig. 11. Mohammed Ahmed Abd er-Rasul (in white) posing with Gaston Maspero (reclining) and Emil Brugsch (holding palm-branch) in front of the royal cachette which he and his brothers had found in 1871 and partly plundered over a ten-year period. Engraving by J. H. E. Whitney of a photograph made by Edward L. Wilson, January 1882, some months after Mohammed had disclosed the location of the tomb and it had been officially cleared. Published as an illustration to Wilson's article 'Finding Pharaoh', *Century Magazine* 34, May 1887, 8.

tafa Aga in practice was untouchable due to his consular status. Two of the Abd er-Rasul brothers were arrested, Abd er-Rasul and Hussein, and the former – who tried in vain to invoke his patron's diplomatic status as protection during the proceedings – was imprisoned, interrogated and apparently beaten in the process, possibly even tortured. Mustafa Aga himself remained a free man throughout and continued his activities as before, almost unaffected by the whole affair.[111]

Consular status also conferred a number of other benefits, and this status, combined with considerable personal wealth, made many of them very powerful; Mustafa Aga, for example, is known to have avoided paying taxes for many years because of his consular status.[112] The overall situation in the 1870-1880s was summed up by Budge as follows:

111. He continued as British consular agent, although Belgium

revoked his consular status as a direct result of his involvement in the affair: Wilson, *Signs & Wonders Upon Pharaoh*, 226.
112. Cf. Capart (ed.), *Letters of Charles Edwin Wilbour*, 377.

Many natives in all parts of Egypt dealt openly in antiquities, and Mariette and his successor [as Director of the Antiquities Service], Maspero, bought from them antiquities for the Bulak Museum, and paid for them with Government money. Some natives had been astute enough to get themselves made Consuls or Agents for European Powers, and they excavated tombs, and bought and sold their contents without let or hindrance; and it was reported that some of these Consular Agents had expelled from their premises certain officials of the Service of Antiquities who attempted to control their business, and thus they were able to make the law as to the possession of and dealing in antiquities a dead letter.[113]

This status not only made it possible for consuls to arrange their own excavations (sometimes legally, at other times illegally) in order to acquire antiquities, but it also made them immune to most attempts by the Antiquities Service to restrict the trade. When Eugène Grébaut, the Director of the Antiquities Service, raided the Luxor dealers in 1888 (cf. p. 143), the consuls were in practice untouchable: 'the houses of the consuls were not entered, and they were permitted, for obvious reasons, to retain their goods in peace'.[114] There are indications that the protection offered by the office of consul, or by affiliation with somebody who held that office, was almost expected to have been acquired by major dealers. In a letter from 1881 Wilbour referred in passing to 'Abd-el-Megid, whose consular protector I do not yet know' (he was in fact the nephew of Mustafa Aga).[115] The office of consul often remained in the same family for generations, in practice being inherited although in principle each new consul-general (appointed by his nation) was free to appoint his own consuls or consular agents in Egypt. Generally Christians seem to have been preferred since the vast majority were

Copts (or in a few cases Armenians),[116] but Muslim consuls are also attested.

There were also a number of European consular agents. One of these was the miller Auguste Frénay who was French consular agent at Akhmim (fl. 1884-1897). Like his Egyptian peers, he too exploited his diplomatic immunity and became involved in the antiquities trade, particularly that which centered on the rich archaeological sites in the vicinity.[117] In reference to the sites that he considered for his fieldwork in 1886, Petrie notes in his archaeological memoirs:

> At Ekhmim there had been great expectations, two or three years before, of results from a large and undisturbed cemetery of all periods; but a French Consul was put there (without any subjects to represent), and he raided and stripped the place under Consular seal, which could not be interfered with.[118]

Being a consular agent was not the only way to be protected against prosecution by the Egyptian authorities – land or buildings could also be designated as sovereign territory, thus barring Egyptian officials from entering without express permission. Jan Herman Insinger, a Dutch citizen who lived at Luxor for nearly forty years, had built a large castle-like residence which was officially regarded as Dutch territory and therefore sported the Dutch flag.[119] The construction was already underway in 1888 when Grébaut carried out numerous raids against antiquities dealers all over Egypt, and Insinger's collection of antiquities was thus left intact. The largest dealer in Luxor at this time, apart from the consular agents, was Mohammed Mohasseb whose business was among those raided that year. A letter written some weeks later by Wilbour, a personal friend of Insinger, mentions that the

---

113. Budge, *By Nile and Tigris* I, III-112.
114. Bell, *A Winter on the Nile*, 242. Even so, a consular agent might still have reasons to hide and disperse his stores; cf. Rhind, *Thebes, its Tombs and their Tenants*, 248, who notes that the stores of Todros Bolos, the Prussian consular agent, were 'hidden away in all kinds of places and friends' houses'.
115. Cf. Capart (ed.), *Letters of Charles Edwin Wilbour*, 48.

116. Cf. Duff-Gordon, *Lady Duff-Gordon's Letters from Egypt*, 19.
117. Ryholt, in Ryholt and Barjamovic (eds.), *Libraries before Alexandria*, forthcoming.
118. Petrie, *Seventy Years in Archaeology*, 75.
119. Demarée, http://www.tawy.nl/insinger-house.html (accessed 28 Feb. 2013); cf. further Raven, *OMRO* 71 (1991), 18. The house is described in Baedeker, *Egypt and the Sudân*, 7th edition, 251, as a conspicuous 'castellated villa of a Dutch resident'.

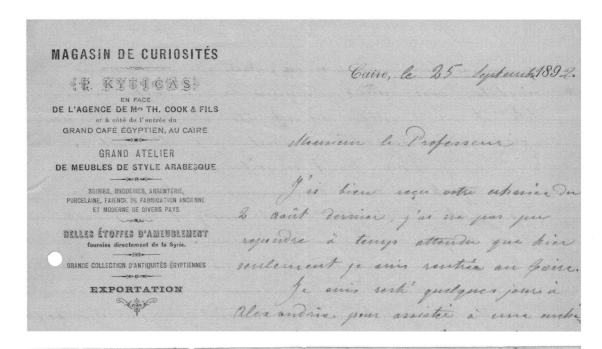

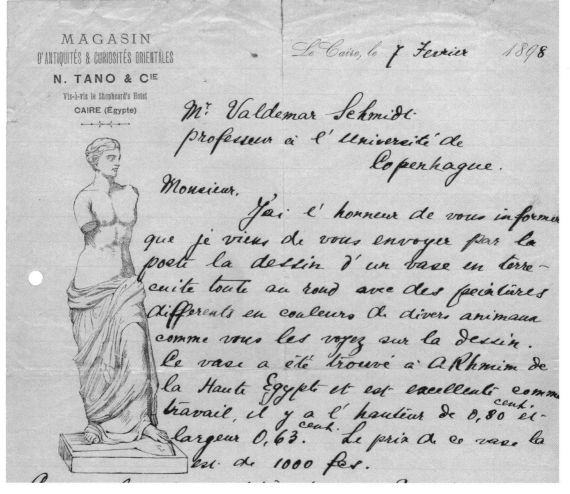

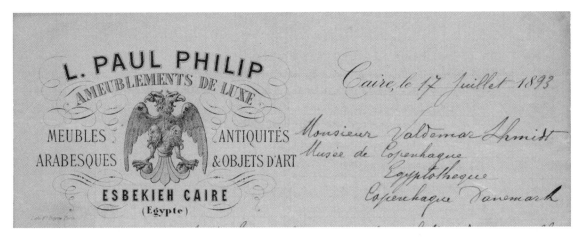

Fig. 12-14. Examples of letterheads of antiquities dealers in Cairo, from letters addressed to Valdemar Schmidt. Opposite page, top: Panayotis Kyticas (25 Sept. 1892). Opposite page, bottom: Nicolas Tano & Co. (8 Febr. 1898). Above: Paul Philip (17 July 1893). In contrast to the later letterheads reproduced in fig. 15-17, these do not include license numbers, which were only introduced with the antiquities law of 1912, and locations are indicated by relation to landmarks (Shepheard's Hotel, Thos. Cook, and Ezbekiya Gardens), rather than street names and numbers. All courtesy of Ny Carlsberg Glyptotek.

latter 'would be willing that M. Mohassib should use it [i.e. his residence] as an antiquarian shop, inviolable under the Dutch flag.'[120] His motive was not entirely 'altruistic'; he had for some years pursued the idea of having a Dutch consular agent installed at Luxor in order to facilitate the acquisition of antiquities, and he found Mohasseb a most fitting candidate.[121] (Incidentally, it may be noted that it was from the aforementioned Frénay that Insinger had purchased the famous papyrus, now named in his honour, that he sold on to the National Museum of Antiquities in Leiden for 4,000 francs in 1895.) The dealer Hussein at Edfu had similarly been hit by Grébaut and subsequently managed to obtain the protection of a Greek who enjoyed diplomatic immunity at Edfu. His identity is not clear, but Wilbour reports that he operated 'a new Greek rum-shop, provided with all the fluvial amenities, including four dancing girls' and that Hussein 'keeps antiquities there under the protection of the blue and white flag'.[122]

A final group consisted of those dealers whose main source of income was the trade in antiquities, but here too this rough categorization encompasses a wide range of possibilities. At the top end of the scale were Cairo dealers like Maurice Nahman and Jean Tano, the former of whom famously inhabited a veritable palace filled with antiquities, and at the bottom end more modest dealers who operated out of shops and stalls, especially in or near the great hotels with their lucrative crop of rich Western tourists (see p. 76) for a discussion of the locations of dealers in the main centres of trade, Cairo and Luxor). These dealers would invest in letterheads (Fig. 12-17), business cards (Fig. 18-21), and other means of advertising (Fig. 22-23, 120).

One of the advantages for customers dealing with such dealers was the flexible financial arrangements they offered, as well as their more European way of conducting business. Valdemar Schmidt, for example, preferred dealing with them because they did not necessarily demand immediate payment, but could offer long-term credit and would accept money transfers through banks. Well-established dealers like Philip, Dingli and Nahman were happy to send objects

120. Cf. Capart (ed.), *Letters of Charles Edwin Wilbour*, 463-464.
121. Raven, *OMRO* 71 (1991), 17-18.
122. Cf. Capart (ed.), *Letters of Charles Edwin Wilbour*, 511.

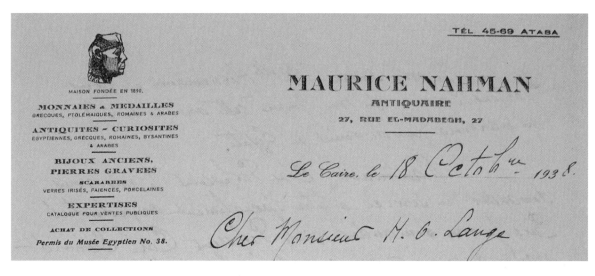

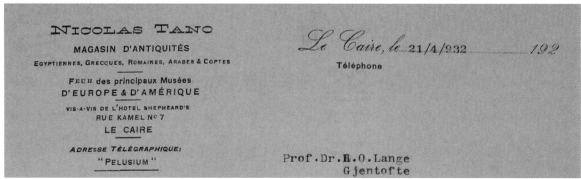

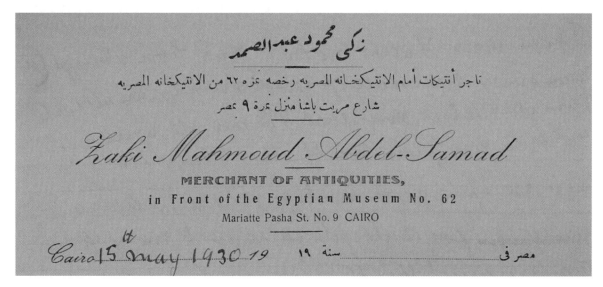

Fig. 15-17. Examples of letterheads of antiquities dealers in Cairo, from letters addressed to Lange. Top: Maurice Nahman (18 Oct. 1938). Middle: Nicolas Tano but used by his successor Phocion Jean Tano after his death (21 April 1932). Bottom: Zaki Mahmud Abd es-Samad (15 May 1930). It may be noted that the Arab dealer chose to include an Arabic version of his address and also gave it first priority, although this would not have been relevant to most of his customers. He was himself illiterate. All courtesy of the Royal Library.

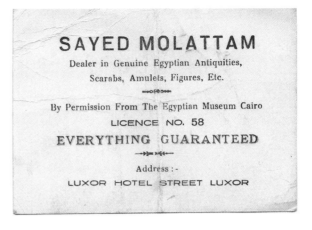

Fig. 18-21. Examples of business cards of antiquities dealers in Cairo and Luxor, circulated c. 1970. Top left: Hefnawy Ismaïl el-Shaer whose family received the first official license to deal antiquities from the Egyptian Museum. Bottom left: Christmas greeting card from *Hajji* Mohammed Abd er-Rahim el-Shaer, the nephew of Hefnawy. The family named is here misspelled 'el Caher' for el-Chaer. Top right: Sayed Molattam with license no. 58. Bottom right: the successors of Philip Elias Mitry, the previous proprietor of the Anglo-American Bookshop which also sold 'certified genuine antiques', with license no. 90. All courtesy of Rob Demarée.

abroad for inspection by potential buyers, and in certain cases had a return policy.[123]

Some of the more successful dealers had shops outside Egypt too, or would travel to Europe or America to trade; the Kalebdjian brothers also had a shop in Paris, for example, as did Dikran Kelekian and Mihran Sivadjian; and dealers like Dingli, Nahman and Tano would occasionally travel to Paris or London to trade. By Lange's second visit in 1929-1930 these professional dealers were accommodated by the legisla-

tion, and they operated under state-issued licenses.[124] Dealers licensed in this way would display their license numbers on the façades of their shops, and as part of their letterheads, but perhaps not surprisingly many retained close relations with colleagues operating under less legal circumstances, and some if not all had supply networks whose legal status was dubious.

---

123. Jørgensen, *How it all began*, 30.

124. For a list of the numbers we have come across, see Appendix 2. These range from no. 1 (Ismail Abdallah el-Shaer) to no. 127 (Hassani Abd el-Galil). All but two of the dealers with licenses that we have identified were based in Cairo.

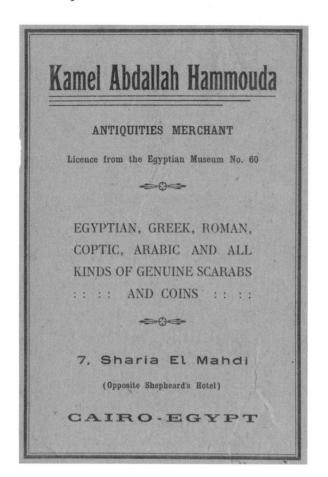
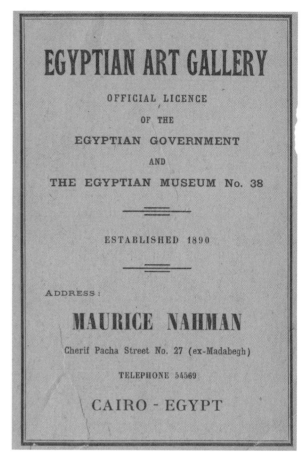

Fig. 22-23. Advertisements by Kamal Abdallah Hammouda and Maurice Nahman (with official license numbers 38 and 60), enclosed with the exhibition catalogue *Exposition d'art copte, Décembre 1944,* Société d'archéologie copte. Both dealers lent objects to the exhibition.

With the legislation of 1912 (cf. Appendix 1), which made it illegal and punishable by law to deal without an official permit, it becomes possible to quantify the legal market in terms of authorized dealers. Maspero reports that the Antiquities Service received 205 applications for licenses, which, then, indicates the number of dealers who at the time considered themselves sufficiently well-established to go through the procedure. Only 76 of those applications were initially approved, but subsequently about twenty more were approved upon re-application, so that by 15 November 1912 there were just under one hundred licensed dealers in Egypt.[125] It was a deliberate decision

at the time to limit licences to those cities that had significant numbers of tourists and to exclude those provincial sites that were most plagued by illegal activities:

> Il m'a paru, en effet, que, seuls, pouvaient être tolérés ceux qui resident dans les villes fréquentées par les tourists, le Caire, Alexandrie, Assiout, Louxor, Edfou, Assouân, et ainsi de suite; les autres sont ou des agents provocateurs au vol ou des receleurs qui ne méritent aucune indulgence. J'ai donc écarté impitoyablement des gens de Guizéh, de Médinét-el-Fayoum, de Béni-Souef, de Mellawi, de Sohag, de Bélianéh (...)[126]

125. Gouvernement égyptien, *Rapport du Service des antiquités pour*

l'année 1912, 18-21; idem, *Rapport ... pour l'année 1913,* 11-13.

126. Gouvernement égyptien, *Rapport du Service des antiquités pour*

It is unclear how many new licenses were granted in the following seventy years before the antiquities trade became prohibited in 1983 and the old licenses were annulled. We have not systematically collected license numbers (the information is hard to come by), but the four dealers with the highest license numbers that we have come across – license nos. 116, 117, 121, and 127 (cf. Appendix 2) – were active in the 1940s until the early 1980s. This may suggest that relatively few new license numbers were issued in the following decades. However, old licenses were not always cancelled by the death or retirement of their proprietors, but might be taken over by their heirs or business associates and thus remain in use. For instance, license no. 1 was taken over by the son of Ismaïl el-Shaer, no. 7 by the son of Joseph Khawam, and no. 116 by the sons of Farag el-Shaer. Although it is unclear how many license numbers went out of use over the years and how many were transferred, there seems to have been a slight decrease in the number of dealers over time. It seems unlikely that the number of active licensed dealers at any given point was much more than a hundred.

How the scale of the legal trade in antiquities compared to illegal trade is impossible to estimate; even if relevant statistical data were available (and it is not), it would depend on a number of problematic parameters: is the number of dealers important (and if so how does one define a 'dealer')? Or should one rather look at the number of traded objects? Or their value? In terms of volume and value, it seems fairly certain that – for the period after 1912 – the activities of licensed dealers represented the bulk of the trade. The number of unauthorized individuals involved in the antiquities trade was presumably higher, but they would typically have fewer resources available (financing for excavations, payment of agents who could scout for material, etc.). Moreover, they were not in a position to demand the same prices as licensed dealers, and there was a risk of both fines and

imprisonment involving hard labour if they were caught. Hence it was safer and, we suspect, more common for such dealers to sell their goods to licensed dealers who then sold the objects on to Westerners, although there would, of course, be exceptions.

Discussing dealers in the way we have done here, grouped according to a series of more or less arbitrary characteristics, may create an impression of a fairly homogeneous set of individuals within each group, but this would be misleading. There are several individuals who are not easily placed within these categories: Grégoire Loukianoff, for example, who in Lange's description 'more or less makes a living out of selling antiquities, but since he is poor he has no store and no shop' (p. 231).[127] He is thus not on the same level as the group of professional dealers with established (and licensed) shops described above, but neither is he comparable to most members of the group of local and semi-professional dealers. Similarly, Oxan Aslanian appears to have made his living primarily from selling antiquities (real and forged), and so may be described as a 'professional' dealer, but he operated out of various hotels rather than from a shop, and travelled widely in Egypt while buying objects directly from locals who had found or looted them, like many of the 'semi-professional' dealers of our second group (p. 200).

One individual, referred to simply as 'Uncle Hassan' (Fig. 24) and interviewed in Maguid Sameda's shop in the late 1950s, described himself as a wholeseller of antiquities. Like Aslanian and others, he did not own his own shop, but functioned as a middle man and supplied other dealers with stock acquired from sites all over Egypt. In the interview, he claims to have been in business for seven years, since the death of his father, and to have known all of Egyptian history by heart, 'better than university professors'.[128]

l'année 1912, 20. The report from the following year adds that further sites were excluded: Saqqara, Meidum, 'et plusieurs sites moins illustres de la Moyenne-Egypte'.

127. Lange, *Dagbog i Ægypten 1929-30*, 279; the entire passage is translated in on p. 173.
128. Clipping from unidentified newspaper, late 1950s, article entitled 'In Relation to the Case of the American Scholar who Stole Egypt's Antiquities' (translated from Arabic).

Fig. 24. 'Uncle Hassan', a self-proclaimed whole-seller of antiquities, photographed in Maguid Sameda's antiquities shop in Cairo. Newspaper clipping, late 1950s; source not located.

Another set of actors on the antiquities market that falls outside the groups outlined above are Western academics whose professional careers were as Egyptologists, archaeologists, or even missionaries. These were in fact key players, both as agents for their home institutions, such as Lange for the Glyptotek and the Danish National Museum, but also as collectors in their own right. The latter circumstance may seem odd today when few archaeologists would tolerate this practice – although it is not unknown even now – but it was the rule rather than the exception in Lange's time. Many such collections were built up around personal research agendas; several philolo-

gists had significant collections of ostraca, for example.[129]

Two prominent Egyptological figures in the antiquities trade were Howard Carter (Fig. 107) and Ludwig Borchardt (Fig. 122). Both used their Egyptological knowledge and experience to position themselves as key agents for Anglo-American and German collectors and museums, respectively. Borchardt, himself a man of independent means through marriage, would often receive a commission to buy at his discretion on behalf of various institutions and he was probably the leading agent for German collections in his time. By way of example, Lange reports that he on one occasion, July 1900, sent no less than 15 boxes of acquired antiquities to the Egyptian Museum in Berlin.[130] Carter, on the other hand, came from a relatively modest background and relied on this 'side business' to secure himself financially. As an agent, he would often negotiate the acquisition of specific objects with prospective buyers, but over the years, as he became comfortable financially and more experienced with the market, he would also build up a personal stock of objects.[131] Some of the deals resulted in quite substantial profits, his usual rate of commission being 15%, and his brokering of the famous gold treasure from the tomb of the three foreign wives of Tuthmosis III earned him no less than £8,000 (five times the yearly salary of the Director of the Antiquities Service).[132] On another occasion, he received a 20% commission (£E 200) on the acquisition of two papyri from Maurice Nahman on behalf of Edward Harkness.[133] Selling objects could be an integral part of the financing of archaeological excavations, and Carter once suggested to Lord Carnarvon that expenses 'might well be

129. Hagen, *JEA* 96 (2010), 71, n. 21; Reeves, in Goring, Reeves, and Ruffle (eds.), *FsAldred*, 242-250.
130. Lange and Lange, *Dagbog fra Ægyptensrejsen 1899-1900*, 753.
131. Reeves, in Goring, Reeves, and Ruffle (eds.), *FsAldred*, 242-250.
132. For a discussion, s.v. Mohammed Mohasseb Bey.
133. Howard Carter diaries 1922/23. Images and transcripts are available though the homepage of the Griffith Institute: http://www.griffith.ox.ac.uk/discoveringTut/journals-and-diaries/season-1/diary.html (accessed 12 Oct. 2015).

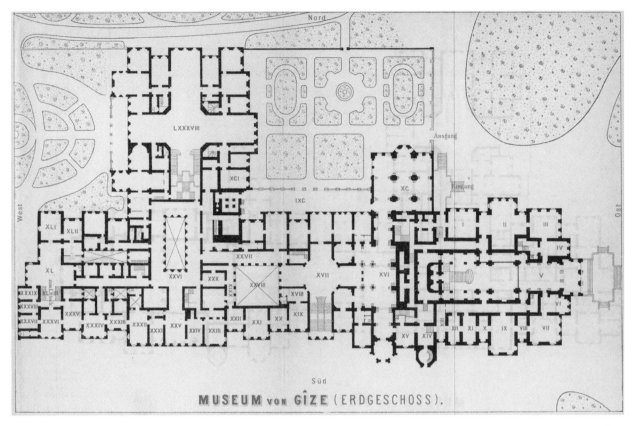

Fig. 25. Plan of the Gizeh Museum. Room XCI, facing the museum garden in its south-western corner, was set up as the official Sales Room (*salle de vente*) where the museum sold surplus antiquities. While the antiquities service had been selling antiquities for years, the idea for an official Sales Room was a direct result of the extensive raids on antiquities dealers by the director of the service, Eugène Grébaut, in early 1888. Baedeker, *Ägypten*, 4th edition, 1898.

defrayed by buying antiques in the bazaar in Cairo or elsewhere to sell them to collectors at a handsome profit'.[134]

Even Petrie, 'the father of Egyptian archaeology', was an active buyer, and in fact bought rather than excavated a surprisingly large proportion of his teaching collection (now in the Petrie Museum in London).[135] The extensive buying and selling in which Borchardt was involved will be discussed in detail in the chapter on the acquisition of papyri below, but

there is no reason to believe that he and Carter were unusual in their level of activity: the line between archaeologist and 'dealer' (or at least customer) was blurred, and it is difficult to envisage any archaeologist working in Egypt in this period not taking an active part in the antiquities trade. For many, in fact, visiting dealers was the first thing they did on arrival in Egypt at the start of a season. Howard Carter, for example, arriving in Cairo in October 1922, spent his first two days in Cairo doing business with Nahman, Tano, and Abemayor, and later visited other dealers, before heading south to Luxor to excavate in the Valley of the Kings (where he would discover the tomb of Tutankhamun that same season).[136] Similarly, Bernard

134. Reeves, *The Complete Tutankhamun*, 47.
135. See Stephen Quirke's forthcoming work on Petrie as a collector (in preparation); he estimates that Petrie bought rather than excavated about 35-45% of his collection (personal communication).

136. Cf. James, *Howard Carter*, 251. The full details of the

Fig. 26. The gardens of the Gizeh Museum. The Sales Room was located in the lower left-hand corner. Lange photograph, 1899. Courtesy of the Royal Library.

Bruyère started his excavation season by visiting local dealers in Luxor before starting work at Deir el-Medina, specifically to buy objects that he thought came from his own site.[137]

The ethnic or national identity of dealers is only occasionally apparent, either from their names or from descriptions in Lange's travel diaries. In purely numerical terms Egyptian dealers appear to account for the majority of individuals (but not necessarily in volume or turnover). In addition to Muslims (these are too numerous to list here, but cf. the list at the back of the book), there were several Copts, such as Todros Bolos and his son Mohareb Todros, as well as the Qena dealers, the brothers Girgis and Abd en-Nur Gabrial, and the Mansoor family. Bedouins were another group heavily involved in the antiquities trade;

Carter's diaries for the dates in question are now available through the homepage of the Griffith Institute: http://www.griffith.ox.ac.uk/discoveringTut/journals-and-diaries/season-1/diary.html (accessed 12 Oct. 2015).
137. Cf. the excavation diary of Bernard Bruyère, accessible online at http://www.ifao.egnet.net/bases/archives/bruyere (accessed 9 Nov. 2012), entry of 16 Feb. 1926.

in their case their particular legal status facilitated operating on the margins of the law (p. 99). The term 'Bedouin' was used quite loosely by most Western travellers, and does not necessarily correspond to local ethnic or juridical identity in a straightforward manner. Another major ethnic group were Jews, represented by such dealers as Joseph Cohen, the Abemayor family and Maurice Nahman (from Syria). Armenians were also well represented, and the Kalebdjian brothers, Dikran Kelekian, A. Pusgul and Oxan Aslanian were all relatively high-profile dealers at the time. European and other Western nationalities were represented by American (R.H. Blanchard), Belgian (Albert Eid), Cypriot (the Tano family), Dutch (Herman Insinger), French (Paul Philip), Greek (Alexandre Dingli), German (Wolfgang Dreiss), Russian (Grègoire Loukianoff, de Rustafjaell) and Swiss (André Bircher, Henri Dufour) dealers. Nationalities and ethnic backgrounds are not always readily identifiable, however; we have made no attempt to expand on this aspect in our work and have simply noted such information where it was preserved in our sources.

The trade in antiquities was dominated by men,

Fig. 27. Example of object sold through the Sales Room of the Egyptian Museum: the base and feet of a sculpture of king Mycerinus made from anorthosite gneiss. Acquired by the British Museum (EA 82331) from Bonhams in 2012. Intermediate owners unknown. Courtesy of the British Museum.

Fig. 28. Detail of object shown in fig. 27. When it was acquired in 2012 its original label from the Egyptian Museum, with inventory number and description, was still preserved intact. The price indicated in handwriting in the upper right corner of the label must have been added after the fragment was removed from the stores and deaccessioned for sale. Courtesy of the British Museum.

and only rarely do women appear as dealers, and then most often as anonymous discoverers of objects who sell them on to more established dealers, rather than as professional dealers in their own right. Information about such individuals is necessarily scarce, and few are known by name; a rare exception is Gindiya, who produced and sold modern copies of mudbricks stamped with the name of Ramesses III near Medinet Habu, and a woman called Sitt el-Amara from Amarna whom Wilbour met.[138] Interestingly, he noted that in his experience (writing in 1883), the antiquities trade at Amarna and Elephantine seemed 'entirely in the hands of the women; the men don't bother with it, except sometimes to see if the money is good'.[139] These details lends some credibility to the report that the famous Amarna cuneiform archive, discovered just a few years later, was found 'by a peasant woman when searching for antiquities' at the site.[140]

The antiquities service as dealer

The Antiquities Service itself also played a significant role in the antiquities trade. It collaborated with the self-established antiquities dealers by issuing licenses to sell or even to excavate, and by inspecting (or verifying) objects and providing export papers; it had also long functioned as a dealer itself. Collectors might approach the Director of the Antiquities Service or the Egyptian Museum concerning the acquisition of single items or the establishment of entire collections. By way of example, the Director of the Metropolitan Museum of Art, Gen. Luigi Palma di Cesnola, engaged the Director of the Antiquities Service, Gaston Maspero (Fig. 11; and, after his retirement, his successor Eugène Grébaut), in the creation of an Egyptian collection in 1886, originally offering $5,000 and later doubling this figure to $10,000.[141]

138. Capart (ed.), *Letters of Charles Edwin Wilbour*, 246, 285, 354.
139. Capart (ed.), *Letters of Charles Edwin Wilbour*, 246.
140. Bezold and Budge, *The Tell El-Amarna Tablets*, 1; cf. further Budge, *By Nile and Tigris* 1, 128-129; idem, *A History of Egypt* 4, 185.

The information provided by Budge is credited to an antiquities dealer whose name is discretely suppressed, possibly Mohammed Mohasseb from whom he is known to have acquired a substantial number of the tablets.
141. Anonymous, 'Relics from Egypt', *New York Times*, 18 Feb. 1887. The episode is also mentioned in one of the Wilbour letters; cf. Capart (ed.), *Letters of Charles Edwin Wilbour*, 349

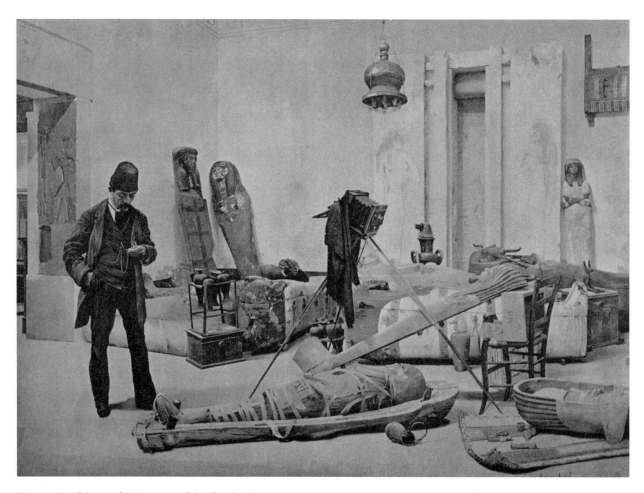

Fig. 29. Emil Brugsch, Director of the Gizeh Museum, photographing mummies and other funerary equipment from the cache of royal mummies that had been cleared in 1881. He was an excellent photographer and is here shown carefully timing the exposure of a close-up shot of the face of a sarcophagus. Engraving of painting by Marius Michel, c. 1890. Clipping from *World's Best Art,* 1894.

This was the equivalent of about £2,000. The project was soon completed and the new Egyptian exhibition opened at the Metropolitan Museum of Art in November 1888.[142] Emil Brugsch (Fig. 11, 29), the Director at the Egyptian Museum, similarly put together a collection for Col. Anthony J. Drexel in 1895 for the

sum of $3,000 (c. £600); this was destined for the Drexel Institute of Art, Science and Industry.[143] Earlier, in 1881 he had also helped Crown Prince Rudolph of Austria establish a large collection (cf. below); while in 1883/84 he had assembled a smaller collection of 399 objects for the Jaipur Museum in India.[144] In the 1880s, he had further secured several coffins and a mummy for the Glyptotek in Copenhagen.[145]

(where the editor misidentifies Cesnola). According to Wilbour, Cesnola had originally contacted one of the curators of the Egyptian Museum, Emil Brugsch, but Wilbour advised him rather to deal with Gaston Maspero. See also David, *Lettres d'Égypte*, 177, 216, 234, and del Vesco, *EDAL* 4 (2013/2014), 247-248.

142. Anonymous, 'Notes', *The Connoisseur* 3 (1888), 47.

143. Benson Harer, in D'Auria (ed.), *Fs Fazzini*, 111-119.

144. Bresciani and Betrò, *Egypt in India,* 67-68, 101-243.

145. Jørgensen, *How it all began*, 17-22, fig. 1-4.

An illustration of the importance of this trade to the operation of the Egyptian Antiquities Service is provided by a letter from its Director, Maspero, to his wife in 1886. In reference to the above-mentioned sale to Cesnola, he remarks that 'je ne sais comment je me serais tiré d'affaire sans les ventes d'objets et de momies'.[146]

Just two years later a formal decision was made to establish a Sales Room (*Salle de vente*) at the Egyptian Museum in order to dispose of surplus material. Its creation seems to have been instituted as a direct result of the extensive raids on antiquities dealers and seizures of their goods by Eugène Grébaut, the Director of the Antiquities Service, which began on New Year's Day in 1888 (p. 143). His raids were regarded as excessive and made him widely unpopular. Within a short time a committee was established to keep him in check, and in April Grébaut informed Wilbour that he had been 'ordered to set up an anteekeh sales room in the Museum'.[147]

A year later, the Egyptian Museum moved to the Khedival harem palace of Ismaïl at Giza and the *Salle de vente* was set up in Room XCI facing the Museum Garden (Fig. 25-28).[148] It is briefly described in the Baedeker guide from 1895:

In Room XCI, beside the exit from the museum, the visitor may purchase antiques, the authenticity of which is vouched for by the museum-authorities. A permit to export is given with each purchase...[149]

Valdemar Schmidt visited *Salle de vente* in February 1892, when he was in Cairo to acquire antiquities on behalf of Jacobsen, but was disappointed and reported back:

Concerning the museum, there is a *Salle de ventes*, but the prices are high and everything is *très inférieure*, intended for tourists. Everything is genuine, that's the only virtue. Larger objects are not sold, but traded.[150]

In 1902, after twelve years, the Egyptian Museum relocated again and was moved to a custom-built building on the north side of Tahrir Square. The new *Salle de vente* was located in the eastern pavilion, just to the right of the entrance, while the western pavilion housed the library (Fig. 78). Here the *Salle de vente* remained until it was shut down, perhaps in the 1950s or 60s.[151] The Greco-Roman Museum in Alexandria, which was founded in 1892, also had an official *Salle de vente*; again it remains uncertain exactly when it closed down, but presumably around the same time as the one in Cairo.[152]

According to various editions of the Baedeker guide, the antiquities sold at the Museum were, at this point in time, cheaper than those sold by the established antiquities dealers.[153] The museum sold nearly all categories of antiquities; papyri, scarabs, ushabtis, coins, bronze figures, mummies, coffins, larger sculptures – even entire tombs could be acquired by museums by special arrangement.[154] An example of the prices is provided by Robert Hubbard who visited the *Salle de vente* in 1894.[155] He reports a mummy and case

146. David, *Lettres d'Égypte*, 234.
147. Cf. Capart (ed.), *Letters of Charles Edwin Wilbour*, 466.
148. A photograph of the façade of the *Salle de vente* from 1898 may be found in Piacentini (ed.), *Egypt and the Pharaohs*, 31.
149. Baedeker, *Lower Egypt*, 3rd edition, 100, cf. also p. 87. The guarantee of authenticity presumably did not stop altogether forgeries from being sold; some objects in the shop had been impounded from dealers and may well have included undetected forgeries. The museum also knowingly 'embellished' objects in some cases, including an Early Dynastic jar which was painted (by Museum staff) with New Kingdom-style decoration and then sold; cf. Fiechter, *Faux et faussaires en art égyptien*, 187-188, and Hardwick, *IA* 3 (2011), 37.

150. Letter from V. Schmidt to C. Jacobsen, dated 24 Feb. 1892 (Ny Carlsberg Glyptotek).
151. Piacentini, *EDAL* 4 (2013/2014), 116-117, lists the year of closure as 1979. While this may be formally correct, a number of colleagues who worked in Egypt and at the museum during the 1970s are adamant that there was no actual shop there at this stage.
152. David, *Gaston Maspero*, 232.
153. E.g. Baedeker, *Egypt and the Sûdân*, 7th edition, 41; idem, *Egypt and the Sudân*, 8th edition, 39.
154. Also unpublished excavated papyri might be removed for sale at *Salle de vente*; e.g. Cairo Museum, Temporary Register, 11/11/30/1 (fragments from Oxyrhynchus).
155. Zimmer, *Curiosities of Central New York*, 55-66.

could be had for £20 or £30 and that scarabs were sold at a price of 5-20 pence a piece. He himself acquired a well-preserved sarcophagus with a mummy for £20 (now in the Cazenovia Public Library, NY). The low prices also seem to be borne out by the official revenue figures. Over a 12-year period, from 1899 to 1910, the *Salle de vente* generated £15,866 – a yearly average of about £1,320.[156] By comparison £1,250 is the price Lange agreed to pay the dealer Girgis for a single bronze (although in 1930) and it must have been a fraction of the sum dealers such as Maurice Nahman or Mohammed Mohasseb would have made in a year. It may also be noted that during the same 12-year period the museum earned about £62,000 on tourist passes and another £10,000 on museum tickets.

Nonetheless, the extra income from the sale of antiquities was sorely needed for the excavation, protection and preservation of sites. The museum was also in need of a good research library, and in 1900 it was decided to allocate £300 of the income generated from the sale of antiquities and tickets for this purpose.[157] As a result, excavations were instituted with the express purpose of gathering objects that might be sold, and the report of the Antiquities Department for 1901 shows that Georges Daressy spent three weeks digging for bronzes at Sais (unsuccessfully), and that the *reïs* Rubi dug for amulets at Saqqara (successfully).[158] A few years later, in 1905, Legrain happily reported to Maspero that he had discovered a great number of 'adorables statuettes de pierre et d'excellents bronzes' at Karnak and that he might be able to provide as many as 500 for the *Salle de vente*.[159] Over the 12-year period from 1899 to 1912, the activity was

expanded and we see a five-fold increase in earnings from the sale of antiquities from the years 1899 and 1900 (with yearly revenues of c. £400) to 1909 and 1910 (at c. £2,100). The increasing activity is also reflected in the report of the Antiquities Department for 1910 where several local inspectors are said to have been sent out to dig for objects that might be sold; Tewfik *Effendi* Bolos at Minya and Assiut, Elias *Effendi* Ghirghis at Sohag, Hassan *Effendi* Hosni at Giza, Mohammed *Effendi* Châban at Mansoura, and Antoun *Effendi* Youssef at Gharbia.[160] In addition to the objects excavated by the Antiquities Service, further material for sale was provided by licensed excavations by Egyptologists and antiquities dealers, illegally traded items seized from dealers and tourists, as well as items seized by the *ghaffirs* who inspected construction projects (such as the excavation of canals or building of railways) and *sebakh* digging. The latter activity, aimed specifically at ancient ruins, was particularly profitable and the report for 1910 mentions that the *Salle de vente* had been filled with several thousand objects secured by careful supervision of *sebakh* digging.[161]

The inspectors involved in acquiring objects for the *Salle de vente* were of the second class and, by way of comparison, the average yearly income of £1,320 from the *Salle de vente* was more than ten times an inspector's yearly salary (cf. Appendix 4). Revenue figures are also available for the period spanning 1911 to 1916/17 where the yearly average was just slightly higher at £1,380. This average obscures a sharp decrease in revenues after the outbreak of the First World War when far fewer tourists visited Egypt and the yearly earnings drop from about £2,000 to just a little over £300.

156. Gouvernement Égyptien, *Rapport sur la marche du Service des antiquités de 1899 à 1910*, xiv.
157. *Ibid.*, 24, 45.
158. *Ibid.*, 39, 40.
159. Jambon, *BIFAO* 109 (2009), 274.
160. Gouvernement Égyptien, *Rapport sur la marche du Service des antiquités de 1899 à 1910*, 319.
161. *Ibid.*, 321.

Year	Income	Year	Income
1899	£E 387	1909	£E 2,117
1900	£E 403	1910	£E 2,101
1901	£E 913	1911	£E 2,503
1902	£E 917	1912	£E 1,774
1903	£E 1,051	1913	£E 1,956
1904	£E 2,476	1914 Jan-Mar	£E 1,500
1905	£E 1,258	1914/1915	£E 610
1906	£E 1,486	1915/1916	£E 306
1907	£E 1,065	1916/1917	£E 319
1908	£E 1,692		

Table 1. Income generated by the *Salle de vente* from 1899 to 1916/1917.[162]

The official figures given above do not give a comprehensive picture of the scale of the trade carried out by the Antiquities Service. Monumental acquisitions, particularly by institutions, are not included, so that, for example, the records do not include the many Old Kingdom chapels bought by western museums during this period (cf. n. 167 below). Acquisitions of larger groups of objects also seem to be excluded; the sale of a number of objects to D. G. Lyon on behalf of the Harvard Semitic Museum in 1902 came to a total of £E 15,990, more than sixteen times the annual income of the *Salle de Vente* that year.[163]

It is interesting to note that in 1912, when the museum sales were at their height, Arthur Weigall, the Chief Inspector of Antiquities for Upper Egypt, submitted a proposal to the authorities stating that museum profits might be significantly increased by broadening the range and quality of antiquities offered for sale in stronger competition with the antiquities dealers.[164] It begins:

> The dealers in Egypt at present make enormous profits each year by the sale of antiquities. From the Sale-Room of the Cairo Museum, however, very small profits are made, owing to the fact that only worthless objects are there to be obtained. The dealers are thus without competition, and all persons who are engaged in buying antiquities for foreign museums or collections go always to them, and never come to us, ... I propose that the sale of the antiquities by the Cairo Museum should be vastly extended, and that the work should be put on business lines.

The plan came to nothing. It involved much stricter control of the division of finds in favour of the Museum and therefore failed to find support among archaeologists working in Egypt, and Weigall also did not have the support of Gaston Maspero, the Director of the Antiquities Service, of whom he was openly critical.

Large-scale monuments were not sold through the *Salle de vente* (and hence the income does not figure in those accounts), but could be acquired by special arrangement. An interesting example is provided by the acquisition of the mastaba of Kaemrehu by the Glyptotek. Jacobsen, the industrialist, above all desired great monuments or, as he put it, *grand monuments*. Schmidt explains the situation to Lange in a letter from 1900 written just after the latter had successfully acquired a well-preserved Ramesside statue of a man and a woman (p. 137).

> He [i.e. Jacobsen] told me to say that what he would particularly like, if possible, is to acquire larger objects or one large object (which should not be too badly preserved or damaged). What you might call *grand monuments*, such as can be found in the Great Hall in the

162. Gouvernement Égyptien, *Rapport sur la marche du Service des antiquités de 1899 à 1910*, xiv; idem, *Rapport du Service des antiquités pour l'année 1911*, 26; idem, *Rapport ... l'année 1912*, 42; idem, *Rapport ... l'année 1913*, 40; idem, *Rapport ... l'année 1914 et 1915*, 59, 62; idem, *Rapport ... l'année 1916*, 9.
163. Letter from G. Maspero to D. G. Lyons, dated 30 Sept. 1902 (Harvard Semitic Museum).

164. Hankey, *A Passion for Egypt*, 181-187.

Louvre, and in the Great Hall in the British Museum. It is naturally not easy to find, and expensive, but it might be possible and he would very much like such objects. Lesser objects he cares less for. Larger objects provide a backdrop for the lesser ones.[165]

One of the larger items that he managed to secure was the main part of the mastaba of Kaemrehu which arrived in Copenhagen in 1911 through the efforts of Valdemar Schmidt. This was sold directly through the Antiquities Service, and a letter from the preceding year gives an example of how a suitable monument might be chosen and acquired:

> Borchardt says to say hello to you, as does Quibell whom I have been with for 3 days. He lives in the desert between the Step Pyramid and Abusir in a newly built inspectors' residence and has made some important finds … I will not make the planned detour to Upper Egypt this year. I have spent 3 days with Quibell in Saqqara to look at mastabas which he has cleared of sand for me to choose from.[166]

In other words, at the prospect of a deal involving a substantial sum of money several mastaba tombs were cleared of sand with the explicit purpose of presenting them to the agent of the prospective buyer.[167]

Schmidt made his choice and the reliefs in the tomb were cut out and brought to the Egyptian Museum. There the Museum decided to keep some scenes which were not considered to be well-represented in its own collection, and the rest of the reliefs were shipped off to Copenhagen.[168]

Although objects sold at the Museum came with a guarantee of authenticity, fakes were occasionally sold; some of these can be linked directly to the notorious Emil Brugsch (brother of the Egyptologist Heinrich Brugsch) who was the Director at the Museum and in charge of the *Salle de vente* (Fig. 11, 29).[169] Lange was none too impressed with him and his description seems worth citing as it provides an impression of this highly influential individual who for many years was in charge of running the Egyptian Museum, including the supervision of divisions of finds and the sale of surplus objects:

> Emil (with emphasis on the E) Brugsch is, in several respects, a rather mysterious person. He is the brother of the deceased, famous Egyptologist Heinrich Brugsch, and was born in Berlin. He must be fifty-odd years old now. Through his brother's influence with Mariette, he came down here to the newly founded Museum in Bulaq. His past was no recommendation; he had wandered about in America and had led an adventurous existence, among other things as the manager of a tavern with female singers, but he had learnt to make photographs, which was the only card on his hand [sc. only relevant skill] when he arrived at the Museum. This type of character flourished down here in Ismaïl Pasha's time. He was married to a rather questionable figure who ended up running away from him a few years ago. But now he is a permanent fixture at

165. Letter from V. Schmidt to H. O. Lange, dated 8 Mar. 1900 (Royal Library, Copenhagen).

166. Letter from V. Schmidt to H. O. Lange, dated 16 Apr. 1910 (Royal Library, Copenhagen).

167. On the practice of buying entire mastabas, see Griffith, *Egypt Exploration Fund, Archaeological Report 1908-09*, 12: 'A scheme has been approved for the sale of entire mastabas from Sakkareh to the museums of Europe and America. It is hoped that when such can be obtained at a moderate figure the directors of museums will be less eager to buy odd blocks and fragments broken out by robbers, and that so the robbers will give up their detestable trade.' In addition to the Glyptotek, museums which also bought Old Kingdom mastabas include the Louvre in Paris (Akhethotep, acquired in 1902/1903), Leiden Museum (Hetepherakhet, 1902), the British Museum in London (Werirenptah, 1904), the University Museum of Philadelphia (Kaipure, 1904), the Museum of Fine Arts in Boston (Sekhemankhptah and Kaiemnofret, 1904), the Musées Royaux d'Art et d'Histoire in Brussels (Neferirtenef, 1906), the Field Museum of Chicago (Unasankh and Netjeruser, 1908), and the Metropolitan Museum of Art in

New York (Perneb, 1913). The acquisition process and correspondence related to the mastaba bought by the MRAH in Brussels is discussed in detail by Bruffaerts, *BMRAH* 76 (2005), 5-36; for the American acquisitions, see Brovarski, in Thomas (ed.), *The American Discovery of Ancient Egypt*, 34-35.

168. Ny Carlsberg Glyptotek, ÆIN 1271: Jørgensen, *How it all began*, 91-98; idem, *Egypt I*, 64-79.

169. Fiechter, *Egyptian Fakes*, 84-85. The image of Brugsch here reproduced in fig. 29 has recently been discussed by Riggs, *Museum Worlds* 1 (2013), 72-74; cf. also Bickerstaffe, *KMT* 26.1 (2015), 18-25.

the museum and second in command according to his seniority and has received the title of Bey, but he is of little use and is rather ignorant.[170]

It may be added that Crown Prince Rudolph of Austria described how Brugsch (who frequently offered to accompany wealthy visitors and notables during their visits to Egypt) assisted him in buying antiquities at Abydos which he knew to be illegally excavated.[171] Brugsch also accompanied him on visits to the consular agents Mustafa Aga and Mohareb Todros, who had large collections of antiquities for sale, and helped him buy 'several valuable articles' from the latter.[172] Clearly he did not see a conflict of interest between his museum post and his role as adviser to buyers of antiquities.

In addition to selling objects, the Egyptian Museum itself also acquired numerous objects from dealers. Detailed information is not readily available in published form, but partial records exist for the six years from 1885 through 1890.[173] These allow us to gain an impression of who were the more important dealers at this time. It must be emphasized that the information is distorted by the fact that most objects bought by the museum are simply recorded as 'achat' without the name of the dealers in question. The figures represent the number of items acquired the year in question.

Dealer	Year and no. of objects
Abd es-Salam	1887 (2), 1888 (1)
Dingli (Alexandre Dingli)	1887 (18), 1888 (16)
Duttil (E. D. J. Dutilh)	1888 (5), 1889 (1)
Farag (Farag Ismaïn)	1885 (30), 1886 (15), 1887 (56), 1889 (1), 1890 (11)
Hamed Ismaïl	1887 (1)
Iconomopoulos	1890 (6)
Jovanovich	1885 (1)
Macri (Pietro Makri)	1885 (1)
Mohammed Ali	1887 (16), 4 (1888)
Mohammed Dakhakhni	1887 (3)
Murad (Ali Murad)	1887 (3)
Philip (Paul Philip)	1887 (5), 1888 (1)
Saïd (Saïd Ismaïn)	1885 (2), 1888 (14)
Soliman (Soliman Abd es-Samad)	1885 (1), 1887 (9), 1888 (2)
Tano (Marius Tano)	1885 (9), 1886 (1), 1887 (2)
Zissiadis	1889 (14)

Table 2. Dealers selling objects to the Egyptian Museum 1885-1890.

During these six years, the largest number of objects from dealers identified by name were acquired from Farag Ismaïn (113 objects), followed by Dingli (34), Mohammed Ali (20), Saïd Ismaïn (16), Zissiadis (14), Soliman Abd es-Samad (12), and Tano (12). Most of the objects in question were, in other words, acquired from dealers based in Kafr el-Haram (sc. Farag Ismaïn, Mohammed Ali, Saïd Ismaïn, and Soliman Abd es-Samad).

The Antiquities Service had inspectors who oversaw, at least in principle, all archaeological excavations in Egypt, but they could apparently also be em-

170. Lange and Lange, *Dagbog fra Ægyptensrejsen 1899-1900*, 221-222. Note that the word 'adventurous' has a distinctively negative connotation in the present context. Lange's description may be compared to the equally negative assessment of Emil Brugsch in autobiography of Erman, *Mein Werden und mein Wirken*, 213-215.

171. Rudolph, *Travels in the East*, 116.

172. *Ibid.*, 125, 130.

173. For the years 1886-1890, see Anonymous, *BIE*, 2nd ser., 7 (1887), i-xxix; 8 (1888), i-xlv ; 9 (1889), i-xli; 10 (1890), i-xxxvii; 3rd ser. 1 (1891), 225-232. Information about year 1885 (including a single entry of 27 Dec. 1884) has been gathered directly from the *Journal d'entrée* of the Cairo Museum: Farag (JE 26423-68424, 26430-26438, 27017-27035); Jovanovich (26415); Saïd (26870-26871); Soliman (26425), Tano (26427, 26719-26720, 26864-26869). In the register the source of the objects was rarely noted before 1885.

ployed, under contract, to conduct excavations on behalf of private individuals. One such example is Sayed Khashaba *Pasha* who was a prominent Egyptian merchant and collector/dealer from Assiut; for several years before the Second World War he had employed Ahmed *Bey* Kamal (then assistant curator at the Egyptian Museum) to excavate various sites in Middle Egypt on his behalf.[74] The price for such work, as recorded by de Morgan – who apparently instigated the practice – in a letter from 1894, was five Egyptian pounds per day:

> J'ai inauguré un système de fouilles qui nous rend de grands services. J'autorise les amateurs à fouiller euxmêmes sous la surveillance d'un de mes employés payé aux frais du fouilleur à raison de 5£ par jour. Tous les objets sont apportés à Gizeh aux frais du fouilleur et partagés. Je ne me montre pas très difficile dans le partage et avec les amateurs je le suis bien moins qu'avec les marchants, bien entendu.[175]

Buying antiquities

Buying antiquities was an integral part of a holiday in Egypt for many tourists, to the extent that already in 1833 one visitor drily remarked that 'a traveller from Egypt cannot decently show his face in Europe without a mummy in one hand and a crocodile in the other'.[176] Guidebooks took account of this, and one of the most popular during Lange's visits to Egypt was Karl Baedeker's *Ägypten und der Sudan: Handbuch für Reisende* (Lange too had a copy). The 1928 edition of the book listed several dealers by location. In Cairo only three dealers warranted a mention, namely Maurice Nahman (27 Sharia el-Madabegh), Nicolas Tano and R. H. Blanchard (both on Sharia Kamel), in addition to the Sale Room (*Salle de vente*) of the Egyptian Museum where surplus antiquities were sold off. For Luxor the guidebook listed a total of seven dealers:

Mohareb Todros (between Luxor temple and the Nile), Mohammed Mohasseb, Hussein Abd el-Megid, Mansur Mahmud and Girgis Gabrial (all on Sharia el-Lukanda), as well as Yussuf Hassan (on Sharia el-Markaz) and Kamal Khalid (in the Winter Palace Hotel). Of these at least three are mentioned by Lange (Mohareb Todros, Abd el-Megid, and Girgis Gubrian who is identical with Girgis Gabrial), but he may well have visited others without naming them, especially if he did not buy anything. The guidebook also mentioned a single dealer in Aswan by the name Mischriky Girgis who apparently could be found in 'die deutsche Sûdân-Pionier-Mission'.[177]

Lange's introduction to the antiquities market in Cairo was facilitated not only by his German colleagues whom he accompanied on his first visits to dealers, but also by his old professor from Copenhagen, Valdemar Schmidt, who by then had a reputation in the trade. Schmidt had been to Cairo several times and had there spent significant amounts of money on objects for the Glyptotek; he returned with his niece in early November 1899 to buy more. Lange went with him on several occasions, and by accompanying Schmidt he got to know the dealers himself. He was presented to them as the person who would be buying on Schmidt's behalf once the latter had returned to Denmark, and while this was a great way to get to know the people and the trade, he suspected – quite rightly – that this would lead to an endless stream of dealers pestering him to buy from them.[178] Just two weeks later he remarks that 'it is curious, but

---

174. Kamal, *ASAE* 13 (1914), 161-178; idem, *ASAE* 16 (1916), 65-114.

175. Cited by Piacentini, *EDAL* 4 (2013/2014), 114.

176. de Géramb, *A pilgrimage to Palestine* 2, 384; cited by Schmidt, *Westcar on the Nile*, 199.

177. Baedeker, *Ägypten und der Sudan*, 8th edition, 38, 260, 368.

178. Lange and Lange, *Dagbog fra Ægyptensrejsen 1899-1900*, 131, 'In the evening Valdemar Schmidt was visited by a Bedouin and his son from the village by the pyramids who wanted to speak to him and sell antiquities. Some years ago he was down here with a lot of money and bought on behalf of [Carl] Jacobsen, and word spread immediately that he was back again, and both at home and on the street he is often sought out by Arab dealers'; *ibid.*, 141-142, 'Through him [i.e. Schmidt] I have become involved with all of these [dealers], and Schmidt promises them that he will write to me about what he wants to buy. The consequence will naturally be that I will be overrun by them, but when dealing with these Arabs one has to take it easy, and certainly not rush things'.

I can now hardly open my front door without bump-ing into my new Arab acquaintances'.[179] In December the same year he complains that he has not yet heard from either Schmidt or from the Director of the Na-tional Museum, and that he therefore has his hands full 'dealing with the Bedouins who are constantly knocking on my door asking if there has yet been word from Schmidt'.[180]

Despite his growing experience with dealers, and – as reported by himself – a reputation for being able to spot fakes, he was occasionally the victim of scams. He recalls one such occasion during his 1899-1900 visit, when he was on the train to Aswan. It made a brief stop at Luxor, and he was waiting for the train to depart again:

> I carried out a minor transaction with a small man, but the ass tried to swindle me. We had agreed on the price for a small object - a single piaster, - I gave him the coin, but instead of handing me the object he ran off with the money, exactly at the same time that the train was leaving.[181]

A railway porter ran after the hustler and eventually managed to retrieve the money for Lange, who then continued on his journey southwards (for other scams, involving fakes, see p. 56 and p. 152).

Initial contact with antiquities dealers could be es-tablished either by visits to their shops, by chance meetings on the street, or, more rarely, by unan-nounced visits, both at the Pension König during the first visit, and at Cecil House during the second.[182] Some shops were well-known and rather ostentatious in terms of architectural style - Maurice Nahman's shop was famously like 'a palace' - while others were more low-profile affairs. The latter could be hidden away in the labyrinth of Cairo backstreets and some-times required the use of guides who brought custom-ers there under cover of darkness. The clandestine at-

mosphere is evoked by Jonna Lange's descriptions of a visit to the shop of Soliman Abd es-Samad in 1900:

> ... we all got dressed and followed them to their house, which was situated in the side street of a side street of an Arabic street. It was strange to walk through these narrow streets, illuminated only by a single oil lamp in a stall or a coffee shop. The young one, Muhammed, had run ahead and came to greet us when the door to the house was opened with a candle. Through a kind of entry area we entered the room where the objects were; there were probably some magnificent objects, but one cannot reveal any particular interest. It was rather fun watching Professor Schmidt and Hans, each with their own candle, crawling around the floor to get at the in-scriptions, and Soliman and Muhammed standing by with ears straining to try and understand what was being said. They are real rascals these Arabs; all of the-se treasures they have stolen from tombs during the night, from who knows where; and if only one could extract the information from them it could be of the highest importance.[183] Their entire business is quite il-legal, of course, and they are very careful about who they allow to see their objects.[184]

A degree of secrecy was no doubt necessary for unli-censed dealers like these - as Jonna remarks, 'their entire business is quite illegal' - but it was frequently exaggerated as part of a strategy to increase the sale price of objects and to put pressure on the buyer to strike a deal, rather than just a way of avoiding atten-tion from the authorities.[185] Hans and Jonna Lange had similar encounters during their second visit in 1929-1930, when some dealers were even more clan-

179. Lange and Lange, *Dagbog fra Ægyptensrejsen 1899-1900*, 136.
180. Lange and Lange, *Dagbog fra Ægyptensrejsen 1899-1900*, 207.
181. Lange and Lange, *Dagbog fra Ægyptensrejsen 1899-1900*, 295.
182. E.g. Lange and Lange, *Dagbog fra Ægyptensrejsen 1899-1900*, 30; Lange, *Dagbog fra Ægypten, 1929-1930*, 95.

183. Jonna's emphasis on archaeological context is interesting but not surprising; the awareness of the importance of provenance is not a modern phenomenon, and the loss of this knowledge was seen as one of the most serious problems of the antiquities trade even at this early stage. Compare the obituary of the famous antiquities dealer Maurice Nahman, where the Egyptologist Jean Capart remarked that 'Si Maurice Nahman avait eu la preoccupation de tenir un journal, les égyptologues y auraient appris bien des secrets qui leur restent fermés'; *CdE* 22 (1947), 300.
184. Lange and Lange, *Dagbog fra Ægyptensrejsen 1899-1900*, 131-132.
185. On this strategy see the insightful comments by Rhind, *Thebes, Its Tombs and their Tenants*, 249.

destine in their operations, partly as a result of new and more stringent legislation (p. 137):

> It was funny seeing how secretive the two men [i.e. the dealers] behaved. Nobody was allowed to see or hear what was going on; we were in a room round the back of the shop, and I was told not to let anyone on the street see the object, and it was thoroughly wrapped up in paper.[186]

Entry into Cairo city from the West bank of the Nile, where one of the centres for the illicit trade in antiquities was located (at the village Kafr el-Haram in Giza), was controlled by the authorities. On one occasion Lange and his wife picked up some stone objects (stelae or reliefs) which they had bought from the Giza dealer Farag Ismaïn, and they had to disguise them and drive them to Borchardt's place for storage until they could be sent home to Copenhagen:

> At 3pm we took a cab and drove out to Giza to pick up some stones which Hans had bought from Farag some time ago. It was a nice trip ... At Farag's place we were naturally offered coffee, and after the stones had been carefully wrapped in paper they were placed in the carriage and covered with Hans' havelock which had been brought along for this purpose. Because it is illegal to transport the stones and we would have to pass a tolling station at the English bridge, we drove instead to Borchardt's where they will be stored.[187]

Lange and Borchardt were good friends by this stage, so to store the objects at the latter's place was an obvious solution to the problem; in fact their friendship lasted for the rest of their lives, and Borchardt even talked of transferring his institute (now the Swiss Archaeological Institute in Cairo) into Danish hands – one of several possibilites – in the years leading up to the Second World War.[188] Crossing the bridge could

be problematic, and several contemporaries mention taking precautions; having presented a box of illicit antiquities to the authorities (in the vain hope that it would be sealed for export without being inspected), the dealer Chauncey Murch actually asked to be accompanied by a man from the Museum 'to see that I would have no difficulty in getting back across the bridge with it [i.e. the antiquity]'.[189] After the introduction of the Antiquities law of 1912 (see p. 137), it was illegal for a dealer to travel with an antiquity anywhere within the borders of Egypt without an explicit written authorisation from the Antiquities Service.[190]

Not all dealers were immediately accessible, especially to European visitors, and Lange described how on one occasion his friend and dealer (and trained Egyptologist) Grégoire Loukianoff, had introduced him to various Arab dealers who did not usually trade directly with Europeans:

> Tuesday 4 March. This morning, when we were heading off for the Museum, we met Loukianoff, who said that he was free until 1pm today to show me around some of the smaller dealers' shops, whom no strangers [i.e. non-Arabs] visit. These shops are where the larger dealers hunt, and purchase their objects cheaply. He had promised me that he would one day show them to me. Although I am loath to let down the Museum like this, I thought I should take the opportunity, and so we followed Loukianoff. He led us down, first to an Armenian near Shepheard's Hotel, then to a Greek, and finally down to the Arab quarter, and this visit was quite an experience. In one of the narrow streets which we entered through a gate where people were drinking coffee and smoking a shisha and polishing boots, we arrived at a doorway in a corridor about one metre wide, with narrow arches above us, which led to a stairway of stone with uncomfortably high steps, and we entered onto the first floor where there was a long corridor running straight through the house, with doors behind which could hear women and children. The floor consisted of down-trodden clay with remains of tiles lying loose on top, so one had to watch one's step. At the end of the corridor there was a door leading into an

186. Lange, *Dagbog fra Ægypten, 1929-1930*, 150.
187. Lange and Lange, *Dagbog fra Ægyptensrejsen 1899-1900*, 229.
188. Schreiber Pedersen, *Fund og Forskning i Det Kongelige Biblioteks Samlinger* 46 (2007), 197-222; von Pilgrim, in Bickel et al. (eds.), *Ägyptologen und Ägyptologien zwischen Kaiserreich und Gründung der beiden deutschen Staaten*, 243-266.

189. Ismail, *Wallis Budge*, 291.
190. Fricke, in Merryman (ed.), *Imperialism, Art and Restitution*, 186.

SCI.DAN.H. 4 · 8

BUYING ANTIQUITIES

apartment with windows onto another street. Here an Arab woman lived with two children, and she had a large collection of Egyptian, Coptic and Arab antiquities. They were all piled up together in the most chaotic fashion and with dust everywhere in the small room where it was difficult to move. Here one had to really dig if one were to locate any genuine finds, as they would be hidden away among the fake and the uninteresting, including modern potsherds ... We spent a whole hour there, and would have stayed longer if we had had more time.[191]

Lange found Loukianoff's tour very useful; he bought a few objects, pleasantly surprised at the prices, and even went back to the Arab woman some days later to buy more.[192]

Chance meetings on the street with various dealers were a regular occurrence and Lange makes many references to such meetings, but rarely with much detail. Dealers congregated anywhere tourists could be found, including outside hotels, at train stations, and on the way to archaeological sites.[193] Once a personal relationship had developed with a dealer, he would often call on Lange at home when he had new objects for sale, or he would bring along colleagues who were hoping to sell and introduce them to Lange. The following passage describes one such encounter, and we quote it *in extenso* for its historical value and the way in which it evokes the atmosphere of such occasions:

Saturday 10 March 1900. When we got home we found a curious party sitting in our living room, namely three Arabs whom we didn't know; they had brought 2 large leather suitcases with them, the contents of which they wanted to sell. The other day one of our oldest acquaintances had come by, a young man by the name Soliman, still quite new in the antiquities trade, accompanied by an old man who was one of the most eccentric-looking I have seen down here. Unfortunately I don't have a photograph of him; a description of

him will only give a vague impression of this extremely curious person. He was tall and thin, his skin quite dark brown, thin greyish full beard, and no teeth. His clothes consisted of a hat (a red cap) with a dirty handkerchief around, a long and dirty old kaftan which had once been blue, and a couple of worn shoes on his otherwise bare feet. He was missing half his index finger on his right hand, and his kaftan was open in front so that one could see his naked, brown, hairy chest all the way down to the navel. He was addressed as 'Sheikh' by Soliman, but looked more like an old rascal. The old man behaved with the inborn courtesy and dignity of the Arabs, and let his toothless mouth gush forth compliments and greetings before taking a seat. Then he dragged forth from some pocket or other in his kaftan a handkerchief from which he unwrapped two statuettes which he praised verbosely. They were both fakes, and Soliman, who still has to learn his profession, watched me closely as I examined them. When the unfortunate judgment fell Soliman apparently became quite distraught, he slapped himself and expressed much disappointment. What was wrong with him I do not know; it was probably just a polite and courteous way to apologise for having brought the old man up to me. The old one was unperturbed, but before he left he said something about coming back with beautiful things. Well, the next morning at 8am he returned, and now he had another man with him that I didn't know. He himself only showed me a handkerchief with scarabs which he said were fake. The other one took out some small objects from a little bag, but we could not agree on the price. He promised however that he would come back with more. It was this person along with two others who were waiting for us when we returned today. The old man was not there, but it wasn't long before he too arrived. It was obviously him that had alerted the others about me. These two, one old and one young, were business partners, and all three were from Upper Egypt and only in Cairo for a few days to sell their objects. Then these two presented their things which almost filled the entire dining room table. There were some exquisite things among them, and my mouth was watering; but I restrained myself to three objects, two heads and some fragments of a papyrus with some of the best drawings I have seen. He wanted 2 pounds for it all, and I offered 15 shilling. Then I let him pack it all away again, and let the other unpack his things; he had some really nice things, including a papyrus roll with a Greek text, pretty well

191. Lange, *Dagbog fra Ægypten, 1929-1930*, 321-322.

192. Lange, *Dagbog fra Ægypten, 1929-1930*, 322 ('less than a third of what one would have had to pay elsewhere'), 330.

193. Lange and Lange, *Dagbog fra Ægyptensrejsen 1899-1900*, 157, 295 (Luxor), 327, 332 (on the way to Deir el-Medina), 345-347 (at Deir el-Bahri), 372-376 (at Abydos).

preserved, a boat of blue porcelain (a very rare piece)[194] and small but interesting stela. For these three pieces he wanted 11 pounds, but I offered 2 while trying not to show how valuable I thought they were, and how much I wanted them. He was quite shocked and started to pack away the things I had bargained for with exaggerated gestures, but I remained calm. Then the old rascal began persuading the man to be reasonable, and he went down to half of the original price. The other happy dealer who had already accepted my gold coins suggested 2½ pounds, but I remained adamant. The old man continued his persuasions but the owner was still upset. The other, who had already suggested 2½ pounds, now lowered the price to 2 pounds 4 shilling, despite the owner's protests. This was my window of opportunity and I put down 2 shining gold coins on the table and refused to pay more. Then these two, who didn't own the objects, closed the deal, 'for another time's sake', as they said. The owner was incandescent with rage and protested with both words and gestures; but the other two said 'Shut up! Finished!', and when I gave him back his objects and demanded my money back he refused, even as he insisted it wasn't half of their true worth. Then the whole party were given cigarettes and left, giving me happy assurances that they would always bring me their most wonderful things. I had done my best deal yet in Egypt. These are the nicest things in my entire museum, and they were extremely cheap.[195]

The transaction is described by Lange as 'typical ...; these people, who are partly cunning and partly like children, have little knowledge of what their objects are worth, but still believe that every object is a treasure'.[196] The passage gives a vivid portrayal of the theatrical aspects of the business transactions conducted by Lange, but also illustrates the personal relationships and reputation that gave him access to a wide range of dealers. The basic pattern described here – Upper Egyptian dealers coming to Cairo to sell antiquities – was common, and once in town they relied on their informal social networks (family, friends, acquaintances and colleagues) for information about potential customers.[197] Word spread quickly about serious buyers, and not just among dealers in the capital: on a trip to Luxor in 1929, Lange found that Zaki Mahmud Abd es-Samad, a Cairo dealer, had sent a letter to a colleague there to alert him of Lange's imminent arrival.[198] Many of the dealers knew each other, and although it is in practice difficult to map such informal networks based on the available material, the overall impression gained from the diaries is that of a complex web where information travelled at speed, and where participants were well connected with each other. A good example of this is the network surrounding the aforementioned Zaki, whom Lange had instructed to look for antiquities on his behalf when he returned to Copenhagen in April 1930. Several of the dealers that Lange stayed in touch with after his return referred to Zaki in their letters, despite few of them having any formal ties with him; Mme Serveux-Sickenberger, who was selling off the Bircher Collection, forwarded greetings from Zaki to Lange in a letter from June 1930,[199] Wolfgang Dreiss men-

---

194. The blue faience boat came to the National Museum as part of Lange's bequest; it now carries the inventory number NM 11740; cf. Hansen, *The Egyptians*, 39. The register of the Lange bequest (p. 80) describes it as a 'Boat-shaped dish with forward-facing jackal heads in both the prow and the stern; faience with blue glaze. Composed of two pieces. A piece has broken off the underside. Length: 12 cm. "New Kingdom" (suspect)'. The skepticism of the register is perhaps justified: Tom Hardwick (personal communication) informs us that this is a well-known category of fakes for which there are no genuine models in the archaeological record.

195. Lange and Lange, *Dagbog fra Ægyptensrejsen 1899-1900*, 418-422. The papyri mentioned here are P. Carlsberg 201 and P. Copenhagen NM 5302; see further above. It may be worth pointing out that Lange's views of Egyptian dealers need to be taken with a pinch of salt; they certainly managed to fool him occasionally by charging 'genuine' prices for objects that were in fact forgeries.

---

196. Lange and Lange, *Dagbog fra Ægyptensrejsen 1899-1900*, 428.
197. Cf. Wakeling, *Forged Egyptian Antiquities*, 126-127.
198. Lange, *Dagbog fra Ægypten, 1929-1930*, 181. Similarly, Cairo dealers had alerted their Luxor colleagues about the arrival of Breasted in 1919-1920 ('News that I was buying had preceded me and I was waited on by rows of finely dressed natives…'); Grant, *OINN* 205 (2010), 7.
199. Letter from F. Serveux-Sickenberger to H. O. Lange, dated 21 June 1930 (Royal Library, Copenhagen); 'Zaki schickt Ihnen und Ihrer werten Familie die besten Grüsse. Er ist ganz

tioned Zaki's shop being unharmed by an incident where some lanterns had caught fire near the Egyptian Museum and burnt some buildings in a letter from August the same year,[200] and Grégoire Loukianoff related having spoken to Zaki in connection with some ostraca that Lange had bought.[201] This is one of the few cases where one can document part of the social network surrounding a dealer.

Many of the established shops were family businesses that were handed down over several generations. The Abemayor and Tano shops are perhaps the best-known (for the latter, see Table 7),[202] but the material surveyed here provides many further examples. Most conspicuous are the great dealers at Luxor, all of whom involved their sons in the business; Todros Bolos, Mustafa Aga, Mohammed Mohasseb, and Abd el-Megid (for the three latter, see Table 4). Girgis Gabrial at Qena similarly worked with both his brother and his son. The largest documented family is that of Zaki Mahmud Abd es-Samad at Kafr el-Haram; this included famous dealers such as his grandfather and granduncle, the brothers Ibrahim and Soliman, as well as Ali Gabri and Ali Abd el-Haj el-Gabri (Table 3). The large el-Gabri family in Cairo was perhaps related to these individuals, while another large Cairo family is that of el-Shaer (Table 6).

Home visits by antiquities dealers were by no means an unusual occurrence, but generally they had either been invited or they were long-standing acquaintances (or both): the sense of surprise expressed in the above passage seems to stem from the fact that many of the individuals were either not known to

Lange previously or only very peripherally so. A more regular evening of visits took place on Monday 12 March 1900:

> ... around 6 the Arabs began to arrive. We had only invited Mansur but first Farag Ali, a good-looking young man whom we have visited on a couple of occasions, arrived. He had to leave without closing a deal, and next up was Mansur; he is a sociable man, very fat and very dark, almost black; he has an unbelievable number of pockets out of which he pulls his treasures, and again and again one thinks that this has got to be the last, but there is still more. He was more expensive than he usually is when we are alone, but he managed to sell a few things, including a faience ring to Dr Speyer and a small bird of stone to Bundgaard. A little after Mansur left, there was a knock on the door, and it was young Soliman and Mahmud, the biggest child of them all, son of the Sheikh from Abusir. He started giving bakshish to everyone in the hope of bribing them, but the whole affair came to little more than 6 piastres. He always talks about his wealth, and speaks incessantly; we had just taken out some of our own objects to show Dr Speyer when he arrived, including the little faience boat that Hans bought the other day for about ½ pound; he was much taken by this and could not understand that we wouldn't sell it to him when he was willing to pay 5 pounds for it.[203]

The situation described here, with dealer after dealer dropping by, seems a common pattern for the visits. The only guest who had been invited was Mansur, but two other groups also dropped by unannounced (Farag Ali; Soliman and Mahmud). The invitation was probably sent out specifically to allow Lange's guests, Dr Speyer and Mrs Bundgaard, to buy objects in the comfort of the Lange residence from a known and trusted dealer; although the fact that they had visitors necessarily pushed the prices up ('he was more expensive than he usually is when we are alone').

There were various ways of being presented with antiquities, some more elaborate than others, depending on the status and resources available to the dealer. A traveller who visited Egypt around the time of

glücklich mit der schönen Uhr, die Sie ihm geschenkt haben!'. Zaki may occasionally have functioned as an agent for Mme Serveux; see under 'Bircher' in the list of dealers at the end of this book.

200. Letter from W. Dreiss to H. O. Lange, dated 1 Aug. 1930 (Royal Library, Copenhagen).

201. Letter from G. Loukianoff to H. O. Lange, undated but written during the autumn of 1930 (Royal Library, Copenhagen): 'Zaki m'a dit qu'il vous ai envoyé 3 ostraca. Il n'a rien à son magasin'.

202. Bierbrier, *Who was Who in Egyptology*, 4th edition, 3, 533-534.

203. Lange and Lange, *Dagbog fra Ægyptensrejsen 1899-1900*, 429.

Table 3. Family tree of one of the main families involved in the antiquities trade at Kafr el-Haram.

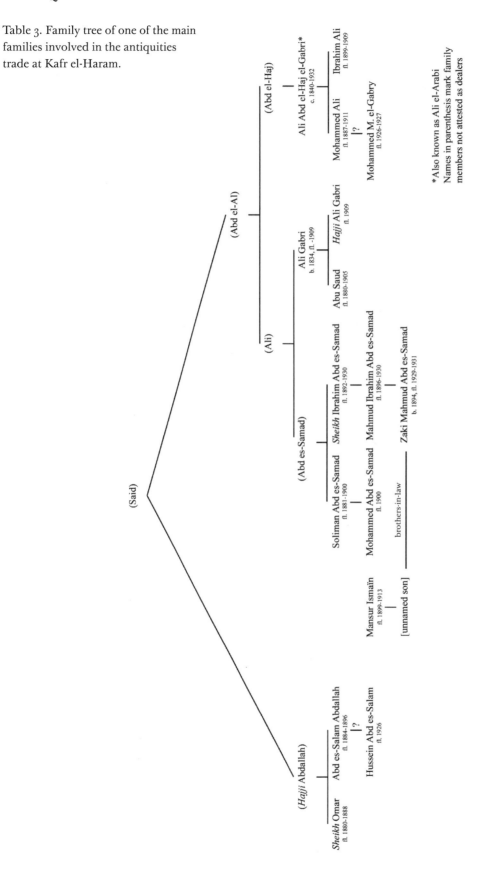

Fig. 30. The house of consular agent Mustafa Aga Ayat in Luxor Temple, being prepared for a formal occasion, probably one of his well-known *fantasiyas*. A portico of palm branches has been set up at the entrance to his residence, with two throne-like chairs in front. Two consular flags, possibly the British and the Russian, can be seen behind the chairs. Commercial photograph by Bonfils, 1880s.

Lange's first visit described a rather ingenious method, employed by an unnamed consul at Luxor, which he had clearly seen through.

> One of them has a celebrated plan. Consul at Luxor of a certain country, he invites any rich strangers he may meet to a dinner in true Arab style. At dessert, the doorbell is heard to ring, and the servants announce that some natives have just arrived with some remarkable antiquities discovered that day. They are brought in, and, on the advice of the Consul, the rich foreigners, unable to resist the temptation, buy what really belongs to the host himself.[204]

Grand dinners accompanied by entertainment, known as *fantasias*, in fact represent a well-documented phenomenon among consular agents at Luxor (Fig. 30).[205] When well-to-do individuals and parties were spotted on their way to Luxor, messengers would inform the consular agents in advance and these would send representatives with dinner invitations. Others would be invited on the spot, had they come unrecognized or unnoticed. These invitations to lavish dinners were by no means altruistic, but a manner of establishing a setting in which some business might

204. de Guerville, *New Egypt*, 205.

205. Several *fantasias* held by Mustafa Aga are mentioned in contemporary travellers accounts; one is vividly described by Edwards, *A Thousand Miles up the Nile*, 2nd edition, 455-459.

hopefully be conducted. Lange himself was also extended such an invitation by the consular agent Mohareb Todros, once it was realized that he was a potential buyer, but Lange had neither the time nor
desire to participate and declined.

> He [i.e. Mohareb Todros] complained severely that our
> stay was so brief, since he wanted to invite us to a din-
> ner at his place. In our minds we did not regret this
> because we had heard from Germans at the hotel, who
> had participated in one of his dinners, that they were
> near-fatal since he always serves around 14 courses of
> food and decorum dictates that one partakes in rich
> measure of each course.[206]

The type of staged encounter between dealers and potential customers was not just employed by consular
agents, but also by other dealers who were wealthy
enough. James Henry Breasted, who travelled to
Egypt to acquire antiquities for the Oriental Institute
in Chicago in 1919-1920, provides an example which
concerns the well-known dealer Yussuf Hassan.

> Old Yussuf Hassan, who is an old aristocrat, had asked
> me to come to [his] house for dinner and to bring a
> group of friends. I asked the friends just mentioned.
> Old Sir Valentine said he had been doing a lot of that
> kind of thing and begged off; but the others came and
> we had a picturesque time, eating endless courses, and
> listening to old Yussuf telling of the great folk with
> whom he had consorted, especially the Duke of Con-
> naught, of whose friendship he was very proud.[207]

Wealthy dealers at Luxor and elsewhere made a point
of talking about renowned clients and acquaintances;
some even had visitor books with signatures and photographs on the walls to show off. The stories they
could relate naturally helped to attract new potential
customers who were curious to hear about this or that
person. The following example is related by a British
colonel who visited Mustafa Aga's house in 1885:

> One of the greatest curiosities in Luxor was the visi-
> tors' book kept there. What hundreds of well-known
> names we saw in it! The Prince of Wales's name occur-
> red twice, the second time being accompanied by that
> of the Princess; and there besides were registered the
> names of very many British officers, written down when
> going, as we were, into the Soudan. Among them was
> the undying name of Gordon, written when passing
> through on his last ill-fated journey to Khartoum.[208]

Even more famous is the visitor book of the German
consular agents in Luxor.[209] It had been begun and
used briefly by Richard Lepsius in 1845, while living
three months in Thebes, and later passed to Todros
Bolos. He and his successors – his son Mohareb Todros and grandson Zaki Mohareb Todros – made rich
use of it, and it includes more than 2,600 entries written by visitors between 1845 and 1973. These include
heads of state and high-ranking notables (e.g. President Theodore Roosevelt of the United States, Grand
Duke Peter Nikolaevich of Russia, the later German
Emperor Wilhelm II), authors (e.g. Rudyard Kipling,
Henrik Ibsen), numerous Egyptologists, and many
other individuals.

Establishing identity and credentials seems to
have been an important first step during most encounters, also for lesser dealers, and in this context
business cards and letters of recommendation played
a key role; dealers collected the cards of professional
Egyptologists who had bought from them in the past
and used them to demonstrate their reliability and experience;

---

206. Lange and Lange, *Dagbog fra Ægyptensrejsen 1899-1900*, 340.
207. Larson (ed.), *Letters from James Henry Breasted*, 149. In
addition to Yussuf Hassan, Breasted visited many of the major
dealers on his trip, including Nahman, Kyticas, and Tano in
Cairo, as well as Mohammed Mohasseb and a Mohammed
Tandrous (sic, presumably Mohareb Todros) in Luxor; Grant,
OINN 205 (2010), 3-7.

208. Haggard, *Under Crescent and Star*, cheap edition[(sic)], 343. The
Prince of Wales visited Mustafa Aga both in 1862 and 1869. A
brief account of the latter visit is given by Grey, *Journal of a Visit
to Egypt*, 50-51, 98-100.
209. For an account of this visitors' book, with examples of
the visitors' entries, see Keimer, *CHE* 7 (1955), 300-314. It is
now in the Egyptian Museum in Berlin (inv. 36103), having
been acquired in 2002.

Fig. 31-34. Two evidently fake royal heads offered for sale by Wolfgang Dreiss in a letter to H. O. Lange dated 22 January 1932. Dreiss had earlier successfully duped Lange into buying a head of an Amarna princess, which was soon discovered to be fake, and this likely influenced his decision not to buy these objects. There was no further correspondence between the two. Unknown photographer. Courtesy of the Royal Library.

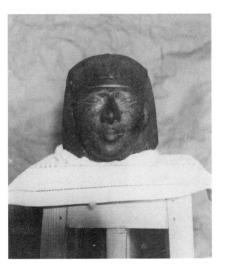
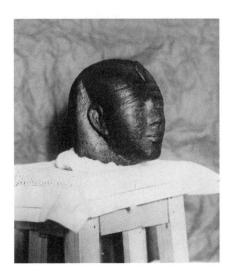

As I was walking down the street an Arab [i.e. Abdallah Mohammed Mohasseb] came up to me and showed me a business card, and asked me if I knew this man; when I said yes he pulled out two more whom I also knew; the three men were Carl Schmidt, Spiegelberg and Schubart. He then invited me to his house, where he kept antiquities.[210]

Once he had examined the dealer's stock, Lange was asked for his own business card which the dealer would 'undoubtedly use in the same way as those of the other Egyptologists'.[211]

Similarly, Lange relates how, during a visit to *Sheikh* Ibrahim Abd es-Samad at Giza in 1930, the dealer proudly showed him letters from Lange's old teacher Valdemar Schmidt, as well as 'several business cards of Egyptologists, which he used as advertisement.'[212] Dealers wanted such letters and recommendations from Lange in his turn, and the dealer Zaki Mahmud Abd es-Samad went as far as to say that a letter of recommendation was all the pay he needed for his work in assisting Lange in his efforts to buy

---

210. Lange, *Dagbog fra Ægypten, 1929-1930*, 194; Carl Schmidt (1868-1938) and Wilhelm Spiegelberg (1870-1930) need no introduction to Egyptologists; 'Schubart' refers to the famous papyrologist Wilhelm Schubart (1873-1960) of the Königlichen Museen zu Berlin.

211. Lange, *Dagbog fra Ægypten, 1929-1930*, 195.
212. Lange, *Dagbog fra Ægypten, 1929-1930*, 97, 124-125.

Kairo. Statuette of Kvarts bos Nahman

Elfenbens - Statuette hos Nahman.

Fig. 35-36. Objects seen by H. O. Lange with Maurice Nahman in Cairo, 1929/1930. Lange sometimes made photographs of objects in which he was interested so that he could send them to Copenhagen or show them to colleagues for evaluation. Above left: 'Statuette of quarts with Nahman.' Above right: 'Ivory statuette with Nahman.' The Middle Kingdom ivory figure was sold to Henry Walters shortly afterwards and is now in the Walters Art Museum (inv. 71.509). The First Intermediate Period statuette presumably derives from Sayed Khashaba's excavations at Assyut; some of his antiquities were sold through Maurice Nahman. Courtesy of the Egyptological Archives, University of Copenhagen.

antiquities.[213] Lange then offered to give him a present as a token of appreciation, and Zaki asked for a watch with an engraved dedication. Such a watch would naturally trump the business cards and letters of reccommendation from customers which many dealers collected. Lange was only too happy to grant him this, and he remarks several times in the diaries that he felt Zaki had really earned it.

213. Lange, *Dagbog fra Ægypten, 1929-1930*, 115, 323. Cf. the entry on Zaki in the list of dealers at the end of the book.

It was not uncommon for lesser dealers and even relatives of important dealers to act as guides for buyers and introduce them to other dealers. While Zaki acted as guide to Lange in Cairo in 1929/30, Mohammed Abd el-Haggag of Sheikh Abd el-Qurna took this role upon himself in Luxor during the same stay in Egypt, and in 1899/1900 Abdallah, a cousin of the major dealer Ali Abd el-Haj, had acted as guide for Lange in Cairo. Zaki also accompanied Friedrich Zucker to Eshmunein and the Fayum on a three day journey some months after Lange had left Egypt in 1930, perhaps on Lange's recommendation. On this occasion

Fig. 37-38. Further items photographed by Lange at Nahman's in Cairo, 1929/1930. Above right: 'Statuette of wax with Nahman.' Above left: 'Cairo. Unguent spoon with Nahman.' The wax figure was last sold at Christie's on 29 October 2003 for £447 (Sale 9723, Lot 149). Courtesy of the Egyptological Archives, University of Copenhagen.

the services of a local dealer, Mohammed Abdallah, were also obtained; having himself operated out of both Eshmunein and Medinet el-Fayum for many years, he undoubtedly had intimate knowledge of the local situation and he was able to lead them to a whole series of local dealers. Mohammed Abdallah spent three days as guide and was paid a fee for his services (100 piastres, in addition to which he would most likely have received a percentage of all sales). By contrast Zaki, whose efforts lead to more important acquisitions, was rewarded with the above-mentioned watch. Such a fine gift may not have been unusual: Charles Lang Freer had, some 25 years earlier, given gold watches both to the antiquities dealer Ali Abd el-Haj and his sons Ibrahim Ali (who had served as his guide

and translator on his visits to Egypt) and Mohammed Ali in return for their services.[214] Earlier examples of dealers acting as guides include Auad who had worked for Champollion and served as guide to Richard Lepsius in Thebes in 1844-45; Saïd Ismaïn, a brother of the dealer Farag Ismaïn at Kafr el-Haram, who travelled

214. Cf. Clarke, in Hurtado (ed.), *The Freer Biblical Manuscripts*, 29, n. 30. Although it is not explicitly stated, we feel fairly confident that Ibrahim Ali should be identified with Ali's like-named son who is said to have an excellent command of English and who was well acquainted with Cairo and the antiquities market (p. 223). Clarke refers to the other son as Mohamed Ali Abdulhi; we have not otherwise come across the latter name in reference to this son, and it is perhaps simply a transliteration of Abd el-Haj.

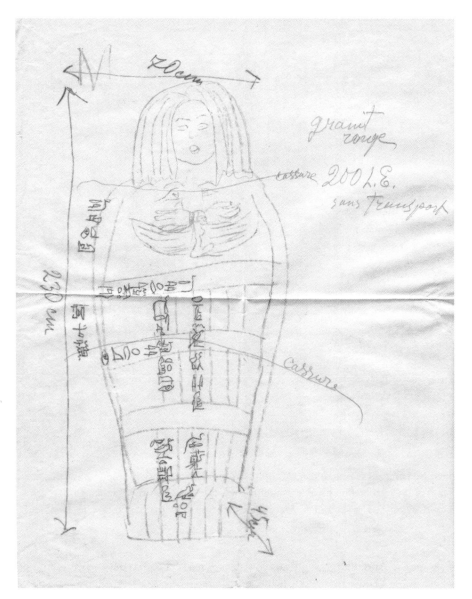

Fig. 39. Red granite sarcophagus offered for sale by Grégoire Loukianoff in a letter to Lange dated 14 January 1931. Having no photograph available, he supplied a sketch instead. The hieroglyphs show that it belonged to a chantress of Amun named Baketamun. Courtesy of the Royal Library.

with Charles Wilbour and functioned as his guide during his visits in 1881-84; and a son of *Sheikh* Ibrahim Ali at Kafr el-Haram who served as a guide to the Crown princess of Sweden, Victoria of Baden, in 1890-91.[215]

Concluding a sale quickly was often important to the dealers, perhaps especially if the status of the object as genuine or fake was disputed,[216] and one strategy used by provincial dealers was to claim that they were leaving Cairo that very evening. Lange mentions one dealer from Luxor who did this and showed him the return ticket as confirmation.[217] It is not clear whether Lange believed him or thought it an elaborate strategy to hasten the sale, but the fact that he remarked on it, as well as the seemingly unprovoked display of the re-

215. For Auad, see Keimer, *CHE* 7 (1955), 300-314, and Bierbrier, *Who was Who in Egyptology*, 4th edition, 28. For the two other individuals, see Saïd Ismaïn and *Sheikh* Ibrahim Ali in the biographical section below.

216. Lange, *Dagbog fra Ægypten, 1929-1930*, 91.
217. Lange, *Dagbog fra Ægypten, 1929-1930*, 318.

turn ticket by the dealer, may suggest a fairly common strategy where documentation was needed to be taken seriously. At other times, dealers would be frustratingly patient if an offer did not meet their expectations and they felt that they might make a better bargain. In such cases they might retain objects for years. An extreme example is offered by Spiegelberg who mentions an interesting group of papyri from Gebelein belonging to Mohammed Mohasseb which he first saw in 1898, but they were unable to agree on a price, and it was not until 1927 – nearly thirty years later – that he finally managed to acquire them.[218]

Some of the major dealers like Nahman, Tano and Kyticas were regularly in contact with Western museums by post, and sales could be initiated over long distances by sending photographs of objects along with short descriptions. It is difficult to judge to what extent this was also true of Egyptian dealers like Ali Abd el-Haj and Farag Ismaïn at Giza, or Mohammed Mohasseb or Abd el-Megid at Luxor; certainly the two former dealers seem to have relied more on personal visits than correspondence. Literacy may have been an issue, but even illiterate dealers could get others to write on their behalf by means of dictation, as in the case of the correspondence between Zaki Mahmud Abd es-Samad and Lange. Occasionally Egyptologists in Egypt would have formal or informal agreements with their colleagues abroad to look for objects on their behalf. Ludwig Borchardt was one such person; he was involved, inter alia, in the German *Papyruskartell* (p. 168), but he also actively sought out objects for Lange. A letter from Borchardt in Luxor to Lange in Denmark illustrates how this was done in practice. Having acknowledged receipt of a cheque as payment for some antiquities, he writes that he will keep the remaining £15 for future acquisitions. One of the objects he has in mind is a stele which he saw at Ali Abd el-Haj's house in Kafr el-Haram before leaving for Luxor:

> Hoffentlich ist die Stele noch bei Ali [sc. Ali Abd el-Haj], wenn ich zurückkomme.

Bei Moharb [sc. Mohareb Todros] ist eine kleine, charakteristische m.R. Statue, 21 cm hoch, stehender Mann, kahler Kopf, langes Gewand, ohne Inschrift. 15 £. Ich habe ihm gesagt, er soll Sie zurückhalten, ich würde ihm schreiben. Wenn Sie sie wollen, benachrichtigen Sie mich.

> Bei Mohammed Mohasseb ist eine <u>schöne</u> Mumie in Papphülle, tadellos erhalten, ein Amonspriester(?) aus der 19ten order 20ten [Dynastie]. Verlangt werden 150 £.[219]

Here Borchardt provides Lange with short descriptions of objects, and their suggested prices, as a starting point for negotiation. If Lange expressed an interest in any of the objects then the next step would be to ask for photographs. There are several examples of such photographs preserved among the Lange material, both photographs sent to him by others (Fig. 31-34) and photographs taken by him in Egypt to send to Danish museums (Fig. 35-38). Photographs were expensive, and unless the dealer had the necessary funds, or the interested party offered to pay for them to be made, the alternative was to send drawings, as in the case of Grégoire Loukianoff who sent Lange drawings of both a papyrus (Fig. 122) and a red granite sarcophagus (Fig. 39).

The geography of the antiquities trade

The main centres of the antiquities trade were Cairo in Lower Egypt and Luxor in Upper Egypt (Fig. 40). Although Luxor was the second centre, Cairo was by far the largest market with the majority of well-established dealers, and local dealers from the south would sometimes prefer to travel to Cairo rather than Luxor to sell their objects.[220] It does not seem unreasonable to assume that perhaps as much as 90 per cent of the

---

218. Spiegelberg, *Die demotischen Papyri Loeb*, v.

219. Letter from L. Borchardt to H. O. Lange, dated 31 May 1901 (Royal Library, Copenhagen).
220. Cf., e.g., the examples of Sadic Girgis Ebed who travelled from Qena (p. 259); Abd en-Nur who travelled from Luxor (p. 185); Hassan Abd er-Rahman who travelled from Assiut (p. 219); Shakir Farag who travelled from Beni Suef (p. 262); and the two dealers who travelled from Upper Egypt and sold items from Akhmim and Gebelein (p. 55).

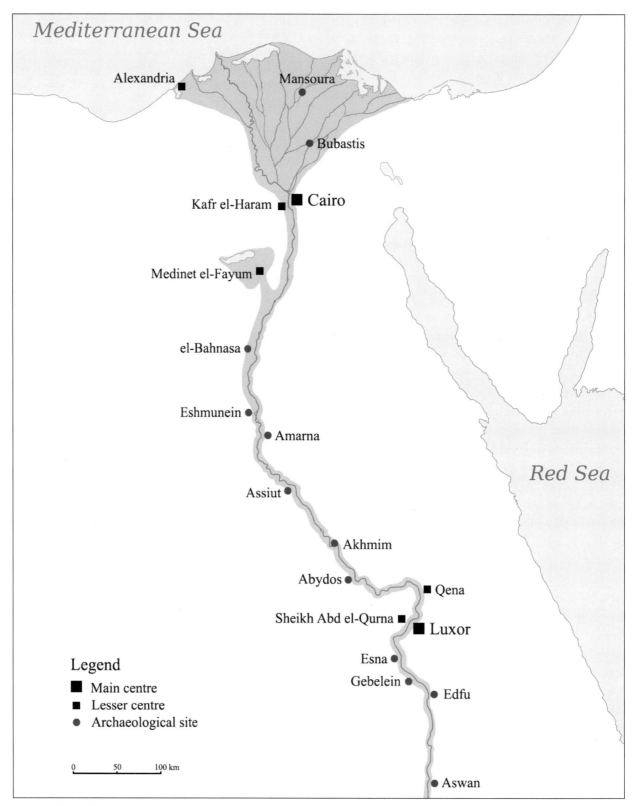

Fig. 40. Map of Egypt indicating the main locations discussed in the book. The more important centres for the antiquities trade are marked with squares. Based on map by Jeff Dahl, Wikimedia Commons, 22. Nov. 2007.

Fig. 41-42. Lange surrounded by antiquities peddlers in
Abydos (above) and at the Ramesseum on the Theban
West Bank (right). Lange photographs, 1929/30. Courtesy
of the Royal Library.

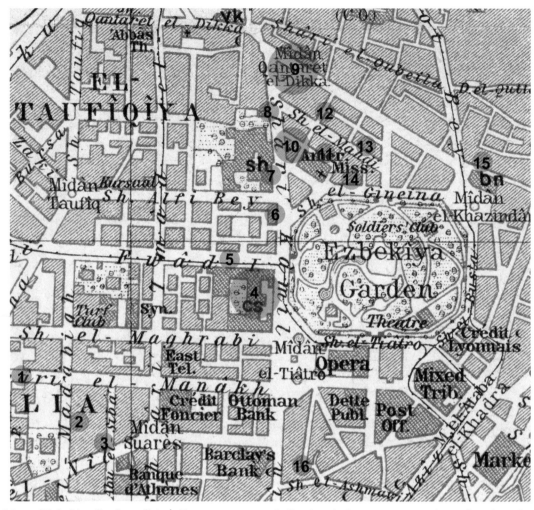

Fig. 43. Map of Ezbekiya Gardens, Cairo's European quarter, indicating the known or approximate location of various dealers, including larger and smaller shops, private apartments, and store rooms. Baedeker, *Egypt* 8th ed., 1928, detail.

(1) Sharia Deir el-Banat*, westward continuation of Sharia el-Manakh: Alexandre Dingli.

(2) Sharia el-Madabegh: Maurice Nahman (later address).

(3) Sharia Sheikh Abu el-Siba: Maurice Nahman (earlier address)

(4) Continental Hotel: Dikran Kelekian, M. A. Mansoor (main address), Elia Pantazi

(5) Sharia Fuad I*: Maguid Sameda (earlier address), Mohammed Shaker

(6) Sharia Kamel: Panayotis Kyticas (later address)

(7) Sharia Kamel, within Shepheard's Hotel: M. A. Mansoor (secondary address)

(8) Sharia Kamel, garden of Shepheard's Hotel: R. H. Blanchard, taken over by H. Dufour

(9) Midan Kantaret el-Dikka: Panayotis Kyticas (earlier address), Nicolas Tano (earlier address)

(10) Sharia Kamel, building across from Shepheard's Hotel: Abemayor family (earlier address), Mohammed M. el-Gabry, Minotto, Philip E. Mitry, Paul Philip, Maguid Sameda (later address), Tano family (later address)

(11) Haret el-Zahar*: Abemayor family (later address), Michel Casira, Ismaïl Abdallah el-Shaer, Mohammed A. el-Shaer

(12) Haret el-Madrastein*: Khawam Brothers (secondary address)

(13) Sharia el-Mahdi*: A. Aly el-Gabry, Kamal A. Hammouda

(14) Sharia el-Guineina*: Grégoire Loukianoff

(15) Arab quarter behind Hôtel Bristol*: Soliman Abd es-Samad

(16) Arab quarter next to Sharia Abdin: Farag Ali

*Approximate location

Fig. 44. The legendary Shepheard's Hotel in the European quarter of Cairo near Ezbekiya Gardens. The well-known shop of R. H. Blanchard, located in the northern part of the hotel garden and facing the main street, Sharia Kamel, can be seen in the foreground. The sign reads 'Blanchard Antiquities'. Postcard issued by Zogolopoulo Frères, Cairo, c. 1930.

Fig. 45. Grand Continental Hotel on Sharia Kamel across from Ezbekiya Gardens and the Opera Square. The hotel housed the Cairo shop of Dikran Kelekian and a second shop of M. A. Mansoor whose main shop was located in Shepheard's Hotel. Other dealers with shops in the vicinity include Maguid Sameda and Mohammed Shaker. Postcard issued by B. Livadas e Coutsicos, no. 547.

Fig. 46. Shops along the southern façade of Shepheard's Hotel facing Sharia Kamel. The antiquities shop of M. A. Mansoor is visible on the left. The sign over the open awning carries the name of the dealer. Postcard issued by Eastern Publishing Company, undated.

Fig. 47. Blanchard's shop was later taken over by Henri Dufour who was the proprietor until its destruction during the revolution in 1952. The head of a colossal statue can be seen set up before the entrance from the front garden of Shepheard's Hotel. Detail of unlabelled photograph. Courtesy of the Egyptological Archives, University of Copenhagen.

Fig. 48. The façade and street entrance to M. A. Mansoor's antiquities shop at Shepheard's Hotel. The sign reads 'Authorised by the Egyptian Museum to sell antiquities as per license No. 85.' Standing to the left is his oldest son Edmond Robert Mansoor (1923-2012). Photograph by J. M. Robinson, Claremont Colleges.

Fig. 49. The large and prominent building right across from the entrance to Shepheard's Hotel on Sharia Kamel (now Sharia Gomehoriya) housed several antiquities shops, including those of the Tano family, the el-Shaer family, and Philip E. Mitry. Photograph by the authors, May 2013.

Fig. 50. Philip E. Mitry ran the Anglo-American Bookshop (est. 1869) from the early 1920s and also dealt antiquities from the shop with an official license until he left for California in the 1960s. It was perfectly situated in the building right across from the grand entrance to Shepheard's Hotel. Photograph c. 1945. Courtesy of *Life*, Time Magazine.

Fig. 51. Haret el-Zahar, a side alley that ran down the left side of the large building with the many antiquities dealers across from Shepheard's Hotel. The entrance to the el-Shaer shop was located at the begining of the alley. Further down on the left side, across from the American Mission (later demolished and replaced by the building visible on the right) was the antiquities shop of Michel Casira. Photograph by the authors, May 2013.

Fig. 52. Shops at Sharia Kamel with Shepheard's Hotel in the background. The shop behind the tree in the foreground is that of the antiquities dealer Panayotis Kyticas. The British Museum acquired several thousand objects through him over the years, mainly through E. A. Wallis Budge, who also stayed with him on at least one of his visits to Egypt. The sign 'P. Kyticas' is partly visible behind the tree. Postcard, early 20th Century.

actual profits were made in these two cities. This is based on the proportional numbers of attested dealers in Cairo (contrasted with other places), our impression of the volume of commodities bought and sold in Cairo, and the price levels conveyed by the materials we have examined, but it remains a rough estimate at best.

Well-established dealers in Cairo and Luxor would often situate their shops as close as possible to up-market hotels where wealthy tourists would congregate. Most prominent was the world famous Shepheard's Hotel at Sharia Kamel, next to Ezbekiya Gardens in Cairo.

Not surprisingly, there seems to have been dealers at almost every larger archaeological site (although few of the local dealers were particularly prominent); San near ancient Tanis, Zagazig near ancient Bubas-

tis, Mallawi near ancient Amarna and Hermopolis, Akhmim at ancient Panopolis, Qena near Dendera, etc.[221] The local centres would typically be located in the closest town with a train station for easy access to tourists and other buyers. The centre for the trade in the Fayum Oasis was Medinet el-Fayum, the only major city and the main train connection.

Locals who chanced upon archaeological material or conducted illicit excavations would typically sell to these local dealers for a relatively low price or, time

221. Lange was based in Cairo during both visits, and so his travel diaries contain information almost exclusively relating to the antiquities market there (as well as in Upper Egypt which he also visited); there is virtually nothing about the Delta (which he only travelled through on his way to and from Alexandria).

Fig. 53. Sharia el-Muski, 21 September 1903. The busy bazaar street ran just off Ezbekiya Gardens and down to Khan el-Khalili. Several established dealers had their shops in the bazaar, including André Bircher and E. Hatoun. Photograph by William Herman Rau.

Fig. 54. Sharia el-Muski, c. 1900. An unidentified antiques shop prominently located on a corner in the bazaar street. Detail from an undated postcard; no. 52, 'Le Caire. Environs du Mousky', of a series marked 'L.J.'

Fig. 56. Leaning against the wall of a side entrance, a business sign from a previous venture of André Bircher in Upper Egypt, *Briqueterie, platriere & poterie*. Detail of last.

Fig. 55. The entrance to André Bircher's residence at Sharia el-Muski in Cairo. Undated photograph. Courtesy of Archiv für Zeitgeschichte, Zürich.

and resources permitting, they might travel to Cairo and Luxor in the hope of obtaining better prices. The local dealers for their part would sell to the occasional visitor or themselves travel to Cairo or Luxor to sell to the larger dealers, or in order to peddle their objects directly to tourists and collectors (Fig. 41-42). Sometimes the reverse might also happen and larger dealers would travel out to search for valuable material

locally, but most of the antiquities seem to have gone through Cairo or Luxor at some stage.

The markets at Cairo and Luxor each had a 'satellite' or secondary centre. In both cases it was located next to a vast archaeological site; Kafr el-Haram at Cairo next to the Giza necropolis and Sheikh Abd el-Qurna at Luxor next to the Theban necropolis. Provincial areas were less likely to have established dealers; in 1930, according to Lange, Aswan had none and even a rich archaeological site such as Abydos had only one.[222] 'Hubs' such as Medinet el-Fayum and

222. Lange, *Dagbog fra Ægypten, 1929-1930*, 247, but note that Baedeker, *Ägypten und der Sudân*, 8th edition, 368, listed a single dealer in Aswan, Mischriky Girgis, who was associated with 'die deutsche Sûdân-Pionier-Mission'. The identity of the

Qena had relatively few established dealers, and Cairo and Luxor remained the areas with the vast majority of established dealers.

The infrastructure of the antiquities market is rarely explicitly discussed by Lange, but he makes some passing comments that draw at least a partial picture:

> The thing is that the Nubians here in Aswan have relatives in the Nubian villages further up along the Nile. When these people find something they bring it down here where it is easier to sell it. But it is rather sad to think that these heads [of granite statues that Lange had seen for sale in Aswan] probably means that these people have found whole statues, and because they cannot transport an entire statue in secrecy, they remove the head which can then be easily concealed in their garments. The rest is then just left there. These excavations, which are carried out under the cover of night by the natives, are illegal, and they are afraid of getting caught and punished by the police. They have no real understanding of the value of these kinds of objects, and always believe that such a head represents a king and that they are in possession of a treasure. Usually they will approach antiquities dealers with their finds but there are no such dealers here in Aswan, and Luxor, where the nearest dealers are, is some distance away, so trade here is difficult.[223]

The antiquities market in Cairo

There were two main clusters of dealers in Cairo: those around Ezbekiya Gardens (which may be termed the 'Ezbekiya dealers') and those at the bazaar (the 'Bazaar dealers'). They were all well-established dealers, but the first group was generally specialized in antiquities, whereas the latter group dealt more broadly in oriental wares.

The majority of the leading antiquities dealers had their shops around Ezbekiya Gardens (Fig. 43), close to the fashionable Shepheard's Hotel and Continental Hotel which lay just one block apart on Sharia Kamel (at no. 8 and no. 2 respectively; Fig. 44-45).[224] Lange was impressed by the area, and remarked already in 1900 that 'Ezbekiya Garden is the centre of the European neighbourhood. It is surrounded by stately broad streets with broad flagstone-covered sidewalks.'[225]

Especially the world-famous Shepheard's Hotel, with its well-to-do clientele, attracted dealers who could afford shops in the quarter.[226] That of M. A. Mansoor (his main shop) was located inside the hotel with a street façade close to its entrance (Fig. 46-47), R. H. Blanchard's was in a small separate building that occupied the northern part of the hotel garden facing the street (Fig. 44, 48), and it was apparently these same premises that later became the shop of H. Dufour. In a large, prominent building directly opposite the hotel (Fig. 49) were the shops of Paul Philip, the Tano family (their later shop), Maguid Sameda (his later shop), and Philip E. Mitry in Sharia Kamel (Fig. 50), with the original shops of Panayotis Kyticas and Nicolas Tano at Midan Kantaret el-Dikka, those of the Abemayor family (their later shop), Michel Casira, Ismaïl Abdallah el-Shaer, and Mohammed Abd er-Rahim el-Shaer in the side street Haret el-Zahar (Fig. 51), Khawam Brothers (their second shop) in the

---

Abydos trader remains unknown.

223. Lange, *Dagbog fra Ægypten, 1929-1930*, 154-155. The practice described here accounts for many of the Egyptian statues in modern museums which lack heads. Perhaps worth mentioning here is the case of the body of a royal statue discovered on the island of Elephantine in 1932, which was found to join a head that had arrived in Vienna some hundred years earlier; Fay, *MDAIK* 44 (1988), 67-77; we are grateful to Stephen Quirke for this reference.

224. Note that nearly all the streets mentioned in the following have since been re-named, because of the changing political situation, especially the Revolution of 1952, and this has led to some confusion where certain dealers are believed to have moved from one address to another, while it is merely the name of the street (and sometimes also the street numbering) that has changed. We generally use the Arabic designation of streets, rather than the colonial English or French, and thus – for example – refer to *Sharia* Kamel instead of *Rue* Kamel or Kamel *Street*. Sharia Kamel was later re-named Sharia Ibrahim Pasha and is now Sharia al-Gomehoriya.

225. Lange and Lange, *Dagbog fra Ægyptensrejsen 1899-1900*, 79.

226. An account of the history of Shepheard's Hotel, and its total destruction during the Revolution in 1952, may be found in Nelson, *Shepheard's Hotel*. The Central Bank of Egypt now stands on the grounds formerly occupied by the hotel.

Fig. 57. One of the rooms in a former Mameluke palace at Sharia el-Muski in Cairo where André Bircher had his residence and kept his large collection of antiquities. In the vaulted niche at the back, behind the small pillar, can be seen a fragment of a tomb relief with a hieroglyphic inscription, lying on its side. Undated photograph. Courtesy of Archiv für Zeitgeschichte, Zürich.

side street Sharia el-Madrasteen, and Kamel Abdallah Hammouda and A. Aly el-Gabri in the side street Sharia el-Mahdi. Opposite Thomas Cook & Son (just north of Shepheard's Hotel at 6 Sharia Kamel) was the shop of Mohammed M. el-Gabri. In the other direction, down Sharia Kamel, were the shops of the Abemayor family (earlier shop), Panayotis Kyticas (later shop, Fig. 52), and Minotto, while Grégoire Loukianoff lived with his family in Sharia el-Guineina. Elia Pantazi, Dikran Kelekian and a further shop of M. A. Mansoor were located at the Continental Hotel further down Sharia Kamel, and next to the Continental Hotel, at 1 Sharia Fuâd I (now Sharia 26 July), were the shops of Maguid Sameda (earlier shop) and Mohammed Shaker. According to a newspaper article published in the late 1950s, there were still some eight major antiquities dealers in the former Sharia Kamel (by then part of Sharia Gomehoriya) at the time.[227]

Also located near Ezbekiya Gardens, but in the Arab neighbourhood to the south, next to Sharia Abdin (now also part of Sharia Gomehoriya), was a 'shop' belonging to Farag Ali from Kafr el-Haram which Jonna describes as 'a little hole' (p. 213). Other dealers from Kafr el-Haram, such as Soliman Abd es-

---

227. Clipping from unidentified newspaper, late 1950s, article entitled 'In Relation to the Case of the American Scholar who Stole Egypt's Antiquities' (translated from Arabic).

Fig. 58. The façade of Elias Hatoun's shop in Sharia el-Muski, around 1920. Hatoun dealt broadly in oriental wares, both ancient and modern. Promotional brochure entitled *What every tourist wishes to know*, E. Hatoun, Cairo, no date.

Samad, *Sheikh* Ibrahim, and Abdallah, similarly had storage facilities or shops in Cairo, but their location is not precisely indicated (although it is mentioned that the storage facility of Soliman was located in a house behind Hôtel Bristol, just north-east of Ezbekiya Gardens). Jonna notes concerning the shop of *Sheikh* Ibrahim: 'we finally took off and drove into the real Arab neighbourhood where the streets are so narrow that a wagon can only just pass; the last distance we had to walk on foot.'[228] A more detailed description of the house in which Abdallah's stores were kept evokes the atmosphere:

He [i.e. Abdallah] led us into the Arab neighbourhood, through one alley after the other, into his house. It was a real Arab house. Right inside the door a number of women and children were sitting on the floor, where a small fire had been lit, their only light, for when the door to the street was closed, it was pitch black. Up four small stairs he led us past doors that were ajar and through which we could see ragged and dirty people sitting and laying on the floor. The small room in which he had his goods was actually neat but rather small;

there was no space for more than the three of us. Two chairs, which were stacked on top of each other in a corner, were brought over. This was the only furniture besides the little cabinet and the shelves where the goods were placed. He does not actually live in Cairo, but out by Giza. A nice carpet or two were lying against the wall so that he can sleep here at night when necessary.[229]

Also Valdemar Schmidt, who much preferred doing business with the European dealers, provides a description of the 'shops' of the Arab and Bedouin dealers in the back alleys of Cairo in a letter from 1894:

My way is blocked by Arabs and Bedouins, and they simply cannot grasp that I do not want to hear anything about 'business'. Even so I cannot refrain from visiting their shops: Rooms in an awful street, which look like a place in which anything could happen – even being murdered, but, notwithstanding, they drag things out towards midnight with their tardiness, so there is nothing to fear – especially since they are so good-natured as to accompany me out of the labyrinth to a more European street.[230]

---

228. Lange and Lange, *Dagbog fra Ægyptensrejsen 1899-1900*, 664.

229. Lange and Lange, *Dagbog fra Ægyptensrejsen 1899-1900*, 133.
230. Letter from V. Schmidt to C. Jacobsen, dated 11 Oct. 1894 (Ny Carlsberg Glyptotek); Jørgensen, *How it all began*, 54.

Another group of dealers were located at the bazaars of Muski and Khan el-Khalili that, by contrast, were much visited by tourists. Sharia el-Muski (Fig. 53-54) began close to Ezbekiya Gardens and ran straight down to Khan el-Khalili. The bazaar was a very different environment to the broad palm-lined streets of the European neighborhood around Ezbekiya. Lange provides a very long description of which a short excerpt may suffice:

> The bazaar quarter is quite large and consists of a number of very narrow streets which are partly covered with cloth (usually rags) or planks with the result that the air is nearly always cool and yet curiously fresh. One would be inclined to think that the narrow streets would be a terrible nuisance, but on a really hot day it is a great pleasure to enter from the broad European streets into the narrow, twisted Arab streets where the sun cannot penetrate. Naturally the smell is not always pleasant where the Arabs live closely packed, but not that many people live in the Bazaar quarter; the merchants merely have their stalls here and live elsewhere in the city. These streets mostly surround large square courtyards with great warehouses where one can see enormous bales of goods stacked up without really understanding how they can have been brought through the narrow streets. ... The section of the bazaar, which the Europeans are usually content with visiting, is called *Khan el Khalil*, and the stalls there are bursting with curios, embroideries, carpets, jewellery, etc.[231]

The dealers in the quarter of Sharia el-Muski included André Bircher (Fig. 55-57) and E. Hatoun (Fig. 58), while Khan el-Khalili included Dimitri Andalaft, Joseph Cohen (Fig. 59), Albert Eid (Fig. 60-61), Mohammed Khattab, and the Khawam Brothers (Fig. 62-67). The latter was the only major antiquities shop in the area by the late 1950s, although antiquities could also be found in shops that had a broader and more general assortment of merchandise.[232]

Fig. 59. Scene from the bazaar of Khan el-Khalili. The entrance to the shop of Joseph Cohen, said to be the largest antiquities shop in the bazaar, can be seen on the left. Undated postcard.

Other dealers were located in the area between Ezbekiya Gardens and the Egyptian Museum. A little further west was the famous shop of Maurice Nahman in 27 Sharia el-Madabegh (now Sherif Pasha; Fig. 68-73), close to Crédit Fonciér Égyptien where he worked as chief cashier for many years. He had earlier conducted business from his apartment at 20 Sharia Sheikh Abu el-Sibâ (now Gawad Honsy; Fig. 74), which ran parallel with Sharia el-Madabegh, less than 100 metres to the east, and at that time had a second shop at Sharia Qasr el-Nil across from the Savoy Hotel, about 500 metres from the Egyptian Museum. Even further west was the shop of Alexandre Dingli in Sharia Deir el-Banat (now Abd el-Khalik Tharwat).

231. Lange and Lange, *Dagbog fra Ægyptensrejsen 1899-1900*, 605-613, also pp. 46-47.

232. Clipping from unidentified newspaper, late 1950s, article entitled 'In Relation to the Case of the American Scholar who Stole Egypt's Antiquities' (translated from Arabic).

Fig. 60. The façade of Albert Eid's (1886-1950) antiquities shop at Khan el-Khalili. Eid is mostly known for his involvement in the sale of the Nag Hammadi codices. The business, which was nationalized in 1956, continued under the general management of Robert Viola for about ten years. Courtesy of Claremont Colleges Digital Libraries.

Fig. 61. Robert Viola, the general manager of Albert Eid & Co., arranging a display case in the gallery. The large 4-sided stela from the reign of reign of Ramesses II was later acquired by the Cairo Museum (inv. JE 89624). Photograph dated 22 September 1960. Courtesy of Lucien Viola.

Fig. 62-63. The shop Khawam Brothers in Khan el-Khalili. The Khawam family runs the longest operating Egyptian anti-quities business; it was founded by Sélim Khawam in 1862 and was active in Egypt until 1977 when it was relocated to Pa-ris, France. The image on the left is earlier in date than the one on the right. Photographs courtesy of Bertrand Khawam.

Fig. 64. The interior of the Khawam Brothers shop in Khan el-Khalili, late 1950s. Newspaper clipping; source not located.

Fig. 65. Joseph Khawam in the family shop, late 1950s. Newspaper clipping; source not located.

Fig. 66-67. Two views of the interior of the Khawam Brothers shop in Khan el-Khalili, c. 1930. The great variety of objects seems typical of antiquities shops at the time (compare the shop of Maurice Nahman, Fig. 70-71). Courtesy of Bertrand Khawam.

Fig. 68. The façade of Maurice Nahman's mansion and
antiquities shop at 27 Sharia
el-Madabegh (now Sherif
Pasha) in the 1930s. Built by
the French architect Baron
Delort de Gléon in the late
19th Century, it was described
as a palace by Lange and was
the largest antiquities shop
in Cairo. Courtesy of Rosario
Pintaudi. Gift from Maurice
Nahman's daughter, Alexandra Nahman Manessero.

Fig. 69. Maurice Nahman
next to the entrance to his
antiquities shop. The entrance
has been decorated on the
occasion of some celebration.
Photo c. 1945. Courtesy of
Lucien Viola.

Fig. 70-71. The main gallery of Maurice Nahman's antiquities shop. The Egyptologist J. H. Breasted describes it in 1919 as 'a huge drawing room as big as a church, where he exhibits his immense collection'. While Nahman is mainly known as a dealer of ancient Egyptian antiquities, his stock evidently also included many Byzantine and Islamic objects. Courtesy of Rosario Pintaudi. Gift from Maurice Nahman's daughter, Alexandra Nahman Manessero.

Fig. 72. Detail of the main gallery of Maurice Nahman's antiquities shop. A female customer is looking at some object, while two uniformed shop attendants are standing in the background. Photo c. 1935. Courtesy of Lucien Viola.

There were also dealers close to the Egyptian Museum, although they are less well documented in our material. Both Zaki Mahmud Abd es-Samad (Fig. 75) and Hefnawy Ismaïl el-Shaer (Fig. 76), as well as a gallery belonging to M. A. Mansoor, were located directly across from the entrance to the Museum in Sharia Mariette Pasha (just around the corner from Cecil House where Lange stayed). The latter also had a shop at the famous Semiramis Hotel which lay between the Egyptian Museum and Garden City (in addition to shops at Shepheard's Hotel and Continental Hotel).

A single dealer, Mohammed Hamed Ibrahim, is known to have had a shop opposite Mena House near the pyramids, but there are likely to have been others located in or around this expensive hotel.[233]

Finally there was the possibility of acquiring surplus antiquities from the Egyptian Museum, first at its location in the khedival harem palace at Giza (Fig. 6, 25-26) and later at its current location north of Tahrir Square in Cairo (Fig. 77-78). Between 1889 and until the 1950s or 60s, antiquities were exhibited and sold from a specific room designated *Salle de vente* (p. 47).

Lange stayed close to the Museum and the dealers during both of his visits to Egypt. The couple's residence during the first half of their stay in 1899/1900 was Pension König, located right next to Ezbekiya Gardens 'between the Place de l'Opéra and the Shâri'a 'Abdîn', and a room cost '8 fr.' per night at the time of Lange's visit.[234] Sharia Abdin was the southward continuation of Sharia Kamel beyond Opera Square, leading to the 'Abdîn Palace, and now part of Sharia al-Gomehoriya. They arrived on Sunday 15 October and were greeted by the proprietor, the Austrian

233. Rob Demarée informs us that there was a small shop at Mena House as late as the mid-1960s, when he himself purchased the lower half of a Ramesside kneeling statue, although he could not recall the name of the dealer. Demarée donated the fragment in question to the Metropolitan Museum of Art in 2009 upon discovering that it possessed the

upper half of the same statue (now MMA 66.99.94 + 2009.253); see Roehrig, *BMMA* 68, no. 2 (2010), 4.

234. Baedeker, *Ägypten*, 4th edition, 24.

Fig. 73. Standard-bearing statue of Ramesses III offered for sale by Nahman to Lange through Johannes Pedersen, the later professor of Semitic Philology at Copenhagen, who was then studying at Al-Azhar University in Cairo. The statue was kept in the basement of Nahman's mansi-on which was also filled with antiquities; note the cabinet in the background with objects inside and jars stored on top. The statue is now in the Museum of Archaeology and Anthropology (inv. E15727) at the University of Pennsylvania. Enclosed with a letter from Pedersen to Lange dated 3 December 1920. Courtesy of the Royal Library.

Fig. 74. 20 Sharia Sheikh Abu el-Sibâ (now Gawad Hos-ny) where Maurice Nahman lived and conducted his early business. He later opened a shop at Sharia Qasr el-Nil, across from the Savoy Hotel. Around 1920 he moved both his business and his residence to the palatial building on Sharia Madabegh, on the opposite side of the same block. Photograph by the authors, May 2013.

Frau König.[235] They were initially somewhat disap-pointed; 'first of all, there was only one room, and sec-ond, it did not look very comfortable; it resembles entirely a well-furnished bedroom.' The room was relatively small, some 4½ by 4½ metres (Fig. 79); 'the

floor has tiles as in most other buildings, which is ef-ficient against vermin, but there are plenty of carpets on the floor.' Yet they immediately took a liking to Frau König herself, who was 'exceptionally helpful, always forthcoming and kind', and they were very pleased with her cooking. They also found the dining hall, which included a balcony, very pleasant.

During the second half of their stay, the Lange couple lived with Borchardt and Schäfer in the spa-cious guestroom of their large six-room apartment (Fig. 80-81) at Sharia Zekki (now Sayed Anbar), which led straight to Ezbekiya Gardens via Sharia Elfi

235. Lange and Lange, *Dagbog fra Ægyptensrejsen 1899-1900*, esp. pp. 37, 68, 122, 151.

Fig. 75. Zaki Mahmud Abd es-Samad in front of his antiquities shop at 9 Sharia Mariette Pasha, Cairo. Photograph given to Lange in 1929. Courtesy of the Royal Library.

Fig. 76. Hefnawy Ismaïl el-Shaer with customers in his antiquities shop across from the Cairo Museum, January 1971. He belonged to a large family of dealers who had recieved the very first official license to sell antiquities when registration became mandatory in 1912. Courtesy of Rob Demarée.

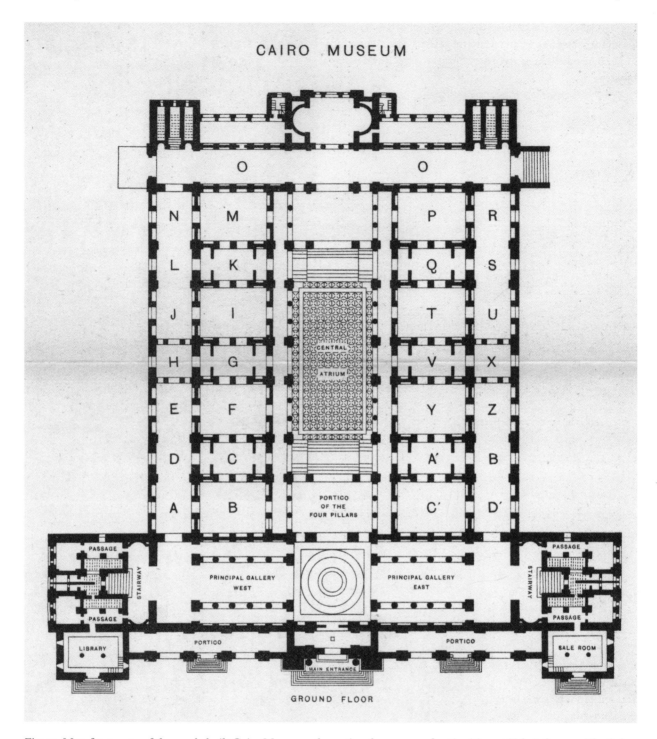

Fig. 77. Map from 1902 of the newly built Cairo Museum, the national museum of antiquities, at Tahrir Square. The Sales Room (*salle de vente*) was located in the eastern pavilion, just to the right of the entrance, while the western pavilion held the library. Maspero, *Guide to the Cairo Museum,* Cairo, 1903.

Fig. 78. The eastern pavilion of the Egyptian Museum at Tahrir Square functioned as the official Sales Room (*salle de vente*) from 1902 until at least 1952. The main street along the museum, named Sharia Mariette Pasha after the founder of the Antiquities Service and just visible to the right in the photograph, housed a series of antiquities dealers just across from the Sales Room. They included Zaki Mahmud Abd es-Samad, Hefnawy Ismaïl el-Shaer, and M. A. Mansoor. Photograph by the authors, May 2013.

Bey. Their two German friends had suggested already in November that they might move into the guest-room as soon as it became available; Georg Steindorff was currently living there but was expected to move out in May.[236] He left some weeks earlier than origi-nally expected and the couple settled in already in March.

During their second visit in 1929/30, they stayed at Cecil House at 4 Sharia Nasr ed-Din (Fig. 82-83), next to the Mohammed Ali Club, which cost '60 Z., P. 70-80 Pi.'[237] Sharia Nasr ed-Din is a little side-street leading north from Sharia el-Bustan (now Sharia Abd el-Salam Aref), almost directly across from the Egyp-tian Museum. Cecil House is said to have been popu-lar among Danes, and one of the more famous Danes to visit it was the playwright and pastor, Kaj Munk, who stayed there in 1934. Lange provides the follow-ing description in their diary:

We have been here a month now, and I have to say that we are exceptionally pleased with Cecil House. The food is really good; the variety they can offer is surpris-ing. We eat at smaller or larger tables. We and Miss H. [sc. Hornemann] have our own table. The service is good and quick, and is handled by 4 servants in white coats with red scarves and red caps, and a similarly dressed one organises the serving and serves soup. The hotel is managed by two sisters, Miss Simons and Mrs. Quedens; they inherited the hotel from an aunt. Mr Quedens [sc. Julius N. Quedens], who is from southern Jutland and has studied theology in Germany and Co-penhagen, is Danish Vice-consul and married to one of the sisters; they have a daughter who is 6½ years. There is space here for about 60 guests. Quite a few live here as pensioners; there are still not many here; the main influx of students only starts in January.[238]

Cecil House was popular amongst scholars in gener-al, and several colleagues stayed there during Lange's visit:

236. Lange and Lange, *Dagbog fra Ægyptensrejsen 1899-1900*, 116.
237. Baedeker, *Ägypten und der Sudân*, 8th edition, 34. The building is now abandoned and partly demolished.

238. Lange, *Dagbog fra Ægypten, 1929-1930*, 110.

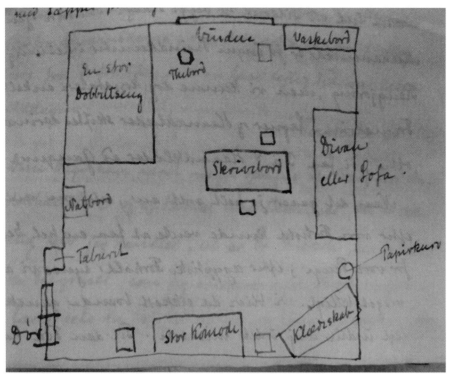

Fig. 79. The Lange couple arrived at Pension König, next to Ezbekiyeh Gardens, on 17 October 1899 and stayed there for about five months. The American Egyptologist G. A. Reisner told Lange during a visit on 7 December that he and his wife had stayed in exactly the same room two years earlier when they first came to Egypt. The room measured just under 20 m². Sketch in travel diary of 1899/1900. Courtesy of the Royal Library.

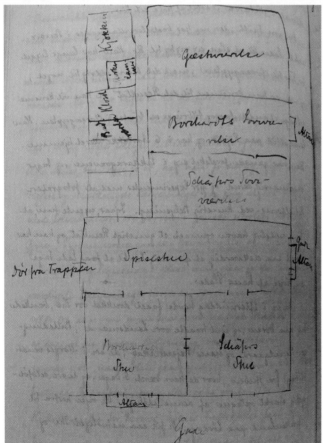

Fig. 80. The six-room apartment shared by Lange's German colleagues and friends, Ludwig Borchardt and Heinrich Schäfer. In March 1900 the Lange couple moved into the guestroom next to Borchardt's bedroom and across from the kitchen. This room was 'significantly larger' than the one they had so far rented from Frau König. Sketch in travel diary 1899/1900. Courtesy of the Royal Library.

Fig. 81. H. O. Lange and Jonna lived for several months with Ludwig Borchardt and Heinrich Schäfer in their six room apartment next to Ezbekiya Gardens, Cairo, during their first visit to Egypt in 1899/1900. In this partially faded photograph they are seen playing cards in the living room (clockwise: LB, HOL, JL, HS). Lange photograph, 1900. Courtesy of the Royal Library.

Cecil House is a real meeting place for Egyptologists and Arabists. In addition to Spiegelberg and de Buck, there is also a young Russian Egyptologist called Piankoff, whom I have met in Paris and London. Of Arabists we have here Wensinck from Leiden, Nallino from Turin, and Dr Schacht from Germany who lectures on Syrian grammar at the university in classical Arabic.[239]

A few years earlier, in 1926, Idris Bell and Francis Kelsey, of the British Museum and University of Michigan respectively, stayed there while hunting for papyri in Cairo.[240] It is not clear whether Lange heard about Cecil House from other Danes, from colleagues, or from the Baedeker guidebooks.

239. Lange, *Dagbog fra Ægypten, 1929-1930*, 317. The Arabists mentioned are Arent Jan Wensinck (1882-1939), Carlo Alfonso Nallino (1872-1938), and Joseph Schacht (1902-1969).

240. Pedley, *The Life and Work of Francis Willey Kelsey*, 375.

Fig. 82. H. O. and Jonna Lange drinking tea on the roof terrace of Cecil House. Lange photograph, 1929. Courtesy of the Royal Library.

Fig. 83. Cecil House at Sharia Nasr ed-Din 4, now abandoned and partly collapsed. Photograph by the authors, May 2013.

The antiquities market in Kafr el-Haram at Giza

The Bedouin village of Kafr el-Haram (Fig. 84-89) was located at Giza near the pyramids and housed a large number of mostly illicit antiquities dealers.[241] With the legislation of 1912 all trade at Kafr el-Haram was effectively banned (p. 40). A few of the dealers received formal licences to open shops in Cairo, while others chose to operate through strawmen because only Egyptian and Turkish nationals could be punished for illicit dealing. One example of this is given by Petrie, who mentioned in 1914 that 'Two of the best-known dealers from the pyramids now have a prominent shop in Cairo with an Italian name over the door'.[242]

The dealers at Kafr el-Haram comprised a large proportion of all the dealers mentioned in the Lange papers: *Sheikh* Hamza, *Sheikh* Ibrahim Abd es-Samad, his brother Soliman and his son Zaki Mahmud Abd es-Samad (who had a shop in Cairo), Ali Abd el-Haj, his sons Mohammed Ali and Ibrahim Ali, the brothers Farag and Saïd Ismaïn, Mansur Ismäin, Ali Gabri, Mangud, and Mansur. A number of the dealers in this relatively small village are known to have been related to each other, either by blood or by marriage (cf. Table 5). In principle many of the inhabitants of Kafr el-Haram may have functioned as dealers on a minor level, but it is clear that some of the dealers listed were better known, and presumably more established, than others.

The dealers at Kafr el-Haram exploited both the steady flow of tourists who came to see the great pyramids and the seemingly endless supply of antiquities afforded by the vast Old Kingdom necropolis. Speaking as a tourist, the US consul general in Cairo, Elbert E. Farman (who accompagnied President Ulysses S. Grant during his visit to Egypt in 1877, just after his retirement) writes:

I have several times visited the village of the pyramid-Arabs, which is on the edge of the desert nearby, in search of antiquities. They are not a bad people, though frequently annoying.[243]

The archaeologist G. A. Reisner, who carried out careful and systematic excavations at Giza over many years, and whom Lange met in Cairo in 1899,[244] was more frustrated. He complained bitterly about the situation at the turn of the century:

the natives of Kafr-el-Haram, the pyramid village, were carrying on an almost systematic series of illicit excavations in the great cemetery: and every year a number of reliefs, offering-stones and private statues from the tombs found their way to European museums.[245]

In another contribution, Reisner described the security measures he found necessary during the excavation of a tomb he had recently discovered:

Three days we had our meals in or beside the tomb and working until late at night. At night the shaft was closed with beams, boards and canvas and guarded by twenty men, who were given unlimited cigarettes and coffee to keep them awake. The heavy guard was necessary as we were working in full view of the loafers of Kafr-el-Haram, who hang about the plateau, people who have been notorious for generations as thieves of antiquities.[246]

Lange himself provides several descriptions of his visits to the antiquities dealers at the village of Kafr el-Haram in 1899 and 1900. These visits included not least the main dealers, Ali Abd el-Haj and Farag Ismäin, who had earlier been partners but had now become rivals (p. 192). During one of his first visits to the village, on 18 November 1899, he had been invited to the homes of the brothers Soliman and Ibrahim Abd es-Samad together with Valdemar Schmidt.

241. A photograph of Kafr el-Haram, taken in 1881 from the rock-cut tombs above the village by Petrie, may be found in Quirke, *Hidden Hands*, 273, fig. 9.3; cf. also the sketch of the village on p. 275, fig. 9.8.
242. Petrie in *Ancient Egypt* I (1914), 128.
243. Farman, *Along the Nile with General Grant*, 47.
244. Lange and Lange, *Dagbog fra Ægyptensrejsen 1899-1900*, 178.
245. Reisner, 'Recent Explorations in Egypt', *The Independent*, New York, 10 Feb. 1910, 303.
246. Reisner, *BMFA* 11 (1913), 59.

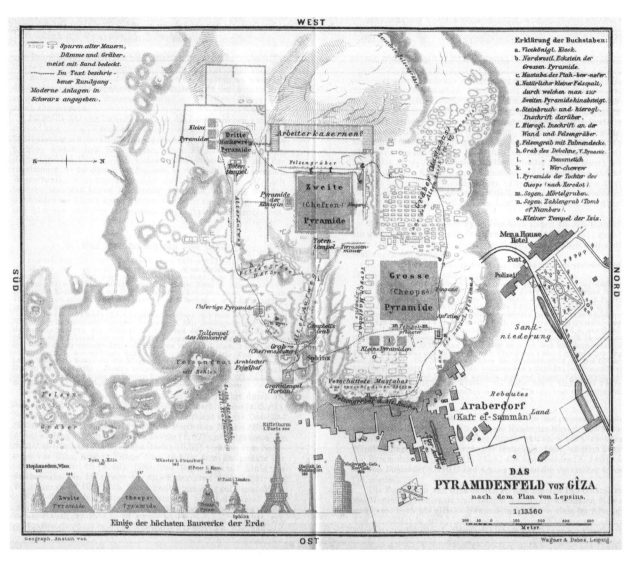

Fig. 84. Map from 1913 indicating the Bedouin village of Kafr el-Haram (here called Kafr es-Sammân), immediately east of the Cheops cemetery below the desert plateau. The village, mostly referred to simply as 'Kafr', functioned as a satellite for the Cairene antiquities trade. Its location next to the vast Old Kingdom archaeological site facilitated the large-scale trade in illicit antiquities here; in fact most local families seem to have been involved on some level. Several of the dealers were well-established, such as Ali Abd el-Haj el-Gabri, Farag Ismaïn, and the Abd es-Samad family. Baedeker, *Ägypten*, 7th ed., 1913.

we walked along, huddled together, as we passed their streets, as it was less than appealing, and at last we got to the house of Soliman which was behind a large wall and partly newly built... we sat in a circular outhouse with coloured glass in the windows and carpets from Mecca on the floor [*Jonna adds a few lines later that the whole family had been to Mecca and Medina*] ... Upon leaving Soliman we went to his brother Ibrahim's house. It too was a two-storey house, newly built; we were gi-

ven coffee and there was an entire museum on display.[247]

A more detailed and picturesque account of a visit to Mohammed Ali on 18 December 1899 reads as follows:

247. Lange and Lange, *Dagbog fra Ægyptensrejsen 1899-1900*, 140-141.

Fig. 85. The road to the pyramids at Giza which would
have been travelled by H. O.
Lange and other visitors. The
whole Bedouin village of Kafr
el-Haram is visible before the
pyramids. Magic lantern glass
slide, 1890s? Private collection, Kim Ryholt (gift from
grandmother's sister).

When we arrived at Giza, a messenger from Muhammed Ali, to whom we were going, was awaiting us. He
led us by a very difficult route up along steep slopes
and through much sand to that part of the village Kafr
where the man lived. Just outside the village we met
Muhammed Ali himself who asked where Schäfer was,
but we had no idea. Our guide was then sent up to the
pyramids to find him and we followed the other. He led
us by the most remarkable route into his house. We had
to crawl up a hencoop ladder onto the roof of a mud
house, walk along the edge of this out of fear that our
legs would fall straight through the ceiling, and then
down another ladder; now we were in his house. This is
still under construction, a huge house, part of which is
intended for visitors, he said; apparently in order to
rent it out. Poor man! He has apparently overextended
himself, for he seems to be in the most horrible need of
money. While we were looking at his stock and drinking coffee, Schäfer came ... We had coffee once more
– it was horrible – and the man invited us to eat lunch
in his house in which case he would slaughter one of

his turkeys for us immediately. But we thanked him
very much; it would have to wait until next time. When
we had seen his stock, he led us to his brother, Ibrahim,
who is the most learned of all the Bedouins; he can
really read parts of the inscriptions and looks very intelligent. There we had coffee once more and Schäfer
purchased from him. It had now gotten late, and we
started to get hungry. In order to get rid of the Bedouins who followed us and carried our things, we sat
outside Mena House and had refreshments.[248]

Lange had a rather similar experience during another
visit to Soliman Abd es-Samad, Mansur, and an unnamed son of Farag Ismaïn on 1 January 1900:

> We then visited three Bedouins in the village: Soliman,
> who has an exceptionally beautiful statue of granite,
> was not himself at home, but his good-looking young

248. Lange and Lange, *Dagbog fra Ægyptensrejsen 1899-1900*,
194-195.

Fig. 86-87. Views of the Bedouin village of Kafr el-Haram at Giza where many Egyptian dealers lived and conducted their largely illicit business. The village was located below the desert plateau with the extensive Old Kingdom necropolis. Smaller tombs cut into the cliffs can be seen in the background. Petrie's assistant Ali Gabri, who lived in the village and dealt with antiquities, kept his stock in one of these tombs. The clearly visible ladder leading to the roof of one of the houses recalls the description by Lange of his visit to the village where he and his company were lead 'by the most remarkable route' to get to the well-hidden antiquities stash of Muhammed Ali, a son of Ali Abd el-Haj el-Gabri: 'We had to crawl up a hencoop ladder onto the roof of a mud house, walk along the edge of this out of fear that our legs would fall straight through the ceiling, and then down another ladder; now we were in his house.' Lange photographs, 1899. Courtesy of the Royal Library.

Fig. 88. Schäfer and Jonna Lange posing with a group of dealers from Kafr el-Haram. The man standing next to Schäfer is perhaps Ali Abd el-Haj (Fig. 127) whom they visited several times. Photograph by Lange, 1899/1900. Courtesy of the Royal Library.

Fig. 89. The courtyard of the house of the antiquities dealer Soliman Abd es-Samad at Kafr el-Haram. Soliman was a granduncle of Zaki's. Jonna Lange, who took the photograph, was worried that it might not turn out well because of the bad lighting. Lange photograph, 1 January 1900. Courtesy of the Royal Library.

son Muhammed showed it to us. It is kept carefully hidden; only after the doors had been locked behind us was it hauled forth with much effort. It was lying under a bed in a room that is not used. It is curious how lovingly they may look at such a nice object, but the fact of the matter is presumably that it is its worth in money which they love.

It is funny in such a house how men and animals live together; on the stairs we met goats, chickens and pigeons, which can really be unpleasant. Down in the courtyard we made a photograph of a whole crowd of small children among whom was a little Negro boy, but the lighting was bad so it will probable not turn out well [Fig. 89].

From Soliman we went to someone whose name is Mansur who also has fine things, especially here in Cairo. We had coffee there, and Hans bought the head of a limestone statue. First he demanded 15 shillings for it, but in the end Hans got it for 5 shillings. Apparently he does not realize how much these things are worth but instead seems to evaluate them according to their size; apart from that, he is probably a man with whom one can do business.

The third, a son of Farag in Giza, had nothing. A fourth, whose name is Mangud, we looked for, but he was unfortunately in Cairo.[249]

The illegal antiquities trade that went on at Kafr el-Haram was not entirely without risk to those involved, but harsh action was rare. On 25 March 1912 George Reisner notes in his diary, not without some glee, that the Faïd family which had been 'favorites of Maspero for over twenty-five years' had received harsh sentences for their theft of reliefs from 'Petrie's tomb' (a Saïte period tomb at Zawyet al-Aryan): 'It is a great satisfaction to me to see that my judgment of these men was correct and to know that a severe lesson has been given to the Kafr-el-Haram thieves.'[250] The head of the family was none less than a government reïs (a local foreman in the Antiquities Service) named Ibrahim

Faïd. He was sentenced to five years hard labor, while other family members and participants received sentences of 25 and 30 months.[251] The men were sentenced on March 24, the day before Reisner wrote his letter, but Maspero personally helped them appeal the case and in a matter of weeks, on May 1, they were fully acquitted and set free. Ibrahim Faïd resumed his function as reïs and a few months later he was involved with Junker's mission at Giza.

Although Maspero intervened on behalf of the Faïd family, he was less favourable towards Kafr el-Haram than Reisner seems to imply. When the antiquities law of 1912 was introduced, he decided explicitly to ban all trade at Kafr el-Haram and very few of the local dealers got permission to conduct business in Cairo. Thus, for instance, Petrie mentions that two of the most important dealers were behind 'a prominent shop in Cairo with an Italian name' (p. 93). Among the licensed dealers from Kafr el-Haram with a shop in Cairo was Zaki Mahmud Abd es-Samad and presumably also Mohammed M. el-Gabri.

Lange records the origins of the village, as related to him by its inhabitants, as follows: some hundred years earlier (so around 1800) a tribe of Bedouins had settled near the pyramids and become permanent residents there. Most of the current inhabitants of Kafr el-Haram were said to be descended from this tribe, and identified themselves as such in contrast to 'the Egyptian people' in Cairo. The inhabitants claimed to be, by virtue of their history, not Egyptian citizens but free people, and, like other Bedouin tribes, under the protection of the French Consul-General. Lange then observes that 'This is the reason why it is so difficult to do anything about their illegal trade in antiquities'.[252] This may be the reason why, according to Lange, they were not allowed to carry out licensed excavations, but there

249. Lange and Lange, *Dagbog fra Ægyptensrejsen 1899-1900*, 220-221. A number of objects seen with these dealers on this particular day are copied into Lange, *Notebook 1899/1900*, 207-208.
250. Der Manuelian, *KMT* 7, no. 2 (1996), 70, 72.

251. Gouvernement Égyptien, *Rapport du Service des Antiquités pour l'année 1912*, 18; cf. also idem, *Rapport du Service des Antiquités pour l'année 1913*, 14-17, and letters cited by David, *Gaston Maspero*, 540, 559. The details provided by Reisner about the sentences differ in some details from this report.
252. Lange and Lange, *Dagbog fra Ægyptensrejsen 1899-1900*, 434.

may have been ways of circumventing the legislation by having others named in the license. Certainly Farag Ismaïn conducted licensed excavations, and Lange too was approached by a Bedouin for a partnership where he would effectively lend his name to the excavation.[253]

The Bedouins settled in Kafr el-Haram belonged to the Najama tribe, and although they were certainly not above the law in any formal sense – as shown by the (temporary) conviction of the Faïd family – they had, historically like all Bedouins, enjoyed an existence on the margins of Egyptian society. This manifested itself in a strong sense of group identity, accompanied by a legal tradition of solving disputes without involving the state; however, Lange's information about them being under the jurisdiction of the French Consul-General has proven difficult to verify.[254] As Bedouin they enjoyed certain privileges like exemption from corvée duty and military service, in return for which they were tasked with the protection and patrolling of Egypt's borders and desert areas, or, in the case of the Najama, the Giza pyramids and the adjacent necropolis.[255] The 1882 census of Egypt reports the presence of six sheikhs (presumably appointed by the Khedive) among the Najama of Giza overseeing around six thousands individuals, although this would have included, in addition to Kafr el-Haram, neighbouring villages such as Nazlat al-Batran.[256]

While the villagers of Kafr el-Haram preferred to solve disputes without outside interference, peaceful solutions were not always possible and sometimes matters came to a head. Lange reports a very dramatic incident that took place in July 1900:

Out in the village of Kafr there is at the moment much violent unrest: the other day there was a big fight which involved about 150 people; eventually they took up firearms, 'a bit of lead', as one of the Bedouins said, and in the end some seven or eight people were killed. It is almost certainly exceptional that things come to this; normally the Arabs are more inclined to use words than than brute force.[257]

The antiquities market in the Fayum

Although the whole Fayum had become the object of an intensive search for papyri and other antiquities in the late 19th century, the region seems to have had few established dealers. Valdemar Schmidt visited Medinet el-Fayum (Fig. 90) in 1894, the largest city in the area, accompanied by his friend, the antiquities dealer Alexandre Dingli, and he refers to just one dealer who was evidently Muslim:

In this town there were three places selling Egyptian antiquities. All three belonged to one and the same man, who in each of the houses had a shop and — a wife, so three in total. A total of four is allowed.[258]

This man was perhaps a certain Khalil who, according to Wilbour, operated what he described as the 'principal anteekeh shop' at Medinet el-Fayum in 1891.[259]

The situation seems not to have changed significantly in the course of the next six years. On 10-11 April 1900 Lange went for a two-day visit to the Fayum in the company of Dr Speyer. At the train station they met the young C. C. Edgar, who was chief inspector of antiquities for Lower Egypt and who joined them in their 2nd class wagon (even though he had purchased a 1st class ticket). The visit included an excursion to Arsinoe, and as usual Lange took the opportunity to provide a brief description of the area and its state of affairs:

253. Lange and Lange, *Dagbog fra Ægyptensrejsen 1899-1900*, 738.
254. Schölch, *Die Welt des Islams* 17 (1976-1977), 46, notes that 'The Egyptian Bedouins as a whole were subordinate to the general jurisdiction of the country, and they had to pay the land- and cattle-taxes if they owned either'. For a general overview of the legal system of Egyptian Bedouins, see Murray, *Sons of Ishmael*, 200-242.
255. Schölch, *Die Welt des Islams* 17 (1976-1977), 46.
256. Quirke, *Hidden Hands*, 112.

257. Lange and Lange, *Dagbog fra Ægyptensrejsen 1899-1900*, 752.
258. Schmidt, *Af et Langt Livs Historie*, 96. It is not entirely clear to us what the em dash (—) is intended to signal; perhaps simply a rhetorical pause.
259. Cf. Capart (ed.), *Letters of Charles Edwin Wilbour*, 580. Wilbour further mentions two lesser dealers at Medinet el-Fayum, *Hajji* Mahmud and Stamati.

Fig. 90. The centre of Medinet el-Fayum, mostly referred to simply as 'Fayum', with the main street running along the canal. Lange photograph, April 1900. Courtesy of the Royal Library.

... sometimes we found a bronze coin or a piece of glass or faience, nothing of value, because the Arabs are thorough in their plundering ... From these heaps of rubble derive especially lots of papyri, mainly Greek; they are found by the Arabs who sift through the ruins in search for <u>Sebakh</u> ... which they use as fertilizer in their fields.[260] The mounds are thoroughly sifted through and the Greek business people in Medine like to run a small-scale side business selling papyri and other antiquities.

Lange was very impressed with the ruins and spent four hours walking around the site, but they still had some time on their hands before supper and tried to make the best of it.

Since there was still some time left before supper could be made ready, we got hold of a boy who could show us the way to a couple of antiquities dealers. One of them was a Greek herb merchant, who brought out a few smaller objects which were without interest, and a large box of papyri; Edgar and I took aside some of these and asked about the price; he demanded 100 Francs which obviously was out of the question. We made no business there. We were led to another merchant, but he was not home. We therefore had nothing else to do than to return home to the hotel and comfort ourselves with the Greek food.[261]

The difficulty in finding antiquities for sale at Medinet el-Fayum marks a striking contrast to Cairo, where Lange almost had to fend off dealers. The situation is

260. On the practice of digging for sebakh, see Bailey, *JEA* 85 (1999), 211-218.

261. Lange and Lange, *Dagbog fra Ægyptensrejsen 1899-1900*, 518.

perhaps explained by the fact that few tourists both-
ered to visit the region. Lange himself stayed at the
recently built Hotel Karun which Grenfell had recommended to him ('one does not need to bring insect
powder'), but he was thoroughly disappointed with
the place and the food, and drily notes that 'I can't
imagine Grenfell would have recommended the hotel
so warmly if he had arrived here directly from Cairo,
rather than from four months in a tent in the desert'.[262]
He ends his description of the Fayum with a note to
the effect that much of the trade in antiquities in Medinet el-Fayum was dominated by Greeks:

> It is often the Greeks in the cities who are behind the
> systematic plunderings, in particular in the Fayum,
> where they are unusually numerous. The Greeks down
> here play a very peculiar role; of the Europeans they are
> unsurpassed in their ability to establish contact with
> the natives and thereby exploit them.[263]

Two established dealers at the time of Lange's visit
was the Copt Yassa Todros (*fl.* 1897-1911), who is
known to have carried out excavations, and Mohammed Abdallah (*fl.* c. 1900-1930), while other dealers
active around the turn of the century are *Hajji*
Mahmud (*fl.* 1891), Mahmud Rifai (*fl.* 1900-1905, same
as the preceding?), and Stamati (*fl.* 1891). The number
of dealers in the region seems to have increased after
the turn of the century and includes Mohammed Saïd
(*fl.* 1910-1912, described by Petrie as the 'main dealer'
of the area at the time), Mohammed Khalil (*fl.* 1907-
1931), Scopelitis (*fl.* 1913), Mohammed Rafar (*fl.* 1920),
and the Copts Andreas Girgis (*fl.* 1920), Todros (*fl.*
1926), and Agaibi Makarios (*fl.* 1930-36).

The antiquities market in Qena

Qena was the largest city in Upper Egypt with a population of c. 27,500 during Lange's first visit to Egypt
(Fig. 91). At this time, the population of Luxor was

just c. 11,000.[264] There were no significant ruins in
Qena, but the city was a hub for the antiquities trade
(based on material from rich archaeological sites
nearby such as Akhmim and Dendera) and linked directly to Luxor which is located some 50 km to the
south. It was therefore natural that Lange would visit
Qena, even though it was off the beaten track for tourists; Thomas Cook tours, for example, who had a vir-
tual monopoly on tourism up the Nile in the 1880s-
1890s, did not usually stop there – they went from
Cairo to Assiut and then directly to Luxor (and then
on to Aswan and Khartoum).[265]

In February 1900 he notes that 'Qena is supposed
to be the largest city in Upper Egypt, but by no means
makes a notable impression. Inside it really looks no
different from the village of Giza or Luxor.'[266] He proceeds to describe his journey on donkey from the train
station through the narrow streets, nearly blocked by
camels loaded with goods, to the river which he has to
cross by ferry. Although his arrival was not expected
and there were no other Europeans present, he was
immediately offered antiquities by several farmers
who had already boarded the ferry (cited in context p.
31); apparently it was common to keep smaller objects
at hand should a chance encounter with a collector
come about. When he visited the city thirty years later
in January 1930, it was still crowded (this time because
of a fifteen day long celebration in honor of the local
saint, *Sheikh* Abd er-Rahim) and Hotel Dendera was
closed (because the owner had died the day before),
but Lange was impressed with the city's new electric
plant which provided 'a magnificent illumination
over the large plaza at the tomb of the holy man (sc.
Abd er-Rahim)'.[267] During his two visits, Lange was in
touch with several Qena dealers, including the brothers Girgis and Abd en-Nur Gabrial, Todros Girgis Gabrial, Sadic Girgis Ebed, and a certain 'Bastra' (pos-

262. Lange and Lange, *Dagbog fra Ægyptensrejsen 1899-1900*, 515.
263. Lange and Lange, *Dagbog fra Ægyptensrejsen 1899-1900*, 524,
cf. pp. 516-517.

264. Baedeker, *Egypte*, 2nd edition, 226, 236.
265. Robert Hunter, *Middle Eastern Studies* 40, no. 5 (2004), 43.
266. Lange and Lange, *Dagbog fra Ægyptensrejsen 1899-1900*, 349.
267. Lange, *Dagbog fra Ægypten, 1929-1930*, 239-243.

Fig. 91. A view of Qena, the capital of the Qena governorate and the largest city in Upper Egypt. The city housed several dealers, among which Girgis Gabrial was the most prominent, but few tourists visited Qena and Girgis often travelled to Cairo and Luxor to do business. Undated postcard issued by A. Bergeret et cie, probably early 20ᵗʰ Century.

sibly Basta Abd el-Melek). The Freer diaries mention two other dealers at Qena, apparently named Tanios Girgis and Morgos Chanher.[268]

The antiquities market in Luxor

In the late 19ᵗʰ Century, the main antiquities dealers at Luxor (Fig. 92-93) - most of them consular agents - dealt from prominent private houses located along the embankment (Fig. 94-96). The house of Mohareb Todros (the German consular agent) was situated between the ancient quay and the Luxor temple,[269] while those of Mustafa Aga (the British consular agent), Shenudi Makarios (the French consular agent), and *Sheikh* Ali Ledid had been built inside the temple itself. Edwin Smith also had a house

inside the temple, built for him by Mustafa Aga. The house of Ali Murad (the US consular agent) was situated on the embankment between the Luxor temple and the Karnak Hotel to the north,[270] and Mohammed Mohasseb had a house on the embankment.[271]

By the time of Lange's first trip, the two consular houses and all other private residences inside the Lux-

268. Gunter, *A Collector's Journey*, 91, 116-117.
269. Baedeker, *Egypte et Soudan*, 4ᵗʰ edition, pl. facing p. 245.

270. Baedeker, *Egypt*, 5ᵗʰ edition, pl. facing p. 233 (marked '1'). By 1906 the house of the US consular agent was located on the embankment south of the Luxor temple on the site where the current Winter Palace Hotel was later built; cf. idem, *Ägypten und der Sudân*, 6ᵗʰ edition, pl. facing p. 239 (marked '1'). Note that the original Winter Palace Hotel stood somewhat further north of its current location; compare idem, *Egypt and the Sudân*, 6ᵗʰ edition, 248, with idem, *Egypt and the Sûdân*, 7ᵗʰ edition, pl. facing p. 251.
271. Baedeker, *Egypte et Soudan*, 4ᵗʰ edition, 247; Budge, *By Nile and Tigris* I, 138.

Fig. 92. Map of Luxor from
1903, around the time of
Lange's first visit to Egypt.
The city expanded rapidly
over the next 25 years, as can
be seen in the map of Luxor
from 1928 (Fig. 93). Baedeker,
Égypte, 2nd ed., 1903.

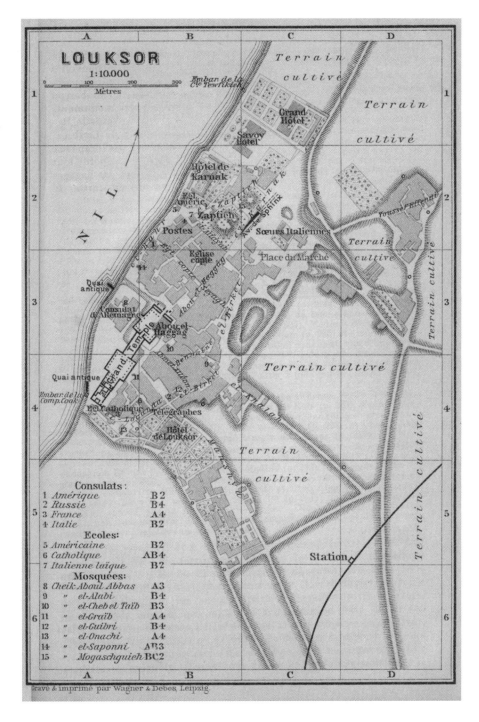

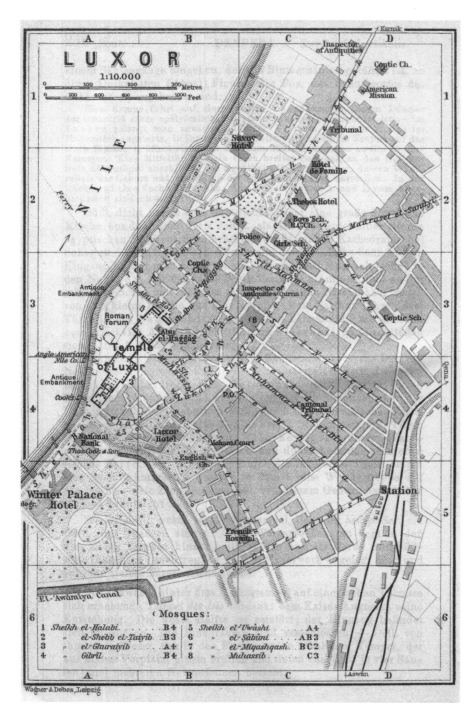

Fig. 93. Map of Luxor from 1928. Most of the established dealers were located in Sharia el-Lukanda (A4, B4), including Muhammed Mohasseb, Abd el-Megid Hussein Aga, Mansur Mahmud, and Todros Girgis Gabrial. The shop of Yussuf Hassan was at Sharia el-Markaz (B3, C2) which is a more or less direct continuation of Sharia el-Lukanda, while the residence and museum-like shop of German consular agent Mohareb Todros was located on the bank of the Nile on the other side of Luxor temple (A3). Kamal Khalid had his stall at the Winter Palace Hotel (A5), and that of Abd er-Rahim was near the same hotel. Hotel du Nil, where Wolfgang Dreiss conducted his early business, was located on the Nile on the other side of the Winter Palace Hotel (off the map). All houses on the west side of Sharia el-Lukanda and Sharia el-Markaz, towards the river bank, have since been demolished. Baedeker, *Egypt*, 8th ed., 1928.

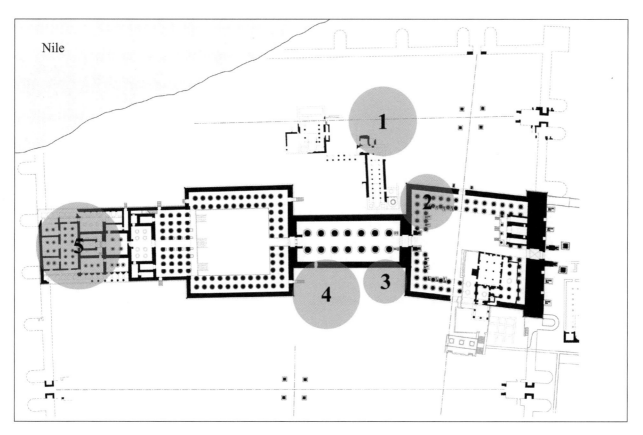

Fig. 94. A map of the approximate locations of the houses of the antiquities dealers at the temple of Luxor in the 1880s. Clockwise from the top: (1) residence of Todros Bolos and later his son Mohareb Todros, German consular agents (Fig. 95-96); (2) house of *Sheikh* Ali Ledid; (3) house of Edwin Smith; (4) residence of Mustafa Aga Ayat, originally consular agent for the US, later for Britain, Russia and Belgium (Fig. 30, 97-98); (5) Maison de France, residence of Shenudi Makarios, French consular agent (Fig. 99-100). Plan by James B. Heidel, courtesy of the Epigraphic Survey, Oriental Institute, University of Chicago.

or temple had been demolished. There had long been a desire to clear the well-preserved temple and make it more accessible, but the residents opposed the plans and the consular agents for their part had diplomatic immunity. Maspero managed to commence an expropriation process in 1881 and after much resistance and many delays, all the houses had been appropriated and demolished by 1886 – except for that of Mustafa Aga (Fig. 97-98), which was removed in 1889.[272] While

Shenudi had been cooperative and agreed to a compensation in land and a cash sum of £120 for the construction of a new house, Mustafa Aga for his part began adding to the house in order to increase his damages, prevented access to the engineer sent to inspect it, and is said to have demanded an exorbitant compensation of £3,000.[273] In the end, the state de-

272. Daressy, obituary of G. Maspero, *ASAE* 16 (1916), 132; cf. also Legrain, *ASAE* 17 (1917), 56; cf. also David, *Gaston Maspero*, 61, 134-135, 173, 178-179, 181-182, 217. In Sept. 2014 a number of letters by Gaston Maspero from 1884-1886 discussing the

appropriation of the houses of Shenudi Makarios and Mustafa Aga (from the Ministry of Public Works) were sold on Ebay.
273. The episode is well documented in the Wilbour letters; cf. Capart (ed.), *Letters of Charles Edwin Wilbour*, passim, esp. pp. 117, 285, 377, 508; cf. also Edwards, *A Thousand Miles up the Nile*, 2nd edition, 143-144, n. 1. The house was built about thirty years earlier in the 1850s; cf. Bell, in Brinkman (ed.), *The Oriental*

Fig. 95. View of Luxor temple from the west, early 1870s. Half-hidden behind the colonnade is the house of the British, Russian and Belgian consular agent Mustafa Aga Ayat. The larger building in the foreground to the left, in the process of being white-washed, is the house of the German consular agent Todros Bolos and his son and successor Mohareb Todros. Both buildings were later expropriated and demolished to clear the temple area, the former in 1888 and the latter in 1914. These were the main venues for the antiquities trade at Luxor at the time. Detail of commercial photograph by Félix Bonfils, inscribed 'Vue générale de Louqsor'. Courtesy of Library of Congress.

Fig. 96. The quay between Luxor Temple and the Nile bank, 1900. The photograph captures the bustling atmosphere of the quayside where local traders, guides, and boatmen congregated to do business with passing tourists. The white-washed house of the German consular agent, Mohareb Todros, can be seen in the background. Schäfer had informed him of Lange's arrival in advance, and Lange visited his huge sales collection which was exhibited in three large rooms within the consular residence. He describes Mohareb as honourable and knowledgeable, but his prices were steep and he acquired only a few smaller objects. Lange photograph. Courtesy of the Royal Library.

Fig. 97. The residence of the consular agent Mustafa Aga Ayat was built within Luxor Temple in the 1850s and made clever use of the great colonnade of Amenhotep III as a monumental portico at its front. The main entrance at the end of a broad staircase is visible between two of the massive columns. Three flag poles are embedded in the soil before the columns and mark his status as consular agent for Britain, Russia and Belgium. The writing above the entrance is not an official sign, but in fact a poster where only the heading 'Palestine' can be made out. Edwin Smith lived in one of the adjacent two-storey houses, which was also owned by Mustafa Aga, until the two men fell out with each other in 1876. Commercial photograph by Antonio Beato, 1870s.

cided to grant £290 but considered deducting it from his tax arrears of £1,200 which he had failed to pay under the protection of his diplomatic immunity as consular agent. He had still not vacated the house by his death in 1887; it was inherited by his son and removed two years later.

The house occupied by Shenoudi Makarios, on top of the Luxor temple (Fig. 99-101),[274] was said to have been built by Henry Salt, the British consul-general, around 1815 and also to have been used by his agent, Giovanni Battista Belzoni. It was later present-

Institute, Annual Report 1980-81, 10-11, w. fig. A detailed description of the house may be found in Ferguson, *Moss gathered by a rolling stone,* 42-44; cf. also Hopley, *Under Egyptian Palms,* 166-167.

274. Edwards, *A Thousand Miles up the Nile,* 2ⁿᵈ edition, 451-454, w. pl. on p. 452; Duff-Gordon, *Lady Duff-Gordon's Letters from Egypt,* revised edition, 84-86, 101-102, w. plate facing p. 101; Bierbrier, *Who was Who in Egyptology,* 4ᵗʰ edition, 164-165 (Duff-Gordon), 363 (s.v. Maunier).

Fig. 98. An earlier view of Mustafa Aga Ayat's residence before the construction of the second floor had been completed. A contemporary visitor provides the following description: the house 'is built in the courts of Amunoph's temple, and boasts of as fine a portico as the Parthenon. Mustafa, with an eye to the dignity of his post, has managed to introduce his porch between two pillars of the great colonnade leading to the adyta, to which his dwelling, a rough roomy structure, hangs as a pendant' (Hopley, *Under Egyptian Palms*, 166). Commercial photograph by Francis Frith, 1858.

ed to the French government by Muhammed Ali and became *Maison de France*. It was used by Champollion and Rosellini in 1829, and two years later by the French naval officers who had been sent to bring one of the Luxor obelisks to the Place de la Concorde. The French consular agent and antiquities dealer V. Galli Maunier resided in the house for about 20 years in the mid 19th century. At this time, French visitors would occasionally stay there, including Gustave Flaubert and Maxime Du Camp in 1850. In the 1860s, the house was rented to Lady Duff-Gordon, before finally becoming the consular residence of Shenoudi Makari-os.[275] The latter showed it to Amelia Edwards in 1873/74; at that time some of the furniture of Lady Duff-Gordon was still there, but it was in a state of disrepair – 'All was very bare and comfortless.'[276] The location on top of the temple was central and commanded good views of the area, making it popular; the Italian antiquities dealer Andrea Castellari (died c. 1848) also lived in a hut on the temple roof.[277]

275. For an overview of Lady Duff-Gordon's stay in the house, see Fagan, *The Rape of the Nile*, 306-307, with an illustration of the house on p. 307.
276. Edwards, *A Thousand Miles up the Nile*, 2nd edition, 454.
277. Bierbrier, *Who was Who in Egyptology*, 4th edition, 107.

Fig. 99. Luxor temple seen from the Nile with *Maison de France* to the right. The consular flag raised from its roof signals its status as French sovereign territory. The house covers the entire southern and innermost part of the temple. Built by Henry Salt around 1815 and used by his agent Belzoni, it was later presented to the French government and housed famous individuals including Champollion, Gustave Flaubert and Maxime Du Camp. It was later let to Lady Duff-Gordon who lived there for several years in the 1860s. The house was demolished in the mid 1880s. Detail of undated commercial photograph by Antonio Beato.

At the time of Lange's first visit, Shenudi Makarios' successor as French consular agent, Basile Bichara, and Mustafa Aga's son Ahmed *Effendi*, who had succeeded him as consular agent to Britain and Russia, both resided in Sharia el-Lukanda which lay less than 100 m from the Luxor temple and more or less across from the Luxor Hotel (Fig. 93, B/4). Shenudi settled next to the Catholic Church,[278] and Ahmed *Effendi* at the corner of Sharia el-Isbilalya.[279] During Lange's two visits to Luxor, nearly all the main antiquities dealers were located in Sharia el-Lukanda. In addition to the two consular agents, they included Mohammed Mohasseb (and later his son Mahmud Mohasseb), Abd el-Megid (Fig. 102), Todros Girgis Gabrial, Mansur Mahmud, and Ahmed Abd er-Rahim, while Yussuf Hassan was located in Sharia el-Markaz which lay in direct continuation of Sharia el-Lukanda.

The house of Mohareb Todros, the German consular agent, was located just outside the Luxor temple, close to the quay, during Lange's first visit (Fig. 95-96). Although it lay within the temple precinct, it had not been the target for appropriation in the 1880s because it was not inside the temple proper. However, when the First World War broke out in 1914 and Mohareb Todros renounced his German consulship – thus losing his diplomatic immunity – it too was immediately appropriated and removed.[280] Mohareb

278. Baedeker, *Egypt*, 5th edition, pl. facing p. 233 (marked '3'); idem, *Egypte*, 2nd edition, pl. facing p. 234 (marked '3'). His son, Iskander Shenudi (consul of Austria-Hungary), later resided next to the Luxor train station; cf. idem, *Egypte et Soudan*, 4th edition, pl. facing p. 247 (marked '2').

279. Baedeker, *Egypt*, 5th edition, pl. facing p. 233 (marked '2'); idem, *Egypte et Soudan*, 3rd edition, pl. facing p. 245 (marked '2').

280. Legrain, *ASAE* 17 (1917), 56-57; Lacau, obituary of G. Legrain, *ASAE* 19, 115.

Fig. 100. Detail of Maison de France situated on top of the Luxor temple showing the terrace which had a magnificent view of the Nile. Photograph by Théodule Devéria, 1859.

Fig. 101. Modern view of the same section of the Luxor temple. Photograph by the authors, May 2013.

Fig. 102. The antiquities shop of Abd el-Megid Hussein Aga, the nephew of Mustafa Aga Ayat and a prominent dealer in Luxor, with the barque of the local saint Abu el-Haggag passing by in procession. The sign reads 'Abd el Megid Hussein Aga, Dealer of Antiquities. Entrance free.' The free entry notice suggests that his shop contained a museum-like exhibit like several of the other large antiquities shops (including that of his competitor Mohareb Todros on the other side of the Luxor temple) and was obviously intended to attract customers. Photo, c. 1913, published by Legrain, *Louqsor sans les pharaons*, pl. 23.

relocated his business to another house of his just a short distance to the north, and also located on the water front, which is described in the Baedeker guide from 1928 as a 'hübsches Museum beim Luxor-Tempel, am Nilufer'. This house, later inherited by his son and successor Zaki Mohareb Todros, was also appropriated and demolished – this time by the city in 1955 – and the business moved to Station Street next to the Luxor train station.[281]

A few further dealers were located in or near the hotels. Abd er-Rahim lived near the Winter Palace Hotel (Fig. 103-104), which lay just south of the Luxor Temple and which became the main hotel in Luxor around the turn of the century. Later both Hassani Abd el-Galil and Kamal Khalid opened shops at this hotel, while Sayed Molattam had his shop next to the entrance of the neighbouring Luxor Hotel, also south of the Luxor Temple. Hôtel du Nil, where Wolfgang Dreiss conducted his business until 1929, was located on the Nile on the opposite side of the Winter Palace Hotel, further away from the city.[282] There was a shop

---

281. Baedeker, *Ägypten und der Sudân*, 8th edition, 260.

282. Baedeker, *Egypt and the Sûdân*, 7th edition, 251 and pl. betw. pp. 254-255.

Fig. 103. Winter Palace Hotel, 1936. The main hotel in Luxor, with a wealthy clientele, it housed several antiquities shops which also attracted passing trade from the corniche. Courtesy of Library of Congress.

Fig. 104. Winter Palace Hotel. The street level of the hotel front, as seen clearly in the photograph above, is lined with shops. Presumably this is where the businesses of dealers such as Hassani Abd el-Galil and Kamal Khalid would have been located. Photograph by the authors, May 2013.

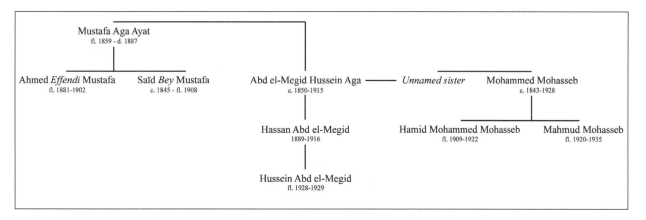

Table 4. Family tree of the main family involved in the antiquities trade at Luxor, c. 1860-1935.

in the Winter Palace Hotel itself which sold antiquities (under the raised front terrace, looking out onto the corniche), and there were also a number of small-time dealers in the Luxor bazaar who simply sold antiquities as a side-business, although the quality of their stock was variable to say the least: one visitor remarked drily that there was nothing new under the sun with the exception of the 'antiquities' sold in the bazaar.[283] Lange visited a number of such petty dealers, some of whom sold small quantities of antiquities out of their homes. Most of these are not mentioned by name, but exceptions include Abdallah Mohammed Mohasseb and Schafi in Luxor as well as Mohammed Abd el-Haggag (at Dra Abu el-Naga) and Abd er-Rasul (next to Deutsches Haus; fig. 105) on the Westbank.

Lange was surprised at the changes Luxor had undergone in the thirty years between his first and second visit, transforming it from a humble village to a modern town:

> I have now made the first excursion to Luxor, which 30 years ago was a dismal village but now has delusions of being a city. There is a water plant, but not to the extent that water carriers do not need to fill their skins down by the Nile… This year saw the arrival of electric lights, but it only works from 5 to 11. Parts of the town look like a typical Egyptian village with low mudbrick houses, stables, palms, and cattle in the dusty streets.

The corniche with the hotels and the Indian merchants' shops is naturally rather posh, and in some quarters nice houses can be found. The town is going through a transitional period.[284]

Owing to a scarcity of sources, the social networks at Luxor are difficult to map, but as in the case of Kafr el-Haram they are likely to have been complex and several of the famous dealers active in the late 19th Century are known to have been related (Table 4).

The antiquities market in Sheikh Abd el-Qurna

While Lange met several dealers on the West Bank in the area surrounding Sheikh Abd el-Qurna (or, more informally, Qurna; Fig. 105-106), this was not an antiquities satellite of Luxor directly comparable to that of Kafr el-Haram in relation to Cairo. Lange makes no mention of established dealers at Qurna, and Bruyère, writing in 1923, states that there was only one 'true' antiquities dealer in Qurna at that time, sc. Molattam. His two sons Ahmed and Saïd Molattam were also involved in the antiquities trade, but they mainly

---

283. Humphreys, *Grand Hotels of Egypt*, 180.

284. Lange, *Dagbog fra Ægypten, 1929-1930*, 177. He makes some brief remarks along the same lines about Cairo, but without much explicit detail concerning the nature of the changes (e.g. p. 32). An exception was his observation that there were much fewer mosquitoes on his second visit, a fact he attributed to the new sewage system (p. 40).

Fig. 105. Deutsches Haus, the centre for German archaeological and cultural activities in Upper Egypt, lay immediately to the south of the village of Sheikh Abd el-Qurna. The original building was destroyed during the First World War, allegedly because 'it was found to be the centre of illicit antiquities trade and otherwise undesirable' (Polz, in Cooke and Daubney, *Every Traveller Needs a Compass*, 149). The new building, shown in the photograph, was inaugurated 1 April 1927. Lange photograph, January 1930. Courtesy of the Royal Library.

Fig. 106. The village of Sheikh Abd el-Qurna situated amongst the tombs of the ancient necropolis on the Theban Westbank. It was said that virtually all the villagers were engaged in the illicit antiquities trade. Many of them excavated objects, sometimes from tombs beneath their houses, which they sold to visiting tourists. The photograph appears to have been taken during a funeral procession. Lange photograph, January 1930. Courtesy of the Royal Library.

sold fakes.[285] Bruyère adds a further list of dealers in Qurna who all primarily sold fakes ('Voici quelques noms de vendeurs de fausses (et à l'occasion de vraies) antiquités') and a single individual based in Medinet Habu: 'Gournah: Mhammed Abou l'Aggag, Hassén Saïd, Mhammed Abdallah Aouiss, Mhammed el Boum, Mhammed Aboul Hadi, Hassén el Gauz, Hassén Laban, Tayeb Mhammed Aouiss, Mhammed Abd el Galil, Mhammed Gouttayé, Mhammed Ago...[?], Saïd Mhammed, Eissé Fouli (mort). Medinet Habou: Abou Zeïd Abdallah Soudani'. Lange met a dealer called Mohammed Abd el-Haggag in Qurna, who is perhaps the same person as the Mohammed Abu el-Haggag mentioned by Bruyère.

Emma Andrews, who accompanied Theodore M. Davis to Thebes in 1890, provides a description of a Qurna which seems not to have changed much by the time of Lange's two visits to the area.

> It is very stirring and exciting to think of the constant digging and searching among the tombs across the river. Every Arab in Goornah I am told spends his night in this way. It is against all law – the government allows no digging or excavations – but they seem powerless to prevent it. It would be difficult to put such extensive territory under sufficient guard . . . In the meantime hundreds of hands are surreptitiously at work at it - valuable things are destroyed and injured by hasty and forbidden search. (...) These men dare not offer what they find for sale openly – either they have to part with them at a moderate price, to two or three dealers in Luxor, who in their turn secrete them until a safe and advantageous opening offers itself – or – they sometimes make a secret sale directly to the tourist. It is soon known among this thriving fraternity, that a tourist is anxious to buy good things, and willing to pay for them – and this accounts for the one or two mysterious men, who are constantly squatting on the bank near us, and who if he catches the eye of us holds up some bag or packet to attract our curiosity.[286]

The antiquities market in Alexandria

Alexandria, being Egypt's main port and transit zone for tourists and a centre of commerce, naturally housed a number of dealers. However, contrary to what one might expect, none of them can be ranked among the more important, and transactions relating to Alexandria are rarely mentioned in the literature. Lange, for his part, did not spent much time in Alexandria and does not discuss the antiquities trade there at all. Petrie records in his notebook from 1884/1885 some instructions, perhaps from Greville Chester, on how to find some antiquities shops in Alexandria.[287] Only one name is mentioned, but it is uncertain whether this refers to a dealer, and the brief note suggests that none of the dealers were sufficiently well-known that they could be found simply by asking for directions. Our list of dealers includes only eight dealers active in Alexandria: Theodor Graf, Dr. Eddé, Elia Pantazi, Pietro Pugioli, Pietro Makri, and Stamati Vinga of the late 19th Century, and the Anawati family and Tawfig Saïd of the mid 20th Century. Among these, Eddé and Graf seem to have been the biggest dealers. Graf's main occupation was carpet-dealing and all of his large-scale antiquities trade – the sale of substantial collections of Fayum papyri, Amarna tablets, and mummy portraits – was conducted from his base in Vienna. Eddé, by contrast, was active in Alexandria for more than 20 years.

The market: seasons, wars, and buyers

Virtually all of the trade in antiquities in Egypt took place during the four winter months, when both professional Egyptologists and tourists would descend on the country, and the dealers would flock to Cairo with their wares.[288] Lange's first visit to Egypt could hardly have been better timed in terms of the avail-

---

285. Excavation diary of Bernard Bruyère, entry of 30 Jan. 1923, accessible on-line at http://www.ifao.egnet.net/bases/archives/bruyere (accessed 16 July 2013).

286. Andrews and Davis, *A Journal on the Bedawin, 1889-1912*, typescript, kept in the Department of Egyptian Art, Metro-

politan Museum of Art. This entry relating to 4 Feb. 1890 is cited by Reeves, *MMJ* 48 (2013), 32, n. 77.

287. Cited in Quirke, *Hidden Hands*, 129.

288. Lange, *Dagbog fra Ægypten, 1929-1930*, 129; cf. Wakeling, *Forged Egyptian Antiquities*, 126.

ability of objects on the market, and in terms of prices, because some of the biggest spenders were unable to come that year:

> They [i.e. the antiquities dealers] have the feeling that this is going to be a bad year here in Egypt because of the plague and the quarantine and the war of the English. All of them also know that one of their best customers, the Englishman Budge from the British Museum, cannot come this winter because of illness, and that another good customer, the English captain Myers, has fallen in Transvaal. They are extremely keen to sell ...[289]

The rumours were correct. Budge had serious problems with his right eye, which had been operated upon but which left him unable to travel. His contacts in Egypt had written to him to enquire about his health; 'The people here and there are asking me [Chauncey Murch] whether you are to be out this year or not. They all represent to me that they have immense interests which are all staked on the matter of your coming'.[290] Other visitors that year reported similar conditions; A. H. Sayce wrote from Luxor and Cairo to say that the Boer War meant there were few English travellers on the Nile and that as a direct consequence of this the antiquities dealers had lots of objects and were prepared to bargain.[291] After the dismal winter season, traditionally the high point of the year in antiquities trading, the dealers were forced to lower their prices. Lange writes in July 1900, shortly before his return to Denmark, that

> ... the biggest customers have hardly bought anything. Everyone had high hopes for the head of the Egyptian Department in the British Museum, as he is the one who pays the most down here, but he had bad eyes and did not come. It was no wonder then that the man whom I had bought the statue from, on behalf of Jacobsen, was ecstatic when I brought him the final hundred pounds of the price, and he asked me to choose anything at all as a souvenir to remember the transaction, and he also wrapped up a couple of beautiful objects which now belong to my museum.[292]

The expected arrival of big spenders would not only drive up prices, but might also lead dealers to keep back certain items for their sake. Thus, for instance, Lord Crawford had acquired all the papyri he could lay his hands on in Cairo the preceding winter, 1898/99, including the entire papyrus stock of the two main dealers, Ali Abd el-Haj and Farag Ismaïn at Kafr el-Haram; from the former he acquired 35 papyrus rolls and 571 folio sheets filled with fragments, and from the latter another 767 folio sheets containing at least 2,300 fragments. He told Grenfell and Hunt that he might return the following winter, to which Hunt replied 'We had better not tell Ali and his confrères that you are

---

289. Lange and Lange, *Dagbog fra Ægyptensrejsen 1899-1900*, 156-157, cf. also p. 736. Budge was a regular visitor to Egypt to purchase antiquities, and according to his autobiography he made thirteen trips between 1892 and 1913, including the winters of 1898 and 1900, i.e. the years before and after Lange's first trip, in addition to several earlier visits; Budge, *By Nile and Tigris* 2, 322, 356; Ismail, *Wallis Budge*, 64-85, 111-119, 185-186, 218. His reputation as reported by Lange matches well his own description in the same autobiography, where he says that 'It only took a couple of winters to teach the dealers that the Trustees of the British Museum always paid fair prices for their purchases, and that they did not expect their servants to deprive a native of the last piaster of his profit ... I have often secured valuable antiquities over the heads of many bidders among the agents for public museums and private collectors, but this was always due to the fact that I offered a fair price, and did not try to obtain a prize below its prime cost. The prices sanctioned by the Trustees were always fair and reasonable, *and often generous*'; Budge, *By Nile and Tigris* 2, 326-328, 364 (our emphasis). The 'Captain Myers' referred to in the text is Major William Joseph Myers, a British officer who spent much of his time in Egypt but who had died in the Boer War (at the battle of Ladysmith) on 30 Oct. 1899; Myers' personal collection of antiquities today forms the core of the Egyptian collection of Eton College. For a short biography, see Spurr, in Spurr, Reeves, and Quirke (eds.), *Egyptian Art at Eton College*, 1-3; Persson, *JHC* 24, no. 1 (2012), 8-9.

290. Letter from Chauncey Murch to Budge, from November 1899; cited by Ismail, *Wallis Budge*, 380 (cf. p. 325 for the operation on his eyes).

291. Ismail, *Wallis Budge*, 381.

292. Lange and Lange, *Dagbog fra Ægyptensrejsen 1899-1900*, 737-738. The statue in question is Ny Carlsberg Glyptotek, ÆIN 935, which was acquired from Maurice Nahman (p. 137).

expected this year, otherwise they will probably insist on keeping everything till your arrival.'[293]

The situation after the conclusion of the First World War is described in a letter from Breasted written in 1919 where he is asking the president of the Art Institute in Chicago for additional funding for the acquisition of antiquities:

> The situation is this. The natives have made a great deal of money on the war. Many of them who never bought antiquities before have done so since last spring and they are holding all they have bought at preposterous prices. Hence very little that is new comes upon the market at all and the dealers are unable to replenish their stocks. Meantime most of them are willing to listen to reason and are disposing of what they still have on hand at practically pre-war prices; although some of them like the native peasant buyers have gone crazy and are asking absurd prices.[294]

Lange was to enjoy circumstances similar to his first visit on his return to Egypt in 1929-1930, when again the then Keeper of the Egyptian (and Assyrian) Department of the British Museum, Henry Hall, was unable to make the trip to Egypt.[295] Prices could also be affected by the personal circumstances of the dealers,

and some were forced to sell cheaply because of debt,[296] occasionally pawning their collections to more well-off colleagues.[297] Such occasions could attract considerable attention; in one instance Lange notes how, in the case of the collection of Mohammed Ali, the Berlin Museum had put in an offer but did 'not need it all, and one has therefore written to Steindorff in Leipzig, to Reisner, to Spiegelberg in Strasbourg, and to Jacobsen [in Copenhagen]' to ask if any of them might be interested in the remaining objects.[298]

Circumstances were often less cordial. There was inevitably an element of competition among buyers both to get the more interesting objects and to obtain the better price, not least in view of the substantial commissions that might be earned by those acting as agents for collectors and institutions. In numerous cases, individuals proudly recount how they secured an object ahead of the competition (e.g. the Bacchylides papyrus, s.v. Ali Farag). Even friends or close colleagues might privately take some glee in the disadvantage of others. An explicit example occurs in a letter from Borchardt to his wife in 1902:

> Von da aus bei Casira, einem Antikenhändler, vorbei gegangen. Einen feinen Spaß erlebt. Vor meinem Urlaub hatte er eine Reihe von Sachen, die für uns Berliner zusammen 120 L kosten sollten. Ich kaufte nur das einzige, für uns brauchbare Stück, das Modell der Ziegelei, für 20 L. Jetzt hat er den Rest für 200 L verkauft an — v. Bissing. *Schadenfreude ist die einzige reine Freude.*[299]

---

293. Barker, *Bibliotheca Lindesiana*, 339, 341; Choat, in Schubert (ed.), *Actes du 26e Congrès international de papyrologie*, 143.

294. Letter from J. H. Breasted to C. L. Hutchinson, dated 4 Dec. 1919. We are grateful to Emily Teeter for bringing this letter to our attention and providing us with a copy; the quote in question can also be found in her article in Hawass and Houser Wegner (eds.), *Fs Silverman*, 308.

295. Lange, *Dagbog fra Ægypten, 1929-1930*, 50, 280. Hall may have been in bad health; he had fallen ill after a visit to Brussels and died shortly after in London on 13 Oct. 1930; Bierbrier, *Who was Who in Egyptology*, 4th edition, 237-238. Tom Hardwick (personal communication) points out that the Great Depression, which started with the Wall Street Crash of October 1929, also affected the ability of some of the major museums to purchase Egyptian antiquities at this time. A concrete example of this is the Tebtunis temple library which was offered for sale from 1930 and the years following; German Egyptologists became aware of these papyri early on but were unable to secure funds for the acquisition and instead turned to H. O. Lange, a close personal friend of Ludwig Borchardt (p. 178).

296. For the dealers Farag Ismaïn and 'Bastra' selling cheaply because of debt, see the entries on them below.

297. Mohammed Ali is said to have pawned his collection to the Swiss dealer André Bircher because of debt problems (see the relevant entries on these individuals below).

298. Lange and Lange, *Dagbog fra Ægyptensrejsen 1899-1900*, 654; eventually Lange bought a piece for 350 Danish crowns from the sale on behalf of the Glyptotek (p. 736).

299. Our italics; it is not clear to us whether the underscore (here indicated by an emdash) that precedes v. Bissing's name indicates a dramatic pause or an omitted expletive. Letter from L. Borchardt to M. Borchardt, dated 28 Dec. 1902 (Swiss Institute, Kairo; transcript kindly provided by Cornelius von Pilgrim, 31 Oct. 2014).

Many years later, Carl Schmidt acquired a large group of papyri for £500 on behalf of Lange; Borchardt had negotiated a price of £800 for the same group, but not yet secured the funding. Carl Schmidt was clearly amused to think what would happen when Borchardt returned and found the papyri already sold and gone – 'Borch[ardt] wird erstaunt sein wenn er von dem Ankauf durch mich erfährt' (p. 180).

Dealers travelling abroad

Outside the tourist season, some of the more renowned and better established dealers would themselves visit European and US cities where a wealthy clientele –

Fig. 107. Maurice Nahman and Howard Carter on the deck of SS Champollion which, sailing from Marseilles to Alexandria and beyond, was the fast line between Cairo and Paris. Nahman regularly visited Paris on business outside the tourist season. Photo c. 1926. Courtesy of Lucien Viola.

both museums and private collectors – might be found. The dealers would arrive laden with those objects they were most likely to sell, together with photographs of what they could not bring along for various reasons, weight and legal risks being the primary concerns. Prior to the Second World War, the main venues were Paris and London, which were regularly visited by dealers such as Maurice Nahman (Fig. 107), the Kalebdjian brothers, and Phocion Jean Tano. Up until 1935, Paris is said to have been particularly attractive to Egyptian dealers because of the free currency rate.[300]

The years following the Second World War saw a boom in this activity, since few tourists had visited Egypt during this more than five-year long period with the result that the antiquities trade had dwindled, and the venues now prominently included also New York and San Francisco. An interesting collector's perspective, written five years after the war, is provided by Albert Gallatin; he had visited Egypt several times and missed the more exotic atmosphere there, but notes:

> There is one advantage in buying in New York from my Cairo friends (sc. antiquities dealers): the headache of how to get the objects out of Egypt and safely into this country is eliminated as far as I am concerned. Owing to the fall in the Egyptian pound and the demand for dollars due to the absence of free-spending Nile tourists, prices are often low for large objects from recent digs which the dealers manage somehow to bring over in their personal luggage, thereby saving expensive packing and ocean freight. They are learning that it does not pay to import trash; the halo which hovered about a bronze god or a glazed ushabti when 'picked up' by a traveller in an antique land is no longer apparent in the New York hotel room, where buyers who venture in are apt to be meticulous in their choice and shrewd in their bargaining.[301]

Among the dealers with whom Gallatin did business in New York after the war are Michel Elias Abemayor,

300. Clipping from unidentified newspaper, late 1950s, article entitled 'In Relation to the Case of the American Scholar who Stole Egypt's Antiquities' (translated from Arabic).
301. Gallatin, *The Pursuit of Happiness*, 172-179; quote from p. 179.

Mansoor, Maguid Sameda and Phocion Jean Tano. Some dealers found business abroad so profitable that they travelled regularly or even established a branch abroad (e.g. the Kalebdjian brothers who founded a second shop in Paris which became their base, or Phocion Jean Tano who installed his nephew Frank John Tano in New York) or moved the entire business out of Egypt (e.g. Michel Elias Abemayor who eventually settled in New York, Philip Elias Mitry who settled in Castro Valley close to San Francisco, the Mansoors who also settled in San Francisco, and Roger Khawam who relocated to Paris).

Objects not bought on the market

Not all of the antiquities that Lange brought back were bought from dealers, and some came via colleagues; Borchardt once let him buy a stela and some 'small objects' upon his return to Cairo, and following a trip to dealers at Giza, Schäfer and Borchardt sold him one Old Kingdom and one Middle Kingdom stela they had purchased there.[302] Like other visitors to Egypt Lange was also not above picking up objects from archaeological sites. While visiting von Bissing's excavation of the sun-temple of Niuserre at Abusir, he took 'a small piece of granite belonging to one of the corner-stones of the gate leading into the courtyard of the temple' and 'a couple of nice little things of clay, which are very old and also completely preserved',[303] and during a trip to Dendera he found 'among the ruins, a piece of an old cooking jar of stone, still black on the outside. Naturally I took it with me to include it in my museum'.[304] Similarly, during a visit to the Ramesseum in Thebes, he described how his wife picked up some mummy bandages:

Among the ruins behind the Ramesseum one observes

the unpleasant sight of masses of human bones, some still wrapped in mummy bandages, which are the remains of large burials of poor people from antiquity. Jonna herself unwrapped some mummy bandages from a bone (to keep) as a memory of the large Theban necropolis.[305]

His trip to the Fayum oasis included a visit to the Hawara pyramid, where 'Amongst the ruins I found a piece of a statue of black granite, which I took with me', while his companion Dr Speyer 'picked up an excellent skull, which he took with him'.[306] Lange was well aware of the similarity between his own actions and the robbing of ancient sites by contemporary Egyptians, and he noted in an aside that 'the Arabs act in a similar vein across Egypt, and the sites which they have plundered are numberless, and the damage thereby done to science is immeasurable,' but there is little further reflection on this issue in his diaries.[307]

Acquiring antiquities through excavations

Many institutions as well as individuals acquired antiquities through excavation as well as buying, and although we are not primarily concerned in this book with the history of archaeology in Egypt, it is perhaps worth mentioning this practice in the context of Lange's work to supply Danish museums with antiquities. The law at the time of his first visit (1899-1900) gave the Egyptian Museum the right to retain half of what had been recovered during a season of excavation, with the other half being handed over to the excavator (who in turn would forward objects to those institutions or individuals who had sponsored the excavations).[308] Although unique and unusual objects might be retained by the Museum, the sponsoring of

302. Lange and Lange, *Dagbog fra Ægyptensrejsen 1899-1900*, 722-723. We have been unable to identify these two stelae.
303. Lange and Lange, *Dagbog fra Ægyptensrejsen 1899-1900*, 93-94. These objects are likewise unidentified.
304. Lange and Lange, *Dagbog fra Ægyptensrejsen 1899-1900*, 360 (object unidentified).

305. Lange and Lange, *Dagbog fra Ægyptensrejsen 1899-1900*, 330. These fragments of linen are now in the National Museum, inv. 12135 (Lange bequest).
306. Lange and Lange, *Dagbog fra Ægyptensrejsen 1899-1900*, 521, 522-523.
307. Lange and Lange, *Dagbog fra Ægyptensrejsen 1899-1900*, 523.
308. For the law of 1891 pertaining to the division of finds (*partage*) from excavations, see Fricke, in Merryman (ed.), *Imperialism, Art and Restitution*, 178.

Fig. 108. Not a well-stocked antiquities shop, but a seasons' worth of finds by Flinders Petrie placed on exhibit for the purposes of division among his sponsors and sale. Petrie referred to the antiquities dealer Farag as 'that brute of a plunderer' on account of his extensive excavations at Hawara in search for mummy portraits, but Petrie too worked at great speed and did not provide much detail about the archaeological context of the individual portraits. Courtesy of the Egypt Exploration Society.

archaeological excavations provided foreign institutions with a convenient way to acquire large quantities of antiquities.

This method was also considered by Lange, and in his 1899-1900 diary he talks at some length about his ideas in this regard:

By several people I have been encouraged to return here to conduct excavations. The cost associated with this would not necessarily be that great, and it would probably be relatively easy to get funding for this from the Carlsberg Foundation. But it is hardly possible in reality. I am unlikely to be able to get away for a whole winter once more from the library. On the other hand I hope to put forward another man for this task. There is

a young man by the name Henry Madsen who these days is starting his studies in Copenhagen, and he came to see me a few times before I departed. The idea is that I will read Egyptian with him this autumn term. He seems a very nice and competent person; he is comfortable financially so he thinks he can afford to study such an unprofitable subject as Egyptology... So perhaps in a few years' time he could be trained to come down and head an excavation. He would need a young engineer with him for the practical stuff; we would need a larger grant of about 10,000 DKK from the Carlsberg Foundation, and through my connections here we could get a suitable and productive site to excavate. I could then have a kind of supervisory role while based in Copenhagen, and oversee the publication of the excavation report and the finds. This plan has matured in my mind

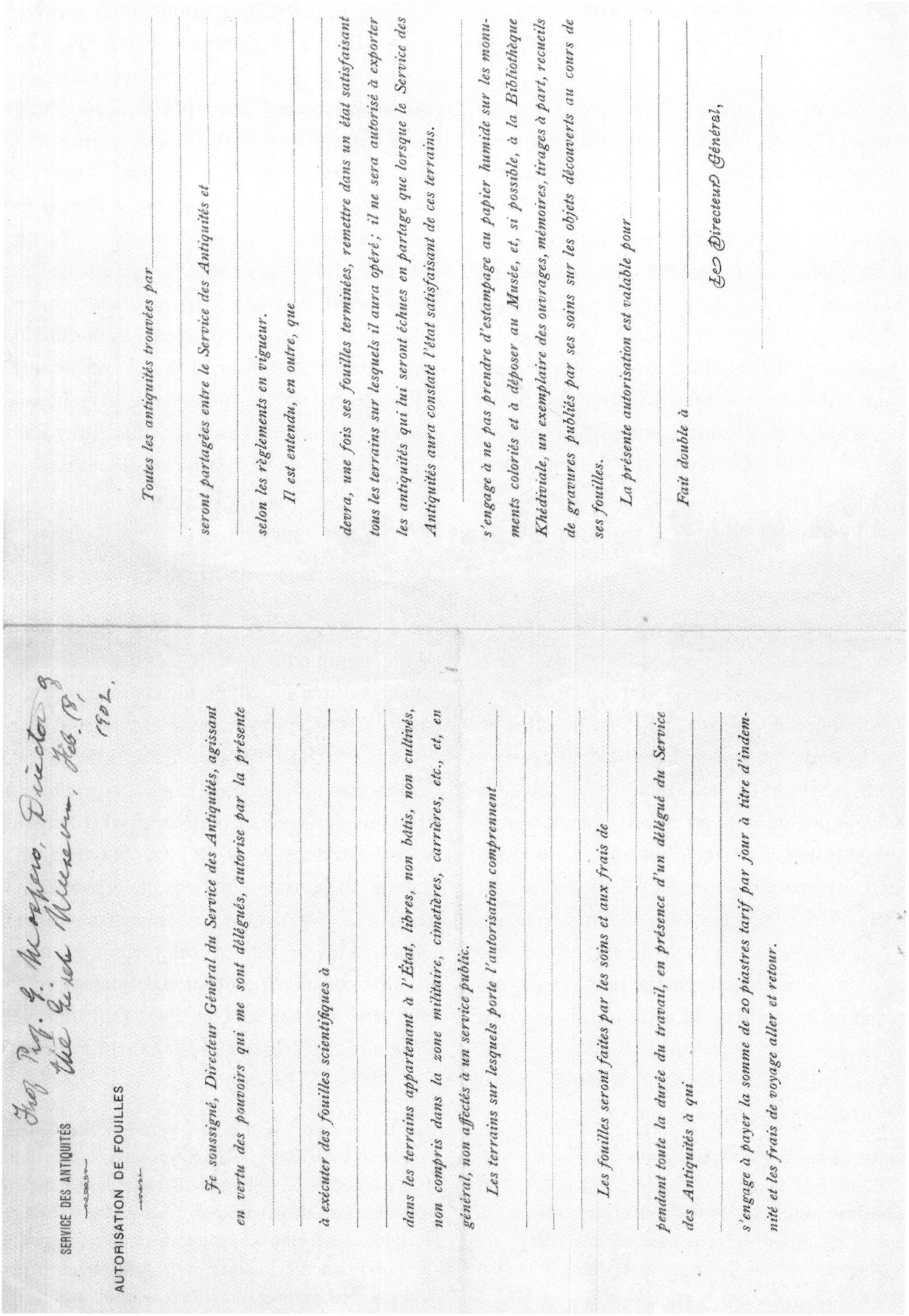

SERVICE DES ANTIQUITÉS

AUTORISATION DE FOUILLES

Je soussigné, Directeur Général du Service des Antiquités, agissant en vertu des pouvoirs qui me sont délégués, autorise par la présente _____

à exécuter des fouilles scientifiques à _____

dans les terrains appartenant à l'État, libres, non bâtis, non cultivés, non compris dans la zone militaire, cimetières, carrières, etc., et, en général, non affectés à un service public.

Les terrains sur lesquels porte l'autorisation comprennent _____

Les fouilles seront faites par les soins et aux frais de _____

pendant toute la durée du travail, en présence d'un délégué du Service des Antiquités à qui _____

s'engage à payer la somme de 20 piastres tarif par jour à titre d'indemnité et les frais de voyage aller et retour.

Toutes les antiquités trouvées par _____

seront partagées entre le Service des Antiquités et _____

selon les règlements en vigueur.

Il est entendu, en outre, que _____

devra, une fois ses fouilles terminées, remettre dans un état satisfaisant tous les terrains sur lesquels il aura opéré ; il ne sera autorisé à exporter les antiquités qui lui seront échues en partage que lorsque le Service des Antiquités aura constaté l'état satisfaisant de ces terrains.

s'engage à ne pas prendre d'estampage au papier humide sur les monuments coloriés et à déposer au Musée, et, si possible, à la Bibliothèque Khédiviale, un exemplaire des ouvrages, mémoires, tirages à part, recueils de gravures publiés par ses soins sur les objets découverts au cours de ses fouilles.

La présente autorisation est valable pour _____

Fait double à _____

Le Directeur Général,

[handwritten: Prof. Prof. G. Maspero, Director of the First Museum. Feb. 18, 1902.]

Fig. 109. Blank application form for permission to excavate sent by Gaston Maspero, the Director of the Antiquities Service, to D. G. Lyon of the Harvard Semitic Museum, dated 18. Feb. 1902. The document lays out the terms and conditions for excavation, including the division of finds. Courtesy of Harvard Semitic Museum.

down here, and I think it makes good sense. I would of course love to do it myself, but I have put that thought completely out of my mind.[309]

Henry Madsen (1881-1921) went on to have a short career in Egyptology, publishing some 16 minor Egyptological articles, alongside his work as a journalist, author and editor, but he never conducted any excavations in Egypt.[310] In fact, the plan came to nothing, and there was never a Danish excavation in Egypt in Lange's lifetime. Jacobsen was reluctant and chose instead to begin contributing funds to Petrie's excavations in 1908 (and later to other British excavations) in order to acquire larger monuments whose export permission was hard to secure outside the division of finds that was allowed excavators.[311] He considered this a better investment 'since Petrie has a unique experience'.

Petrie, for his part, had his own fixed system of rewarding his contributors. At the end of each excavation season, and after the authorities of the Egyptian Antiquities Service in Cairo had selected their share of objects for the Egyptian Museum, he would return to London and organise a public exhibit of his results (Fig. 108). In addition to the publicity, this gave his sponsors the opportunity to assess the objects in person and present their wishes, and the finds would then be allocated according to the size of their financial contributions. This approach also encouraged an element of competition among the sponsors, since they would get a direct impression of the kind of fine objects they might have obtained if they had provided more funds.

Lange eventually abandoned the idea of a Danish excavation, and although he had a couple of possible fieldwork projects in mind during his second visit thirty years later,[312] the creation of the Papyrus Carlsberg Collection was to provide a different focus for Danish Egyptology. In a dossier labelled 'The future of Egyptology in our country', a handwritten document authored by Lange around 1938, he sets out what he sees as important for the future of the subject. This includes infrastructure (library resources, a photographic archive of papyri), its international position ('the central place in the Nordic countries'), but also research profile and agenda; here there is no mention of archaeological fieldwork of any kind, but an insistence on the importance of the papyrus collection and associated lexicographic projects.[313]

Dealers' methods of obtaining antiquities

In addition to looking at how collectors from the West acquired antiquities, it is instructive also to look at the manner in which dealers in Egypt might come into possession of the material they sold on.

One method was to conduct official excavations. This seems to have been particularly common among the consular agents in the south who sometimes excavated extensively. While the activities of consular agents at Luxor are especially well-documented (above all those of the British consular agent Mustafa Aga and the French consular agent Shenudi Makarios), the consular agents at other sites were also active, including the French consular agent at Girga, Abd en-Nur, and the British consular agent at Aswan, Musta-

309. Lange and Lange, *Dagbog fra Ægyptensrejsen 1899-1900*, 704-706.
310. Dahl and Engelstoft, *Dansk skønlitterært forfatterleksikon 2*, 261; Svanholm (ed.), *Skagenleksikon*, 112; some letters from Madsen to Lange are preserved in the Royal Library in Copenhagen.
311. The nature and the results of this collaboration is discussed in detail by Jørgensen, *How it all began*, 69-126; Bagh, *Finds from W.M.F. Petrie's Excavations in Egypt*; and eadem, *Finds from the Excavations of J. Garstang in Meroe and F.Ll. Griffith in Kawa*.

312. Lange made loose plans to approach the Rask-Ørsted fund to finance the excavations of Junker at Merimde (at Junker's request), which would have provided the opportunity to train a Danish archaeologist; Lange, *Dagbog fra Ægypten, 1929-1930*, 305. Another project that never materialised was the idea of conducting a survey of the Edfu temple in cooperation with the Service des Antiquités (discussed with its Director, P. Lacau), which he thought the Ny Carlsberg Foundation might have financed (pp. 94-95).
313. H. O. Lange, *Ægyptologiens Fremtid i vort Land*, c. 1938 (University of Copenhagen, Egyptological Archive, E102).

fa Shakir. Other dealers who obtained official permits to excavate include Ali Abd el-Haj, Farag Ismaïn, Girgis Gabrial, Paul Philip, Pietro Makri, Sayed Khashaba *Pasha*, Soliman Abd es-Samad, and Yassa Todros, as well as small-timers like Abu Gamb and the son of Ali Kamuri.[314]

In return for excavation permits, whether granted to dealers, collectors, or institutions, the Egyptian Museum claimed the right to half of the excavated objects as well as any object of unique value or interest. The rest of the objects would go to the excavator who was free to dispose of them as he saw fit. This practice was already established in the 1880s, if not earlier, and was formalized by law in 1891 (Fig. 109).[315] In practical terms, the excavator would often get more than half, since the Egyptian Museum had neither room nor interest in many of the smaller objects. According to a letter written by Arthur Weigall, the Chief Inspector of Antiquities for Upper Egypt, to Alan H. Gardiner in 1912, the division of finds at that time (and perhaps in general) was a somewhat disorganized affair and not to the advantage of the Museum; it was neither sufficiently supervised nor conducted in a manner that would necessarily secure the proper items.[316]

> [In Upper Egypt], I generally made the selection of what the Museum wanted, visiting the excavations for this purpose and going through the finds in the rough before they were cleaned or shown to advantage. I had no idea what the Cairo Museum required ... in any one class of objects, for my work gave me very little opportunities for visiting the Museum; and I therefore made a quite casual selection ... of what happened to strike me as being needed by us. Other excavators, considering that I was severe in my selection, preferred to take their finds to Cairo, where often only a few boxes were

unpacked for inspection. Other excavators did not show their finds at all, but the selection was made at Cairo by means of photographs.

Many of the excavations conducted by dealers were extensive and, inevitably, the focus on the types of objects that might be sold for a profit, combined with the lack of both proper archaeological training and any form of documentation of the sites and the finds in question, meant that countless archaeological areas were subject to large-scale destruction and forever lost to science. It is therefore not surprising that several Western excavators expressed their frustration with the numerous excavation permits issued to dealers. By way of example, Petrie referred to Farag Ismaïn as 'that brute of a plunderer' in relation to his excavations at Hawara and Amarna, and Quibell called Farag's excavation at Deir el-Bersha an 'extraordinary concession to vandalism'.[317] Excavation permits, for dealers and scholars alike, were obtained by annual application to the Director of the Antiquities Service, and Quibell rejoiced when Victor Loret in 1898, soon after his appointment as Director, decided to refuse any new permits for dealers to excavate. The change in policy proved very short-lived; Loret had at the same time introduced tighter restrictions on the division of finds (with, for instance, all royal name objects going to the Antiquities Service) and, now widely unpopular with both archaeologists and dealers, he was soon let go. Maspero returned as Director in 1899 and resumed his liberal policy of granting excavation permits to dealers, including, as before, for historically important and promising sites. In a private letter from 1911, Arthur Weigall, expresses his frustration over these ongoing excavations which, in his view, represented 'nothing more nor less than legalized plundering'.

> The worst case of this occurred lately at Assiut. A native named Said Bey [sc. Saïd Bey Khashaba] obtained a permit to excavate from our Department ... Ahmed Bey

---

314. For references to the excavations mentioned here, see the entries for each individual at the back of the book. See also the entry on Grégoire Loukianoff who may represent a similar case; he excavated with some associates at Lake Mariut near Alexandria, although the references to his excavations are sometimes couched in a language that makes it difficult to ascertain the details of the arrangements.

315. Fricke in *Imperialism, Art and Restitution*, 178.

316. Hankey, *A Passion for Egypt*, 185.

317. Cf. Petrie, *Seventy Years in Archaeology*, 90 (Hawara); Drower, *Flinders Petrie*, 191 (Amarna); Griffith, *Egypt Exploration Fund, Archaeological Report* 1898-99, 19-20.

Kamal, an old Egyptian employee at the Museum, half blind and not having rudimentary knowledge of scientific methods, was told to go and look after him. Magnificent antiquities were found, and Ahmed Bey was allowed to make the division himself with Said Bey who was to sell his half, which at least put a grave temptation in the way of both men to make a deal with the balance on the side of the originator of the scheme. Said Bey's share of the spoil was sold for hundreds of pounds. One statue alone fetched £300. No record was made of the work, but as a sop to the archaeologists a brief catalogue of the antiquities was drawn up – of no use to anybody. This really scandalous piece of work was authorized by our Director General [sc. Gaston Maspero].[318]

Despite Maspero's liberal policy, Cecil Firth (later Inspector of Antiquities at Saqqara) arrived to excavate what he considered an important site in Lower Nubia that same year, only to find himself forestalled by a Luxor dealer who had apparently cleared most of the site with a fake permit in hand:

This cemetery had been an important Early Dynastic burying place, but the graves had been very thoroughly rifled by a Luxor dealer who had showed the villagers a paper purporting to be a permit from the Department of Antiquities to excavate for archæological material. This cemetery was one of the few in which there were clear traces of modern plundering, the pottery in the graves having been wantonly smashed. Only a very few graves had escaped.[319]

While fake permits may have been out of the ordinary, many dealers were involved in illegal excavations. Even well-established dealers abroad might be tempted to set up illegal excavations. A documented example from 1913 concerns Joseph Brummer, at the time the proprietor of Brummer Gallery in Paris (later relocating to New York), who acquired a house at el-

Araba el-Madfuna and conducted excavations at the local temple of Seti I, before this was brought to the attention of the Egyptian Antiquities Service and stopped.[320]

At other times, the involvement was more indirect. Often dealers were able to provide reliable information about the provenance of a given item or group of items, and they must have been aware that their providers had no license to excavate that particular site. However, by turning a blind eye they were able to acquire illegally obtained objects at a relatively low price (since they might be dangerous for the excavators to vend directly) and to sell these at a profit. In such cases the dealers effectively served as fences and the practice was very common. Moreover, this was not just a case of finders bringing material to the dealers. Rumours of great discoveries would inevitably attract dealers, not least the wealthier dealers and their agents. Thus, for example, C. C. Edgar reports that after the discovery of the great treasure of Bubastis in 1906, 'Zagazig [sc. the modern city] was infested by the bigger antiquity-dealers, and during the winter several gold and silver vases were shown and sold in Cairo, quite openly, as part of the stolen treasure.'[321]

Another type of fencing was the acquisition of objects stolen from excavations by workmen. This was also an extremely common occurrence and affected most excavations (p. 30). Few dealers seem to have had any qualms about acquiring such looted material, although some rare exceptions are praised in contemporary reports (p. 157). Indeed some dealers would openly admit to these illegal dealings. Thus, for instance, Phocion Jean Tano sold a painted limestone bust to Albert Gallatin in New York after the Second World War, and informed him that it was 'from a house in Deir el Medinah, one of the finest from the excavations of 1934-35', i.e. the official excavations of Bruyère which were plagued by thefts.[322]

318. Cited after Hankey, *A Passion for Egypt*, 168-169, except for the explanatory notes. For Saïd Bey Khashaba and his excavations at Assiut, see p. 260. It may be noted that Ahmed Bey Kamal was not just any old employee, but in fact the most senior Egyptian archaeologist at the time and second to Emil Brugsch at the Cairo Museum.
319. Firth, *The Archæological Survey of Nubia*, 213.

320. Gouvernement Égyptien, *Rapport du Service des Antiquités pour l'année 1913*, 13.
321. Edgar, *Le Musée égyptien* 2 (1907), 94.
322. Gallatin, *The Pursuit of Happiness*, 178.

Engaging in illegal excavations always involved the risk of being discovered and subjected to confiscation and punishment. The reporting of illegal activities to the authorities often seems to have been motivated by competition or the greed of other interested parties rather than moral considerations. An example of how an illegal excavation may come about and unfold is the chance discovery of a cemetery of Ptolemaic date at Gamhud (Beni Suef governorate) by a local man in 1907.[323] The man immediately contacted a nearby antiquities dealer at Biba, Farag Todros, and proposed that they should conduct an (illicit) excavation together on the condition that all objects found be split between them. A number of Bedouin who inhabited the area at first consented to the activities, which implies that they got or expected to get some remuneration, but soon two of the Bedouin reported them to the authorities and the antiquities were seized. Farag Todros quickly contacted a Hungarian archaeological mission working close by and told them of the discoveries, undoubtedly desperate not to lose his golden egg and hoping for collaboration, but when they soon after received official permission to excavate the site it naturally excluded his participation.

Many dealers sold antiquities on behalf of others, thus earning money by taking a commission, but most seem to have bought objects themselves in order to sell them on.[324] This meant that even high profile dealers like Maurice Nahman and Jean Tano were in a reciprocal relationship with the diggers and fellaheen who brought them objects, and would sometimes find

themselves having to buy objects that they did not feel inclined to acquire, simply to keep them as loyal suppliers:

> The Arabs think every piece is worth its weight in gold, and the antiquities dealers have to keep their suppliers sweet by buying what they offer, lest they go to a competitor when they find a particularly nice object.[325]

Petrie found himself in a somewhat similar situation already during his early years in Egypt. In a letter from 1884, while working at Tanis, he noted:

> Today a man brought in some antikas from the neighbourhood, a tell a few miles off. There was nothing of interest, ...; as however I want to encourage the dealers about here to bring things in, and want to open relations with them, I bought them seeing that he was well content with about half of the Cairo value or a quarter of the English rate.[326]

Another way to acquire antiquities was to lend money against antiquities as security, of which there are many examples. The American Edwin Smith, who lived in a house within the Luxor temple provided by Mustafa Aga, earned a living as money-lender and antiquities dealer.[327] He would sometimes receive antiquities in return for outstanding debt. André Bircher conducted a similar business in Cairo, lending money to Bedouins at Kafr el-Haram and taking antiquities as security (p. 201), and also Jan Herman Insinger, the above-mentioned Dutch business man at Luxor, engaged in both money-lending and the antiquities trade. This money-lending for antiquities may well have been a relatively common phenomenon; Lange, for instance, mentions that there were many Greek antiquities dealers and also that many Greeks made an income on the side through money-lending.[328] This is perhaps the reason why Jonna Lange originally thought that Bircher might be Greek.

---

323. Kamal, *ASAE* 9 (1908), 8-9.

324. '[Many of] these Bedouins come from around the pyramids where they have learned English from tourists, and language is the secret of their business. They do not dig up the objects themselves but function as agents for the finders or are in cahoots with them; they walk up and down outside the hotels with small objects, including many fakes, which they sell to tourists, and also try to find collectors and Egyptologists who are what one of them termed "collection men" (museum people). If they find one of these they think their luck is made ...'; Lange and Lange, *Dagbog fra Ægyptensrejsen 1899-1900*, 157.

325. Lange, *Dagbog fra Ægypten, 1929-1930*, 87.

326. Drower, *Letters from the Desert*, 51.

327. Wilson, *Signs & Wonders Upon Pharaoh*, 52-57.

328. Lange and Lange, *Dagbog fra Ægyptensrejsen 1899-1900*, 524, cf. pp. 516-517.

High profile dealers would regularly travel around the country to visit lesser dealers, not least if it was rumoured that there were valuable objects available. As objects passed through lesser dealers to the top-tier dealers, prices increased dramatically. Thus, for instance, Newberry saw a gold pendant from the illicitly discovered tomb of Queen Sobekemsaf with an Edfu dealer in 1895; he later saw the same object with Mohareb Todros in Luxor 'but his price was even more prohibitive than that of the Edfu dealer'.[329] The evaluation of the financial value of antiquities could sometimes be a tricky business and most dealers were naturally keen to avoid selling a valuable object too cheaply, or to invest good money in a worthless object. An interesting episode of this kind, which took place in 1888, is reported by Wilbour. Emin *Bey*, a lesser dealer from Akhmim, had come to Luxor to dispose of an exceptionally fine commemorative scarab of Amenhotep III.[330] The Cairo dealer Marius Tano, who was also in Luxor to do business, considered the scarab worth $200 and devised a plan to get it at very low cost. He met with Emin and arranged for a man to bring some scraps of Coptic papyrus for which he paid £1. Concealing his identity, he then sent another dealer, Idris, to acquire the scarab from Emin through a trade against an Abyssinian liturgy. Emin thought he could sell the liturgy to Tano at a great price, seeing that the latter had just paid quite well for a mere few fragments. He therefore consented to a trade with the scarab and even threw in $10. He will have learned that Tano (for obvious reasons) was uninterested in the liturgy, but managed to sell it to Luxor dealer Abd el-Megid for $125 instead, receiving $25 up front and with a promise of another $100 which Abd el-Megid would borrow from his brother-in-law, the dealer Mohammed Mohassib. The latter, sceptical about the value of the liturgy, sent it for evaluation with an Abyssinian monk who

judged it to be worth a mere $2. The shrewd Abd el-Megid managed to trick Emin to take the liturgy back by claiming he would have to wait half a year for the money, something to which he evidently expected Emin would not consent.

It is important to note that dealers would often travel far to sell or acquire antiquities; the mere fact that an object was sold at a certain location is no indication that it was also found there. To provide just a few examples, Mohammed Mohasseb at Luxor acquired gold pieces from Fayum, statuettes from Meir, and mummies from Gebelein.[331] Similarly, Mohareb Todros at Luxor sold many of the Old Kingdom decrees that had been excavated at Coptos. In another example, two pieces of a single 26th Dynasty statue were purchased some 100 km and four years apart.[332]

Travelling with funds to pay for antiquities was itself a risk – if robbed one could not seek judicial redress, as is so entertainingly described in the story *Haj Hamid and the Brigand* (cf. Appendix 5) – but even transporting the objects themselves could be dangerous when the Antiquites Service got wind of their existence:

> Mohammed Ali el-Gebri got [the artefact]. Mohammed [Mohassib] of Luxor sent his boys down and they made a pretty high bid on it, but the owners were not willing to deliver it even at a boat on the river. The Museum people got wind of the affair then they made a strong effort to get hands on it. Watchmen undertook to get possession of it when it should be taken away from the village. Native boats were searched as they passed Nag Hamadi Bridge. Natives were watched and

329. Newberry, *PSBA* 24 (1902), 285. Both the location of the tomb and the present whereabouts of the pendant remain unknown, while a few other objects from her burial are now in the British Museum.

330. Cf. Capart (ed.), *Letters of Charles Edwin Wilbour*, 461.

331. Gold pieces from Fayum: p. 291; Meir statuettes: Bull, *JAOS* 56 (1936), 166; Gebelein mummies: Capart (ed.), *Letters of Charles Edwin Wilbour*, 291-292.

332. Mohareb Todros demanded an exorbitant sum of £1,500 for the group of Old Kingdom decrees which Breasted saw in 1920; cf. Emberling (ed.), *Pioneers to the Past*, 141-142. Borchardt saw these decrees already in 1911 (cf. letter from L. Borchardt to M. Borchardt, dated 6 Jan. 1911, Swiss Institute, Cairo) and it is clear that Mohareb was patiently waiting for someone willing to meet his price. For the 26th Dynasty statue (BM EA 1132 + 1225), purchased at Luxor (1893) and Edfu (1897), see Russmann, *Eternal Egypt*, 234-237 (no. 129); we are grateful to Tom Hardwick for this reference.

searched when they got off the cars at Luxor. Mohammad Ali hired a small steam launch from Cook at [£?]
per day; and while native craft were being searched he
steamed down the river with his treasure unmolested.[333]

Here the Luxor dealer Mohammed Mohasseb had
sent representatives north to Abu Tig (near Assiut) in
order to negotiate a price for an unspecified object
with a local dealer. Although some of the details are
obscure, it demonstrates not only the lengths to which
the Antiquities Service would go in its efforts to stop
the trade, but also the manoeuvres undertaken by
dealers trying to avoid detection.

During a visit to Maurice Nahman's shop in Cairo
in 1930, Lange got talking to him about the provenance of an object he had for sale:

> He told me that to buy the crocodile [of a green stone,
> allegedly prehistoric] he had travelled for 16 hours and
> spent eight hours from 3 until 11 in a mud-brick hut in
> a village, fighting with five fellaheens about the price;
> during that time they drank coffee and smoked cigaret-
> tes. It is often the case that it isn't one single man who
> owns an object; several are involved when they have
> found it together; and then it is naturally more difficult
> to get them all to agree on the same price.[334]

Although the story may have been primarily intended
to justify the price of the object from Nahman's point
of view, it seems to illustrate a common situation
where several illegal excavators would own 'shares' in
an object, which necessarily complicated the process
of negotiation and made it more difficult to close a
deal.

Many objects travelled through very complex
routes from finder to collector. A good example is offered by two significant groups of papyri from Tebtunis that were discovered by locals in 1930; one was the
remains of the temple library and the other a large

number of discarded documents from the temple archives.[335] The papyri were believed to derive from two
illicit excavations organized by either a reïs (foreman)
or a ghafir (watchman) attached to the Italian mission
that held the concession to the site. The papyri were
then split up and sold on, most of them ending up
with the dealer Mohammed Khalil in Medinet el-Fayum, the regional capital, where they were thus partially re-united again. This dealer, in turn, sold the
majority of his papyri to the two main dealers in Cairo,
Maurice Nahman and Jean Tano, but other fragments
ended up with lesser dealers such as Dr Kondilios,
Grégoire Loukianoff, and Zaki Mahmud Abd es-Samad. Borchardt saw the material in the possession of
Nahman and Tano and soon realized that much of it
belonged to a temple archive. Because funding could
not be found in Germany, it was instead offered to his
friend Lange and most of it was acquired for him
through Ludwig Borchardt and Carl Schmidt who systematically searched Cairo dealers for further fragments (p. 180). Thus much of the material was once
again re-united, although it had passed through many
hands at this point. A comparable example is offered
by the famous Nag Hammadi codices.[336]

Another instructive example concerns the famous
head of Queen Tiye in Berlin.[337] In 1905 Otto Rubensohn met the dealer Michel Casira, who was re-
turning to Cairo from Beni Suef, on the train in Ash-
ment. Casira showed him the head which he felt sure
that Borchardt would be interested in. He informed
him that it had been excavated at Gurob and sold to a
small-time dealer at Illahun. It was next acquired by a
consortium of four men in Beni Suef, from whom he
himself had acquired it. He further informed Rubensohn that he was in a partnership with Maurice
Nahman and that Borchardt would be able to see the
head at the home of the latter. Rubensohn passed

333. Letter from Chauncey Murch to Budge, British Museum,
Department of the Middle East Correspondence 1901, 526;
cited by Ismail, *Wallis Budge*, 381 (Ismail's transcription has
been retained here).

334. Lange, *Dagbog fra Ægypten, 1929-1930*, 253-254.

335. A study of the acquisition of these two groups of papyri is
in preparation by Kim Ryholt.

336. Robinson, in Barc (ed.), *Colloque international sur les textes de
Nag Hammadi*, 21-58; idem, *The Facsimile Edition of the Nag Hammadi
Codices*, 3-14; idem, *The Nag Hammadi Story*.

337. Arnold, *The Royal Women of Amarna*, 27-35.

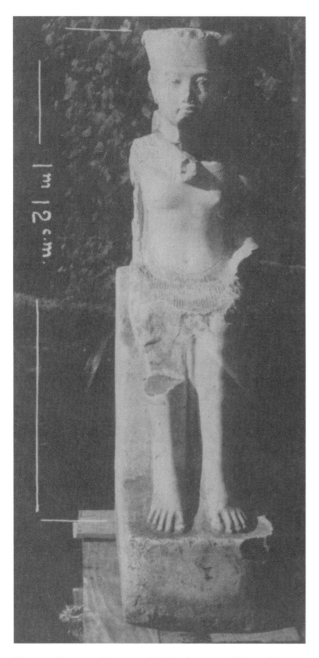

Fig. 110. Statue of Amun with the features of Tutankha-mun offered for sale by Grégoire Loukianoff in a letter to Lange dated 14 January 1931. It eventually ended up in the Badisches Landesmuseum (inv. 65/15) in Karlsruhe, Germany, having passed through the hands of several dealers. Courtesy of the Royal Library.

word on to Borchardt who saw the piece and immediately contacted Berlin. Within 24 hours, it had been arranged through the telegraph that the head would be acquired by the philanthropist James Simon who later donated it to the Egyptian Museum in Berlin.[338] We have here two joint ventures; the four unnamed individuals in Beni Suef and the partnership between Casira and Nahman. It was by no means uncommon for well-established dealers to join forces or to buy or sell to each other, and Maurice Nahman had many such connections.

Dealers might also act as agents on behalf of others, selling objects that were not in their own possession (Fig. 110-111). A straightforward example is the dealer Pusgul who sought to sell Lange a papyrus owned by an unnamed professor (p. 174). Sometimes the situation was more complicated. In January 1930 Loukianoff offered Lange a statue of Amun with the features of Tutankhamun.[339] He states that he himself found the sculpture, but it remains somewhat unclear whether he merely identified its nature or actually discovered it somewhere. He further mentions that it had been acquired by another dealer, but should this be taken to imply that he had sold it on?

> J'éspère de gagner quelque chose sur la statue de Tou-tankhamon en dieu Amon, que j'ai trouvé l'année pas-sée et qui a été acheté par un antiquaire. Il m'a promis me donner une partie de ses benefices, quand il la ven-dera. Il demande 3000 L.E. avec le transport à la place. Je Vous envoie le photo, peut être cela Vous interesser. Seulement ne la montrez pas aux autres personnes.

Other documentation that has recently emerged indicates that the statue changed hands several times in

---

338. Information summarised from Borchardt, *Der Porträtkopf der Königin Teje.*
339. Letter from G. Loukianoff to H. O. Lange, dated 14 Jan. 1931 (Royal Library, Copenhagen). The statue is now in the Badisches Landesmuseum (inv. 65/15) in Karlsruhe and has most recently been published in Albersmeier, *Ägyptische Kunst,* 154-157, and frontispiece. We are grateful to Marianne Eaton-Krauss for tracking down the statue and providing us with this reference (email of 9 Nov. 2012).

and outside Cairo over the next thirty-five years.[340] In 1962 it received permission for export through the *Salle de vente* of the Egyptian Museum; it was then in the possession of Kamel Abdallah Hammouda, whose antiquities shop was located just around the corner from Loukianoff's apartment. Before this point it is said to have formed part of the estate of Dikran Kelekian whose shop was also located very close to Loukianoff and who died in 1951. The buyer in 1962 was the Swiss antiquities dealer Ernst E. Kofler, and three years later it was acquired by the Badisches Landesmuseum in Karlsruhe, apparently through a German dealer.

Dealers generally found it difficult to keep up with the demand for antiquities; there were never enough objects to go around. The mass production of fakes from the early 19th Century onwards was one very tangible result of this situation. Pressed to find new material some dealers are known to have travelled all the way to Europe and bid at auctions, only to bring the antiquities back to Egypt for resale. The apparent paradox that Egyptian antiquities were actually more expensive in Egypt than abroad is described in an account by Fairholt already in 1862:

> all antiquities are dearer at Thebes than in London, and less likely to be genuine; for the demand is sometimes greater than the genuine supply. Most persons would buy at Thebes, and at a large price, what they would not purchase at a moderate in London. The most absurd sums are given by travellers for what dealers at home would be only too glad to get rid of for a trifle.[341]

The psychological effect of buying antiquities in their cultural context should, of course, not be underesti-

Fig. 111. Part of a royal statuette offered for sale by Loukianoff to Lange. The back of the photograph is inscribed 'Un buste de XVIII dyn de calcaire hauteur 35 cm. Le prix 200 L.E. [cancelled out]. Reduit à 75 L.E.' Undated photograph, c. 1931. The statuette has changed hands several times over the years; cf. Eisenberg, *Art of the Ancient World* 25, 76-77, no. 171. It was sold once more in 2014 and is currently in a private collection in London. Courtesy of the Egyptological Archives, University of Copenhagen.

mated. An excellent example of dealers who engaged in this type of enterprise are the Kalebdjian brothers (p. 225) who are known to have purchased objects at several large-scale auctions in Europe; these include the Amélineau Collection in 1904, the Hilton Price Collection in 1911, the MacGregor Collection in 1922, and the Hearst Collection in 1939; the former in Paris and the three latter at Sotheby's in London.[342] The

340. Piacentini, 'The Antiquities Path: from the Sale Room of the Egyptian Museum in Cairo (ca 1890-1970), through Dealers, to Private and Public Collections', *Forming Material Egypt*, UCL Institute of Archaeology, Annual Conference, 20-21 May 2013, pre-circulated draft of paper, later published as Piacentini, *EDAL* 4 (2013/2014), 105-130. Note that only the pre-circulated copy includes the part about the Karlsruhe statue.

341. Fairholt, *Up the Nile and Home Again*, 266-267.

342. Hardwick, *JHC* 23, no. 1 (2011), 179-192, esp. pp. 181-182; idem, 65 (2012), 7-52, esp. pp. 17, 47; cf. further Larson (ed.), *Letters from James Henry Breasted*, 72, for the Amélineau collection.

sums were sometimes considerable, and the brothers spent c. £1,400 at the MacGregor sale, acquiring some 138 lots with more than 450 objects. Another dealer who participated in both the MacGregor and Hearst auctions was Albert Abemayor, but his spending at the former was rather insignificant; he acquired merely two lots with ten objects for £10¼.

The sale of the Hilton Price Collection to Egyptian dealers is mentioned in a letter written by Breasted to his family from Cairo in 1919. The letter clearly conveys his feeling of urgency in the face of a diminishing supply of antiquities.

> Now is the last chance! It is evident that as a place to buy, Egypt is nearly exhausted. Why the dealers here have gone to London and purchased the Hilton Price collection when it was auctioned off there, and I have bought some of his best pieces here in Cairo! I must get some more money for use this season ... [343]

Collections might also sometimes be acquired locally. Also in 1919, the dealer Kyticas acquired the 'collection of magnificent predynastic flints' belonging to Captain C. S. Timmins who, according to Breasted, had become tired of Egypt and wished to dispose of his antiquities.[344] Breasted himself had hoped to purchase the collection directly from Timmins and was furious that he had sold it to a dealer for a lesser sum that he had himself proposed. He ends his description of the incident with the words: 'I have since learned that Timmins is an ass who doesn't know enough to feed his face straight, but as I thought I was dealing with a normal person, I have lost 50 pounds.' Some years earlier Kyticas had gone to Greece and acquired objects from another private collection which had belonged to a Persian diplomat.[345]

Another example is Michel Abemayor – the father of the above-mentioned Albert Abemayor – who acquired most of the collection of Tigrane *Pasha* d'Abro (d. 1904) which numbered more than five hundred items.[346]

Dealers' handling of antiquities

Although antiquities represented a financial value, they were not always appropriately cared for and suffered damage. Much of the damage incurred was incidental; many excavators lacked the skills and means to preserve fragile objects and to transport them in a secure manner. In the case of larger objects, transport from the site of discovery to the nearest city or railroad was usually by donkey or camel. Thus, for instance, wooden coffins, mummies and inscribed stones might be fastened with ropes to the sides of camels.[347] Smaller objects were sometimes packed in leather suitcases (p. 55), but more often transported in soft cloth, such as bags, handkerchiefs, or any handy material such as an 'apron-like piece of cloth' with 'individually tied corners' (p.31). Needless to say, this mainly affected organic materials (such as wooden objects and papyri) and soft stones.

The Lange material provides several examples of the treatment that might befall papyri. In Cairo a man arrived with papyri in his pockets (cited in context p. 55) which he had brought all the way from Upper Egypt. Similarly, Farag Ismaïn at Kafr el-Haram showed Lange papyrus fragments simply bundled in a rag, presumably the manner in which they had been brought to him (cited in context p. 166). Such handling of papyri will inevitably have resulted in damage, and many of the fragments acquired by and for Lange can in fact be joined together to form larger pieces. Papyri were, moreover, often deliberately broken up to be divided into portions among the find-

343. *Ibid.*, 91.
344. Letter from J. H. Breasted to his family, dated 5 Dec. 1919 (Oriental Institute, Chicago); edited by *ibid.*, 111, cf. also p. 97. Timmins also owned a fine scarab collection which was published in Newberry, *The Timins Collection of Ancient Egypt Scarabs and Cylinder Seals*; he notes that the seals in the collection at that time comprised about 580 objects.
345. Cf. Devonshire, *The Burlington Magazine* 35 (1919), 241.

346. Jones, *Minerva* 17, no. 3 (2006), 5. A concise catalogue of the Tigrane *Pasha* collection was published by Pasha, *Collection d'Antiquités égyptiennes de Tigrane Pacha d'Abro*; cf. further Bierbrier, *Who was Who in Egyptology*, 4th edition, 541.
347. Cf. Drower, *Letters from the Desert*, 187; cf. Quirke's forthcoming work on Petrie as a collector.

ers.[348] One example is represented by some papyrus fragments acquired by Lange which are now known to represent the outer section of a Ptolemaic Book of the Dead that had been wrapped around the chest of a mummy; Lange's fragments were clearly torn from the mummy while the rest remained *in situ* on the mummy at the time it was sold (p. 167). There are also many examples of papyri that were deliberately cut up. Often the damaged outer parts of papyri were trimmed away, so that the remaining roll would look more intact. Hence it is not uncommon to find the first columns of a papyrus missing. The outer fragments were sometimes sold separately. An example is P. Carlsberg 488 which consists of the first four columns of a Book of the Dead. And sometimes they, like other fragmentary papyri, were used to manufacture 'fake' papyrus rolls (cf. p. 148). Such papyrus rolls are a well-known phenomenon and can be found in most major collections. The National Museum in Copenhagen includes several examples that were acquired in the 1850s.[349]

Lange himself describes further cases of accidental damage to objects, two of which are cited here. One concerns two brothers from Qena, one apparently named Basta, whose house he visited in February 1900.

> In the middle of the floor in his living room there was a small three-legged table, on top of which a huge board had been placed. This had been covered with a large exhibition of mostly fragile things. Immediately the younger brother, in his rush to show me his brother's

treasures, bumped into it, and the whole exhibition fell to the floor in a mess. The brothers threw themselves down amidst the now partly broken treasures with laments, but with typical Egyptian fortitude they collected themselves quickly and started to gather the pieces.[350]

The other incident took place a month later in March and concerns 'young Soliman':

> Between 7 and 8, then, we had a short visit from the young Soliman, who had something new to show us, but it was an unlucky one for him because just as he was leaving, without having made a sale, he dropped his bundle and a rather nice alabaster dish broke into many pieces. He took the whole thing calmly, even though just a moment ago he had valued it at 8 shillings; he now offered it to Hans for 4 but he would have none of it. Then negotiations started anew; a small jar which Hans had made an offer on was pulled out again, and it ended up with us, along with the pieces of the other one, for a total of 6 Piastres.[351]

Morals and ethics in the antiquities trade

Lange was a man with strong moral principles, a campaigner against alcohol consumption and a Christian activist, but he seems to have been less concerned with the ethics of trade in antiquities than one might have expected. He was certainly well aware of the issues, in particular the lamentable loss of information that accompanied any illegal excavation, but at the same time he felt that the problems were unsolvable in the local context where such activities were often tacitly accepted – and sometimes even organised – by government officials: 'naturally the Arabs' excavations are illegal, but they dig at night, and they also bribe the local officials to look the other way; it also sometimes happen that they are in partnerships with the officials.'[352] In support of this assertion he describes an incident that had taken place in the Fayum just before his visit:

---

348. A recent example is P. Baldwin (= BM EA 10061) and P. Amiens, the upper and lower half of a document containing the grain accounts of a fleet of ships from the temple of Amun-Re at Karnak (found and torn in two c. 1882, probably at Assiut), published by Janssen, *Grain Transport in the Ramesside Period*. Also a number of the famous tomb robbery papyri have been torn in two: examples include Papyrus Léopold II (= Brussels E 6857) + papyrus Amherst VII (now Pierpont Morgan Library Amh. Egy. Pap. 7), Papyrus Abbott (= BM EA 10221), and P. BM EA 10383. Cf. Capart and Gardiner, *Le papyrus Léopold II*; Peet, *The Great Tomb-Robberies*.

349. Four of these are included in Christiansen and Ryholt, *The Carlsberg Papyri 13*, Texts 9-12.

350. Lange and Lange, *Dagbog fra Ægyptensrejsen 1899-1900*, 365.

351. Lange and Lange, *Dagbog fra Ægyptensrejsen 1899-1900*, 430. The bowl is now in the National Museum, inv. 12594 (Lange bequest).

352. Lange and Lange, *Dagbog fra Ægyptensrejsen 1899-1900*, 523.

The station manager of a small railway station, so a state employee, used to supplement his income by conducting illegal excavations; during the night he would go out into the desert with a group of people and dig as much as he could. But the *ghafirs* came across them one night, and while the majority managed to flee, they succeeded in capturing the station manager; they bound him up and handed him over to the police for further action. What happened? The station manager was released, and the *ghafirs* were accused of assaulting a state employee, and <u>sentenced</u> to jail. They went to their superior, the native inspector of the Fayum, a man who speaks French and who belongs to the upper class down here. They knew he could help them to appeal the case; they brought him the necessary money, and he accepted it and promised them that he would take care of things. The deadline for appeal passed without an appeal being made, and the *ghafirs* were convicted for having done their duty. I have this story from Quibell, who has had to become acquainted with the circumstances because of his office.[353]

There can be no doubt that Lange was less than impressed with what he saw as a general lack of civil responsibility and integrity in Egypt, but although there are occasionally observations that look crassly colonial to the modern reader, most of his descriptions nonetheless seem to suggest an individual with a lot of sympathy for the country and its inhabitants:

It is quite a strange feeling, wandering as the only Europeans down these Arab alleyways among these brown, yellow and black people, half-naked children and veiled women; quite naturally one is inclined to become a little uneasy and to breathe more easily upon seeing a European or upon exiting onto a broader street; but in reality one walks safer among Arabs here in Cairo than most places in Middle- and South Italy. They are extremely decent and friendly people through and through, and one never comes across an intoxicated native, and it is after all the intoxicating drink which makes so many Europeans dangerous to their fellow man. [354]

The tendency to abstain from alcohol was, to Lange, one of the endearing aspects of Egyptian culture, very much in line with his own convictions, but he also makes a point of comparing Egyptians favourably with southern Europeans – an attitude not shared by many of his colleagues at the time.

The loss of information that accompanies any object removed from its archaeological context was a concern for Lange, and his experiences with the antiquities trade brought this concern into focus on several occasions. During his second visit in 1930 he notes that:

One often finds oneself annoyed at objects available on the market. Nahman, for example, has a collection of c. 150 clay seals from wine-jars with royal names of the first and second dynasties. Flinders Petrie found many such seals in the royal tombs at Abydos. Now it seems that the fellaheen down there have found new tombs which they rob, depriving science of its proper share thereof. It's even worse at Tell el-Amarna. The English have been digging there for years and found very little, but still there are constantly new objects from there available in the shops.[355] The farmers down there know, in other words, of places which the excavators have no knowledge of, and no one knows how much is lost to science by this transgression. During the excavations themselves much is also stolen. The day before yesterday I was offered pieces of alabaster dishes, which Zaki [Mahmud Abd es-Samad] confessed came from the government's excavation at Tura, east of Cairo; and it is said that when Montet excavated Byblos in Syria, over half of the objects found were stolen by his own workers who sold them to antiquities dealers and collectors. Petrie in his time introduced a system whereby he gave his workers *bakshish* for each piece that they brought him, and the size of the *bakshish* depended on the value of the object. Now that the price of antiquities have increased so much this system, which was adopted by all excavators, is simply not feasible anymore.[356]

---

353. Lange and Lange, *Dagbog fra Ægyptensrejsen 1899-1900*, 523-524; Quibell was at the time employed by the Antiquities Service as Inspector-in-Chief of Lower Egypt.

354. Lange and Lange, *Dagbog fra Ægyptensrejsen 1899-1900*, 81.

355. This increase in Amarna-period statues and reliefs on the market was due principally to the considerable production of fakes, represented primarily by the work of Oxan Aslanian; see Fiechter, *Faux et faussaires en art égyptien*, 27-29; idem, *Egyptian Fakes*, 124-131.

356. Lange, *Dagbog fra Ægypten, 1929-1930*, 87-88.

Lange saw illegal excavations as a big problem, but recognised that it would be difficult if not impossible to stop them. His own pragmatic position was that by buying objects from such illegal excavations they would at least become available for study by Egyptologists, and so whatever moral qualms he may have had they certainly did not interfere with his purchasing activities; five of the clay seals he mentioned as examples of looting he later had Nahman set aside for him to buy on behalf of the National Museum.[357] A certain amount of what by modern standards might be called hypocrisy was presumably the norm at the time, and Lange would have been unremarkable in this. A rather telling example is the distinguished Assyriologist A. H. Sayce, who in passing mentioned, in his autobiography, that 'As I was in part responsible for the law for the prevention of illicit excavations I could not go myself to Ali Farag [a dealer at Kafr el-Haram]'. To avoid announcing his hypocrisy publicly he instead got an archaeologist to explore the dealer's stock on his behalf, and then report back.[358] Lange's own moral stance regarding the antiquity trade may perhaps be described as utilitarian, but he had clear instructions from the Glyptotek not to buy looted objects.[359] As a philologist he was particularly concerned about papyri, and was annoyed at the common habit of illegal excavators of tearing papyrus rolls in two before putting them onto the market,[360] and he also lamented the fact that because of their modest size papyri were often smuggled out by dealers and tourists who simply put them in their pockets when they left Egypt.[361] Lange's attitude to the antiquities trade in general was in other words sympathetic (in that he accepted the basic premise of antiquities being sold by dealers), and he even felt that institutions like the Egyptian Museum would do well to capitalise on their holdings by selling dupli-

cates in their collections as a way to fund its activities.[362]

Laying down the law: attempts to curb the trade

The first legislation against the export of antiquities from Egypt had appeared as early as 1835, with a decree from the then ruler of Egypt, Muhammad Ali.[363] This was apparently issued partly as a reply to complaints from Champollion (in 1830) that in the three decades since Napoleon's expedition had first systematically started to record monuments, a full thirteen temples had disappeared. He appealed to Muhammad Ali in the name of science and begged him to do something, but as the latter placed a large proportion of the blame for the destruction on Europeans, the decree of 15 August 1835 was mainly aimed at the export of antiquities to Europe, and instead ordered such objects to be brought to Cairo, where a museum was to be built to house them (this was never realised under Muhammad Ali).[364] The decree was 'one of the first pieces of legislation passed by any country to pre-

357. Lange, *Dagbog fra Ægypten, 1929-1930*, 118; the transaction seems never to have been completed.
358. Sayce, *Reminiscences*, 334; cf. Ismail, *Wallis Budge*, 297-299.
359. Lange, *Dagbog fra Ægypten, 1929-1930*, 274.
360. Lange, *Dagbog fra Ægypten, 1929-1930*, 107.
361. Lange, *Dagbog fra Ægypten, 1929-1930*, 325.

362. Lange, *Dagbog fra Ægypten, 1929-1930*, 325; 'There is a large number of duplicates in the Museum; these should be sold to fund a better administration and more museum positions. But such ideas are not popular down here ...' (compare the similar comments on pp. 42-43). It is not obvious how this comment should be understood: the Egyptian museum in Cairo already had a *Salle de vente* at this point where tourists could buy genuine antiquities that were surplus to requirements in the Museum (discussed above, p. 47), and Lange would have been familiar with this shop. Perhaps his point is to do with scale – he may be thinking of a more large-scale and long-term clearance policy.
363. For a historical overview of the legislation pertaining to the trade in antiquities in Egypt, see Table 5 below. A convenient summary is also provided by Ikram, in Silverman (ed.), *Contested Cultural Heritage*, 142-144.
364. Reid, *Whose Pharaohs?*, 54-56; Colla, *Conflicted Antiquities*, 101-103, 116-118. This and other decrees relating to antiquities were published by Tagher, *CHE* 3 (1950), 13-26; see also Khater, *Le regime juridique des fouilles et des antiquités en Égypte*, 37-79. On the role of Champollion, see now also Gady, in Goyon and Cardin (eds.), *Proceedings of the Ninth International Congress of Egyptologists*, 767-775.

serve its cultural heritage, and a pivotal moment in the history of imperial collecting,' whereby Egypt proclaimed independence from the claims of European powers upon its past.[365] The decree dealt with the export of antiquities as part of more general measures to protect the ancient monuments, but any tourist who attempted to take antiquities out of Egypt without the authority of governors and toll officials would now see these objects impounded by the state – at least in principle. As a direct consequence, J. G. Wilkinson could report just a few years later, in 1843, that the city of Cairo included:

> a collection of antiquities belonging to Mohammed Ali, which is occasionally increased by those seized at the Custom-house, in the possession of persons unauthorised by special favour to take them out of the country. It was to have formed part of a museum to be erected in the Uzbekéëh [i.e. Ezbekiya]; but the formation of a museum in Egypt is purely Utopian.[366]

This was presumably not a blanket ban even in theory: the official decree states that 'having taken these circumstances into account [viz. the destruction and loss of antiquities], the government has decided to maintain the ban on the export of such antiquities as are to be found in the old monuments of Egypt, and which are of a particularly high value'.[367] What this value would be is not specified, and there are signs that it could be interpreted quite liberally: in a letter from October the same year (shortly after the publication of the decree), Muhammad Ali stated that an Englishman's attempt to bring a wooden coffin with a mummy onto a ship bound for India was not to be hindered, 'Because the decree on antiquities is silent on the subject of mummies of the unbelievers … and so there does not exist a formal ban'.[368] In theory any object found by locals should be handed over to the local *nazir* who would then send it on to Cairo, and anyone found selling objects would be severely punished. In practice, however, sales and illicit excavations continued, more or less with the approval of local officials; consuls for various European countries even sent out people to dig under their diplomatic seal which made them virtually impossible to stop.[369]

Lange rarely mentions export licenses or administrative procedures relating to the trade in antiquities in the diary from his first visit in 1899-1900, but the procedure is described as follows in a general guidebook from 1906:

> On leaving the country luggage is liable to be examined, and no traveller should attempt to export Egyptian antiquities without a special authorization to do so. Antiquities should be submitted to the authorities of the Egyptian Museum, who will assess their value for export duty, and have them duly sealed with the official seal, and will give the owner a signed permit addressed to the Mudir of the Customs, instructing him to allow the objects to leave the country.[370]

---

365. Jasanoff, *Edge of Empire*, 300. Greece had passed a law to the same effect only the year before, in 1834; Avgouli, in Kaplan (ed.), *Museums and the Making of "Ourselves"*, 247. Another early attempt to legislate against the looting and export of antiquities was a papal decree of 1802 which sought to protect the monuments and archaeological sites of Rome; this 'represented the most comprehensive archaeological protection law up to that point', although it had only a limited effect. It was followed, in 1820, by a more elaborate decree which is considered to be a precursor to both the Greek and later Italian efforts to legislate the antiquities trade: Dryson, *In Pursuit of Ancient Pasts*, 22.

366. Wilkinson, *Modern Egypt and Thebes* 1, 264. Wilkinson's comments notwithstanding, the collection was established at Ezbekiya, and subsequently transferred to the Cairo Citadel, although not for long; it was sold (or given, according to some sources), to the Archduke of Austria, Ferdinand Maximillian, on a state visit to Egypt in 1855; Saleh and Sourouzian, *The Egyptian Museum Cairo*, 9; Hamernik, in Lazar and Holaubek (eds.), *Egypt and Austria V*, 229-234.

367. Tagher, *CHE* 3 (1950), 21; 'Ayant pris en considération ces faits, le gouvernement a jugé à propos de défendre l'exportation à l'étranger des objets d'antiquités qui se trouvent dans les édifices anciens de l'Égypte, et qui ont une si grande valeur…'.

368. Khater, *Le régime juridique*, 45

369. Tagher, *CHE* 3 (1950), 22; cf. p. 31. For an analysis of the legal situation as it applied to the state-sanctioned export of antiquities, see Osman, *Columbia Journal of Transnational Law* 37 (1999), 969-1002, with a discussion of the 'inconsistent' enforcement of the 1835 decree on p. 989.

370. Budge, *Cook's Handbook for Egypt and the Sûdân*, 20.

We have been unable to find much archival information about these procedures. However, a photograph of a page from the export license register of the Egyptian Museum from 1959 survives in Milan and provides an example of how such information was recorded by the museum at the time. The register is arranged chronologically and provides information on the date, the identity of the seller (the antiquities dealer), the identity of the buyer (a collector, an institution, or another dealer), as well as a description and one or two inserted photographs of each object. The page in question lists dealers such as Joseph Khawam (3 entries), Kamel Abdallah Hammouda (1 entry), Abd el-Megid Hussein (1 entry), Albert Eid & Co. (1 entry), Hefnawy ismaïl el-Shaer (2 entries), Mohammed Abd el-Rahim el-Shaer (3 entries), and Sayed Molattam, Luxor (1 entry).[371]

The instructions about the export of antiquities quoted above were written by Sir E. A. Wallis Budge, a man who today has a rather dubious reputation in regard to his own acquisition practices for the British Museum ('scandalous' according to one commentator),[372] and the irony of his insistence on following the proper procedure will not be lost on modern Egyptologists – a case of 'do as I say and not as I do' if ever there was one. His description nonetheless sums up the main points; an export license had to be acquired from the Egyptian Museum, which would then seal the package (Fig. 112-113) and provide the necessary documents for presentation to the relevant customs officials on departure. The inclusion of such advice in contemporary guidebooks may reflect individual editorial decisions rather than government pressure, but there is no doubt that the government also publicised the legislation, to the extent where one visitor in 1909 remarked that 'The government forbids the sale or export of antiquities and posts placards to this effect in all public places.'[373]

Although boxes with antiquities were supposed to be inspected by qualified staff from the Antiquities Service before being sealed and approved for export, in practice this was not always done. It depended on the diligence of the people in charge, but also on the personal relationship between the owner and the official in question. The strict Director of the Antiquities Service, Eugène Grébaut, would personally inspect and approve antiquities for export. Schmidt reports to Jacobsen in 1892:

> Some of the objects are already packed. They then had to be presented at the *Musée de Guizeh* to M. Grèbaut solo, to be unpacked item by item – and then the box is sealed and marked for export, all by Mr. Grèbaut solo. *Permesso* is charged at 100 Piastre.[374]

If the circumstances were more favourable one could persuade (or bribe) representatives of the Service to seal a box without opening it; how common this would have been is difficult to say. A letter from Chauncey Murch to Budge, dated 6 March 1887, cites a conversation that the former had with Emil Brugsch, about a box with an illegally excavated Old Kingdom statue which they were afraid would be denied an export permit:

> [Brugsch:] Well, Mr. Murch, I'll tell you how it is. It is impossible for me to pass anything more without opening the boxes. Mr. Budge told me that he had nothing of the Old Empire, and I believed what he said. The truth [however] is that he bought a fine piece from Dingli. Dingli had bought it from Suleiman; and the result will be that we will have Suleiman's house watched or searched. Everyone knows what Budge got, and the result is that hereafter I will not take the responsibility of passing anything without opening it.[375]

---

371. Published by Piacentini, *Egypt and the Pharaohs*, 36-37; idem., *EDAL* 4 (2013/2014), pl. 12. Note that she interprets the document – incorrectly in our view – as a register of sales from the *Salle de Vente*.

372. Ismail, *Wallis Budge*, xvi-xvii, and passim.

373. Carson, *From Cairo to Cataract*, 196.

374. Letter from V. Schmidt to C. Jacobsen, dated 27 Feb. 1892 (Ny Carlsberg Glyptotek).

375. Reproduced in its entirety by Ismail, *Wallis Budge*, 290-292; the box was eventually smuggled out by Dingli without an official seal and export permission.

Fig. 112-113. Mummy of a child approved for export by the Egyptian Museum and with the original seal preserved intact. Museum Schleitheim. Courtesy of Gemaindearchiv, Schleitheim.

The passage seems to imply that Brugsch had previously not been averse to passing boxes for export without actually having opened them; later in the letter he is also said to have claimed that 'if it was even his brother he could not *after this* pass anything unless he first saw it' (our italics). The obvious conclusion is that he had in fact done precisely this in the past, and we can see no reason to suppose that he had favoured Budge uniquely in this regard.[376]

Although many objects were smuggled out of Egypt one way or another, the Antiquities Service was not generally regarded as lax with regard to the inspection of objects submitted for export permits; indeed some found that it was too bureaucratic, such as Charles Lang Freer who expresses his frustration in a letter from 1907:

The red tape in this land surpasses that of all other countries. And as for getting antiquities out of Egypt, it's worse than getting oneself out of Hades.[377]

Towards the end of the first visit, in the middle of the summer of 1900, Lange set about getting the antiquities he had bought ready for transportation; his collection was packed down in a box on 16 July:

The smaller objects had already been individually wrapped in paper and put into metal canisters that we had put aside for this purpose; old tea containers, biscuit tins and cigarette boxes. It was strange watching all my wonderful things, heavy and light, solid granite pieces and fragile jars of pottery, disappear into the gaping mouth of the box; I wonder if I shall see them again in Copenhagen? Can they manage the long journey? Or will the large ones grind down the small ones, as so often happens with humans? All manner of precautions have been taken to prevent this, and Domenico is an experienced porter ...[378]

376. He is reported to have done precisely this, notably after his claim to Murch and Budge that he had changed his ways, for E. E. Ayers who was shipping out several boxes of antiquities for the Field Museum in Chicago; Ismail, *Wallis Budge*, 294.

377. Cited by Clarke, in Hurtado (ed.), *The Freer Biblical Manuscripts*, 52, n. 94.
378. Lange and Lange, *Dagbog fra Ægyptensrejsen 1899-1900*, 729.

A single crate was more than enough for his personal collection of antiquities because most of what he had bought were small objects. But the objects he had acquired for the museums were often more monumental in nature – statues and reliefs – and required sturdier boxes because of their size and weight. Some had already been sent home, like the limestone statue of a man and a woman (Fig. 114) that he had bought for the Glyptotek,[379] while others were packed in two large wooden crates that were shipped separately from the rest of his luggage.[380] As he was leaving he was approached by several dealers with business proposals:

> One wanted me as a business partner for excavation work; he would fund the undertaking, and my role would be to get a concession from the Museum since a Bedouin cannot hold one, and then we would share the spoils. They're all rascals, these Bedouins; there are perhaps a couple of reasonably decent men once in a while, for example Mansur and the young Farag Ali, but then they are not the largest either [i.e. among the dealers].[381]

He accepted none of these proposals, and returned to Copenhagen without ever becoming involved in excavations in Egypt.

By the time of Lange's second visit in 1929-1930, new legislation had been introduced to curb the market: Law No. 14 of 12 June 1912.[382] This bill, along with Ministerial Order No. 50, issued just five months later (8 December 1912) formalized the procedures surrounding the excavation, trade and export of antiquites. Dealers had to register with the Antiquities Service, and were given license numbers, and all export of antiquities from Egypt was banned, unless one obtained a special permit from the head of the Antiqui-

Fig. 114. Group statue of a man and his wife, acquired by Lange from Maurice Nahman on 20 February 1900. This was Lange's first major acquisition. Ny Carlsberg Glyptotek, ÆIN 935. Courtesy of Ny Carlsberg Glyptotek.

ties Service.[383] Amongst other things, the law now recognised two separate categories of state-authorised dealers; on the one hand there were those with a proper shop (with a license number), and on the other there were stall-keepers (vendeurs à l'étalage) who were only allowed to sell objects worth five Egyptian pounds or less. The former had to apply to the Antiquities Service centrally at the Egyptian Museum 'on paper with 3 piastres worth of stamps', stating 'the last name, first name, and domicile … the premises where [the applicant] would like to do business' and

Compare the chapter on packing in Petrie's influential *Methods and Aims in Archaeology*, 105-113.

379. Lange and Lange, *Dagbog fra Ægyptensrejsen 1899-1900*, 591.
380. Lange and Lange, *Dagbog fra Ægyptensrejsen 1899-1900*, 743.
381. Lange and Lange, *Dagbog fra Ægyptensrejsen 1899-1900*, 738.
382. For an English translation see Fricke, in Merryman (ed.), *Imperialism, Art and Restitution*, 181-192; cf. Anonymous, *ASAE* 12 (1912), 245-251.

383. Lyons, *JEA* 1 (1914), 45-46; Wakeling, *Forged Egyptian Antiquites*, 7.

Year	Law	Summary
1835	High Order of Mu-hammed Ali of 15 August 1835	An order forbidding, amongst other things, the export of antiquities from Egypt without an export license.
1869	High Order of Ismail Pasha of March 1869	This included regulations regarding excavations with a view to stop the unauthorised export of antiquities, with the exception of coins; objects discovered on private land were said to belong to the owner of the land.
1880	Decree of Muhammed Tewfik of 19 May 1880	This expanded the prohibition on export to include coins.
1912	Law no. 14 of 12 June 1912	An extensive update of the older legislation after years of discussion, this included more wide-ranging laws governing the antiquities trade, including the introduction of state licenses for dealers. For extracts of the text relating to the antiquities trade (as discussed above p. 137; cf. further Appendix 1).
1951	Law No. 215 of 31 October 1951	The law strictly regulated private ownership of antiquities, but made provisions for dealers who already possessed collections (article 22.1), and for museums who might wish to sell objects (article 22.6). As in previous laws dealers were allowed to trade but would need government authorisation (article 24), and export was prohibited without a special license (article 26).
1973	Signing of the UNESCO agreement of 1970	The UNESCO agreement, formally known as the Convention on the Means of Prohibi-ting and Preventing the Illicit Import, Export and Transfer of Ownership of Cultural Property and which came into force on 24 April 1972, is generally seen as the first serious international attempt to curb the trade in illicit antiquities.
1976	Charte culturelle de l'Afrique	A pan-African initiative by the Organisation of African Unity (precursor to the African Union) to safeguard African culture and history, including archaeology, amongst other things by aiding UNESCO and by adhering to its rules and regulations.
1983	Law no. 117 of 6 August 1983	The principal law governing cultural heritage in Egypt today (with amendment of 2010, see below), it forbade any trade in antiquities in Egypt, and gave current dealers a one year period of grace in which to dispose of their stock (article 7), although private ownership of antiquities in some cases was accepted (article 8), and these could be disposed of by securing a special permission in writing as long as the object did not leave the country (article 9). In practice the law made the operations of antiquities dealers illegal.
2010	Law no. 3 of 14 February 2010	Amendment of Law no. 117 of 1983; there were no substantial changes to the articles governing the (by now officially non-existing) antiquities trade.

Table 5. An overview of legislation relating to the trade in antiquities in Egypt.[384]

384. The data in the table was mainly summarised from the UNESCO *Database of National Cultural Heritage Laws*, which is available online at http://www.unesco.org/culture/natlaws/ (accessed 10 Jan. 2013). Amongst the other sources we have utilised, the most useful have been Nakhla, Beshai, and Mahmoud, 'Cultural Heritage Legislation in Egypt', an article setting out the legal background for cultural heritage issues in Egypt on behalf of the Cultural Policy Research Institute; available online at http://www.cprinst.org/cultural-heritagelegislation-in-egypt (accessed 10 Jan. 2013) and Khater, *Le regime juridique des fouilles et des antiquitiés en Égypte* (for pre-1960 legislation, compare Fricke, in Merryman (ed.), *Imperialism, Art and Restitution*, 175-192). French translations (with no judicial authority) of the original Arabic documents can be accessed through the UNESCO database; the information provided in our table is based on this material and not on the original text in Arabic. For a modern interpretation of Law 117 of 1983 in an international context see Yasaitis, *International Journal of Cultural Property* 12 (2005), 103-104.

'a certificate of the requesting party's criminal record'. Stall-keepers, on the other hand, needed only the approval of 'the local directorate of the Service', a much less complicated procedure, relying on 'the opinion of the local authority'.[385]

The new law naturally led to an increase in the bureaucracy surrounding both archaeological excavation and the trade in antiquities, and several Egyptologists were provoked by it; many if not most both excavated and bought objects on the market,[386] and they viewed the change in the legislature as a major inconvenience. In 1914, shortly after the new law was introduced, W. M. F. Petrie devoted two pages to it in his journal *Ancient Egypt*. In this rather polemical article he laid out his own view of the law and the implications it would have:

The New Law on the Antiquities of Egypt

Unfortunately for archaeology, the legal questions of the claims of Government on antiquities, and the complications of dealers and valuers, are continually interfering with the progress of science. Perhaps no other subject of research is hampered with equal restrictions, legal and social. The discoverer in chemistry, in geology, in astronomy, has no Government imposing licenses and demanding half or the whole of the results of his labour. If the chemist or electrician makes a discovery of commercial value, he may have both his honours and his cash for it; but an archaeologist who made any personal profit would lose caste at once.

The entire prohibition of all export of antiquities in Turkey or Greece, only produces a permanent and well-organised, though hidden, route to every European museum. The bar on exportation from Italy is almost as effective in maintaining a systematic transport. In Egypt, since M. MASPERO began in rule in 1880, a more rational claim has prevailed. The Government has only barred export of objects really needed for the Cairo Museum, and returned the purchase money to the owner. Excavation in private land was free; and in Government land permission was given to excavate on half shares with the Museum.

Last year a new codification of the law was issued, which is of much importance to both excavators and purchasers of antiquities. The new principle which is most surprising in this law is the claim of the Government to appropriate all antiquities under the soil, in private as well as public land. This seizure of all such property, formerly private, is unexampled in any other country. Hitherto the whole returns from such sites as Memphis and Heliopolis were a scanty reward for the difficult and expensive task of working under water. If only half of the proceeds may be received, all such work is arrested.

In the beginning of the new law it is stated that the penalties laid down only apply to persons of Egyptian or Turkish nationality. The immediate result has been the transfer of dealing, really or nominally, to foreigners. Two of the best-known dealers from the Pyramids now have a prominent shop in Cairo with an Italian name over the door. The effect of the stringent law, only applicable to natives, will be to put the whole of the dealing in the hands of Greeks, Italians and others; and to throw all native dealers into foreign partnerships. A nominal partnership will confer immunity from the law on any native, as he can then plead agency, the property of being foreign. This is altogether an unsatisfactory state of affairs.

The definitions of antiquities are of the most sweeping kind; they include all manifestations and products of arts, sciences, literatures, religions, manners and industries, of all ages down to Coptic. This definition is expanded in detail to cover not only all it might be supposed to include, but also scattered blocks or bricks, chips of stone, sand, chips of pottery, and earth from towns (*sebakh*). But the law allows that objects already in private collections, or subsequently shared with the discoverers by the Government, may be sold.

The Government is entitled to expropriate any land containing antiquities, on paying a valuation, and ten per cent. over. Any discoverer of a fixed monument is bound to inform the department, and wait six weeks to know if it is claimed.

Any portable object, accidentally found, must be given up within six days, the finder to receive half the value. If not settled by consent, this half will be settled by the

---

385. Fricke, in Merryman (ed.), *Imperialism, Art and Restitution*, 185-187.

386. See e.g. Quirke, *Hidden Hands*, 128-131. A full study of W. M. F. Petrie as a buyer of antiquities is under way by Stephen Quirke; we are grateful to him for sharing some of his preliminary results with us.

Department arranging two halves, and giving the finder the choice. Or if the Department requires to keep more, then it may name a value, and, if accepted, it will then pay half to the finder; or if not accepted, the finder must name a value, and the Department will pay half and keep the objects, or require the finder to pay half and take the objects. This procedure also applies to all discoveries made by scientific excavators.

For dealers, a permit is requisite. Every dealer must keep a day book with entry of every object over £5 in value, with all details of dimensions, material, colour, etc.; the purchaser's name to be filled in, and every page of the register to be sealed by the Inspector of Antiquities. Nothing may be sold outside of the shop licensed, or carried about without an authorization of the Department. The Inspector may, by day or night, raid every place belonging to a dealer, to verify his stock and register. All of this seems to have been devised without a reference to practical conditions.

Regular excavations must be sanctioned by the Minister of Public Works, on the proposal of the Director, after acceptance by the Committee of Egyptology. Temporary searches for less than a month may be sanctioned by the Director. Permission will only be granted to *savants* delegated by public bodies, or to private persons who may present sufficient guarantees. This is a wide term, which has already included native dealers and other most unsatisfactory diggers. Only two sites may be held by the representatives of one body; a proviso which is already neglected. Every permit must be worked for at least two months in each season, on one or both of the sites.

Taking wet squeezes, or any other damaging process, is prohibited; but no bar is laid on tracing or dry squeezes. Many formal and minor regulations are also laid down; but those quoted here will suffice to show the main points where a purchaser or an intending excavator will come in touch with the law.

W.M.F.P.

Petrie's summary of this new law, which in his opinion was 'continually interfering with the progress of science', is interesting not just as an example of how the law was viewed by someone involved in the activities

it was attempting to control,[387] but also because he included anecdotal evidence of how the antiquities market was affected, based on his own experiences. Some of this confirms or contextualizes Lange's comments in his travel diary of 1929-1930: for example, Petrie's reference to dealers 'from the Pyramids' (i.e. the village of Kafr el-Haram) having shops in Cairo, and the absurdities resulting from the strict distinction between Egyptians and foreigners in the law – exemplified by the two local dealers operating under the auspices of an Italian.

The new legislation imposed unwelcome restrictions on the trade in antiquities – 'an altogether unsatisfactory state of affairs', according to Petrie – and Jean Tano, one of the largest Cairo dealers, complained bitterly to Lange about it:

> The Museum can appear on the scene [i.e. in a shop] and confiscate any object which one of its staff members has seen previously in its place of origin, or which a dealer has bought from a farmer who has stolen it. Objects which are sold to overseas buyers can be withheld by the Museum, or the export license can be delayed for months.[388]

In a slightly later semi-autobiographical account, Alan Rowe describes his own authority as the Director of the Graeco-Roman Museum in Alexandria (1941-1949) vis-à-vis the local antiquities trade:

> My work included inspecting shops of the Registered Antiquity Dealers in Alexandria and also dealing with alleged illicit holders of antiquities in the city; my ef-

---

387. However, it is clear that Petrie's perspective needs to be interpreted in the light of his decade-long struggle against what he saw as meddling from the Antiquities Service, a conflict that had its origins in the strained relationship he had with one of the directors of the Service, E. Grébaut; cf. Drower, *Flinders Petrie*, 196.

388. Lange, *Dagbog fra Ægypten, 1929-1930*, 57. Tano's reaction is, not surprisingly, very much in line with that of Luxor dealers reported by Budge some forty years previously; Budge, *By Nile and Tigris* I, 111. Unhappiness with government interference will have been a common attitude amongst dealers in all periods.

forts were much helped, in the latter respect, because I had the legal right to enter suspected premises without a search-warrant. ...[389]

Combined with the need to keep a journal of all objects above five pounds in value – noting the material, dimensions and even details of buyers – and the ability of representatives of the Antiquities Service to 'enter, at any moment and in every part, premises assigned to the trading of antiquities',[390] the market was subjected to strict regulations. Lange also found the new laws to be an irritating obstacle in his quest to purchase antiquities, and on at least one occasion the Egyptian authorities refused to supply him with the necessary export license for some objects that he had bought from Maurice Nahman:

> The discomforting thing is that the Museum has forbidden me to export the best of the objects that I have bought for the Glyptotek. The rules of the Egyptian Museum are quite nonsensical; the rule is that anything taken from temples or tombs cannot be exported, neither can objects that the Museum itself does not possess. But nobody can tell just by looking at an object whether it has been found in the sand or whether it has been broken off from a wall, and the Museum is quite incapable of saying where a relief is from, and of putting it back in its rightful place. Those objects that the museum does not possess it cannot always buy because they lack the funds, and that leaves the dealer with a lot of capital tied up. Madame Serveux has a Horus of bronze which she had sold for £2,000, but the Museum stopped its export license because it did not possess a statue of a comparable size; and what is it

worth now? It is no wonder that masses of antiquities are being smuggled out of the country.[391]

Such events were not uncommon. Wealthy buyers were especially interested in objects of aesthetic or historical value, and precisely this type of archaeological material could naturally be claimed to be of national interest. Albert Gallatin tells of similar problems in relation to a quartzite relief of Akhenaten which he acquired from Maurice Nahman in 1939:

> Nahman had managed to get himself into considerable trouble with the government over getting the large Akhenaten stele, fragments of which later appeared in Paris and New York, out of the country and so would do nothing about arranging for the export of this one [sc. the quartzite relief] should I purchase it from him. So I took it to the Museum myself, along with some minor material, hoping that it would be passed easily. But it was held; the heads of the Museum were called in, and it ended with their holding it till they could compare it with all known published monuments in order to make sure that it had not been broken off of one of them. Several weeks later Nahman cabled me at Naples that it had been cleared and I sent him my cheque and it arrived in New York safely; the cutting of it is of gem-like quality. Nahman had a big slab of a relief of mourners from an Amarna tomb at this time, but its export was too big a proposition for me to tackle, and Nahman refused to attempt it.[392]

In such situations, with the right connections, pressure might sometimes be brought to bear on the Antiquities Service. One example contemporary with Lange's account concerns a fine sarcophagus with a mummy which had been acquired for the Wayne County Historical Museum in Richmond (Virginia) from Hatoun in the Sharia el-Muski; the Antiquities Service declined to release the objects, but when the US State Department was contacted and intervened,

---

389. Rowe, *Some Details of the Life of Olga Serafina Rowe (A.D. 1905-1958)*. A copy of this unpublished manuscript was sent to I. E. S. Edwards of the British Museum and is preserved in the archives of the Egyptian Department. Despite its title, it is largely an autobiographical account of his own career. We are grateful to Patricia Usick for bringing the manuscript and the relevant passage to our attention.

390. Fricke, in Merryman (ed.), *Imperialism, Art and Restitution*, 186.

391. Lange, *Dagbog fra Ægypten, 1929-1930*, 258.

392. Gallatin, *The Pursuit of Happiness*, 48-49, pl. 4. The relief is now in the Metropolitan Museum of Art, inv. 66.99.41.

an export license was swiftly granted.[393] In another case some 74 boxes of antiquities which Budge wanted to send to the British Museum were apparently only approved and sealed after political pressure from Lord Cromer, the British Consul-General and '*de facto* ruler of Egypt',[394] and Sir William Garstin, of the Ministry of Public Works.[395]

An alternative, undoubtedly much more widespread, was smuggling. Smuggling could take various forms, from the simple concealment of small objects in the baggage of travellers to more elaborate schemes: one dealer explained to Lange that for statuary, one way of acquiring such a license without the Museum prohibiting the export was to present the statue in separate pieces; 'the head and one arm are sent separately, and later one takes along the body and the seat'.[396] Papyri, on the other hand could easily be carried out of the country as part of one's personal baggage, or alternatively simply posted out: Budge related how he, in several cases, cut up and concealed fragments of papyri (which he knew the authorities would never approve for export) among the pages of books of tourist photographs, and then simply posted the parcels to the British Museum.[397] It is clear that much material made its way out of Egypt illegally in the late 19th and early 20th Century, but it is equally clear that the ways of effecting such unofficial exports were not usually committed to paper, so the details are often unknowable today. An anecdotal account of how methods were discussed and transmitted between Western buyers operating in the Egyptian market was provided by Budge, who during his first visit to Cairo in 1886 spent an evening in the Hotel du Nil (Sharia el-Muski) where he was introduced, by the Rev. W. J. Loftie, to 'Walter Myers, Henry Wallis, the Rev. Greville Chester, a couple of dealers, and several other men who were interested in Egyptian antiquities'. These individuals had between them consider-

able expertise and experience of the market, and it seems from Budge's uncharacteristically cagey account that he picked up some of the tricks of the trade from them; he makes reference to having 'learned many things about the "antiquarian politics" of Cairo' which he found 'most useful in later days'.[398] The veiled reference to "antiquarian politics" (singled out by his own use of quotation marks) suggests knowledge of a less prosaic kind than the usual tips on how to bargain.[399]

If an export license was granted, this was accompanied by an export tax, payable by the person wishing to send the object out of Egypt. In the law of 1912, this was set at 1.5% of the stated value of the object, but it was increased to 2.5% by 27 January 1916.[400]

Petrie was very critical of the right to raid in his open letter of 1912. Dealers had in fact been exposed to the possibility of raids since the first Antiquities law was passed, but they had not so far proved very effective and the Antiquities Service had found it was difficult to curb the largely illegal trade. One example consists of the comprehensive raids by Eugène

393. Gaar, *Indiana History Bulletin* 8 (1931), 363.

394. Reid, in Daly (ed.), *The Cambridge History of Egypt* 2, 219.

395. Ismail, *Wallis Budge*, 323-324.

396. Lange, *Dagbog fra Ægypten, 1929-1930*, 128.

397. Budge, *By Nile and Tigris* 2, 154, 351-352.

398. Budge, *By Nile and Tigris* 1, 82-83. Compare also Budge's amusement at and admiration for the expertise of Greville Chester in smuggling antiquities (from Egypt, Turkey, Syria and Greece) expressed on pp. 84-85, n. 1; cf. Ismail, *Wallis Budge*, 71-74.

399. It is worth keeping in mind that Budge often had accomplices. The involvement of some representatives of the British authorities in the transport of antiquities is particularly noteworthy in this context. Budge describes, in a private letter, how the boxes of antiquities (more than 24 in total) from his first trip (1886/7) were transported back to England via troop ship on the order of General Montmorency, thus 'circumventing the attentions of the Bulaq Museum'; Ismail, *Wallis Budge*, 81-83. In another letter Budge describes an occasion when some papyri were packed into boxes marked as government property, and then taken out of the country by a British Major (pp. 116-117); compare too the export of antiquities from the Sudan (also formally under the authority of the Antiquities Service at the time), in connection with which Lord Cromer offered his support (p. 334).

400. Fricke, in Merryman (ed.), *Imperialism, Art and Restitution*, 187-188; cf. Lyons, *JEA* 1 (1914), 46; Larson (ed.), *Letters from James Henry Breasted*, 148; Baedeker, *Egypt and the Sûdân*, 8th edition, xvi.

Grébaut, the Director of the Antiquities Service, in 1888.[401] His main objective was the hope of securing the cuneiform tablets that had been discovered at Tell el-Amarna in late 1887 and which were being dispersed, illegally, on the market.

The raids started on 1 January and were well-planned. On just one day, Grébaut seized the antiquities of several major dealers in different cities; these included Sidrac at Akhmim, Hanna Kerass at el-Manshah, Abd en-Nur at Girga,[402] Mohammed Mohasseb, Abd el-Megid, and Mahmud Ledid, the latter three at Luxor, as well as Hussein at Edfu. Other targeted individuals included the principal dealer (unnamed) in Medinet el-Fayum and Khalil at Akhmim. The dealers at Luxor soon met and discussed the situation and undoubtedly took their precautions against future raids. They would have been wise to do so since the raids continued throughout the year and some dealers were targeted more than once. Thus, for instance, Sidrac was raided both in January and December; his main local competitor Khalil was thought to have instigated both raids, as an informer, apparently because he was conveniently away from Akhmim during the first raid (which implies that his own shop was not raided on that occasion).[403] In the end Grébaut was forced or pressed to pay a compensation for the antiquities he seized, and Wilbour reports that 'the principal anteekeh shop' at Medinet el-Fayum was paid £70, while other major dealers received lesser amounts; Abd el-Megid £50, Mohammed Mohasseb £40, and

Sidrac £29. Wilbour heard various rumours as to the results of the raids in Luxor:

> I think Grébaut got all A[bd el] Megeed's antiquities. You know he kept them all in the room he slept in. But M[ohammed] Mohassib used to go out of his shop and bring in better things from other rooms. So when the police sealed up his shop, they got only the poorest things. Or, they say, he paid the police two hundred pounds to open the room and take out the best things. Or, as they say, he had notice some hours before the police came.[404]

Wilbour had a relatively balanced view of Grébaut and found the British attacks on him 'malignant', but at the same time he personally felt that Grébaut's methods were rather harsh and sometimes unfair. 'Grebaut is quite a convert to the methods of Mariette and wishes the Koorbash still swung' – the *koorbash* being a whip made from hippotamus hide. He also noted that Grébaut had seized all Abd en-Nur's antiquities, 'even those which were his half, digging on shares for Maspero.' He was also critical of the practical results and noted in a sarcastic tone:

> His efforts to stop antiquity dealing are so successful that Budge sent nine tons, they say, to the British Museum, through General Grenfell, who himself is creating a private Museum, and whose sendings to England pass the custom-house unchallenged.[405]

---

401. This account is based on the Wilbour letters; cf. Capart (ed.), *Letters of Charles Edwin Wilbour*, cf. esp. pp. 455, 458, 461, 462, 465, 466, 488, 511, 580. Budge, *By Nile and Tigris* I, 138-150, similarly describes these events, but his account is heavily biased and also seems dramatized; he was clearly out to ridicule the Frenchman Grébaut and presented himself as both shrewd and influential – perhaps more so than he really was. A further contemporary account may be found in Bell, *A Winter on the Nile*, 242.

402. Presumably Abd en-Nur was not yet a consul at this stage (p. 185), otherwise his diplomatic status ought to have protected his business.

403. Cf. Capart (ed.), *Letters of Charles Edwin Wilbour*, 456, 488.

404. Cf. Capart (ed.), *Letters of Charles Edwin Wilbour*, 461-462. Wilbour's contemporary account may be contrasted with that of Budge, *By Nile and Tigris* I, 150, n. 1 (cf. also Ismail, *Wallis Budge*, 117-118), who reports: '[Grébaut] went to 'Abd al-Majid's house and entered it, and went through room after room, but found no antiquities of any kind. He then went on to Mohammed [Mohasseb]'s house, broke the seals, and entered, and went through all the rooms but found no antiquities.' Budge's account seems quite unreliable; it should be recalled that it was written more than thirty years after the incident and that Budge was very critical of the French antiquities administration and of Grébaut in particular. Moreover, the claim that Grébaut found no antiquities with Abd el-Megid and Mohasseb is contradicted by Wilbour's assertion that he later paid both of them compensation for antiquities that had been seized.

405. Cf. Capart (ed.), *Letters of Charles Edwin Wilbour*, 463.

Fig. 115. A large group of servant statuettes from the Old Kingdom tomb of Nykauinpu displayed on a table in the private residence of the dealer Nicholas Tano in Heliopolis. The man on the left is William Edgerton. The statuettes were subsequently acquired by J. H. Breasted for the Oriental Institute, Chicago. Courtesy of The Oriental Institute, University of Chicago.

The right of the authorities to raid dealers and individuals and the risk of having antiquities confiscated inevitably resulted in a continual game of cat and mouse. Lange provides several examples of how antiquities were stored away in obscure locations around Cairo and Kafr el-Haram (cf. above). He also cites an example from his visit to Luxor in 1930, where a petty dealer named Abd er-Rasul had a wooden sarcophagus which he had dismantled and hidden away in his granary (p. 187). Established dealers also frequently hid objects that they wished to keep from the attention of the authorities. Breasted reported in 1919 that Nicolas Tano had come into possession of an exceptionally fine Book of the Dead, 'a perfectly intact roll as thick as a roll of wall paper with the outer wrap-

pings of cover papyrus still around it'.[406] This papyrus was kept hidden in the shop of a rug dealer across the street, undoubtedly to avoid entering it into the required protocol; this was a direct violation of the Antiquities law of 1912, which stated that 'None of the objects available for sale by the merchant shall be kept outside of the premises where he is authorized to conduct his business'.[407] Two months later, Nicolas

406. Cf. Larson (ed.), *Letters from James Henry Breasted*, 96-97, cf. further pp. 100, 148. The papyrus, which turned out to be more than ten metres long, is now in the Oriental Institute Museum (inv. 10486, 'Papyrus Milbank') and has been published by Allen, *The Egyptian Book of the Dead*.
407. Fricke, in Merryman (ed.), *Imperialism, Art and Restitution*, 186.

Tano showed Breasted a group of 25 'remarkable statues of limestone' which had been excavated – by implication illicitly – at Giza; also these were not kept in his shop, where they would have to be registered, but instead at his private residence in Heliopolis (Fig. 115).[408] Similarly, in her diary of 1890 Emma Andrews, who accompanied Theodore M. Davies, observed that 'These men [i.e. the antiquities dealers] never keep their best things on exhibition – nor do they produce them unless they are very sure of their customers. They keep them in safe hiding either in or out of the house'.[409]

The introduction of the new Antiquities law of 1912, though ambitious in its attempt to limit and regulate the growing antiquities trade, seems to have had relatively limited impact. One of the main problems was the fact that the courts continued to show little interest in cases involving antiquities trade, and hence much illicit activity went unpunished or merely resulted in token action. As a result, people did not refrain from illicit antiquities trading, and Lange repeatedly reports how he was surrounded by fellahin and children openly peddling antiquities at every site he visited, despite it being illegal to do so without a license.

In 1920, several years after the institution of the new law, Reginald Engelbach was appointed Chief Inspector of Antiquities for Upper Egypt. With the enthusiasm of a newly appointed official, he published an account of his activities at the end of first year of duty (the only one he published; indeed such reports were unfortunately all too infrequent).[410] Engelbach had been active in reporting a number of

cases to the courts and was evidently hoping that they would set a precedent:

> The year has produced a fair crop of cases in the Courts. The majority of these are concerned with illicit diggings, dealing in antiquities without licenses, thefts in a small way and assaults. Some cases are of considerable importance as they serve to establish precedents which may be of value in future cases. Of these, two may be cited:

> On the 19 February 1920 two natives were condemned to one month's imprisonment for not reporting a find of sculptors' models, made in digging a well on their own property at Karnak. The objects were confiscated.

> At the Parquet at Qena, on the 11th April 1920 two other persons were condemned to six months imprisonment for selling imitation antiquities as genuine, and to two months' imprisonment for trying to sell a genuine antiquity – namely a bronze Osiris – without a license.

The sentences reported here – one month for failing to report an archaeological discovery, two months for attempting to sell a bronze, and six months for selling forgeries – may seem harsh. They were, in fact, out of the ordinary and did not set a precedent. In the same report, for instance, Engelbach mentioned that another petty unlicensed dealer at Luxor was found with a wooden ushabti-box in his possession; 'the case was taken before the tribunal and resulted in a fine of P.T. 50 and the confiscation of the box'. Like other inspectors, he was soon frustrated with the situation. A few years later, he reported on 'one of the all too rare instances where the Department of Antiquities has recovered objects without catching the plunderers in the act'.[411] It turned out that a certain family had long been selling bronzes. Although the police managed to catch the culprits on this occasion, many of the bronzes had reached the antiquities shops in Cairo, and Engelbach drily remarked that 'Bitter experience has taught us the absolute futility of attempting to recover these'. Evidently catching criminals through actual investigation was not the *forte* of the

408. Larson (ed.), *Letters from James Henry Breasted*, 139-140, cf. further pp. 145-146, 147; Grant, *OlNN* 205 (2010), 5-6. The statuettes represent the largest known assemblage of servant figures from a single tomb, the Old Kingdom tomb of Nykauinpu; cf. Teeter, *Ancient Egypt*, 21-25.

409. Andrews and Davis, *A Journal on the Bedawin, 1889-1912*, typescript, kept in the Department of Egyptian Art, Metropolitan Museum of Art. This entry relating to 4 Feb. 1890 is cited by Reeves, *MMJ* 48 (2013), 32, n. 77.

410. Engelbach, *ASAE* 21 (1921), 61-76; for the passages cited here, see pp. 63, 67.

411. Engelbach, *ASAE* 24 (1924), 169-177.

authorities, and there was much money to be made from the trade with antiquities. Engelbach summed up the situation as follows:

> The prospect of a reward out of all proportion to the labour expended in getting it, the fun of dodging the policeman and the slight element of risk (though the Courts are very lenient), all combine to make illicit excavation the most delightful sport which the country can offer the *fellâh* [sc. the peasants].

It is symptomatic of the situation that Hakim Abou-Seif, another Inspector of Antiquities, similarly uses the word 'lenience' in relation to the courts in the same publication from the Antiquities Department. He had been transferred from Karnak to the Tanta district about a year earlier, and commented on the problem with illicit excavations at his new station.[412]

> On looking over the dossiers of previous convictions for illicit excavations, I was amazed at the leniency of the sentences by the Parquet. Though this is occasionally due to the 'don't care' attitude often adopted by the judges in matters relating to antiquities, or even a lack of knowledge of the terms of the Antiquities Law, it is more often than not the fault of the agents of the Antiquities Department, who have not, in the past, made a careful distinction between the acts of merely taking *sebakh* without a license, for which the maximum fine is P.T. 50, and digging for antiquities or taking *sebakh* from an area not authorised for this purpose, for which a very stiff fine, or even imprisonment with hard labour, can be awarded.

When Lange visited Egypt for the second time, in 1929-1930, the most recently published Baedeker guide (1929) described the process – changed in view of the 1912 law that had come into effect since his last visit – which he had to go through in order to get the objects he had bought exported to Denmark:

> For the export of antiquities a permit from the Department of Antiquities is necessary. Applications for leave to export should contain a complete description of the objects, with a statement of their value and the name of the port through which they are to be sent. The objects should be sent to the Cairo Museum for examination in the cases in which they are to be exported, but the lids should not be fastened down. A sealing fee of 60 Mill[imes] per box and an export duty of 2½% on the value are charged.[413]

In late March 1930 he took stock of the objects he had bought, and he had considerably more antiquities to send back than after the first visit. The practicalities, including the purchase of wooden boxes, the presentation of objects to the Museum for export licenses, and the physical packing of the crates, were handled by Lange's friend, the dealer Zaki Mahmud Abd es-Samad, in his shop. The whole business was surprisingly expensive: 'Boxes are extremely dear here, as all wood has to be brought in from afar. The box for the paper casts [of inscriptions] cost 14 Danish Crowns and the one for our private stuff 18'.[414] Finally the eleven boxes (ten of which contained antiquities) were stored in the basement of the hotel where they were staying (Cecil House) until they could be sent by ship to Port Saïd, and from there on to Europe.[415] To facilitate the transport, as well as the passage through customs in Denmark, Lange wrote letters to the Glyptotek and to the Chief Customs Officer in Copenhagen, but did not expect much interest from their side; 'it will probably receive only a summary examination'.[416] His hunch proved correct, and the objects seem to have arrived at the museums without any problems.

---

412. Abou-Seif, *ASAE* 24 (1924), 147-148.

413. Baedeker, *Egypt and the Sûdân*, 8th edition, xvi. The sealing fee had originally been set at four piastres in 1912, and this was then increased to six piastres in 1916; Fricke, in Merryman (ed.), *Imperialism, Art and Restitution*, 187-188.
414. Lange, *Dagbog fra Ægypten, 1929-1930*, 327.
415. Lange, *Dagbog fra Ægypten, 1929-1930*, 313, 324-327, 330. For comparison, Budge allegedly sent back some 24 boxes of antiquities after his first four-month stay in Egypt (1886-1887), 45 boxes in 1887-1888, 55 boxes in 1888-1889, and 74 boxes in 1898-1899; Ismail, *Wallis Budge*, 80-84, 297, 314, 323.
416. Lange, *Dagbog fra Ægypten, 1929-1930*, 334-335.

Fakes and forgers

At the time of Lange's first visit to Egypt in 1900 the antiquities market was full of forgeries – as it had been for decades – produced primarily to deceive tourists and visitors but also museum representatives, and he often mentions encountering fakes; virtually all dealers appear to have had such objects for sale. The scale of the antiquities trade, both in genuine and fake objects, had been considerable even as early as the mid-19th Century.[417] An American traveller describes a visit, in 1855, to a 'laboratory' in Luxor where fakes were mass-produced on behalf of one of the leading antiquities dealers, the Copt Ibrahim:

> We made a sally in the moonlight to the village and the house of Ibrahim. Passing through the narrow and silent streets, we entered a dark passage into the mud walls, and going to the rear of his house, mounted a crazy flight of steps and entered his sanctum. It was a queer hole, not unlike the rooms of antiquarians that I have seen in America. Masses of stuff, broken coffin-boards, and mummy-cloths, lay piled in heaps around, while on shelves, and tables, and chairs, were the relics of Ancient Egypt. The old fellow frankly confessed that nine-tenths of all that we saw was modern Arab manufacture, and the ingenuity of the laborers is deserving of all praise. The astonishment of my friends was increased fourfold when they recognized numbers of articles which, they said, had been offered for sale at the steamer that same afternoon, and *fac-similes* of which had been purchased at enormous prices by travelers in their company. One article, in particular, attracted the attention of one of the gentlemen. He had been bargaining with an Arab for one precisely like it, and an Englishman had bought it before his eyes at the native's price, whereat my friend had been decidedly and justly offended. He now saw its counterpart lying here, and asked Ibrahim if that were modern? The fellow took out a box and showed him a dozen precisely likely it. 'It's a favorite, and sells well,' said he. It was a beautiful thing; and when I asked for the original from which the copy was made, he produced it from a secret place, and asked me ten pounds for it. It was but a piece of stone, four inches by five, with a figure in relief on one side.[418]

A guidebook roughly contemporary with Lange's first visit described the situation as follows:

> In the purchase of 'antikas' great care should be exercised, for genuine antiquities are scarce, and forgeries abound. Imitation scarabs are often well made, for the Egyptian workman has learned how to cut the commonest cartouches with great success, and also how to melt the glaze chipped from ancient beads and to lay it on his modern steatite scarabs by means of a blowpipe. Genuine antiquities are now rare, and their prices have risen so greatly that the traveller has to pay nowadays as many pounds for a genuine scarab of good colour as francs were paid in 1883, or piastres in 1870.[419]

The number of forgeries available made a lasting impression on Lange; on stopping by Luxor on his way back from Aswan, he laconically observes that 'half of Luxor makes a living from manufacturing fake antiquities, and the other half from selling them.'[420] The phrasing may have been influenced by a common saying; the first edition Baedeker's guide to Egypt from 1892 similarly states that 'Half the population of Luxor is engaged in traffic with antiquities, and the practice of fabricating scarabaei and other articles frequently found in tombs is by no means unknown to the other half'.[421] Not all forgeries were Egyptian products, however; some were produced as far away as Italy and England.[422]

417. A marked increase from around 1850 to 1860 was noted by Rhind, *Thebes, Its Tombs and Tenants*, 247. Contemporary guidebooks also remark on the numerous fakes offered for sale; see e.g. Wilkinson, *Handbook for Travellers in Egypt*, 324-325 (cited below).

418. Prime, *Boat Life in Egypt*, 363-364.

419. Budge, *Cook's Handbook for Egypt and the Sûdân*, 465. Some of the forgers were well-known even at this stage: in 1862 'the arch-forger at Thebes' was a certain Ali Kamuri, specialising in metal objects and scarabs; Rhind, *Thebes, Its Tombs and their Tenants*, 253 (there called Gamooni).

420. Lange and Lange, *Dagbog fra Ægyptensrejsen 1899-1900*, 316.

421. Baedeker, *Ober-Ägypten*, 1st edition, 116; idem, *Upper Egypt*, 1st edition, 103.

422. Fiechter, *Faux et faussaires en art égyptien*, 12-13; cf. Rhind, *Thebes, Its Tombs and their Tenants*, 252 (bronzes from Italy); de Guerville, *New Egypt*, 191 (antiquities from Birmingham).

Particularly widespread was the production of scarabs, sculptures - both in the round (nearly always with heads) and in relief - and papyri. The situation is well described already in 1858 in Wilkinson's *Handbook for Travellers in Egypt*:

> Those who expect to find abundance of good antiques for sale at Thebes will be disappointed. Occasionally they are found, and brought to travellers; and those who understand them and know how to make a judicious choice, not giving a high price for the bad, but paying well for objects of real value, may occasionally obtain some interesting objects. The dealers soon discover whether the purchaser understands their value; and if he is ignorant they will sell the worst to him for a high price, and false ones, rather than the best they have. Indeed a great portion of those sold by dealers are forgeries; and some are so cleverly imitated, that it requires a practised eye to detect them; particularly scarabæi. Papyri are made up very cleverly, on a stick, enveloped in fragments, or leaves; the outer covering being a piece of real papyrus, and the whole sealed with clay. Good papyri are broken up to obtain these outer coatings to false ones; and unless a papyrus can be at least partly unrolled, it is scarcely worth while for a novice in antiques to purchase it.[423]

Yet the production was not confined to costly objects, but included anything that might allow even the smallest profit. A good example was recorded by Wilbour on a visit to Medinet Habu in 1884:

> I visited the woman Gindeeyeh, who showed me the (modern) stamp from which she moulds and bakes the round brick stamps of Ramses III, that are always offered you in his temple at Medinet Haboo. She lives next north of Yussuf and I encouraged her industry; it saves monuments from destruction.[424]

The forgers did not limit their work to objects they had before them, but also made good use of images and publications. Thus, for instance, Ahmed Fakhry reports that he, while Inspector of Antiquities at Luxor in 1932-1936, visited known forgers and 'saw in their houses some parts of publications in hand drawing, especially the book of Percy Newberry on the scarabs [sc. *Scarabs*, 1906], as well as other books and they were using them as models for their forgeries'.[425]

According to H. R. Hall, later Keeper of Egyptian Antiquities at the British Museum, most of the production took place during the height of the inundation in preparation for the winter:

> During the height of the inundation the agricultural population is left without its usual occupation for some weeks. The ingenious inhabitants of many of the villages utilise this period of enforced leisure in manufacturing forged antiquities to sell to tourists during the ensuing winter.[426]

Lange himself claims repeatedly that in the majority of cases he was able to spot fakes relatively easily due to his Egyptological training and his extensive experience in working with the collections of the Egyptian Museum. Not infrequently, however, he found himself unable to decide on the authenticity of objects, and in those cases he was, understandably, unwilling to commit himself financially.[427] It is notoriously difficult to evaluate such autobiographical claims about the ability to spot fakes because there is rarely any corroborative evidence to back it up - objects thought to be fake (and therefore not purchased) do not make it into the museum registers, and most scholars only mention specific objects in exceptional cases.[428] The

423. Wilkinson, *Handbook for Travellers in Egypt*, 324-325. Perhaps significantly, this passage is not present in the earlier edition of 1847.
424. Capart (ed.), *Letters of Charles Edwin Wilbour*, 285, cf. also p. 354: 'El Gindeeyeh, the old woman who bakes bricks with the seal of Ramses III for the benefit of the *Khawagas* [i.e. foreigners], gave me a bit of an ostraca which bore a fragment of a romance in Hieratic with red periods.' One of the stamped round 'bricks' can be found in Bolton Museum (inv.

no. 1983.1.211); a photograph of this is reproduced by Hardwick, *IA* 3 (2010), 39, Abb. 1.
425. Lilyquist, *The Tomb of the Three Foreign Wives of Tuthmosis III*, 270.
426. Hall, *Handbook for Egypt and the Sudan*, 11th edition, 27.
427. Lange, *Dagbog fra Ægypten, 1929-1930*, 91, 96, 266.
428. Compare the case of Petrie, who 'had an extraordinary instinct for something that was not genuine', but who was still misled by the famous forgeries of the Necho and Akhenaten

insistence on being in possession of such skills may be central to the social identity of 'expert', providing a convenient criterion for distinguishing oneself from others with less knowledge. Certainly several of the objects Lange bought for both the Ny Carlsberg Glyptotek and the National Museum were later viewed as 'suspicious' by curators, including objects from categories that he would have been intimately familiar with, such as stelae.[429]

Occasionally objects which he recommended to the Glyptotek for purchase were turned down because the curator at the time, Maria Mogensen, thought them suspect, but this appears to have been rare, and Lange expressed his 'surprise' when it happened.[430] An example of this was a wooden ibis which he had bought from Zaki Mahmud Abd es-Samad before the Museum was able to reply.[431] Having received a negative answer from the Museum he attempted to cancel the transaction, which Zaki agreed to do providing he could find another buyer for it. Lange seems not to have managed this, and ended up bringing it back to Denmark where it appears to have been accepted by the Museum after all; a wooden ibis in the Glyptotek (ÆIN 1670) is recorded as having been bought in Egypt in 1930 by Lange, for £150.[432] Another case is a 'quite exceptional' ivory statue that Lange saw for sale at Maurice Nahman's shop, which the Glyptotek declined to buy (Fig. 36).[433]

Statue de prisonnier du Nouvel Empire.

Statue de prisonnier du Nouvel Empire.

Fig. 116. An unusual sculpture of a bound foreigner offered to Lange at Luxor in 1929. The piece interested him, but he felt unsure about its authenticity because of the palaeography of the inscription and eventually declined the offer. The object is now in the Luxor Museum. It was published by Keimer, *ASAE* 49 (1949), pls. II, IV.

A further instance where the status of the object (as genuine or fake) was uncertain concerned a black granite offering table (Fig. 116);

> It is a so-called offering table. Behind the tied-up foreigner there is a depression which ends in two small canals by his feet. One would pour water over the fi-

scarabs; Drower, *Flinders Petrie*, 298-299, 330; cf. Fiechter, *Faux et faussaires en art égyptien*, 75-79, 254-255.

429. The most well-known fakes include ÆIN 1674 and 1677 at the Ny Carlsberg Glyptotek; cf. Fiechter, *Faux et faussaires en art égyptien*, 134-135, 142. Stelae in the National Museum labelled as 'suspect' by the Museum inventory include inv. no. 11580, 11581, and 11582 (all supposedly Middle Kingdom, the very period which his catalogue volume for the Egyptian Museum dealt with).

430. Lange, *Dagbog fra Ægypten, 1929-1930*, 324.

431. Lange himself had not been entirely certain whether the ibis was genuine; *Dagbog fra Ægypten, 1929-1930*, 266.

432. Cf. Koefoed-Petersen, *Catalogue des statues et statuettes égyptiennes*, 21, pl. 33, no. 32.

433. Lange, *Dagbog fra Ægypten, 1929-1930*, 312; Lange photographs 147-149. This appears to be genuine, and is now in the Walters Art Museum (71.509), having been bought directly

from Nahman by Henry Walters in 1930. We are grateful to Tom Hardwick for identifying the object.

THE ANTIQUITIES TRADE IN EGYPT

SCI.DAN.H. 4 · 8

gure and this would collect itself in the depression and run off via the two canals. It is the libation offering that is presented to the deceased this way. The deceased was a count and high priest, but I cannot yet read his name.[434] (...)

The question of whether it is a genuinely ancient object must be considered carefully. It is a given that such a piece even the best forger cannot compose out of his own mind, but he would be capable of copying an original if it was in front of him. If the statue of the foreigner is a copy, then the original must exist or must have existed here in Luxor, and it would be well worth tracking it down.[435]

It was offered for sale for a mere £20; Lange considered this 'a laughably low price for a genuinely ancient object of this kind, which of course arouses suspicion', and did not buy it.[436] About five years later Ludwig Keimer saw the same statue in the hands of the antiquities dealer Mahmud Mohassib *Bey* in Luxor, and in 1938 or 1939 it was acquired by Moïse Lévi de Benzion in Cairo.[437] The object later came to the Luxor Museum where it is now on display, said on the label to be a 'Statue of a prisoner. New Kingdom. Qasr el-Koba (Cairo). Grey Granite', and to have 'an offering prayer dedicated to a man named Peninhery'. Although Keimer's publication read the name in the offering formula differently (Khnumhat rather than Peninhery) and the object has somehow come to be associated with Qasr el-Koba, the photographs show it to be the same object. His titles 'count' (*ḥȝty-ˁ*) and 'high priest' (*imy-r ḥmw-nṯr*) are also the same as those read by Lange.

Even when several experienced Egyptologists examined an object it was not always evident whether it was a forgery or a genuinely ancient artefact. An example is the above-mentioned ivory statuette:

At Nahman's there is an ivory statuette which is quite exceptional if it is genuine. And there's the rub: it has been taken to the Museum where they kept it for a whole day to examine it.[438] The conclusion was reached that it was suspicious, and Lacau [sc. the Director of the Antiquities Service] declared that he would allow it to be exported. The price asked for was £1,000. Since then Capart has seen it, and he considers it genuine beyond doubt, Jéquier has his doubts, while Nahman, who doesn't own it but is simply selling it for the owner, considers it genuine, and he has a lot of experience. I have studied it for over half an hour, and I have consulted similar statues in the Museum, and I cannot believe otherwise than that it is genuine. One of Jéquier's arguments is only valid if it should be dated to the 6th Dynasty, but not if – as I believe – it should be dated to the 12th Dynasty. But the amazing thing is that it looks like it had been made yesterday. The Museum's judgment is not decisive; both Lacau and Gunn [Assistant Curator at the Museum at the time] are pure philologists, and Engelbach [Assistant Keeper at the time] is an engineer; there isn't really an archaeologist at the museum.[439]

Ludwig Borchardt, certainly one of the most experienced buyers in his time, was also sometimes deceived. An interesting episode is described by him in a letter to his wife in 1903:

Am Sonnabend früh, sehr früh sogar, fuhren wir nach Qeneh, die Alterthumshändler besuchen. Es war nicht rechtes dort. Nur eins fiel mir auf u. ich nahm es mit. Ein Stein mit Inschrift u. einem Skorpion en relief. Als ich ihn in Luqsor Mohareb Todrus zeigte, sagte er, es sei falsch. Steindorff u. ich glaubten es nicht u. nun liessen wir alle bekannten Fälscher von Steinsachen aus Luqsor u. vom Westufer kommen, um den Stein zu begutachten. Der erste sagte, er sei echt. Zwei andere

---

434. Lange, *Dagbog fra Ægypten, 1929-1930*, 185.
435. Lange, *Dagbog fra Ægypten, 1929-1930*, 190-191.
436. Lange, *Dagbog fra Ægypten, 1929-1930*, 190.
437. Keimer, *ASAE* 49 (1949), 37-39. A colour photograph can be found in el-Shahawy and Atiya, *Luxor Museum*, 102-103.

438. The Egyptian Museum had for a long time offered a service whereby one could bring an object to them to establish its authenticity, but this practice had stopped several years earlier; Wakeling, *Forged Egyptian Antiquities*, 67. On this occasion the purpose of the presentation seems to have been to try to secure an export license, and the authenticity question, although highly relevant, was not the main reason for the visit.
439. Lange, *Dagbog fra Ægypten, 1929-1930*, 265-266.

hielten Theile für falsch, u. der vierte erklärte es kurzweg für die Arbeit des zuerst gefragten. Er gab Indicien an, die auch mir einleuchteten, so dass ich auch jetzt das Ding für eine sehr geschickte Fälschung halte. Wir versuchten dann noch vergeblich aus dem vermutlichen Verfertiger ein Geständniss herauszulocken. Jedenfalls hat Steindorff u. mir diese ganze Untersuchung viel Freude gemacht.[440]

The quality of the forgeries seems to have risen by the time of Lange's second visit to Egypt in 1930, when he makes the following remark:

> They are incredibly good at producing fake antiquities of every kind here in Luxor. What I have seen on the stalls here surpass any description, but in general it is possible to tell the fake from the genuine. The difficulties arise when they copy, with great skill, a good original. Dreiss says that they always find it difficult to copy a hieroglyphic inscription.[441]

When his lack of experience with certain categories of objects meant that he had little faith in his ability to identify forgeries, he was systematic in his approach and would scour the museum collections for parallels and potential models; for example, when he was offered a pair of golden earrings in 1930, he went straight to the museum to look at their collection of similar objects to familiarise himself with the category,[442] and on a later occasion he did the same with the above-mentioned ivory statuette.[443]

By 1930 it seems as if there were also more categories of fakes available to buy than there had been dur-

ing his first visit, and while staying in Thebes he describes the following encounter:

> A couple of fellaheens turned up at tea time to sell some objects. Borchardt pointed out to them that virtually everything they were selling was fake. One of them had a couple of arrowheads in flint which were also fake. There are now some people who are extremely good at imitating prehistoric flint objects. As it happens forging antiquities is big business here. [444]

Part of the subterfuge of selling fake antiquities was to come up with a plausible provenance for a piece, and such stories could be fairly elaborate, sometimes involving significant effort on the part of the dealers. The most famous example is the story about a dealer who was presented with an allegedly sealed tomb and who was offered the opportunity to buy everything in it. Having inspected the tomb the dealer agreed and paid a large sum of money to the 'discoverers', and arranged to have all the contents delivered to his storehouse. This was done gradually under the cover of darkness, and once completed the dealer waited patiently for the winter trading season to begin, looking forward to making a handsome profit on the collection. When he finally presented the objects to rival dealers and Egyptologists, the unanimous verdict was that every single piece was a forgery, and that the poor man had been duped. Slightly different versions of the story are recorded, and although the historicity is difficult to confirm, it may illustrate the extraordinary lengths to which dealers and forgers would go to construct a plausible provenance for forged objects.[445]

The invention of provenances was ubiquitous, both in the case of forgeries and genuine antiquities. Elaborate stories and settings were used to provide objects with backgrounds that would make them more attractive to buyers; in the case of forged objects it was done to establish a plausible origin, and in the case of genuine objects it could be a way to increase their value, or to cover dubious acquisition practices.

---

440. Letter from L. Borchardt to M. Borchardt, dated 26 Apr. 1903 (Swiss Institute, Cairo). We are grateful to Cornelius von Pilgrim for bringing this letter to our attention.

441. Lange, *Dagbog fra Ægypten, 1929-1930*, 190. For the dealer Wolfgang Dreiss, see the list at the end of the book.

442. Lange, *Dagbog fra Ægypten, 1929-1930*, 103. He appears to have bought these (p. 215), but we have been unable to locate them in Copenhagen; they need not be genuine, as Lange himself admitted that 'It is a mystery that the man [Mohammed Abd el-Haggag] wants to sell these earrings so cheaply' (p. 103). On the manufacturing of fake ancient Egyptian jewellery at this time, see Wakeling, *Forged Egyptian Antiquities*, 11-36.

443. Lange, *Dagbog fra Ægypten, 1929-1930*, 265.

---

444. Lange, *Dagbog fra Ægypten, 1929-1930*, 224.

445. Fiechter, *Faux et faussaires en art égyptien*, 16-17; idem, *Egyptian Fakes*, 34-35; Wakeling, *Forged Egyptian Antiquities*, 119-122.

A famous example is the apparent invention of an underground chapel beneath Karnak temple as the fictional provenance of several statues and stelae which Budge persuaded the British Museum to buy. It has been suggested that the 'chapel' was a modern construction, perhaps arranged by Mohammed Mohasseb, in order to raise the price and to provide a convenient single provenance for an otherwise disparate group of objects.[446] Already in 1862, Rhind reports concerning bronze figures that they abound at Saqqara and that 'inferior specimens, which there overstock the market, are occasionally consigned to Tadrous [sc. the Prussian consular agent Todros Bolos at Luxor], to be sold with the prestige of having been found under the shadow of the Theban temples.'[447] Conversely, objects might also be assigned to the locations where they were common; thus, for instance, 'Akhmim became synonymous with high-quality textile finds and dealers used the site as a selling point, attributing to it almost any "Coptic" textiles, even when these had been excavated elsewhere.'[448]

A different type of subterfuge was sometimes employed in order to stage finds for visiting dignitaries. In these cases genuine antiquities were acquired, mostly through excavations, and then reburied in convenient locations in order to be 'discovered' at the appropriate time. One such staged find concerned the visit of a cousin of the emperor Napoleon III, prince Napoleon, whose plans for a trip to Egypt in 1857 was prefaced by an elaborate programme of excavation and reburial. The Khedive Saïd Pasha had instructed Mariette to proceed up the Nile on his own viceregal steamer, and had provided him with the necessary workforce to arrange a suitable programme of discovery. The Khedive wanted 'every step of the visiting prince to sprout antiquities', but although objects were excavated for this purpose at Giza, Saqqara, Abydos, Thebes and Elephantine, the prince never ac-

tually came to Egypt.[449] There may have been similar events in connection with other royal visits at the time, but the evidence is rarely as detailed as the case above. The visit by the Prince of Wales (the future King Edward VII) in 1869, during which some 30-odd mummies and coffins were acquired, has been interpreted as such a 'staged' find,[450] but recent work has suggested that this is unlikely, based on contemporary eyewitness accounts.[451]

Stories like these illustrate the theatrical aspects associated with the antiquities trade, and the extraordinarily elaborate schemes involved in the transmission of antiquities, both genuine and forged. The efforts and resources expended were considerable because there were correspondingly large sums at stake, and deception could rely as much on personalities and social relationships as on the quality of the forgeries themselves. Both buyers and dealers were acting out their roles, trying to get the better of their opponents in the transactions, and the lure of a good bargain clouded the judgment of specialists and tourists alike.

A Tale of Two Heads

In the travel diaries Lange repeatedly stresses his ability to spot fakes (p. 148), and although he was certainly competent in view of his considerable experience with museum collections, he was also taken in on several occasions. One of these was to play a central role not just in Lange's narrative of himself and his career as an antiquities buyer, but also in terms of his relation to the Ny Carlsberg Glyptotek and the Carlsberg Foundation which had funded his acquisitions. During his second trip to Egypt in 1930, he was presented with an impressive granite head (Fig. 117):

... consisting of two pieces of extremely black granite of superior craftsmanship. The nose, both ears and one eye were damaged, as was one chin, the break passing

446. James, *Bulletin de la Société française d'égyptologie* 75 (1976), 7-30. However, for a divergent view, interpreting the find as genuine, see Eaton-Krauss, *JEA* 85 (1999), 117-120.
447. Rhind, *Thebes, Its Tombs and their Tenants*, 253.
448. Persson, *JHC* (2010), 1.

449. See Winlock, *JEA* 10 (1924), 259-260, with references.
450. Adams, *DE* 18 (1990), 5-19.
451. Sheikholeslami, in Fortenberry (ed.), *Souvenirs and New Ideas*, 151.

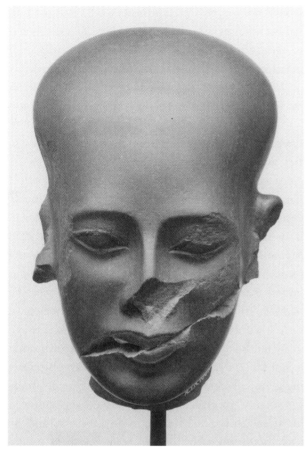

Fig. 117. Fake head of an 'Amarna princess', acquired by Lange from Todros Girgis Gabrial, February 1930, for the price of £61. Ny Carlsberg Glyptotek, ÆIN 1669. Courtesy of Ny Carlsberg Glyptotek.

Fig. 118. Fake head of an 'Amarna princess', acquired through Lange from Wolfgang Dreiss, November 1930, for the price of £1,500. Ny Carlsberg Glyptotek, ÆIN 1677. Courtesy of Ny Carlsberg Glyptotek.

straight through the mouth, and the bottom part of the face was defective; but in spite of the damage the head was impressive as a piece of art. There was no doubt that one was standing before the work of a great sculptor of the Amarna age.[452]

The head was shown to Lange in Cairo by the dealer Todros Girgis Gabrial from Luxor, with whom Lange had dealt in the past. Girgis claimed to have met a man on the train to Cairo, who in the course of their conversation happened to mention that he had some antiquities that he was bringing to the capital to sell: 'Girgis admitted to being a dealer and told the other

that he would lead him to a good friend in Cairo who was a professor and might want to buy the head he had shown him'. Girgis went on to say that it was 'a remarkable head with a strange face'. He also mentioned that the owner was from Mallawi, the closest station to Tell el-Amarna, and that it had been bought from a local official. Lange immediately thought – as he was no doubt meant to – of the 'strange' Amarna style, and was pleasantly surprised when Girgis miraculously seemed oblivious to the value that this provenance would imply.[453] (Girgis had in fact been

452. Lange, *Dagbog fra Ægypten, 1929-1930*, 271.

453. 'It was evident that Girgis had no idea of the real value of the head'; Lange, *Dagbog fra Ægypten, 1929-1930*, 272. Several

providing the dealer M. A. Mansoor in Cairo with pieces in this distinct style for several years, cf. p. 268). After much negotiation they agreed on a price (£61) which was so low that Lange later described it as 'ridiculously cheap', 'like a fairytale'.[454] Upon his return he sold it on to the Glyptotek, who quickly published it as a recent acquisition 'par une hazard unique'.[455] This head was itself very similar to one (Fig. 118) that Lange had seen in the possession of Wolfgang Dreiss, a hotelier and dealer from Luxor that he had gotten to know well when staying at his hotel.[456] Dreiss had been looking to sell his head for some time (for £8,000), and Lange was hoping to purchase it for the Glyptotek. Along with the head he had bought from Girgis, the two would be like 'sisters': 'And then the Glyptotek would be able to boast of possessing two of the finest pieces of art from ancient Egypt, including the largest known head from Tell el-Amarna'.[457]

Despite the different stone, the two were remarkably similar; so similar in fact, that Lange thought they had been made by the same sculptor.[458] Ironically he may well have been correct in his suggestion that the sculptor of both objects was the same individual, although it seems to have been a modern artist, not an ancient one. Exactly who this was is difficult to pin down as the evidence is contradictory. On the one hand a photograph of the head bought by Lange in Egypt (ÆIN 1669) was found in the archive of the infamous forger Oxan Aslanian after his death, suggesting that perhaps the 'Berlin Master' had been its creator. On the other hand, Borchardt reported that Paul

Dingli, the forger turned informant who assisted him in his enquiries into the production of fakes, claimed in 1930 that he himself had produced it – so around the same time as Lange actually bought the head.[459]

Lange foresaw a potential problem with the export of the head in that the Egyptian Museum would be unlikely to let such a magnificent piece out of Egypt, but his worry turned out to be misplaced – in fact the Museum seems to have recognised that the piece was a fake, and so did not object to its export.[460] Lange expresses his surprise at Girgis' inability to recognise the value of the piece several times,[461] particularly since the much less experienced dealer Zaki Mahmud Abd es-Samad, to whom Lange showed the piece after having bought it, immediately priced it at no less than £1,000, and thought it 'the best piece he had seen this season'.[462] This too should perhaps have been a warning sign to Lange; he had himself previously remarked that a ridiculously low price was often a sign that a dealer was unconvinced of an object being genuinely ancient.[463] Pride in having made an exceptionally good deal seems to have overshadowed his usual suspicion and alertness, however, and he was ecstatic when he heard the news that the Museum would not in fact be prohibiting the export of the piece:

Today has been a great day for us. The inconceivable has happened: the black head has been shown to the Museum and has not been blocked [for export]. This is certainly in large parts due to Zaki's diplomacy and

Amarna heads were being produced around the same time; see Steindorff, *The Journal of the Walters Art Gallery* 10 (1947), 55-56.

454. Lange, *Dagbog fra Ægypten, 1929-1930*, 291, 297.

455. This is ÆIN 1669; cf. Mogensen, *BIFAO* 30 (1930), 461-464, pl. III.

456. See the entry on him below.

457. Lange, *Dagbog fra Ægypten, 1929-1930*, 178, 291, 297.

458. Lange, *Dagbog fra Ægypten, 1929-1930*, 290, 297. The head in Dreiss' possession was said to have been found at Thebes rather than Amarna, but Lange explained this by suggesting that the artist 'worked in Tell el-Amarna, while it was still the royal residence, but then moved to Thebes, when Tutankhamun moved the residence there' (p. 297).

459. Fiechter, *Faux et faussaires en art égyptien*, 46 (Dingli as creator), 164-165 (for Aslanian as possible creator). Fiechter does not discuss the contradictory nature of the sources, but it is worth bearing in mind that Dingli and Aslanian were part of the same *milieu* of forgers; in one case Dingli used a genuine royal head (perhaps Brooklyn 53.75) in the possession of Kalebdjian as a model for a forgery (BM EA 1641). Kalebdjian in turn was the uncle of Aslanian, and the latter worked in the former's shop, and so presumably knew Dingli. For the objects, see now Hardwick, *IA* 3 (2011), 32-33.

460. Lange, *Dagbog fra Ægypten, 1929-1930*, 311-312.

461. Lange, *Dagbog fra Ægypten, 1929-1930*, 272, 299.

462. Lange, *Dagbog fra Ægypten, 1929-1930*, 299.

463. Lange, *Dagbog fra Ægypten, 1929-1930*, 190.

methods. I had impressed upon him how important it was for me to get it home, and he said that if the Museum blocked it, he would find another way of getting it to Copenhagen. This morning he then brought the head on my behalf, and presented it to Engelbach, who asked where I had bought it. Zaki answered 'From Girgis in Luxor'. This was true as I had paid the money to Girgis. Zaki then told him a tall tale about having seen the head in the bazaar last summer, but that it had not sold because "it is not a very real piece" (a way of saying that it was considered fake). Engelbach has evidently believed this and not looked at the head very closely; he can hardly have had it in his hands or even out of the box, as he would then undoubtedly have seen the marvellous technique and Tell el-Amarna style. He accepted Zaki's suggesting about there being something not quite right about it, as he told me this morning. But still, there remained for it to be show to Lacau, or, as he was absent today, to Gauthier. Then Zaki made the decisive move. By paying suitable bakshish he got one of the native gentlemen who deal with the sealing of antiquities for export to seal the box without it being shown to Gauthier. This is the usual way with the administration down here, where almost anything can be achieved by bakshish ... It is unbelievable that Engelbach did not block the head for export immediately. It may be because any object which is extraordinary, which one has never seen the like of, is always considered suspect ... But then Engelbach is not a connoisseur, although he is an excellent administrator.[464]

Reviewing the results of this second trip to Egypt, and the antiquities he had bought, he says – somewhat inappropriately with hindsight – that he thinks that 'The black head is most definitely the most important object; it alone more than repays our trip'.[465]

The brown or yellowish 'sister' head was offered to the Glyptotek by Dreiss and his sister for the sum of 90,000 Reichsmark, and initially declined. After some negotiations, however, the Museum agreed to pay the reduced price of 1,500 Egyptian Pounds for it. In the letter-correspondence between Lange, Dreiss and Dreiss' sister which document the negotiations, now

preserved in the Royal Library in Copenhagen, the alleged provenance of the piece is explained in some detail:

> Vom Besitzer dieser Felder [on the Theban West Bank], 'Hassan' Abdel Meghid wurde dieser Kopf direkt vom Fellahin c. Zt. 1908/9 eingehandelt. Dieser Hassan kam sehr oft zu mir als ich noch das Hotel du Nil besass, da sein Vater Abdel Meghid der Grundbesitzer des Hotels war, war er mir sehr gut bekant & brachte mir Hassan von anderen Seite des öfteren sehr schöne Stücke.[466]

In a letter written some two weeks later, Dreiss elaborated on this first written account:

> Der <u>detaillierte</u> Hergang des Fundes ist folgender: Im Herbst 1908 von Medinet Habu kommend, traf ich Hassan Abdel Meghid auf seinen Feldern (südlich den Memnon Kolossen & östl. von Medinet Habu gelegen) mit Abladen von Säcken beschäftigt, welche mit Tempelschutt gefüllt waren & auf Eseln herbeigeschafft wurden um als Dünger auf die Felder gestreut zu werden. Einer von diesen Leuten nahm Hassan auf die Seite, öffnete einen Sack & brachte den Kopf zum Vorschein. Ich liess mir nichts anmerken, nur beim Wegreiten gab ich Hassan zu verstehen, dass ich Interesse für das Stück hätte, & denselbigen Tag nach Sonnenuntergang brachte er mir das Stück ins Hotel du Nil.

> Der Kopf war mutmasslich einstmals übertrücht, aber durch tausende von Jahren langes im Schutt vergraben liegend [(sic)] & Regengüsse waren sicher auch nicht ausgeblieben, war von Tünche nichts verblieben. Von mir wurde der Kopf nur mit weicher Bürste & wollenen Lappen gereinigt. Zur selbigen Zeit wurde meistens des Sabbach-Schutt südwestl. von Medinet Habu herbeigeschafft, ungefähr in der Gegend wo früher der Palast des Amenophis d. III. gestanden haben dürfte. Heute wenn Sabbach geschürft wird, werden die Leute streng überwacht, was vor dem Krieg wenig beachtet wurde.[467]

---

464. Lange, *Dagbog fra Ægypten, 1929-1930*, 311-312.
465. Lange, *Dagbog fra Ægypten, 1929-1930*, 312.

466. Letter from W. Dreiss to H. O. Lange, dated 23 May 1930 (Royal Library, Copenhagen). Abd el-Megid ('Abdel Meghid') was one of the main antiquities dealers in Luxor until his death c. 1915.
467. Letter from W. Dreiss to H. O. Lange, dated 6 June 1930 (Royal Library, Copenhagen).

This may be compared to the story which Dreiss had told Lange already in December of 1929 concerning the provenance of a unique statue depicting a bound foreigner.[468]

> He could tell me the background of this piece. It had been the property of a man by the name Hussein Abd el-Megid, who was the son of an old and rich antiquities dealer who owned some land between Medinet Habu and the Memnon colossi, where are the sorry remains of a large mortuary temple of Amenophis III. Hussein also dealt in antiquities, and during the war the surveillance was bad, and they could no longer sell [antiquities] to foreigners, so the dealers were stuck with a lot of stock … The statue in question was probably found in the mortuary temple of Amenophis III, perhaps on Hussein's own land, and has now ended up with Mansur [sic: for Schafi], who probably hasn't given £30 for it. Dreiss was extremely keen to buy it, as he considers it worth £5,000 on the market in Paris because this three-dimensional statue is quite unique and in perfect condition.[469]

Curiously Lange does not seem to have connected the two stories. Once the Glyptotek agreed to the reduced price, the head was posted to Copenhagen from Stuttgart by Wolfgang Dreiss' sister, Eugenie Dreiss, who was to receive 30% of the price paid by the Museum.[470]

The head, catalogued as ÆIN 1677, is probably a fake,[471] and Dreiss seems to have been involved in selling objects produced by the famous 'Berlin Master', Oxan Aslanian, who may have sculpted it. J-J. Fiechter cited a note in the archives of the Royal Museum of Art and History in Brussels where Valdemar Schmidt reported that it was 'l'oeuvre d'un sculpteur arménien qui a fait ses études en Europe et qui travaillé notamment pour l'antiquaire Dreiss, hôtelier à Louqsor'.[472] This is presumably a reference to Oxan Aslanian and would seem to suggest that Dreiss was involved in selling Aslanian's forgeries.

Although the Glyptotek eventually agreed to buy the second head (ÆIN 1677), known informally as 'the brown head', it is clear that not everyone there was convinced of the authenticity of the piece even at this early stage: Maria Mogensen felt it necessary to state in the Museum register that the object 'was bought by the Ny Carlsberg Foundation without my knowledge and against my advice'. It is difficult to reconstruct the details of the negotiations and manoeuverings that must have taken place behind the scenes, but there can be no doubt that Lange thought the head genuine, and that he was instrumental in convincing the Ny Carlsberg Foundation to pay for it. However, he may have come to regret this decision. In a letter addressed to him by the then head of both the Ny Carlsberg Glyptotek and the Foundation, Frederik Poulsen, the latter declines to buy some antiquities that the Museum had been offered through Lange (from the collection of Bircher in Cairo). The letter, dated 29 January 1931, is relatively polite in its phrasing, but below the typed message Poulsen has added in his own pen the following pointed question: 'Can I now get an egyptological article from you about the Brown Head?'.[473] The question hints at previous cor-

468. For this object, see (p. 149).

469. Lange, *Dagbog fra Ægypten, 1929-1930*, 182-183.

470. Letter from E. Dreiss to H. O. Lange, dated 23 May 1930 (Royal Library, Copenhagen). Note that Fiechter, *Faux et faussaires en art égyptien*, 134, 164, seems to have inadvertently switched the background information relating to the two heads, including the provenance: ÆIN 1669 (the slightly damaged one) was the one bought by Lange for c. £60, whereas ÆIN 1677 was bought from Dreiss for £Eg. 1500. The first provenance that Fiechter lists for ÆIN 1669 (i.e. that it was acquired in 1895 by V. Schmidt) - which should in any case really be associated with ÆIN 1677 - is patently not true, as shown by the correspondence between Wolfgang (and his sister Eugenie) Dreiss and Lange. Similarly, Fiechter lists an article by Maria Mogensen as publishing ÆIN 1677 (p. 135), whereas the article in fact refers to ÆIN 1669; cf. Mogensen, *BIFAO* 30 (1930), 461-464, pl. III. The provenance question, and in particular the year of acquisition, is relevant to his argument in favour of seeing ÆIN 1669 as genuine since he

argues that 1895 is implausibly early for Amarna fakes (cf. p. 165).

471. Fiechter, *Faux et faussaires en art égyptien*, 134-135.

472. Fiechter, *Faux et faussaires en art égyptien*, 164, referring to ÆIN 1669.

473. 'P.S. Faar jeg saa en ægyptisk Artikel af Dem om det brune Hoved?'; letter from F. Poulsen to H. O. Lange, dated 29 Jan. 1931 (Carlsberg Foundation, Copenhagen).

respondence where an academic article on this expensive object had been asked for, and the apparent lack of replies that must have followed. The letter seems to mark the end of Lange's activities as a buyer of antiquities for the Glyptotek, which may or may not be coincidence; certainly the acquisition of the two fake Amarna heads for the Museum provides an arresting *leitmotif* in the story of his career as a purchaser of ancient Egyptian objects.

Honest dealers: Building up a reputation

While fake antiquities flooded the market and will have passed through each and every dealer, wittingly or not, some of the better established ones found it profitable to develop a respectable reputation in order to attract wealthy customers. There were different ways to do so. Some were relatively inexpensive, although they did include a potential loss of profits, such as not selling too many obviously looted items and not selling too many obvious fakes. Mohareb Todros, for example, the German consul at Thebes, had a separate display case with fake antiquities in his house which he showed to visitors as examples of forgeries. This was part of a strategy to instill a sense of security in customers, who were then prepared to pay higher prices knowing that that they were dealing with a knowledgeable and honest dealer.[474] Another way to allay the fears of potential buyers would be to issue certificates of authenticity. Many professional dealers had printed individually numbered certificates which would be filled out and signed upon completion of a transaction (Fig. 119).

A willingness to provide reliable and useful information about the provenance and context of a given object to important buyers was greatly appreciated, and some dealers would even help finance the activities of the Antiquities Department. The more common method was to conduct licensed excavations where the museum would get a share of the objects

found, without having to pay any of the expenses (p. 122), but dealers might also help with the restoration or protection of monuments.

Mohammed Mohasseb at Luxor was particularly successful in establishing a solid reputation for himself.[475] Hall wrote the following about him in a guide from 1907:

> There are several resident antiquity dealers in Luxor: el-Hagg Mohamed Mohassib is the most reliable, and is always extremely careful with regard to the genuineness of his antiquities; the same cannot, however, be said of all the Luxor dealers, though several are desirous of securing as good a reputation as Mohamed Mohassib's in this respect.[476]

His reputation came not just from his efforts to avoid fake antiquities, but also from his long-standing collaboration with excavators and his refusal to buy antiquities stolen from official excavations. Already more than twenty years earlier, in 1895, Quibell had reported the following in relation to his own excavations at the Ramesseum in Thebes:

> a large part of the winter's energies was spent in the continual struggle with the dealers; their success would have meant the destruction of the scientific value of all our work. It is a pleasure, therefore, to recognise the good feeling of one dealer, Mohammed Mohassib of Luxor, who refused to buy anything stolen from us on the ground that he would not make a profit from the robbery of his friends. And, whenever our other dealer friend, Girgis, came from Qeneh, his actions were above suspicion, as we have always found them.[477]

The following year Petrie, also during excavations at Thebes, had had to fire his whole local workforce from Sheikh Abd el-Qurna because of the extensive looting:

474. Lange and Lange, *Dagbog fra Ægyptensrejsen* 1899-1900, 316. For the context of the quotation see the entry on Mohareb Todros in the list at the back of the book.

475. His favourable reputation was not confined to the antiquities trade. Legrain, *Louqsor sans les pharaons*, 15, in reference to the Muslims at Luxor, singles out Mohasseb 'que tout le monde révère ici, à quelque religion qu'il appartienne'.
476. Hall, *Handbook for Egypt and the Sudan*, 11th edition, 379.
477. Quibell, *The Ramesseum*, 1. Drower, *Flinders Petrie*, 220, mistakenly attributes the statement to Petrie.

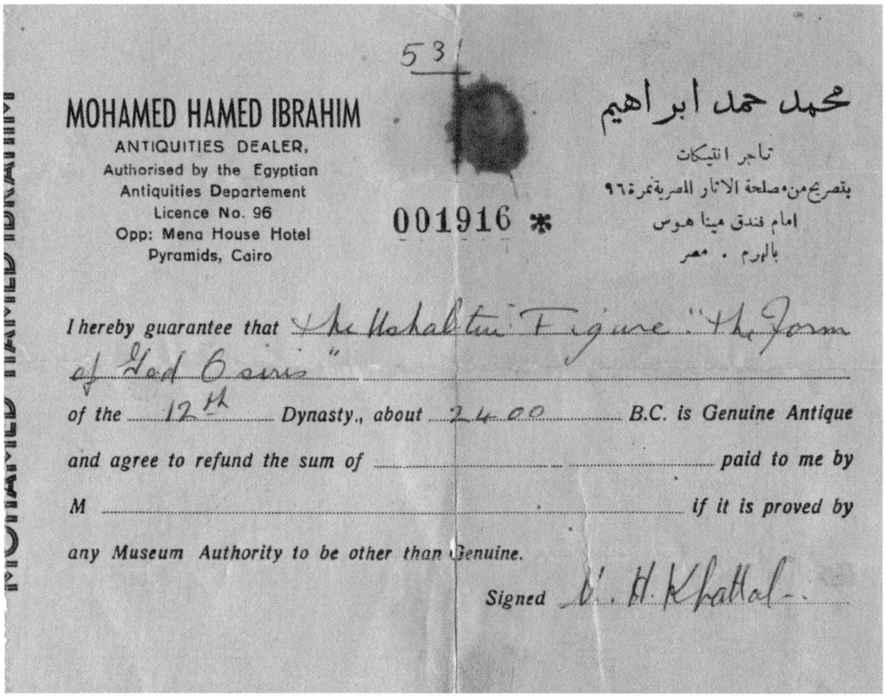
53

MOHAMED HAMED IBRAHIM
ANTIQUITIES DEALER,
Authorised by the Egyptian
Antiquities Departement
Licence No. 96
Opp: Mena House Hotel
Pyramids, Cairo

محمد حمد ابراهيم
تاجر انتيكات
بتصريح من مصلحة الاثار المصرية نمرة ٩٦
امام فندق مينا هوس
بالهرم . مصر

001916 *

I hereby guarantee that the Ushabtu Figure "the Form of God Osiris"
of the 12th *Dynasty., about* 2400 *B.C. is Genuine Antique*
and agree to refund the sum of .... *paid to me by*
M .... *if it is proved by*
any Museum Authority to be other than Genuine.
Signed M. H. Khattab

Fig. 119. Undated certificate of authenticity issued by Mohammed Hamed Ibrahim, 1940s. It is signed by a M. H. Khattab who is presumably identical to the later dealer Mohammed Khattab. Courtesy of the Egyptological Archives, University of Copenhagen.

> Half or more of what they found was abstracted for their old friends [i.e. the antiquities dealers] ... for two months, we completely defeated the endless machinations of the Luxor and Qurneh dealers, and the petty terrorism which they tried to exercise. So long as I had Qurneh men, I heard within twenty-four hours of what was stolen, through reports sent to me from Luxor; so soon as I dismissed them, I never heard of anything else going astray, nor had my good and honest old friend Muhammed Mohassib at Luxor any knowledge of anything reaching there.[478]

Moreover, when Arthur Weigall, then Chief Inspector of Antiquities for Upper Egypt (and just 27 years old), undertook a systematic attempt to protect the tombs of Sheikh Abd el-Qurna by clearing them and fitting them with iron doors in 1907 and 1908, Mohammed Mohasseb – among other dealers, individuals, and institutions – stepped forth to help with financial aid. The dealers included Abd el-Megid (protection of Theban Tomb 59), the brothers Girgis and Abd en-Nur (TT 87), Mohammed Mohasseb (TT 88, TT 89), and Yussef Hassan (TT 90, TT 91).[479] Both of the two latter were singled out in a report concerning on looting among the Theban tombs written by Weigall the following year:

> Certain dealers, such as Muhammed Muhassib and Yusuf Hassan, behave very loyally to the Department; and in such cases as this robbery from the tomb discovered by Lord Carnarvon one may be sure that the stolen pieces would not be purchased by them.[480]

In spite of his outstanding reputation, several fakes did pass through Mohasseb, but whether he was aware that they were not authentic cannot now be known. These include the statuette of Queen Tetisheri (acquired by Wallis Budge in 1890 for the British Museum) and the gold-covered heart scarab of Akhenaten (acquired by Alfred Percival Maudslay, also in

478. Petrie, *Six Temples at Thebes*, 2.

479. Weigall, *ASAE* 9 (1908), 118-136. We assume that 'Girgis Abd en-Nur' is a slip of the pen for Girgis *and* Abd en-Nur, the well-attested brothers who had shops in both Qena and Luxor (p. 216).

480. Letter from Weigall cited by Griffith in *Egypt Exploration Fund, Archaeological Report* 1908-09, 13.

1890, and later donated to the British Museum), as well as various other objects.[481] Moreover, Mohasseb also on occasion dealt with objects known to have been stolen, such as a gold earring inscribed with the name of Queen Tawosret that had been found during Theodore Davis' excavation in Theban Tomb 56 in 1908 (also now in the British Museum, acquired in 1919).[482]

Dealers would sometimes allow prospective buyers to copy objects themselves. At the time of Lange's visits this was mostly done by hand-copy, although photography and paper squeezes were also used. All three methods were employed by Lange. It could not be taken for granted that permission would be given freely, although valued customers are naturally likely to have been treated with more courtesy than strangers. Lange himself is happy to report in December 1929, during a visit to Luxor, that 'I have been granted permission to copy inscriptions at a couple of the more important dealers'.[483]

Although permission to copy interesting items might help attract customers, dealers were not always accommodating. In one case, Ali Abd el-Haj offered Lange some interesting sculptures at a very high price, but was nonetheless unwilling to let him have photographs that he might forward for an evaluation (p. 194). In such a situation, one cannot help wonder if the dealer suspected or knew that the objects in question were fakes.[484] There may also have been situations where dealers were afraid that certain objects might be confiscated by the authorities, should they come to their attention.

Sometimes it might also have taxed the patience of a dealer to have a visitor sitting around all day in order to copy one or more objects. In 1929 Lange became very interested in the statue of a bound foreigner in the hands of Schafi, a dealer at Luxor, but he felt unsure about its authenticity because of the palaeography of the inscription (p. 149). He needed an accurate copy, something better than a hand-copy, so that he could consult with colleagues. In these early days it was a cumbersome process to have photographs taken and developed, so he was permitted to make squeezes of the text, a process which in this case also turned out to be rather time-consuming. He had apparently arrived in the morning, and reports that:

> Since the paper was very thick, it took an unreasonable amount of time to dry, and it was not until 6:30 in the evening that I could remove the paper and make the print of the other side. The paper will hopefully dry tonight so that I can remove it again.[485]

481. The acquisitions are mentioned in the letters of Wilbour; cf. Capart (ed.), *Letters of Charles Edwin Wilbour*, 509 (statue of Tetisheri) and 558 (heart scarab of Akhenaten); cf. also Budge, *By Nile and Tigris* 2, 291, w. plate, who proudly singles out the statue as one of most noteworthy results of his fourth mission. The authenticity of the statue (BM EA 22558) is discussed by Davies, *The Statuette of Queen Tetisheri*, and that of the heart scarab (BM EA 58801) by Fiechter, *Faux et faussaires en art égyptien*, 254-255, who also lists other examples; 183 (a 'predynastic' female figurine), 182 (a 'predynastic' jar), 244 (a set of canopic jars).
482. BM EA 54459; cf. letter from Howard Carter to Lord Carnarvon, dated 20 Nov. 1912, cited in Reeves and Taylor, *Howard Carter before Tutankhamun*, 119. It has been suggested that Mohammed Mohasseb also brokered a deal that allowed Theodore Davies to buy back some objects that had been stolen from his excavation of KV 55; Adams, *The Millionaire and the Mummies*, 170-171.
483. Lange, *Dagbog fra Ægypten, 1929-1930*, 181. A few days later he notes, 'Incidentally I have copied a couple of inscriptions at another dealer' (p. 192). During this visit Lange also copied stelae in the possession of Girgis Gabrial (pp. 243-244). Some of these copies survive in the notebooks kept here in the Department at the University of Copenhagen, including several stelae held by the aforementioned Girgis Gabrial, as well as Hussein Abd el-Megid; Lange, *Notebook Thebes, Dec. 1929 - Jan. 1930*, 6-7, 12, 65-58. Similarly, a notebook from the first

trip shows him copying inscriptions on objects with a variety of dealers, including Farag Ismaïn, Alexandre Dingli, Mansur, Soliman, Mohammed Ali, and others; Lange, *Notebook 1899/1900*, 41-42, 210-226.
484. On another occasion Lange was allowed to make photographs of a royal sculpture in the possession of *Sheikh* Hamza which was undoubtedly fake, but this may not have been known to him or he may simply have been willing to risk it (p. 218).
485. Lange, *Dagbog fra Ægypten, 1929-1930*, 193. A paper squeeze of a stele in the possession of the dealer Loukianoff, kindly brought to our attention by Thomas Christiansen, survives among Lange's collection of squeezes (Royal Library). The

SALE OF ANCIENT EGYPTIAN, GREEK, ROMAN, COPTIC, MOSLEM ANTIQUITIES

Fig. 120. Advertisement by Maurice Nahman. His bold claim to have supplied 'all museums in Europe and America' was not far from the truth as far as Egyptian collections are concerned. Published in Blattner (ed.), *Le Mondain Egyptien 1941*.

Whether some fee or *baksheesh* was expected on such occasions is not clear, and although Lange does not mention any this was at least occasionally the case: Wilbour mentions an example where 'Ahmed the Crazy', as he calls a dealer in Hu, demanded a guinea for a stele or half a dollar for permission to copy it.[486]

Another less common approach to building a reputation as a knowledgable dealer was through publications that might impress potential customers. Thus,

for instance, R. H. Blanchard published a *Handbook of Egyptian Gods and Mummy Amulets* (Cairo, 1909) and Philip E. Mitry compiled an *Illustrated Catalogue of the Egyptian Museum* (Cairo, no date).[487] An exceptional character in this respect is Robert de Rustafjaell who published three books on objects from his own collection.[488] The volumes all served to promote interest in objects he had for sale or had recently sold. On several occasions he also managed successfully to issue press releases that were widely circulated about important discoveries, all of which similarly pertained to objects in his own collection which were available for immediate acquisition. Three such press releases concern collections of Coptic, Demotic, Greek, and Nubian manuscripts (press releases in 1907 and 1912),[489] and a well-preserved painted textile from the Hathor sanctuary at Deir el-Bahri (press release in 1912).[490] The press releases are easily seen as products of a shrewd dealer seeking to drive up prices for his stock. In the press reports concerning manuscripts from 1907, it is stated concerning a group of Coptic parchment manuscripts that they were found at Edfu:

> The native sold them to an Arab dealer for a few dollars, and the Arab resold them to a Copt for $2,500. Then the find came into the hands of Mr. De Rustafjaell, a well-known explorer, who brought it to England.

Rustafjaell attempts, in other words, to set the tone for negotiations; by implication, he would have paid

---

majority of squeezes in this collection were made from objects in the Egyptian Museum.
486. Cf. Capart (ed.), *Letters of Charles Edwin Wilbour*, 490.

487. Mitry, *Illustrated Catalogue of the Egyptian Museum*. It must have been published in or before 1965 as it appears in the *Annual Egyptological Bibliography* as AEB 1965.0258 (= OEB 11354).
488. de Rustafjaell, *Palaeolithic vessels of Egypt*; idem, *The Light of Egypt*; idem, *The Stone Age in Egypt*.
489. Manuscripts of 1907: cf. Dijkstra, *BASP* 44 (2007), 197-202. This paper is mainly concerned with the Patermouthis archive from Aswan, and it does not refer to the press reports which mainly concern the Edfu manuscripts. Examples may be found in *The New York Times* 21 July 1907 and *The Omaha Sunday Bee* 11 Aug. 1907. Manuscripts of 1912: Ryholt, *ZPE* 190 (2014), 173-187.
490. D'Auria, in Der Manuelian (ed.), *Fs Simpson* 1, 169-176. The paper does not cite any of the press reports. Examples may be found in *The San Francisco Call* 24 Nov. 1912 and *The Evening Standard* 7 Nov. 1912.

Fig. 121. On 26 January, the so-called Black Saturday, the 1952 revolution broke out and Shepheard's Hotel, which had become a symbol of the British occupation, was burnt to the ground. The two photographs dated 25 and 27 January 1952 bear witness to the destruction of the former antiquities shop of R. H. Blanchard in the hotel garden (Fig. 44) which had been taken over by Henri Dufour around 1940 (Fig. 47). The shop of M. A. Mansoor (Fig. 46-47), located at the other end of the hotel, was also lost. Newspaper clipping; source not located.

more than $2,500 for this group, and so the buyer would naturally be expected to pay even more. The press release about the painted textile ends with the paragraph:

> Before he (sc. Rustafjaell) left Luxor with the painting an American traveler offered the finder a large sum for the work, but at that time he was determined to keep it for his own collection and refused to part with it. Since his return, however, the offers have been raised to such a figure that he has consented to negotiate for its sale. Rustafjaell declares that the most tempting offers have been by the London agents of American collectors, and he feels sure that the painting will be sent across the Atlantic.

In fact he had acquired a whole cache of these textiles, not just a single and – again by implication – unique item; this, too, was a deliberate strategy to drive the price up.

The top dealers had less need of subterfuge. Thus, without any pretence at modesty, Nicolas Tano referred to himself as 'Feur des principaux Musées d'Europe and d'Amérique' on his letterhead (Fig. 16) and Maurice Nahman cited 'all museums in Europe and America' as reference on his advertisements (Fig. 120).

The aftermath

About twenty years after Lange's second visit to Egypt, the antiquities trade in Egypt would change significantly. The system of consular agents had been abolished (officially in 1949) and it was no longer possible to offer protection to antiquities dealers or conduct large-scale illegal excavations under the protection of diplomatic immunity (p. 33).

Even greater change was brought about by the Second World War and the Revolution. In 1942 the British had forced King Farouk, to appoint (under military threat) an emergency government consisting of anti-Facists; the evident lack of national independence and autonomy gave rise to widespread nationalism and anti-British sentiment, and repeated mass-demonstrations followed in the wake of the war.

During the political turmoil, in 1946, the antiquities dealer Michel Abemayor left Egypt for the United States. Two years later the grand old man of the antiquities trade, Maurice Nahman, died and most of his remaining antiquities were auctioned off soon thereafter.

The unstable political situation culminated with the Revolution of 1952. During this dramatic event, Shepheard's Hotel was burned to the ground by anti-British rioters (with the loss of the antiquities shops inside) and several hundred other buildings were destroyed (Fig. 121). A number of Westeners were also killed and the following years inevitably saw a further reduction in the number of tourists, which hurt the antiquities market.

In an interview given in the late 1950s, Philip Mitry, whose shop was located right across the entrance to Shepheard's Hotel (Fig. 50), states that the antiquities trade had more or less ceased since the destruction of the hotel in 1952 and the 'last war', i.e. the Tripartite Invasion of Egypt by Israel, Britain, and France in 1956 which led Egypt to expel many foreign nationals; children were now playing soccer on the site where the famous hotel had stood and there were few tourists.[491] He thought a new market for antiquities trade might eventually develop around the Hilton Hotel or the New Shepheard's Hotel (this was not to happen) and adds that the trade in Luxor was equally affected.

The expulsion of foreign nationals also affected dealers and in the process the shop of at least one large dealer, Albert Eid, was nationalized by the government. In an interview included in the aforementioned article, just a few years later, the Deputy Director of the Antiquities Service, Abd el-Fattah Hilmy, describes plans to nationalize the entire trade in antiquities and prohibit all private sale; 'We will sell [antiquities, ed.] at reasonable prices in halls accessible to the public.'

---

491. Clipping from unidentified newspaper, late 1950s, article entitled 'In Relation to the Case of the American Scholar who Stole Egypt's Antiquities' (translated from Arabic).

Another dealer, 'uncle Hassan', also interviewed in the article, points to another factor that had considerable impact on the supply of antiquities. Informing the journalist somewhat cryptically that 'chemicals have ruined the trade', he explains that the increasing use of fertilizer had put a stop to the extensive *sebakh* digging which had been such a rich source of objects.

The final blow to the antiquities trade came with Law No. 117 of 1983 which effectively prohibited all future trade and export of antiquities (cf. Table 3 above). The anticipation of this radical revision of the antiquities laws, which was already in preparation during the 1960s,[492] led further dealers to leave Cairo, including the prominent Khawam Brothers who left for Paris in 1977. The Egyptian Museum itself had ceased to deal in antiquities when it closed down the *Salle de vente* (p. 47), perhaps in the 1950s or 60s.

492. The aforementioned newspaper clipping cites the deputy general director of the Antiquities Service, Abd el-Fattah Hilmy, as stating that the law is in the process of being approved.

The Hunt for Papyri

For Lange, the acquisition of papyri was of particular interest, and eventually resulted in the formation of two papyrus collections in Copenhagen, the story of which is told below. The Papyrus Carlsberg Collection, which mainly consists of hieratic and demotic documents, has been kept at the Egyptology Department (then known as 'the Egyptological Laboratory') of the University of Copenhagen since 1938. The Papyrus Hauniensis Collection, which contains most of the Greek papyri, has been kept by the Department of Greek and Latin at the same institution since the 1930s. Both collections were financed by the Carlsberg Foundation, and are today housed in the same room at the Department of Cross-Cultural and Regional Studies.

While there have been no studies of the acquisition history of pharaonic papyri as a category of antiquities in itself, accounts of Jewish, Arabic and Graeco-Roman papyri exist, albeit only in a summary form.[493] The following account is therefore necessarily narrow in focus, with little comparative material to draw on, but it does provide a reasonably detailed account of how such collections could be formed.

The beginning

In 1887 the 24-year old H. O. Lange received a stipend from the Ministry of Culture to study with Adolf Erman in Berlin. These studies would have a profound impact on Lange, and the two men developed a life-long friendship.[494] Lange had long had a passion for philology, a subject in which his old Danish professor Valdemar Schmidt had little interest, and he was now finally able to acquire the necessary skills to study papyri. He soon developed a talent for reading hieratic and he is one of just two colleagues – the other being Wilhelm Spiegelberg – acknowledged with providing 'very important corrections and remarks' in F. Ll. Griffith's seminal edition of the Middle Kingdom papyri from Lahun published in 1898.[495]

Wish for a papyrus collection

In view of Lange's philological interest and his professional employment as a librarian – he had been hired by the Royal Library in 1885 at the age of just 22 – it is hardly surprising that he would wish to form a papyrus collection that could become a focus for Egyptological research in Copenhagen. His first visit to Egypt in 1899 brought him within tantalizing reach of the material he so desired. However, to his regret the National Museum was not interested in papyri.

> Occasionally my thoughts wander home to the Library; the other day I wrote to Justice Council Bruun and suggested to him that a few hundred Crowns should be spent on Greek and Coptic papyri which I would then be able to purchase, now that I know all the good sources. Vald[emar] Schmidt should also try to get some rich person in Copenhagen interested, who might then be willing to spend a thousand Crowns on the acquisition of such papyri.[496]

Justice Council Chr. W. Bruun was the Head Librarian of the Royal Library and it was he who had encour-

---

493. E.g. Volkoff, *Á la recherche de manuscrits en Égypte*. We are grateful to Tom Hardwick for this reference. See also Baikie, *Egyptian papyri and papyrus-hunting*, 47-60, 225-251; as well as Preisendanz, *Papyrusfunde und Papyrusforschung*; Turner, *Greek Papyri*; Montevecchi, *La papirologia*; and Bagnall (ed.), *The Oxford Handbook of Papyrology*.

494. The great esteem in which Lange held Erman emerges clearly from their correspondence and his incomplete *Memoirs*,

cf. also his obituary of Erman published in *ZDMG* 91 (1937), 484-5.

495. Griffith, *Hieratic Papyri from Kahun and Gurob*, vi.

496. Lange and Lange, *Dagbog fra Ægyptensrejsen 1899-1900*, 188-189.

aged the young Lange, while working for the University Library, to seek employment with the Royal Library.[497] Lange remained with the Royal Library for nearly forty years, and was himself Head Librarian from 1901 to 1924.

Lange evidently also contacted his old teacher Valdemar Schmidt, who wrote in reply:

> I still have not gotten my project about papyri up and running... 'Papyrus' he says [Sophus Müller, the director of the National Museum], 'is not part of the Museum's collections', and Bruun says yes, if a nice piece with an extract of a Greek writer could be had for a reasonable sum then he might buy it, but not accounts and such.[498]

Acquisitions of papyri during the first visit to Egypt 1899/1900

Although his funds were very limited, Lange was able to make a few modest acquisitions during his first visit to Egypt in 1899/1900. His travel diary provides details of several occasions on which Lange studied papyri and ostraca offered for sale by antiquities dealers. He does not seem to have come across any substantial amount of papyri which is not surprising since, probably unbeknownst to Lange, Lord Crawford had acquired all the papyri he could lay his hands on during the preceding winter and thus exhausted all existing stocks (p. 116).

The first visit, recorded by Jonna Lange, went to a certain Ali at Giza who is easily identified as the well-established dealer Ali Abd el-Haj.

(Wednesday, 22 November 1899:) During the trip to Gizeh on Monday we were quite a few; Dr Thiersch, a remarkably pleasant young man,[499] was with us, so we were five in addition to our guide, Abdallah. He is a cousin of Ali and was to act as interpreter because Ali, a very fine old gentleman, didn't speak English. We had coffee twice at Ali's place, immediately after arrival and then again just before leaving. Hans was given a gift there; the dealers are much taken with him, probably because they think he has lots of money, even though Hans assures them that this is not the case. There was a pile of potsherds there with texts, which Hans and Thiersch had been examining; he took aside a lovely piece with a particularly beautiful Demotic inscription (Late-Egyptian), which he cannot yet read, and asked how much it would cost. Abdallah asked Ali, and after some negotiation Abdallah put it in Hans' pocket and told him that it was a gift from Ali.[500]

The ostracon is presumably to be identified with O. Copenhagen NM 11685, an intact Demotic potsherd ostracon with 14 well-preserved lines of writing.[501] The next day Lange went out with Dr Thiersch to look at some papyri in the possession of 'Mr. Birker' (sc. André Bircher), but there is no indication that he purchased anything on this occasion. Again in the hand of Jonna Lange:

> Yesterday was another busy day for the gentlemen. After some time at the Museum, I made tea for Hans and Dr Thiersch from Munich who has been here about a week. I had also expected two Englishmen who were joining the expedition, but they had gone ahead to see the papyri. The visit concerned a certain Mr Birker who seems to be Greek. They left at 4½. He lives here in Cairo, so it was not far away, but it was 7½ before they returned.[502]

---

497. Lange's gratitude to Chr. W. Bruun emerges clearly from the very incomplete draft of his *Memoirs* which he commenced on 15 Feb. 1939; it comprises seven pages describing his childhood and his gratitude towards his parents, a single paragraph where he had begun to describe his gratitude towards Adolf Erman, and a single paragraph describing his gratitude towards Chr. W. Bruun. In drawing up these pages he evidently, and not surprisingly, focussed on the three main components of his identity: his Christian life, his career as the head of the Royal Library, and his career as an Egyptologist.
498. Letter from V. Schmidt to H. O. Lange, dated Feb. 1900 (Royal Library, Copenhagen).

499. Sc. Hermann Thiersch, who was 25 years old at the time, would later become Professor of Classical Archaeology at Göttingen.
500. Lange and Lange, *Dagbog fra Ægyptensrejsen 1899-1900*, 143.
501. Cf. Hagen, in Nyord and Ryholt (eds.), *Fs Frandsen*, 90. The only other Demotic ostracon in the Collection from the Lange bequest is O. Copenhagen NM 11684, a small tax-receipt with just three lines of writing.
502. Lange and Lange, *Dagbog fra Ægyptensrejsen 1899-1900*, 142-143.

About a week later Lange went back to Giza to visit Farag Ismaïn where some modest acquisitions were made.

> (Tuesday, 28 November 1899:) For nearly 3 hours we rummaged through his papyri and further antiquities ... Suddenly he held forth a rag which contained a mass of papyrus fragments and said that they had been found together in one spot. I untied the piece of cloth the four corners of which were bound together and immediately saw that there were several pieces of a letter from the Middle Kingdom, a period from which papyri are very rare and precious; there were moreover some Greek bits among them. I was very careful not to show any emotion and reveal that this was something important since I would then have to pay more expensively; but I was immediately aware that I had to try and acquire this rag and its contents. I sought out something more which I could use to hand back in order to drive down the price, this is a common trick here. Finally it was time for us to negotiate; he demanded 15 Pounds Sterling; then I put a part back and offered 2 Pounds for the rest, among which the bundle; he squirmed pathetically but eventually went down to 5 Pounds and then to 3 Pounds, then I took out 2 blank gold pieces and placed them before him, got up and made as if to take back the money and leave; then he could resist no further, but accepted, and I brought away the treasure with pleasure. When I came home with it some time before noon, I singled out the Greek pieces and showed them to Dr. Thiersch. He found them very interesting with the result that I traded them with him in return for some Coptic and Egyptian bits, which were more interesting for me, and as a result I have obtained something both valuable and interesting in return for my 36 Crowns. This is not an acquisition for the Museum but for myself, for the Museum does not want to acquire papyri.[503]

This is likely to have been the most exciting personal acquisition by Lange at this point, but fate was soon to play a trick on him and the papyri would only remain in his possession for a short time. Earlier the same year a large quantity of papyri from the temple archive of Lahun had appeared on the antiquities market. The lion's share of these had been acquired in 1899 by Dr Reinhardt for the papyrus collection in Berlin, while other lots were acquired by Heinrich Schäfer and B. P. Grenfell and given to the Cairo Museum. A further group of fragments was acquired by Lange's friend Ludwig Borchardt from Ali Abd el-Haj on 6 November, and it turned out that they had been sold to Ali by the same Mansur from whom Lange acquired his fragments a week earlier.[504] Borchardt soon after set out for Lahun where he succeeded in locating the source of the papyri and excavated what still remained *in situ*. This material too went to Berlin.[505] Seeing that the fragments purchased by Lange similarly belonged to this archive, he felt obliged to hand over his material to Borchardt so that it could be re-united with the material in Berlin.[506]

As far as the Coptic 'bits' are concerned, they are perhaps identical with 15 parchment fragments which Lange was later able to assemble into two bifolia of a codex (P. Carlsberg 52). The codex was inscribed with Coptic and Greek magical texts, and Lange presented his study of the former in honour of Griffith in his *Festschrift* of 1932.[507]

Lange had not had much opportunity to buy papyri and his wife sympathized with him. When, on 20 February 1900, he was able to able to close the deal on

503. Lange and Lange, *Dagbog fra Ægyptensrejsen 1899-1900*, 154-156.

504. Borchardt diary, Sept. 1899 - Jan. 1900, entry 5 Dec. 1899 (Swiss Institute, Kairo; transcript kindly provided by Cornelius von Pilgrim, 21 Jan. 2015).

505. For an account of these papyri and their discovery, see Borchardt, *ZÄS* 37 (1899), 89-90, and Kaplony-Heckel, *Ägyptische Handschriften* 1, ix-xx. The latter account does not explicitly mention the Lange fragments which were perhaps handed in together with the rest of the material excavated by Borchardt and not recorded separately.

506. Lange, *Dagbog i Ægypten 1929-30*, 107, 'Personally I acquired in 1899 a number of fragments from the same find from the old Farag in Gizeh which I naturally handed over to Borchardt for Berlin.'

507. Lange in *Fs Griffith*, 161-166. The text is re-edited in Meyer and Smith, *Ancient Christian Magic*, 237-9, no. 118. The Greek text is published by Bülow-Jacobsen and Brashear in *Magica Varia*, 16-62. In his edition Lange merely states that he acquired the papyrus in Egypt 'vor Jahren', i.e. years ago. In view of the publication date, it will therefore have been acquired during his first visit to Egypt.

a statue for £10 less than the sum Jacobsen had put at his disposal (p. 254), she recorded in the diary:

(22 February 1900:) Now *I* think at least that Hans should be allowed to dispose of the £10, which he has saved Jacobsen, in order to acquire papyri for the Library, for instance; but whether J. thinks likewise is probably dubious.[508]

Three weeks later he finally purchased two papyri with which he felt very satisfied. The relevant section of the diary is cited in full elsewhere (p. 55) and we cite here only the description of the papyri and the immediate context. Two dealers from Upper Egypt had come to Cairo for a few days to sell their objects and had called upon Lange at his place of residence.

(Saturday, 10 March 1900:) Then these two presented their things which almost filled the entire dining room table. There were some exquisite things among them, and my mouth was watering; but I restrained myself to three objects, two heads and some fragments of a papyrus with some of the best drawings I have seen. He wanted 2 pounds for it all, and I offered 15 shilling. Then I let him pack it all away again, and let the other unpack his things; he had some really nice things, including a papyrus roll with a Greek text, pretty well preserved, ...[509]

In the end Lange managed to purchase both of the papyri and some other objects at what he considered a reasonable price. The two papyri are easily identified. The first-mentioned is P. Carlsberg 201, which is inscribed with a Ptolemaic copy of the Book of the Dead in hieroglyphs. The text belonged to a Min priest from Akhmim named Totoes. It has recently been discovered that this Book of the Dead originally was physically wrapped around the chest of a mummy and that the fragments now in Copenhagen formed its outermost section. The mummy, its coffin and the parts of the papyrus that remained *in situ* on the mummy somehow ended up in the Liebieghaus Museum in

Frankfurt.[510] Curiously, an X-Ray study of the mummy indicates that it is that of a grown woman rather than a man as indicated by the name and titles in the Book of the Dead.

The other papyrus is P. Copenhagen NM 5032, a Greek deed of sale dated to 99 BC. The text was edited for publication by Christian Blinkenberg at the National Museum immediately after Lange's return to Denmark.[511] Concerning its provenance, the Egyptian who sold the papyri to Lange informed him that they came from Akhmim.[512] This is certainly true of the Book of the Dead, but as regards the Greek papyrus, Blinkenberg rightly felt sceptical because the internal evidence relates the text directly to Gebelein. It was not uncommon for texts to have been written in one place and later moved to another. It may incidentally be noted that this same Blinkenberg many years later, in 1923, would help Lange create the graduate programme in Egyptology (cf. below).

Also two smaller Greek and Coptic papyrus fragments (P. Copenhagen NM 5033 and 5034) were given to the National Museum by Lange in November 1900. Since they are described in the register as having been 'purchased from an Arab antiquities dealer from Upper Egypt who said they derived from Akhmim', it seems reasonable to assume that they were purchased on the same occasion as the two aforementioned papyri. They are not mentioned in the diary, however, but this could be because they were considered too insignificant to merit a special mention.

Lange went on a two-day excursion to the Fayum about a month later (described above p. 99), during which he visited a local dealer in the company of C. C. Edgar. The dealer had a large box with papyri, and

---

508. Lange and Lange, *Dagbog fra Ægyptensrejsen 1899-1900*, 394. The pronoun 'I' is underscored in the original.

509. Lange and Lange, *Dagbog fra Ægyptensrejsen 1899-1900*, 420-1.

510. The Liebighaus fragments of the Book of the Dead are described in Bayer-Niemeier et al., *Liebighaus - Museum Alter Plastik II*, pp. 254-293, which includes images that show the remaining fragments *in situ* on the mummy before they were removed. The acquisition details remain unclear. The Carlsberg fragments are published in Christiansen and Ryholt, *The Carlsberg Papyri 13*, Text 4.

511. Published by Blinkenberg in *Oversigt over det kongelige danske Videnskabernes Selskabs Forhandlinger,* 119-126, pl. 2.

512. So Blinkenberg, *ibid.*, 119.

the two colleagues inquired about a selection of them, but the price demanded was much too high and no business was conducted.

No further papyri seem to be mentioned during the remaining half year of his stay in Egypt, perhaps because Lange was mainly occupied with his task of cataloguing the Middle Kingdom stelae at the Egyptian Museum together with Schäfer, and in September he returned to Denmark.

Lange as Head Librarian

The following year, in 1901, the Head Librarian of the Royal Library, Chr. W. Bruun died, and Lange became his successor. He was now in a better position to acquire papyri and turned to his friend Borchardt for help (Fig. 122). He seems to have been very insistent in his approach as hinted at by this typically sarcastic reply from Borchardt which was written on 14 December 1903 in Cairo.

> Nun zu den Papyruskäufen. Zur Zeit besorge ich Papyri für: Berlin, Leipzig, Giessen, Strassburg, Würzburg und Königsberg, welche sich zu gemeinsamen Kaufen (sic) vereinigt haben. Halten Sie es da für möglich, dass ich dann <u>gleichzeitig</u> für die Kopenhagener Bibliothek kaufe? Ich schreibe sehr gern in meinen Jahresbericht: 'Auch wurden einige Ankäufe für die Kopenhagener Königl. Bibl. vermittelt, da deutsche Sammlungen für diese Erwerbungen nicht mit concurrierten.' Aber dieses Mal, fürchte ich, concurrieren deutsche Sammlungen mit. Wenn Sie warten können, bis sich die Papyruswuth in Deutschland etwas gelegt hat, dann kann ich mit gutem Gewissen auch für Sie sorgen.[513]

The collections which Borchardt lists had entered a formal collaboration to acquire papyri, known as the *Deutsche Papyruskartell*, which was active from 1902 until the outbreak of the First World War in 1914.[514]

Lange also tried to involve Valdemar Schmidt, who regularly travelled to Egypt and was an experienced buyer of antiquities. These efforts were to no avail, albeit for entirely different reasons. Schmidt had never had much interest in papyri and probably lacked both the necessary connections and qualifications to obtain the kind of material Lange desired. Nonetheless he made an effort, as shown by his correspondence with Lange, including this letter from 1903:

> Of papyri I have seen a good Greek one, almost complete (with only a few fragments missing in a fold), but seemingly from a rather late period; Byzantine. It is with Dattari. Costs about £10. I intend to buy it.[515]

Two letters from 1910 shows that the hunt for papyri was still in progress at that time. They both concern the well-known dealer Girgis Gabrial.

> I have written to Girgis in Qena that I will not be able to come this year and that I do not have as much money as I would like to acquire papyri. There is hardly any great competition for this sort of 'cat in the bag'!! Ali caught up with me in the street. He sat in a closed carriage and asked me to come out to him in Giza. I said I would be able to come before 3 o'clock. He said he had a papyrus. His papyrus is probably not very important, but if only it is something relatively well-preserved then I suppose a little (if it is not too expensive) is better than nothing. I shall proceed with caution and not be wasteful.[516]

Four days later:

> At noon I received a telegram from Girgis in Luxor and Qena that he would come to Cairo this morning for business and that he would bring the papyrus. I telegraphed back that I would be home between 1 and 3 o'clock so that we could talk things over. I will be able to borrow some money here if this will improve the price, since I expect in any case to get most of it refunded after my return.[517]

---

513. Letter from L. Borchardt to H. O. Lange, dated 14 Dec. 1903 (Royal Library, Copenhagen). Borchardt had already explained the situation concerning the acquisition of papyri in an earlier letter to Lange dated 29 Jan. 1903 (Royal Library, Copenhagen).
514. The history of this institution is discussed by Primavesi, *ZPE* 114 (1996), 173-187; cf. further Martin, in Bowman et al. (eds.), *Oxyrhynchus: A City and Its Texts*, 40-49.

515. Letter from V. Schmidt to H. O. Lange, dated 30 Oct. 1903 (Royal Library, Copenhagen).
516. Letter from V. Schmidt to H. O. Lange, dated 16 Apr. 1910 (Royal Library, Copenhagen).
517. Letter from V. Schmidt to H. O. Lange, dated 20 Apr. 1910 (Royal Library, Copenhagen).

Fig. 122. The Lange couple
with Ludwig and Mimi
Borchardt on the rooftop of
Deutsches Haus in Thebes.
Lange photograph, January
1930. Courtesy of the Royal
Library.

Schmidt's use of the idiom 'cat in the bag' in the second letter demonstrates all too clearly how he felt about buying papyrus. It corresponds to the English 'pig in a poke' and describes the act of buying something without really knowing what it is. It remains uncertain whether any of these papyri were acquired.

Not being able to journey to Egypt himself, Lange had little real opportunity to acquire papyri until the end of the war, and it would be many years before his dream of creating a substantial papyrus collection came true.

The Formation of the Papyrus Hauniensis Collection

The first breakthrough came in 1920 when Johannes Pedersen (1883-1977), who later became Professor of Semitic philology at the University of Copenhagen and president of the Royal Academy of Sciences and Letters, went to Egypt to study at al-Azhar University. Lange seized this opportunity to secure funds from the Carlsberg Foundation for the acquisition of pa-

pyri on behalf of the Royal Library, and the task was entrusted to Pedersen.

Pedersen was very conscientious in his assignment. However, not being an Egyptologist himself, it was almost impossible for him to discern what was worth buying and he therefore sought help among colleagues in Cairo. He arrived in Egypt 10 October and reported to Lange two weeks later:

(25 October 1920:) About 14 days ago, I approached the Museum people. Mr. Quibell was engaged, but I spoke to Mr. Edgar who promised to assist me. Since then I have looked around for papyri. Today I went to the Museum & met both Mr. Quibell & Mr. Edgar. Mr. Quibell was pleased to receive your greeting & inquired about you. However, he declared that it was not possible for him or anyone else from the Museum to offer me direct assistance concerning acquisitions, because it would not be compatible with the relationship they have in respect of their positions at the Museum in relation to the antiquity dealers. Yet he helped me by referring me to an expert on papyri who is not here at the moment, but who could come soon. Grenfell is not

here and is not expected to come.[518] As concerns papyri, they have become very expensive. Partly few are said to have appeared in the last years, and partly the American acquisitions have forced up the prices. Ali al Arabi, whom I've been to twice, once with Capt. Davidsen, had some very beautiful rolls, but he demanded £500 for three of them and two small pages! Naturally this price could be lowered considerably, but Edgar told me that Grenfell made no acquisitions from him last year because he was too expensive. For a single one of the fragmentary pages he demanded £30. Another, Abdallah Isma'il, who lives across from Shepheards Hotel, has 12 boxes full of fragments and demanded £10 for each. Most fragments were minor pieces. The boxes were ordinary letter boxes. Moreover, he had a case with a lot, perhaps 30-40 leaves which, in contrast with the aforementioned, were separated and neatly arranged. For these he demanded £40. His prices were thus at any rate significantly more reasonable than Ali's.[519]

Two months later he could report that he had spent nearly half the money (£E 89 of 189,75) buying two groups of papyri from Abdallah Ismaïl and Maurice Nahman with the help of the Norwegian Professor of Classical Philology Samson Eitrem.[520] He stated that he would like to spend the remaining £E 100 on a collection of more than a hundred Arabic papyri in the possession of Nahman, doubtlessly because of his personal academic interests. Nahman demanded £E 300, but he hoped to reduce the price to £E 100. Lange approved this suggestion, 'Such a collection will always be of considerable interest'.[521] However, on 17 February, he reported with regret: 'Concerning papyri, I will make purchases when a good opportunity arises. I will not get the Arabic collection which Nach-

man has; he now quotes a price that is 3-4 times higher than before.'[522] Lange replied: 'I am sorry we will not get the Arabic papyri. We have to console ourselves with the Greek. Are there no Coptic fragments to be had? I don't suppose there are many competitors this winter in Egypt.'[523] The next letter, written in Luxor on 28 March, briefly noted that 'Here in Luxor there are no papyri. I will spend a day going out to Assiut to see if there might be anything there.'[524] No documentation has been found concerning the remainder of his stay, except that on 1 May 1921, he reported that the acquired papyri had been sent in a lead-sealed box to the Foreign Ministry in Copenhagen through the Danish consulate.[525]

The papyri acquired by Pedersen were mainly Greek, although they also contained a number of Coptic, some Arabic, three Demotic, two hieratic, and a single Latin one.[526] The collection was donated by the Carlsberg Foundation to the University of Copenhagen the following year and was deposited in the Department of Greek and Latin, where it became the Papyrus Hauniensis Collection. Two further significant additions, though on a more limited scale, were made in 1929 and 1930 with the aid of Wilhelm Schubart and Friedrich Zucker respectively and once again with means provided by the Carlsberg Foundation.[527]

518. Grenfell is the famous papyrologist: cf. Bierbrier, *Who was Who in Egyptology*, 4th edition, 225-226.

519. Letter from J. Pedersen to H. O. Lange, dated 25 Oct. 1920 (Royal Library, Copenhagen).

520. Letter from J. Pedersen to H. O. Lange, dated 3 Dec. 1920 (Royal Library, Copenhagen). Prof. Eitrem published a brief account of his hunt for papyri in 1920 in his *Ved Nilens Bredder for et Par Tusen År Siden*, 164-171. It does not mention his meeting with Lange nor provide any other noteworthy details.

521. Letter from H. O. Lange to J. Pedersen, dated 21 Dec. 1920 (Royal Library, Copenhagen).

522. Letter from J. Pedersen to H. O. Lange dated 17 Feb. 1921 (Royal Library, Copenhagen).

523. Letter from H. O. Lange to J. Pedersen, dated 8 Mar. 1921 (Royal Library, Copenhagen).

524. Letter from J. Pedersen to H. O. Lange dated 28 Mar. 1921 (Royal Library, Copenhagen).

525. Letter from J. Pedersen to H. O. Lange, dated 1 May 1921 (Royal Library, Copenhagen).

526. One of these papyri, the Middle Kingdom letter P. Haun. inv. Hierat. 1, was published by Frandsen, *JARCE* 15 (1978), 25-31, pls. 5-8. Another hieratic and two demotic papyri are included in Christiansen and Ryholt, *The Carlsberg Papyri 13*, Texts 20-22.

527. For the documentation concerning the acquisitions in 1929 and 1930, see now Bülow-Jacobsen, *Aegis* 12 (2012), 1-60. The acquisitions in 1929 are mentioned below in relation to Ali Abd el-Haj and Maurice Nahman, and those in 1930 in Agaibi Makarios, Mohammed in Eshmunein, Shakir Farag, and Zaki Mahmud Abd es-Samad.

Other acquisitions

Further acquisitions between Lange's two visits to Egypt seem to have been relatively limited. Perhaps the most important took place in 1924 when Lange succeeded in acquiring a beautiful Book of the Dead of the Theban priest Amenhotep which was not only complete, but in a remarkable state of preservation (c. 1000 BC).[528] It had previously belonged to a collection of rare manuscripts owned by the Saffroy brothers who ran an antiquarian bookshop in Paris, and its sale is likely to have been directly related to the dissolution of their partnership in 1923. It was originally kept at the Royal Library and was later transferred to the Papyrus Carlsberg Collection where it is now inventoried as P. Carlsberg 250.

Acquisitions during the second visit to Egypt 1929-30

The more than twenty years as Head Librarian, with the many official duties involved, had not afforded Lange the leisure to re-visit Egypt. However, 1924 saw the fulfillment of one of his great ambitions with the establishment of a graduate programme in Egyptology and the foundation of an Egyptological Institute at the University of Copenhagen.[529] Lange retired from the Royal Library to become the first lecturer of the Institute. Yet it was not until 1929 that he had the opportunity to undertake another visit to Egypt. During this second visit, Lange, now 66 years of age, would once again try to acquire a collection of papyri. This time he had better access to resources, in view of his prominent academic standing, but he did not have much success in finding interesting material.

Although neither a papyrus nor an ostracon, it may be worth mentioning that the first text offered to Lange, on 9 November 1929, was in fact a cuneiform tablet.[530] The dealer was Zaki Mahmud Abd es-Samad with whom Lange would become friends and conduct much business. The tablet had been brought by a man from Amarna and Zaki had it in commission; it might in fact have belonged to Ali Abd el-Haj (his great uncle) or Farag Ismaïn, both of whom lived in the same village and are known to have been in possession of other Amarna tablets.[531] Zaki said the man wanted £30, but Lange offered £6 to which he agreed and said that he would get it for him. There seems to be no further mention of the tablet and it is unclear whether this settled the deal or whether the tablet went elsewhere.

One of the acquisitions that initially caused Lange much excitement was a group of fragments in a fine hieratic hand which he saw with Maurice Nahman. He got the impression that the text was not part of the Book of the Dead and thought the fragments might belong to the Chester Beatty papyri.

> (Friday, 22 November 1929:) On the way home we dropped by Nahman's who once again had new beautiful things to show. Naturally we had coffee, and he showed me a group of fragments from a hieratic papyrus with religious content, which I could ascertain was not from the Book of the Dead. He offered it to me for £4. I could imagine that they might belong to one of the curious Beattie [sic] papyri which were acquired down here two years ago. Newberry told me yesterday that the papyri themselves were not purchased from Nahman, but that Gardiner last year found a few fragments with Nahman which belonged to them. I will have to purchase them one of these days, and I hope to get them for £3, which in my estimate is quite a bargain, seeing that hieratic papyri from such a good [sic] period like these pieces are very rare. If it turns out that they belong to one of Beattie's papyri, it would be a 'grand coup', since they would obviously have to be

528. The papyrus is included in Christiansen and Ryholt, *The Carlsberg Papyri 13*, Text 1.
529. Cf. Iversen in *Københavns Universitet 1479-1979*, 630; Sander-Hansen in *Universitetets Festskrift*, 134.

530. Lange, *Dagbog i Ægypten 1929-30*, 35. The tablet may have been found around the time of the excavations of the Egypt Exploration Society at Tell el-Amarna; the online Amarna database lists one tablet found in 1921, and a handful from 1933; see http://www.amarnaproject.com/pages/recent_projects/material_culture/small_finds/database.shtml (accessed 21 Sept. 2012).
531. Cf. Knudtzon, *Die El-Amarna-Tafeln*, 6.

given to the British Museum which has received all of Beattie's collection.[532]

The term *grand coup*, taken from the card game Bridge, might require a brief comment. It is here used in the sense that Lange would have something good on his hand, the papyrus fragments in question, but that he would be forced to pass them on to the British Museum, and thus lose them, if indeed they would turn out to belong to the Chester Beatty papyri in that collection. Evidently this seemed to him the only decent thing to do, just as he had handed over the Lahun fragments to the Egyptian Museum in Berlin.

> (Saturday, 23 November 1929:) On the way home we collected 10 excellent photographs, and I slipped in to Nahman's and offered him £3 for the papyrus fragments to which he agreed. When we got home, we immediately began trying to join some of the larger fragments and we had amazing success, so that we already now have considerably larger pieces than we had dreamt about. It is a very beautiful hieratic script from the 22nd Dynasty, and this must be said to be an inexpensive purchase. I believe that these fragments do not belong to any of Beattie's [(sic)] papyri in the British Museum like I had supposed.[533]

It has since become clear that the fragments in fact do belong to a Book of the Dead. They represent the remains of the first four columns of a single manuscript which had evidently been cut off from the rest of the manuscript in modern times, presumably by those who found it or the dealer. The papyrus, which is now designated P. Carlsberg 488, belonged to a chantress of Amun named Neskhons.[534] It can be attributed to Thebes and dated to c. 950 BC on account of its style.

The following Friday and Saturday Lange returned to Nahman once again.

> (Saturday, 30 November 1929:) At 6 o'clock we went over to Nahman who always has something new to show us. Yesterday he showed us the remains of a Coptic book on papyrus from the 6th Century AD; a large box full of larger and smaller fragments which could probably be fitted together. He also had another Coptic book on parchment which has been half consumed by fire so that only half of each page is preserved. His prices are terribly high.[535]

No manuscripts seem to have been acquired during these visits. About a month later, Lange found himself in Thebes. He found no suitable papyri, but the acquisition of a number of ostraca was considered interesting enough to merit a brief description in his diary.

> (Thursday, 26 December 1929:) Yesterday I purchased from Abd er-Rahim, who lives near the Winter Palace Hotel, a beautiful Coptic limestone ostracon, which has writing on both sides, for 20 Piastre, which I was very happy about. I got it for that price, as he said, 'because you are my friend.'[536]

> (Tuesday, 31 December 1929:) On the way there [i.e. to Dra Abu el-Naga] a man came with a hieratic ostracon with a small and rather nice hand. I purchased it for 5 Piastre.[537]

> (Thursday, 2 January 1930:) At 11 o'clock I left this tomb and met Muhamed Abd el-Haggag ... Muhamed brought me over to one of his uncles who sold me a Coptic lamp, decorated with a frog, and a hieratic ostracon for 5 Piastre.[538]

> (Thursday, 16 January 1930:) In the afternoon I went over to the old Girgis – the young one had stayed in Qena – to copy some stelae in his storeroom and to rummage through three baskets full of junk to find hieratic ostaca. I found none but instead a number of Demotic ones. I sought out 12 Greek and Coptic ostraca, which I got for 5 Piastre a piece.[539]

532. Cf. Lange, *Dagbog i Ægypten 1929-30*, 86. For the Chester Beatty gift, see Hall, *British Museum Quarterly* 5 (1930), 46-47; Gardiner, *Chester Beatty Gift*, v, vii. One of the papyri (P. Chester Beatty I) was given to the Chester Beatty Library in Dublin: Gardiner, *The Chester Beatty Papyri, No. I.*

533. Cf. Lange, *Dagbog i Ægypten 1929-30*, 92.

534. Christiansen and Ryholt, *The Carlsberg Papyri 13*, Text 2.

535. Lange, *Dagbog i Ægypten 1929-30*, 109.

536. Lange, *Dagbog i Ægypten 1929-30*, 194.

537. Lange, *Dagbog i Ægypten 1929-30*, 211.

538. Lange, *Dagbog i Ægypten 1929-30*, 215-216.

539. Lange, *Dagbog i Ægypten 1929-30*, 243-244. The stelae copied

'Old Girgis' is presumably the older of the two dealers by the name Girgis Gabrial. It is evident from his description that Lange had no interest in Demotic texts at this point in time. This would change just one year later, when he would personally take up Demotic studies and begin to build up Copenhagen as a centre for Demotic studies. All the ostraca here mentioned are now in the National Museum.[540]

The most expensive papyrus purchased during this visit to Egypt was acquired from the dealer Grégoire Loukianoff, a Russian exile with whom Lange also developed a friendship. The hieratic papyrus was purchased for the sum of £200 and must therefore have been substantial. Regrettably it has now disappeared. It is presumably this papyrus which was inventoried as either P. Carlsberg 10 or P. Carlsberg 11, both of which disappeared from the Collection many years ago.[541] Loukianoff was under the impression that the papyrus might preserve part of P. Leiden I 348, a New Kingdom manuscript preserving magical texts,[542] which may or may not provide a reliable indication of its date and subject matter.

(Thursday, 30 January 1930:) Yesterday I had a visit by a Russian refugee, Loukianoff, who has studied Egyp-

tology but mostly makes a living buying and selling antiquities. He has a hieratic papyrus which seems to be part of a papyrus in Leiden (J. 348). He would like to sell it but he demands £300 for it and this seems to me an impossible price.[543]

Two weeks later:

(Wednesday, 12 February 1930:) Yesterday we had the pleasure of receiving a telegram from Prof. Drachmann to the effect that the Carlsberg Foundation had granted £200 so that I could purchase a hieratic papyrus which is owned by the Russian Loukianoff. When he showed it to me some weeks ago, he said that his price was £300, this price was set by the antiquities dealer Blanchard; he had himself obtained it for a very modest sum, but it was important for him to turn it into cash ... He had so far in vain offered his papyrus for sale, first and foremost to the museum in Leiden, which has a larger part of the same manuscript, which has been there for about 100 years; he has also offered it in Germany through Borchardt. Now it is his hope that I would buy it, and he said that if the sale could be realized soon, he might be able to reduce the price to £250; and when he left, he said, that he would talk to his wife about whether they perhaps should reduce the price further in order to get it sold. The next time he came to me to show me some things, which he had sniffed out, he said that they had now agreed to sell the papyrus for £200. Since it is now the situation that I did not need the 20,000 Crowns which the Carlsberg Foundation had granted for the eventual purchase of the three papyri which Newberry had shown me, I wrote to Drachmann and suggested that Loukianoff's papyrus might be purchased for 4,000 Crowns and asked for an answer through the telegraph and the money through a telegram. The matter has now been resolved, and I am extremely pleased for the little Russian family. Loukianoff more or less makes a living out of selling antiquities, but since he is poor he has no store and no shop.[544]

Prof. A. B. Drachmann was the chairman of the Carlsberg Foundation. Another three weeks later Lange was offered more papyrus fragments, but he had no funds left.

---

during this visit can be found in one of his notebooks; Lange, *Notebook Thebes, Dec. 1929 - Jan. 1930*, 56-58.

540. The 'beautiful Coptic limestone ostracon' is O. Copenhagen NM 11683; the two hieratic ostraca can be identified with O. Copenhagen NM 11677 and 11679 respectively; cf. Hagen, in Nyord and Ryholt (eds.), *Fs Frandsen*, 94-102. The '12 Greek and Coptic ostraca' are presumably identical with twelve ostraca designated O. Copenhagen NM 11682 (limestone) and 11686-96 (pottery), since these are the only ostraca from Lange's collection which are not otherwise accounted for. They are all described as Coptic in the register, but have not yet been studied.

541. P. Carlsberg 11 was the subject of a doctoral thesis submitted to the University of Copenhagen by E. Iversen, but in a letter dated 16 Oct. 1952 to the Faculty of Philosophy he withdrew the thesis and in its place handed in his work *Canon and Proportion in Egyptian Art*. For this reason no copy of the original thesis was deposited in the archives and we have been unable to discover any direct information on the nature of the papyrus.

542. Edited by Borghouts, *The Magical Texts of Papyrus Leiden I 348*.

543. Lange, *Dagbog i Ægypten 1929-30*, 260-1.

544. Lange, *Dagbog i Ægypten 1929-30*, 279.

(Monday, 3 March 1930:) When we came home there was not much time before lunch at 1 o'clock, but what time there was was taken up by a visitor, Muhamed Abd el-Haggag from Qurneh on the Theban Westbank ... He had some papyrus fragments and small objects for sale and finally brought forth a very beautiful head of an ivory statuette of remarkably good execution and undoubtedly genuine.[545]

On the way out we met, by the Qasr en-Nil military barracks by the great Nile bridge, Zaki who delightedly shook our hands and immediately said: 'Really, why you put yourself in such great debt in order to give me a watch?' I did not understand why he said this and answered: 'But you have helped me so well during my stay.' Zaki's next words gave me the explanation: 'I have acquired the papyrus fragments for 10 Shilling.' In other words, Muhamed had gone straight from us down to Zaki and had told him everything, that I had no money, etc.[546]

Zaki had by this point helped Lange for more than three months, and although the passage seems to indicate that he purchased the papyrus fragments very cheaply on Lange's behalf, it is not explicitly recorded whether they were actually given to Lange.

Some disappointments

Although Lange had better access to funding during his second visit, he was in for other occasional disappointments of a kind that many buyers would probably have been familiar with. We offer here two illustrative examples.

The first gives an example of his great expectations and hope of finding something exceptional. On 4 December 1929 he records his excitement at the prospect of acquiring a rare medical papyrus which was in the possession of an unnamed professor in financial trouble.

There is an Armenian antiquities dealer named A. Pusgul. He is our good friend ... He told me that tomorrow he would show me photographs of a medical papyrus which a professor here in Cairo, who is in financial em-

barrassment, wants to sell. Naturally I am very excited about this. If it is good it would be a rare item of the highest interest.[547]

Two days later he notes that the papyrus was not in fact medical but magical and badly worn, and that an outrageous price had been demanded.

The so-called medical papyrus, of which I saw photographs yesterday evening at Pusgul's, turns out to be a magical papyrus 50 cm. long and quite worn. £300 was demanded for it; so I will let that bird fly without regret.[548]

The other example concerns a regular practice by the dealers. Often a price would be negotiated – partially or completely – with the understanding that the potential buyer would then contact some third party, who would provide financial means, and enquire whether the item or/and the price was acceptable. The third party would typically be a collection, a collector, or a sponsor. While this communication went on the item in question was put on reserve.

In the present example, Lange had come across an interesting group of papyri which had been reserved by Percy E. Newberry on behalf of Alan H. Gardiner. He lost no time in his attempt to secure the necessary funds in case Gardiner should decide to decline the material.

(Wednesday, 4 December 1930:) In the afternoon I was invited for tea at Newberry's who wanted my opinion about some papyri which he had at his home for study. They were three rolls from the 10th-12th Dynasty which apparently contained religious texts, quite extraordinary pieces.[549]

From two later entries in the diary, both cited below (p. 175), we surmise that it was apparently unclear whether Newberry could find a buyer for the papyri and whether Gardiner would wish to purchase them. And so Lange contacted Professor Drachmann and

545. Lange, *Dagbog i Ægypten 1929-30*, 318-9.
546. Lange, *Dagbog i Ægypten 1929-30*, 320.

547. Lange, *Dagbog i Ægypten 1929-30*, 116.
548. Lange, *Dagbog i Ægypten 1929-30*, 118.
549. Lange, *Dagbog i Ægypten 1929-30*, 114.

asked if the Carlsberg Foundation would provide the necessary funds in case the papyri became available. Drachmann replied that the Carlsberg Foundation would provide him with a sum of 20,000 Danish Crowns, the equivalent of £1,000.

> (Thursday, 26 December 1930:) But the greatest event of the day is that I have received a letter from Drachmann with these words: 'Dear Lange! Yes, you can count on the Direction helping with the acquisition and handling of the papyri with a sum of up to 20,000 Crowns, in case the deal really comes through.' This means that if Gardiner cannot provide the money to purchase them, then I can purchase them for Denmark. We will know when we come to Cairo.[550]

Already on New Year's Day, before the return to Cairo, Newberry kindly wrote to Lange that Gardiner had decided to purchase the papyri.[551] The reception of the letter is recorded in the diary, and Lange seems not to have been overly distraught.

> (Friday, 3 January 1931:) Newberry wrote to me yesterday that he had acquired the aforementioned papyri for Gardiner at the price of £800; accordingly there will be no need for the 20,000 Crowns from the Carlsberg Foundation which I have informed Prof. Drachmann about. Though I would not hesitate to take action should some other important papyrus turn up.[552]

The three papyri can be identified with P. Gardiner II-IV, all substantial papyri preserving copies of the Coffin Texts.[553] The longest measures about 10 metres in length. Their date remains uncertain; they have recently been assigned to the late 6th Dynasty or early First Intermediate Period.[554]

A later entry in the diary provides a few details about the three papyri which are perhaps worth noting. Lange is describing a meeting with his old friend, the Coptologist Carl Schmidt, with whom he had become acquainted some forty years earlier during his first visits to Berlin,[555] and notes:

> (Friday, 14 March 1930:) The day before yesterday we met Professor Carl Schmidt (called Carlchen Schmidt) on the street, whom I have known since my first visits to Berlin forty years ago. He is a very experienced buyer of papyri down here; he knows all the dealers down here. Dr Stier told me that when Nahman saw him, he gave him a brotherly kiss on the cheek. He is a funny eccentric and it is curious that he is informed about all sorts of matters relating to the Egyptological world. He told me that Beatty's papyri derive from Medamud, and he knew that Newberry in great secrecy had purchased three papyri from Tano which also derive from Medamud.[556]

In other words, the seller was the infamous Jean Tano, one of the more important dealers in Cairo, and the sale was apparently conducted in secrecy. Since the Chester Beatty papyri are certainly from Deir el-Medina, his information about the provenance seems unreliable. In principle he or his source (or perhaps even Lange) could have confused Medina with Medamud in the case of the Chester Beatty papyri, but the three rolls with the Coffin Texts are much earlier in date and therefore unlikely to derive from this Ramesside community. Moreover, Gardiner was apparently informed that they were found at Saqqara.[557]

Acquisitions after the second visit to Egypt

Shortly before his departure from Egypt, Lange felt confident that he had established good connections in the country and that he might be able to continue to acquire interesting material.

---

550. Lange, *Dagbog i Ægypten 1929-30*, 196.

551. Letter from P. E. Newberry to H. O. Lange, dated 1 Jan. 1930 (Royal Library, Copenhagen).

552. Lange, *Dagbog i Ægypten 1929-30*, 219.

553. In 1933 Gardiner donated the three papyri to the British Museum (EA 10676 = P. Gard. II), Chicago Oriental Institute (OIM 14059-87 = P. Gard. III), and the Louvre (E 14703 = P. Gard. IV).

554. Gestermann, in Hawass (ed.), *Egyptology at the Dawn of the Twenty-first Century* 1, 206.

555. The relationship between Lange and Schmidt is discussed by Giversen, in Nagel (ed.), *Carl-Schmidt-Kolloquium*, 49-58.

556. Lange, *Dagbog i Ægypten 1929-30*, 336.

557. Gestermann, in Hawass (ed.), *Egyptology at the Dawn of the Twenty-first Century* 1, 206.

(23 March 1930:) I have now secured good connections for the Glyptothek down here. Dreiss and Loukianoff will keep me *à jour* about the good things which come to their attention. Zaki and Girgis will collect hieratic ostraca for me, and through Zaki I will probably be informed about whatever noteworthy material the Bedouins might find by the pyramids.[558]

He does not mention papyri on this occasion, perhaps because good manuscripts were few and far between, and as far as ostraca were concerned, he evidently preferred hieratic ones.

Loukianoff for his part did in fact offer Lange a series of objects in the course of the following year, including several papyri. The first was a large hieratic Book of the Dead measuring 4 metres of which 320 cm were covered with vignettes, some 90 figures with six in colour. He adds 'Vous y aurez 7 lignes sur le 3 mètres de longueur sous les scènes et 13 lignes du texte après les scènes. Je ne doute pas, que c'est une livre des morts, mais ils ont tous les variants bien intéressants.' The papyrus had belonged to a museum in Jerusalem which sought to sell off its Egyptian collection (p. 232). It was first offered to Lange in April of 1930, and in May Loukianoff placed it in the Danish *légation* in Cairo in the hope that Junker or Schott would inspect it for Lange.[559] He was still trying to sell the papyrus to Lange in August;[560] when the offer was rejected he instead offered it, in November, to Marija Rudzinskaitė-Arcimavičienė in Lithuania with whom he had become acquainted some years earlier.[561] The asking price in her case was £E 50.

In the autumn, he offered Lange two further papyri.[562] One was extraordinarily expensive: 'On m'a sig-

nalé à Luxor un grand papyrus en rouleau, mais le prix est bien élévés (800 L.E.)'. The other, by contrast, rather cheap; 'Si cela Vous interesse, je Vous propose un papyrus démotique, que Mr. Spigelberg(sic) a trouvé très interessant. Le prix est 5 L.E. Je peux l'envoyer en lettre récommandé, si Vous approuvez son achat.' The claim that the renowned Wilhelm Spiegelberg had found the papyrus interesting was clearly intended to make the piece attractive, but given the low price one might imagine that the German scholar would have acquired the papyrus himself if this was really the case.

Finally, in a letter dated 14 January 1931, Loukianoff offered Lange a batch of papyrus fragments and included a partial handcopy of one of the larger (Fig. 123-124).[563] These fragments, whose nature was unknown at the time, represent the first documented batch of papyri from the Tebtunis temple library offered for sale on the antiquities market. Along with further material offered for sale by other dealers, they were later secured for Copenhagen (p. 178).

As for Zaki Mahmud Abd es-Samad, he thanks Lange – in a letter from 15 May 1931 – for a cheque for £10 and also mentions that he has recieved £50 for 'Mr. Zuider'; the £10 cheque relates to the acquisition of a small box of fragments from the Tebtunis temple library.[564] Zaki was himself illiterate and therefore had to turn to the assistance of others, but the writer was certainly neither a native English speaker nor familiar with Lange or Egyptology. The letter is addressed to 'K. O. Langer' at the 'Yuniversity of Copenhagen'. Zaki had promised to look for hieratic ostraca, and the letter ends with an amusing *post scriptum* after being signed 'I am your obediented servant, Zaki Mahmud':

558. Lange, *Dagbog i Ægypten 1929-30*, 346.
559. Letters from G. Loukianoff to H. O. Lange dated 20 Apr., 30 Apr., and 28 May 1930 (Royal Library, Copenhagen).
560. Letter from G. Loukianoff to H. O. Lange dated 22 Aug. 1930 (Royal Library, Copenhagen).
561. Letter from G. Loukianoff to Marija Rudzinskaitė-Arcimavičienė dated 24 Nov. 1930, cited by Snitkuvienė, *Acta Orientalia Vilnensia* 10 (2009), 191.
562. Letter from G. Loukianoff to H. O. Lange, undated but certainly autumn of 1930 from internal evidence (Royal Library, Copenhagen).

563. Letter from G. Loukianoff to H. O. Lange, dated 14 Jan. 1931 (Royal Library, Copenhagen).
564. Letter from Z. M. Abd es-Samad to H. O. Lange, dated 15 May 1930 (Royal Library, Copenhagen). The year is apparently a slip of the pen for 1931, since Lange was still in Cairo at May 1930 and it emerges from other letters that the papyri in question were offered to Lange in March of 1931. The identity of 'Mr. Zuider' remains unclear.

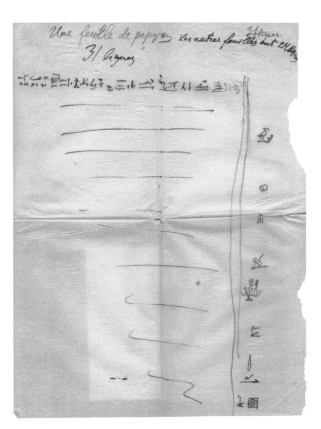

Fig. 124. Loukianoff's sketch of the same sheet of papyrus in a letter to Lange dated 14 January 1931 where he offers this and other papyri for sale. Courtesy of the Royal Library.

Fig. 123. Papyrus Carlsberg 7, a hieroglyphic dictionary with hieratic commentary from the Tebtunis temple library (1st/2nd Century AD). The papyrus was eventually acquired, but not directly from Grégoire Loukianoff. Courtesy of the Papyrus Carlsberg Collection.

P.S. Ostrich Stone I am still looking for it as soon as found I shall gladly send it to you.

Clearly Zaki had intended to communicate that he was still looking for ostraca for Lange and that he would send whatever material he could find. Zaki did indeed send three ostraca to Lange. This emerges from a letter which was written in a different hand than the preceeding one and bears no date, but which seems to have been written soon after.

Moreover, I found 3 pieces of ostraks & sent them to you as you told me while in Cairo. Also a square piece has the name of the Goddess Isis & I hope that you will

receive them safely. The 3 pieces of ostraks have been seen by Mr. Alfred Sakkor & Mr. Lhont [?], they said that they will send a letter to the man they knows to examine the ostraks & the prices is depend on you & then you will send me the money for the things ...[565]

All three ostraca were Demotic, which must have been disappointing to Lange. They are now in the Papyrus Hauniensis Collection (O. Haun. inv. Demot. 1-3); the Papyrus Carlsberg Collection, where they would have found a more natural setting, had not yet been formed and Lange and his students had little interest in Demotic at the time, so there was little reason for him to hold

565. Letter from Z. M. Abd es-Samad to H. O. Lange, undated (Royal Library, Copenhagen). In the last dated letter from Zaki, dated 20 Sept. 1931, he stated that he had not heard from Lange 'for a long time'.

on to them personally. As in the case of Loukianoff, the communication with Zaki and Girgis also seems to cease in 1931 to judge from the extant documentation.[566]

Among the more significant acquisitions after his return to Copenhagen are two Coptic codices which were acquired through Carl Schmidt. Schmidt regularly visited Egypt and made a business out of acquiring papyri from various dealers and re-selling them at a profit, sometimes after they had been conserved and made more presentable by the skillful hands of Hugo Ibscher at the Egyptian Museum in Berlin (who was also commissioned by other dealers for such work).[567] The first of the two manuscripts is a Fayumic papyrus codex (P. Carlsberg 300) which preserves the *Apology for Lack of Faith* and part of the *Dispute with Stratonicus*, both works of Agathonicos, bishop of Tarsus.[568] This manuscript had been purchased by Schmidt in 1927, partly in the Fayum and partly in Cairo, and it was acquired by the Carlsberg Foundation in 1931.[569] It was published with remarkable speed by Lange's student Wolja Erichsen in the following year.[570] The other was a medical parchment codex (P. Carlsberg 500)

which Schmidt is said to have purchased from an antiquities dealer in Cairo in the early 1930s.[571] This text was acquired in 1936/37.[572]

The formation of the Papyrus Carlsberg Collection[573]

Lange's big break came early in 1931, less than a year after his return from Egypt. On February 18 Siegfried Schott informed Lange about an important discovery of papyri which, in Borchardt's opinion, derived from a temple library.[574] It had proved impossible to get funding from Germany for the acquisition and instead Lange was now approached. He must have gone straight to the Carlsberg Foundation since the deal was closed just two weeks later. The Foundation provided a generous sum sufficient for the full acquisition – the first batch at £1,000 and the following batches amounting to a total in excess of £1,250 (the exact sum remains unclear).

The material was truly remarkable. As was soon discovered, the papyri derived from the site of Tebtunis and the bulk of them represents nothing less than the remains of the only extant temple library from ancient Egypt.[575] The library is, at the same time, the

566. The last item in their correspondance is a letter from Z. M. Abd es-Samad to H. O. Lange, dated 20 Sept. 1931 (Royal Library), which ends with the *post scriptum*, 'P.S. I thought that you will answer my letters, but now I am forgotten. Please write me.'

567. An example is P. Haun. 11 which belongs to the Demotic/Greek archive of Amenothes son of Harsiesis from Thebes; see Bülow-Jacobsen, *Aegis* 12 (2012), 47.

568. Erichsen, *Faijumische Fragmente der Reden des Agathonicus Bischofs von Tarsus*; Andersen, Holmen, and Tait, *Enchoria* 25 (1999), 1-19, pls. 1-16. The well-preserved codex was beautifully re-mounted in 2010 by the kind offices of Myriam Krutzsch who now holds Hugo Ibscher's former position as conservator of the Papyrussammlung in Berlin.

569. The details of its acquisition by C. Schmidt emerges from a letter to H. O. Lange, dated 24 Jan. 1930 (Royal Library, Copenhagen) where he offers the papyrus for sale. Lange was still in Egypt at the time. In another letter dated 22 Feb. 1931 (Royal Library, Copenhagen), Schmidt thanks Lange for his decision to purchase the papyrus and informs him that he has passed the papyrus on to Hugo Ibscher.

570. The information on the acquisition of the papyrus provided by Erichsen, *Faijumische Fragmente*, 3, is not entirely correct as shown by the letters from Schmidt.

571. Erichsen, *AcOr* 27 (1963), 23.

572. Cf. letters from W. Erichsen to H. O. Lange, dated 17 Nov. 1935, 2 Sept. 1936, 22 Dec. 1936, and 1 Feb. 1937 (Royal Library, Copenhagen).

573. A detailed account of the acquisition of the material from the Tebtunis temple library will be published separately. The substantial addition to the Papyrus Carlsberg Collection made by Aksel Volten in 1954 with means provided by the Carlsberg Foundation, which included papyri from Hawara and other sites (mainly in Demotic, but also some Greek; purchased from Robert Nahman, Jean Tano, and a certain 'Kamal', presumably Kamel Abdallah Hammouda), is not relevant to the present publication and will therefore not be further mentioned on this occasion. Nor will the recent acquisition of the Adler Papyri (i.e. the Demotic-Greek archive of Horos son of Nechutes) in July 2012 through the support of the Augustinus Foundation and the Carlsberg Foundation.

574. Letter from S. Schott to H. O. Lange, dated 18 Feb. 1931 (Royal Library, Copenhagen).

575. Another important group of papyri represents the remains of an archive that included a great number of so-called

Fig. 125. Papyrus Carlsberg 1, *The Book of Nut*, from the Tebtunis temple library (1st/2nd Century AD). Acquired 1931 from Maurice Nahman through Ludwig Borchardt. Courtesy of the Papyrus Carlsberg Collection.

largest assemblage of ancient Egyptian literary papyri discovered to date. The details of its contents have been outlined elsewhere, and it will therefore suffice only to include a few remarks here.

The library pertains to the temple of Soknebtunis, the main deity of Tebtunis, and it was discovered very close to the sanctuary in two underground cellars.[576] It had been abandoned in the early 3rd Century and its contents date to the 1st and 2nd Century AD. It included several hundred papyri inscribed with literary texts, including cultic works (such as rituals, hymns, and compendia of priestly knowledge), scientific works (espe-

cially of divinatory nature such as astrology and dream interpretation, but also much medical), and many narratives about historical figures from the past (such as Djoser and Imhotep). Adding to the significance of the corpus is the fact that most of the texts are unique. The majority are written in demotic and hieratic, but there are also a number of scientific works in Greek as well as a few hieroglyphic texts.

One of the best preserved papyri was an astronomical treatise written in a mixture of hieratic and demotic (P. Carlsberg 1; Fig. 125). Lange was so keen on publishing this papyrus that he undertook the study of Demotic at the age of 68. The publication, written in collaboration with a German-Jewish colleague, Otto Neugebauer, who had sought refuge from the Nazis in Denmark, appeared in 1940.[577]

The acquisition of the temple library proved no easy task. It soon became clear that the papyri had reached the hands of many dealers with the result that parts of the individual papyri had been split up. For more than a year Borchardt made an effort to track

self-dedications. They pertain to the same temple but date to the 2nd century BC. The phenomenon of self-dedications is discussed by Ryholt, in Nyord and Ryholt (eds.), *Fs Frandsen*, 329-350, pl. 8.
576. For the complex excavation history and the archaeological context of the papyri, see Ryholt, in Ryholt and Barjamovic (eds.), *Libraries before Alexandria*, forthcoming; Gallazzi, in idem., *Tebtynis VI: Scripta Varia*, forthcoming. Surveys of the extensive material may be found in Ryholt, in Lippert and Schentuleit (eds.), *Tebtynis und Soknopaiu Nesos*, 141-170; von Lieven in *ibid.*, 57-70; Quack, in Ryholt (ed.), *The Carlsberg Papyri 7*, 1-7. For the Greek texts, see Ryholt, *ZPE* 187 (2013), 233-238.

577. Lange and Neugebauer, *Papyrus Carlsberg No. 1*. The text has since been re-edited by von Lieven, *The Carlsberg Papyri 8*.

down as much of the material as possible and to secure it for Lange. In 1932 Carl Schmidt also got involved. He had come across new batches and complained to Lange that Borchardt was offering the dealers far too much money for them. Borchardt and Schmidt had long conducted a similar business and there seems to have been some competition and slight rivalry between them, although Borchardt generally concentrated on older Egyptian texts and Schmidt on Coptic and Greek texts. In the present case, Schmidt claimed that Borchardt had offered a dealer £800 for a large batch of Tebtunis papyri, but that he had just secured it for the price of £500 after hours of negotiation. He ended the report with the words 'Borch[ardt] wird erstaunt sein wenn er von dem Ankauf durch mich erfährt.'[578]

Many new batches of papyri from the temple library appeared on the market for years after the initial purchase. This forced Lange to apply to the Carlsberg Foundation for further funding over and over. Fortunately, the Foundation remained patient with him and he was able to acquire all the relevant material that came to his attention. From 1931 onwards, he concentrated his efforts on these papyri and no more acquisitions were made for the Papyrus Hauniensis Collection. His last acquisition of Tebtunis papyri was made in 1938 and that same year the Carlsberg Foundation officially donated the collection to the University of Copenhagen. It was deposited in the Egyptology Department and became the Papyrus Carlsberg Collection, and for Lange and his students it became the focal point of Danish Egyptology for years to come.

Refraining from further acquisitions

The acquisition of the Tebtunis papyri in 1931 had not come cheaply, and Lange largely refrained from the temptation to seek more funding from the Carlsberg Foundation when new, unrelated material was offered to him. This would prove a wise move since, as it turned out, he would need much further funding to secure the further groups of material from the temple library that would appear on the market for several years to come.

An interesting example of the type of material he felt compelled to decline is provided by a letter from Borchardt from December 1931.

Vorgestern Abend kam ein Qurnaui zu mir, der noch zwei von den Papyris aus dem letztjährigen Funde demotischer Kontrakte hatte. Es war ein griechischer und ein demotischer. Der griechische war etwa 12 cm hoch, noch zugerollt, schöner gelber Papyrus, die Rolle etwa 2 cm dick. Ich konnte rd. 150 cm glatt entrollen, dann stiess ich auf den zugebundenen und gesiegelten Kern der Rolle. Das Siegel war, soviel ich erkennen konnte, ein Ptolemäerkopf ... Die demotische Rolle ist etwa doppelt so hoch und etwa 5 cm zusammengerollt dick. Sie ist, wie die erste, nur einseitig, innen beschrieben. Beim Aufrollen steht aber, etwa nach Abrollen einer Windung, eine schmale Spalte auf der Rückseite, etwa 3 cm breit und etwa 16 cm hoch. Auf der Innenseite stehen, u.zw. ziemlich dicht am Anfang (also Ende der Zeilen) der Rolle, 4 demotische Zeilen in der Mitte des Blattes, das ich etwa 150 cm weit aufwickelte. Also wie bei den bekannten demotischen Kontrakten. Ich kann etwa 1/3 der Rolle nur aufgewickelt haben, ich schätze ihre Länge auf 4 m! Da der Besitzer weiss, dass die anderen Stücke aus diesen Funde, den er übrigens genau so beschrieb, wie im Vorjahre der Besitzer des anderen Teiles des Fundes, mit etwa 50 LE verkauft worden sind, so verlangte er für den Griechen 100 LE und für den demotischen Papyrus 200 LE.[579]

Another example is a hieratic ostracon which Carl Schmidt offered to Lange in a letter written in November of 1931.[580] He had purchased the ostracon in Edfu and found out that it belonged to a larger group

578. Letter from C. Schmidt to H. O. Lange, dated 6 Apr. 1932 (Royal Library, Copenhagen). One may perhaps also detect a slightly sarcastic tone in the casual manner in which Borchardt refers to Schmidt in a letter to Lange written some years later, dated 22 Apr. 1937 (Royal Library, Copenhagen): 'Carlchen Schmidt ist wieder hier im Lande und besucht die Händler. Ich kümmere mich aber um seine Geschäfte nicht.'

579. Letter from L. Borchardt to H. O. Lange, dated 25 Dec. 1931 (Royal Library, Copenhagen). Lange's rejection is mentioned in Borchardt's next letter written 30 Jan. 1932.
580. Letter from C. Schmidt to H. O. Lange, dated 12 Nov. 1931 (Royal Library, Copenhagen).

Fig. 126. Papyrus Carlsberg 6, *The Teaching for Merikare* (12th Century BC). Acquired 1937 from Ludwig Borchardt who offered it to Copenhagen in reaction to the *Berufsverbot* issued by the Nazi regime in Germany. Courtesy of the Papyrus Carlsberg Collection.

of which others had ended up in the Cairo Museum. The ostracon had a rubric in the first line of the front and the verso was inscribed with a text which he thought might be an account. The asking price was 45 Deutschmark.

Antisemitism – Merikare comes to Copenhagen

In addition to the temple library, Lange made one notable acquisition in the last ten years of his life. This was a copy of the *Teaching for King Merikare* (Fig. 126) of which only one other version was then known, and the story behind this acquisition is extraordinary.

On 7 April 1933 the Nazi government in Germany issued the *Gesetz zur Wiederherstellung des Berufsbeamtentums*, and its effects caused widespread shock and anger, not least in the academic world where many scholars of Jewish descent were barred from using institutional libraries. Ludwig Borchardt felt rejected and particularly the situation of his and Lange's old friend and teacher, Adolf Erman, worried him. In a direct response he decided to stage his own version of the *Berufsverbot*. A few years before, he had made a very valuable acquisition – a beautiful and well-preserved section of a papyrus inscribed with the *Teaching for King Merikare*.[581] He knew that this would be a

prize for any Egyptologist to edit and therefore decided to make it the object of his personal protest, announcing that only a German scholar of Jewish or Semitic descent would be allowed to publish the text. After some years, he realized that this was impossible and decided to sell the papyrus to his old friend Lange instead. He described the situation in a letter from April 1937.

> 1933, gleich nach dem Umbruch, zog ich die damals in Berlin befindliche Handschrift aus Deutschland heraus und nahm mir vor, sie nur von einem jüdischen Deutschen bearbeiten zu lassen, da ich selbst wohl nicht mehr dazu kommen würde. Von diesem Grundsatz abzugehen habe ich um so weniger Grund, als neulich einem gar nicht schlechten deutsch-jüdischen Gelehrten meiner Bekanntschaft in Berlin die Benutzung einer von ihm besuchten Bibliothek verboten worden ist ... So liegt die Sache also heute. Haben Sie einem Jüdisch-Deutschen, oder Semitisch-Deutschen, oder selbst desgl. Dänen oder anderer Nationalität, so können Sie den *Mry-kȝ-rˁ* ohne Weiteres von mir zur Bearbeitung bekommen, d.h. dass dieser ihn macht. Ich bin gewiss kein Rassenfanatiker, aber unter den heutigen Umständen sehe ich keinen Grund, von meinem oben angeführten Vorsatz abzugehen. Eine andere Möglichkeit, die mir eben einfällt, wäre noch die, dass ich den Papyrus durch Verkauf loswerde und damit auch meinen Vorsatz. Aber das wird Ihnen wohl etwas zu teuer werden. Sehen Sie noch eine andere Möglichkeit?[582]

---

581. Borchardt in *Allerhand Kleinigkeiten*, 45, pl. 15. The papyrus is included in the modern synoptic edition of the text, Quack, *Studien zur Lehre für Merikare*.

582. Letter from L. Borchardt to H. O. Lange, dated 22 Apr. 1937 (Royal Library, Copenhagen).

That this was no mere joke or private political gesture is indicated by a footnote in Alexander Scharff's commentary on the historical section of *The Teaching for Merikare*, where he expressed evident regret at not being allowed to cite Borchardt's papyrus. This is all the more noteworthy since Scharff himself was known to be strongly opposed to National Socialism; in fact Georg Steindorff placed him first in his list of German Egyptologists 'who have proved themselves men of honour' during the Nazi era.[583]

> Zweitens besitzt Borchardt eine Handschrift, von der bisher leider nur eine Seite bekannt gemacht ist ... Der Besitzer gestattete mir bei meinem Aufenthalt in Kairo im Spätherbst 1935 auch die Photographien der übrigen Seiten anzusehen, untersagte aber ausdrücklich jegliche Benutzung.[584]

In August of 1937 Borchardt wrote to Lange and made him a direct offer.

> Wenn Sie ihn haben wollen, und er wäre bei Ihnen in guten Händen, was wäre Ihnen nicht zu viel dafür? -- Ist LE 150 = 153/15/- engl.Pfd. über Ihr Können? Teuer war das Ding damals, und Ibscher hat es bereits bearbeitet, auch sind benutzbare Photographien, die als Unterlagen für die Veröffentlichung in Lichtdruck dienen können, bereits vorhanden. Mehrkosten würden also nicht für Sie oder den Erwerber entstehen.[585]

The Carlsberg Foundation was immediately contacted and a month later the aforementioned Johannes Pedersen, who had become its chairman, informed Lange that it had decided to grant the sum of £150.[586] The deal was struck and the papyrus sent off to Copenhagen. It emerges from a later letter by Borchardt that he had apparently enquired about the safe arrival of the papyrus, but that Lange had re-

plied something about the financial matter. The letter is worth citing for the light it sheds on the funding situation in Germany at this point in time during the Nazi regime.

> Vielen Dank für Ihren freundlichen Brief vom 3.11.37. Meine Frage betraf aber nicht Ihre Devisenschwierigkeiten, sondern, ob der Papyrus <u>gut</u> angekommen wäre. Hoffentlich können Sie sich davon bald überzeugen und es mir dann mitteilen. -- Dieselben Schwierigkeiten haben übrigens auch alle anderen Museen und Institute. Man wundert sich eigentlich über jeden Pfennig, der heute noch für Wissenschaft ausgegeben wird, es sei denn in Deutschland für Vorgeschichte und Rassenforschung. Aber in Deutschland wundert man sich schon lange über nichts mehr.[587]

Assessment of papyrus acquisitions

With the formation of the Papyrus Carlsberg Collection and Papyrus Hauniensis Collection, Lange had secured a substantial group of ancient manuscripts for Danish Egyptology and Papyrology. The bulk of the material was slightly later in date than he would have preferred; his first priority had always been hieratic texts of the earlier periods. He did, however, manage to acquire the *Teaching for Merikare* and the (now lost) Loukianoff Papyrus, as well as some other minor items of New Kingdom date. It seems appropriate, with hindsight, that Lange, who had been Head Librarian for most of his life, managed to acquire the remains of the only surviving, large-scale temple library from ancient Egypt. As one of the most important discoveries of papyri ever made in Egypt, it continues to be a focal point for Danish and international Egyptological research; a fitting memorial to one of Denmark's most distinguished Egyptologists.

583. Schneider, *JEgH* 5 (2012), 145, cf. further pp. 147-150.
584. Scharff, *Der historische Abschnitt der Lehre für König Merikare*, 6, n. 1.
585. Letter from L. Borchardt to H. O. Lange, dated 9 Aug. 1937 (Royal Library, Copenhagen).
586. Letter from J. Pedersen to H. O. Lange, dated 17 Sept. 1937 (Royal Library, Copenhagen).
587. Letter from L. Borchardt to H. O. Lange, dated 13 Nov. 1937 (Royal Library, Copenhagen).

The Antiquities Dealers

The history of Egyptology is much more than the history of Egyptologists, but it is relatively rare to find the diverse 'supporting cast' (workmen, photographers, financiers, etc.) treated in any depth in the Egyptological literature; two recent exceptions are Stephen Quirke's study of the workmen who assisted Petrie and others in their excavations,[588] and Wendy Doyon's ongoing work on Reisner's use of Egyptian workmen.[589] In the following section we provide a brief but similar attempt to identify the individuals involved in the antiquities trade in Egypt, primarily during the years 1899-1930. Lange encountered numerous dealers during his two visits to Cairo, and he described many of them in detail. Although the list below is reasonably exhaustive in relation to the Lange files we have made no systematic attempt to correlate the information with other archival material elsewhere.[590] We have, however, supplemented it with other references, including the (little-known) autobiography in Danish by his teacher Valdemar Schmidt from whom Lange had learnt first-hand about the Egyptian antiquities trade.[591] We have included much information from Wilbour's published letters which cover the years 1880-1891, which were both readily available and highly relevant. We have excluded dealers whose activities fall entirely before 1880, unless they are mentioned elsewhere in the book. We have also excluded Western scholars such as Ludwig Borchardt and Howard Carter, who were prominent dealers alongside their academic careers.

The list is in alphabetical order based on last names for non-Arabs and first names for Arabs, following normal conventions. A word of caution is in order when using the list and the information it contains, as it may in some cases be incorrect. There are three main sources for potential errors. The first is that Egyptians did not have family names as such until around the turn of the 20th Century, but traditionally used their father's name as a second name. In contrast to Westerners, they would therefore usually be referred to by their first names. Thus the sons of Ali Abd el-Haj were named Mohammed Ali and Ibrahim Ali, and the three individuals would usually be referred to simply as Ali, Mohammed, and Ibrahim, as were so many Egyptians. This is not always realized in the literature where the names by which the dealers are referred are sometimes assumed to be family names as in the Western tradition. We have, moreover, found many examples where we suspect that dealers with identical names are confused, such as Ali Abd el-Haj and Ali Farag who would both have been called simply Ali. Another difficulty is the question of family relationships, where it is clear that often terms like 'brother' or 'grandfather' might simply refer, respectively, to a person from the same village or any elderly relative.[592] It is also clear that some unlicensed Arab dealers did not give their real names to Westerners; a certain Mahmud, for example, was in the habit of calling himself Hassan, allegedly because he

---

588. Quirke, *Hidden hands.*

589. Doyon, in Carruthers (ed.), *Histories of Egyptology*, 141-156.

590. Other archives undoubtedly contain significant information about dealers at the time, but a survey of all such material would fall outside the scope of this book. References can be found e.g. in the personal papers and letters from prominent Egyptologists at the time, of which few are readily accessible to scholars, but cf. Capart (ed.), *Letters of Charles Edwin Wilbour*; Larson (ed.), *Letters from James Henry Breasted.* Particularly useful in this regard is presumably the Herbert Winlock correspondence and the diaries of Emma B. Andrews (mistress of Theodore Davies) at the Metropolitan Museum of Art, and the papers of Ludwig Borchardt at the Swiss Institute in Cairo. Relevant material is also discussed by Fiechter, *Faux et faussaires en art égyptien*, esp. pp. 13-17; cf. Wakeling, *Forged Egyptian Antiquities.*

591. Schmidt, *Af et Langt Livs Historie.*

592. Lange and Lange, *Dagbog fra Ægyptensrejsen 1899-1900*, 494; Lange, *Dagbog fra Ægypten, 1929-1930*, 34.

thought Germans found this easier to 'understand'.[593] These issues all introduce a margin of error in our identifications of individuals and their families, and we have occasionally been in doubt ourselves as to whether we were looking at one or several individuals.

The years in brackets (*fl.* = *floruit*) refer to approximate periods of activity; only in exceptional cases are we able indicate date of birth or time of death. The dates are approximate and should not be interpreted as setting out the limits of their period of activity.

***

A. Ali el-Gabri (date uncertain)

Cairo dealer of uncertain date who ran a shop at 11 Sharia el-Mahdi, near Shepheard's Hotel, with antiquities license no. 84.[594] The name suggests that he is a member of the el-Gabri family of Kafr el-Haram.

Abbas Mohammed Ali el-Arabi (*fl.* 1933)

Antiquities dealer who lived at Giza and assisted Carl Schmidt in his enquiries into the production of forged antiquities in Egypt in 1933.[595] He may have been a relative of Ali Abd el-Haj (more often known as Ali el-Arabi) to judge from his name.

Abd el-Al (*fl.* 1904)

A dealer in Eshmunein who sold a number of papyri to the German papyrus cartel.[596]

Abd el-Aziz (*fl.* 1881)

Antiquities dealer at Abusir visited by Wilbour.[597]

Abd el-Megid Hussein Aga (c. 1850-1915)

Abd el-Megid Hussein Aga (Table 4), known universally as simply 'Abd el-Megid', was one of the main dealers in Luxor at the turn of the century.[598] In 1929, many years after his death, Wolfgang Dreiss described him to Lange as a rich antiquities dealer whose estate had included land holdings between Medinet Habu and the mortuary temple of Amenhotep III and that he had also been the proprietor of the land on which the Hôtel du Nil (earlier managed by Dreiss himself) was located.[599] Maspero evidently took a dislike to him, at least in 1884, writing to his wife: 'Abdoulméguid est plus bête que jamais: il se confit chaque jour dans sa stupidité.'[600] His shop was located in Sharia el-Lukanda opposite the Luxor temple (Fig. 103).

Abd el-Megid was closely tied to two other prominent antiquities dealers as the nephew of the British consular agent at Luxor, Mustafa Aga,[601] and the brother-in-law of Mohammed Mohasseb whose sister he married around 1868.[602] Not being a consul he had no diplomatic immunity, and he was arrested at least once, during the campaign of raids on dealers in 1888,

593. Lange and Lange, *Dagbog fra Ægyptensrejsen 1899-1900*, 162; obviously operating under an alias might also have certain advantages for an unlicensed dealer.
594. A scarab, accompanied by a certificate from the dealer, was sold by Cordier Auctions on 5 Nov. 2011, lot 284; cf. http://www.invaluable.com/auction-lot/gold-swivel-mounted-egyptian-scarab-ring-284-c-379693f5d2 (accessed 6 Dec. 2013). The header of the certificate reads 'A. Aly el-Gabry, Antiquities Dealer, (Licence No. 84 - No Branches.) R. C: 48948', and the description of the object is followed by the printed declaration: 'The above mentioned antiquities are guaranteed genuine by the merchant. If the above antiquities are proved false by any expert, of any museum, I am willing to refund the price of antiquities and expense to the holder of this Certificate' (accessed 13 Sept. 2013).
595. Fiechter, *Faux et faussaires en art égyptien*, 43.

596. Martin and Primavesi, *L'Empédocle de Strasbourg*, 327.
597. Cf. Capart (ed.), *Letters of Charles Edwin Wilbour*, 89.
598. His full name emerges from the façade of his shop in Luxor, 'Abd el Megid Hussein Aga. Dealer of antiquities. Entrance free.' Cf. Legrain, *Louqsor sans les pharaons*, pl. 23 (reproduced here in Fig. 102).
599. Lange, *Dagbog fra Ægypten, 1929-1930*, 182; two letters from W. Dreiss to H. O. Lange, dated 23 May and 6 June 1930, respectively (Royal Library, Copenhagen).
600. David, *Gaston Maspero*, 47, cf. further p. 134.
601. Cf. Capart (ed.), *Letters of Charles Edwin Wilbour*, 59.
602. Cf. Capart (ed.), *Letters of Charles Edwin Wilbour*, 496, 497.

despite his connections.[603] During his time in custody Grébaut, then the head of the Antiquities Service, ransacked his Luxor home and confiscated a number of antiquities for which Abd el-Megid was later paid £50 in compensation (p. 143).

His business and the shop at Sharia el-Lukanda was inherited by his son Hassan Abd el-Megid (1889-1916), by a second wife,[604] and later by his grandson Hussein Abd el-Megid. Dreiss informed Lange that Hassan Abd el-Megid died in 1916 when his house collapsed, killing the entire family except for an infant son 'who lived with his grandmother'; the entire estate went to his under-age son, Hussein Abd el-Megid, but it was looked after by the state judicial system during Lange's visit because the boy was apparently still under-age in 1929. This agrees with the fact that the Baedeker guides from 1928 and 1929 list a Hussein Abd el-Megid among the antiquities dealers in Luxor.[605]

Among much else, he is known to have sold a large quantity of the so-called el-Hibeh papyri to Spiegelberg in 1895.[606]

Abd en-Nur (fl. 1881-d. 1890)

Abd en-Nur at Girga was a French consular agent; later he became consular agent for the United States and his brother took over the former consulship.[607] He carried out whole-sale licensed excavations by

agreement with Maspero and later Grébaut, including the temple of Ramesses II at Mesheikh, but was nonetheless among those dealers who had their antiquities seized by the latter in 1888 (p. 143). He died in July 1890.

Abd en-Nur Gabrial (fl. 1894-1911)

Brother of Girgis Gabrial, q.v.

Abd er-Rahim (fl. 1930)

Abd er-Rahim was a dealer who lived 'near the Winter Palace Hotel' in Luxor, from whom Lange bought a Coptic ostracon (NM 11683, unpublished).[608] He and Dreiss also aided Lange with the inspection of a monument in the possession of the dealer Schafi.[609]

Abd er-Rahman Ahmed Abd er-Rasul

Brother of Abd er-Rasul Ahmed Abd er-Rasul, q.v.

Abd er-Rahman es-Sadiq (fl. 1943-late 1940s)

Licensed dealer at Hehia who sold objects from other sites in the Delta including Athribis, Qantir, and Tell el-Moqdam.[610] In 1943 he presented a few minor objects to the Egyptian Museum.[611]

Abd er-Rasul Ahmed Abd er-Rasul (c. 1820-1910)

The five brothers Abd er-Rasul Ahmed Abd er-Rasul, Mohammed A. A., Hussein A. A., Abd er-Rahman A.

603. Budge, *By Nile and Tigris* 1, 145.

604. Cf. Capart (ed.), *Letters of Charles Edwin Wilbour*, 497, 588.

605. Baedeker, *Ägypten und der Sûdan*, 8th edition, 38-39; idem, *Egypt and the Sûdân*, 8th edition, 268. In 1959 a dealer named Abd el-Megid Hussein received permission from the Egyptian Museum to export a stele; cf. the export register (sic, not a purchase register as stated in the publication) reproduced in Piacentini, *Egypt and the Pharaohs*, 36-37; idem, *EDAL* 4 (2013/2014), 106, pl. 7, no. 1. If he is identical with Hussein Abd el-Megid, which seems not very likely in view of the reversal of the two names, the latter would still have been active some thirty years after Lange's visit to Egypt, but the person in question is perhaps more likely to be a son.

606. Spiegelberg, *ZÄS* 53 (1917), 1.

607. He is mentioned repeatedly in the Wilbour letters; cf. Capart (ed.), *Letters of Charles Edwin Wilbour*, 593 (index); cf. also Bouriant, *RT* 9 (1887), 89.

608. Lange, *Dagbog fra Ægypten, 1929-1930*, 194-195. This is presumably not the forger Abd er-Rahmin mentioned by Fiechter, *Faux et faussaires en art égyptien*, 15-16, who lived at Qus and specialised in gold jewellery.

609. Lange, *Dagbog fra Ægypten, 1929-1930*, 190.

610. Habachi, in Johnson and Wente (eds.), *Fs Hughes*, 88; Clarysse and Yan, *CdE* 82 (2007), 84-85; Wagner, *ZPE* 106 (1995), 126-130.

611. Cairo Museum, Temporary Register, s.v. 23/10/43/1-5.

A., and Soliman A. A. (all named Ahmed Abd er-Rasul after, it may be assumed, their father) were among the more notorious dealers in Western Thebes in the late 19th and early 20th Century. Four of the brothers (but apparently not Abd er-Rahman) were involved in the discovery of the famous cache of royal mummies in 1871. The sale of high-end items from the cache in the following years, including magnificent Books of the Dead, led to their detection by the authorities in 1881.[612] Abd er-Rasul was soon arrested, but the investigation was partly obstructed by the fact that the brothers were under the protection of the consular agent Mustafa Aga and that the son of the latter was the chief of police at Qena, the capital of the governorate. As for the details of what went on, the account published by Budge is usually cited, but it is heavily biased by his critical attitude towards the French antiquities administration which he frequently sought to ridicule. Moreover, he did not witness any part of the affair personally. His first visit to Egypt only took place several years afterwards and his account was written and published decades later. He dramatically recounts that:

> All the men of the family, young and old, were dragged to Kana in 1880, and tied to posts and well beaten ... One of the two brothers, Abd ar-Rasûl, died under this torture, and the other, when I saw him, still bore the scars of the burns which he received from the heated pots on his forehead, face, and neck.

By contrast, it is explicitly stated by Maspero, who was directly involved in the affair as the Director of the Antiquities Service, that it was just two of the brothers, Abd er-Rasul and Hussein, who were sent to Qena and that only the former was imprisoned. This is corroborated by Wilbour who was also in Egypt at the time

and who knew several members of the Abd er-Rasul family; only Abd er-Rasul was imprisoned at Qena, and Mohammed, who had originally found the tomb, was not arrested. Abd er-Rasul, whom Budge claims died from torture, in fact lived for many years after the interrogation and even demanded compensation for the (in his view) false imprisonment. When Abd er-Rasul was released after some months in prison, he felt – according to Maspero's sources – entitled to more than a fifth share of the loot because of his suffering; he now claimed half or he would collaborate with the authorities. At this point his brother Mohammed (Fig. 11) decided to forestall him. He handed over a number of the items that had been removed from the tomb, and the rest of the rich contents that still remained in the tomb was cleared in a two-day operation under the supervision of Emil Brugsch. Mohammed was afterwards rewarded with £500 and the job as a government reïs, and it was also he who pointed out to Emil Brugsch the location of the other rich cache of priestly mummies at Deir el-Bahri in 1891.[613]

In 1901 the tomb of Amenhotep II was partly robbed and Howard Carter, then Chief Inspector of Antiquities for Upper Egypt, had strong reason to suspect four of the brothers – Abd er-Rasul, Abd er-Rahman, Mohammed, and Soliman (the two former having been identified by the guards of the tomb and the third by the imprint of a foot) – but none of them could be convicted.[614]

Wilbour frequently interacted with Abd er-Rasul and Mohammed in the years 1880-1890 during his visits to the Theban West Bank where they would guide him around the tombs. He reports that the former had built a house (perhaps with proceeds from the royal cache), called the White House, at Sheikh Abd el-Qurna and that the contents of the tomb, which Mohammed had discovered, were rumoured to be

---

612. For the story of the discovery of the royal cache of mummies, and the role of the Abd er-Rasul family, see Maspero, *MMAF* 1 (1889), 511-788, and the letters of Wilbour edited by Capart (ed.), *Letters of Charles Edwin Wilbour*, 34, 48, 65, 66, 67, 71, 73-74, 78, 107, 115, 123, 148, 156, 187-188, 189. The accounts by Budge, *By Nile & Tigris* 1, 113-114, and Wilson, *Signs & Wonders Upon Pharaoh*, 81-84, should both be used with caution.

613. Daressy, *ASAE* 1 (1900), 141. It was also Mohammed Ahmed Abder er-Rasul, in 1883, who removed the obelisk from the pyramid tomb of Antef Nubkheperre and lost it in the Nile; cf. Capart (ed.), *Letters of Charles Edwin Wilbour*, 214-215.
614. Carter, *ASAE* 3 (1902), 115-121; Reeves and Taylor, *Howard Carter before Tutankhamun*, 60-63.

Fig. 127. Abd er-Rasul Ahmed
Abd er-Rasul with his aging
mother (said to be 120 years
of age) and his daughter and
grandchild. Photograph by
R. de Rustafjaell, taken in
or shortly before 1909, and
published in *The Light of Egypt*,
pl. XXIX.

worth £40,000. In 1886 Abd er-Rasul carried out excavations on behalf of General Grenfell at Sheikh
Abd el-Qurna.[615]

Lange met Abd er-Rasul in 1900 during a visit to
Medinet Habu:

> ... an old grey-bearded Arab came who said his name
> was Abd er-Rasul. He is the most knowledgeable local
> when it comes to tombs in western Thebes; for it was he
> who long ago found the many royal mummies, and just
> these days it is said that he has found another two
> tombs. He told a long story of which I understood pre-
> cious little.[616]

Abd er-Rasul was still alive in 1909 when Robert de
Rustafjaell took two photographs of him on the Theban West Bank, one in the company of his mother
Fendia, a daughter, and a granddaughter (Fig. 127),
and the other at the entrance to the royal cache. He

comments: 'He is still alive, and nearly ninety years
old, and dependent on charity; his mother died a few
months ago at the age of 120.'[617] Such accounts are
unlikely to be entirely accurate; Abd er-Rasul himself
told Wilbour in 1886 that he was 73 years old.[618]

Abd er-Rasul (*fl.* 1930)

Lange was introduced to a dealer named Abd er-Rasul by Mohammed Abd el-Haggag; he lived in Thebes where he was Borchardt's next door neighbour.
Lange did not purchase anything from him but relates
how he:

> led me, in the greatest secrecy, into the room in which
> he stores his corn; there he showed me an anthropoid
> coffin which had been dismantled but seemed comple-
> te. It was well preserved and belonged to a woman cal-
> led ⌂𓄿𓇋𓏲 (*K3-iri-rw*) who was a priestess of

615. David, *Gaston Maspero*, 146.
616. Lange and Lange, *Dagbog fra Ægyptensrejsen 1899-1900*, 336.

617. de Rustafjaell, *The Light of Egypt*, 55, pls. 28-29.
618. Cf. Capart (ed.), *Letters of Charles Edwin Wilbour*, 353.

Hathor of Dendera and chantress of Amun-Re. I had no interest in it.[619]

Abd es-Salam Abdallah (fl. 1884-1896)

Dealer at Kafr el-Haram (Table 3), the son of *Hajji* Abdallah and brother of *Sheikh* Omar, and said to be a cousin of Soliman Abd es-Samad, all of whom were also involved in the antiquities trade.[620] He assisted Petrie with his excavations at Tanis in 1884-85, and is known to have sold a few objects to the Egyptian Museum in 1887 and 1888 (p. 51); he was still dealing antiquities in 1896.[621] In view of his name and date, he might be the father of the Cairo dealers Hassan Abd es-Salam and Hussein Abd es-Salam.

Abd el-Wahed (fl. 1906)

A dealer in Illahun who sold a number of papyri to the German papyrus cartel.[622]

Abdallah (fl. 1886-1900)

Abdallah was one of the first antiquities dealers visited by Lange in 1899; he lived in Kafr el-Haram and had a small storage depot in Cairo which Lange saw on 13 November.[623] He was a cousin of the major deal-

er Ali Abd el-Haj and became a guide for Lange. It was presumably the same Abdallah who similarly introduced Lord Crawford to Ali at Giza, described as 'his aged relation', a few months later.[624]

He is mentioned already several years earlier by Schmidt who writes to Jacobsen in 1894 that Abdallah had, 'hidden away in his stable or outbuilding out by the Pyramid', seven directly joining, two-three meter wide relief blocks of a similar quality to those in the Tomb of Ti.[625] It might also be this Abdallah who kept a store at the house of Mohammed *Effendi* in Cairo which Wilbour saw in 1886 (p. 244).

Abdallah Abd el-Djanat el-Gabri (fl. 1900)

This name is recorded by Lange in his notebook during a visit to Kafr el-Haram in 1900.[626] The name suggests that he was a member of the prominent el-Gabri family of dealers in this village.

Abdallah Ismaïl (fl. 1920)

In 1920 during his quest for papyri on behalf of Lange, Johannes Pedersen (p. 169) visited a dealer whom he refers to as Abdallah Ismaïl (Table 6). He notes that he 'lives across from Shepheards Hotel' and the wording suggests that he sold his antiquities from his home.[627] Pedersen adds that his prices were 'significantly more reasonable' than those of Ali Abd el-Haj, whom he had also visited, and he acquired a larger group of Greek papyri from him.[628] These papyri, together with a further group purchased from Maurice Nahman at the same time, form the bulk of the Papyrus Hauniensis Collection (p. 169). In view

619. Lange, *Dagbog fra Ægypten, 1929-1930*, 219-220.
620. According to a letter by Petrie (EES Archive XVII d 47) cited by Quirke, *Hidden Hands*, 63-64, cf. also. 130, 131, 132-133 (the family relation is incorrectly indicated in the table on p. 133). A further brother of Abd es-Salam was Abd el-Gowi Abdallah.
621. A stele acquired from Abd es-Salam for the Egyptian Museum in 1887 is published by Jansen-Winkeln, *Orientalia* 67 (1998), 159-163, pl. 9.
622. Martin, in Bowman et al. (eds.), *Oxyrhynchus: A City and Its Texts*, 42.
623. Lange and Lange, *Dagbog fra Ægyptensrejsen 1899-1900*, 133-134, 135. The photoalbum includes an image (dated 30 Nov. 1899) of Jonna and four young Egyptians, one of which was a son of Abdallah. This Abdallah is perhaps the same as the Abdallah *Effendi* from whom Josef Strzygowski acquired some antiquities in March 1901; cf. Mietke et al., *Josef Strzygowski und die Berliner Museen*, 12.

624. Cf. Choat, in Schubert (ed.), *Actes du 26e Congrès international de papyrologie*, 143.
625. Letter from V. Schmidt to C. Jacobsen, dated 7 Oct. 1894 (Ny Carlsberg Glyptotek).
626. Lange, *Notebook 1899/1900*, 1.
627. Letter from J. Pedersen to H. O. Lange, dated 25 Oct. 1920 (Royal Library, Copenhagen). Cited above p. 169 in context.
628. Letter from J. Pedersen to H. O. Lange, dated 3 Dec. 1920 (Royal Library, Copenhagen).

Table 6. Family tree of the el-Shaer family in Cairo, c. 1920-2005.

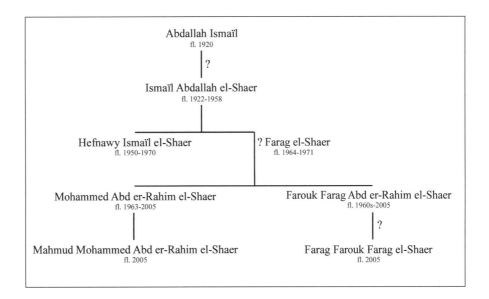

of his names, date, and address, Abdallah Ismaïl is likely to be the father of Ismaïl Abdallah el-Shaer.

Abdallah Ismaïn (*fl.* 1896/97-1900)

Dealer in Cairo who sold Petrie a group of objects in 1896/97.[629] In 1900 he and Mansur Ismaïn, perhaps a brother of his, brought Borchardt to Darb el-Nubi in the Muski quarter to inspect a fine stele.[630] He is possibly identical with Abdallah Ismaïl.

Abdallah Mohammed Mohasseb (*fl.* 1930)

Abdallah Mohammed Mohasseb was a small-time Luxor dealer. In order to gain Lange's attention, he showed him three business cards inscribed for Carl Schmidt, Wilhelm Spiegelberg, and Wilhelm Schubart (p. 61). He had no shop but sold antiquities from his modest dwelling:

> a mudbrick hut with a bed, a mastaba, a chair, a fireplace in the middle of the floor, a clay container for grain, and a Zir (large water jar). There were no win-

dows, and the roof consisted of a couple of planks and straw, and you could see the blue sky right through it. Perhaps there were other rooms in the rear. I had to sit in the open doorway to see the things which he placed on the mastaba one by one. It was all rubbish without any interest; a bronze bowl, for which he demanded £1, I got for 15 Piastre 'because you are my friend and you have visited my house'.[631]

Abdul Mossum (*fl.* 1926)

Dealer in Cairo who sold papyri to Idris Bell in 1926.[632]

Abemayor, Elie Albert (1883-1941)

Elie Albert Abemayor, 'who was said to be a Jew', belonged to an Egyptian-American family of antiquities dealers who ran one of the oldest and most expensive shops in Cairo.[633] The shop was founded by his father

629. Cf. Quirke, *Hidden Hands*, 131 ('Abdullah Smain').
630. Borchardt diary, Sept. 1899 - Jan. 1900, entry 3 Jan. 1900 (Swiss Institute, Cairo; transcript kindly provided by Cornelius von Pilgrim, 21 Jan. 2015).

631. Lange, *Dagbog fra Ægypten, 1929-1930*, 195-196.
632. Emmel, 'The Yale Papyrus Collection. Catalog Introduction', 1993, with additions by R. Duttenhofer 1996, available on-line http://www.library.yale.edu/ beinecke/brblsear/ aboutpap.htm (accessed 24 July 2012).
633. Bierbrier, *Who was Who in Egyptology*, 4th edition, 3. Note, however, that the Abemayor shop was not ranked among the more important shops in the Baedeker guide until the last

Michel Abemayor in 1888 and was later run by Elie Albert and his brother Joseph, before it passed to his son, Michel E. Abemayor (1912-1975). The stall was originally located in 9 Sharia Kamel just across from Shepheard's Hotel and later moved around the corner to the side alley of Haret el-Zahar.[634] The son, Michel E. Abemayor, left Egypt for the United States after the Second World War and established a new shop on Madison Avenue in New York.

The family actively acquired objects from private collections, obtaining most of that belonging to Tigrane *Pasha* d'Abro (d. 1904) and also attending the MacGregor and Hearst auctions in 1922 and 1939 (p. 130). Lange visited Albert Abemayor in 1929, but bought nothing from him, despite the quality of his objects:

> He displayed one item after the other at quite fantastic prices. There were excellent objects, which one would really have desired, but the prices were quite impossibly high, clearly aimed at American millionaires staying at Shepheard's Hotel. Even if the prices could be halved, I would not be able to close a deal on these objects.[635]

Abu Bakr esh-Sheikh (*fl.* 1928)

Antiquities dealer based at Giza, presumably Kafr el-Haram.[636]

Abu Gamb (*fl.* 1883- d. 1890)

Abu Gamb was a neighbour of Ali Kamuri at Sheikh Abd el-Qurna and conducted excavations with his son (p. 197).[637] Wilbour frequently bought antiquities from him. In 1890 he was mugged and killed on his way to Qena with antiquities.

Abu Lifa (*fl.* 1888)

Dealer at Durunka, located a few kilometers south of the Assiut necropolis; Wilbour provides a curious story about him:

> At Dronkah, Omar [sc. Wilbour's donkey boy] tells me, lives Aboo Leefa, who is the anteekeh man of his region and has been in prison for it, which seems to add to a man's reputation. He is not afraid o' nights because he has a ring, which he does not put on in the day time, and which makes his heart like iron. He knows all the tombs and all the ancient and terrible places, for he has a book from his father which has maps of them all. Aboo Leefa says he has a golden chicken (farrooga) for which he will take a thousand guineas; when one asks to see it, he says: 'Show me the money first.' Omar seems a little skeptical about the chicken.[638]

Abu Saud (*fl.* 1880-1905)

The son of Ali Gabri, Abu Saud of Kafr el-Haram (Table 3) followed in his father's footsteps and assisted Petrie during his excavations at Giza (1880-81) and Tanis (1883-84), while in 1905 he is recorded as dealing in antiquities.[639]

Abu Zeïd Abdallah Soudani (*fl.* 1923)

A minor dealer at Medinet Habu who mainly sold fakes, according to B. Bruyère.[640]

English edition published in 1929 (p. 287).

634. Information from Howard Carter's address book; Reeves, in Goring, Reeves, and Ruffle (eds.), *FsAldred*, 248. The letterhead of a letter to H. R. Hall of the British Museum, dated 14 Feb. 1930, reads 'E. A. Abemayor', 'Antiquaire en face l'entrée du Shepheard's Hôtel, Rue Kamel', 'Maison fondée en 1888', 'Grand choix des antiquités egyptiennes, grecques, romains', 'Scharabées pour collections, Amulette porcelaine et bronze, Monnaies et médailles, or, argent et bronze pour collection et des Bijoux Ancient', 'Antiquaire & frand choix d'article chinois'. A small collection of objects acquired from Elie Albert and Joseph Abemayor in 1938 is now in Baroda Museum and Picture Gallery in India: Bresciani and Betrò, *Egypt in India*, 250-261.

635. Lange, *Dagbog fra Ægypten, 1929-1930*, 129.

636. von Briskorn, *Zur Sammlungsgeschichte afrikanischer Ethnographica im Übersee-Museum Bremen 1841-1945*, 292.

637. Cf. Capart (ed.), *Letters of Charles Edwin Wilbour*, 593 (index).

638. Cf. Capart (ed.), *Letters of Charles Edwin Wilbour*, 493.

639. Quirke, *Hidden Hands*, passim.

640. Diary entry dated 30 Jan. 1923; http://www.ifao.egnet.net/bases/archives/bruyere/ (accessed 11 Sept. 2013).

Agaibi Makarios (fl. 1930-1936)[641]

A Coptic dealer in Medinet el-Fayum. He was visited in 1930 by Friedrich Zucker who was seeking papyri on behalf of the Papyrus Hauniensis Collection. Zucker reported to Carsten Høeg:

> Ich kaufte eine unversehrt erhaltene byzantinische Urkunde grösseren Umfangs und wählte ausserdem aus einer grossen Zahl von Fragmenten einige aus, die mir nicht unwichtig zu sein schienen, darunter ein lateinisches und ein paar zusammenhörige griechische literarische. Die unmässige Preisforderung von 200 £.E. drückte ich auf 40 £.E. herab. Der Verkäufer versprach mir, mich nach meiner Rückkehr in Cairo aufzusuchen, und stellte mir ein Angebot besonders wertvoller Papyri in Aussicht. In der Tat erschien er am 20. Sept. in meiner Wohnung und brachte einen anderen Händler, Shâkir Farag aus Benisuwêf, mit, mit dem er vermutlich durch Kompagnie-Geschäfte verbunden ist. Über die Papyri, die mir dieser Shâkir Farag vorlegte und deren Preis meinen Kredit überstieg, berichte ich in Anlage a) zu diesem Schreiben mit einem Vorschlag für etwaige Erwerbung.[642]

He is presumably identical with the Fayum dealer 'Izabi' from whom the Yale Papyrus Collection acquired a number of papyri in 1931,[643] and was still active in 1936 when he sold a small alabaster coffin to the Cairo Museum.[644]

Ahmed Abd er-Rahim (fl. 1929)

Ahmed Abd er-Rahim had an antiquities shop at Sharia el-Lukanda in Luxor and was included in the Baedeker guide of 1929.[645]

Ahmed Abdallah (fl. 1881-1890)

Antiquities dealer from Salmiya (just north of Nag Hammadi); Wilbour met him in 1888 when he came south to Luxor to do business.[646]

Ahmed Ali (fl. 1904)

Son of Ali Murad, q.v.

Ahmed Molattam (fl. c. 1922)

Brother of Sayed Molattam, q.v.

Ahmed Effendi Mustafa Ayat (fl. 1881-1902)

Ahmed Mustafa (Table 4) was a younger son of Mustafa Aga Ayat and succeeded him as consular agent for Britain and Russia (1887-1902).[647] He had been educated by Lady Duff-Gordon and was said to speak excellent English.[648] Wilbour reported in 1881 that he was the secret business partner and protector of Mohammed Mohasseb.[649]

Ahmed Yussuf (fl. 1889-1899)

Antiquities dealer at Luxor; entered a partnership with the dealer Khaled in 1889.[650] He was still active in October 1899 when Borchardt records visiting him.[651] He might be identical with – or related to – a dealer who had a shop opposite the British consular agent at

641. His names are also cited as Aqaibi and Maqarûs/Maqarius.
642. Letter from F. Zucker to C. Høeg, dated 2 Oct. 1930 (Papyrus Hauniensis Collection). Cited in toto by Bülow-Jacobsen, Aegis 12 (2012), 36-40, cf. p. 36.
643. Emmel, 'The Yale Papyrus Collection. Catalog Introduction', 1993, with additions by R. Duttenhofer 1996, available on-line http://www.library.yale.edu/ beinecke/brblsear/aboutpap.htm (accessed 24 July 2012).
644. Cairo Museum, Journal d'entrée, s.v. JE 66573A.
645. Baedeker, Egypt and the Sûdân, 8th edition, 268.

646. Cf. Capart (ed.), Letters of Charles Edwin Wilbour, 497.
647. Cf. Capart (ed.), Letters of Charles Edwin Wilbour, 48. On 22 Dec. 1897 Ahmed Effendi was visited by the Maharajah Sayaji Rao III at Luxor and presented him with a small faience figure of Thoth, and it may well have been from him that the Maharajah acquired two stelae and a relief on that same day: Bresciani and Betrò, Egypt in India, 68, 255.
648. Edwards, A Thousand Miles up the Nile, 2nd edition, 455; cf. Capart (ed.), Letters of Charles Edwin Wilbour, 47.
649. Cf. Capart (ed.), Letters of Charles Edwin Wilbour, 48.
650. Cf. Capart (ed.), Letters of Charles Edwin Wilbour, 508.
651. Borchardt diary, Sept. 1899 - Jan. 1900, entry 13 Oct. 1899 (Swiss Institute, Kairo; transcript kindly provided by Cornelius von Pilgrim, 21 Jan. 2015).

SCI.DAN.H. 4 · 8

Luxor and whose name Petrie recorded as 'Yusef Ahmed (?)' with a query in 1893; presumably Petrie had the name second-hand and was unsure about its correct form.

Albert Tawdros (*fl.* 1963 - d. 1978)

Albert Tawdros [sc. Todros] was a grandson of Girgis Gabrial, and presumably the son of Todros Girgis Gabrial; he took over the family shop in Sharia el-Lukanda near the Luxor Hotel.[652]

Ahmed 'the Crazy' (*fl.* 1887-1888)

An obscure dealer at Hu. The nick name 'the crazy' (Arabic *magnoon*) was coined by Wilbour because he had refused to sell him a stela.[653]

Ali Abd el-Haj el-Gabri, *aka* Ali el-Arabi (c. 1840-1932)

Ali Abd el-Haj el-Gabri (Fig. 128) was one of the two main dealers at Kafr el-Haram. He was mostly referred to simply as 'Ali in Giza' or as 'Ali el-Arabi' by his customers; the latter should be understood as 'Ali the Bedouin' and refers to his ethnicity and by implication – like 'Ali in Giza' – to his residency in the Bedouin village of Kafr el-Haram.[654]

Ali Abd el-Haj was the former business partner and later competitor with the other main dealer at Kafr el-Haram, Farag Ismaïn, and for many years the two controlled much of the antiquities trade. They are described as the 'Magi o Cerberi' of Kafr el-Haram in relation to a visit in 1903, suggesting something of

their importance in the market, while Erman refers to them – with a hint of sarcasm? – as 'das edlen Paares Ali und Farag in Gizeh.'[655] Farag had earlier, in the 1880s, been the most important Arab dealer in Egypt, but by 1897 Petrie refers to Ali as 'the main dealer at Gizeh'.[656] Lange similarly describes him, a couple of years later, as 'the largest Arabic antiquities dealer', who 'in truth had a whole museum, but also extortionate prices'; 'a very rich man ... his prices are utterly ludicrous, but he does have the nicest things.'[657] Farag, for his part, is said to run 'the second largest antiquities shop here in Egypt'. The break between the two came about in 1896 according to a contemporary letter by Murch to Budge:

> I think I told you in a previous letter that Ferag and Ali have parted company. They became such unprincipled and brazen-faced thieves that they could not refrain from robbing each other. The result is they can no longer do business together ...[658]

In an account contemporary with Lange's, Grenfell and Hunt refer – more discreetly, without providing names – to Farag as 'the ablest and most enterprising of the Gizeh dealers' and to Ali, with whom earlier collaborated, as 'his now more ambitious and success-

652. Ehlebracht, *Haltet die Pyramiden fest!*, 305, 333. Several antiquities acquired from Albert Tawdros by J. J. Clère in 1963-64 were sold by Pierre Bergé & Associates, Auction of 26 Nov. 2013, lots 17, 21-22; cf. www.pba-auctions.com (accessed 5 Dec. 2013), lot 21 realizing €170,000; cf. also on-line sales-catalogue *Jacques Jean Clère* [www.kunicki.eu], 4, 7, 14, which cites notes by Clère on his acquisitions.

653. Cf. Capart (ed.), *Letters of Charles Edwin Wilbour*, 490.

654. He is also, less commonly, referred to Ali el-Bedawi which similarly means 'Ali the Bedouin'.

655. Breccia, *Aegyptus* 15 (1935), 258, who also notes (p. 260) that Ali Abd el-Haj died three years before the article was written and was said to be 'nearly a hundred years old'; Erman, *Mein Werden und mein Wirken*, 213.

656. Petrie, *Journals*, December 1897, where it is noted that he had acquired from him an 'ebony negress' (UC14210) the year before; cf. Quirke's forthcoming work on Petrie as a collector. The statuette is published in Petrie, *Man* 1 (1901), 129, where it is also explicitly mentioned that he acquired the object from 'Ali Arabi', i.e. Ali Abd el-Haj; cf. also Petrie, *Seventy Years in Archaeology*, 167.

657. Lange and Lange, *Dagbog fra Ægyptensrejsen 1899-1900*, 142, 156, 783.

658. Letter from C. Murch to E. A. W. Budge, dated 23 May 1896, cited by Ismail, *Wallis Budge*, 294. The latter is, in our view, mistaken in identifying Ali with Ali Farag (*ibid.*, 296); the latter is more likely a son of Farag Ismaïn. The date for the break given by Murch agrees with the fact that Farag and Ali are still described as partners in letters from V. Schmidt to C. Jacobson, dated 6-8 and 27 Oct. 1894 (Ny Carlsberg Glyptotek).

Fig. 128. Ali Abd el-Haj el-Gabri (1840-1932), often referred
to as 'Ali in Giza' or as 'Ali el-
Arabi'. He is here seen seated
in a studio photograph from
1907 by P. Dittrich, Cairo,
together with Charles Lang
Freer and his companion, Dr.
Frederick W. Mann. Standing
between Ali and Freer is Ali's
son Ibrahim Ali who spoke
English very well and acted
as Freer's guide. Courtesy of
the Smithsonian Institution,
Washington D.C.

ful rival'.[659] Ali is indeed known to have sold numerous high-quality objects, including important papyri,
to western Egyptologists from the late 1880s onwards,
and he is even recorded as selling royal statuary from

Memphis.[660] He is perhaps best known for his sale of

659. Grenfell, Hunt, and Hogarth, *Fayûm Towns and Their Papyri*,
18.

660. Bolshakov, *Studies on Old Kingdom Reliefs*, 5-6 (Ali Abd
el-Haj); cf. also Mazza, in Schubert (ed.), *Actes du 26e Congrès
international de papyrologie*, 506 (where he is referred to as 'Schech
Aly Abdelhay el Gabri'). Ali Abd el-Haj selling papyri to G.
Vitelli in 1903: Breccia, *Aegyptus* 15 (1935), 260.

the now famous 'Freer Biblical Manuscripts', and Charles Lang Freer rewarded both Ali and his sons Ibrahim Ali and Mohammed Ali with gold watches for the service they rendered him in Egypt (p. 63).[661]

Valdemar Schmidt first visited Ali at Kafr el-Haram in 1892 and provides the following brief description in his memoirs:

> In the village of Giza lived an Arab dealer called Ali, who was the only one of the Arab dealers I met who was somewhat Europeanised. He too had no official licence to sell antiquities, and he therefore dealt only with people he knew from previous visits.[662]

Lange would similarly visit Ali at his home in Kafr el-Haram on several occasions during his first stay in Egypt, 1899-1900.[663] According to Breccia, his house was located centrally in the village, meaning that the route to it was labyrinthine and difficult to manoeuvre – it is described as providing 'un ambiente di puro carattere orientale'. It was relatively big (two storeys) and included an open courtyard and an imposing façade with a great wooden door facing the street; access was not easily gained by the casual visitor.[664] Lange describes Ali as an 'old Bedouin' who was 'a very nice old gentleman who spoke no English', and

Jonna adds that he 'looks like an old fox when he laughs'.[665]

Erman provides the following description of him in his autobiography:

> Ali, der wie ein alter polnischer Jude aussah, (...) Er war ein intelligenter Mann und hatte sich zum Mittelpunkte des Antikenhandels gemacht; wo immer Ausgrabungen im Gange waren oder wo sonst Altertümer zutage traten, da waren auch seine Spione und Diebe dabei, und es geschah wohl, daß man bei Ali nachher kaufte, was in der eigenen Grabung gestohlen war. Er selbst konnte würdevoll aussehen, wenn er den Käufer in seinem großen Hause in Gizeh emfing und ihn mit Kaffe mit Rosenwasser bewirtete, aber der gemeine Schacherer kam dann doch heraus, und es tat der Freundschaft auch keinen Abbruch, wenn man ihn einmal einen Lügner nannte. Wir haben damals und später gute Geschäfte mit ihm gemacht und besonders auch griechische Papyrus von ihm gekauft.[666]

Ali was also visited several times by Johannes Pedersen in 1920 in his quest for papyri on behalf of Lange (p. 170). In one letter he complained bitterly about his prices.

> Ali al Arabi ... had some very beautiful rolls, but he demanded £500 for three of them and two small pages! Naturally this price could be lowered considerably, but Edgar told me that Grenfell made no acquisitions from him last year because he was too expensive. For a single one of the fragmentary pages he demanded £30.[667]

In another letter, he complained about the fact that Ali demanded an outrageous price for some sculptures and at the same time prevented him from obtaining photographs of them which might be sent to Copenhagen for evaluation. Naturally such behaviour should have raised some suspicion about their authenticity.

---

661. Cf. Gunter, *A Collector's Journey*, 97-98 et passim, and Clarke, in Hurtado (ed.), *The Freer Biblical Manuscripts*, 28-29 et passim. Ali Abd el-Haj el-Gabri was also among the dealers frequented by Carl Schmidt in his search for papyri; cf., e.g., Meyer, *Griechische Texte aus Ägypten*, Berlin, 1916, iii.

662. Schmidt, *Af et Langt Livs Historie*, 90. Schmidt wrote his memoirs in his late 80s, relying on his memory alone, and there are many minor inconsistencies. As an example, licences were not in fact required in 1892, but when they were introduced 20 years later, Ali Abd el-Haj was not given a licence since he did not have a shop in Cairo proper (p. 137).

663. It might have been on this occasion that Lange acquired the small fragment of Papyrus Spiegelberg now in the Papyrus Carlsberg Collection, since it was the same Ali who sold the bulk of the papyrus to Wilhelm Spiegelberg a few years later: Ryholt, in Dodson, Johnson, and Monkhouse (eds.), *Fs Tait*, 271-278.

664. Breccia, *Aegyptus* 15 (1935), 259. We are grateful to Luigi Prada for this reference.

665. Lange and Lange, *Dagbog fra Ægyptensrejsen 1899-1900*, 143-144, cf. also p. 156.

666. Erman, *Mein Werden und mein Wirken*, 213.

667. Letter from J. Pedersen to H. O. Lange, dated 25 Oct. 1920 (Royal Library, Copenhagen). Cited above p. 170 in context.

Ali al Arabi had ~~some~~ [sic] two human portrait busts of which one in Eitrem's judgement was very interesting. He would sell the two & a third, in Eitrem's opinion uninteresting, statue, for £5,000! I sought to have them photographed, but came twice in vain & had to content myself with poor excuses.[668]

Nearly ten years later, in 1929, Wilhelm Schubart purchased a number of Greek papyri from Ali at the more reasonable price of £E 80 for the Papyrus Hauniensis Collection.[669] Lange mentions Ali only in passing in connection with his own, second stay in Egypt, 1929-1930. He was then reputedly in his nineties and died soon after.

From a family tree drawn up by Petrie in 1887, we learn that Ali Abd el-Haj (Table 3) was the paternal cousin of Ali Gabri and also related to the brothers Soliman and Ibrahim Abd es-Samad.[670] His own two sons, Mohammed Ali and Ibrahim Ali, were also involved in the antiquities trade, as was an unnamed grandson whose father is not identified. The grandson was a small child in 1903 and then a grown man in 1935, and he continued the family business with a shop in front of Shepheard's Hotel. He was said to have developed European tastes and habits (perhaps from a stay in Paris), with the associated costs that this implies; he seems to have spent a considerable proportion of his inheritance on this lifestyle, and even had a portrait of himself in the shop, but he carried a more limited stock than his father and grandfather.[671] The description would suit Mohammed M. el-Gabri in view of his name, his date, and the location of his shop by Shepheard's Hotel. Zaki Mahmud Abd es-Samad claimed that Ali was his grandfather. Lange doubted this was literally true: '"Grandfather" probably only means an old uncle'.[672] This assumption was

correct; Ali was in fact a cousin of Zaki's great-grandfather. Another cousin of Ali's, Abdallah, served as a guide to Lange (p. 188).

Ali el-Arabi

Another name for Ali Abd el-Haj el-Gabri, q.v.

Ali Farag (fl. 1896)

An 'antika-dealer at Giza [sc. Kafr el-Haram]' who sold a Greek papyrus inscribed with poems of Bacchylides which Budge acquired for the British Museum in 1896 in bitter competition with Fraser, Naville, Petrie, and Sayce, and which had to be smuggled out of Egypt.[673] He is possibly identical with the unnamed son of Farag Ismaïn (q.v.) whom Lange visited in 1890.

Ali Gabri (I) (1833/34-1904)[674]

Ali Gabri (Table 3; Fig. 129) of Kafr el-Haram was born c. 1834 according to the family tree drawn up by Petrie in 1887.[675] He had allegedly worked as a basket carrier at the age of just four years for Howard Vyse in 1837; he was Piazzi Smyth's assistant in 1864 and Petrie's in 1880-82 during their researches on the Giza pyramids and later at Tanis.[676] Ali was also an active dealer and Petrie notes in 1880 that he used a tomb in the cliffs behind the village as storage for his antiqui-

668. Letter from J. Pedersen to H. O. Lange, dated 3 Dec. 1920 (Royal Library, Copenhagen). For Samson Eitrem, cf. p.170 above.
669. Bülow-Jacobsen, *Aegis* 12 (2012), 22.
670. Quirke, *Hidden Hands*, 132-134.
671. Breccia, *Aegyptus* 15 (1935), 260-1.
672. Lange, *Dagbog fra Ægypten, 1929-1930*, 34.

673. Ismail, *Wallis Budge*, 296-301; cf. also Sayce, *Reminiscences*, 334; Drower, *Letters from the Desert*, 95. That same year Pierre Jouguet copied a Greek inscription written on a plaque of white marble in the possession of the same Ali: Jouguet, *Bulletin de correspondance hellénique* 20 (1896), 398-399.
674. His surname is spelled variously Gabri and Jabri by Petrie, Gabree by Wilbour, and Dobree by Piazzi Smyth.
675. Cf. Quirke, *Hidden Hands*, 132-134; according to the family tree, Ali Gabri was 53 years old in 1887. Petrie, *The Pyramids and Temples of Gizeh*, 6, states that Ali Gabri was four years old in 1837. He died in December 1904.
676. Petrie, *Seventy Years in Archaeology*, 20, 21, 42; Quirke, *Hidden Hands*, passim. Cf. also Drower, *Flinders Petrie*, 37, 94; idem, *Letters from the Desert*, 13-14, 15, 50-51.

Fig. 129. Ali Gabri (I) of Kafr el-Haram. Detail of photograph by Petrie from 1881, inscribed 'The faithful Ali. Gizeh.' Petrie Album 7, no. 386. Courtesy of The Griffith Institute, University of Oxford.

Fig. 130. *Hajji* Ali Gabri (II), as a child, with his father Ali Gabri (I). Photograph from the 1890s published by Ward, *Pyramids and Progress*, 3.

ties.[677] He was the paternal uncle of the brothers Soliman and Ibrahim Abd es-Samad at Kafr el-Haram, the first cousin of Ali Abd el-Haj, and the father of Abu Saud and *Hajji* Ali Gabri. He may also have been related to Farag Ismaïn with whom he had – at least at one point – some form of partnership in the antiquities trade.[678]

Hajji Ali Gabri (II) (*fl.* 1907-9)

Hajji Ali Gabri (Table 3; fig. 130) was a younger son of Ali Gabri, born late in his life.[679] In 1909, he sold a

valuable collection of antiquities, including a root-emerald statue of an official and a gold mask, to the British Museum for the sum of £1,300 through Budge and after two years of negotiation.[680] That same year he guided the brothers John and Morton Edgar around the Great Pyramid, and he features in a series of photographs shot by them.[681]

Ali Halabata (*fl.* 1907)

Dealer at Qena who sold papyri to the German papyrus cartel.[682]

677. Quirke, *Hidden Hands*, 271/276; cf. also p. 60 for Ali Gabri's role as an antiquities dealer.
678. Cf. Capart (ed.), *Letters of Charles Edwin Wilbour*, 80, 81, 416.
679. In a photograph of *Hajji* Ali Gabri and his father from the 1890s, he appears to be less than ten years old; cf. Ward, *Pyramids and Progress*, 3.

680. Ismail, *Wallis Budge*, 385-386.
681. Edgar and Edgar, *The Great Pyramid Passages and Chambers*, 103, 107, 113, 118, 149, 169, 300, pl. 29, 55, 56, 64, 65, 102.
682. Papyrus und Ostraka Projekt - Halle, Jena, Leipzig

Ali Jussuf (*fl.* 1930)

A dealer and forger in Luxor, Ali Jussuf occurs in the 1929-1930 diary only peripherally, where he is said to be an associate of the dealer Schafi; he is characterised as 'the proficient forger', perhaps suggesting a certain level of notoriety.[683]

Ali Kamuri (*fl.* 1842-1888)

Ali Kamuri, described by Rhind as 'the arch-forger at Thebes' and by Wilbour as 'the best maker of false things', lived at Sheikh Abd el-Qurna. He was a (silver?) smith who specialised in the manufacture and sale of fake scarabs. Interestingly, some of these were sold to Nubians, rather than to tourists, who wore them as amulets; when encountered by Westerners in this setting (i.e. worn by Nubians) they were thus rarely suspected of being forgeries. He was elaborate in his deceptions, which included the forging of hieroglyphic inscriptions with some skill: on one occasion he explained how he had copied a genuine text from Medinet Habu, but substituted a royal name in the cartouche with a rarer one in order to get a better price.[684] He gave Wilbour 'a very pretty little statue, the finest piece of modern Egyptian art I have yet seen', and Wilbour later returned the gesture by sending the old man a pair of spectacles from Cairo; when he met him again the following year, he noted with satisfaction 'the spectacles I sent him have enabled him to do some very good work', i.e. producing further fakes. Wilbour was not the only Westerner to 'aid' Kamuri in his forgeries; one foreigner had furnished Ali ... with broken penknives and other appliances to aid his already manifested talent, in the somewhat fantastic hope of flooding the local marked with 'curiosities', and so saving the monuments from being laid under contribution. The patron might have been surprised had he learned the growing aptitude of the protégé ...[685]

Ali Kamuri's son (no name given) and their neighbour Abu Gamb conducted some legal excavations at Thebes in the 1880s, since Wilbour mentions that they went to divide their finds with Maspero.

Sheikh Ali Ledid (*fl.* 1882-1891)

The brothers *Sheikh* Ali Ledid, Mahmud Ledid, and Mohammed Ledid, were antiquities dealers based in Akhmim, Qena, and Luxor, while at one point *Sheikh* Ali also had a number of antiquities for sale that were kept in a house at Coptos.[686] *Sheikh* Ali's house at Luxor was located inside the Great Court of Ramesses II of the Luxor Temple and was demolished in 1886.[687] That same year Wilbour saw 'near a hundred mummies' in his house at Akhmim; 'he had three rooms full'. He was rumoured to be involved in the production of fake antiquities at Luxor.

Ali Mahmud (*fl.* 1928-1929)

Dealer at el-Bahnasa (ancient Oxyrhynchus) who sold several batches of papyri to Leiv Amundsen for the Oslo Papyrus Collection in 1928-1929.[688]

on-line (http://papyri.uni-leipzig.de, s.v. Ali Halabata; accessed 7 Dec. 2013).

683. Lange, *Dagbog fra Ægypten, 1929-1930*, 189.

684. Rhind, *Thebes, Its Tombs and their Tenants*, 251-253 (called Ali Qamooni); Wilbour letters (called Aly Qamoory/Kamoory), cf. Capart (ed.), *Letters of Charles Edwin Wilbour*, 603 (index); Budge, *By Nile and Tigris* I, 114 (called Alî Kamûrî); Prime, *Boat Life in Egypt*, 216 (called Achmet-el-Kamouri, but Achmet is very likely a slip of the pen for Ali, given the matching description, unless a relative of his).

685. Rhind, *Thebes, Its Tombs and their Tenants*, 254-255.

686. Cf. Capart (ed.), *Letters of Charles Edwin Wilbour*, III, 241, 272, 298, 349, 456, 461, 496, 501, 584. For Mahmud Ledid, see further Louis, in Bosson and Boud'hors (eds.), *Actes du huitième congrès international d'études coptes* I, 106; David, *Gaston Maspero*, 132.

687. David, *Gaston Maspero*, 134, 137, 142.

688. Anonymous, 'Acquisition history of the Oslo Papyrus Collection', available on-line http://ub-fmserver.uio.no/Acquisition.html (accessed 30 July 2012).

Ali Murad (fl. 1870-1902)

Antiquities dealer based in Luxor and the US consular agent at Luxor, succeeding Mustafa Aga in 1871.[689] A visitor in 1875 describes him as 'a well-featured, bronze-complexioned Arab of good family (I think of the Ababdehs), whose brother is Sheykh of a tribe at Karnak. He cannot speak English, but he has a pleasanter smile than any other American consul I know.'[690] He was involved in the affair of the famous Deir el-Bahri royal cache, where he apparently reported the Abd er-Rasul brothers to the Antiquities Service.[691] It was rumoured that he financed the production of fake antiquities by a brother of his at Sheikh Abd el-Qurna.[692] His business was carried on by his son Ahmed Ali (fl. 1904).[693]

Ali Ramadan (fl. 1926)

Antiquities dealer in Cairo who is described by Borchardt as a 'kleine Händler'.[694]

Anawati, Alfred and Edouard C. (fl. 1940s)

The brothers Alfred and Edouard C. Anawati ran an antiquities shop named 'Khan Khalil' at 32-34 Fouad I Street (now Sharia el-Horreya) in Alexandria under antiquities license no. 117; they were involved in the sale of the Nag Hammadi codices.[695]

Andalaft, Dimitri (fl. around 1906/09)

Dimitri Andalaft, with a prominent shop in Khan el-Khalili, dealt broadly in oriental wares, both ancient and modern.[696]

Andreas Girgis (fl. 1920)

Dealer at Medinet el-Fayum who sold papyri to Francis Kelsey in 1920, a Copt to judge by his name.[697]

Askren, David Leslie (1875-1939)[698]

American physician specialized in gynaecology (Fig. 131). He went to Egypt in 1899 as a medical missionary and practiced at the United Presbyterian Hospital in Assiut for a few years before settling in Medinet el-Fayum, at Sharia Sekka el-Hadid el-Gharbi, where he practiced until his death. He got involved in the antiquities trade soon after his arrival in the Fayum through *fellahin* patients of his engaged in *sebakh* digging and the discovery of papyri. Over the years he became one of the central providers of papyri for American collections, and with his intimate knowledge of the Fayum and activities in the region, he assisted buyers such as Francis Kelsey and Idris Bell in travelling around the local villages in the search for papyri. He also participated in the American excavations at Karanis and Soknopaiou Nesos.

Aslanian, Oxan (1887-1968)

Aslanian was perhaps the most infamous forger of Egyptian antiquities in the history of Egyptology. His

689. For his date of appointment, see United States Department of State, *Register of the Department of State 1893*, 40. Ali Murad is mentioned repeatedly in the Wilbour letters edited by Capart (ed.), *Letters of Charles Edwin Wilbour*, 594 (index); cf. further David, *Gaston Maspero*, 175, 179.
690. Warner, *My Winter on the Nile*, 195-196. Also Peters, *Die Klimatischen Winterkurorte Egyptens*, 40, notes that he only spoke Arabic.
691. Wilson, *Signs & Wonders Upon Pharaoh*, 83-84.
692. Cf. Capart (ed.), *Letters of Charles Edwin Wilbour*, 146.
693. Legrain, *ASAE* 6 (1905), 130.
694. von Briskorn, *Zur Sammlungsgeschichte afrikanischer Ethnographica im Übersee-Museum Bremen 1841-1945*, 285.
695. Robinson, in Barc (ed.), *Colloque international sur les textes de Nag Hammadi*, 49; idem, *The Facsimile Edition of the Nag Hammadi Codices*, 7; idem, *The Nag Hammadi Story*, 358.

696. Sladen, *Oriental Cairo*, 97-98, 99; Gunter, *A Collector's Journey*, 90, 152, n. 19. His name is variously spelled Andalaft and Andalft.
697. Pedley, *The Life and Work of Francis Willey Kelsey*, 271.
698. Pedley, *The Life and Work of Francis Willey Kelsey*, passim; Clarke, in Hurtado (ed.), *The Freer Biblical Manuscripts*, 33-34; Boak, *The Quarterly Review* 66, no. 10 (1959-1960), 35-42; Blattner (ed.), *Le mondain égyptien: The Egyptian Who's Who 1939*, 167; obituary in *Bedford Times-Press*, 9 Feb. 1939. Early trade with papyri: cf. Willis, *BASP* 25 (1988), 99.

life and career were studied recently by J.-J. Fiechter,[699] and apart from some basic facts we only provide information from Lange's 1929-1930 travel diary where it adds to or corroborates the presentation given by Fiechter. Aslanian is best known to Egyptologists as 'The Berlin Master', the very successful forger of Egyptian antiquities who specialised in Old Kingdom and Amarna Period art. Born in Thessaloniki (Salonica) in Greece to Armenian parents, he had lived in both Syria and Egypt before settling in Berlin just after the First World War (c. 1920); there he remained until 1947, when he moved on to Hamburg and then finally to Munich (where he died in 1968). His extended family had been involved in the antiquities trade in Egypt for some time, and when Lange first visited Egypt in 1899-1900, Aslanian was working for his uncle Kalebdijan in his Cairo shop, where he initially seems to have been responsible for restorations of, and perhaps also the sale of, genuine artefacts.[700] Although Lange did not meet him on that occasion, he met him during the second visit in 1929-1930, when he was very impressed by the objects Aslanian had for sale and recommended some for the Ny Carlsberg Glyptotek to buy.[701] His wife Jonna was uncharacteristically keen on some of the minor objects Aslanian had for sale, and quickly closed a deal with him; she paid 'a high price, but not too high', according to Lange, who notes his 'great surprise' at the transaction; Jonna herself was 'very proud' of her acquisition.[702] Lange seems to have been unaware of Aslanian's identity as the Armenian master forger,

Fig. 131. Dr. David Askren with his family at his home in Medinet el-Fayum where he practiced until his death in 1939. Courtesy of the Kelsey Museum of Archaeology, University of Michigan.

although he had probably seen some of his products: two of his pieces had been bought in good faith by the Ny Carlsberg Glyptotek in 1919 and 1927.[703] Even in later years he need not have been aware of whom he had met, as Egyptologists frequently avoided referring to Aslanian by name, using circumlocutions like 'that talented Armenian', even in letters written to close friends: Ludwig Borchardt, for example, wrote to Lange on 6 April 1931 (so not long after Lange's

---

699. Fiechter, *Faux et faussaires en art égyptien*, 29-44; idem, *Egyptian Fakes*, 92-118; cf. Herzer, *Objets* 4-5 (1971), 39-46.

700. Fiechter, *Faux et faussaires en art égyptien*, 30 ; idem, *Egyptian Fakes*, 72.

701. Lange, *Dagbog fra Ægypten, 1929-1930*, 65; the objects he recommended for the Museum were 'a head from Tell el-Amarna (in relief) ... a lovely little hand of sandstone, holding a dove; it ends in a tap, whereby it would have been attached to a statue. Also a nice relief in granite with a representation of the god Amun. These four pieces I will recommend for the Glyptotek to buy; but the price will be about 50.000 Danish crowns'. None of these were bought by the Museum.

702. Lange, *Dagbog fra Ægypten, 1929-1930*, 67.

---

703. Glyptotek inv. no. ÆIN 1536 and 1655; Fiechter, *Faux et faussaires en art égyptien*, 126-127 (no. I.10, limestone head of a woman, Old Kingdom style), 133-134 (no. I.22, limestone head of a princess, Amarna style).

return from Egypt) about his work in tracking down forgers and their products in Egypt and beyond, and he explicitly refused to disclose names: 'Nomina sunt odiosa'.[704]

Lange and his wife spent well over three hours in the company of Aslanian, whom they appear to have found a charming conversationalist, and Lange subsequently wrote down a lengthy description of him in his diary:

> A man like this Armenian lives a rather peculiar life. Every summer he comes to Egypt already in the month of May; then he travels around the Nile valley, visiting the villages that are close to the most important archaeological sites, seeing his old contacts among the Fellaheen and making new contacts, paying in cash whatever he buys, and then has to transport frail objects that cannot withstand rough handling, by train or by automobile; this year he brought a piece from Mallawi to Cairo in a car; it was a journey of about 83 Danish miles [sc. 830 km]. He has his own way of getting objects out of the country, without the Museum stopping them. This summer he was bedridden with a fever in the strong heat. Occasionally it happens that his cash reserves are inadequate to buy the best objects; then he joins up with some business man or other, who then becomes part owner of the object in question, and they agree on a reserve price together. When he buys a fragment from a farmer he gives him an advance on the

remaining [i.e. missing] parts which he instructs him to look for, and sometimes it appears some 2-3 years down the line. He has numerous such fragments lying around and waiting to be joined. So far he has not been selling to other museums than Berlin. He always presents his objects to Schäfer, so that he can buy whatever he wants first.[705] Then he offers them to antiquities dealers but not to collectors, the reason being that he needs money for his next round of purchases which necessitates a quick turn-over. I have implored him to enter into a direct relationship with the Glyptotek, which could benefit greatly therefrom, and the Glyptotek is lacking in good connections for Egyptian objects.[706]

It is not clear to what extent the objects Aslanian presented to Lange were fakes or genuine antiquities; Lange was no novice on the antiquities market and could frequently identify forgeries when presented with them, but he was also fallible, even when the objects were from categories that were particularly well known to him, like Middle Kingdom stelae (p. 22). It does not seem unreasonable to suggest that some of Aslanian's stock may have been genuine, because it is known that Aslanian possessed genuine objects which he used as models for his forgeries.[707] The description he gave Lange of his activities was presumably not entirely true, but his reputation as 'just' a forger may be somewhat inaccurate, and his contacts throughout Egypt could well have furnished him with genuine antiquities. The dealer Loukianoff (see above) told Lange that he had personally tracked down a statue for Aslanian which the latter subsequently offered for sale on the market; this confirms that he did also occasionally deal in genuine objects.[708]

704. Fiechter, *Faux et faussaires en art égyptien*, 34. As Fiechter gives no context for the quotation, we provide that here: 'Ist Frl. Mogensen [Maria Mogensen, curator at the Ny Carlsberg Glyptotek] immer noch so böse auf mich? Das täte mir sehr leid. Aber die Reinigung unserer Museen geht bei mir persönlichen Gefühlen vor. Leider muss ich sie schon wieder kränken, oder vielmehr die Glyptotek. In meinen Aufzeichnungen über Unterhaltungen mit den Fälschern steht nämlich Folgendes: "Am Dienstag, den 31.3.31, kommt A.B. (Nomina sunt odiosa) wieder ... Dabei spricht er wieder von anderen Sachen, die er früher, allein oder mit anderen zusammen gemacht habe ... An ... habe er auch einen Kopf aus grünem Stein verkauft, der gleich der alte Voldemar [sic] Schmidt für Kopenhagen erstanden habe. Die Beschreibung dieses Kopfes scheint auf den MR-Kopf mit Krone von Oberägypten in der Glyptotek zu Kopenhagen zu stimmen. Da sei das Gesicht, die Augen usw., neuzeitlich."' (letter from L. Borchardt to H. O. Lange, dated 6 Apr. 1931; original spelling and typography has been retained; Royal Library, Copenhagen).

705. The fact that Schäfer, as the Director of the Egyptian Museum in Berlin, bought a number of objects from Aslanian is well documented, as is the conflict between him and Borchardt, who thought that many of them were fakes; Fiechter, *Faux et faussaires en art égyptien*, 38-42.
706. Lange, *Dagbog fra Ægypten, 1929-1930*, 65-67.
707. Fiechter, *Faux et faussaires en art égyptien*, 34, 43.
708. Lange, *Dagbog fra Ægypten, 1929-1930*, 280: 'The statue that Aslanian had offered for sale for £2000 in the autumn had originally been found by Loukianoff in a private collection here in Cairo'. On Aslanian as possessor and dealer of genuine

Basta ('Bastra(?)') (fl. 1900)

'Bastra', whose name is followed by a question mark in Lange's diary, was a dealer living in Qena.[709] He had spotted Lange being led away by his rival dealers Girgis and Abd en-Nur at Qena (see below), and 'came running … highly jealous of his competitors'. Lange consented to seeing his wares, but was disappointed by the number of fakes:

> He and his brother dragged out one thing after another. First they brought in one fake after the other, with the most urgent insistence on their genuine nature and high value. There were large limestone stelae with long inscriptions, which were all fake but which could probably be foisted upon American tourists at an appropriate occasion. When I immediately told him that they were false he admitted it and then finally the real pieces appeared. He was obviously in need of money quickly, and could not understand that I didn't buy half his shop on the spot. A nice complete stela which he wanted 2 pounds for I offered 8 shillings for, and when I stuck to my offer I ended up getting it along with some other minor objects for a total of 12 shillings.

Lange proceeds to describe an accident he witnessed at their house (cited in context p. 131).

The name 'Bastra', as marked with a question mark, is likely a mistake either for Boutros, in which case we might be dealing with Boutros Abd el-Melek at Qena, or for Basta. The latter name is associated with another antiquities dealer from Qena, Zaki Basta, who is known to have been active from the 1940s onwards; in view of this date he could have been a son or some other relative of the dealer whom Lange met.

Bayoumi (fl. 1883)

Antiquities dealer living at Saqqara who was visited a few times by Wilbour.[710]

Bircher, André (1839-1925)[711]

Bircher (Fig. 132) was a Swiss trader and antiquities dealer in Cairo, as well as a founding member and the first president of the Swiss Club ('Cercle Suisse') in Cairo in 1894.[712] He lived with his family in a former Mameluk palace from the 14th Century, which he had acquired in the late 1870s, at Sharia esh-Sharawy el-Barany (a continuation of Sharia Bein es-Surein) in the Arab quarter north of Muski; the building has since been demolished.[713] As early as 1885 he had brought a sarcophagus 'direkt aus einer Ausgrabung' back to Switzerland (Aargau), but it is not clear whether this excavation was organised by Bircher himself.[714] Lange visited him during his first trip to Egypt in order to look at some papyri but does not mention buying anything.[715] Bircher acted as a moneylender to Bedouins at Kafr el-Haram, and would take antiquities as security; sales arranged by the owners of the objects then had to be approved by him.[716] Prior to Lange's second trip, Bircher had taken possession of the collection of a dealer called Mohammed Ali because of the latter's debts. There is little information about him in the diaries, but Lange notes initially that he (sc. Mohammed Ali) 'had some nice pieces that I would like to buy for the Museum at home, but he

antiquities, see Fiechter, *Faux et faussaires en art égyptien*, 34, 43.

709. Lange and Lange, *Dagbog fra Ægyptensrejsen 1899-1900*, 363-365.

710. Cf. Capart (ed.), *Letters of Charles Edwin Wilbour*, 194, 253 ('Bayoomi').

711. Bierbrier, *Who was Who in Egyptology*, 4th edition, 60. The short sketch of his life in Sigerist, *Schweizer in Ägypten*, 23-33, is informative but only makes a passing mention of his activities as collector and dealer of antiquities (pp. 28-29).

712. The remains of the archive of the Cercle Suisse are now kept in the Swiss Archaeological Institute in Cairo.

713. *Annuaire égyptien, administratif et commercial, 1891-1892*, 86.

714. Sigerist, *Schweizer in Ägypten*, 28.

715. Lange and Lange, *Dagbog fra Ægyptensrejsen 1899-1900*, 142-143. Prior to meeting him, Jonna thought he might be Greek. She records his name as 'Birker', but this is corrected to 'Bircher' in the index to the travel journal.

716. Lange, *Dagbog fra Ægypten, 1929-1930*, 59-60. A Middle Kingdom coffin in Leiden (inv. F 1930/6.1) appears to have been seen by Lange at Farag Ismaïn's house at Kafr prior to it being purchased by Leiden from Bircher (via L. Keimer; cf. p. 215), but it is not clear whether Bircher had taken this as security for a loan – it could also have been a straightforward sale.

Fig. 132. André Bircher. Detail of undated photograph. Courtesy of Archiv für Zeitgeschichte, Zürich.

insists on some rather meaningless prices.' As Mohammed Ali got more desperate to sell, the whole collection was eventually offered for the reasonable price of 250 pounds.[717] Borchardt visited Bircher's house for the first time on the same day as Lange, accompagnied by Mohammed Ali, and recorded in his diary (before proceeding to describe the antiquities he examined):

> Früh mit Moh. Ali Gabri zu Bircher, dort Lange getroffen. Birchers Haus besichtigt. Prachtvolle Holzdecken, gefalze, zusammengesetzte Thüren, Steinmosaiken etc. ...[718]

Bircher had died by the time of Lange's second visit in 1929-1930, and his collection was being sold off from his house. During this visit Lange describes the house as:

> one of the fine old Patrician's houses ... where his second wife lives as a widow, with a lady who is the daughter of a German professor Sickenberger and who was previously married to a Frenchman, Madame Serveux, who was in Bircher's house for 33 years. It is the latter who in the testament was charged with selling the collection, and as a sort of pension she received 10% of the income therefrom.[719]

Bircher's home and his collection is also described in a letter written by Breasted in 1919:

> The house lay in a little side street off the Muski ... It is an ancient house built some 450 years ago, with wonderful old Saracen carving and antique glass in the open work of the fretted stone windows. Here Anton (sic) Bircher has lived for nearly fifty years, conducting a little office just off the spacious court below, and carrying on there an importation business in which he has amassed a fortune. For nearly forty years he has been buying antiquities and he has an immense mass of stuff. He has an elderly woman as curator to look after it all, and after serving us oriental coffee under the afternoon light coming through the wonderful ancient glass and shimmering over a fountain in marble mosaic in the floor, he left us to go back to the office where he has spent half a century, and the lady took us around the collection. Nine tenths of the stuff is junk. Of the other tenth, he has sold off much that was valuable.[720]

Bircher's collection was said to be considerable with several thousand objects, although mostly minor ones like scarabs, amulets, faience pieces, bronzes and small terracotta figures. According to Breasted, the huge

---

717. Lange and Lange, *Dagbog fra Ægyptensrejsen 1899-1900*, 187, 654.
718. Borchardt diary, Sept. 1899 - Jan. 1900, entry 11 Dec. 1899 (Swiss Institute, Kairo; transcript kindly provided by Cornelius von Pilgrim, 21 Jan. 2015).

719. F. Serveux-Sickenberger also wrote to potential buyers using André Bircher's letterhead which reads 'André Bircher. Le Caire (Egypte). Succursale à Alexandrie.'
720. Letter from J. H. Breasted to his family, dated 14 Dec. 1919 (Oriental Institute, Chicago); edited by Larson, *Letters from James Henry Breasted*, 116.

collection contained 'over 17,000 numbers' in 1919,[721] and even if the majority were minor pieces it included exquisite examples of statuary, including an 18th Dynasty princess (Isis, daughter of Amenhotep III).[722] In fact by 1900 the collection was too big to be housed in the Mameluke palace where he lived, so he had to store some of it in a neighbouring building.[723] The sale was going slowly, partly because it was on display off the beaten track ('where the tourists never go'), and partly because the professional dealers did their best to discourage potential customers about the value and integrity of the collection.[724]

Towards the end of his stay, Lange and his wife were invited by the custodian of the collection, Mme Serveux, to view a secret part of the collection that only J. H. Breasted and L. Borchardt had so far seen, and about which she dared not inform the Egyptian Museum; this was 'a silver treasure ... a number of objects of solid silver, which are rather unique', and which Mme Serveux claimed came from the Step Pyr-

amid of Djoser. The price for the entire silver hoard was 120,000 Danish Crowns, and Lange said in his diary that Mme Serveux would send him photographs of the objects later.[725] In a letter from her dated 9 April 1930, she again made reference to photographs that she would send to him, adding that they do not do justice to the beauty of the objects, but remarks that he has in any case already seen them in person. The letter is also interesting because it reveals that Lord Carnarvon had seen the silver treasure while Bircher was still alive, and had offered him £E 8,000 for it, but that Bircher had declined the offer. Mme Serveux then proposes to sell the lot to Lange for £E 5,800, but is also prepared to sell pieces individually, as shown by the inclusion of a list of the main objects, with prices:

1. Silbertopf £E 2500
2. Zauberteller 2200
3. Teller mit Lotus 350 [Nur diese 2 Teller zusamen £E 2400]
4. Sistrum 600
5. Griff mit Sperberkopf 300
6. Relief der Cleopatra III 1500
7. Hierzu gehörende Kartusche aus Elektron (Philometores Soteres)[726]

The photos clearly arrived at some point, perhaps even with the above letter (although we have found no trace of them), as shown by a letter to Lange written some four years later (15 October 1934), where she announced a 'sale' (the price of many objects in the collection had been halved by then). She also said that she still hoped to sell the 'silver treasure' to Copenhagen:

Auch mit dem Ausstellen des sogenannten Silberschatzes, von dem Sie Photos haben, dürfte es keine Schwierigkeiten mehr geben. Über Preis und Zahlungsweise könnte man sich sicher auch verständigen; nur möchten wir nicht, dass hiesige Händler sich in die Sache mischen würden.[727]

---

721. Letter from J. H. Breasted to his family, dated 30 Dec. 1919 (Oriental Institute, Chicago); edited by Larson, *Letters from James Henry Breasted*, 126.

722. The statue is currently in the George Ortiz collection; http://www.georgeortiz.com/ortiz_test/indexv. asp?itemid=v039 (accessed 14 Nov. 2013). It was published by van de Walle, *CdE* 43, no. 85 (1968), 36-54. We are grateful to Tom Hardwick for these references.

723. Sigerist, *Schweizer in Ägypten*, 29.

724. Letter from F. Serveux-Sickenberger to H. O. Lange, dated 15 Oct. 1931 (Royal Library, Copenhagen); in addition to other dealers who were hostile and did 'not stop at anything' to damage the reputation of the collection, Borchardt is also explicitly mentioned as expressing his dislike, despite Serveux-Sickenberger's claims of 'not having done him anything wrong'. Similarly, some of the papyri in the collection were thought to be forgeries at the time; Pedley, *The Life and Work of Francis Willey Kelsey*, 375-376. It is difficult to judge how much of the collection was authentic and how many objects were forgeries without a full and illustrated catalogue at our disposal, but it would be naïve to think that there were no forgeries at all. Borchardt's views are not easily dismissed as he was the foremost expert on forgeries at the time, and Sigerist's apologetic aside that 'über deren authentische Herkunft kein Zweifel bestand' rings rather hollow; Sigerist, *Schweizer in Ägypten*, 29.

725. Lange, *Dagbog fra Ægypten, 1929-1930*, 86, 89-90, 342, 350.

726. Letter from F. Serveux-Sickenberger to H. O. Lange, dated 9 Apr. 1930 (University of Copenhagen, Egyptological Archive, B137).

727. Letter from F. Serveux-Sickenberger to H. O. Lange,

Fig. 133. Silver incense burner, acquired by the Carlsberg Glyptotek through Lange in 1930 from Mme Serveux-Sickenberg. It was said to be part of a large silver treasure, found at the site of the Step Pyramid. Ny Carlsberg Glyptotek, ÆIN 1678. Courtesy of Ny Carlsberg Glyptotek.

Mme Serveux had by then already sold an object to the Glyptotek, delivered by her in person in Copenhagen in late July 1930; this was a silver incense-burner (Fig. 133, presumably the 'Griff mit Sperberkopf' in the list above), which was bought for £E 300 according to the museum records.[728] During her visit she wrote to Lange that:

> Da die Glyptotek sich nicht für die andern (sic) silbernen Stücke interessiert, habe ich in Abwesenheit der Herrn Direktors der ägyptischen Abteilung im Prinsens Palais mit dessen Assistent Herrn Nielsen (sic) Breitenstein[729] von den Silbersachen und andern Beständen der Bir-

cher Sammlung gesprochen, (nicht aber von den Köpfen) und ihn gebeten, sich bei Ihnen nach den Sachen und nach uns zu erkundigen. Seien Sie so gütig, den Herren Auskunft zu geben.[730]

The phrase 'die *andern* silbernen Stücke' (our emphasis) is clearly a reference to the 'silver treasure'.[731] Mme Serveux clearly wanted to make sure that few people knew of the existence of the 'treasure', and the reference to anonymous 'hiesige Händler' who should be kept ignorant of any potential transaction also suggests a degree of secrecy;[732] unfortunately we have found no further references to this 'silver treasure'.

In January of 1931, Mme Serveux sent Lange a letter with photographs of a number of sculptures which she sought to sell (Fig. 134-139).[733] They comprised the following. Item 1: The marble head of a woman, 28 cm tall (Bircher inv. 240). 'Der Kopf wurde vor 52 Jahren in der Nähe von Alexandria gefunden u. von Kennern, darunter auch Herr Professor Schubart aus Berlin, auf 1,000 £E geschätzt.' She asks for £E 800.

dated 3 Feb. 1934 (Royal Library, Copenhagen). Words underlined in the original letter, presumably for emphasis.
728. Cf. M. Jørgensen, *Egypt V*, 288-289, no. 99.2. This sales price also emerges from a letter from Zaki Mahmud Abd es-Samad to Lange, undated but received 6 Sept. 1930 (Royal Library), where both Mme Serveux and Mme Bircher are credited with the sale.
729. 'Prinsens Palais' is the building which houses the National Museum. Niels Breitenstein was a notable Danish classical scholar specialising in numismatics; he was employed at the National Museum in Copenhagen 1927-1961 (from 1949 as Head of the Department of Classical and Near Eastern Antiquities).

730. Letter from F. Serveux-Sickenberger to H. O. Lange, dated 27 July 1930 (Royal Library, Copenhagen); written at the Hotel Terminus in Copenhagen, on the hotel's letterhead.
731. Zaki Mahmud Abd es-Samad makes a reference to this transaction in a letter written to H. O. Lange later that year: 'I am satisfied that you bought this piece of silver from Mme. Sarvé & Mme. Birkher for 3 hundred pounds. As I see your letter I saw your letter (sic) first with Mme Sarvé & if you please you remember that you have promised me that you are going to give me ten percentage when the sale is finished. Kindly therefore send me the 30 pound because I am in much need to it' (letter from Z. M. Abd es-Samad to H. O. Lange with original spelling preserved; undated but received in Copenhagen on 6 Sept. 1930; Royal Library, Copenhagen).
732. The reference to 'hiesigen Händler' probably included Zaki Mahmud Abd es-Samad, who in a letter to Lange claimed a 10% commission on the transaction that Mme Serveux had conducted with the Glyptotek; keeping the potential sale of the larger silver treasure secret may have been a way to avoid paying such a commission on that sale too; for the quotation, see the footnote above. Their business arrangement is also explicitly acknowledged by Mme Serveux in the letter of 9 Apr. 1930 cited above.
733. Letter from F. Serveux-Sickenberg to H. O. Lange, dated 17 Jan. 1931 (Royal Library, Copenhagen).

Item 2: Marble head of a man wearing a diadem, 30 cm tall (Bircher inv. 235), £E 150. Item 3: A Serapis bust in alabaster, 26 cm tall (Bircher inv. 197), £E 100. Item 4: An incomplete head of an Egyptian priest, said to have been found in Memphis, limestone, 20 cm tall (without inv. no.), £E 500. Item 5: A Roman-period head of a man in bronze, said to have been found in the Fayum, 34 cm tall, £E 800.

Lange immediately contacted the Ny Carlsberg Glyptotek and the Carlsberg Foundation, but the offer was rejected by the Director of the Museum with the explanation that 'We consider the prices too high and none of the objects are of any particular interest to the Glyptotek.'[734]

The sale of Bircher's collection went slowly, much to the annoyance of Bircher's heirs in Switzerland. There was no love lost between his children and Mme Serveux; she denounced them as philistines ('die gar nichts von Antiken verstehen und trotz ihrem Reichtum sehr habgierig sind'), and they held her responsible for Bircher's divorce from his first wife and the marriage to his second, eventually branding her an 'Erbsleicherin'.[735] Apparently Bircher's heirs took Mme Serveux to court in 1931 to force her to sell,[736] but this seems only to have had a limited effect because as late as 1934 she was still trying to get rid of the collection, although at much reduced prices.[737] Objects were sold to numerous collectors and museums, including the Metropolitan Museum in New York, the Ägyptisches Museum in Berlin, and the

Cinquantenaire Museum in Brussels.[738] In 1977 the remains of the collection, then in the hands of Bircher's granddaughter, the geologist Warda Hermine Bircher-Bleser (1905-2006), was impounded by the Egyptian police, including some ancient Egyptian reliefs that had been embedded in the façade of an old family home in Maadi.[739]

Blanchard, Ralph Huntington (1875-1936)

The American R. H. Blanchard, who came to Egypt in 1905 to work in the consular service, became one of the major antiquities dealers in Cairo.[740] He seems to have begun collecting antiquities (above all scarabs and seals) soon after his arrival in Cairo, and he was elected a member of the Society of Biblical Archaeology in 1907.[741] He is known to have been relatively close to the famous forger, Oxan Aslanian, and to have bought many objects from him.[742] His shop, established in 1910, was located at Shepheard's Hotel where he leased a separate building in the northern part of the hotel garden facing Sharia Kamel (Fig. 44, 48).[743] The sign of his later shop read 'Blanchard Antiquities' and his stationary reads, somewhat boldly, 'Blanchard's Egyptian Museum. Sharia Kamel, Cairo, Egypt.' He lived at 9 Sharia Ismaïl Pasha, Garden City, Cairo.

734. Letter from F. Poulsen to H. O. Lange, dated 29 Jan. 1931 (Royal Library, Copenhagen). Whether these issues were the real reason for the Glyptotek to decline the purchase is not clear; certainly they had recently spent a considerable amount of money, on the advice of Lange, on an object that turned out to be fake, and this appears to have soured their relationship considerably (see ooo).
735. Letter from F. Serveux-Sickenberger to H. O. Lange, dated 15 Oct. 1931 (Royal Library, Copenhagen); Bussmann, *Die mutige Pionierin*, 7.
736. Letter from F. Serveux-Sickenberger to H. O. Lange, dated 15 Oct. 1931 (Royal Library, Copenhagen).
737. Letter from F. Serveux-Sickenberger to H. O. Lange, dated 3 Feb. 1934 (Royal Library, Copenhagen).

738. Bussmann, *Die mutige Pionerin*, 8.
739. Sigerist, *Schweizer in Ägypten*, 32.
740. Bierbrier, *Who was Who in Egyptology*, 4th edition, 64; and esp. Cooney, *BCM* 62, no. 1 (1975), 13-14; Wordsworth, Marr Johnson, and Shaw, 'Re the Estate of Ralph Huntington Blanchard, Deceased', *The London Gazette* 7 Feb. 1939, 910.
741. Membership of the Society of Biblical Archaeology: *PSBA* 29 (1907), 90. Antiquities collection: cf. Nash, *PSBA* 30 (1908), 293.
742. Fiechter, *Egyptian Fakes*, 74.
743. His home address was apparently Sharia Qasr el-Aini, south of Tahrir Square or Mîdân Ismaʿîlîyeh as it was then called, since several objects formerly in his possession have a label reading 'Estate R. H. Blanchard. 113, Rue el Kasr el Aini. Cairo - Egypt'; cf. auction catalogue of Michael Malter, *Ancient Art from Around the World* (http://www.liveauctioneers.com/catalog/20589, accessed 13 June 2013), lots 51 and 52.

He is mentioned once in passing by Lange as having fixed the price of a large hieratic papyrus for Loukianoff. Somewhat surprisingly, Lange does not record visiting his shop, although it is described in the Baedeker guide from 1928 as one of three places where one may acquire fine antiquities at a reasonable price.[744]

Boutros Abd el-Melek (*fl.* 1893/94-1899)

Coptic antiquities dealer from Qena. Borchardt met him at Michel Casira's shop in Cairo in 1899, where he was apparently conducting business, and purchased some objects directly from him.[745] He is likely identical with the dealer whom Petrie refers to as Basta Abd el-Melek and whose antiquities he saw while working at Qift in 1893/94.[746]

Cabulla Ali Soliman (*fl.* 1926)

Dealer in el-Bahnasa (ancient Oxyrhynchus) who sold papyri to Idris Bell in 1926.[747]

Casira, Michel (*fl.* 1898- d. 1911)

Michel Casira had a shop at Haret el-Zahar, across from the American Mission, just around the corner from Shepheard's Hotel.[748] He was one of the main dealers in Cairo at the turn of the 19th Century,[749] and was involved, together with Maurice Nahman, in the sale of the famous head of Queen Tiye from Gurob in 1905 (p. 127).

According to a letter from Borchardt to Lange, written in 1931 when he was investigating forgeries, Valdemar Schmidt had – at some unspecified date – acquired a fake head in Cairo soon after it was produced.[750] Based on the description (a royal head wearing the white crown), Lange was worried that this might be the famous Black Head, which had been acquired from Alexandre Dingli by Schmidt and which was the pride of the Egyptian collection at the Glyptotek, but Borchardt wrote back in his usual slightly sarcastic tone:

> Wegen des Kopfes [sc. the Black Head] ... können Sie (bis auf Weiteres) beruhigt sein. Ich habe soeben wieder einmal den Besuch meines Gewährsmannes gehabt und ihn gefragt, ob er etwa 1895 schon gearbeitet habe. Seine Antwort war ein klares Nein; damals sei er noch auf der Kunsthochschule in .... [sic, deliberately suppressed] gewesen.

He adds that the head in question was made of 'green basalt' and that this one was acquired by Schmidt from Michel Casira.[751] He is also known to have sold other fakes.[752]

Castellari, Andrea (d. c. 1848)

Castellari was an Italian antiquities dealer who lived on the roof of Luxor temple in the mid-19th Century.[753]

---

744. Baedeker, *Ägypten und der Sûdan*, 8th edition, 38-39.

745. Borchardt diary, Sept. 1899 - Jan. 1900, entry 29 Dec. 1899 (Swiss Institute, Kairo; transcript kindly provided by Cornelius von Pilgrim, 21 Jan. 2015).

746. Quirke, *Hidden Hands*, 130, 131.

747. Emmel, 'The Yale Papyrus Collection. Catalog Introduction', 1993, with additions by R. Duttenhofer 1996, available on-line http://www.library.yale.edu/ beinecke/brblsear/ aboutpap.htm (accessed 24 July 2012).

748. Eaton-Krauss, in Gabra and Takla (eds.), *Christianity and Monasticism in Upper Egypt* 2, 204.

749. Botti, *Rapport sur le Musée Gréco-Romain*, 23 (donation to the Greco-Roman Museum in Alexandria in 1898, called 'Michel Casyra'); Persson, *JHC* 24, no. 1 (2010), 6 (textiles acquired from Casira in 1898); David, *Gaston Maspero*, 387, 403; Gunter, *A Collector's Journey*, 91. According to Paul Dingli, Michel Casira

died 20 June 1911; cf. Fiechter, *Faux et faussaires en art égypten*, 47, and also Spiegelberg, *ZÄS* 51 (1913), 79.

750. Letter from L. Borchardt to H. O. Lange, dated 6 Apr. and 19 May 1931 (Royal Library, Copenhagen).

751. We have not been able to identify this object in the Museum.

752. Voss, in Fitzenreiter, Kirchner, and Kriseleit (eds.), *Authentizität*, 57.

753. Bierbrier, *Who was Who in Egyptology*, 4th edition, 107; Jackson, in Fortenberry (ed.), *Souvenirs and New Ideas*, 63-64.

Chanher, Morgos (fl. around 1906/09)

Obscure dealer in Qena mentioned in the Freer diaries.[754]

Cohen, Joseph (fl. 1891-1914)

Joseph Cohen, who had a prominent shop in Khan el-Khalili, dealt broadly in oriental wares, both ancient and modern.[755] Lange mentions his shop in passing as 'one of the largest and most expensive shops in the whole bazaar', and this is confirmed by other contemporary accounts.[756] It was 'Established 1891' according to the sign in front of the shop (Fig. 59).

Dattari, Giovanni (1858-1923)

Giovanni (aka Giannino) Dattari was an Italian collector and dealer in Cairo who specialised in coins and glass, but who also, on occasion, sold papyri and other antiquities.[757] Dutilh provided the following description of him in 1895:

> M.r G. Dattari personnifie l'antiquaire passionné, et le travailleur infatigable ; il a su réunir en très peu de temps, une très intéressante série de monuments égyptiens ; ses Collections Numismatiques seront bientôt les plus riches du Pays. Gentleman parfait, il est très accessible et s'estime heureux lorsqu'on lui fournit l'occassion de faire les honneurs de ce qu'il appele son sanctuaire.[758]

During a trip to Egypt in 1903 Valdemar Schmidt writes to Lange that Dattari, whose collection he had seen on an earlier occasion, had put up an important collection of antiquities for sale, and that he was considering the acquisition of a knife with an ivory handle and gold inlay, a quiver with bow and arrows with their stone heads infact, a well-preserved model boat with crew from Deir el-Bersha, a couple of predynastic vases, and some bronze tools.[759]

Dattari donated several large collections of coins to *Società numismatica italiana* from 1893 (when he became a member) onwards, the two largest consisting of no less than 1,000 and 2,000 items respectively, and in 1907 he donated a stele of King Haremhab to the Cairo Museum.[760] His daughter, Maria Dattari (d. 1981), was later involved in the sale of the Nag Hammadi codices.[761]

Dingli, Alexandre (fl. 1887-1903)

Dingli was an old acquaintance of Lange's teacher Valdemar Schmidt who mentions him in his autobiography in relation to a visit to Egypt in 1894:

> I made an excursion to the Fayum with my friend, the Greek Alexander Dingli, who had previously earned his living by trading in ostrich feathers, a trade which the rebellion of the Mahdi had made impossible, and he had then turned to antiquities trading ... With Dingli's help I bought, among other things, a particularly nice collection of terracotta figures at an outstandingly low price.[762]

754. Gunter, *A Collector's Journey*, 91.

755. *Annuaire égyptien, administratif et commercial, 1891-1892*, Cairo, 1891, 91; Sladen, *Oriental Cairo*, 97-98; Reynolds-Ball, *Cairo of To-Day*, 1st edition, 22; 5th edition, 24; Baedeker, *Ägypten*, 4th edition, 28; idem, *Egypt and the Sûdân*, 7th edition, 41.

756. Lange, *Dagbog fra Ægypten, 1929-1930*, 301.

757. Lucchelli, *Rivista italiana di numismatica* 110 (2009), 537-542; Bierbrier, *Who was Who in Egyptology*, 4th edition, 143. Active as dealer already in 1894: Forrer, *Description Catalogue of the Collection of Greek Coins* 3, no. 2, 866, 869, 870, 873; cf. also Dutilh, *BIE* 6, 3rd ser. (1896), 227.

758. Dutilh, *Rivista italiana di numismatica* 8 (1895), 96 w. note 1.

759. Letter from V. Schmidt to H. O. Lange, dated 30 Oct. 1903 (Royal Library, Copenhagen). The records of the Egyptian collection at the Louvre Museum preserve a correspondance with Dattari concerning the material offered for sale in 1903 under the heading 'M. G Dattari propose à l'acquisition un important lot d'antiquités (plusieurs planches photographiques les montrent). août-octobre 1903 [24 p.]'.

760. Cf. Anonymous, 'Atti della Società numismatica italiana', *Rivista italiana di numismatica* 6 (1893), 511, and subsequent volumes; Legrain, *ASAE* 8 (1907), 57-59.

761. Robinson, in Barc (ed.), *Colloque international sur les textes de Nag Hammadi*, 27-28; idem, *The Facsimile Edition of the Nag Hammadi Codices*, 10-11; idem, *The Nag Hammadi Story*, passim.

762. Schmidt, *Af et Langt Livs Historie*, 96. These are now in the Ny Carlsberg Glyptotek and are published by Fjeldhagen, *Graeco-Roman Terracottas from Egypt*. Several other objects acquired during this visit to Fayum are in the same collection.

Fig. 134-139. Sculptures from the estate of André Bircher offered for sale by Mme Serveux-Sickenberg in a letter to Lange, dated 17 January 1931. Their inventory numbers in the Bircher collection were, clockwise from the top left, nos. 235, 197, 525, no number recorded (Egyptian male), 240 (back view), 240 (front view). Courtesy of the Royal Library.

Surprisingly, Schmidt makes no mention of the fact that he also acquired from Dingli during that same visit to Egypt the so-called Black Head, one of the most famous works of royal art from the Middle Kingdom, believed to depict Amenemhet III.[763] Nor does he mention the three magnificent, well-preserved marble busts of Augustus, Tiberius, and Livia – said to have been found at a Roman amphitheatre in the Fayum – whose acquisition from Dingli he facilitated just a few months later, in 1895.[764]

---

763. Jørgensen, *Egypt I*, 168-169; idem, *How it all began*, 56/61, fig. 54.

764. Jørgensen, *How it all began*, 61-62, fig. 55-57.

In a letter from 1900, Schmidt recalled another time when Dingli did him a favour; 'With the help of Dingli I stayed at Hotel Karnak-Cook at half price.'[765] Schmidt had first befriended him in Cairo in 1892, and in 1893 he acquired a perfectly preserved Late Period statue from Dingli in Paris where he also did business.[766]

Alexandre Dingli is also mentioned once in Lange's 1899-1900 diary where he is described as 'a Greek' who in his home had 'some particularly wonderful objects'.[767] No transaction took place at the time. Just after his return to Copenhagen Schmidt, who had visited Dingli together with Lange, writes to the latter that he would like photographs of the two Old Kingdom items they had seen and that he has informed Dingli about this.[768] In his following letter, he notes 'Jacobsen complains of a lack of funds – would probably otherwise have bought the Dingliana'.[769] A few months later, he writes that Jacobsen finds the items too expensive, but that they should try to make an offer for one of them. He adds that if they had been larger, Jacobsen would probably have bought them even if they were more expensive.[770]

Dingli was active already in 1887 and 1888 (p. 135), when he sold a statue of King Niuserre (CGC 38) and other objects to the Egyptian Museum,[771] he is further known to have been visited several times by Wilhelm Fröhner in 1893,[772] and to have donated sculptures to the Graeco-Roman Museum in Alexandria.[773] In 1896 he assisted Budge in smuggling antiquities out of Egypt.[774] By 1904 he had left Egypt with his family and re-settled in Larnaca, Cyprus, where he was directly involved with the smuggling of a valuable archaeological treasure, a case which also involved the well-known dealers Nicolas Tano and Mihran Sivadjian.[775] He seems to have retained the shop in Cairo since Charles Freer apparently visited it during his trips to Egypt between 1906 and 1909.[776]

Alexandre Dingli was the father of Paul Dingli (see below), according to whom he sometimes worked alone and sometimes in partnership with other dealers such as Paul Philip and Michel Casira.[777]

Dingli, Paul [Paolo] (*fl.* 1910s-1930s)

Paul Dingli (also known as Radamès Dingli, Fig. 140), the son of Alexandre Dingli, was born in Egypt, but held British citizenship and was of Maltese extraction.[778] He lived at 6 Sharia Deir el-Banat in Cairo. He dealt in antiquities, but worked mainly as a forger. In the 1920s and 1930s he assisted Borchardt in his quest to identify fakes and forgers. Dingli had learned his trade in the Restoration Department of the Egyptian Museum in Cairo, alongside Mario Rescigno with whom he sometimes collaborated. As restorers they had access to genuine antiquities as models, and after they established their own atelier at Sharia Maruf (which runs parallel to Sharia Deir el-Banat, a little to the south towards the Egyptian Museum), they continued working from originals, in one case a genuine head belonging to the Kalebdjian Brothers.

765. Letter from V. Schmidt to H. O. Lange, dated Feb. 1900 (Royal Library, Copenhagen).

766. Jørgensen, *How it all began*, 51-53; cf. also idem, *Egypt IV*, 108-109.

767. Lange and Lange, *Dagbog fra Ægyptensrejsen 1899-1900*, 142. Some objects seen with Dingli are copied in Lange, *Notebook 1899/1900*, 217-218.

768. Letter from V. Schmidt to H. O. Lange, dated 7 Dec. 1899 (Royal Library, Copenhagen).

769. Letter from V. Schmidt to H. O. Lange, dated 1 Jan. 1900 (Royal Library, Copenhagen).

770. Letter from V. Schmidt to H. O. Lange, dated 26 Apr. 1900 (Royal Library, Copenhagen).

771. Borchardt, *Statuen und Statuetten von Königen und Privatleuten*, 36.

772. Bakhoum and Hellmann, *Journal des savants* 1992, 163-164.

773. Cf. Botti, *Catalogue des monuments exposés au Musée gréco-Romain d'Alexandrie*, 158, 159.

774. Ismail, *Wallis Budge*, 290-294.

775. Merrillees, *The Tano Family*, 9-13.

776. Gunter, *A Collector's Journey*, 91.

777. Fiechter, *Faux et faussaires en art égyptien*, 45-48.

778. Fiechter, *Faux et faussaires en art égyptien*, 45-48, 91; idem, *Egyptian Fakes*, 80-81, 84, 87-89. Cornelius von Pilgrim informs us that the photograph included in the latter publication (p. 81) does not in fact show Paolo Dingli, as indicated by the caption, but another forger named Mario Rescigno.

Fig. 140. Paul Dingli, a petty antiquities dealer who is better known as a forger of sculptures. This photograph, which he gave to Ludwig Borchardt on 10 February 1931, shows him working on a small sculpture at his home. Courtesy of the Borchardt Archives, Schweizerisches Institut für Ägyptische Bauforschung und Altertumskunde, Cairo.

Dingli later helped Borchardt identify several fakes – some made by himself – including objects in the Ny Carlsberg Glyptotek in Copenhagen, although none of these were bought by Lange. His own fakes were apparently often sold through Maurice Nahman's shop, but also other dealers like Michel Casira.

Diniacopoulos, Vincent (1886-1967)

Diniacopoulos was a Greek-Canadian dealer with shops in Egypt and Paris. Borchardt and others had suspected him of forging objects, and he was once

thought to have been responsible for the famous forgery of the Louvre harp's head.[779]

Dreiss, Wolfgang (*fl.* 1904-1932)

Dreiss was a German who managed a hotel in Luxor (with his sister Eugénie) where Lange stayed in December 1929.[780] Before the First World War he had run the Hôtel du Nil near the Winter Palace.[781] During the war, he was rounded up and sent to an internment camp in Malta because of his German citizenship, only to return to Egypt after the war.[782] By February 1930 he had been forced to leave his position as hotel manager at the Thebes Hotel because of problems with the owner.[783] When Lange met him he already had 25 years' worth of experience of the local antiquities market as a buyer and collector, and claimed to

779. Fiechter, *Faux et faussaires en art égyptien*, 65-70 (for the Louvre harp's head), 97, 147 (for Diniacopoulos). Cf. Bierbrier, *Who was Who in Egyptology*, 4th edition, 154-155.

780. The travel journal of a young American called Hall Lippincott, who passed through Luxor in March 1929, also describes staying at the hotel, and gives a lengthy description of Dreiss. He confirms his interest in antiquities, but paints a picture of a rather eccentric figure who played with, fondled and talked to his statues 'as one would to a small child' behind closed doors. We are inclined to ascribe this to poetic license on Lippincott's behalf, rather than take it at face value: certainly Lange makes no mention of any irregular behaviour, and Lippincott's descriptions seem in general to be coloured by a tendency to dramatise: 'The truth of the matter is that several men who evidently work in excavating sell him pieces that are either stolen or smuggled out. I cornered him one night and learned this. However, he keeps it all dark that he collects and nobody knows it in Luxor. Thus all the secrecy ... Strange Arabs come and go, always carrying on their business behind locked doors.' (http://www.halllippincott. info/?p=1530, accessed 13 May 2011).

781. For the location of the hotel (south-west of the Winter Palace), see e.g. Baedeker, *Egypt and the Sûdân*, 7th edition, 251; not to be confused with the popular Cairo hotel of the same name, for which see Humphreys, *Grand hotels of Egypt*, 50, 59.

782. Lange, *Dagbog fra Ægypten, 1929-1930*, 236.

783. Lange, *Dagbog fra Ægypten, 1929-1930*, 291; 'he said he had had to close the hotel because of harassment from the owner, and because he had spent too much money'. For the name of the hotel, see p. 244.

know several contemporary Egyptologists, including Maspero, Naville, Carter, Borchardt, Steindorff and Legrain. Lange got to know him and his sister well during his stay, when they became involved in a drawn-out story about a local dealer (Schafi, whom Lange initially called 'Mansur') who had deceived Dreiss with a granite statue of a kneeling prisoner with his head on the ground and the arms tied behind his back. The dealer had accepted Dreiss' advance on the price but never delivered, and had subsequently offered Lange the same object; the two then joined forces in trying to acquire the object.[784] When Lange left Egypt he considered Dreiss one of two agents that he could rely on for information about new objects that came onto the market (the other was Loukianoff; see below).[785]

Dreiss' personal collection included 'a lovely group of objects from Deir el-Bahri', as well as the head of an Amarna-period princess which Lange admired and eventually persuaded the Glyptotek to buy upon his return to Denmark (see above, p. 154).

Having given up his career as a hotelier in 1930, Dreiss wrote to Lange that he intended instead to earn his living as a full-time antiquities dealer in the future, and for this purpose he moved to Aswan, where he wanted to set himself up as the 'sole ruler' (Alleinherrscher) of the antiquities market from Nubia to Edfu;[786] four months later he was in Aswan trying to sell a significant amount of antiquities, including granite and limestone statuary.[787] The final letter from him to Lange arrived a year later, in January 1932, and was also written from Aswan.[788] Dreiss forwarded photographs of two sculptures which he evidently hoped to sell; the head of a king, 24 cm tall in black

basalt, 'wohl eines der besten Stücke bis dato', and the head of a queen without further specification (Fig. 31-34). Both are obvious fakes and there is nothing to indicate that Lange took further action, perhaps because of the embarrassment already caused by the Amarna head.

Dufour, Henri (fl. 1923-1964)

Dealer in Cairo of Swiss origin. He is recorded selling antiquities already in 1923, but only seems to have become an established dealer around 1940; in 1939 he is listed as a *rentier* in *Le mondain égyptien*, but from 1941 onwards as an *antiquaire*.[789] He took over the antiquities shop formerly run by R. H. Blanchard (until his death in 1936) in the garden of Shepheard's Hotel, facing Sharia Kamel, where he changed the sign to read simply 'Antiquités' (Fig. 121). The shop was destroyed by fire during the revolution in 1952, when the hotel was burnt to the ground, but Dufour continued his business for at least another 12 years. He sold and donated several objects to the Musée d'Art et d'Histoire in Geneva where he was born. He lived in Heliopolis at 5 Rue Chéops.

Dutilh, Ernest Daniel Jean (1836-1905)

Dutch consul in Cairo, numismatist, and antiquities dealer. He sold a whole collection to the Egyptian Museum in Berlin in 1878 (through the German consul in Cairo, Gustav Travers) and some further objects to the Egyptian Museum in 1888 and 1889 (p. 51).[790]

784. For the story of this object, now in the Luxor Museum in Egypt, see above.

785. Lange, *Dagbog fra Ægypten, 1929-1930*, 181, 189-190, 193-194, 236, 346.

786. Letter from W. Dreiss to H. O. Lange, dated 24 Oct. 1930 (Royal Library, Copenhagen).

787. Letter from W. Dreiss to H. O. Lange, dated 27 Feb. 1931 (Royal Library, Copenhagen).

788. Letter from W. Dreiss to H. O. Lange, dated 22 Jan. 1932 (Royal Library, Copenhagen.

789. Wild, *JEA* 37 (1951), 12; Blattner (ed.), *Le mondain égyptien: The Egyptian Who's Who 1939*, 167; idem, *Le mondain égyptien: The Egyptian Who's Who 1941*, 133; idem, *Le mondain égyptien: The Egyptian Who's Who 1952*, 312; idem, *Le mondain égyptien et du Proche-Orient 1953*, 318; Deonna, *Genava: Bulletin du Musée d'Art et d'Histoire de Genève* 2 (1924), 52; Karageorghis, *Ancient Cypriote Art in the Musée d'Art et d'Histoire, Geneva*, 11, 109, 196.

790. Königliche Museen zu Berlin, *Ausführliches Verzeichniss der Aegyptischen Altertümer, Gipsabgüsse und Papyrus*, ix et passim. His name is recorded as 'Duttil' in *BIE* 9, 2nd ser. (1889), xxvi, xxxv; 10 (1890), xiii. The latter refers to Cairo Museum JE 28795. This object is published by Reisner, *Amulets*, 101, who

He also donated several objects to the Graeco-Roman Museum in Alexandria, where he was the Keeper of the Numismatic Collection,[791] as well as over 300 objects to the Leiden Museum during the years 1875-1877. He was a member of the *Institut Égyptien*, and is listed as the author of nine articles in the *Online Egyptological Bibliography* between 1893 and 1905, mostly in the Bulletin of the Institute. Erman provides the following description of him in his autobiography:

> Da war der gute Monsieur Dutilh; der war einst in den Tagen des Suezkanals ein reicher Kaufmann und Konsul gewesen und hatte zusammen mit einem niederländischen Prinzen eine Handelsgesellschaft gegründet; jetzt ernährte er sich kümmerlich als Vermittler zwischen Sammlern und Händlern. Er war ein braver Mann, und ich habe später zu meiner Freude gehört, daß man ihm eine Stelle an einem der Museen gegeben hätte.[792]

Dr Eddé (*fl.* 1898-1920)

Numismatist and antiquities dealer in Alexandria.[793] In 1902 he acquired the bulk of a great gold treasure discovered at Abukir, including 600 Roman *aurei*, 20 Alexander medallions, and 18-20 stamped bars of gold.[794] He sold most of his private collection through Hôtel Drouot in 1911, where Valdemar Schmidt acquired a sphinx for the Glyptotek.[795]

Edris *Effendi*, see Idris *Effendi*

Eid, Albert (1886-1950)

The son of a Belgian consul to Egypt, Albert Eid (Fig. 141) was born in Cairo and ran an antiquities shop at Sikket el-Bâdistân in Khan el-Khalili under the name 'Albert Eid & Co.' with antiquities license no. 112 (Fig. 60).[796] The large shop was located in a former mosque dating back to the 14th Century. Bernard Bothmer noted in 1950, the year Albert Eid died, that he 'had a big place, but nothing much to show.'[797]

He is mostly known for his involvement in the sale of the Nag Hammadi codices. He was indicted for smuggling one of the codices out of Egypt and, having passed away by the time of his conviction, a £6,000 fine was imposed on his estate.[798] As a result part of his stock was confiscated in 1950.[799] His business was continued by his widow Simone Eid (née van Lierde) with Robert Viola, a son of Maurice Nahman, as the general manager (Fig. 61). In 1956, when many foreigners were asked to leave Egypt as a result of the Tripartite Invasion, the shop was nationalized by the Egyptian government. Viola was asked to help liquidate the inventory and he continued as general manager, now on behalf of the government, until he left Egypt in 1963. The sale of antiquities continued as before; 'Albert Eid & Co.' is mentioned in the export register of the Egyptian Museum of 1959,[800] and in

corrects the name to 'Dutilh' (but mistakenly identifies the object as JE 28395 and the year of acquisition as 1890).

791. Cf. Botti, *Catalogue des monuments exposés au Musée gréco-Romain d'Alexandrie*, 116, 117, 120, 545, 556, cf. also pp. 159-160; idem, *Rapport sur le Musée Gréco-Romain*, 25; Revillout, *RevEg* 11 (1904), 105.

792. Erman, *Mein Werden und mein Wirken*, 213.

793. Bakhoum and Hellmann, *Journal des savants* 1992, 167-168, 176; Botti, *Rapport sur le Musée Gréco-Romain*, 25; Forrer, *Description Catalogue of the Collection of Greek Coins* 3, no. 2, 845, 902.

794. Eddé, *Bulletin de Numismatique* 13 (1906), 78-82. For a recent discussion of the treasure, see Dahmen, *AJN* 20, 2nd Ser. (2008), 493-546, pls. 100-110.

795. Hôtel Drouot, *Collection de M. le Docteur Eddé d'Alexandrie*; Jørgensen, *How it all began*, 107, fig. 96.

796. Lucien Viola (personal communication, 8 Dec. 2014); Bierbrier, *Who was Who in Egyptology*, 4th edition, 175; Robinson, *The Nag Hammadi Story*, passim. The sign on his storefront (Fig. 60) reads 'Albert Eid & Co. antiquites. Permis du service des Antiquités no. 112.' in French, with the same text repeated in Arabic.

797. Bothmer, *Egypt 1950: My First Visit*, 110.

798. Pagels, *The Gnostic Gospels*, xxvi.

799. These objects include Temporary Register 8/4/70/1-12, a group of well-preserved bronze figures and an alabaster pot and a fragment of a relief. Certain objects are said to have been 'purchased' by the Cairo Museum from Eid's collection; cf. Zayed, *RdE* 16 (1964), 193 (Cairo JE 89624). Other objects from Eid's collection in the Egyptian Museum include JE 89623-89624 and 89781-783.

800. Cf. the pages reproduced in Piacentini (ed.), *Egypt and the Pharaohs*, 36-37.

1961 a large collection of antiquities purchased from Eid was exhibited in Texas.[801] (The highest inventory number in the part of his collection that went on exhibit in Texas was 4294; the numbers may have been assigned for the purposes of the journal which dealers were obliged to keep.) The business was carried on under new management after 1963 until it was finally closed down around the late 1960s; by 1972 the large shop had been sold by the government and turned into a bazaar.

Eissé Fouli (d. 1922/3)

A minor dealer at Sheikh Abd el-Qurna who mainly sold fakes, according to B. Bruyère.[802]

Emin *Bey* (*fl.* 1888)

Dealer from Akhmim whom Marius Tano tricked out of an exceptionally fine commemorative scarab of Amenhotep III in 1888 (p. 126).[803]

Farag Ali (*fl.* 1900-1901)

This dealer, described as a pleasant young man, had a 'shop' – or rather a storeroom; Jonna describes it as 'the little hole' – in a house in an Arabic neighbourhood conveniently located a few minutes away from Ezbekiya Gardens, although it was only reached by passing through 'the most horrible alleys'.[804] Lange and his wife visited this storeroom on both 27 November 1899 (alone) and again the day after (in the com-

Fig. 141. Albert Eid at his desk. Courtesy of Claremont Colleges Digital Libraries.

pany of Borchardt, Schäfer, and Thiersch). It emerges from the diary of Borchardt, who briefly mentions the latter visit, that the 'shop' in question was close to Sharia Abdin, the direct southward continuation of Sharia Kamel (both streets now renamed Sharia Gomehoriya).[805] Farag Ali came and peddled antiquities again in March of 1900 (cited in context p. 57), and Schäfer is mentioned as closing a deal with him in June.[806] Towards the end of his stay, Lange refers to him as an example of 'a reasonably decent' Egyptian dealer (cited in context p. 137).[807]

801. Zayed, *Egyptian Antiquities*. The purpose of the catalogue is not stated in the preface, but the collection may well have been exhibited for sales purposes.
802. Diary entry dated 30 Jan. 1923; http://www.ifao.egnet.net/bases/archives/bruyere/ (accessed 11 Sept. 2013).
803. Cf. Capart (ed.), *Letters of Charles Edwin Wilbour*, 461.
804. Lange and Lange, *Dagbog fra Ægyptensrejsen 1899-1900*, 158-159; cf. also Mietke et al., *Josef Strzygowski und die Berliner Museen*, 12, where Farag Ali is recorded selling objects to Josef Strzygowski in 1901 (note that he is not identical with the two older dealers Farag and Ali in Giza who must surely be Farag Ismaïn and Ali Abd el-Haj).

805. Borchardt diary, Sept. 1899 - Jan. 1900, entry 28 Oct. 1899 (Swiss Institute, Kairo): 'Nachmittags mit Schäfer, Lange u. Frau u. Thiersch zu Farag Ali (r.v. Abdin-Strasse) ...'; transcript kindly provided by Cornelius von Pilgrim (21 Jan. 2015).
806. Lange and Lange, *Dagbog fra Ægyptensrejsen 1899-1900*, 429, 664.
807. Lange and Lange, *Dagbog fra Ægyptensrejsen 1899-1900*, 738.

Farag Ismaïn (born c. 1830, *fl.* 1881-1900)[808]

Farag Ismaïn, a Bedouin living at Kafr el-Haram, was one of the main antiquities dealers in Egypt and was generally known simply as Farag. He was a former partner of the other main dealer at Kafr el-Haram, Ali Abd el-Haj, but their collaboration came to an end in 1896 and they became rivals (p. 192). Lange describes him as 'an old Arab ... who has the second largest antiquities shop here in Egypt' and who lived 'in the village of Giza'.[809] Jonna notes that he 'had a voice so coarse that one can scarcely understand what he says',[810] a characteristic which is also recalled by Adolf Erman in his autobiography, describing him as 'ein hagerer langer Mann mit heiserer Stimme'.[811]

Farag had earlier enjoyed much success and apparently used to buy antiquities wholesale from smaller dealers. An example is provided by a letter from 1881 where Wilbour describes a visit to Saqqara, 'I found some stones on the site of Memphis, but hardly anything to buy; Farrakh had bought everything, they said'.[812] He was one of the local dealers who somehow, as a Bedouin, still managed to acquire an official permit to conduct excavations, in return for providing the Gizeh Museum with a share of the discoveries; the sites included Hawara (1888),[813] Soknopaiou Nesos (1890 and 1891, in collaboration with Ali Abd el-Haj),[814] Assiut (1894, poss. in collaboration with Ali Abd el-Haj, discoveries included the tomb of Mesehty with its famous wooden models),[815] Deir el-Aizam at Assiut (1897, in collaboration with Yassa Todros),[816] and Deir el-Bersha (1897).[817] He is also known to have sold objects to Maspero and the Boulaq Museum in the 1880s.[818] In 1886, Wilbour described his collection as 'the finest in any Arab's hands'.[819] In his biography from 1894, Heinrich Brugsch also referred to Farag and his role in the antiquities trade: 'Mein noch heutigen Tages lebender Freund, der Beduine Farag Ismail(sic), gegenwärtig ein sehr reicher Mann, leistete Großartiges darin, denn seiner Spürnase entging beinahe nichts'.[820] G. Vitelli, who bought a number of papyri from him just after 1900, described him as an imposing figure; the 'Cerberus' of Giza (one of two described this way – the other was Ali Abd el-Haj).[821]

---

808. His surname is sometimes spelled Farrakh (Schmidt, Wilbour).

809. Lange and Lange, *Dagbog fra Ægyptensrejsen 1899-1900*, 154.

810. Lange and Lange, *Dagbog fra Ægyptensrejsen 1899-1900*, 196.

811. Erman, *Mein Werden und mein Wirken*, 213.

812. Cf. Capart (ed.), *Letters of Charles Edwin Wilbour*, 81.

813. In the late 1888 Farag received permission to excavate at the site of Hawara from Eugène Grébaut, the Director of the Antiquities Service, much to the regret of Petrie: 'old Farag, the Arab dealer, was allowed to work at Hawara. He was there for two and a half months, but he only got four or five portraits it is said, beside a lot of the common gilt masks'; Petrie, *Seventy Years in Archaeology*, 90-91; cf. Drower, *Flinders Petrie*, 143, 187, 191 (where Petrie refers to him as 'that brute of a plunderer'), and Quirke, *Hidden Hands*, 69, 123-124 (citing two letters that mention Farag's work at Hawara). Petrie was nonetheless one of his regular customers and acquired the famous Revenue Papyrus from him (cf. Drower, *op. cit.*, 207).

814. Cf. Grenfell, Hunt, and Hogarth, *Fayûm Towns and Their Papyri*, 18 (that Ali Abd el-Haj and Farag Ismaïn, both unnamed, 'received permission in two succssive winters to excavate at Dimê'); Grenfell, Hunt, and Goodspeed, *The Tebtunis Papyri II*, 348; É. Bernand, *Recueil des inscriptions grecques du Fayoum I*, 121-122; Davoli, *Atene e Roma 1-2* (2008), 104.

815. Letter from V. Schmidt to C. Jacobsen, dated 6-8 Oct. 1894 (Ny Carlsberg Glyptotek).

816. Cf. Maspero, *ASAE* 1 (1900), 109.

817. Fowler et al., *AJA* 2, 2nd ser. (1898), 101. Daressy, *ASAE* 1 (1900), 17-43, reports on these excavations, but does not mention the involvement of Farag Ismaïn. Griffith in *Egypt Exploration Fund, Archaeological Report* 1897-98, 19, mentions that 'numerous large wooden sarcophagi have been found by the Arab dealer, Farag, in the wells of the El Bersheh tombs, and taken to the Gîzeh Museum'; the sarcophagi in question clearly represents the Museum's share of the division of finds; cf. further Reisner, *ZÄS* 37 (1899), 64, n. 4.

818. Cf. Capart (ed.), *Letters of Charles Edwin Wilbour*, 308; Bolshakov, *Studies on Old Kingdom Reliefs*, 6. See further p. 51.

819. Cf. Capart (ed.), *Letters of Charles Edwin Wilbour*, 416.

820. Brugsch, *Mein Leben und Wandern*, 2nd edition, 163.

821. Breccia, *Aegyptus* 15 (1935), 258-9. We are confident that the man to whom Breccia refers as Farag Ali is identical with Farag Ismaïn, and that the identity given – 'Farag Ali' – is a *lapsus memoriae*; dealers were known by their first names only and it should be noted that Breccia wrote his account thirty years after the visit to Egypt. There was in fact a dealer named Farag Ali at Kafr el-Haram, but he was a young man at the time and the fact

He spoke a little English, and was said to have particularly good Greek and Coptic papyri when Lange visited in November 1899, although the only transaction recorded by Lange concerns fragments of a Middle Kingdom letter (see further above p. 166). At the time, rumour had it that Farag was in debt and therefore was willing to sell his antiquities at reasonable prices (in contrast to Ali Abd el-Haj).[822] This seems to be confirmed by Erman who notes that Farag, having used part of his fortune to build a Mosque, gambled the rest away.[823]

Lange and Heinrich Schäfer made further, unspecified purchases from him in December 1899, the former on behalf of Ny Carlsberg Glyptotek.[824] In March of 1900, Lange records that they photographed the reliefs 'that I acquired some time ago from the old Farag for £7, 20 piastre; I will send the photographs home to Vald[emar] Schmidt so that he may enquire whether the Museum or Jacobsen wants them. In that case my money would become disposable for me again and I could buy other things for myself.' Just a few days before their departure from Egypt in 1900, on August 9, Farag came by their hotel and mentioned that he had acquired 'some new things which he would like to present', and the Lange couple went out to see him at Kafr el-Haram. Here Jonna met his wife for the

first time, 'a young, very heavyset, but quite pretty woman', in her private quarters; she had borne Farag Ismaïn two children that had both died young. She was in her twenties and Farag around 70.[825]

His brother Saïd Ismaïn also dealt in antiquities and so too did a son of his. Lange visited the son at least once at his home in Kafr el-Haram; he records in his diary on 1 January 1900 that 'he had nothing' (cited in context p. 95).[826] This unnamed son might well be Ali Farag who sold a famous papyrus to Budge a few years before. Farag Ismaïn also had some kind of business (and family?) relationship with Ali Gabri; Wilbour recorded them storing and selling objects together.[827]

Farag el-Shaer (fl. 1964-1971)

A relative of Mohammed Abd er-Rahim el-Shaer, q.v.

Farag Todros (fl. 1907)

Coptic dealer at Biba, c. 20 kilometres south of Beni Suef, who conducted an illegal excavation at a previously unknown cemetery at Gamhud (p. 125).[828]

Farouk Farag Abd er-Rahim el-Shaer (fl. 1960s-2005)

Son of Mohammed Abd er-Rahim el-Shaer, q.v.

Fodi (fl. 1881-1886)

Antiquities dealer living at Saqqara and visited several times by Wilbour.[829]

that the experienced buyer Heinrich Schäfer was unaware how to find him, as it emerges from Lange's diary, shows that this cannot have been the famous Farag (p. 213). We assume that it was similarly Farag Ismaïn who sold his entire collection of papyri to Lord Crawford in 1899 (now in the Rylands Library), rather than Farag Ali as suggested by Choat, in Schubert (ed.), *Actes du 26e Congrès international de papyrologie*, 143; the letter he cites records simply the name Farag and no patronym.
822. Lange and Lange, *Dagbog fra Ægyptensrejsen 1899-1900*, 154-156.
823. Erman, *Mein Werden und mein Wirken*, 213.
824. Lange and Lange, *Dagbog fra Ægyptensrejsen 1899-1900*, 196, cf. also p. 229. Some objects seen with Farag are listed in Lange, *Notebook 1899/1900*, 215, 226; on one visit he saw a 'Sarcophagi, 12th Dynasty', including a 'very large one for a woman' named Sat-Ipi, and another complete one for a general named Sep, and also a canopic box, while on another the material included some Old Kingdom reliefs and the stela of a Sekeby. The coffin of Sat-Ipi is probably Leiden inv. F 1930/6.1, which was bought from André Bircher via Ludwig Keimer; van Wijngaarden, *OMRO* 24 (1943), 11-14 (we are grateful to one of our peer reviewers for this identification).

825. Lange and Lange, *Dagbog fra Ægyptensrejsen 1899-1900*, 781-782.
826. Lange and Lange, *Dagbog fra Ægyptensrejsen 1899-1900*, 221. Lange, *Notebook 1899/1900*, 207, includes a single object seen during this particular visit, a large offering table of a certain *Bw-nfry*. Lange does not mention the name of Farag Ismaïn's son, but refers to him as 'a son of Farag in Gizeh' and 'Farag's son in Kafr'.
827. Cf. Capart (ed.), *Letters of Charles Edwin Wilbour*, 80, 81, 416.
828. Kamal, *ASAE* 9 (1908), 8-9.
829. Cf. Capart (ed.), *Letters of Charles Edwin Wilbour*, 89, 194, 253, 386.

Frénay, Auguste (fl. 1884-1897)

The superintendent of the French flour mills at Akhmim, with residence in Alexandria, and French consular agent between 1884 and 1897.[830] He was deeply involved with the antiquities trade in the region of Akhmim (p. 35); famous objects that passed through his hands include Amarna tablets, the demotic Papyrus Insinger, and more than a thousand leaves of Coptic manuscripts.[831]

Galil (fl. 1899)

Antiquities dealer at Luxor; Borchardt visited him on 13 October 1899 on a round trip that also included Mohammed (Mohasseb), Mohareb (Todros), Abd el-Megid, Ahmed Yussuf, and others.[832]

Gindi Faltas (fl. 1901-1910)

Coptic dealer at Akhmim who is recorded selling papyri to the German papyrus cartel between 1901 and 1910.[833]

Gindiya (fl. 1884)

Woman living at Qurnet Murai on the Theban West Bank who specialised in the production of fake stamps with the name of Ramesses III which she sold at Medinet Habu (p. 45).[834]

Girgis and Abd en-Nur Gabrial (fl. 1884-1930)

Lange notes in 1900 that the Coptic brothers Girgis Gabrial and Abd en-Nur Gabrial were said to be 'the most significant dealers in Qena' and that they sometimes journeyed to Cairo to meet prospective clients; Lange had met Abd en-Nur when the latter came on such a visit to see Schäfer, and recognised him while passing through Qena on his way back to Cairo. He was introduced to his brother Girgis, 'the most beautiful Egyptian I have ever seen', and shown to their house which was located next to a school: 'Girgis was a decent man, and immediately pointed out the fakes to me, and when I pointed a fake out to him he put it aside at once.'[835]

Charles Wilbour already bought objects from Girgis between 1884 and 1890, and refers explicitly to him having an antiquities shop at Qena in 1890.[836] Petrie first made his acquaintance in January 1887 and regularly did business with him for many years.[837] He notes, in passing, that Girgis had earlier had a permit to excavate a cemetery at Dendera, where he himself excavated in 1897, but that the dealer found all the tombs empty.[838] He first mentions dealing with the brother of Girgis, Abd en-Nur, in 1898. Quibell mentioned him as an example of an honest and trustwor-

830. Cf. Capart (ed.), *Letters of Charles Edwin Wilbour*, 204, 348; Meurice, in Immerzeel and J. van der Vliet (eds.), *Coptic Studies on the Threshold of a New Millennium* 2, 964.

831. Amarna tablets: Sayce, *AJSL* 33, no. 2 (1917), 89-90. Papyrus Insinger: Ryholt, in Ryholt and Barjamovic (eds.), *Libraries before Alexandria*, forthcoming. Coptic manuscripts: Louis, in Bosson and Boud'hors (eds.), *Actes du huitième congrès international d'études coptes* 1, 99-114; David, *Gaston Maspero*, 149-150; Maspero, *Lettres d'Égypte*, 131. Cf. further Golénischeff, *RT* 11 (1889), 96; Bouriant, *RT* 11 (1889), 146. Frénay is the unnamed French consul from whom Budge purchased some 200 vellum leaves of early Coptic manuscripts at Akhmim in January 1888; cf. Ismail, *Wallis Budge*, 112-113.

832. Borchardt diary, Sept. 1899 - Jan. 1900, entry 13 Oct. 1899 (Swiss Institute, Kairo; transcript kindly provided by Cornelius von Pilgrim, 21 Jan. 2015).

833. Martin and Primavesi, *L'Empédocle de Strasbourg*, 327, n. 3; cf. also Mietke et al., *Josef Strzygowski und die Berliner Museen*, 65-66 (selling Coptic textiles in 1900/1901).

834. Cf. Capart (ed.), *Letters of Charles Edwin Wilbour*, 285, 354.

835. Lange and Lange, *Dagbog fra Ægyptensrejsen 1899-1900*, 363-364. For Abd en-Nur, cf. also Quirke, *Hidden Hands*, 131.

836. Cf. Capart (ed.), *Letters of Charles Edwin Wilbour*, 271, 298, 350, 559, 560.

837. Petrie, *Seventy Years in Archaeology*, 169, 230; cf. Quirke's forthcoming work on Petrie as a collector.

838. Petrie, *Seventy Years in Archaeology*, 169.

thy dealer in 1895 (cited in context p. 157),[839] and Budge dealt with him in 1896.[840]

Abd en-Nur Gabrial, for his part, is known to have been involved in the sale of the Patermouthis archive in 1907-1908 together with the dealer Hamed Abd el-Hamid from Edfu.[841] The following year he sold the only extant Coptic version of the *Apocalypse of Paul* in collaboration with Maurice Nahman.[842]

The two brothers also had a shop in Luxor, at least from 1911.[843] In the Baedeker guides from 1928 and 1929, the younger brother ('Girgis Gubrian') is included among the reliable antiquities dealers in Luxor and the shop is said to be located on Sharia el-Lukanda.[844] Lange visited the shop in 1930 and copied various stelae in his possession, and also bought 12 Greek and Coptic ostraca, for 5 piastres each.[845] At that time, the shop was tended both by 'the old Girgis' (Girgis Gabrial) and his son, 'the young Girgis' (Todros Girgis Gabrial). The shop was later run by Albert Tawdros, the grandson of Girgis Gabrial and presumably a son of Todros Girgis Gabrial.

Graf, Otto Theodor (1840-1903)

Austrian merchant who came to Egypt, after his education, to head the branch of a trading company in Alexandria (Fig. 142).[846] He soon got involved in the trade of carpets and antiquities, dealing first from his address in Alexandria (Maison Monferrato at Rue du

Fig. 142. Theodor Graf, a Viennese carpet dealer with offices in Alexandria and Cairo who enjoyed considerable success in antiquities trade in the 1870s and 1880s. Photo dated 1897. Courtesy of Österreichische Nationalbibliothek.

Café Paradis) and later opening a shop in Vienna with a branch in Cairo. He enjoyed considerable success in the late 1870s through the 1890s, securing thousands of papyri from the Fayum, the bulk of the Fayum portraits, the majority of the Amarna tablets, and important groups of mainly Late Antique textiles. Between 1888 and 1893 he toured internationally with a sales exhibition of his vast collection of mummy portraits, and Jacobsen acquired five examples in 1892 when it reached Copenhagen.[847] Most of his antiquities trade was conducted from Vienna.

839. Quibell, *The Ramesseum*, 1.

840. Ismail, *Wallis Budge*, 294.

841. Dijkstra, *BASP* 44 (2007), 199, 205-206, n. 1.

842. Cf. Layton, *Catalogue of Coptic Literary Manuscripts in the British Museum*, 134.

843. Cf. Spiegelberg, *ZÄS* 51 (1913), 81.

844. Baedeker, *Ägypten und der Sûdan*, 8th edition, 38-39; idem, *Egypt and the Sûdân*, 8th edition, 268.

845. Lange, *Dagbog fra Ægypten, 1929-1930*, 243-244.

846. Bierbrier, *Who was Who in Egyptology*, 4th edition, 219-220; Bernhard-Walcher, in Seipel (ed.), *Bilder aus dem Wüstensand*, 27-35. For the Alexandria office, cf. *Annuaire égyptien, administratif et commercial, 1891-1892*, 186; Ebers, *ZÄS* 18 (1880), 58, and Budge, *PSBA* 10 (1888), 541. A series of letters concerning Graf's trade in antiquities are published by Hunger, *Aus der Vorgeschichte der Papyrussammlung der Österreichischen Nationalbibliothek*.

847. The five mummy portraits cost DM 10,000; Graf eventually offered all 90 exhibited portraits to Jacobsen for a total of DM 37,500, but the latter felt that five were enough for his collection. Jørgensen, *How it all began*, 45-46, fig. 41-45; cf. also idem, *Egypt III*, 330-331, 334-341.

Habib Tawadrus (*fl.* 1945-48)

Antiquities dealer, apparently a Copt to judge from his name. He sold objects to the Egyptian Museum in 1945, and in 1948 he gave the Egyptian Museum 34 stelae from Kom Abu Billo (as well as some minor fayence objects from Qantir) in exchange for antiquities from Tuna el-Gebel.[848]

Hamed Abd el-Hamid (*fl.* 1908-1930)

Hamed Abd el-Hamid (occasionally called Hamed Hamid) was a dealer based at Edfu. Lange visited him on 23 December 1929 and described him as 'an older and distinguished gentleman', whose collection was displayed at his house in 'a living room with glass display cases around the walls, where good and bad, genuine and fake, stood next to each other'.[849] His collection included local stelae mentioning Edfu, and 'black-topped predynastic vases, lovely alabaster objects that are so sought after by tourists, as well as prehistoric schist palettes'. Lange bought one such palette in the shape of a bird, for 20 piastres. He had clearly been informed about him prior to his visit to Edfu, because the day before he arrived he noted his intention to seek him out, and mentions him by name.

Hamed Abd el-Hamid is otherwise known to have been active between 1908 (when he was involved in the sale of the Patermouthis Archive with Abd en-Nur Gabrial)[850] and 1926.[851]

Hamed Ismaïl (*fl.* 1887)

Obscure dealer who sold an object to the Egyptian Museum in 1887 (p. 51).

Hamid Mohammed Mohasseb (*fl.* 1909-1922)

Son of Mohammed Mohasseb *Bey*, q.v.

Sheikh Hamza (*fl.* 1930)

Sheikh Hamza was a Cairo dealer living in the village Kafr el-Haram near Giza, who on one occasion used Zaki Mahmud Abd es-Samad as an agent to try to sell Lange a statue of a king for £200 (Fig. 143).[852] Hamza claimed that he had not shown the statue to anyone else and that he wanted to sell it 'in secret'. Lange was initially excited about the item and immediately contacted the Ny Carlsberg Glyptotek, having agreed to a price of £150 after some bartering. Nonetheless he later declined the offer as he found the statue 'suspicious', perhaps having conferred with colleagues on the matter. On another occasion Lange was offered a granite head of a king for £50 by Hamza, which he also declined for unstated reasons; this same head was later sold to the Danish diplomat Niels Peter Arnstedt (1882-1954) in a transaction with Zaki Mahmud Abd es-Samad that was facilitated by Lange.[853] Lange for his part instead acquired some fragmentary alabaster objects from Hamza's son.

Hanna Kerass (*fl.* 1887-1890)

Antiquities dealer at el-Manshah (Gr. *Ptolemais Hermou*) who also ran a protestant school which he opened around 1887.[854] He was among the dealers whose antiquities were seized by Grébaut in 1888 (p.

848. Cairo Museum, Temporary Register, s.v. 6/2/46/1-21, 22/2/48/1-34 and 26/2/48/1-8.
849. Lange, *Dagbog fra Ægypten, 1929-1930*, 171, 174. The palette is now in the National Museum, inv. 11621 (Lange bequest).
850. Dijkstra, *BASP* 44 (2007), 199.
851. Emmel, 'The Yale Papyrus Collection. Catalog Introduction', 1993, with additions by R. Duttenhofer 1996, available on-line http://www.library.yale.edu/ beinecke/brblsear/ aboutpap.htm (accessed 24 July 2012); cf. also Kruit and Worp, *BASP* 39 (2002), 47.

852. Lange, *Dagbog fra Ægypten, 1929-1930*, 127-129, 183-184, 250, 266.
853. Lange, *Dagbog fra Ægypten, 1929-1930*, 350.
854. Cf. Capart (ed.), *Letters of Charles Edwin Wilbour*, 428, 456, 461, 490, 526, 528, 544, 560, 561.

Fig. 143. Royal statue offered for sale by *Sheikh* Hamza at Kafr el-Haram in December 1929. Lange, initially excited by the small sculpture, records in his travel diary on 20 January: 'I arrived at the stop at Kafr at 10 o'clock. Zakki [sc. Zaki Mahmud Abd es-Samad] was waiting for me there and immediately brought me to the house of *Sheikh* Hamzah where I took three photographs of his statue.' Some days later, on 2 February, he briefly notes, 'I give up on the royal statue at Hamzah's. It looks suspicious to me.' Lange photographs. Courtesy of the Egyptological Archives, University of Copenhagen.

143). In 1889 he was accused and acquitted of the murder of the local postmaster.

Sheikh Hassan (*fl.* 1895-1896)

Antiquities dealer from Kafr el-Haram who excavated the greater part of the necropolis of el-Hiba in 1895/96; Grenfell and Hunt report that 'from the assertions of an inhabitant of Hibeh who was then employed as a *reis*, it appears that the dealer met with much success'.[855] Papyri from this excavation were acquired by Grenfell and Hunt as well as Carl Reinhardt on the antiquities market in Cairo in 1896.[856]

Hassan Abd el-Megid (1889-1916)

Son of Abd el-Megid, q.v.

Hassan Abd er-Rahman (*fl.* 1930)

Little is known about Hassan Abd er-Rahman. On one occasion he sold Lange a glass bowl for 50 piastres,[857] and on another he contacted him on behalf of a man from Assiut who has arrived in Cairo with the head of a princess ('broken just below the breast, with a uraeus and a lovingly crafted wig, complete without a splinter missing'); Lange was uncertain whether the head was genuine and declined the offer.[858]

Hassan Abd es-Salam (*fl.* 1913)

Cairo dealer with whom the numismatist Edward T. Newell is said to have traded extensively.[859] Possibly a son of the dealer Abd es-Salam from Kafr el-Haram.

855. Grenfell and Hunt, *The Hibeh Papyri* 1, 2.
856. Goodspeed, *Classical Philology* 7, no. 4 (1912), 512.

857. Lange, *Dagbog fra Ægypten, 1929-1930*, 47.
858. Lange, *Dagbog fra Ægypten, 1929-1930*, 90-91, cf. p. 28.
859. Metcalf, *Revue belge de numismatique* 122 (1976), 70.

Hassan el-Gauz (*fl.* 1923)

A minor dealer at Sheikh Abd el-Qurna who mainly sold fakes, according to B. Bruyère.[860]

Hassan Ibrahim Anwad (*fl.* 1926)

A dealer at Sheikh Abd el-Qurna from whom Borchardt, in 1926, acquired a stool said to have been found at Moalla.[861]

Hassan Laban (*fl.* 1923)

A minor dealer at Sheikh Abd el-Qurna who mainly sold fakes, according to B. Bruyère.[862]

Hassan Mohammed Mahmud (*fl.* prior to 1974)

Luxor dealer with antiquities license no. 92.[863]

Hassan Saïd (*fl.* 1923)

A minor dealer at Sheikh Abd el-Qurna who mainly sold fakes, according to B. Bruyère.[864]

Hatoun, Elias (*fl.* 1893-1930s)

Elias Hatoun, who had a prominent shop at Sharia el-Muski (Fig. 58), dealt broadly in oriental wares, both ancient and modern.[865] One tourist described his large shop as 'really a museum of ancient and modern Oriental articles'.[866] Another described the acquisition for the Wayne County Historical Museum, in Richmond, of

> a mummy and a fine case covered with hieroglyphs. ... It had been on exhibition in Cairo for forty years, in the store of E. Hatoun, and we were fortunate to secure it. The Bureau of Antiquities declined to release it until the State Department took up the matter; it reached Richmond eleven months after being purchased.[867]

Sometime in the early 1930s the shop changed name from 'E. Hatoun' to 'E. Hatoun & Sons', and it later became 'E. Hatoun's Sons'. It was still active in 1963.[868]

Hefnawy Ismaïl el-Shaer (*fl.* 1950-1970)

Hefnawy Ismaïl el-Shaer (Table 6; Fig. 76, 144) was the son of Ismaïl Abdallah and took over his father's business. He was active at least from 1950.[869] By 1969/70 the shop was located at 11 Sharia Mariette Pasha, across from the Cairo Museum, and a business card obtained there reads (Fig. 18):

> H. Ismail el Shaer. Dealer in Genuine old Egyptian Antiquities. Licence No. 1. 11, Mariette Pasha St. obest. Egyptian Museum. Cairo (Egypt).

Ismaïl el-Shaer was the uncle of Mohammed Abd er-Rahim el-Shaer and possibly the brother of Farag el-Shaer.

Heras (*fl.* 1884)

Dealer at Qena briefly mentioned by Wilbour.[870]

860. Diary entry dated 30 Jan. 1923; http://www.ifao.egnet.net/bases/archives/bruyere/ (accessed 11 Sept. 2013).
861. von Briskorn, *Zur Sammlungsgeschichte afrikanischer Ethnographica im Übersee-Museum Bremen 1841-1945*, 195.
862. Diary entry dated 30 Jan. 1923; http://www.ifao.egnet.net/bases/archives/bruyere/ (accessed 11 Sept. 2013).
863. Bonhams, Antiquities, Auction catalogue of 23 Oct. 2013, London, 2013, 16, which includes a photograph of Hassan Mohammed Mahmud in front of his shop.
864. Diary entry dated 30 Jan. 1923; http://www.ifao.egnet.net/bases/archives/bruyere/ (accessed 11 Sept. 2013).
865. Sladen, *Oriental Cairo*, 70, 97; Reynolds-Ball, *Cairo of To-Day*, 1st edition, 22; 5th edition, 24; Baedeker, *Ägypten*, 4th edition, 28; idem, *Egypt and the Sûdân*, 8th edition, 43; Gunter, *A Collector's*

Journey, 90, 115, 151, n. 7. He was active already in 1893, cf. Gottheil, *JAOS* 30 (1910), 60.
866. Carson, *From Cairo to Cataract*, 96.
867. Gaar, *Indiana History Bulletin* 8 (1931), 363.
868. Bresciani, *EVO* 18 (1995), 19.
869. Christie's auction of 30 Sept. 2003 (sale 5062, lot 50; cf. http://www.christies.com (accessed 24 Sept. 2013).
870. Cf. Capart (ed.), *Letters of Charles Edwin Wilbour*, 298.

d'Hulst, Riamo (*fl.* 1870-1921)

Count d'Hulst, a former German officer, excavated in Egypt for the Egypt Exploration Fund 1886-1893 (mainly as an assistant to Édouard Naville) and later became an antiquities dealer based in Cairo; he may have been the 'middle man' dealer in the acquisition of an obsidian head of King Senwosret III now in the Museum Calouste Gulbenkian, Lisbon (inv. no. 238).[871] He was a keen photographer and is said to have created a collection of some 15,000 images, some of which were exhibited abroad.

Hussein (*fl.* 1887-1889)

Antiquities dealer based at Edfu.[872] He was among the dealers who had their antiquities seized by Grébaut in 1888 (p. 143). He subsequently obtained the protection of an unidentified Greek who enjoyed diplomatic immunity and operated a local rum-shop in which Hussein stored antiquities (p. 37).

Hussein Abd el-Megid (*fl.* 1928-1929)

Grandson of Abd el-Megid, q.v.

Hussein Abd es-Salam (*fl.* 1926)

Cairo dealer who sold papyri to Idris Bell in 1926.[873] Possibly a son of the dealer Abd es-Salam from Kafr el-Haram.

Fig. 144. Hefnawy Ismaïl el-Shaer in his antiquities shop, January 1971. Courtesy of Rob Demarée.

Hussein Ahmed Abd er-Rasul

Brother of Abd er-Rasul Ahmed Abd er-Rasul, q.v.

Ibrahim (*fl.* 1855)

The Copt Ibrahim was one of the main dealers at Luxor in the 1850s; he ran a 'laboratory' at his house (described in p. 147), where several forgers mass-produced objects for sale, and he is also recorded acquiring antiquities at el-Kab.[874]

Sheikh Ibrahim Abd es-Samad (born *c.* 1838, *fl.* 1892-1930)

Ibrahim Abd es-Samad (Table 3) was the brother of Soliman Abd es-Samad. The Lange couple first went

871. Bierbrier, *Who was Who in Egyptology*, 4th edition, 268-269; Hardwick, *DE* 65 (2012), 9-10; Jefferson, *JHC* 21, no. 1 (2009), 125-142; idem, in Outhwaite and Bhayro (eds.), *Fs Reif*, 171-200.
872. Cf. Capart (ed.), *Letters of Charles Edwin Wilbour*, 461, 462, 511, cf. also p. 424 w. plate, for the Elephant Hunt Inscription acquired from Hussein in 1887.
873. Emmel, 'The Yale Papyrus Collection. Catalog Introduction', 1993, with additions by R. Duttenhofer 1996, available on-line http://www.library.yale.edu/ beinecke/brblsear/ aboutpap.htm (accessed 24 July 2012).

874. Prime, *Boat Life in Egypt*, 216-217, 229-230, 363-364.

to see him at his newly built two-storey house at Kafr el-Haram in November 1899. His collection of antiquities was considerable, 'a veritable museum' according to Jonna.[875] They also received him at their own home.[876]

Jonna provides several descriptions of Ibrahim. The longest informs us that he was:

> a learned man, circumstances considering; he can read royal names in inscriptions, and enjoys a considerable reputation for that reason in the village. He gets his knowledge from a couple of books which the Arabic assistant in the museum, Ahmed Bey [i.e. Ahmed *Bey* Kamal], has written for his compatriots.[877]

Later he is described as 'a handsome old man, 61 or 62 years old; he speaks English best among them all, where he learnt it, I don't know', 'the learned one' and 'really a handsome man ... very elegantly dressed'.[878] Ibrahim had performed the Hajj with his whole family, including his brother Soliman, and had printed business cards that proclaimed his status as *Hajji* which he handed out to customers and acquaintances.[879]

Lange's friend Dr Tiescher once bought a fake lead figurine from him, which Lange went to return to him in the village on Tiescher's behalf on 13 June 1900. Ibrahim was 'very sorry to hear that it was fake, but had evidently not known it himself'; he readily agreed to let Lange choose a replacement from his shop in Cairo the next day.[880] At the end of the trip to Egypt in 1899/1900, Lange included him in a list of three 'reasonably decent' Egyptian dealers.[881]

The Lange couple visited Ibrahim Abd es-Samad again thirty years later during their second visit to Egypt. He must now have been around 90 years old (if his age as reported by Jonna was correct), but was still very active in the trade. Once more he is described as 'the learned Ibrahim' and 'the only one among the Bedouins at Kafr who knows a bit of Egyptian history and who can also read some hieroglyphs.'[882] On one visit they were presented with a large block of diorite inscribed with the royal names of Sahure, which the aged Ibrahim and his son Mahmud pulled out from somewhere, but the price was much too high; 'He demanded £100, so I won't rob him of this item', Lange wrote.

Ibrahim and his brother Soliman are also mentioned in the autobiography of Lange's old teacher Valdemar Schmidt in a passsage describing the antiquities trade at Giza around 1892:

> Most of the inhabitants of the little Arab village by the great pyramids would only display their antiquities after dark, when they would drag them in the dark from one hiding-place to another. The most famous dealers were the brothers Soliman and Ibrahim Abd-el-Samon.[883]

Sheikh Ibrahim continued to have dealings with Valdemar Schmidt, who had furnished him with a letter of recommendation in 1914 that was proudly showed to Lange upon his return to Egypt in 1929.[884]

The brothers Ibrahim and Soliman were related to the antiquities dealer Ali Gabri and are included in his elaborate family tree which was recorded by Petrie in 1887 and traces the family back to an ancestor who left Tunis about two centuries earlier; it emerges that Ibrahim and Soliman were sons of Ali Gabri's brother

875. Lange and Lange, *Dagbog fra Ægyptensrejsen 1899-1900*, 141.

876. Lange and Lange, *Dagbog fra Ægyptensrejsen 1899-1900*, 662-669.

877. Lange and Lange, *Dagbog fra Ægyptensrejsen 1899-1900*, 739.

878. Lange and Lange, *Dagbog fra Ægyptensrejsen 1899-1900*, 481, 662-663.

879. Lange and Lange, *Dagbog fra Ægyptensrejsen 1899-1900*, 141; cf. also Lange, *Dagbog fra Ægypten, 1929-1930*, 87 (El Hagg Ibrahim Abd es-Samad). Abd es-Saman is a variant translitteration of Abd es-Samad.

880. Lange and Lange, *Dagbog fra Ægyptensrejsen 1899-1900*, 656. Lange, *Notebook 1899/1900*, 206, records seeing fragments in black granite from a temple of Nectanebo I depicting at least two nomes (the nomen and prenomen of the king copied out in hieroglyphs toghether with the names of the two nomes)

with 'Old Ibrahim in an old courtyard in Cairo.'

881. Lange and Lange, *Dagbog fra Ægyptensrejsen 1899-1900*, 738-739.

882. Lange, *Dagbog fra Ægypten, 1929-1930*, 96, 124-125.

883. Schmidt, *Af et Langt Livs Historie*, 90.

884. Lange, *Dagbog fra Ægypten, 1929-1930*, 87, 124-125.

Abd es-Samad and hence his nephews.[885] Two of Ibrahim's sons were also involved in the antiquities trade: Mahmud Ibrahim Abd es-Samad, whom the Lange couple regarded as a childish man, and another unnamed son, whom they describe as:

> the most attractive individual one could imagine (...) we bought from him for £3. He has guided the Crown Princess of Sweden on the Nile three times, and can usually be found at Mena House, where he apparently does very profitable business; his entire collection was also exceptional, only meant for persons of standing.[886]

It is perhaps the same *Sheikh* Ibrahim, 'who spoke very good English', whom Wilbour met at Giza during his first visit to Egypt in 1881 and who assisted Petrie during his work at Giza 1880-1882.[887]

Ibrahim Ali (*fl.* 1899-1909)

Ibrahim Ali (Table 3) was a son of Ali Abd el-Haj el-Gabri and, in contrast to his older brother Mohammed Ali, whom the Lange couple despised, Jonna Lange took a liking to Ibrahim. Hans and Jonna went to see him at his house at Kafr el-Haram in 1900 and Lange acquired 'some small objects', while Jonna was given three little figures.[888] She describes him, on an-

other occasion, as 'the most learned of all the Bedouins; he can really read parts of the inscriptions and looks very intelligent.'[889]

It was presumably the same Ibrahim Ali (Fig. 128) who had served as a guide and translator for Charles Lang Freer during his visits to Egypt 1906-9 and who received a gold-watch for his services along with Ali Abd el-Haj el-Gabri and Mohammed Ali (p. 63).

Ibrahim Faïd (*fl.* 1885-1912)

Ibrahim Faïd (Fig. 145), a native of Kafr el-Haram, was a government *reïs* (i.e. foreman) attached to excavations between Cairo and Fayum, a function he held at least as early as 1900.[890] In 1912 he and several members of his family were convicted of illegal trading in antiquities, although they had for many years – according to Reisner – been under the protection of Maspero (p. 98).[891] Ibrahim Faïd himself was sentenced to five years' hard labour, but appealed with the aid of Maspero and was almost immediately acquitted. Soon after he became involved with Junker's excavations at Giza.

Ibrahim Hamid (*fl.* 1900)

Dealer who showed Borchardt some antiquities in Cairo in 1900; Borchardt described them as 'useless'.[892] He is perhaps identical to a like-named antiquities dealer who had a shop in Luxor in 1901.[893]

---

885. Quirke, *Hidden Hands*, 132-134.
886. Lange and Lange, *Dagbog fra Ægyptensrejsen 1899-1900*, 657. The Crown Princess referred to here is Victoria of Baden (1862-1930) who had an abiding interest in Egyptian archaeology. She travelled extensively in Egypt in 1890-1891, and the objects acquired during the trip were later donated to Uppsala University where they named a museum after her (Victoriamuseet); Alm and Johansson, *Resan till Egypten*, 170-171. She published an illustrated account of her travels: *Vom Nil: Tagebuchblätter während des Aufenthalts in Ägypten im Winter 1890-1891*; visits to antiquities dealers are mentioned on pp. 138 (in Luxor; a mummy is bought, said to be for the collection of her parents in Karlsruhe) and 152 (in Cairo, accompanied by Emil Brugsch). Her excavations at Aswan included the famous Old Kingdom tomb of Harkhuf; cf. Schiaparelli, *Una tomba egiziana inedita della VIª dinastia*, 5.
887. Cf. Capart (ed.), *Letters of Charles Edwin Wilbour*, 11-13; Quirke, *Hidden Hands*, 51, 55.
888. Lange and Lange, *Dagbog fra Ægyptensrejsen 1899-1900*, 655.

889. Lange and Lange, *Dagbog fra Ægyptensrejsen 1899-1900*, 195.
890. Covington, *ASAE* 6 (1905), 194; Barsanti, *ASAE* 7 (1906), 260-261; cf. also Kamal, *ASAE* 9 (1908), 85; Barsanti, *ASAE* 8 (1908), 205, 207, 209; idem, *ASAE* 12 (1912), 58; Edgar and Edgar, *The Great Pyramid Passages and Chambers*, 115, photograph on p. 175; Der Manuelian, *KMT* 7, no. 2 (1996), 70, 72; idem, in Spiekermann (ed.), *Fs Schmitz*, 34.
891. Reisner's claim about Maspero seems corroborated by Wilbour's statement that 'he employs from preference the Bedaween of the Gizeh pyramids', sc. the Bedouin from Kafr el-Haram; cf. Capart (ed.), *Letters of Charles Edwin Wilbour*, 92.
892. Borchardt diary, Sept. 1899 - Jan. 1900, entry 3 Jan. 1900 (Swiss Institute, Kairo; transcript kindly provided by Cornelius von Pilgrim, 21 Jan. 2015).
893. Wakeling, *Forged Egyptian Antiquities*, 24-25, 45, 66, 80-81. He

Fig. 145. Ibrahim Faïd of Kafr el-Haram, 1909. Published by Edgar & Edgar, *The Great Pyramid Passages and Chambers*, 175.

Ibrahim Mohasseb (*fl.* 1881-1886)

The dealer Ibrahim Mohasseb was the neighbour of Mohammed Ahmed Abd er-Rasul at Sheikh Abd el-Qurna.[894] Wilbour mentions that Ibrahim on one occasion acquired an expensive papyrus on behalf of Mohammed Mohasseb, and in view of their identical patronyms and his date, he is likely to have been a brother of his. Wilbour further reports that it was this

Ibrahim who first told him, in April 1881, about the Abd er-Rasul brothers' discovery of the famous royal cache, that they believed its contents to be worth £40,000, and that he himself had personally seen 36 papyri from the tomb.

Iconomopoulos (*fl.* 1890)

Individual from whom the Bulaq Museum acquired some objects in 1890 (p. 51); perhaps identical with the physician D. Iconomopoulos who published *Le cholera en Égypte en 1883* in 1884 or the railway engineer Léonidas D. Iconomopoulos who published *Cairo: A Guide Book for Visitors to the Capital of Egypt* in 1894; both were stationed in Cairo.

Idris *Effendi* (*fl.* 1887 - d. 1898)

Dealer living at Dra Abu el-Naga visited by collectors including Wilbour, Budge, Petrie, and Myers; Newberry rented his house during work in the area in 1895.[895] Petrie notes in 1893 that he had a shop in Luxor located opposite that of Abd el-Megid.[896]

Insinger, Jan Herman (1854-1918)

Dutch business man who came to Egypt for reasons of health in 1879; from 1889 (or 1884?) until his death in 1918 he lived in Luxor.[897] He engaged in both money-lending and the antiquities trade from the castle-like residence which he had constructed (p. 35, 125) and which was apparently considered sovereign Dutch territory. This meant in practice that no Egyptian official could enter the premises without permission, a fact which saved him and his collection during Grébaut's raids (p. 143). He had been trying to get the

refers to him as 'Hamid Ibrahim' at one point, but otherwise simply as Ibrahim which indicates that the name was rather Ibrahim Hamid.

894. Cf. Capart (ed.), *Letters of Charles Edwin Wilbour*, 65, 297, 371; David, *Gaston Maspero*, 134.

895. Bierbrier, *Who was Who in Egyptology*, 4th edition, 273 (w. photo). He was active already in 1887; cf. Miatello, *ZÄS* 139 (2012), 158.
896. Quirke, *Hidden Hands*, 129.
897. Raven, *OMRO* 71 (1991), 13-27; Bierbrier, *Who was Who in Egyptology*, 4th edition, 273; Raven (ed.), *J. H. Insinger: In het land der Nijlcataracten (1883)*, 1-16; cf. further David, *Gaston Maspero*, passim.

prominent dealer Mohammed Mohasseb appointed as a Dutch consul, but the Dutch government refused.

Ishak Migallah (*fl.* 1943)

Dealer at Akhmim who sold the base of a black basalt statue to the Egyptian Museum in 1943.[898]

Iskander Farag (*fl.* 1931)

Dealer who sold a demotic manual on meterological omina to the Egyptian Museum on 4 February 1931.[899]

Ismaïl Abdallah el-Shaer (*fl.* 1907-1958)

Ismaïl Abdallah el-Shaer (Table 6) was active in the antiquities business for more than fifty years. He was originally based at 'Giza' (sc. Kafr el-Haram) where he is recorded selling papyri to the German papyrus cartel in 1907.[900] He later operated a shop across from Shepheard's Hotel which he may have inherited from Abdallah Ismaïl if the latter is corrected identified as his father. A business card of his from 1922, inscribed on the reverse with a certificate of authenticity concerning a scarab, reads:

> Ismail Abdallah el-Shaer. Dealer in genuine old Egyptian Antiquities, Real old Scarabs, Amulets, Figures and such Curiosities. By Permission from the Egyptian Museum Cairo. Licence No. 1. Every thing guaranteed. Harat el-Zahar Opposite Shepheard's Hotel Cairo.[901]

He was still active in January 1958.[902] His business was continued by his son Hefnawy Ismaïl el-Shaer.

Jovanovich (*fl.* 1885)

Individual from whom the Bulaq Museum acquired some objects in 1885 (p. 51).

Kalebdjian, Hagob and Garbis (*fl.* 1900-1956)

The Armenian brothers Hagob Kalebdjian and his younger brother Garbis (b. 1885) ran the shop 'Kalebdjian Frères' in Cairo at Rue el-Méligui from around 1900; in 1905 they opened a second shop in Paris at 12 Rue de la Paix, later relocating to 21 Rue Balzac and thence to 52 Avenue d'Iéna.[903] A visit to the latter in 1919 is described by Breasted:

> I found two Armenian brothers, Kalebdjian Frères, with an antiquity shop in the Rue de la Paix. They turned out to be wealthy antiquity dealers with a place also in Cairo. Over in the region where Benjamin Hart lived they also had an entire house filled with wonderful things which they were offering for sale, – their main stock indeed. They had quite a number of things from the old Amélineau sale ...[904]

They were active at least as early as 1900, at which point their nephew, the famous forger Oxan Aslanian,

---

898. Cairo Museum, Temporary Register, s.v. 24/7/43/1; Journal d'entrée 86634.

899. Cairo Museum, Temporary Register, s.v. 4.2.31.1. For a discussion of the text, see now Collombert, in Depauw and Broux (eds.), *Acts of the Tenth International Congres of Demotic Studies*, 15-26.

900. Giessener Papyri- und Ostrakadatenbank on-line (http://digibib.ub.uni-giessen.de/cgi-bin/populo/pap.pl, s.v. Ismain Abdallah el-Sair; accessed 7 Dec. 2013). Further papyri were acquired from him in 1926 by Idris Bell from his shop in Cairo; cf. Emmel, 'The Yale Papyrus Collection. Catalog Introduction', 1993, with additions by R. Duttenhofer 1996, available on-line http://www.library.yale.edu/ beinecke/brblsear/aboutpap.htm (accessed 24 July 2012); cf. also Pedley, *The Life and Work of Francis Willey Kelsey*, 375.

901. Offered for sale by Live Auctioneers on 30 May 2006, cf. http://www.liveauctioneers.com/item/2056915 (accessed 24 July 2012). We are uncertain if the certificate is genuine, since a number of other fake certificates are known to have been fabricated.

902. De Meulenaere, *BIFAO* 60 (1960), 118, n. 7.

903. Schröter, *Stoff für Tausend und Ein Jahr*, 214-223; cf. also Musée du Louvre, *Les Donateurs du Louvre*, 240; Gunter, *A Collector's Journey*, 35, fig. 2.7, 38, fig. 2.10, 91. Leiden Museum bought 54 objects from their Paris shop during the years 1949-1956 (Maarten Raven, personal communication).

904. Cf. Larson (ed.), *Letters from James Henry Breasted*, 72.

worked at their Cairo shop; the Paris shop, at which they were based, was later notorious for selling forgeries.[905] They are known to have purchased objects at various large-scale auctions of Egyptian antiquities in Europe, including the Amélineau Collection in 1904, the Hilton Price Collection in 1911, the MacGregor Collection in 1922, and the Hearst Collection in 1939 (p. 129). They were still active after World War II; the Leiden Museum purchased a magical statue fragment from them in 1950.[906]

Kalemkarian, Trifon H. (fl. 1926-1935)

Dealer in Cairo recorded selling papyri in 1926-1927; by 1935 he had moved his business to Palestine where he was a licensed dealer.[907]

Kamel Abdallah Hammouda (fl. 1944-1972)

Kamel Abdallah Hammouda, a dealer in Cairo, had his shop at 7 Sharia el-Mahdi, close to Shepheard's Hotel.[908] He was active at least since 1944, in 1962 he was involved in the sale of an Amun statue from the reign of Tutankhamun now in Karlsruhe (p. 129), and he was still in business in 1972.[909] It is presumably the

same Kamel in Cairo from whom Aksel Volten acquired a number of papyri for the Papyrus Carlsberg Collection in late 1954.[910]

Kamal Khalid (fl. late 1920s)

Kamal Khalid had an antiquities shop in one of the stalls at the Winter Palace Hotel at Luxor and is mentioned in the Baedeker guides of 1928 and 1929 (p. 287).[911]

Kelekian, Dikran Garabed (1867-1951)

Prominent Armenian antiquities dealer (Fig. 146) who began his career in Istanbul, 1892; later settled in New York, becoming a US citizen in 1898, and opened a shop on Madison Avenue called *Le Musée de Bosphore*.[912] He opened two further branches, in Paris at 12 Place Vendôme and Cairo at Continental Hotel, the latter in 1910.[913] The Egyptian venue was, according to the collector Albert Gallatin, 'only a small shop which he (sc. Kelekian) occupied on his visits to Cairo'.[914] Kelekian had been a friend of Oxan Aslanian and was able to provide useful information on him and his

905. Fiechter, *Faux et faussaires en art égyptien*, 30-32; idem, *Egyptian Fakes*, 71-73.

906. Klasens, *A Magical Statue Base*, 1.

907. Emmel, 'The Yale Papyrus Collection. Catalog Introduction', 1993, with additions by R. Duttenhofer 1996, available on-line http://www.library.yale.edu/ beinecke/brblsear/ aboutpap.htm (accessed 24 July 2012, s.v. Kalimkurion); Kersel, *Jewish Quarterly* 33 (2008), 34; Pedley, *The Life and Work of Francis Willey Kelsey*, 378.

908. Cf. advertisement enclosed with the exhibition catalogue of the Société d'archéologie copte, *Exposition d'art copte, Décembre 1944*, (here reproduced in Fig. 22); also reproduced by Bénazeth, *BIFAO* 97 (1997), 47. It reads, 'Kamel Abdallah Hammouda. Antiquities merchant. Licence from the Egyptian Museum No. 60. Egyptian, Greek, Roman, Coptic, Arabic and all kinds of genuine scarabs and coins. 7, Sharia El Mahdi. (Opposite Shepheard's Hotel). Cairo - Egypt.' The building has since been demolished and new construction work is presently taking place here.

909. The auction catalogue Zeeuws Veilinghuis, *Kunst- en antiekveiling, 8-10 juni 2010*, 20-21, 22, lists two objects acquired

from Hammouda in 1964, while a further number of objects acquired by Leighton A. Wilke from Hammouda in 1970 were sold by Bonhams on 26 Apr. 2007 (Auction 15215, lots 173-176, 188-189, 191), 26 Oct. 2007 (Auction 15216, no. 66), and 23 Jan. 2008 (Auction 15679, lot 38); cf. http://www.bonhams.com (accessed 6 Feb. 2013). A royal head in sunk relief cut from a temple wall was conceded to the Cairo Museum, 6 Dec. 1972; Cairo Museum, Temporary Register, s.v. 30/12/72/1.

910. Information inscribed on the paper folders originally used to store and sort the papyri in the collection.

911. Baedeker, *Ägypten und der Sudân*, 8th edition, 260; idem, *Egypt and the Sûdân*, 8th edition, 268; Clère, *BIFAO* 28 (1929), 190-192, 199, 200 (selling objects from Deir el-Medina).

912. Cf. Bierbrier, *Who was Who in Egyptology*, 4th edition, 292-293; New York, Southern District Index to Petitions for Naturalization, 1824-1941, accessed 13 June 2013 through *FamilySearch* (https://familysearch.org/pal:/MM9.1.1/XGNL-6YJ). His descendants still possess Egyptian objects; cf. Kelekian, *GM* 209 (2006), 43-47.

913. *American Art News* 9, no. 10 (Dec. 17, 1910), 5.

914. Gallatin, *The Pursuit of Happiness*, 178.

forgeries to H. E. Winlock in 1920.[915] His business was continued by his son Charles Dikran Kelekian (1899-1983). The Egyptian shop was nationalized in 1952 and the Paris shop closed in 1953, with business continuing in New York until the 1980s.

Khaled (*fl.* 1881-1893)

Antiquities dealer with a shop in Luxor; Wilbour mentions objects acquired by Khaled from both Akhmim and el-Manshah (both Sohag Governorate) and that he became a partner of the dealer Ahmed Yussuf in 1889.[916]

Khalifa (*fl.* 1881-1888)

Antiquities dealer living on the Theban West Bank often visited by Wilbour whose exploration of the area he would facilitate as a guide or provider of transportation.[917] Wilbour notes that he owned ten acres of land as well as three camels and five donkeys, and provides the following description of the man whom he sometimes refers to as 'old leather-face':

> Khaleefeh is a little dried up old man, the patriarch of a group of houses behind the Colossi half way from Medinet-Abu to Goornah.

He further mentions that Khalifa would fetch gilded mummies (and at least once also a stela) from tombs near the el-Kharga Oasis for sale at Thebes.

Khalil (*fl.* 1886-1889)

Antiquities dealer at Akhmim.[918] He was thought to have been involved in Grébaut's raids against Sidrac,

Fig. 146. Dikran Garabed Kelekian. Studio photograph from 1902 on the occasion of his appointment as Persian Consul in New York, where his art gallery came to serve as the Persian consulate. Courtesy of the Armenian Memory Institute.

another antiquities dealer at Akhmim, in 1888, but he himself also had antiquities seized.

Khalil (*fl.* 1891)

Antiquities dealer who ran what Wilbour described as the 'principal anteekeh shop' at Medinet el-Fayum in 1891.[919] He might be the father of Mohammed Khalil, a later dealer in this city.

915. Fiechter, *Faux et faussaires en art égyptien*, 33-34.
916. Cf. Capart (ed.), *Letters of Charles Edwin Wilbour*, 65, 105, 273, 508, 523, 557, 565; Kraeling, *The Brooklyn Museum Aramaic Papyri*, 10, fig. 1.
917. Cf. Capart (ed.), *Letters of Charles Edwin Wilbour*, 55, 58, 107, 115-116, 135, 136, 144-145, 210, 211, 224, 225, 273, 275, 351, 353, 354, 355, 356, 458, 463, 497 ('Khaleefeh', var. 'Khalifeh').
918. Cf. Capart (ed.), *Letters of Charles Edwin Wilbour*, 379, 456, 465, 488, 489, 526.
919. Cf. Capart (ed.), *Letters of Charles Edwin Wilbour*, 580.

Fig. 147. Sélim Khawam. Courtesy of Bertrand Khawam.

Fig. 148. Joseph Khawam. Courtesy of Bertrand Khawam.

Khawam Brothers (1912-)

Sélim Khawam (c. 1840-1900; Fig. 147), a Christian Syrian, founded an antiquities business in Cairo in 1862.[920] When the antiquities law of 1912 was issued, which required dealers to obtain an official license, his sons Jean (d. 1918), Amin (1875-1944), Faragallah (1884-1956), and Joseph (1883-1964; fig. 65, 148) – who had all become involved in the business – founded Khawam Brothers and received antiquities license no.

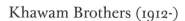

920. Bierbrier, *Who was Who in Egyptology*, 4th edition, 294; Pierre Bergé & associés, *Bibliothèque de l'Égyptologue Roger Khawam*; idem, *Archéologie*; Waxman, *Loot: The battle over the stolen treasures of the ancient world*, 123-129; http://www.khawam-brothers.com/en/historique (accessed 8 Jan. 2013); cf. also Musée du Louvre, *Les Donateurs du Louvre*, 241; personal information Bertrand Khawam.

7. The brothers had two shops; one at Sharia el-Madrastein and the other at Khan el-Khalili. Joseph's son Roger Khawam (1922-2016, Fig. 149) became manager of the business in 1952. Facing severe restrictions in the export of antiquities, he decided to close the business in Cairo in 1977 and move to Paris where it re-opened under the name Galerie Khepri. His son Bertrand Khawam took over the management in the early 2000s and the younger son Roland also joined the business (Fig. 149). Part of the remaining collection and the library of Roger Khawam was sold over two days at an auction in Paris, 29-30 November 2012, at the 100th anniversary of the founding of Khawam Brothers.

In an interview from the late 1950s, Roger Khawam describes how business was dwindling and had been much better in the past when their clientele had included five US millionaires. One of them was Henry Walters who had allegedly spent around £40,000 annually at their shop.[921] One of their most famous sales is the statue depicting General Haremhab, the future king, as a royal scribe which was acquired by the Metropolitan Museum of Art in 1923.[922] In November 1954 Aksel Volten acquired from Roger Khawam, at the shop in Khan el-Khalili, a group of intact papyrus rolls from Hawara.[923]

Khodary M. el-Gabri (*fl.* 1964-1970)

Dealer in Cairo; perhaps a descendant of Mohammed M. el-Gabri.[924]

Kondilios, A. N. (*fl.* 1921-1938)

'Dr Kondilios' - as he is usually called - was an antiquities dealer living at Zeitun, about 10 km north of Ezbekiya Gardens and outside Cairo proper. According to Ludwig Borchardt and Erik Iversen, he was a Greek physician.[925] Francis Kelsey, who visited him in Zeitun, reports that he was apparently educated in Paris and Athens, had a 'shrewd face', and was regarded as a 'sharper' (i.e. a swindler) by Maurice Nahman

Fig. 149. Roger Khawam with his sons, Bertrand (right) and Roland (left). Courtesy of Bertrand Khawam.

and David Askren.[926] He is mainly associated with the sale of papyri from the Fayum and was involved in the sale of fragments from the Tebtunis temple library.[927] A number of letters and business cards of his are preserved in the Bentley Historical Library; these refer to him most fully as 'Dr. A. N. Kondilios' and provide the address 'Zeitoun (near Cairo), Telephone no. 412'.[928]

Kyticas, Panayotis (*fl.* 1890-1924)

One of the main dealers in Cairo. His original shop was located at Midan Kantaret el-Dikka, diagonally

921. Clipping from unidentified newspaper, late 1950s, article entitled 'In Relation to the Case of the American Scholar who Stole Egypt's Antiquities' (translated from Arabic).

922. MMA 23.10.1: Freed et al., *Pharaohs of the Sun*, 191, 277; acquisition details provided by the Metropolitan Museum of Art online database, search '30.10.1' (accessed 12 Oct. 2015).

923. Letter from C. E. Sander-Hansen to the Carlsberg Foundation, dated 4 Nov. 1954 (Carlsberg Foundation, Copenhagen). The papyri were edited by Lüddeckens, *Demotische Urkunden aus Hawara* (P. Carlsberg 34-39); Bülow-Jacobsen, *BICS* 29 (1982), 12-16 (P. Carlsberg 46-48); and idem, *BICS* 32 (1985), 45-48 (P. Carlsberg 51).

924. Christie's auction of 11 Dec. 2009 (sale 2232, lot 30; cf. http://www.christies.com (accessed 24 Sept. 2013).

925. Letters to H. O. Lange from L. Borchardt, dated 9 Mar. 1931, and from E. Iversen, one not dated [Feb./Mar. 1938] and the other dated 8 Mar. 1938 (Royal Library, Copenhagen). The 1928 edition of the Baedeker guide makes no mention of him in relation to physicians in Cairo, presumably because he was not actually located in central Cairo.

926. Cited after Francis Kelsey, see Pedley, *The Life and Work of Francis Willey Kelsey*, 317 with n. 17.

927. Cf. the letters cited in the previous footnote for his sale of fragments from the temple library. A 'Report on Papyri Purchased from Dr Kondilios: March 8, 1927' at the Papyrology Collection, University of Michigan, mentions acquisitions of papyri from Kondilios as early as 1921 (http://www.lib.umich.edu/papyrus-collection/acquisitions-reports, accessed 5.2.2013).

928. We are grateful to Margaret A. Leahy, volunteer reference librarian at the Bentley Historical Library, for looking through the correspondence for us. It includes 17 pages of letters in French, English, and Greek, most of which are handwritten. One mentions a visit to London by Kondilios in 1925.

across from Shepheard's Hotel and directly opposite Thomas Cook & Sons; in 1896 he relocated to the Halim Pasha Buildings, the block just south of Shepheard's Hotel on the same side of the street (Fig. 52).[929] He was described by Valdemar Schmidt as 'a Greek by birth, but fully European in every way'.[930]

> In his rather small shop one could often find interesting and important antiquities at appropriately high prices. Around closing time Cairo archaeologists tended to drop by Kytikas, where one could often find officials from the Egyptian Museum. Consequently Kytikas' shop was a place to get good information about antiquities finds and discoveries all over Egypt.[931]

This is confirmed by diary entries by Borchardt from 1899/1900 where he records meeting Quibell, the Chief Inspector of Antiquities for Lower Egypt, at Kyticas' shop and being informed that the dealer Abd en-Nur from Qena had some interesting objects for sale (a stone knife with gold handle, a porphyry knife, and some wood carvings) and that they had been offered to Budge; two days later he meets Reisner there, who informs him that Petrie hopes to find royal tombs at Abydos and that Quibell have seen some in plain sight.[932]

According to Petrie, Kyticas, whom he describes as 'the principal dealer for fine things in Cairo', did good business with the Egyptian Museum.[933] Among the most famous objects acquired from Kyticas, though rarely credited, are three fragments of the Old Kingdom annals which were secured by Emil Brugsch for the Museum in 1910.[934] Kyticas was one of the main suppliers for the British Museum when Budge was Keeper of the Egyptian collection, and around 3,000 objects were acquired through him.[935] The close relationship between the two men is well-illustrated by the fact that Budge – during at least one trip to Egypt, in 1919 – actually lived in Kyticas' home, as recounted by Breasted:

> I found some beautiful things at Kyticas's house. ... Old Budge is coming out next week, and by George, the old fox puts up at Kyticas's house! I saw the room where he is to stay. He had already pinched an almost life size statue which the old man has there, and which he values at 1,000 pounds.[936]

That same year Kyticas acquired the 'magnificent' collection of predynastic flints belonging to Captain C. S. Timmins who, according to Breasted, had become tired of Egypt and wished to dispose of his antiquities (p. 130). His son Denis P. Kyticas (fl. 1913-1930) continued the business after his father's death in 1924.

Loukianoff, Grégoire (1885-1945)

Loukianoff was a Russian refugee who had studied Egyptology in his youth, and he remained an active

---

929. *Annuaire égyptien, administratif et commercial, 1891-1892*, 103; cf. also Baedeker, *Egypt and the Sûdân*, 7th edition, 41. This is the same individual as the 'Pierre' Kyticas mentioned by Volait, *Fous du Caire*, 40, 144, 197. The change in addresses emerge from a series of letters from P. Kyticas to V. Schmidt from the 1890s (Ny Carlsberg Glyptotek).

930. Cf. further Bierbrier, *Who was Who in Egyptology*, 4th edition, 304; Gunter, *A Collector's Journey*, 89, 90-91, 93-94; David, *Gaston Maspero*, 281, 321, 333, 341, 376, 387, 403.

931. Schmidt, *Af et Langt Livs Historie*, 90.

932. Borchardt diary, Sept. 1899 - Jan. 1900, entries 7 Dec. 1899 and 9 Dec. 1899 (Swiss Institute, Kairo; transcript kindly provided by Cornelius von Pilgrim, 21 Jan. 2015).

933. Petrie, *Seventy Years in Archaeology*, 75.

934. Gauthier, *Le Musée Égyptien* 3 (1915), 29, where the sources of the three fragments are simply said to be 'un marchand d'antiquités du Caire'. The identity of the dealer as Kyticas is provided by von Bissing, *Historische Zeitschrift* 113, no. 2 (1914), 333.

935. According to a search for 'Kyticas' on the British Museum online database (accessed 13 Nov. 2012). One transaction between Kyticas and Budge from 1909, the sale of a collection including an Old Kingdom statue from Giza and estimated at c. £800, is briefly mentioned in Ismail, *Wallis Budge*, 385.

936. Letter from J. H. Breasted to his family, dated 11 Nov. 1919 (Oriental Institute, Chicago); edited by Larson, *Letters from James Henry Breasted*, 92. According to some letters of Lord Crawford from 1900, Budge had at that time a low personal opinion of Kyticas which he himself shared; cf. Choat, in Schubert (ed.), *Actes du 26e Congrès international de papyrologie*, 143. Apparently Budge's opinion improved over the years or he adopted a pragmatic approach to this important dealer.

'amateur' Egyptologist for much of his life, giving lectures and publishing academic papers in various journals.[937] He had come to Egypt in 1920, a few years after the Russian Revolution, and died there in 1945.[938] When Lange met him in 1929 he made his living from selling antiquities.[939] Lange described him as 'an enthusiast, for whom the hunt for antiquities is a sport. Even back in Russia he was a keen collector, and collected paintings and walking sticks among other things.'[940] Lange bought several objects from him while in Egypt, including a substantial hieratic papyrus for £200, and a granite piece for £30 for the Glyptotek,[941] as well as some objects after his return to Denmark.[942] Grégoire and his wife Elisabeth (Fig. 150) made quite an impression on Lange, and he and Jonna saw them often socially. At the time of Lange's visit they lived in Heliopolis at 9 Sharia Fayoum with their nine year old daughter Iréne (who attended the English school in Cairo; fig. 151), having escaped from the Bolsheviks; Loukianoff's brother was murdered by them, and his sister had disappeared during the unrest.[943] During the summer he and his family stayed in Cyprus, some 22 hours of travel from Cairo at the time, where they rented a house from a Greek farmer

for four to five months of the year;[944] they must have enjoyed the area as by 16 July 1930 Grégoire writes that they have bought some land there.[945] In early 1931 the family moved to an appartment in Cairo, right next to Ezbekiya Gardens in 8 Sharia el-Guineina (now Ali el-Kasar); Loukianoff's wife and daughter were still living at the latter address in 1950, several years after his death.[946]

Loukianoff made his money primarily from the sale of antiquities, but had no funds to build up a stock of objects, and consequently had no shop,[947] at least when Lange was in Cairo. He also functioned as an agent for collectors who wanted to sell, and got a commission for each transaction he facilitated on their behalf, but the income from this was meagre. One example of this was the lid of a red granite sarcophagus inscribed for a 'Mistress of the House and Chantress of Amun, Baketamun' about which he wrote to Lange. Perhaps because he had limited resources available, he sent a drawing rather than a photograph, to which he added the measurements (70 x 230 cm), a short description of the state of the object (broken across the chest and the waist), and a copy of some of the hieroglyphic inscriptions (Fig. 39). The price of the object would be 200 £E, but this was 'sans transport'; the object was never bought by a Danish museum, as far as we know.[948]

His antiquities trading was not sufficient to sustain his family, and so they had been forced to sell his wife's collection of lace and jewellery over the years;

937. For the lectures, see e.g. the letter to H. O. Lange dated 14 Jan. 1931 (Royal Library, Copenhagen) where he writes that he is giving one entitled 'Le dieu Ched, evolution de son culte dans l'ancienne Égypte' to the Institute d'Égypte; this was later published under the same title in BIE 13 (1931), 67-84. The Online Egyptological Bibliography lists 12 other articles published between 1924 and 1956. He also published a study of one of King Fouad's predecessors, for which he was thanked in a letter from the king's chamberlain (letter from G. Loukianoff to H. O. Lange, dated 14 Jan. 1931; Royal Library, Copenhagen). Also his wife, Elisabeth Loukianoff, gave lectures and published academic papers, including The Orthodox Icon and the Collection of the Greek Monastery of Saint George in Old Cairo.
938. Bothmer, Egypt 1950: My First Visit, 154; Snitkuvienė, Acta Orientalia Vilnensia 10 (2009), 187.
939. Lange, Dagbog fra Ægypten, 1929-1930, 260.
940. Lange, Dagbog fra Ægypten, 1929-1930, 300.
941. For the papyrus, see above p. 173.
942. Including P. Carlsberg 7, part of the Tebtunis temple library; see above.
943. Lange, Dagbog fra Ægypten, 1929-1930, 275.

944. Lange, Dagbog fra Ægypten, 1929-1930, 285.
945. Letter from G. Loukianoff to H. O. Lange, dated 16 July 1930 (Royal Library, Copenhagen).
946. Letter from G. Loukianoff to H. O. Lange, dated 10 Jan. 1931 (Royal Library, Copenhagen); Bothmer, Egypt 1950: My First Visit, 154-155. The building has since been demolished and replaced by a new concrete building.
947. Lange, Dagbog fra Ægypten, 1929-1930, 280.
948. Despite our best efforts we have been unable to track down the current whereabouts of the object (but we are grateful to John Taylor and Aidan Dodson for their kind help). For another occurrence of this name and title, although not necessarily referring to the same individual, see the Ramesside stela BM EA 351; Bierbrier, Hieroglyphic texts from Egyptian stelae, pls. 66-67.

Fig. 150. Elisabeth Loukianoff. Photograph given to Lange, 1929/30. Courtesy of the Royal Library.

they had also run a hostel in Cairo for a few years before moving to Heliopolis.[949] Lange was impressed by Loukianoff's keen eye for antiquities and his Egyptological knowledge, and he explained how Loukianoff would go round the Cairo dealers 'sniffing out the good objects whose true value the dealers do not recognise, buying them and then selling them on to collectors or European buyers';[950] he also evaluated objects for dealers in return for a fee.[951] He stated in a letter to Lange that he preferred to sell his objects to museums, but it is unclear whether this was an idealistic wish to ensure access to the objects or simply a sales technique to convince Lange and the Glyptotek to buy from him.[952]

Loukianoff had a considerable number of contacts among the antiquities dealers in Egypt, partly through his own role as agent and consultant to other dealers

and collectors, but he also knew small-time dealers who were closer to the supply-chain than many of the high-profile dealers; on one occasion he introduced Lange to several of these smaller dealers, including some that allegedly did not usually deal directly with Europeans.[953]

Loukianoffs network was also international. He bought Greek antiquities (vases and sculptures) from a dealer in Rhodes for sale in Egypt,[954] and several inscribed Himyarite stelae from Yemen.[955] Loukianoff also had contacts in Palestine, where he had been asked to prepare a catalogue for a small museum in Jerusalem run by Russian monks; they had lost their financial support from Russia after the revolution, and were now trying to sell their collection of antiquities.

949. Lange, *Dagbog fra Ægypten, 1929-1930*, 285.
950. Lange, *Dagbog fra Ægypten, 1929-1930*, 280.
951. Lange, *Dagbog fra Ægypten, 1929-1930*, 300.
952. Letter from G. Loukianoff to H. O. Lange, dated 30 Apr. 1930 (Royal Library, Copenhagen).

953. Lange, *Dagbog fra Ægypten, 1929-1930*, 321-322; the passage is cited in translation on p. 54 above.
954. Lange, *Dagbog fra Ægypten, 1929-1930*, 285. Lange found two of his Greek sculptures particularly striking and acquired photographs of these to try and persuade the Glyptotek to buy them upon his return to Copenhagen (p. 299).
955. Letter from G. Loukianoff to H. O. Lange, dated 14 Jan. 1931 (Royal Library, Copenhagen).

He showed the catalogue to Lange, who thought several pieces worth buying; Lange then instructed a Danish friend, Ms Bodil Hornemann,[956] to photograph certain objects in the collection during her forthcoming visit to Jerusalem. Loukianoff promised to get permission for photography for her from the monks,[957] but there is unfortunately no further information about this endeavour in the travel diary. Upon his return to Copenhagen Lange wrote a letter to Loukianoff to thank him for all his help during his stay in Cairo and to ask him to keep an eye out for any antiquities that might be of interest to Danish museums; a draft copy of this is preserved as part of the Lange correspondence at the Royal Library in Copenhagen.

There are also ten letters and postcards from Loukianoff to Lange in the same archive, dating from 20 April 1930 to 14 January 1931, which provide further details about his activities. He seems to have been involved in official excavations at Lake Mariut near Alexandria, but these came to an abrupt end 'parce que mes chers associés après m'avoir laissé à part, se brouillèrent entre eux pendant quelques jours de fouilles. Maintenant le propriétaire du terrain m'invite de nouveau reprendre entièrement les fouilles, mais je me refuse'.[958] There is a further reference to him being involved in excavations in the letters, but without the context (presumably known to Lange) it is not clear which excavations it might refer to:

> Dr. Junker, que j'ai rencontré pour la première fois après l'affaire des fouilles, était charmant et nullement trouble. Il m'a dit, qu'il ne voulait pas me déranger dans la première phase de nos fouilles, mais il ne les continuera pas, parce qu'elles deviennent trop chères. Je lui ai répondu que je suis de même avis, étant un peu au courant de l'affaire des fouilles. Ainsi nous avons réglé cette affaire douteuse, et nous sommes de nouveau des bons amis. Tout mieux.[959]

Here it seems as if Junker was involved in one of Loukianoff's previous excavation activities (the same as those alluded to above?), and that things did not end well; certainly Loukianoff appears to have had reason to expect him to be hostile because of this 'questionable affair'.

Loukianoff's trade in antiquities seems to have picked up following Lange's departure from Egypt, and he related how he had sold to several large museums since, including Berlin,[960] Copenhagen, London, Vienna and Chicago.[961] Loukianoff also explained that when Henry R. H. Hall, the Keeper at the British Museum, died on 13 October 1930, the news was received only a day or two later in Cairo, where it was a sad day for both Egyptologists and dealers, including Loukianoff himself; he had in fact received a letter from Hall on 10 October confirming a sale of an object for £60, which now hung in the balance; 'Maintenant je dois attendre la nomination de son successeur'.[962]

Lange seems to have asked Loukianoff to keep an eye out specifically for hieratic ostraca:

> Pour les ostraca, si j'aurai un peu d'argent libre, j'irai à Luxor, où je sais les places de les trouver. Je vous ai dis, que j'ai donné en cadeau à un Musée une cinquantaine des ostraca avec le texte hiératique. J'ai traduis une seule ostracon avec 4 premières lignes des maximes d'Amenemhet...

---

956. Hornemann is mainly known in Egyptology for her publication, *Types of Ancient Egyptian Statuary*, 7 vols.

957. Lange, *Dagbog fra Ægypten, 1929-1930*, 300.

958. Letter from G. Loukianoff to H. O. Lange, dated 30 Apr. 1930 (Royal Library, Copenhagen).

959. Letter from G. Loukianoff to H. O. Lange, dated 28 May 1930 (Royal Library, Copenhagen).

960. Letter from G. Loukianoff to H. O. Lange, dated 28 May 1930 (Royal Library, Copenhagen).

961. Letter from G. Loukianoff to H. O. Lange, dated 14 Jan. 1931 (Royal Library, Copenhagen). In 1935 he had also attempted to sell a cuboid statue (Cairo JE 37361) to the Cairo Museum, but the sale was cancelled when the Museum discovered that it had in fact been stolen from Legrain's excavations at Karnak in 1904; Loukianoff had apparently sourced the object from a Cairo dealer (http://www.ifao.egnet.net/bases/cachette/?&os=344; accessed 8 Nov. 2011). He subsequently published the object himself; Loukianoff, *ASAE* 37 (1937), 225-226; cf. De Meulenaere, in Gabolde (ed.), *Fs Goyon*, 304-305.

962. Letter from G. Loukianoff to H. O. Lange, undated but written during the autumn of 1930, sometime after 15 October but before the start of the winter trading season on internal evidence (Royal Library, Copenhagen).

Fig. 151. Irene Loukianoff aged 9 posing against a background of antiquities in the family home. Photograph given to Lange, 1929/30. Courtesy of the Royal Library.

off what remained of his collection from their home near Ezbekiya Gardens.[964]

M. Hassani Abd el-Galil (*fl.* 1958-1980)

Luxor dealer who ran a shop at the Winter Palace Hotel with Antiquities license no. 127.[965] Perhaps a relative of Mohammed Abd el-Galil.

Maguid Sameda (*fl.* 1944-1968)

Abd el-Maguid Sameda (also referred to simply as Maguid Sameda; Fig. 152) was a Cairo dealer who held the official Antiquities license no. 108. He was for a time based at 1 Sharia Fuâd I, next to Continental Hotel, but moved to 55 Sharia Ibrahim Pasha (later re-named Sharia al-Gomehoriya), the well-known building across from Shepheard's Hotel (Fig. 49), already before 1945.[966] The latter shop was called 'Art Gallery Maguid Sameda', and it was later taken over by his son, Sultan Maguid Sameda.[967]

Albert Gallatin did some business with Maguid Sameda when he came to New York to sell antiquities after the Second World War; he remarks that 'his small hotel room ... contained more Scotch whisky bottles than antiques – Sameda is not an orthodox Mussulman'.[968] Not too long after, in 1950, Bernard Bothmer visited him in Cairo; he noted that the dealer

The gift of some 50 hieratic ostraca to an unspecified museum is probably to be considered as *bakshish* in order to drum up business, and although the final line seems to indicate that he could read a little hieratic (and was able to identify *The Instruction of Amenemhat*), he clearly lacked experience as shown by a largely illegible 'facsimile' of the first line of P. Carlsberg 7 included in the letter to Lange where he initially offered this papyrus for sale (Fig. 123).[963]

In 1950, five years after the death of Gregoire Loukianoff, his widow and daughter were still selling

964. Bothmer, *Egypt 1950: My First Visit*, 154-155.

965. Haring, *JEA* 90 (2004), 219 (ostracon seen with dealer in 1958). Sotheby's auction of 11 June 2010 (lot 56, object purchased from dealer in 1961); cf. http://www.sothebys.com (accessed 13 Sept. 2013). Bonham's auction of 21 Apr. 2005 (Auction 11597, lots 10, 30, 43, 53, 58, 68; objects with dealer's official export permit dated 23 Nov. 1980); cf. http://www.bonhams.com (accessed 13 Sept. 2013).

966. A certificate of authenticity dated to 1945 carries the original address and has the later address added below; it is reproduced in Gravett, *A Critical Analysis of Selected Egyptian Bronze Artefacts*, 118. Note also that a certain Mohammed Shaker apparently dealt from 1 Sharia Fuâd I by 1951.

967. Robinson, *The Story of the Bodmer Papyri*, 41, 82, 102, 124-125, 201.

968. Gallatin, *The Pursuit of Happiness*, 177.

963. Letter from G. Loukianoff to H. O. Lange, dated 14 Jan. 1931 (Royal Library, Copenhagen).

during the first visit 'told me a good many interesting stories', and on the second 'took me to his place and showed me some exquisite pieces of relief; he gave me much useful information.'[969]

He had a close collaboration with the Swiss antiquities dealer Ernst E. Kofler and his wife Martha who acquired Egyptian antiquities through him and used him as a consultant when acquiring material through other dealers.[970] The Boston Museum of Fine Arts, the Brooklyn Museum, and the Metropolitan Museum of Art acquired several objects from him, some of them gifts; he was elected 'Fellow for Life' 1958/1959 at the latter Museum and he was still active in 1968/69 when he and Kofler donated a 'Statuette of an emaciated old man' to the same museum.[971]

Hajji Mahmud (*fl.* 1891)

Antiquities dealer at Medinet el-Fayum, near the French Consulate, visited by Wilbour.[972] He is perhaps identical with Mahmud Rifai.

Mahmud Abu Hassan (*fl.* 1893)

Anquities dealer at Luxor mentioned by Petrie in 1893/94.[973] He may be identical with the Luxor dealer *Sheikh* Mahmud Hassan listed below.

Fig. 152. Maguid Sameda in his shop. Newspaper clipping, late 1950s; source not located.

Mahmud Abdallah (*fl.* 1906)

A dealer in Eshmunein who sold a number of papyri to the German papyrus cartel.[974] He might have been a brother of Mohammed Abdallah of Eshmunein, minding his shop after the latter had relocated to Medinet Fayum and opened a second business there.

Mahmud Ali (*fl.* 1904)

Dealer at Eshmunein who sold papyri to the German papyrus cartel.[975]

Sheikh Mahmud Hassan (*fl.* 1900)

Antiquities dealer at Luxor; a painted sarcophagus acquired from him in 1900 was sold at Christie's for

969. Bothmer, *Egypt 1950: My First Visit*, 152, 153.
970. Lucien Viola (personal communication, 8 Dec. 2014); cf. further Bierbrier, *Who was Who in Egyptology*, 4th edition, 300 (s.v. Kofler).
971. *BMMA* 18, no. 2, new ser. (1959), 72; Fischer, *BMMA* 28, no. 2, new ser. (1969), 70. The Brooklyn Museum has correspondence between Maguid Sameda and John Cooney covering the years 1948-1962 (not seen). A Middle Kingdom statuette sold by Maguid Sameda in the late 1950s is published by Wild, *BIFAO* 69 (1969), 90-97, pls. 17-18; another statue seen with this dealer is mentioned on p. 109, no. 8.
972. Cf. Capart (ed.), *Letters of Charles Edwin Wilbour*, 580.
973. Quirke, *Hidden Hands*, 129.

974. Martin, in Bowman et al. (eds.), *Oxyrhynchus: A City and Its Texts*, 42.
975. *Ibid.*, 46-49.

more than $1,000,000 in 2006.[976] He may be identical with the Luxor dealer Mahmud Abu Hassan listed above.

Mahmud Ibrahim Abd es-Samad (fl. 1896-1930)

Mahmud Ibrahim Abd es-Samad (Table 3) was the son of the Sheikh of Abusir, Ibrahim Abd es-Samad, and father of Zaki Mahmud Abd es-Samad. Lange met him on both his visits to Egypt, and during the first they visited him at his home in Abusir.

During the earlier visit Lange repeatedly refers to him as the 'son of the Sheikh of Abusir', and Petrie similarly calls him 'Mahmud son of Shekh', so this must have been an important part of his identity.[977] His first encounter with Mahmud took place on 4 December 1899:

> Saturday afternoon we had a precious scene up in our room. There is a so-called Bedouin by the name Mahmoud, who is a son of the Sheikh of Abusir; he is a dealer and is, in the case of some larger objects, in business with one of the largest native dealers, a man from the village Kafr [el-Haram] by the pyramids. Smaller objects he trades on his own … [here follows a long description of his visit] … He did not leave until 8 o'clock, when we were going to dinner; but he was entertaining, really just a big child. [978]

The description of Mahmud as a big child is naturally a reference to his character rather than his age. He was already at this time a father, his son Zaki having been born around five years earlier. After another visit by several antiquities dealers some three months later, on 16 March 1900, Lange provides a similar description of Mahmud, calling him 'the biggest child of them all'. On this occasion, Mahmud 'started giving bakshish to everyone in the hope of bribing them, but the whole affair came to little more than 6 piastres. He always talks about his wealth, and speaks incessantly ...'[979]

Jonna provides an example of one of the more curious conversations with Mahmud.

> Mahmud asked me whether we might not be able to come out to Abusir sometime like we had promised. And then he told me in a very secretive manner why he longed so much for this. His wife should look at me and then wish that her next child would be a boy who would be just as fair, in other words just as white as me. He finished with the words, 'This is a good deal for you and for her, right?' I answered with a smile that I couldn't really comprehend how this might be such a good deal for me which amused him greatly.[980]

Mahmud's companion was Soliman 'the young' who often visited Lange with him.[981] The epithet of Soliman, 'the young', serves to distinguish him from the older Soliman Abd es-Samad who was also an antiquities dealer based at Kafr el-Haram and Mahmud's paternal uncle. Soliman may well have been a brother or cousin of Mahmud's. Mahmud also occasionally appears on his own as a dealer, but generally only with small unspecified objects.[982]

During Lange's second visit to Egypt, Mahmud played a lesser role. At this time he was involved, but perhaps only marginally so, in the businesses of his father and then his son.[983]

Mahmud Ledid (fl. 1886-1889)

Mahmud Ledid was a dealer at Luxor and the brother of *Sheikh* Ali Ledid (q.v.); he was raided by Grébaut in

976. Christie's auction of 7 Dec. 2006 (sale 1734, lost 26; cf. http://www.christies.com (accessed 19 Dec. 2013).

977. Lange and Lange, *Dagbog fra Ægyptensrejsen 1899-1900*, 167, 429 (where he is simply called 'Mahmud' and 'son of the Sheikh of Abusir'), 482; Lange, *Notebook 1899/1900*, 1 (where his name is more fully recorded as 'Mahmud Abd es-Samman, son of the Sheikh of Abusir'); Quirke, *Hidden Hands*, 130-131.

978. Lange and Lange, *Dagbog fra Ægyptensrejsen 1899-1900*, 167-169.

979. Lange and Lange, *Dagbog fra Ægyptensrejsen 1899-1900*, 429. Cited in context above p. 57.

980. Lange and Lange, *Dagbog fra Ægyptensrejsen 1899-1900*, 482.

981. Lange and Lange, *Dagbog fra Ægyptensrejsen 1899-1900*, 429.

982. Lange and Lange, *Dagbog fra Ægyptensrejsen 1899-1900*, 167-169, 494-495.

983. Lange, *Dagbog fra Ægypten, 1929-1930*, 34, 124-125, 129.

1888 (p. 143). He excavated sites in the vicinity of Hiw.[984]

Mahmud Mansur

See under Mansur Mahmud

Mahmud Mohammed (*fl.* 1881-82)

Antiquities dealer from Girga with whom Wilbour did some business.[985]

Mahmud Mohammed Abd er-Rahim el-Shaer (*fl.* late 1960s-2005)

Son of Mohammed Abd er-Rahim el-Shaer, q.v.

Mahmud Mohasseb Bey (fl. c. 1920-1935)

Son of Mohammed Mohasseb, q.v.

Mahmud Rifai (*fl.* 1900-1905)

Antiquities dealer in Medinet el-Fayum.[986] He did business with the German papyrus cartel 1901-3,[987] and is perhaps identical with the dealer *Hajji* Mahmud (q.v.) whom Wilbour visited in 1891.

Hajji Mahran (*fl.* c. 1905-1910)

A dealer in Eshmunein who sold a number of papyri to the German papyrus cartel.[988]

Makri, Pietro (*fl.* 1885-1892)

Greek antiquities dealer based in Alexandria; the *Journal d'entrée* of the Cairo Museum mentions a single object acquired from him in January 1885 (p. 51). He excavated with official license at both Abukir and Tell Timai in the mid-1880s and was active at least until 1892.[989] Wilbour mentions in 1886 that 'Pietro Makri, who used to have nice things, has gambled away his goods, and now has no sign; he told me he spent fifteen thousand francs digging at Abookeer ...'[990]

Mangud (*fl.* 1900)

In January 1900 Lange went to visit this dealer at his home in Kafr el-Haram, but he was away in Cairo and he is not otherwise mentioned.[991]

Mansoor, Mansur Abd el-Sayyid (1881-1968)

The Copt Mansur Abd el-Sayyid Mansoor was a former employee of the railroad.[992] He became a major dealer in Cairo with a shop inside Shepheard's Hotel (Fig. 153-154); the shop was established in 1906 after Mansoor had been allowed to display a couple of

984. The shipment of various objects to the Egyptian Museum by Mahmud Ledid seems to imply that at least some of the family's excavations were official; Anonymous, *BIE* 9, 2nd ser. (1889), xxiii; von Bissing, *Fayencegefässe*, 33, no. 3709.
985. Cf. Capart (ed.), *Letters of Charles Edwin Wilbour*, 94, 99, 100, 104.
986. Strzygowski, *ZÄS* 40 (1902), 54; Lefebvre, *Recueil des inscriptions grecques-chrétiennes d'Égypte*, 20-21, nos. 86-93; Łajtar, *ZPE* 97 (1993), 230, 231.
987. Information submitted by J. Keenan to the Papy mailing list on 23 June 2012 (http://lists.hum.ku.dk/pipermail/papy/2012-June/000888.html, accessed 5 Dec. 2013).

988. Hickey, *AfP* 49 (2003), 199; Essler, in Frösén, Purola, and Salmenkivi (eds.), *Proceedings of the 24th International Congress of Papyrology*, 294, n. 17; Martin, in Bowman et al. (eds.), *Oxyrhynchus: A City and Its Texts*, 42.
989. Ryholt, *The Carbonized Papyri from Tanis and Thmuis*, forthcoming.
990. Cf. Capart (ed.), *Letters of Charles Edwin Wilbour*, 338.
991. Lange and Lange, *Dagbog fra Ægyptensrejsen 1899-1900*, 221.
992. Bierbrier, *Who was Who in Egyptology*, 4th edition, 354; Robinson, *The Nag Hammadi Story*, 45-46; cf. further Robinson, *BA* 42, no. 4 (1979), 216, with a photograph of the shop on p. 215, top left. The façade read: 'M. A. Mansoor Antiquities. Authorised by the Egyptian Museum to sell Antiquities per License N° 85.'

Fig. 153. Mansur Abd el-Sayyid Mansoor. Detail of undated photograph. Courtesy of Claremont Colleges Digital Library.

showcases with antiquities for a year and a half. He is also said to have had shops at the Continental Hotel and the Semiramis Hotel, as well as a gallery in front of the Cairo Museum.[993] In the 1940s his son Edmond Robert Mansoor (Fig. 154) joined the business, and after his younger brothers also became involved, it was renamed 'M. A. Mansoor and Sons'. The shop in Shepheard's Hotel was totally destroyed when the hotel was burnt to the ground during the revolution in 1952. The Mansoors did much business in the United States after the Second World War, including auctions in New York in 1947 and 1952 and an exhibition in Dallas in 1950, and they later relocated permanently to San Francisco.[994] Edmond Robert Mansoor

(1923-2012, with name change from Edmond Mansour Abdel-Sayed) became a naturalized citizen in 1965.[995] The family is perhaps best known to Egyptologists today as the owners of a large collection of Amarna pieces, widely believed to be fake.[996]

Mansur Ismaïn (fl. 1899-1913)

Dealer at Kafr el-Haram (Table 3) known to have been active between 1900 and 1913.[997] Lange refers to him several times in his diary, always as simply Mansur. He visited his home at Kafr el-Haram in January 1900 and, noting that he had fine objects, ended up buying the head of a limestone statue from him (cited p. 98).[998] Towards the end of his stay, he refers to him as an example of 'a relatively decent' Egyptian dealer but not among the more important (quote in context p. 137).[999] He is described as 'a sociable person, very fat and very dark, almost black' (quote in context p. 57).[1000] Borchardt similarly referred to him as 'Der dicke Mansur' in a letter from 1902 where he informed Lange that Mansur had a large false door with well-preserved colours for sale at the price of £150.[1001] Ten years later, in 1912, Borchardt acquired papyri from him for the German papyrus cartel.[1002]

993. Fiechter, *Egyptian Fakes*, 112; Mansoor, *The Scandal of the Century*, chap. 1.

994. Bierbrier, *loc. cit.*; Gallatin, *The Pursuit of Happiness*, 175-177; Dallas Museum of Fine Arts, *5000 Years of Egyptian Art and Civilization*, with credit on the last page 'This exhibition loaned to the Dallas Museum by M. A. Mansoor and Sons, Cairo and New York'.

995. California, Northern U.S. District Court Naturalization Index, 1852-1989; accessed 13 June 2013 through *FamilySearch* (https://familysearch.org/pal:/MM9.1.1/K8ZQ-MDD).

996. E.g., Fiechter, *Egyptian Fakes*, 160-167. For a defence of the Collection, see Mansoor, *The Scandal of the Century*.

997. Borchardt, *ZÄS* 42 (1905), 83; Malek, *Topographical Bibliography* 8, entry 802-020-400; Gundel, *Papyri Gissenses*, 2nd edition, 9; Giessener Papyri- und Ostrakadatenbank on-line (http://digibib.ub.uni-giessen.de/cgi-bin/populo/pap.pl, s.v. Mansur Ismaim [sic]; accessed 7 Dec. 2013).

998. Lange and Lange, *Dagbog fra Ægyptensrejsen 1899-1900*, 221.

999. Lange and Lange, *Dagbog fra Ægyptensrejsen 1899-1900*, 738. Some objects seen with Mansur are copied in Lange, *Notebook 1899/1900*, 207, 216.

1000. Lange and Lange, *Dagbog fra Ægyptensrejsen 1899-1900*, 429.

1001. Letter from L. Borchardt to H. O. Lange, dated 30 May 1902 (Royal Library, Copenhagen).

1002. Cf. Martin, in Bowman et al. (eds.), *Oxyrhynchus: A City and Its Texts*, 42.

Fig. 154. Mansur Abd el-Sayyid Mansoor (right) with Edmond Robert Mansoor (middle) and a younger son, standing next to an exhibition cabinet at a hotel in Cairo. Detail of undated photograph. Courtesy of Claremont Colleges Digital Library.

During Lange's second visit in 1930 he met Mansur's son at Giza; he was Zaki Mahmud Abd es-Samad's brother-in-law and was said to speak good English.[1003] One one occasion, in 1900, Mansur is mentioned alongside a certain Abdallah Ismaïn who may well have been his brother.[1004] Mansur might also be related to the brothers Saïd and Farag Ismaïn who were similarly dealers at Kafr el-Haram.

Hajji Mansur Mahmud (*fl.* 1914-1928)

A dealer based in Luxor (p. 109).[1005] In 1924 he sold the Greek/Demotic Archive of Horos son of Nechutes, a soldier based at the military colony of Gebelein, to Lord Adler; these papyri are now part of the Papyrus Carlsberg Collection.[1006]

Maunier, V. Galli (*fl.* 1840-1875)

French consular agent at Luxor for about twenty years; he resided in *Maison de France* within the Luxor temple (p. 108) and excavated extensively in the Theban area.[1007]

1003. Lange, *Dagbog fra Ægypten, 1929-1930*, 97.
1004. Borchardt diary, Sept. 1899 - Jan. 1900, entry 3 Jan. 1900 (Swiss Institute, Kairo; transcript kindly provided by Cornelius von Pilgrim, 21 Jan. 2015).
1005. Baedeker, *Egypt and the Sûdân*, 7th edition, 252; idem, *Ägypten und der Sudân*, 8th edition, 260; idem, *Egypt and the Sûdân*, 8th edition, 268; Lilyquist, *The Tomb of the Three Foreign Wives of Tuthmosis III*, 111, 289. Clère, *BIFAO* 28 (1929), 178-182, 186-187, 188-189, mentions the sale of objects from Deir el-Medina, and two stelae acquired by Clère in 1926-28 were sold by Pierre Bergé & Associates, Auction of 26 Nov. 2013, lots 33-34 (cf.

www.pba-auctions.com, accessed 5 Dec. 2013); cf. also on-line sales-catalogue *Jacques Jean Clère* [www.kunicki.eu], 6, 9, which cites notes by Clère on his acquisitions. Both Clère and Lilyquist refer to the dealer as Mahmud Mansur rather than Mansur Mahmud, and it is unclear whether this is merely an example of the common mistaken inversion of Arabic names or whether we might be dealing with a son of Mansur Mahmud; we have assumed the former.
1006. Adler et al., *The Adler Papyri*, 3.
1007. Bierbrier, *Who was Who in Egyptology*, 4th edition, 363.

Michael and Raphael (*fl.* 1890-1891)

A certain Michael and his son Raphael were antiquities dealers at Akhmim with whom Wilbour conducted some business; he mentions that they were 'called
the Soodaneeyeh because they have lived in the
Soodan'.[1008] Their names indicate that they were
Christians, perhaps Copts.

Minotto (*fl.* 1899-1901)

Antiquities dealer located in Sharia Kamel 'next to
the Gas Company'. Borchardt records a visit in December 1899, finding nothing but 'utter trash', but
nonetheless buying cheap two lamps out of pity, while
Strzygowski acquired some antiquities from him in
March 1901.[1009]

Mishriky Girgis (*fl.* 1927-28)

Coptic dealer associated with the 'Deutsche Sûdân-
Pionier-Mission' at Aswan.[1010]

Mitry, Philip Elias (1896-1981)

Cairo dealer (Fig. 155) of Lebanese origin.[1011] Around

1925 he took over the 'Anglo-American Bookshop' in
Sharia Kamel (established 1869; Fig. 50), conveniently situated right opposite the grand entrance to Shepheard's Hotel, and, having obtained an official antiquities license (no. 90), expanded its activities to
include a significant antiquities trade. According to
an interview given in the late 1950s, he had already
been active as an antiquities dealer for ten years by the
time he acquired his license and the shop. In the early
1960s, frustrated with the situation in Egypt, he mi-
grated to the United States. Settling in Castro Valley,
California, he continued the trade in antiquities and
became a naturalized citizen in 1969, while his business in Cairo was continued by a third party under the
name 'Anglo-American Bookshop. Philip E. Mitry
Succs.' By this time the address had become 55 Sharia
al-Gomehoriya. Mitry compiled an *Illustrated Catalogue
of the Egyptian Museum*, which was published at an unknown date in Cairo.[1012]

Hajji Mohammed (*fl.* 1908, d. 1909?)

Dealer from Kafr el-Haram who assisted Ali Abd el-
Haj in providing Charles Lang Freer with manu-
scripts; the latter describes him as 'a giant of an
Arab'.[1013]

Mohammed Abd el-Galil (*fl.* 1923)

A minor dealer at Sheikh Abd el-Qurna who mainly
sold fakes, according to B. Bruyère.[1014] Perhaps a relative of Hassani Abd el-Galil.

1008. Cf. Capart (ed.), *Letters of Charles Edwin Wilbour*, 561, 562, 584.
1009. Borchardt diary, Sept. 1899 - Jan. 1900, entry 6 Dec. 1899
(Swiss Institute, Kairo; transcript kindly provided by
Cornelius von Pilgrim, 21 Jan. 2015); Mietke et al., *Josef
Strzygowski und die Berliner Museen*, 12.
1010. Baedeker, *Ägypten und der Sudân*, 8th edition, 368, 369. A
single object from this dealer, a scarab, was acquired by the
British Museum in 1927 (inv. EA 58440): British Museum online
database, search 'Mashriki Girgis' (accessed 12 Oct. 2015).
1011. Personal information Rob Demarée (11 Apr. 2013);
clipping from unidentified newspaper, late 1950s, article
entitled 'In Relation to the Case of the American Scholar who
Stole Egypt's Antiquities' (translated from Arabic); Kaper, in
Zivie-Coche and Guermeur (eds.), *Fs Yoyotte* 2, 625-632. For
Mitry's business in the late 1960s, cf. Sotheby's, New York
auction 5 June 2008, lots 100, 104 (www.sothebys.com,
accessed 26 Apr. 2013). Personal information: California,
Northern U.S. District Court Naturalization Index, 1852-1989,
accessed 13 June 2013 through *FamilySearch* (https://family-

search.org/pal:/MM9.1.1/K8ZW-R5R); California, Death
Index, 1940-1997, accessed 13 June 2013 through *FamilySearch*
(https://familysearch.org/pal:/MM9.1.1/VGB2-FJ9).
According to the death record, he was born 21 July 1896 and
died 5 Sept. 1981, and his mother's maiden name was Meyer.
1012. Mitry, *Illustrated Catalogue of the Egyptian Museum*. It must
have been published in or before 1965 as it appears in the
Annual Egyptological Bibliography as AEB 1965.0258 (= OEB 11354).
1013. Cited by Clarke, in Hurtado (ed.), *The Freer Biblical
Manuscripts*, 52-61.
1014. Diary entry dated 30 Jan. 1923; http://www.ifao.egnet.
net/bases/archives/bruyere/ (accessed 11 Sept. 2013).

Mohammed Abd el-Haggag (*fl.* 1923-1932)

Mohammed Abd el-Haggag was an Arab dealer who lived 'in one of the nicest houses in Dra abu'l Neggah' on the Theban West bank 'just north of Der el-Bahari'; his young wife was 'not shy like other women, she came and said "Hello": she was dressed well and had a gold ring in the right nostril'.[1015] Mohammed often travelled to Cairo to sell antiquities, which is where Lange first met him and purchased a pair of earrings. Lange visited him at his house during a trip to Luxor, where Mohammed introduced him to local residents with objects to sell, including an uncle who sold him 'a Coptic lamp decorated with a frog, and a hieratic ostracon for 5 piastres'.[1016] Lange was also introduced by Mohammed to the dealer Abd er-Rasul. Mohammed subsequently contacted Lange in Cairo whenever he had objects to sell, and had, according to Lange, virtually 'appointed himself assistant and agent [for me in Luxor]'.[1017] Although he occasionally bought from him, Lange did not trust him; he described him as 'a wholly unappealing person, untrustworthy in every way'.[1018] Bruyère, writing in 1923, includes Mohammed Abd el-Haggag at the head of a list of Sheikh Abd el-Qurna dealers who mainly sold fakes, and as late as 1932 he lists objects seen with this dealer.[1019] He might be identical with the Sheikh Abd el-Qurna dealer 'Mohammed Hagag' who was active as early as 1913.[1020]

Mohammed Abd es-Samad

Son of Soliman Abd es-Samad, q.v.

Fig. 155. Philip Elias Mitry in his shop. Newspaper clipping, late 1950s; source not located.

Hajji Mohammed Abd er-Rahim el-Shaer (*fl.* 1963-2005)

Mohammed Abd er-Rahim el-Shaer (Table 6), a nephew of Hefnawy Ismaïl el-Shaer, ran a shop in Cairo with his relatives Farouk and Mahmud Mohammed.[1021] It was located at 53 Sharia al-Gomehoriya, next to the shop of Phocion Jean Tano but with an entrance just around the corner of the main street in the side alley. An undated greeting card reads (Fig. 20):

> Merry Christmas and Happy New Year. El Hage Mohamed Abd El Rahim El Caher [sic] & Sons. Antiquity Dealer. 53 Gamhouria Street. Cairo Egypt.[1022]

The shop at one point had the sign 'Sons of Farag El Chaer, Antiquities Dealer' and operated under Antiquities license no. 116.[1023] Farag el-Shaer is known to

1015. Lange, *Dagbog fra Ægypten, 1929-1930*, 215.
1016. Lange, *Dagbog fra Ægypten, 1929-1930*, 216.
1017. Lange, *Dagbog fra Ægypten, 1929-1930*, 221.
1018. Lange, *Dagbog fra Ægypten, 1929-1930*, 320. The acquisitions from Mohammed Abd el-Haggag included an ivory head (Ny Carlsberg Glyptotek, ÆIN 1672) for which Lange paid £10 via Zaki Mahmud Abd es-Samad; *ibid.*, 318-323. For the head, see Jørgensen, *Egypt II*, 278-279, no. 114.
1019. Excavation diary of Bernard Bruyère, entries for 30 Jan. 1923 and 25 Feb. 1932, accessible on-line at http://www.ifao.egnet.net/bases/archives/bruyere (accessed 16 July 2013).
1020. Tooley, *JEA* 82 (1996), 173.

1021. Rob Demarée (personal communication).
1022. The name Shaer is sometimes written Chaer, but Caher seems to be a typographical error. We are grateful to Rob Demarée for showing us the card and for providing additional background information on him.
1023. Robinson, in Barc (ed.), *Colloque international sur les textes de Nag Hammadi*, 27-28; idem, *The Nag Hammadi Story*, 18; idem, *The Story of the Bodmer Papyri*, 126. Two ushabti figures with certificates from Farag el-Shaer, dated 1971, were offered for sale by Museum Surplus in 2013 (www.museumsurplus.com, accessed 4 Dec. 2013).

have been active in 1964-1971 and also held license no. 116, and he was presumably the father or brother of Mohammed Abd er-Rahim el-Shaer.

In the late 1960s, the family is known to have sold larger objects to Japanese buyers for considerable sums. In 2004/2005 the family was convicted of running one of the largest smuggling operations in modern times with objects reaching Australia, England, France, Germany, the Netherlands, Switzerland, and the United States.[1024] Officials estimated that the family had illegally exported about 41,000 pieces, and about 57,000 objects stolen from official state Antiquities storage magazines were reportedly recovered after the arrests. The value of the items was estimated at $55,000,000. Mohammed 'was jailed for 55 years for smuggling artefacts, bribery and encouraging officials to forge documents', while his relatives received sentences from 15 to 42 years; Farouk Farag Abd er-Rahim el-Shaer 'was jailed for 42 years for illegal possession of trade in artefacts', Mahmud Mohammed Abd er-Rahim el-Shaer 'was jailed for 30 years for smuggling hundreds of artefacts out of Egypt', and Farag Farouk Farag el-Shaer 'received a prison sentence of 15 years for his role in smuggling the artefacts recovered in London'. Also convicted for collaborating with the family was Dr Abdul Karim Abu Shanab, a senior employee of the Antiquities Service, who had provided certificates to the effect that the genuine artefacts were replicas so that they could be exported legally.[1025]

Mohammed Abdallah (*fl.* 1905-1930)

A dealer in Eshmunein simply referred to as 'Mohammed' is briefly mentioned in a report by Friedrich

Zucker to Carsten Høeg on a three-day journey with Zaki Mahmud Abd es-Samad to Medinet el-Fayum and Eshmunein in 1930 to look for papyri for the Papyrus Hauniensis Collection. Mohammed was paid a service fee of 100 piastres 'für Vermittlung von Händlerbekanntschaften' at Eshmunein, but Zucker reports that he found absolutely nothing, although he visited 'eine ganze Reihe von Händlern'.[1026]

This Mohammed is probably identical with the well-attested dealer Mohammed Abdallah of Eshmunein (*fl.* 1905-1930). According to Otto Rubensohn's travel diaries, he had already been in the trade for some time by 1905; originally based at Eshmunein, he moved his business to Medinet el-Fayum around this time, but eventually returned to Eshmunein again where he remained active for many years.[1027] He is mainly known from his trade in papyri; one of the last batches was a group of papyri sold in 1928 to the papyrus cartel operated by the British Museum.[1028]

Mohammed Abdallah Aouiss (*fl.* 1923)

A minor dealer said to live at Sheikh Abd el-Qurna, mentioned by B. Bruyère.[1029]

1024. This was widely reported in the media at the time; cf. the short summaries published by Eisenberg, *Minerva* 15, no. 4 (2004), 7; idem, *Minerva* 17, no. 1 (2006), 7.
1025. Shyllon, in Manacorda and Chapell (eds.), *Crime in the Art and Antiquities World*, 136; http://feeds.caironews.net/?rid=odo1c 2ddacae7d92&cat=d7006824400aaac1&f=1. Interesting background on this story can be found in Tokeley, *Rescuing the Past*, 239-243, who questions – probably rightly – the figures involved.
1026. Letter from F. Zucker to C. Høeg, dated 2 Oct. 1930 (Papyrus Hauniensis Collection). Cited *in toto* by Bülow-Jacobsen, *Aegis* 12, 36-40, cf. p. 40.
1027. Essler, in Frösén, Purola, and Salmenkivi (eds.), *Proceedings of the 24th International Congress of Papyrology*, 294, n. 17.
1028. For this cartel, which operated from c. 1920 to the mid 1930s, see Keenan, in Bagnall (ed.), *The Oxford Handbook of Papyrology*, 66-67. Some of the papyri purchased in 1928 were acquired by the Oslo Papyrus Collection: Anonymous, 'Acquisition history of the Oslo Papyrus Collection', available on-line http://ub-fmserver.uio.no/Acquisition.html (accessed 30 July 2012). Papyri acquired by the German papyrus cartel: Giessener Papyri- und Ostrakadatenbank on-line (http://digibib.ub.uni-giessen.de/cgi-bin/populo/pap.pl, s.v. Mohammed Abdallah; accessed 7 Dec. 2013). For a number of papyri sold to the German papyrus cartel, see Martin, in Bowman et al. (eds.), *Oxyrhynchus: A City and Its Texts*, 42.
1029. Diary entry dated 30 Jan. 1923; http://www.ifao.egnet. net/bases/archives/bruyere/ (accessed 11 Sept. 2013).

Mohammed Abu-el-Hadi (fl. 1923)

A minor dealer at Sheikh Abd el-Qurna who mainly sold fakes, according to B. Bruyère.[1030]

Mohammed Adim (fl. 1904)

Dealer at Eshmunein who sold papyri to the German papyrus cartel.[1031]

Mohammed Ago…? (fl. 1923)

A minor dealer at Sheikh Abd el-Qurna who mainly sold fakes, according to B. Bruyère.[1032]

Mohammed Ahmed Abd er-Rasul

Brother of Abd er-Rasul Ahmed Abd er-Rasul, q.v.

Mohammed Ali el-Gabri (fl. 1887-1911)

Mohammed Ali el-Gabri (Table 3) was a dealer based in the village of Kafr el-Haram near Giza. He was a son of the Giza dealer Ali Abd el-Haj el-Gabri, the brother of Ibrahim Ali, and presumably the father of Mohammed M. el-Gabri.

Lange visited his home and that of his brother in December 1899, together with Heinrich Schäfer, in order to see their antiquities (p. 95).[1033] Having built a grandiose house, Mohammed found himself in serious debt at the time, but Lange made no acquisitions and Schäfer only purchased a few items from the brother. By June half a year later, he had, as a result of his debt, pawned his collection of antiquities to the Swiss dealer André Bircher (p. 117); he tried to sell the

whole lot for 250 pounds which was 'really cheap'.[1034] Lange, Schäfer and Mohammed Ali went to Bircher's house in June 1900 in order to close a deal, but at the last moment the dealer tried to persuade his customers that he had been talking about Egyptian rather than English pounds all the time (which were worth a fraction more), supporting his argument by saying that the document drawn up when he pawned his collection to Bircher was also in Egyptian pounds. The bluff was called, the document brought out, and the dealer was proved wrong, upon which Schäfer got very angry and scolded him severely in Arabic. Lange and Schäfer then left without buying anything, only to have Mohammed Ali return a few hours later to beg them to rethink, but Schäfer would have none of it and was resolved to put him on ice for a week or two.[1035] It was around this time, sometime in 1900, that Schäfer acquired the famous Amarna relief known as *Spaziergang im Garten* from Mohammed Ali on behalf of the Egyptian Museum in Berlin.[1036] The year following, Mohammed Ali successfully competed for some artifact found at Abu Tig against the major Luxor dealer Mohammed Mohassib (p. 126).[1037]

Mohammed Ali was described by Jonna Lange as 'a real creep' and 'one of the most repulsive individuals on earth, sycophantic, lying, swearing with every other word'.[1038] Lange himself shared Jonna's impression of the man, and thought him 'the most repulsive

---

1030. Diary entry dated 30 Jan. 1923; http://www.ifao.egnet.net/bases/archives/bruyere/ (accessed 11 Sept. 2013).

1031. Papyrus und Ostraka Projekt - Halle, Jena, Leipzig on-line (http://papyri.uni-leipzig.de, s.v. Mohammed Adim and Mohamed Adinn; accessed 7 Dec. 2013).

1032. Diary entry dated 30 Jan. 1923; http://www.ifao.egnet.net/bases/archives/bruyere/ (accessed 11 Sept. 2013).

1033. Lange and Lange, *Dagbog fra Ægyptensrejsen 1899-1900*, 194-195.

1034. Lange and Lange, *Dagbog fra Ægyptensrejsen 1899-1900*, 654, 737, 783. For André Bircher, see the entry below. Several objects seen with Mohammed Ali and his brother Ibrahim are copied in Lange, *Notebook 1899/1900*, 41-42, 214; to give some examples, these include a New Kingdom stela of a 'high steward of Ptah, Ptahmose' (no price specified), a relief fragment naming a 'king's son Khaemwaset' (asking price £E 30), the 'stela of a false door' of Idu (£E 50), and an offering table of Khufu-ankh (£E 300).

1035. Lange and Lange, *Dagbog fra Ægyptensrejsen 1899-1900*, 662-3.

1036. Krauss, *PJAEE* 6, no. 1 (2009), 1, where Mohammed Ali el-Gabri is confused with his father.

1037. Ismail, *Wallis Budge*, 381.

1038. Lange and Lange, *Dagbog fra Ægyptensrejsen 1899-1900*, 654, 663.

of all Bedouins'.[1039] He is reported to have had a drinking problem which affected his business[1040] and this may have been what provoked the uncharacteristically negative comments about him by Hans and Jonna Lange who were tee-totallers. Their harsh view was evidently not shared by Valdemar Schmidt who, in a letter from 1903, wrote to Lange:

> Today I had a visit by Mohamed Ali who eagerly enquired about 'Mr. and Mrs. Lange'. Mohamed Ali is one of the nicest and most reasonable of the Bedouins.[1041]

A few years later, Charles Lang Freer rewarded both Mohammed Ali and his father and brother with gold watches for the service they rendered him in Egypt (p. 63). He was active as early as 1887 (p. 51) and as late as 1911 the Glyptotek acquired a false door and a series of other objects from him.[1042]

Mohammed el Boum (*fl.* 1923)

A minor dealer at Sheikh Abd el-Qurna who mainly sold fakes, according to B. Bruyère.[1043]

Mohammed Dakhakhni (*fl.* 1887-1888)

Obscure dealer who sold a few objects to the Egyptian Museum in 1887 (p. 51) and was met by Petrie in 1888; the name *Dakhakhni* means 'tobacconist' which might indicate that the antiquities trade was not his primary or original occupation.[1044]

Mohammed *Effendi* (*fl.* 1881-1886)

Dealer in Cairo visited several times by Wilbour; on one occasion in 1884 also the dealers Soliman (presumably Soliman Abd es-Samad) and 'Shookr Homer' showed Wilbour their stores at the house of Mohammed *Effendi*, and on another occasion in 1886 Soliman and Abdallah did the same (presumably the same Abdallah Lange met in 1899).[1045]

Mohammed Gouttayé (*fl.* 1923)

A minor dealer at Sheikh Abd el-Qurna who mainly sold fakes, according to B. Bruyère.[1046]

Mohammed Hamed Ibrahim (*fl.* 1944)

Cairo dealer with Antiquities license no. 96, located opposite Mena House Hotel next to the Pyramids (Fig. 119).[1047]

Mohammed Khalil (*fl.* 1907-1931)

According to a letter from the Coptologist Carl Schmidt to Lange, Mohammed Khalil was a dealer in Medinet el-Fayum who had sold on to the major antiquities dealers Maurice Nahman and Jean Tano in Cairo the majority of those papyri from the Tebtunis temple library that were found during the illicit exca-

1039. Lange and Lange, *Dagbog fra Ægyptensrejsen 1899-1900*, 736.
1040. Bolshakov, *Studies on Old Kingdom Reliefs*, 5-6.
1041. Letter from V. Schmidt to H. O. Lange, dated 30 Oct. 1903 (Royal Library, Copenhagen).
1042. For the false door, Ny Carlsberg Glyptotek ÆIN 1437+1445, see Bolshakov, *Studies on Old Kingdom Reliefs*, 65-69, pls. 20-21. Mogens Jørgensen informs us (personal communication 11 Apr. 2013) that the transaction included 26 objects.
1043. Diary entry dated 30 Jan. 1923; http://www.ifao.egnet.net/bases/archives/bruyere/ (accessed 11 Sept. 2013).
1044. Quirke, *Hidden Hands*, 130.

1045. Cf. Capart (ed.), *Letters of Charles Edwin Wilbour*, 76, 167, 312.
1046. Diary entry dated 30 Jan. 1923; http://www.ifao.egnet.net/bases/archives/bruyere/ (accessed 11 Sept. 2013).
1047. A certificate of authenticity, accompanying an ushabti figure (University of Copenhagen, Egyptological Archive, E504). The certificate, which is not dated, has a letterhead in both English and Egyptian. The English reads 'Mohamed Hamed Ibrahim. Antiquities dealer. Authorised by the Egyptian Antiquities Departement. Licence No. 96. Opp: Mena House Hotel. Pyramids, Cairo.' The signature at the bottom reads 'M. H. Khattal.' Another similar certificate from this dealer, seen on the Internet, is dated 1944. Hamada, *ASAE* 47 (1947), 15, refers to 'the shop of Ḥamad Ibrâhîm the dealer in antiquities opposite Mena House Hotel at the Pyramids' which must surely refer to the same business.

vations in 1930.[1048] He sold papyri to the German papyrus cartel as early as 1907.[1049] In view of his 'surname' he might be a son of the Khalil who ran the principal shop at Medinet el-Fayum in 1891 according to Wilbour.

Hajji Mohammed Khattab (*fl.* 1950s)

Licensed antiquities dealer with a shop in Khan el-Khalili; he formed a personal collection in the 1950s which he donated to the Supreme Council of Antiquities in 1999 after an attempted burglary – the gift comprised 400 objects.[1050] He is perhaps identical with M. H. Khattab who worked in the shop of Mohammed Hamed Ibrahim in the 1940s (Fig. 119).

Mohammed Ledid (*fl.* 1884)

Brother of *Sheikh* Ali Ledid and Mohammed Ledid, q.v.

Mohammed M. el-Gabri (*fl.* 1926-1927)

Cairo dealer with a shop which was located 'Opposite Thos. Cook & Son' (just north of Shepheard's Hotel, at 6 Sharia Kamel) according to his stationary.[1051] He

was very likely the son of Mohammed Ali el-Gabri and grandson of Ali Abd el-Haj el-Gabri, and perhaps also related to Khodary M. el-Gabri.

Mohammed Mohasseb *Bey* (1843-1928)[1052]

Mohammed Mohasseb (Table 4), who designated himself *Hajji* after his pilgrimage in 1888[1053] and later received the title of *Bey*, was one of the most prominent antiquities dealers in Luxor. He opened his shop in Sharia el-Lukanda in the late 1880s, where it remained until his death, but was active in the trade already many years earlier. He also had a house on the waterfront which had been demolished by 1920.[1054]

Emma Andrews, the life-long companion of Theodore Davis, recorded in her diary their first meeting with Mohammed Mohasseb in Luxor in Febuary 1890. She describes him as 'the most prominent dealer in antiquities in Luxor' and 'a really interesting old man, speaking English imperfectly but intelligibly – with such a gentle respectful manner. I am beginning to look upon him in the light of a friend.'[1055] He enjoyed an outstanding reputation among Egyptologists and collectors alike (p. 157); he sold more than 1,000 objects to the British Museum, and his customers included millionaires such as Charles Wilbour, J. P. Morgan,[1056] and Adolph Sutro.[1057] He is famous, amongst other things, for having sold most of the gold jewellery from the looted tomb of the three foreign wives of Tuthmosis III to Howard Carter (fund-

1048. Letter from C. Schmidt to H. O. Lange, dated 15 Mar. 1932 (Royal Library, Copenhagen).

1049. Papyrus und Ostraka Projekt - Halle, Jena, Leipzig on-line (http://papyri.uni-leipzig.de, s.v. Mohamed Chalil, Mohammed Chalil, and Mohamed Kahlil [sic]; accessed 7 Dec. 2013).

1050. *Al-Ahram Weekly* on-line, 22-28 Apr. 1999 (accessed 16 Sept. 2013); Eisenberg, *Minerva* 13, no. 3 (2002), 7.

1051. Letter from Mohammed M. el-Gabri to Harry Raibourne, dated 11 Nov. 1926 (University of Copenhagen, Egyptological Archive, B613). The letter and its envelope both have the same printed address 'Mohamed M. Elgabry, Antiquities merchant, Opposite Thos. Cook & Son, Cairo', while the signature of the letter reads 'Moh. M. El Gabry'. He was visited by Idris Bell and Francis Kelsey in 1926; Pedley, *The Life and Work of Francis Willey Kelsey*, 375. On 11 Jan. 1927 he sold two papyri to W. L. Westermann; cf. Emmel, 'The Yale Papyrus Collection. Catalog Introduction', 1993, with additions by R. Duttenhofer 1996, available on-line http://

www.library.yale.edu/ beinecke/brblsear/aboutpap.htm (accessed 24 July 2012).

1052. Bierbrier, *Who was Who in Egyptology*, 4th edition, 376-377. This is the 'veteran dealer in antiquities who was known to, and esteemed by, all Egyptologists', whose death was reported by Newberry, *JEA* 14 (1928), 184.

1053. Cf. Capart (ed.), *Letters of Charles Edwin Wilbour*, 494-495; Budge, *By Nile and Tigris* 1, 138, n. 1.

1054. Budge, *By Nile and Tigris* 1, 138.

1055. Reeves, *MMJ* 48 (2013) 7-36; Lilyquist, *The Tomb of Three Foreign Wives of Tuthmosis III*; cf. Hoving, *Tutankhamun*, 20.

1056. Satterlee, *J. Pierpont Morgan*, 507-508.

1057. Cf. Capart (ed.), *Letters of Charles Edwin Wilbour*, 293 (Sutro buying 'a room of antiquities' for a sum of 2,500 fr., c. £100, in 1884).

ed by the Earl of Carnarvon), now in the Metropolitan Museum of Art in New York.[1058]

In the early phase of his career as a dealer, Mohasseb was, according to Wilbour, in a secret partnership with Ahmed *Effendi* Mustafa who was also his protector; the latter was the son of the consular agent Mustafa Aga and later became consular agent himself.[1059] In 1886 and the following years, Jan Insinger made efforts to have Mohasseb installed as a Dutch consular agent, in order to facilitate the acquisition of antiquities, but nothing came of these plans (p. 225). As a result he had to rely on his own wealth and status when accused of illegal dealings, and was in fact arrested in Luxor and sent to Qena in irons at least once (1887/8), although he was not convicted or even much inconvenienced by this – in fact he afterwards successfully sued for wrongful arrest, through the intervention of Budge (who personally disliked Grébaut), but only received a relatively modest £40 in compensation.[1060]

Mohasseb became a very wealthy man and over the years, although he remained the most prominent dealer in Luxor, the antiquities trade may have turned into a side business. Breasted recounted the following conversation with one of his sons in 1919:

> Old Mohammed Mohasseb ... owns nearly a thousand acres of land and has an income from these lands, of nearly 20,000 pounds Egyptian a year. These dealers are men of wealth, to whom the profits from such dealing in antiquities is but part of a much larger income. Old Mohammed Mohasseb's son said to me: 'What does this antiquity business which we run for a while in the winter amount to, when we make out of it only a beggarly 1,000 pounds or possible 2,000 pounds a year, when we have our lands with cotton and sugar cane and wheat bringing ten times what they used to bring?'[1061]

The quote suggests that his wealth was not simply based on his trade in antiquities, but the sums mentioned by his son may be an understatement. It is impossible to calculate Mohasseb's exact income, but at the time of his involvement in the sale of the royal jewellery mentioned above his contemporaries estimated that he had been paid somewhere in the region of £1100-£1740 for the first and largest lot of objects.[1062] For comparison, it is known that the total cost to the Metropolitan Museum, which shortly afterwards bought most of the objects from Lord Carnarvon (through Howard Carter who earned a 15% commission), was approximately £53,000.[1063] For Mohasseb, the income from the jewellery would of course have been complemented by other sales, and the British Museum, amongst other institutions, bought numerous objects from him, often for considerable amounts of money.[1064] For example, Budge had arranged to buy one of his collections in several separate lots for budgetary reasons to spread the cost over several years; of these the third lot, consisting of a granite statue, went for £1500, and the fourth lot, a pair of statues, went for £1600.[1065] In any case the antiquities trade was clearly more than an accidental side-business where he just acquired objects brought to him; in 1909/1910 he even tried to buy part of the land on which the temple of Karnak stood, in order to excavate there and then sell the finds.[1066]

Mohammed Mohasseb was the brother-in-law of Abd el-Megid who had married his sister around 1868. He was assisted in the antiquities business by his son *Hajji* Hamid Mohammed Mohasseb (Fig. 156)

1058. Lilyquist, *The Tomb of Three Foreign Wives of Tuthmosis III*; cf. Hoving, *Tutankhamun*, 129-136.

1059. Cf. Capart (ed.), *Letters of Charles Edwin Wilbour*, 48.

1060. Budge, *By Nile and Tigris* 1, 145-146, 149-150; Ismail, *Wallis Budge*, 117-118.

1061. Letter from J. H. Breasted to his family, dated 25 Jan. 1920 (Oriental Institute, Chicago); edited by Larson, *Letters from James Henry Breasted*, 141.

1062. Reported by Lansing (£1700), Carter (£1100), and Carnarvon (£1740); Lilyquist, *The Tomb of Three Foreign Wives of Tuthmosis III*, 37, 40-41.

1063. Hoving, *Tutankhamun*, 135.

1064. At a more modest level, it was also Mohammed Mohasseb who sold the important early demotic archive of the businessman Djekhy to August Eisenlohr in the winter of 1884/85 (now in the Louvre): Donker van Heel, *Djekhy & Son*, 11-12.

1065. Ismail, *Wallis Budge*, 384-386.

1066. Ismail, *Wallis Budge*, 386; whether he ever actually acquired the land is not known.

and apparently also by a brother Ibrahim Mohasseb (q.v.). In 1922 Winlock published a detailed account of a daring trip undertaken by the young Hamid to the Fayum to acquire a pot of gold coins recently found there (cited in full in Appendix 5).[1067] Budge describes another occasion when he travelled to the Kharga Oasis in 1909 with a son of Mohasseb whom he calls *Hajji* Mohammed and who is perhaps the same.[1068] Another son of his who dealt in antiquities (*fl.* c. 1920-1935), and apparently took over the father's shop in Sharia el-Lukanda, is Mahmud Mohasseb *Bey*; he later became a senatorial member of the Parliament.[1069] His oldest son had some mental problems, apparently believing that his family was trying to poison him, and committed suicide in 1903.[1070] The latter may be the son whom he was 'bringing up to the business' already in 1890, according to the diary of Emma Andrews.[1071]

Hajji Mohammed Mohasseb (*fl.* 1909)

Son of Mohammed Mohasseb *Bey*, q.v.

Mohammad Rafar (*fl.* 1920)

Dealer at Medinet el-Fayum who sold papyri to Francis Kelsey in 1920.[1072]

Fig. 156. A young Mohammed Mohasseb, possibly the son of Mohammed Mohasseb *Bey*, holding the head of a statuette excavated at the Mut temple in Karnak. Photo, 1890s, published by Benson and Gourlay, *The Temple of Mut in Asher*, pl. 13.

Mohammed Saïd (*fl.* 1910-12)

Dealer at Medinet el-Fayum who sold papyri to the German papyrus cartel; he is described by Petrie as the 'main dealer' of the area.[1073]

1067. Winlock, *Scribner's Magazine* 71 (1922), 287-292.
1068. Budge, *By Nile and Tigris* 2, 376-381. A photograph of a Mohammed Mohasseb, perhaps the son of the elder Mohammed Mohasseb, is published by Benson and Gourlay, *The Temple of Mut in Asher*, pl. 13.1.
1069. Baedeker, *Egypt and the Sûdân*, 8th edition, 268; Keimer, *ASAE* 49 (1949), 37; Lilyquist, *The Tomb of Three Foreign Wives of Tuthmosis III*, 36, 111, 270. He is also included among the dealers whose objects were copied by J. J. Clère (papers now in the Griffith Institute, Oxford) and L. Keimer; for the latter, see Kircher, *MDAIK* 25 (1969), 44, no. 121. A certificate of authenticity signed by Mahmud Mohasseb on 3 Jan. 1935 has recently been published by Brandl, in Flossmann-Schütze et al. (eds.), *Fs Kessler*, fig. 11.
1070. Ismail, *Wallis Budge*, 381-382.
1071. Reeves, *MMJ* 48 (2013), 21; Lilyquist, *The Tomb of Three Foreign Wives of Tuthmosis III*; cf. Hoving, *Tutankhamun*, 21.
1072. Pedley, *The Life and Work of Francis Willey Kelsey*, 271.

1073. Quirke, *Hidden Hands*, 253; Giessener Papyri- und Ostrakadatenbank on-line (http://digibib.ub.uni-giessen.de/cgi-bin/populo/pap.pl, s.v. Jasso Tadros; accessed 7 Dec. 2013); cf. also Gundel, *Papyri Gissenses*, 2nd edition, 9.

Fig. 157. Todros Bolos. Photo, c. 1868, published by Keimer, *Cahiers d'histoire egyptienne* 7 (1955), pl. II.

Fig. 158. Mohareb Todros. Photo, c. 1930, published by Ehlebracht, *Haltet die Pyramiden fest!*, fig. 58.

Mohammed Shaker (*fl.* 1951)

Cairo dealer with Antiquities license no. 121 and a shop at 1 Sharia Fuâd I, next to Continental Hotel; active in 1951.[1074]

Mohareb Todros (c. 1847-1937)

Mohareb Todros (Fig. 158), a Copt 'who spoke excellent German', was the German consular agent in Luxor until the outbreak of the First World War in 1914

(p. 109).[1075] Lange met him in February 1900 and notes that 'He is the most important antiquities dealer in Luxor, which says a lot'; at this time Mohareb Todros still lived in his large consular house, right next to the Luxor temple, which would be expropriated and demolished in 1914 (p. 109). He still had a prosperous business in later years, and the Baedeker guide from 1928 describes his new residence, which he had built a

1074. So according to the description of a bronze figure sold by Artfact on 7 Feb. 2009; cf. http://www.artfact.com/auction-lot/egyptian-bronze-figure-of-god-thoth,-xviii-dynast-1-c-8dgycdszde (accessed 12 June 2013).

1075. Lange and Lange, *Dagbog fra Ægyptensrejsen 1899-1900*, 316, 340. For the family of Todros Bolos, Mohareb Todros, and Zaki Mohareb Todros, see also Keimer, *CHE* 7 (1955), 300-314, and further Ehlebracht, *Haltet die Pyramiden fest!*, 301-309, with photographs of Mohareb Todros and Zaki Mohareb Todros (called Sakim Harrib), 236, fig. 58-59. A studio photograph of Mohareb as a very young man with his daughter has recently been published by Gertzen, *Boote, Burgen, Bischarin*, 32.

Fig. 159-160. Zaki Mohareb Todros. Photo on the left, c. 1935, published by Ehlebracht, *Haltet die Pyramiden fest!*, fig. 59. Photo on the right, January 1971, courtesy of Rob Demarée.

little to the north of the former consulate, as a 'hübsches Museum beim Luxor-Tempel, am Nilufer'.[1076] Erman, who met Mohareb Todros already in 1885, mentioned that his wealthy father had sent him to a missionary school and that he spoke both German and English and had European habits.[1077] He presumably owed his English skills to his classes with Lady Duff-Gordon during her long stay in Luxor.[1078] Through his consular role, he enjoyed a special rela-

tionship with the Germans, sometimes also of social nature; Schäfer records in his diary how they got slightly drunk together at a bar during a visit in 1900.[1079]

Mohareb Todros had inherited both his office of consular agent and the business from his father, Todros Bolos (*d.* 1898; fig. 157) who was active at least from 1856 and a prominent dealer by 1862; in the catalogue of the Egyptian Museum in Berlin from 1894 he is credited for his gifts to the Collection.[1080] As con-

1076. Baedeker, *Ägypten und der Sudân*, 8th edition, 260; Keimer, *CHE* 7 (1955), 314.

1077. Erman, *Mein Werden und mein Wirken*, 218-219. Also Wilbour reports that 'young Todros ... speaks English and German very well'; cf. Capart (ed.), *Letters of Charles Edwin Wilbour*, 61; as does Peters, *Die Klimatischen Winterkurorte Egyptens*, 40.

1078. Duff-Gordon, *Last Letters from Egypt*, 81.

1079. Gertzen, *Boote, Burgen, Bischarin*, 32.

1080. For Todros Bolos, see Bierbrier, *Who was Who in Egyptology*, 4th edition, 542. He and his son Mohareb Todros are mentioned repeatedly in the Wilbour letters; cf. Capart (ed.), *Letters of Charles Edwin Wilbour*, 613 (index), and note that the

sular agents, they were well placed to control the antiquities market at Luxor, and Wilbour reported that the father got 'nearly all the antiquities found there of value'; even the Egyptian Museum in Cairo bought from him.[1081] He was also responsible for selling some of the royal jewellery from the tomb of the three foreign wives of Tuthmosis III discussed above (p. 245), although he played a minor role compared to Mohammed Mohasseb *Bey* on this occasion.[1082] His uncle was the Patriarch Todros who ran 'the one house of Presbyterian Christianity among the Tombs' at Thebes.[1083]

Mohareb Todros seems to have been something of an expert on fakes; Lange reports that:

> The first room [in his house] which he ushers customers into has, on the left, a large display of fake antiquities which he takes great pride in showing visitors. It is actually pretty canny from a business point of view, because then one is more inclined to pay the high prices he demands, happy in the knowledge that one is dealing with an honourable and knowledgeable man.[1084]

A similar description is provided by a visitor in 1895:

> Er besitzt eine selbst von Archäologen sehr geschätzte Kenntnis der ägyptischen Altertümer und weiß, wie wenige, das Echte vom Falschen zu unterscheiden. ... Sehr interessant ist ein Zimmer des Konsuls, in dem auf der einen Seite echte, auf der anderen gefälschte 'Altertümer' ausgestellt sind.[1085]

That Mohareb had a good knowledge and collection of forgeries is no surprise; he is known to have worked with Oxan Aslanian.[1086] Lange continues his description:

> Then he showed me his objects, 3 large rooms filled with them, and he also told me the prices of some but these were so outrageously high that I could only allow myself to buy a few minor objects, and these were expensive enough.

Mohareb's business was carried on by his second son, Zaki Mohareb Todros (1901-1978; Fig. 159-160), first from the house just north at the Luxor Temple and, after its appropriation and demolition due to official city sanitation in 1955, from a house at 44 Station Street which had also been built by the father.[1087] Zaki Mohareb came under observation by the Antiquities Service in the 1970s and his storage facility was sealed on his death and later confiscated.[1088]

Molattam (*fl.* 1922)

Father of Sayed Molattam, q.v.

Moses Isak (*fl.* 1892)

Jewish dealer in Cairo from whom Valdemar Schmidt acquired several objects in 1892; he came recommended by Emil Brugsch as 'one of the most *raisonnable*'.[1089]

father is called 'Todros' while the son is usually 'young Todros'; cf. also the letters edited by David, *Gaston Maspero*, 133, 134, 142, 147, 170. For Todros Bolos as a prominent dealer by 1862, cf. Rhind, *Thebes, its Tombs and their Tenants*, 253, cf. also p. 248. Gifts for the Egyptian Museum in Berlin: Königliche Museen zu Berlin, *Ausführliches Verzeichniss der Aegyptischen Altertümer, Gipsabgüsse und Papyrus*, ix et passim; a scarab acquired from him was accessioned by the Ägyptisches Museum in Berlin (inv. 9518) as early as 1856.
1081. Cf. Capart (ed.), *Letters of Charles Edwin Wilbour*, 60-61, 115, 354.
1082. Lilyquist, *The Tomb of Three Foreign Wives of Tuthmosis III*, 111.
1083. Cf. Capart (ed.), *Letters of Charles Edwin Wilbour*, 53.
1084. Lange and Lange, *Dagbog fra Ægyptensrejsen 1899-1900*, 316. The family seems to have been less forthright with non-specialist buyers; the father Todros Bolos is said to have sold fake scarabs at 'a rattling price: £5 to £10 each'; Drower, *Flinders Petrie*, 47.

1085. Sabersky, *Ein Winter in Ägypten*, 140.
1086. Fiechter, *Faux et faussaires en art égyptien*, 43.
1087. Keimer, *CHE* 7 (1955), 313-314; Ehlebracht, *Haltet die Pyramiden fest!*, 301-309.
1088. Some of these objects have since been published: el-Noubi, *SAK* 25 (1998), 251; Gabolde and el-Noubi, *RdE* 51 (2000), 262; el-Khadragy, *SAK* 27 (1999), 223; el-Noubi, *GM* 202 (2004), 11. Eisenberg, *Minerva* 13, no. 3 (2002), 7, notes that the heirs of Zaki Mohareb Todros 'have given their long-held accumulation of over 17,000 objects to the government.'
1089. Letters from V. Schmidt to C. Jacobsen, dated Feb. and Mar. 1892 (Ny Carlsberg Glyptotek).

Fig. 161. Mustafa Aga Ayat, at a relatively young age, posing with his children by the ancient hypostyle hall behind which he had constructed his consular residence. Photographer and date unknown. Courtesy of the British Library Board.

Musa (fl. 1881-1886)

Dealer living on the Theban West Bank mentioned by Wilbour.[1090]

Musa Mohte Metiar (fl. 1890)

Dealer at Zagazig (ancient Bubastis) involved in the sale of the carbonized papyri from Thmuis.[1091]

Mustafa (fl. 1883)

Antiquities dealer living at Saqqara visited a few times by Wilbour.[1092]

Mustafa Aga Ayat (fl. 1855- d. 1887)

Prominent antiquities dealer (Table 4; Fig. 161) based in Luxor and for many years simultaneously consular

agent for Britain, Russia, and (until 1881) also Belgium at Luxor;[1093] he had earlier served as consular agent for the United States (at least from 1855) and was succeeded in this office by Ali Murad in 1871.[1094] Valdemar Schmidt briefly describes a large well-preserved statuette of Harpokrates which he attempted to acquire for the National Museum in Copenhagen in the winter of 1860/61, during his first visit to Egypt, but for which he was unable to get the necessary funding.[1095]

1090. Cf. Capart (ed.), *Letters of Charles Edwin Wilbour*, 57, 354.
1091. De Meulenaere and MacKay, *Mendes II*, 219, no. 26.
1092. Cf. Capart (ed.), *Letters of Charles Edwin Wilbour*, 194, 253.

1093. Bierbrier, *Who was Who in Egyptology*, 4th edition, 394. He is mentioned repeatedly in the Wilbour letters; cf. Capart (ed.), *Letters of Charles Edwin Wilbour*, 606 (index). Another very detailed source is Ferguson, *Moss Gathered by a Rolling Stone*, passim. We are grateful to Sylvie Weens for providing us with the reference to the image reproduced in Fig. 161.
1094. For his role as US consular agent, cf. Ames, *Life and Letters of Peter and Susan Lesley*, 52; Sommerville, *Engraved Gems*, 179; Fairholt, *Up the Nile and Home Again*, 266; Ferguson, *Moss Gathered by a Rolling Stone*, 42; Prime, *Boat Life in Egypt*, 210, 213-214.
1095. Schmidt, *Af et Langt Livs Historie*, 88.

Mustafa Aga carried out numerous excavations at Thebes.[1096] An example of the scale is provided by a conversation recounted by a visitor of his in 1868:

'If you will stay till another sunset', he said, 'I can show you a newly-opened sepulchre. The fact is, I have some twenty Arabs quarrying at the western mountain for tombs. We find a good many, and I have lighted upon a fresh one to-day. There are two coffins in separate chambers of the rock, as yet untouched. My men had strict orders neither to handle a pick nor remove a stone till to-morrow morning. You shall see the sleepers *in situ*.'[1097]

Mustafa Aga is mentioned in many contemporary travellers' accounts, and already in 1855, when he was still consular agent for the United States, one traveller remarks that 'I am confident that no American traveller on the Nile has failed to experience his hospitality and kind attentions'.[1098] His popularity with prominent European visitors is further reflected by the fact that his death merited an obituary in the British press.

Death of a Distinguished Egyptian. – Advices from Egypt report the death, at an advanced age, of one of the oldest and best known Consular officials in the East. Mehemet Mustapha Agha was appointed British Consular Agent at Thebes in 1859, and since that time his proverbial hospitality to travellers of all ranks and nationalities has been regarded as one of the attractions of the Nile trip. Among his guests he numbered the Prince of Wales, the Empress Eugénie, and members of most of the Royal families of Europe. A native of Egypt, he had yet travelled in India and gone round the world. His death occurred on the 17th ult., within a few days of the completion of his 28th year of service.[1099]

Another traveller notes that 'Mustapha could neither read nor write, yet he could speak Arabic, Turkish, Persian, Hindostanee, French, Italian, and English; the latter two almost perfectly. He had travelled everywhere, – from London to Calcutta, from Cape Town to Persia.'[1100]

Although popular with most wealthy travellers to Luxor, on account of his hospitality, grand feasts (*fantasias*), and lavish entertainment (cf. p. 59), he seems to have had a more dubious reputation among those who knew him more intimately. Maspero described him as 'un ancient marchand d'esclaves, qui a fait tous les métiers honteux et les fait encore aujourd'hui.'[1101] Mustafa Aga's reputation with the Antiquities Service had been severely tarnished by his role in the plundering of the cache of royal mummies during the 1870s, where he exploited his diplomatic immunity by offering protection to the Abd er-Rasul brothers and facilitating their illegal activities (p. 33). As a direct consequence he was deprived of his Belgian consulship; he also feared for his British consulship, but Wilbour noted that 'It is not likely that the English Government will revoke Mustafa, for it is he who sells antiquities to Englishmen whence they come after a few years into the British Museum' and indeed the British authorities decided to take no action.[1102] Wilbour also reported that Mustafa Aga used forced labour to build a new path to his house, in order to impress Lord Dufferin during his visit in 1883.[1103] Moreover, when the rumour spread that Mustafa Aga's compensation for the expropriation of his house in the Luxor temple would be counted against his substantial tax arrears, Wilbour remarked that 'Luxor will rejoice, for there are few people there whom Mustafa has not made to bleed.' The rumour, as it turned out, was true. Yet Mustafa Aga managed to maintain good relations with influential people, and as late as 1886, the year before he died, he obtained permission to excavate at Quft against Maspero's wishes.[1104]

1096. In 1855 Mustafa Aga also supervised fifty men excavating at Luxor for a wealthy traveller in the absence of the latter; Prime, *Boat Life in Egypt*, 218-219, 347, 350.

1097. Hopley, *Under Egyptian Palms*, 173, cf. further pp. 187-194 for a description of the tomb and its contents. The discovery of another tomb by Mustafa Aga is mentioned *ibid.*, 99-103.

1098. Prime, *Boat Life in Egypt*, 214.

1099. *Manchester Evening News*, 10 Aug. 1887.

1100. Ferguson, *Moss Gathered by a Rolling Stone*, 47. Also Peters, *Die Klimatischen Winterkurorte Egyptens*, 40, notes that he spoke English and Italian well.

1101. Letter by G. Maspero dated 26 Feb. 1886, cited by David, *Gaston Maspero*, 126.

1102. Cf. Capart (ed.), *Letters of Charles Edwin Wilbour*, 67.

1103. Cf. Capart (ed.), *Letters of Charles Edwin Wilbour*, 327, 377.

1104. David, *Gaston Maspero*, 146.

Mustafa Aga's famous house, which had welcomed so many distinguished visitors, was located next to the great colonnade of Amenhotep III inside the Luxor temple (Fig. 29, 97-98);[1105] it was built in the early 1850s and a visitor in 1855 provided the following descriptions:

> His house is the most comfortable private house in Upper Egypt. It is all on one floor, and covers a large space. The halls are roomy and airy, the chambers papered, dark and cool, the furniture plain and comfortable, while the grand front of ancient columns gives it a more royal appearance than the citadel of Cairo.
>
> (*and later in the book:*) Mustapha has the grandest front to his house of any man, private or public, in the world. It is not much of a house; something of a pile of mud, but clean and white-washed within, consisting of five or six rooms, all on one floor, around an open court in which he has some few trees and shrubs. But he has selected for the location of his house the interior of the grand court of the temple, and the doorway is between two of the large columns, while the huge architrave towers above it.[1106]

It was expropriated and demolished in 1889 by the Antiquities Service (p.105). Mustafa Aga was the uncle of the well-known dealer Abd el-Megid Hussein Aga, and his eldest son Saïd *Bey* Mustafa Ayat served as governor of Luxor, at least since 1877,[1107] while his younger son Ahmed *Effendi* Mustafa succeeded him as British and Russian consular agent; Saïd took over from his younger brother as consular agent in 1903.

Mustafa Shakir (*fl.* 1885)

British consular agent at Aswan. In 1885 he recieved permission to excavate the necropolis at Qubbet el-Hawa and produced such significant findings that the British took over the excavations.[1108] According to Budge, the antiquities found by the British were left with Mustafa Shakir to be divided between the British Museum and the Bulaq Museum, but all the objects somehow disappeared and neither museum ever received its share.

Nagyr (*fl.* 1882)

Antiquities dealer in Luxor mentioned in passing by Wilbour.[1109]

Nahman, Maurice (1868-1948)

Maurice Nahman (Fig. 69, 162), a one-time chief cashier of Crédit Fonciér Égyptien (located at 35 Sharia el-Manâkh, around the corner of his mansion), was one of the main antiquities dealers of the time.[1110] His famously premature obituary was published in *Chronique d'Égypte* in 1947,[1111] and some of his papers, including his visitors' book, are now in the Wilbour Library of Egyptology in Brooklyn.[1112]

Nahman's business was established in 1890.[1113] He originally dealt from his apartment at 20 Sharia Sheikh Abu el-Sibâ (now Gawad Hosny, Fig. 74), close to Crédit Fonciér Égyptien, and later opened a shop at Sharia Qasr el-Nil, across from the Savoy Hotel and about 500 metres from the Egyptian Museum.[1114] Around 1920 he moved his business to a large house at 27 Sharia el-Madabegh (now Sherif Pasha, Fig. 68-73) which he had acquired several years earlier in 1914.[1115]

1105. Weens, *EA* 45 (2014), 36-38.
1106. Prime, *Boat Life in Egypt*, 214, 374.
1107. Edwards, *A Thousand Miles up the Nile*, 2nd edition, 455.
1108. Budge, *PSBA* 9 (1887), 78; idem, *PSBA* 10 (1888), 4-40; idem, *By Nile and Tigris* 1, 74-75, 89; von Bissing, *ASAE* 15 (1915), 1-2, n. 1.

1109. Cf. Capart (ed.), *Letters of Charles Edwin Wilbour*, 146.
1110. Bierbrier, *Who was Who in Egyptology*, 4th edition, 397.
1111. Capart, *CdE* 44 (1947), 300-301.
1112. 'Maurice Nahman. Visitor book and miscellaneous papers. 1909-2006 (inclusive)', call number N362 N14; listed at http://www.brooklynmuseum.org (accessed 26 Mar. 2010).
1113. Cf. advertisement enclosed with the exhibition catalogue, Société d'archéologie copte, *Exposition d'art copte, Décembre 1944*, (here reproduced in fig. 23).
1114. Cf. invoice from M. Nahman to Breasted, dated 22 Nov. 1919, depicted on the cover of *The Oriental Institute News & Notes* 205 (2010); Baedeker, *Egypt and the Sûdân*, 7th edition, 41; cf. also Dattari, *Journal International d'Archéologie Numasmatique* 8 (1905), 103, n. 3, who refers to Nahman as 'the well known dealer of Sharia Kasr El Nil'.
1115. As late as 1919 he apparently still ran his business from

One of Lange's earliest visits to him took place on Thursday 20 February 1900, which Lange's wife Jonna describes as follows:

> Tuesday [i.e. 20 February] was a great day. In the afternoon, after we had developed our photographs from that morning, we went and bought a lovely statue for brewer Jacobsen from a man called Nahman. He is a cashier in a bank in town, but also an antiquities dealer on the side, and he only deals in first class objects. He had wanted 150 pounds for it, and Jacobsen was willing to pay said sum, but Hans negotiated well, even though it was in French, and we ended up getting it for 140. The wonderful thing about it is that the colours are incredibly well preserved; it is a double statue, man and wife [Fig. 114].[1116]

Lange seems to have been fortunate in his timing; Borchardt records in his diaries a couple of months earlier that Nahman was in need of money at the time and was keen to sell.[1117]

In 1909, when Jacobsen personally visited Nahman during his only trip to Egypt, he was well on his way to becoming one of the leading dealers in Cairo. The scope of his business and logistical abilities may be illustrated by two early Ptolemaic stone sarcophagi which Jacobsen ordered through Schmidt after his return to Copenhagen. Schmidt wrote to Jacobsen's secretary that 'they are very heavy, 7,000 kiloes, and could not be loaded at Port Saïd where there were no cranes', but a solution was found and they arrived in Copenhagen safe and sound some weeks later.[1118]

His shop was also visited several times by Johannes Pedersen on behalf of Lange in 1920. In one letter he describes two monuments for sale:

> Nahman has a statue of Ramesses II that is 112 cm tall [Fig. 73]. It is placed in a basement so it was difficult to photograph it, but I have obtained a picture which can give an impression of it. It was made by a Danish lady, Miss Hornemann, who is down here. ... Nahman demands £500 for it. He also has a basin. I did not get the measurements, but it is about 3/4 [metre] long. For this he demands £200.[1119]

Whether Pedersen purchased any monuments from Nahman remains uncertain. Lange wrote back to him that he had passed one of the enclosed photographs to the Glyptotek for further consideration, but noted that it was difficult to raise money.[1120] In a later letter Lange writes that 'The Glyptotek will not need Nachman's Ramesses-statue since there is little money available'.[1121] Pedersen did, however, acquire a group of Greek papyri which became part of the Papyrus Hauniensis Collection (p. 170).[1122]

By 1929, when Lange himself next visited Nahman, he was firmly established as the leading dealer in Cairo and a first port of call for most Egyptologists looking to buy objects.[1123] He was now located at Sharia el-Madabegh and Lange found the house impressive:

> He lives in a palace, which used to be an Italian club. In a huge hall there was an imposing collection of Egyptian, Coptic and Arabic antiquities, and from the

---

Sharia Qasr el-Nil and Sharia Sheikh Abu el-Sibâ; cf. the invoice cited in the previous note.

1116. Lange and Lange, *Dagbog fra Ægyptensrejsen 1899-1900*, 393-394. The object in question is the Ramesside limestone statue Ny Carlsberg Glyptotek, ÆIN 935; Jørgensen, *Egypt II*, 274-275; idem, *How it all began*, 64, fig. 58, Manniche, *Egyptian Art in Denmark*, 188, fig. 83. Several other objects seen with Nahman in 1900 are listed in Lange, *Notebook 1899/1900*, 210-212.

1117. Borchardt diary, Sept. 1899 - Jan. 1900, entry 21 Dec. 1899 (Swiss Institute, Kairo; transcript kindly provided by Cornelius von Pilgrim, 21 Jan. 2015).

1118. Jørgensen, *Egypt III*, 244-247; idem, *How it all began*, 100, fig. 88-89.

1119. Letter from J. Pedersen to H. O. Lange, dated 3 Dec. 1920 (Royal Library, Copenhagen).

1120. Letter from H. O. Lange to J. Pedersen, dated 21 Dec. 1920 (Royal Library, Copenhagen).

1121. Letter from H. O. Lange to J. Pedersen, dated 8 Mar. 1921 (Royal Library, Copenhagen).

1122. Letter from J. Pedersen to H. O. Lange, dated 3 Dec. 1920 (Royal Library, Copenhagen).

1123. Nahman's shop was also one of only three Cairo dealers' shops recommended to tourists by the Baedeker guidebook; Baedeker, *Ägypten und der Sudân*, 8th edition, 38-39; the other two were those of N. Tano and R. H. Blanchard.

sides he kept on bringing more things out. Down in the basement there were also nice things.[1124]

The house had been built for the French architect, Baron Delort de Gléon (1843-1899), and was earlier known as *Hôtel du Baron Delort de Gléon*.[1125] The latter lived more than twenty years in Egypt and was also responsible for several other buildings in Cairo, including Crédit Foncier Égyptien where Nahman worked, but perhaps received his greatest publicity when he constructed the *Rue de Caire*, including a down-scaled copy of the minaret of Qayt Bey, for the Exposition Universelle in Paris in 1889.[1126] His widow bequeathed an important Islamic collection to Musée du Louvre in 1912 and a hall was named in their honor as *Salle Delort de Gléon*.

Nahman's status necessitated going there early, and Lange notes in his diary 'I was the first Egyptologist to visit Nahman [this season]; one has to be quick, as the Museum representatives are already starting to appear ... speed is of the essence.'[1127] Nahman's success was well known, and shortly before February 1930 he had been awarded the *Légion d'honneur* (perhaps during a trip to Europe from which he had returned in November 1929); Lange describes him as being 'in a state of vexation, because he is pestered daily by beggars who want to exploit the occasion by extracting money from him'.[1128] Nahman regularly travelled to Paris to do business (Fig. 107).[1129]

Because of Nahman's reputation and the size of his business, he had a significant network in Egypt as well as in Europe and America; 'They come to him from all over the country with their objects, and he sells to museums all over the world, and to tourists.'[1130] His objects were priced accordingly, and Lange thought them 'terribly' expensive.[1131] He nonetheless made several purchases from Nahman in person during both his visits. On 12 February 1929, he notes 'Yesterday I completed a larger transaction with Nahman concerning six items, in addition to which I received a seventh as a bonus. They will now be sent to Copenhagen.'[1132]

After his return to Denmark, between 1931 and 1938, Lange further purchased several large batches of papyri from the Tebtunis temple library from Nahman with the help of Ludwig Borchardt and Carl Schmidt.[1133]

Maurice Nahman was married twice, first to Antoinette Cerra and later to Concetta Viola who were sisters and Italian.[1134] The children from the first marriage were surnamed Nahman and those of the second Viola. Nahman had a son from each marriage named Robert – Robert Nahman and Robert Viola – each of whom assisted him in the antiquities trade and became independent dealers.

1124. Lange, *Dagbog fra Ægypten, 1929-1930*, 50. Another description is provided by J. H. Breasted in 1919: 'Nahman is a wealthy Syrian, first cashier of the Credit Foncier, and lives in a palatial house with a huge drawing room as big as a church, where he exhibits his immense collection'; cited in Alexander, *Art Institute of Chicago Museum Studies* 20 (1994), 12.

1125. A short obituary was published in *Bulletin de l'Association amicale des anciens élèves de l'Ecole des Mines,* juin 1900; cf. also Musée du Louvre, *Les Donateurs du Louvre*, 187.

1126. Reid, *Whose Pharaohs?*, 252.

1127. Lange, *Dagbog fra Ægypten, 1929-1930*, 50. Nahman had returned to Cairo from Europe just five days before Lange's visit (p. 51), so Lange's claim to be the first may well be true.

1128. Lange, *Dagbog fra Ægypten, 1929-1930*, 268.

1129. Thus, for instance, M. I. Rostovtzeff acquired papyri for the Yale Papyrus Collection from Nahman in Paris, Sept. 1931,

June 1933, and July 1935; cf. Emmel, 'The Yale Papyrus Collection. Catalog Introduction', 1993, with additions by R. Duttenhofer 1996, available on-line http://www.library.yale.edu/beinecke/brblsear/ aboutpap.htm (accessed 24 July 2012). See also the (premature) obituary of Maurice Nahman by Capart, *CdE* 22 (1947), 301.

1130. Lange, *Dagbog fra Ægypten, 1929-1930*, 51.

1131. Lange, *Dagbog fra Ægypten, 1929-1930*, 109.

1132. Lange, *Dagbog fra Ægypten, 1929-1930*, 131. The objects are not specified, and seem not to have made it to Denmark: later on in the diary he says that 'unfortunately the Museum has prohibited the export of the best things I had bought for the Glyptotek... my entire business with Nahman has now come to nothing'; p. 258.

1133. See above p. 127.

1134. Lucien Viola (personal communication, 8 Dec. 2014).

Fig. 162. Maurice Nahman in the main gallery of his antiquities shop, 1940s. Courtesy of the Brooklyn Museum.

Fig. 163. *Sheikh* Omar of Kafr el-Haram. Detail of a
photograph by W. M. F. Petrie, 1881, inscribed 'My friend
Shekh Omar holding a levee in a sunny corner. Gizeh.'
Petrie Album 7, no. 432. Courtesy of The Griffith Institute, University of Oxford.

Nahman, Robert Maurice (1901-1954)

The son of Maurice Nahman, Robert Maurice Nahman was involved in his father's business for many
years and took it over upon his father's death in
1948.[1135] The bulk of the inherited collection was put
up for auction in Paris in 1953. In late 1954 a batch of
papyri was acquired by Aksel Volten from his estate,
for the Papyrus Carlsberg Collection, and further batches were acquired by H. Ludin Janssen, for the Oslo
Papyrus Collection, and the antiquities dealer Erik

von Scherling that same year.[1136] His wife Iris and two
of his sisters, Sally and Alice, left Egypt with their inheritance after his death and settled in France where
they put some of their antiquities up for sale. His two
other sisters, Sandra and Solange, stayed in Egypt, as
did his half-brother Robert Viola.[1137] Sandra Manesse-
ro-Nahman sold a New Kingdom relief in Geneva as
late as 1993 (now Leiden F 1993/8.1).[1138]

1135. Bierbrier, *Who was Who in Egyptology*, 4th edition, 397;
Blattner (ed.), *Le mondain égyptien: The Egyptian Who's Who 1939*,
298; idem, *Le mondain égyptien: The Egyptian Who's Who 1941*, 224;
idem, *Le mondain égyptien: The Egyptian Who's Who 1943*, 204;
Gallazzi, in Hoogendijk and Muhs (eds.), *Fs Worp*, 1, n. 3.

1136. Information inscribed on the paper folders originally used
to store and sort fragments in the Papyrus Carlsberg Collection;
Anonymous, 'Acquisition history of the Oslo Papyrus Collection', available on-line http://ub-fmserver.uio.no/Acquisition.
html (accessed 30 July 2012); von Scherling, *Rotulus* 7, 15.
1137. Lucien Viola (personal communication, 8 Dec. 2014).
1138. Raven and Schneider, *OMRO* 74 (1994), 177 and pl. 1.1.

Sheikh Omar (fl. 1880-1888)

Dealer at Kafr el-Haram (Table 3; fig. 163) who did business with Petrie; he was once in the employ of Petrie who kindly acknowledged him in the introduction to the report of his work at Giza as 'my old friend Shekh Omar, of the Pyramid village, shrewd, sharp, and handsome'.[1139] Apparently a man of some authority in the area, he settled in 1885 a case concerning a number of bronzes removed from Petrie's excavation at Nabira (Naukratis) which involved several men from Giza.[1140] He was the brother of the dealer Abd es-Salam Abdallah.

Pantazi, Elia (fl. 1886-1901)

Dealer, possibly of Greek origin, with shops in Alexandria and Cairo, the latter at 2 Sharia Kamel.[1141]

Philip, L. Paul (fl. 1887-1909)

Paul Philip was one of the main dealers in Cairo at the turn of the century with a shop was located in Sharia Kamel, across Shepheard's Hotel.[1142] An advertisement printed in 1891 reads:

> L. Paul Philip. Antiquités – objets d'art. Collections d'étoffes anciennes. Fabrique de Meubles Style Arabe. Le Caire. En Face L'Hotel Shepeard (sic).[1143]

Philip is first mentioned by Lange in a letter to Schmidt that same year, when he was studying with Erman in Berlin:

> In any case the real reason for my writing is that Erman has made me aware that the dealer Phillip in Cairo has a large granite statue for sale, the head is missing, it portrays a certain 𓎼𓏏𓀀 and has inscriptions. Erman would have bought it for the Museum if he had the money but he is still paying for the Tell el-Amarna find. I wonder if Jacobsen would like it? Brugsch saw it in Cairo in the winter, and the price at that point was exceptionally cheap (2,000-3,000 Mark). Wilbour has allegedly published the inscriptions in a 'feuille volante'.[1144]

Schmidt replied that he will contact Jacobsen as soon as possible, and adds 'How can one ascertain the name of the aforementioned antiquities dealer, whether it is really *Phillip*??'[1145] During his next visit to Egypt in 1892, Schmidt sought out Philip and wrote back to Lange that he had acquired the sculpture for the Glyptotek together with some other items.[1146] Valdemar Schmidt also refers to this visit in his biography where he briefly describes Paul Philip as 'originally a French carpenter's apprentice, who had turned to trading in antiquities'.[1147]

Philip was active already in 1887 (p. 51) and is known to have excavated in 1892-3 at Heliopolis with an official permit.[1148] In 1899 he sold a large group of

1139. Petrie, *The Pyramids and Temples of Gizeh*, 8; Quirke, *Hidden Hands*, 55; Drower, *Letters from the Desert*, 30; cf. Quirke's forthcoming work on Petrie as a collector.

1140. Quirke, *Hidden Hands*, 66-67, 116-118, 276.

1141. Cf. Capart (ed.), *Letters of Charles Edwin Wilbour*, 338, 386; *Annuaire égyptien, administratif et commercial, 1891-1892*, 112; Quirke, *Hidden Hands*, 130; Mietke et al., *Josef Strzygowski und die Berliner Museen*, 11.

1142. Philip is briefly mentioned in Bierbrier, *Who was Who in Egyptology*, 4th edition, 431; cf. further Bakhoum and Hellmann, *Journal des savants* 1992, 162. There is a detailed correspondence with and concerning Philip in the Ny Carlsberg Glyptotek.

1143. *Annuaire égyptien, administratif et commercial, 1891-1892*, [144]; cf. also Baedeker, *Ägypten und der Sudân*, 6th edition, 34.

1144. Letter from H. O. Lange to V. Schmidt, dated 26 June 1891 (Royal Library, Copenhagen).

1145. Letter from V. Schmidt to H. O. Lange, dated 30 June 1891 (Royal Library, Copenhagen). One *l* has later been deleted with pencil from the name Phillip.

1146. Letter from V. Schmidt to H. O. Lange, dated 25 Feb. 1892 (Royal Library, Copenhagen). The statue is Ny Carlsberg Glyptotek, ÆIN 661, for which see Jørgensen, *Egypt II*, 80-81, no. 20; Manniche, *Egyptian Art in Denmark*, 121, fig. 51. The other items included two wooden figures attributed to the 5th Dynasty and an offering table.

1147. Schmidt, *Af et Langt Livs Historie*, 88-89.

1148. Griffith, *Egypt Exploration Fund, Archaeological Report* 1892-93, 25; Frothingham, *American Journal of Archaeology and the History of the Fine Arts* 8, no. 1 (1893), 103.

carbonized papyri from Thmuis to Lord Craw-ford.[1149]

Around the turn of the century he moved to Paris and opened a shop at 35 Boulevard Bonne Nouvelle, with the shop in Cairo becoming a 'branch' (succursale). He later returned to Cairo where he was active at least until 1909.[1150] The return to Egypt may have taken place in 1905 when he sold off a large part of his collection – perhaps the stock of his Paris shop – at Hotel Drouot.

Pugioli, Pietro (1831-1902)

Italian collector and antiquities dealer in Alexandria where he also carried out excavations.[1151] Parts of his collection were sold to Bologna, Vienna and New York prior to 1890.[1152] In 1888 the Egyptian Museum (then at Bulaq) purchased a collection of nearly 100 vases and a few other objects from him, and in 1892, shortly after its foundation, he donated a group of monuments to the Greco-Roman Museum in Alexandria.[1153] Borchardt visited him a few years before his death, but found that he had nothing of interest for sale besides two large Roman busts.[1154]

Pusgul, A. (fl. 1930)

Pusgul (first name only indicated with the initial A.) was an Armenian dealer who had a shop in Cairo.[1155] Lange had a favorable impression of him:

> He is our good friend, and when we pass his shop on evening strolls, he hauls us in for a chat and to show us something or other.

Lange bought a 'very nice statuette of sandstone' from him for the Ny Carlsberg Glyptotek.[1156] Pusgul also acted as an agent for others, and on one occasion was trying to sell a magical papyrus (c. 50 cm long, priced at £300) for an unnamed professor in Cairo (p. 174).

Raphael (fl. 1890-1891)

Son of 'Michael', q.v.

Rescigno, Mario (fl. 1910s-1930s)

Mario Rescigno (var. Riccinio), born near Brindisi and educated at the local Accademia di Belle Arti di Napoli, was a professional restorer and forger who sometimes collaborated with Paul Dingli (q.v.); both had previously worked in the Conservation Department of the Egyptian Museum in Cairo and later opened an atelier together.[1157] He specialized in marble, but also worked in wood.

1149. Choat, in Schubert (ed.), Actes du 26e Congrès international de papyrologie, 143.

1150. On the printed letterhead of a letter from P. Philip to V. Schmidt, dated 3 June 1909 (Ny Carlsberg Glyptotek), the Paris address has been crossed out and 'Paris' has been replaced by 'Le Caire'. The letter is personally signed by Philip.

1151. Bierbrier, Who was Who in Egyptology, 4th edition, 446.

1152. Botti, Catalogue des monuments exposés au Musée Gréco-Roman d'Alexandrie, iv. The objects now in the US (a collection of about 75 vases) were originally acquired by the US consul general in Cairo, Elbert E. Farman, who sent them to New York and later sold most of them to the Metropolitan Museum of Art; Cook, Inscribed Hadra Vases in the Metropolitan Museum of Art, 12-18.

1153. 1888 acquisition: Anonymous, BIE 9, 2nd ser. (1889), iv-xii (JE 28210-28309); cf. also Edgar, Greek Vases, iv, 37-50. 1892 donation: Botti, Rapport sur le Musée Gréco-Romain, 36-37; cf. also idem, Catalogue des monuments exposés au Musée Gréco-Roman d'Alexandrie, 59, 80, 243, 253, 260, 261, 262, 272, 277, 299, 557, 560.

1154. Borchardt diary, Sept. 1899 - Jan. 1900, entry 18 Dec. 1899 (Swiss Institute, Kairo; transcript kindly provided by Cornelius von Pilgrim, 21 Jan. 2015).

1155. Lange, Dagbog fra Ægypten, 1929-1930, 116-118. This Pusgul is likely to be the same person as the Cairo dealer mentioned by Bahrami, Transactions of the Oriental Ceramic Society 20 (1944-1945), 40 n. 4, who apparently had donated some objects to the Museum of Islamic Art in Cairo (cf. pl. 16, no. c, 'Collection Pusgul au Musée Arabe du Caire'); at least one of these was exhibited already in 1931; cf. Blair, Muqarnas 25 (2008), 171.

1156. We have been unable to identify this object in the Museum records.

1157. Fiechter, Faux et faussaires en art égyptien, 45-49; idem, Egyptian Fakes, 84, 87-89. Cornelius von Pilgrim informs us that the photograph included in the latter publication (p. 81) does not show Paolo Dingli, as indicated by the caption, but in fact Mario Rescigno. Rescigno is identical with the 'the Italian marble-worker' who showed Borchardt 'all about the

de Rustafjaell, Robert (1859(?)-1943)

Deliberately deceptive about his background and changing his name, origin, and date of birth on several occasions, the Russian born Robert 'de Rustafjaell' (also known as Smith, Fawcus-Smith, Orbeliani, d'Orbeliani-Rustafjaell, etc.) was active as a collector and dealer of Egyptian antiquities c. 1905-1915.[1158]

Large parts of his collection was put up for auction in London in 1906 and 1907. In 1909 he opened an antiquities shop in the main street at Luxor which he called Museum of Practical Archaeology; according to Borchardt it included a considerable number of fakes.[1159] He later put more material up for auction in London (1913), Paris (1914), and New York (1915). The five auctions between 1906 and 1915 lasted a total of fourteen days, while a posthumous auction in New York (1949) also included material from his collection. He further promoted his business through sensational press releases and publications, thus marketing his antiquities; these included two large batches of papyrus rolls and codices from Aswan and Edfu, and a cache of well-preserved textiles from the Hathor sanctuary at Deir el-Bahri.[1160]

Sadic Girgis Ebed (*fl.* 1930-1931)

Sadic Girgis Ebed was a dealer from Qena and a relative of Todros Girgis Gabrial.[1161] The latter accompanied Lange on a trip to Qena in 1930 to show Sadic's 'storeroom of antiquities', but many of them turned out to be fake in Lange's opinion (a 6th Dynasty stele was thought worth photographing by Lange).[1162] His

prize object was a bronze statue in pieces 'of a Roman emperor or prefect' from Dendera. About a week after Lange's visit to Qena, Sadic came to Cairo to show Lange this statue which he was desperate to sell: 'he has a considerable amount of money invested in it, and he has had it lying around for nine years, so the cost in interest is considerable'. Some letters from Ebed to Lange in the Royal Library in Copenhagen, all from the autumn and early winter of 1930, reveal that the Glyptotek had agreed to buy the statue for the sum of £1250 and that it had been given an export license by the Egyptian Museum in Cairo, but for some reason the transaction was never completed. The statue was eventually acquired by the Egyptian Museum the following year for £1,000 and was sent to the Alexandria Museum on 4 March 1931; it is described as a 'statue, possibly of the Emperor Hadrian. Head perfect; body in many fragments. Bronze.'[1163]

Ebed wrote in proficient English and even, in one case, included an English translation of a letter in Arabic that he had received from the Antiquities Service regarding the bronze statue that he wanted to sell.[1164] In view of his name, Sadic Girgis Ebed might be a son of Ebeïd, the French consular agent at Qena.[1165]

Saïd-Allah (*fl.* 1950s)

Antiquities dealer at Baliana involved in the sale of the Pachomian Monastic Library.[1166]

Saïd Ismaïn (*fl.* 1881-1888)

Saïd Ismaïn was the brother of well-known Farag Ismaïn. In January 1881, he invited Charles Wilbour to his home at Kafr el-Haram and he soon became a

technique of his forging', as reported in an anecdote told by Borchardt's wife, recorded by Steindorff, *The Journal of the Walters Art Gallery* 10 (1947), 56.

1158. Bierbrier, *Who was Who in Egyptology*, 4th edition, 479-480.
1159. Voss, in Fitzenreiter, Kirchner, and Kriseleit (eds.), *Authentizität*, 57.
1160. Textiles: D'Auria, in Der Manuelian (ed.), *Fs Simpson* 1, 169-176. Papyri: Ryholt, *ZPE* 190 (2014), 173-187.
1161. Lange, *Dagbog fra Ægypten, 1929-1930*, 239-42, 255-256.
1162. Lange, *Dagbog fra Ægypten, 1929-1930*, 239-242.

1163. Cairo Museum, *Journal d'entrée*, s.v. JE 55593.
1164. The three letters from S. Girgis to H. O. Lange are dated to 17 Aug., 12 Oct., and 21 Nov. 1930 (Royal Library, Copenhagen).
1165. Baedeker, *Egypte et Soudan*, 3rd edition, 237.
1166. Robinson, *The Story of the Bodmer Papyri*, 120-121.

kind of assistant or agent for him. He functioned in this role during Wilbour's visits to Egypt 1881-1884, bringing dealers to him, independently acquiring antiquities on his behalf, and twice even accompanying him on travels to Upper Egypt.[1167] It is very likely the same Saïd who sold a number of objects to the Egyptian Museum in 1888 (p. 51).

Saïd *Bey* Mustafa Ayat (born c. 1845 – *fl.* 1908)

Saïd *Bey* Mustafa Ayat (Table 4), a son of Mustafa Aga Ayat, served as Governor of Luxor at least from 1877 and took over from his younger brother Ahmed *Effendi* Mustafa as consular agent of Britain and Russia, as well as Belgium, from 1903. He was 'nineteen or twenty at most' in 1864, when his father suggested to Lady Duff-Gordon that Saïd might marry a woman discreetly designated 'S'.[1168]

Saïd Mellawi (*fl.* 1914)

Dealer, possibly at Eshmunein or at Mellawi, which lies a few kilometers to the south, who sold some lead tablets to the German papyrus cartel.[1169]

Saïd Mohammed (*fl.* 1923)

A minor dealer at Sheikh Abd el-Qurna who mainly sold fakes, according to B. Bruyère.[1170]

Sawiris (*fl.* 1945)

Antiquities dealer at Qena.[1171] In 1945 he was offered two of the Nag Hammadi codices for £3½, an offer which was immediately rejected and the manuscripts were brought to another dealer.

Sayed Khashaba *Pasha* (*fl.* 1910-1950)

Sayed Khashaba *Pasha* (earlier Sayed *Bey* Khashaba) was an Egyptian merchant (in 1941 also Vice-President of *Société royale d'agriculture* in Cairo) and collector/dealer from Assiut. He conducted official excavations between 1910 and 1914, especially in Middle Egypt (Assiut, Meir, Deir el-Gabrawi, Tihna, but also Soknopaiu Nesos in the Fayum), employing Ahmed *Bey* Kamal, then Assistant Curator at the Egyptian Museum, as a contract excavator.[1172] His share of the finds was kept in a private museum in Assiut. Khashaba's museum was listed in the most recent Baedeker guide during Lange's second visit, with the following directions:

> Close to the post office, in a side-street off the Sharia el-Mahatta, which diverges w[est] from the square, is the Egyptian Museum of Saiyid Khashaba Pasha, a wealthy resident of Asyut, who excavated ancient cemeteries at Asyut and Meir in 1910-1914. Adm[ission] on application to the owner's private house in the Manshiya quarter.[1173]

1167. Cf. Capart (ed.), *Letters of Charles Edwin Wilbour*, passim; note that Saïd is called Essaid in the earliest letters.

1168. Duff-Gordon, *Lady Duff-Gordon's Letters from Egypt*, 174.

1169. Gundel, *Kurzberichte aus den Giessener Papyrussammlungen* 27 (1968), 5.

1170. Diary entry dated 30 Jan. 1923; http://www.ifao.egnet. net/bases/archives/bruyere/ (accessed 11 Sept. 2013).

1171. Robinson, *The Nag Hammadi Story*, 75-76.

1172. Kamal, *ASAE* 13 (1914), 161-178; idem, *ASAE* 16 (1916), 65-114; Gouvernement Égyptien, *Rapport sur la marche du Service des antiquités de 1899 à 1910*, 325; idem, *Rapport du Service des Antiquités pour l'année 1911*, 17; idem, *Rapport du Service des Antiquités pour l'année 1913*, 20; idem, *Rapport du Service des Antiquités pour l'année 1914 et 1915*, 27; Moje, *The Ushebtis from Early Excavations in the Necropolis of Asyut*, 7. A typescript catalogue of the Khashaba collection was made in 1950 by W. C. Hayes of the Metropolitan Museum of Art (*Selective Catalogue of Egyptian Antiquities from the Collection of Sayed Pasha Khashaba*); he is also mentioned in passing by Bothmer, *Egypt 1950: My First Visit*, 92, 94. Vice-President of *Société royale d'agriculture*: Blattner (ed.), *Le mondain égyptien: The Egyptian Who's Who 1941*, 52. A large group of wooden objects from the excavations at Meir was acquired by the Metropolitan Museum of Art between 1910 and 1915, some through Sayed Khashaba himself, some through the dealers Michel Casira and Maurice Nahman, and various objects from Assiut in 1915, 1917 and 1933, again through Sayed Khashaba himself (http://www.metmuseum.org/collections, s.v. Khashaba; accessed 18 Nov. 2013).

1173. Baedeker, *Egypt and the Sudân*, 8th edition, 227; cf. Riggs,

The museum building was completed in 1912. The official report of the Egyptian Antiquities Service from 1913 and 1914 shows that it had originally pressed for the museum to be a (semi-)public institution, financed and administered by Sayed Khashaba and his descendants, but already by the following year, it became clear that Sayed Khashaba intended that it should be private; as a consequence, the Service decided not to grant him further excavation permits, arguing that it could not authorize excavations for the purposes of enriching a private museum.[1174]

Objects from his excavations and the museum were gradually sold over time, culminating in a large-scale dispersal in the 1970s. What remains of his collection in now in the Salam Modern School in Assiut, an American-founded institution formerly known as the American College in Assiut. Other pieces are in the Metropolitan Museum of Art, the Royal Scottish Museum, and in private hands.[1175]

Sayed Molattam (*fl.* 1917-1977)

Sayed Molattam (Fig. 164), with a shop next to the entrance of the Luxor Hotel and Antiquities license no. 84, was active for sixty years and became one of the leading antiquities dealers in Luxor.[1176] As a boy or young man he had apparently worked on Petrie's excavations in Thebes. Also his brother Ahmed and their father Molattam were involved in the antiquities trade; according to Bruyère, writing in 1923, the father

Fig. 164. Sayed Molattam. Photo, 1970s, published by Ehlebracht, *Haltet die Pyramiden Fest!*, fig. 64.

was an honest and trustworthy dealer in Sheikh Abd el-Qurna, while the sons Ahmed and Sayed primarily sold fakes.[1177] Sayed played what seems to have been a duplicitous role in Carl Schmidt's attempt to map networks of forgers in 1933.[1178]

Schafi (*fl.* 1930)

Schafi (whose name Lange originally took to be Mansur) was a dealer based in Luxor with whom Lange and

The Beautiful Burial in Roman Egypt, 110 n. 20.

1174. Gouvernement Égyptien, *Rapport du Service des Antiquités pour l'année 1912*, Cairo, 1913, 10; idem, *Rapport du Service des Antiquités pour l'année 1913*, 35-36; idem, *Rapport du Service des Antiquités pour l'année 1914 et 1915*, 47-48, 61.

1175. Lapp, *Särge des Mittleren Reiches aus der ehemaligen Sammlung Khashaba*.

1176. Bothmer, *Egypt 1950: My First Visit*, 38, 42; Drower, *Flinders Petrie*, 311; Reeves, *Valley of the Kings*, 32, n. 106; Hagen, *JEA* 96 (2010), 75-76; cf. further Ehlebracht, *Haltet die Pyramiden fest!*, 332, fig. 64. Sayed Molattam was active as a dealer at least from 1917 when he sold a Third Intermediate Period coffin to the Metropolitan Museum of Art (inv. 17.2.7a, 1-2): http://www.metmuseum.org/collections, s.v. Melattam; accessed 18 Nov. 2013; further objects, s.v. Molattam.

1177. Excavation diary of Bernard Bruyère, entry of 30 Jan. 1923, accessible on-line at http://www.ifao.egnet.net/bases/archives/bruyere (accessed 16 July 2013). This reference was kindly brought to our attention by Rob Demarée.

1178. Fiechter, *Faux et faussaires en art égyptien*, 43-44.

Wolfgang Dreiss were involved in a scheme to buy a kind of offering table in granite depicting a foreign prisoner in a kneeling position. Dreiss claimed that Schafi was 'the greatest swindler in Thebes' and in league with a well-known forger called Ali Jussef so Lange was apprehensive about making a deal and eventually declined.[1179] This Schafi may well be the same individual as 'Schafeï Ahmed' who was similarly based in Luxor and who is known to have sold a lot of fakes.[1180]

Scopelitis (*fl.* 1913)

Dealer in Medinet el-Fayum, apparently of Greek origin, who sold papyri to the German papyrus cartel.[1181]

Selim *Bey* Kahil (*fl.* 1894-1901)

Collector and dealer in Cairo. According to Dutilh he had, by 1895, built up 'a magnificent collection' of Ptolemaic and Alexandrian coins; he is recorded selling coins in 1894 and was still active in 1901.[1182]

Serveux-Sickenberg, F. (*fl.* 1926-1934)

Madame Serveux (-Sickenberg) was the housekeeper of A. Bircher for 33 years, and upon his death was charged with selling his collection of antiquities (for her work in this regard, see above p. 203). She was the daughter of the German botanist Dr Sickenberg, a professor at the University of Cairo and a friend of A.

Bircher for many years.[1183] In 1926 Idris Bell and Francis Kelsey examined some papyri she had for sale, but they concluded that they were forgeries.[1184]

Shakir Farag (*fl.* 1930)

An obscure dealer from Beni Suef. Having been alerted by the dealer Agaibi Makarios from Medinet el-Fayum to the fact that Friedrich Zucker was seeking papyri on behalf of the Papyrus Hauniensis Collection, he came to Cairo in 1930 to offer a group of 'interesting' papyri. Zucker described his asking price as 'insane' (*den unsinnigen Preis*) and no acquisition was made.[1185]

Shookr [= Shakir?] Homer (*fl.* 1883-1884)

Dealer from Kafr el-Haram; Wilbour acquired objects from him on a few occasions and describes him both as 'one of the Pyramid Arabs' and as 'a sheikh of El Azhar'.[1186]

Shenudi Makarios (1837-1904)

French and Austro-Hungarian consular agent at Luxor.[1187] He spoke a little French but no other foreign language.[1188] Originally residing in *Maison de France* within the Luxor temple, he moved to Sharia el-Lukanda after its expropriation in 1884 and subsequent demolition (p. 107). He carried out official excavations at Thebes (which led to the discoveries of KV39 and KV42 in the Valley of the Kings) and elsewhere. He was succeeded as Austro-Hungarian consular agent by his son Iskander Shenudi who retired from

1179. Lange, *Dagbog fra Ægypten, 1929-1930*, 182-195.
1180. Fiechter, *Faux et faussaires en art égyptien*, 49; idem, *Egyptian Fakes*, 89.
1181. Giessener Papyri- und Ostrakadatenbank on-line (http://digibib.ub.uni-giessen.de/cgi-bin/populo/pap.pl, s.v. Scopilites; accessed 7 Dec. 2013); Gundel, *Kurzberichte aus den Giessener Papyrussammlungen* 27 (1968), 5.
1182. Dutilh, *Rivista italiana di numismatica* 8 (1895), 95 w. note 2; Forrer, *Description Catalogue of the Collection of Greek Coins* 3, no. 2 ('Selim Kabil'), 886; Mietke et al., *Josef Strzygowski und die Berliner Museen*, 47.

1183. Sigerist, *Schweizer in Ägypten*, 28.
1184. Pedley, *The Life and Work of Francis Willey Kelsey*, 375-376.
1185. Letter from F. Zucker to C. Høeg, dated 2 Oct. 1930 (Royal Library, Copenhagen). Cited *in toto* by Bülow-Jacobsen, *Aegis* 12 (2012), 36-40, cf. pp. 36, 38.
1186. Cf. Capart (ed.), *Letters of Charles Edwin Wilbour*, 184, 312.
1187. Bierbrier, *Who was Who in Egyptology*, 4th edition, 507; Weens, *EA* 44 (2014), 27-28.
1188. Peters, *Die Klimatischen Winterkurorte Egyptens*, 40.

this office at the outbreak of the First World War in 1914; his consular house was located next to Luxor train station (p. 109).

Hajji Sidi Mohammed Ahmed el-Gabri (*fl.* 1912-1914)

Dealer at Kafr el-Haram. In 1912 he was a key witness for the State against the government *reïs* Ibrahim Faïd and his associates who stood accused of having plundered and sold a series of reliefs from 'Petrie's Tomb'.[1189] Maspero reported that Sidi bragged at court about how much he had profited from the theft and sale of antiquities, but this statement is likely biased since Ibrahim Faïd had long stood under the protection of Maspero who, after his conviction, helped him appeal and achieve a full acquittal. Moreover, he attempted – in vain – to prosecute Sidi after the Ibrahim Faïd trials.

Sidrac (*fl.* 1888-1906)

A Coptic dealer based at Akhmim.[1190] He was involved in the trading of the Amarna tablets and his antiquities were seized by Grébaut in January and December 1888; he was given a compensation of £29 for the antiquities confiscated during the first raid (p. 143). Some years later, in 1894, he assisted Robert Forrer in his excavations at Akhmim.[1191]

Simonian, Simon Ohan (*fl.* 1980)

Dealer of Armenian extraction who sold a stele with a building inscription of Ptolemy III to the Cairo Museum in 1980.[1192]

Sivadjian, Mihran (*fl.* 1894-1908)

A Turk of Armenian origin, Mihran Sivadjian had his main antiquities shop in Paris, at 17 Rue Le Peletier; he had a another shop in Cairo, at least for some time, and frequently travelled to Egypt to conduct business or acquire material for sale elsewhere.[1193] He sold coins to the Cabinet des Médailles in Paris, as well as many smaller objects to the British Museum between 1896 and 1904. In 1904 he was involved in the smuggling of a rich archaeological treasure in Cyprus in partnership with the dealers Nicolas Tano and Alexandre Dingli (q.v.).

Smith, Edwin (1822-1906)

An American who resided at Luxor between 1857 and 1876, and made a living from the antiquities trade and money-lending (p. 125).[1194] For several years he lived in a two-storey house built for him by Mustafa Aga next to his own within the Luxor temple (p. 102, Fig. 97), which suggests that he was under the protection of this consular agent. In 1862 he guided the Prince of Wales during his visit to Luxor – presumably alongside Mustafa Aga in whose visitors' book the Prince

---

1189. Gouvernement Égyptien, *Rapport du Service des Antiquités pour l'année 1912*, 18-19; idem, *Rapport du Service des Antiquités pour l'année 1913*, 14-17.

1190. He is mentioned repeatedly in the Wilbour letters; cf. Capart (ed.), *Letters of Charles Edwin Wilbour*, 611 (index); cf. also Lefebvre, *Recueil des inscriptions grecques-chrétiennes d'Égypte*, 55-56; idem, *ASAE* 9 (1908), 178; and Mietke et al., *Josef Strzygowski und die Berliner Museen*, 12.

1191. A sketch of him on a donkey, ahead of a small cavaran transporting excavated mummies, may be found in Forrer, *Mein Besuch in El-Achmim*, pl. 9.

1192. Cairo Museum, Temporary Register, s.v. 2/4/80/1.

1193. Bakhoum and Hellmann, *Journal des savants* 1992, 165-166; Merrillees, *The Tano Family*; Wessely, *CdE* 6 (1931), 367; Vandorpe, *Reconstructing Pathyris' Archives*, 66-68 (w. photograph of the letterhead of the Paris shop). An advertisement for his shop in Paris from 1908 reads 'Mihran Sivadjian. Expert. Egyptian, Assyrian, Greek, and Roman Antiquities, Jewels, Arabian and Persian Potteries and Rare Objects for Collection'; *American Art News* 6, no. 34 (1907), 6.

1194. Ferguson, *Moss Gathered by a Rolling Stone*, 50; Auwers, *Bericht über die Beobachtung des Venus-Durchgangs*, 124; Warner, *My Winter on the Nile*, 17th edition, 356-357; Wilson, *Signs & Wonders Upon Pharaoh*, 52-57; Bierbrier, *Who was Who in Egyptology*, 4th edition, 515; Voss, *MDAIK* 65 (2009), 373-376.

of Wales left his name (p. 60). The relationship between Mustafa Aga and Smith seems to have been uneasy; several conflicts between the two men are recorded in contemporary accounts.[1195] After an alleged assasination attempt by a servant of Mustafa Aga, he moved over to the German consular agent Todros Bolos who lived just across from Mustafa Aga. Mohareb Todros, the son of the latter, described Smith as a peculiar man (he often sat in a chair by the river with his bare feet in the water, and his main nourishment was milk) and in 1876 he suddenly 'vanished' from Egypt. He is mainly known for his acquisition of the medical Papyrus Edwin Smith from the New Kingdom, although he is also rumoured to have been involved in the production of fake antiquities.[1196]

Soliman 'the young' (fl. 1900)

Soliman 'the young' lived at Kafr el-Haram, but there is little information about him in Lange's diaries. He is at one stage described as 'one of our oldest acquaintances, a young man named Soliman, still quite new in the antiquities trade ... who often acted as an agent for others'.[1197] He visited the Lange residence once as a representative of a dealer who waited outside on the street.[1198] He is also known to have been a companion of Mahmud Abd es-Samad.

Soliman Ahmed Abd er-Rasul

Brother of Abd er-Rasul Ahmed Abd er-Rasul, q.v.

Soliman Abd es-Samad (fl. 1881-1900)

Soliman Abd es-Samad (Table 3), an Arab dealer who lived at Kafr el-Haram, features several times in the first Lange diary (where he is sometimes called Soliman 'the elder'); he was the brother of Ibrahim Abd es-Samad and apparently also a relative of Abd es-Salam Abdallah, and he had at least one son, the 'nice young' Mohammed.[1199]

He had a storeroom with antiquities both at Kafr el-Haram and in Cairo. The latter was conveniently located in a side street behind Hôtel Bristol at the north-eastern corner of Ezbekiya Gardens, just five minutes away from Shepheard's Hotel (and from Pension König where Lange stayed). Lange visited the Cairo storeroom together with Valdemar Schmidt on 12 November 1899 (described above, p. 53) and again 16 February 1900.[1200] At this meeting he gave Jonna and her friend Mrs Müller 'a little divine image' each, of which they were 'very proud'.[1201] It was presumably the same storeroom in Cairo that Borchardt and Steindorf visited on 23 November 1899, since they went straight to Michel Casira afterwards, whose shop was a few minutes away, and then to Panayotis Kyticas around the corner.[1202]

Lange visited Soliman's home at Kafr el-Haram (Fig. 89) more than once; the first time on 18 November 1899 (p. 93). In January 1900, he went to inspect a granite statue. Soliman himself was not home; the statue was shown to him by Soliman's son Mohammed instead and Lange provides a brief but noteworthy description of how he lived (cited p. 98).[1203] In a

1195. Ames, *Life and Letters of Peter and Susan Lesley*, 59 (a 'Mr. Hale' attempting to settle 'the long quarrel between Smith and Mustafa', in 1868); de Forest, *BMMA* 16 (1921), 193 (Mustafa Aga, Smith, and a dragoman 'rolling on the ground and beating each other with their fists while cries arose from the crowd', in 1870). Cf. Raven (ed.), *W. de Famars Testas: Reisschetsen uit Egypt 1858-1860*, 231 (index); Raven, in Volait (ed.), *Émile Prisse d'Avennes*, 199-200, 202-203.

1196. The rumour persisted even after the departure of Smith from Egypt; cf. Gyllanhaal, in Hawass and Houser Wegner (eds.), *Fs Silverman*, 182-183, citing sources from 1878.

1197. Lange and Lange, *Dagbog fra Ægyptensrejsen 1899-1900*, 418-419.

1198. Lange and Lange, *Dagbog fra Ægyptensrejsen 1899-1900*, 481.

1199. Lange and Lange, *Dagbog fra Ægyptensrejsen 1899-1900*, 132, 136.

1200. Lange and Lange, *Dagbog fra Ægyptensrejsen 1899-1900*, 131-132, 386.

1201. Lange and Lange, *Dagbog fra Ægyptensrejsen 1899-1900*, 132.

1202. Borchardt diary, Sept. 1899 - Jan. 1900, entry 23 Nov. 1899 (Swiss Institute, Kairo): transcript kindly provided by Cornelius von Pilgrim (21 Jan. 2015).

1203. Lange and Lange, *Dagbog fra Ægyptensrejsen 1899-1900*, 220. Some objects seen at the home of Soliman at Kafr el-Haram are copied in Lange, *Notebook 1899/1900*, 207-208. Josef Strzygowski visited Soliman at Giza the following winter; cf.

later letter, Schmidt refers to a visit he and Lange had paid to both Soliman and his brother Ibrahim; he asks whether Soliman still has a certain relief from the 5th Dynasty and remarks that Ibrahim 'had many things, but nothing worth paying for, nothing characteristic or good.'[1204]

Lange records in his diary during July that Soliman possessed 'a unique and remarkable granite statue' that Valdemar Schmidt and he had examined on a prior occasion. Soliman would now like Schmidt to buy it, 'but he really only wants to sell it together with his whole stock and he demands an absolutely ludicrous price for it.'[1205] As Lange was about to return to Denmark, Soliman made him a business proposal whereby he offered to let him buy the entire collection in return for his services as a European agent; Lange would then get a cut of anything that reached a certain price.[1206] There is no indication that Lange seriously considered the proposal.

Valdemar Schmidt first visited Soliman in 1892 and describes him and his brother Ibrahim as the most famous dealers at Kafr el-Haram. He also did business with him in 1894, after Soliman had just returned from a trip up the Nile where he had been acquiring antiquities from local dealers.[1207]

Soliman is known to have sold objects to the Egyptian Museum between 1884 and 1888 (p. 51),[1208] and Petrie, who first mentions him in 1881, notes in 1889 that Soliman had obtained permission from Grébaut to excavate at Tell Defenna.[1209] Is very likely the same Soliman 'from the Pyramids' who is mentioned several times by Wilbour between 1881 and 1886, twice in connection with Mohammed *Effendi*.[1210]

Stamati (*fl.* 1891)

Antiquities dealer at Medinet el-Fayum visited by Wilbour, apparently of Greek origin.[1211]

Sultan Maguid Sameda (*fl.* 1970s)

Son of Maguid Sameda, q.v.

Tayeb Mohammed Aouiss (*fl.* 1923)

A minor dealer at Sheikh Abd el-Qurna who mainly sold fakes, according to B. Bruyère.[1212]

Tanios Girgis (*fl.* around 1906/09)

Coptic dealer in Qena mentioned in the Freer diaries.[1213] The name might be a mistranslitteration or misreading of Tadros/Todros Girgis.

Tano, Frank John (*fl.* 1940s)

Frank John Tano (Table 7), a nephew of Phocion Jean Tano, was stationed in New York by his uncle after the Second World War to facilitate trade with US clients and later seems to have settled in New Jersey.[1214] His name may represent an Anglicized version of Phocion Jean Tano; in this case he would have the same name as his uncle.

Tano, Nicolas George (1866-1924)

Nicolas Tano (Table 7), a nephew of Marius Tano, took over his antiquities business in 1889.[1215] The shop

Mietke et al., *Josef Strzygowski und die Berliner Museen*, 88-89.

1204. Letter from V. Schmidt to H. O. Lange, dated 19 Apr. 1900 (Royal Library, Copenhagen).

1205. Lange and Lange, *Dagbog fra Ægyptensrejsen 1899-1900*, 738.

1206. Lange and Lange, *Dagbog fra Ægyptensrejsen 1899-1900*, 738.

1207. Jørgensen, *How it all began*, 39/44.

1208. An object sold in 1884 is mentioned in Vernier, *Bijoux et orfèvreries* 1, 111.

1209. Cf. Quirke's forthcoming work on Petrie as a collector.

1210. Cf. Capart (ed.), *Letters of Charles Edwin Wilbour*, 76 ('Seliman'), 312 ('Suleeman'), 340 ('Sleeman').

1211. Cf. Capart (ed.), *Letters of Charles Edwin Wilbour*, 580.

1212. Diary entry dated 30 Jan. 1923; http://www.ifao.egnet. net/bases/archives/bruyere/ (accessed 11 Sept. 2013).

1213. Gunter, *A Collector's Journey*, 91, 116-117, 151 n. 7, 153 n. 70, fig. 4.22.

1214. Robinson, *Manuscripts of the Middle East* 5 (1990-1991), 31; Gallatin, *The Pursuit of Happiness*, 178; Sotheby's auction of 5 June 2008, lot 61; cf. http://www.sothebys.com (accessed 10 Dec. 2013).

1215. Merrillees, *The Tano Family*; cf. also Bierbrier, *Who was Who in Egyptology*, 4th edition, 534.

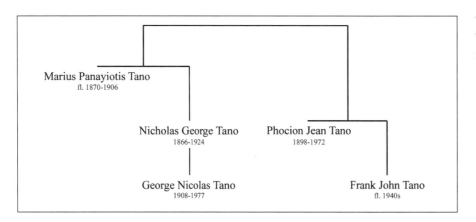

Table 7. Family tree of the Tano family in Cairo, c. 1870-1977.

was located on Sharia Kamel at Midan Kantaret el-Dikka, diagonally across Shepheard's Hotel to the north and just opposite Thomas Cook & Sons.[1216] At his death thirty-five years later, the business was so well-established that his successors retained the name 'Nicolas Tano' (Fig. 16). While much of his business may have been legitimate, he also occasionally operated outside the law. In 1904 he was involved in the smuggling of a valuable archaeological treasure in Cyprus in partnership with the dealers Alexandre Dingli and Mihran Sivadjian, and in 1906 he was involved in the sale of statues stolen from Legain's excavations at Karnak.[1217] Breasted reported two interesting incidents in 1919-1920 which involved Nicolas Tano. The first concerned a thick and intact Book of the Dead roll which Tano had hidden with a rug dealer across the street (p. 144) and the second a large group of 25 limestone servant statuettes from the Old Kingdom which he kept at his private residence at Heliopolis (p. 145), in both cases in order to avoid official registration. Another well-preserved papyrus inscribed with more unusual mortuary texts, the demotic Papyrus Harkness, was sold by Nicolas Tano to Howard Carter in 1922, just months before the discovery of the tomb of Tutankhamun; this was clearly an investment by Carter who later sold it (in London) to Edward S. Harkness.[1218]

Tano, Marius Panayiotis (fl. 1870-1906)

Marius Tano (Table 7), who was born in Cyprus and came to Egypt as a young man, was the founder – in 1870 – of one of the oldest and most successful antiquities businesses in Cairo.[1219] In 1889 Marius returned to Cyprus, where he was also involved in the antiquities trade, and entrusted his business in Cairo to his nephew Nicolas George Tano; it was later run by the younger cousin of the latter, Phocion Jean Tano. Marius Tano sold several objects to the Egyptian Museum in the 1880s (p. 51). An example of how he tricked a lesser dealer to trade a valuable commemorative scarab of Amenhotep III against a nearly worthless Abyssinian liturgy is recounted above (p. 126).

Tano, Phocion Jean [Phokion Ioannis] (1898-1972)

At the death of Nicolas Tano in 1924, his antiquities shop was inherited by his 16-year old son George Nicolas Tano (Table 7), but it was effectively run by Phocion Jean Tano ('Jean Tano'; Fig. 165), a younger cousin of his father, who had already assisted with the business for some years.[1220] In the early 1940s, Jean ac-

---

1216. Annuaire égyptien, administratif et commercial, 1891-1892, 120.

1217. David, Gaston Maspero, 386-388.

1218. Smith, Papyrus Harkness, 1. The papyrus was, in turn, presented by Harkness to the Metropolitan Museum of Art.

1219. Merrillees, The Tano Family; Kapera, Studies in Ancient Art and Civilization 12 (2008), 92-93; cf. also Bierbrier, Who was Who in Egyptology, 4th edition, 533-534, and David, Gaston Maspero, 21, 86, 201, 237.

1220. Merrillees, The Tano Family. Robinson, The Nag Hammadi Story, 1, notes that 'His full name was Phokion J. Tanos ... in French his last name was pronounced without the final 's', and

quired the shop from George and continued to run it until his death in 1972, having renamed it 'Phocion J. Tano Antiquities Gallery.' The shop was described in the Baedeker guide from 1928 as one of the three shops where one might acquire fine antiquities at a reasonable price, and was located on 7 Sharia Kamel (now 53 Sharia al-Gomehoriya) in front of Shepheard's Hotel (Fig. 49).[1221]

Jean Tano remained one of the most important dealers in Cairo and he is perhaps best known for his central role in the sale of the Nag Hammadi codices (found in 1945) and the Pachomian Monastic Library (the 'Dishna Papers', found in 1952); he is even said to have funded an illegal excavation at the latter site, apparently in the hope of finding further documents.[1222] As with other dealers, fakes occasionally passed through his store.[1223]

Lange visited him on several occasions in 1929/30, 'he had some good pieces which I will report to the Glyptotek', but seems not to have bought anything during this stay in Egypt.[1224] He would later, from 1931 to 1933, purchase large batches of papyri from the Tebtunis temple library from Tano with the help of

Fig. 165. Portrait photograph of Phocion Jean Tano, undated. Courtesy of Claremont Colleges Digital Library.

Ludwig Borchardt and Carl Schmidt (p. 180). Further papyri were acquired from Tano by Aksel Volten in late 1954 for the Papyrus Carlsberg Collection.

Tawfik (*fl.* 1926-1927)

Antiquities dealer in Cairo from whom Borchardt acquired some obejcts in 1926 and 1927.[1225]

---

so was usually written Tano. The French pronunciation of his first name was Phoqué, which was the usual way one referred to him'. The letters we have are mostly, and more formally it would seem, signed 'Ph. Jean Tanos'.

1221. Baedeker, *Ägypten und der Sudân*, 8th edition, 38-39. The letterhead of his shop (Fig. 16) reads 'Nicolas Tano. Magasin d'antiquités Egyptiennes, Grecques, Romaines, Arabes & Coptes. Fournisseur des principaux Musées d'Europe & d'Amérique. Vis-a-vis de l'Hotel Shepheard's, Rue Kamel N° 7, Le Caire. Adresse Télégraphique: "Pelusium".'

1222. Nag Hammadi codices: Robinson, in Barc (ed.), *Colloque international sur les textes de Nag Hammadi*, 21-58; idem, *The Facsimile Edition of the Nag Hammadi Codices*, 3-14; idem, *The Nag Hammadi Story*, passim. Pachomian Monastic Library: idem, *The Pachomian Monastic Library*; idem, *Manuscripts of the Middle East 5* (1990-1991), 26-40.

1223. A high-end example is a reserve head (Oriental Institute Museum inv. 13944) which was acquired from Jean Tano in 1929: Teeter, *The Oriental Institute News & Notes* 196 (2008), 9, fig. 6.

1224. Lange, *Dagbog fra Ægypten, 1929-1930*, 57, 123.

1225. von Briskorn, *Zur Sammlungsgeschichte afrikanischer Ethnographica im Übersee-Museum Bremen 1841-1945*, 319.

Tawfiq Fam (*fl.* 1940s)

Antiquities dealer based in Luxor until 1943 when he moved his business to Cairo/Giza.[1226] He is said to have been in frequent contact with Albert Eid and was involved in the sale of the Nag Hammadi codices.

Tawfiq Saïd (*fl.* 1952)

Antiquities dealer based at Alexandria where he operated the shop named 'Tewfik Saad et Fils' at 19 Rue de France.[1227] He was involved in the sale of the Pachomian Monastic Library. He shop was later taken over by his son Émile Saïd who identifed himself as a 'Bijoutier antiquaire' on his business card.

Toby Moursi (*fl.* late 1920s)

Dealer based at Luxor, visited by Clère in 1926/27 or 1927/28.[1228]

Todros (*fl.* 1926)

Coptic dealer at Medinet el-Fayum who sold papyri to Idris Bell in 1926.[1229]

Todros Bolos (*fl.* 1856- *d.* 1898)

Father of Mohareb Todros, q.v.

Todros Girgis Gabrial (*fl.* early 1920s-1941)

Todros Girgis Gabrial, whom Lange also refers to as 'Girgis the younger', was a Coptic antiquities dealer based in Luxor and the son of Girgis Gabrial. He accompanied Lange on a trip to Qena in January 1930 to show him the store of antiquities belonging to his relative Sadic Girgis Ebed.

In February 1930 Girgis came to Cairo to introduce Lange to a 'one-eyed' acquaintance from Mallawi, who was trying to sell the head of an Amarna Period statue;[1230] that transaction was described in detail by Lange, who eventually bought the head (p. 154).[1231] Girgis wanted no commission as an agent in the sale, but instead asked for a letter of recommendation from Lange, who also intended to send him 'a good piece of Copenhagen porcelain' upon his return to Denmark as a thank-you for his services.[1232] This head, as it turned out, was a fake and it is now known that Girgis was the main source of numerous Amarna sculptures and reliefs in a similar style. His dealings went back at least to the early 1920s when he first offered two sculptures to Maurice Nahman; the latter immediately concluded that they were not genuine, but they were soon acquired by M. A. Mansoor.[1233] Girgis would return to Mansoor time and again until 1941, each time bringing new Amarna pieces, and in the course of the two decades Mansoor acquired from him around 75 pieces in all. Girgis' cover story was that he got the sculptures from a *fellah* who had found them buried near Tell el-Amarna and that the latter sold them off one by one when he needed more money.

Verdakis (*fl.* 1906)

Antiquities dealer, presumably of Greek origin, at Zagazig (ancient Bubastis); in 1906 he falsely claimed ownership of two precious items belonging to the

1226. Robinson, in Barc (ed.), *Colloque international sur les textes de Nag Hammadi*, 48; idem, *The Facsimile Edition of the Nag Hammadi Codices*, 7; idem, *The Nag Hammadi Story*, 59.
1227. Robinson, *Manuscripts of the Middle East* 5 (1990-1991), 37, cf. also p. 30; idem, *The Nag Hammadi Story*, 113; idem, *The Story of the Bodmer Papyri*, 125-6, 175.
1228. Clère, *BIFAO* 28 (1929), 188.
1229. Emmel, 'The Yale Papyrus Collection. Catalog Introduction', 1993, with additions by R. Duttenhofer 1996, available on-line http://www.library.yale.edu/ beinecke/brblsear/ aboutpap.htm (accessed 24 July 2012).

1230. Lange, *Dagbog fra Ægypten, 1929-1930*, 269.
1231. For the story, see under *Fakes and forgers*, above (= ÆIN 1669).
1232. Lange, *Dagbog fra Ægypten, 1929-1930*, 274, 290.
1233. Fiechter, *Egyptian Fakes*, 163; cf. Mansoor, *The Scandal of the Century*, chapters 2 and 3.

Bubastis Treasure and lost the case at court.[1234]

Vinga, Stamati (*fl.* 1883- d. 1894)

Antiquities dealer and collector in Alexandria, apparently of Greek origin. A visitor to Alexandria in 1895 provides the following description of him:

> Dans la rue Chérif-Pacha se trouve le magasin de l'antiquaire bien connu, M. Stamati-Vinga, qui pendant nombre d'années avait recueilli, de tous côtés, une très belle collection d'objects antiques de toutes sortes, statuettes de Chypre, Tanagras d'Athènes, bronzes égyptiens, momies, scarabées, etc. Cet antiquaire émérite était décédé depuis plusieurs mois, lors de mon passage à Alexandrie.[1235]

His widow, Helène Stamati Vinga, continued to sell objects from the collection several years after his death; Borchardt visited her in 1899, but found that she had nothing worth buying.[1236]

Viola, Robert (1919-2005)

Robert Viola (Fig. 61, 166) was the second son of Maurice Nahman and, like his half-brother Robert Nahman, assisted his father in the antiquities trade.[1237] In the early 1950s, after Albert Eid's death, he became the general manager of Albert Eid & Co. and quickly went on to become the business partner of Eid's widow. Among other things, Viola sold a complete chapel from an Old Kingdom mastaba from the excavations of Sayed Khashaba to the Calouste Gulbenkian Foun-

Fig. 166. Portrait photograph of Robert Viola, dated 20 March 1943. He was, at the time, working for his father, Maurice Nahman. Courtesy of Lucien Viola.

dation. He continued as general manager when the shop was nationalized by the Egyptian government in 1956. In 1963 he left Egypt with his family. His son, Lucien Viola (b. 1948), later opened L'Ibis Gallery Ltd. in New York which specialized in Egyptian art and was in business between 1974 and 1995. He was at one time married to the granddaughter of the Swiss antiquities dealer Ernst E. Kofler and appraised his collection after his death; part of the collection went to Qatar while he personally acquired the other part.

Vita (*fl.* 1904)

Antiquities dealer in Cairo with whom Maspero did business in 1904.[1238]

1234. Gouvernement Égyptien, *Rapport sur la marche du Service des antiquités de 1899 à 1910*, 207.

1235. Deschamps, *A travers l'Égypte*, 50; cf. also Botti, *Catalogue des monuments exposés au Musée Gréco-Romain d'Alexandrie*, 260. In 1883 he sold some bronzes to the British Museum (EA 12587-12592).

1236. Borchardt diary, Sept. 1899 - Jan. 1900, entry 18 Dec. 1899 (Swiss Institute, Kairo; transcript kindly provided by Cornelius von Pilgrim, 21 Jan. 2015). Cf. further Dutilh, *Journal international d'archéologie numismatique* 5 (1902), 93 (who refers to Stamati Vinga as 'un autre de ces laveurs de sable'); Mietke et al., *Josef Strzygowski und die Berliner Museen*, 58.

1237. Lucien Viola (personal communication, 8 Dec. 2014).

1238. David, *Gaston Maspero*, 327, 341-342.

Fig. 167. Yussuf Hassan (right) in his garden with American visitors (from left); Ludlow Bull, Mrs. Ethel Collier (née Huxley), Miss Huxley, and John Collier. Detail of photograph by J. H. Breasted, January 1920. Courtesy of The Oriental Institute, University of Chicago.

Yassa Todros (*fl. 1897-1911*)

Coptic antiquities dealer active at both Medinet el-Fayum and Assiut. He conducted licensed excavations at Deir el-Aizam at Assiut in 1897 (with Farag Ismaïn) and Deir el-Bersha in 1900,[1239] and sold papyri to the German papyrus cartel in 1911.[1240]

Yasin Mahmud (*fl. 1904*)

Antiquities dealer at Karnak. In 1904 he persuaded two youths employed by the Antiquities Service to provide him with objects; they stole three worthless statues and were immediately caught. The youths were each punished with ten strokes of the cane and Yasin Mahmud with twenty-five.[1241]

Yussuf (*fl. 1882-1886*)

Forger living at Qurnet Murai on the Theban West Bank who, according to Wilbour, made exceptionally fine scarabs.[1242]

Yussuf Ahmed, see Ahmed Yussuf

Yussuf Hassan (*fl. 1907-1928*)

Yussuf Hassan was a Luxor dealer with a house in Sharia el-Markaz.[1243] Breasted referred repeatedly to Hassan as an old man in 1919 and described several visits to his house. During one visit for business:

1239. Deir el-Aizam: Maspero, *ASAE* 1 (1900), 109. Deir el-Bersheh: idem, *BIE* 1, 4th ser. (1901), 225; Gouvernement Égyptien, *Rapport sur la marche du Service des Antiquités de 1899 à 1910*, 17.
1240. Giessener Papyri- und Ostrakadatenbank on-line (http://digibib.ub.uni-giessen.de/cgi-bin/populo/pap.pl, s.v. Jasso Tadros; accessed 7 Dec. 2013).
1241. Gouvernement Égyptien, *Rapport sur la marche du Service des antiquités de 1899 à 1910*, 126-127; Legrain, *ASAE* 5 (1904), 279.

1242. Cf. Capart (ed.), *Letters of Charles Edwin Wilbour*, 141, 211, 285, 354.
1243. Baedeker, *Ägypten und der Sudân*, 8th edition, 260; Clère, *BIFAO* 28 (1929), 185-186 (selling object from Deir el-Medina). He was already active in 1907 (p. 158). According to Fiechter, *Faux et faussaires en art égyptien*, 16-17, the name Ibrahîm Suleyman was used as an alias for 'un vieil antiquaire de Louxor' called Yussuf Hassan who had been duped into buying an 'intact' tomb, which actually contained only forgeries. This might be the same individual.

He rummaged in a crazy old safe built into the thickness of the walls of his house and brought out one treasure after another.[1244]

Another visit in January 1920 was a social gathering, although obviously designed to promote business (Fig. 167).

Old Yussuf Hassan, who is an old aristocrat had asked me to come to [his] house for dinner and to bring a group of friends ... we had a picturesque time, eating endless courses, and listening to old Yussuf telling of the great folk with whom he had consorted, especially the Duke of Connaught, of whose friendship he was very proud. He was a conceited old chap, – Yussuf I mean, and proudly took us to look about through his gardens and houses, for he is well-to-do.[1245]

He was one of several major dealers involved in the sale of objects from the tomb of the three foreign wives of Tuthmosis III.[1246]

Zaki Basta (b. 1897, fl. 1943-1978)

Coptic dealer (Fig. 168) at Qena who was involved in the sale of the Nag Hammadi codices in 1945.[1247] J. M. Robinson reports that he

had a one-fourth interest in the Qinā's Cinema Firyāl (named after King Farouk's daughter) until it closed. However, his main business was to circulate among the villages and antiquities sites of the region collecting antiquities for the small shop upstairs in his home on their way to the antiquities market of Cairo.[1248]

Fig. 168. Portrait photograph of Zaki Basta, c. 1935. Courtesy of Claremont Colleges Digital Library.

Zaki Ghali (fl. 1930s-50s)

Goldsmith and antiquities dealer in Luxor said to have been involved in the production of forgeries and to have collaborated with Mahmud Mohasseb; he was also involved in the sale of the Pachomian Monastic Library.[1249]

1244. Letter from J. H. Breasted to his family, dated 25 Jan. 1920 (Oriental Institute, Chicago); edited by Larson, *Letters from James Henry Breasted*, 140.
1245. Letter from J. H. Breasted to his family, dated 18 Feb. 1920 (Oriental Institute, Chicago); edited by Larson, *Letters from James Henry Breasted*, 149.
1246. Lilyquist, *The Tomb of Three Foreign Wives of Tuthmosis III*, 386.
1247. Robinson, *The Facsimile Edition of the Nag Hammadi Codices*, 4, n. 1, 9-10; idem, *The Nag Hammadi Story*, 43, 44-45, 62-63, 65, 75-77; idem, *The Story of the Bodmer Papyri*, 122, 126, 202.
1248. Robinson, *The Facsimile Edition of the Nag Hammadi Codices*, 4, n. 1, 9-10; idem, *The Nag Hammadi Story*, 44.

1249. Lilyquist, *The Tomb of Three Foreign Wives of Tuthmosis III*, 270; Robinson, *Manuscripts of the Middle East* 5 (1990-1991), 29; idem, *The Story of the Bodmer Papyri*, 112, 126, 159, 202.

Fig. 169. The antiquities dealer Zaki Mahmud Abd es-Samad with his six-year old son Mahmud at Kafr el-Haram. Lange photograph, 1929/30. Courtesy of the Royal Library.

Zaki Mahmud Abd es-Samad (b. 1894, still active 1931) [1250]

Zaki Mahmud Abd es-Samad (Table 3; Fig. 75, 169) was the son of Mahmud Ibrahim Abd es-Samad;[1251] at the time of Lange's visit he was 36 years old and had

two sons, aged five and two.[1252] He spoke good English but could not read the language,[1253] and letters written from him to Lange after the latter's departure from Egypt (preserved in the Royal Library in Copenhagen) were presumably written by dictation: the hands are all different. He was a Cairo dealer who lived in the village of Kafr el-Haram near Giza and had a shop opposite the Egyptian Museum, licensed by the authorities;[1254] the location of his shop meant that he saw Lange virtually every day, and the two struck up a business relationship and, eventually, a cautious friendship. Initially Lange was somewhat reserved, observing that Zaki was a cunning businessman with a talent for acting, 'so one has to preserve a certain distance', but he soon warmed to his personality and described him as 'one of the most charming of our Arab friends'.[1255] Lange and his wife visited Zaki at home on several occasions, and saw him and his family socially;[1256] unlike many Arab women his wife, Lange noted, 'did not wear a veil'.[1257] On one occasion Zaki took Hans and Jonna Lange to see 'some Arabic song, music and dance', consisting of 'two female Arab dancers who performed some national dances accompanied by music'. This, Lange notes afterwards, perhaps with some ambivalence, 'was not appealing, but they demonstrated an extraordinary con-

---

1250. We have in general made little attempt to standardise the transliteration of Arabic surnames, but here we record Zaki Mahmud under 'Abd es-Samad' according to the spelling practices of the other members of his family, although the forms given by Zaki Mahmud's own sign and letterhead (cf. below) and by Lange's diaries, is 'Abdel Samad'. The surname is also found transliterated as Abd es-Samat (Lange), Abd es-Saman (Schmidt, Zucker), es-Samman (Lange), and Abd es-Samon (Schmidt).

1251. Lange, *Dagbog fra Ægypten, 1929-1930*, 28.

1252. Lange, *Dagbog fra Ægypten, 1929-1930*, 52.

1253. Lange, *Dagbog fra Ægypten, 1929-1930*, 326.

1254. Lange, *Dagbog fra Ægypten, 1929-1930*, 44, 52; a letter from him to Lange includes his shop's letterhead (Fig. 17), which bears the inscription 'Zaki Mahmoud Abd es-Samad, Merchant of Antiquities, in Front of the Egyptian Museum No. 62, Mariette Pasha Street No. 9, Cairo' (in English and Arabic). The letter is stamped with the words 'License from the Egyptian Museum No. 62. Opp. Museum, Cairo' (letter from Z. M. Abd es-Samad to H. O. Lange, undated but received 6 Sept. 1930; Royal Library, Copenhagen). The sign in front of his shop (Fig. 75, only partly visible in the photograph) read 'Zacky Mahmoud Abdel[-Samad]' and 'Old Antiquities Licen[se] Forum of Egyptian Mu[seum]'.

1255. Lange, *Dagbog fra Ægypten, 1929-1930*, 115-116, cf. 320-321.

1256. Lange, *Dagbog fra Ægypten, 1929-1930*, 52, 97, 259-260.

1257. Lange, *Dagbog fra Ægypten, 1929-1930*, 97.

trol over all their muscles'.[1258] In 1930 Zaki was an inexperienced dealer, and he often relied on Lange to tell him whether objects he had acquired were genuine, as well as their value;[1259] he developed an understanding of the types of objects Lange was looking for, and seems to have offered these to him first before making them generally available on the market.[1260] There is no doubt that this was part of a clear business strategy by Zaki, although he assured Lange that his main interest was not in fact money, but a letter of recommendation from him that he could use to drum up business.[1261] The relationship between Lange and Zaki was characterized by trust, and when, on one occasion, Zaki was short of cash, Lange lent him the not inconsiderable sum of £50,[1262] a favour that Zaki was prepared to return later in the year.[1263]

In addition to selling his own antiquities to tourists and Egyptologists,[1264] Zaki also acted as an agent for others,[1265] and earned a commission on any sale he closed on his clients' behalf. In one case, cited below (p. 274), the commission was 15%; this may have been the usual rate. An apparently failed attempt to get a double commission concerns the sale of a statue by *Sheikh* Hamza. Lange provides the following description of the closing of the deal:

> I maintained my offer despite all of Hamza's sighing and Zakki's [(sic)] mediation attempts, and in the end Zakki suggested that Hamza should shake my hand and accept, which he did. Zakki then said with his smiling face: '*And what shall I have as commission?*' I answered: '*You get your commission from Sheikh Hamza!*' <He replied:> '*But from you?*' I: '*Only my recommendation.*' The venerable

Sheikh then said: '*And your recommendation is worth more than any commission.*' I answered: '*I hope so.*' And Zakki agreed.[1266]

He also occasionally bought from other dealers on Lange's behalf in order to keep the price low for him,[1267] and when Lange left for Luxor, Zaki – perhaps not entirely altruistically – wrote letters to the local dealers to alert them of his arrival.[1268] Lange, in turn, helped Zaki drum up business from tourists, partly by lending his academic reputation to his shop, but also in a more practical sense: on one occasion he led one of the Danish diplomats in Cairo, a certain Arnstedt, to the premises.[1269] The diplomat showed an interest in one particular object and enquired after its price, upon which Zaki declared that he could have it for free, out of respect for his friendship with Lange. Lange himself interpreted the gesture as a shrewd business strategy, and drily remarks in his diary that 'Naturally Zaki now assumes that the diplomat will make sure that all Danes in Cairo become his customers'.[1270]

Towards the end of his stay in the early summer of 1930 it was, not surprisingly, Zaki whom Lange asked to oversee the packing of all the antiquities he had bought in Egypt, to present them to the Museum authorities in Cairo (to acquire the necessary export licenses), and to ship them to Copenhagen; he was then paid a bonus when the objects arrived safely.[1271] Upon leaving Egypt for the final time, Lange wrote the promised letter of recommendation for Zaki, and gave him a watch with the inscription 'Zaki Mahmoud from Prof. & Mrs. Lange'; in return Zaki gave him a silver ring inset with a scarab for his son, and a wristband for his daughter.[1272] As they left Cairo

1258. Lange, *Dagbog fra Ægypten, 1929-1930*, 331-332.

1259. Lange, *Dagbog fra Ægypten, 1929-1930*, 115-116, 281.

1260. Lange, *Dagbog fra Ægypten, 1929-1930*, 292-293, 324.

1261. Lange, *Dagbog fra Ægypten, 1929-1930*, 52, 116, 125. For a discussion of the use of such letters of recommendation and business cards in the antiquities trade, see above.

1262. Lange, *Dagbog fra Ægypten, 1929-1930*, 281.

1263. Lange, *Dagbog fra Ægypten, 1929-1930*, 230.

1264. Several Egyptologists visited the shop while Lange was present, including Siegfried Schott (p. 313) and Wilhelm Spiegelberg (p. 322).

1265. Lange, *Dagbog fra Ægypten, 1929-1930*, 50.

1266. Lange, *Dagbog fra Ægypten, 1929-1930*, 128. The use of italics in our translation signals text written in English in the diary.

1267. Lange, *Dagbog fra Ægypten, 1929-1930*, 322.

1268. Lange, *Dagbog fra Ægypten, 1929-1930*, 181.

1269. Niels Peter Arnstedt (1882-1954), a Danish diplomat ('gesandt og befuldmægtig minister'), had been stationed in Cairo since 1928.

1270. Lange, *Dagbog fra Ægypten, 1929-1930*, 343.

1271. Lange, *Dagbog fra Ægypten, 1929-1930*, 291.

1272. Lange, *Dagbog fra Ægypten, 1929-1930*, 323, 332.

SCI.DAN.H. 4 · 8

for good, Hans and Jonna Lange were seen off at the train station by Zaki with a large bunch of roses and a fruit hamper, and as a final gesture of friendship he instructed an acquaintance of his who worked on the train to look after their every need during the journey to Alexandria.[1273]

Later the same year, Zaki helped Friedrich Zucker to obtain Greek papyri on behalf of the Papyrus Hauniensis Collection.[1274] One group was purchased directly through Zaki from an unknown dealer on September 13, and later the same day Zaki brought Zucker to Medinet el-Fayum and Eshmunein on a three-day journey to look for further papyri. They took the train together, Zucker travelling 2nd class

and Zaki 3rd class. In Fayum, Zucker purchased another group of papyri from Agaibi Makarios for the price of 4,000 piastre (or £E 40) for which Zaki was paid a 600 piastres commission (i.e. £E 6), so about 15% of the price.

Zaki Mohareb Todros (1901-1978)

Son of Mohareb Todros, q.v.

Zissiadis (fl. 1889)

Obscure dealer who sold some objects to the Egyptian Museum in 1889 (p. 51).

1273. Lange, *Dagbog fra Ægypten, 1929-1930*, 352.
1274. Letter from F. Zucker to C. Høeg, dated 2 Oct. 1930 (University of Copenhagen, Papyrus Hauniensis Archive, B134-B136). Cited *in toto* by Bülow-Jacobsen, *Aegis* 12 (2012), 36-40, cf. p. 39, 40.

Conclusions

During his trips to Egypt in 1899-1900 and 1929-1930, the Danish Egyptologist H. O. Lange bought a number of objects for Danish museums, as well as for himself, and his detailed travel diaries, preserved at the Royal Library in Copenhagen, provide a fascinating description of the antiquities trade in Egypt at this time. Lange was a keen haggler, and seems to have enjoyed the prolonged negotiations that were necessary before a deal could be struck: several passages in the diaries describe such occasions. These passages evoke the social aspects of the antiquities trade in a manner not usually found in published accounts, and we cited several at length for their historical value – the clandestine nature of the transactions with dealers without an official license, the slow build-up of personal relationships with dealers, Lange's joy in striking a good bargain, and his wife Jonna's role as an interpreter in those cases where the dealers spoke only Arabic.

Buying antiquities was a complicated process that depended on contacts, reputation, personality, bargaining skills, knowledge and of course luck and timing. In the case of Lange it is possible to trace the history of his acquisitions in the form of a personal history: from his early days as an observer, introduced to the dealers and the market by more experienced colleagues like Borchardt, Schäfer, and his old teacher Valdemar Schmidt, via his role as an assistant to other buyers – his bargaining skills were apparent to his colleagues from very early on – to a fully-fledged buyer in his own right, building networks and seeking out dealers all over Egypt. During his two visits to Cairo he was, in addition to undertaking research, effectively an agent for Danish museums, and word of this spread rapidly among the dealers. He was constantly approached by dealers wanting to sell objects, and often received them at home in the company of his wife, his servant, and any guests that might be visiting. He also visited shops, including famous ones like Nahman's and Tano's, as well as more obscure establishments where he and Jonna would be led down dark back-alleys to investigate potential objects by candlelight. Arab dealers with licensed shops in Cairo would frequently live outside the city itself, some at the village of Kafr el-Haram near Giza, and here they would have more antiquities in storage – these were available for inspection by those with the right contacts. Lange made several such visits, and relished the opportunity to examine these collections. He relates on one occasion how he was introduced to small-time dealers who rarely dealt directly with Westerners by his friend Loukianoff, a trained Egyptologist who made a living from buying and selling antiquites: this made quite an impression on him, and he happily reports that he paid much less for the objects bought this way than what he would normally have had to pay in the shops catering to tourists and museum representatives.

The informal networks of the dealers (colleagues, friends, acquaintances and business partners) was remarkably efficient in terms of transmitting information, and word spread quickly and across great distances when a 'museum man' arrived on the scene. They were particularly concerned about whether the big buyers would turn up, and when the personal health of Budge from the British Museum prevented him from coming during the winter of 1899-1900, this was known in advance by many if not most of the dealers. Lange was often approached by dealers who had heard from other dealers that he was looking to buy objects, and in one revealing example the Cairo dealer Zaki Mahmud Abd-es Samad wrote to a colleague of his in Luxor, telling him to keep an eye out for Lange as he set out on a journey southwards; the dealer was then able to identify Lange when he visited his shop. Social aspects of the trade are also described by Lange, including the identification and the establishment of one's authority and credentials, so central to such transactions, and in particular the practice of dealers presenting potential customers with examples of cards that they had acquired from Western academics in the past (and all the examples mentioned in the diaries concern academics). Lange stayed in touch with several dealers after his return to Denmark, and remarks that he felt he had provided both the Glyptotek and the National Museum with useful contacts for the future, although his correspondence from this period – also preserved at the Royal Library – indicates that the contact did not, in most cases, last more than a few years.

Virtually all the trade in antiquities in Egypt took place during the four winter months, and during both of these visits Lange seems to have been lucky because his presence coincided with the absence of some of the major buyers at the time, which impacted negatively on the market in the form of price levels going down. Other factors which affected prices were the personal circumstances of dealers, and Lange's diaries provide examples of dealers who found themselves over-stretched financially, who had to sell off their collections quickly, or, in one case, had to pawn the collection to a fellow dealer and money-lender.

The licensed dealers seem to have been concentrated in Cairo and Luxor, but every site on the tourist trail would have smaller-scale, semi-professional groups of dealers hanging around, and train stations and hotels also attracted unlicensed dealers *en masse*. The tourist market was considerable, and the most popular guidebook at the time, Baedeker's, listed the shops of the more successful dealers like Nahman, Tano and Blanchard in Cairo, as well as a number of dealers in Luxor, along with advice to tourists about procedures for export. Places like Abydos and Aswan seem to have had few or no official dealers; in general provincial areas, not surprisingly, had fewer established dealers. People who had antiquities to sell would therefore often bring them to other urban centres, in some cases over considerable distances, and then sell to professional dealers there or leave the objects with them to sell for a commission. A side-effect of this pattern of trade was that even professional dealers found themselves buying objects they did not

necessarily want to take on, because they needed to maintain their contacts and make sure that they kept bringing them antiquities. A significant group of dealers were the consuls or consular agents of various Western nations; these were numerous, stationed in many of the urban centres in the Nile valley, and – crucial for their business as dealers – possessed a degree of diplomatic immunity. They organised illicit excavations, bought illegal antiquities from others, but also, occasionally, conducted licensed archaeological excavation in their own right (and shared their finds with the Antiquities Service). Whatever the legal status of their dealings, their office, which was often kept in the family for generations, as well as their financial situation – many were among the richest inhabitants in their area – protected them from any repercussions from the Egyptian State.

Lange had an ambivalent attitude to the trade itself. On the one hand he lamented again and again the amount of knowledge lost by the illegal excavation of archaeological sites, but he was also pragmatic and seems to have had no qualms about his own involvement: in one telling instance he complained that some clay sealings that he saw in Nahman's shop were clearly stolen from Petrie's excavation of the royal tombs at Abydos, but did not hesitate to ask Nahman to put five of them aside for him to buy later.

Lange's training as an Egyptologist meant that he had extensive experience with a wide range of material objects, not least as a result of his work in the Egyptian Museum in Cairo. While this made him able to recognise many fakes with relative ease, he occasionally found himself unable to decide on the antiquity of objects offered for sale. In such cases he was methodical, and would examine the relevant category of objects in the Egyptian Museum with a view to building up a feel for such artefacts, but it was not just the appearance of the objects that played a part in his deliberations. As a philologist he examined any inscription with a keen eye, and he observed that he rarely if ever came across examples of texts forged to a standard that equalled the forgers' skills with the material objects. The circumstances of the sale were another factor that played a part in the decision-making process – he found a rush to close a deal on the part of the seller suspicious – and the price itself could be a potential give-away: if he thought something was suspiciously cheap he would in most cases back out of the transaction. Despite his extensive knowledge he appears to have been the victim of scams on several occasions, including in connection with object categories where his own experience should have made him a difficult target for forgers, such as stelae. In fact, the acquisition he himself considered to have been his best buy, a head of black granite allegedly from Amarna (Ny Carlsberg Glyptotek ÆIN 1669), seems to be a forgery.

Both of Lange's travel diaries provide first-hand accounts of the practicalities of export of antiquities from Egypt, although it is the diary from the second visit in 1929-1930 that is most informative. By then the Egyptian government had introduced more restrictive legislation to curb the illegal trade and export of antiquities. Representatives of the Egyptian Museum in Cairo had been given the authority to seize any object which they had previously seen *in situ*, or which a dealer had bought from individuals carrying out illegal excavations. In addition to this, any object for which an export license was sought had to be presented to the Egyptian Museum and the head of the Antiquities Service, who then decided whether or not to allow it to leave the country; if the object was otherwise obtained legally it might still be refused a license if the Museum did not possess a similar item. There were ways of avoiding this, and in once case Lange related a method of getting a statue out which was explained to him by a dealer: by breaking it into several pieces, the different parts could be presented on separate occasions, thus ensuring that the authorities would not recognise it as a complete statue. When the pieces had been exported they could then be reunited and the statue restored.

Although the main focus of the book is H. O. Lange and his activities, it is clear from his diaries that his wife, Jonna Lange, was instrumental in many of the transactions, and she built up a modest collection of antiquities herself. She was considerably better at speaking Arabic than her husband and often interpreted for him when he was buying antiquities, and she also worked side by side with him on the project to publish the Middle Kingdom stelae in the Egyptian Museum (where she photographed most of the objects).

The final part of the book presents a list of the dealers Lange described in his diaries, as well as others we have referred to in the course of the text. Dealers are rarely mentioned in the Egyptological literature, with the exception of high-profile – and largely Western – individuals, and although our list is limited, it represents an attempt to make them visible in the historical record. This focus on individuals whose identities and activities have frequently fallen outside the research agenda of Egyptologists is echoed by Stephen Quirke's work on the Arab workers who assisted Petrie in his excavations.[1275] As he argued in that book, an understanding of the circumstances surrounding the origin of the objects being studied, in our case the various aspects of the trade in antiquities, is important if we are to understand how collections have been formed, what motives and priorities dictated the acquisition of certain objects, and not least if we are to understand the early history of our discipline. Further archival work would no doubt add substantially to the list – most major museums have documentation that would throw more light on several of the dealers we mention – but it is our hope that colleagues working with objects in museums will find the list useful, such as it is.

1275. Quirke, *Hidden Hands*.

APPENDIX 1:

Extracts of the 1912 law governing the sale and export of Egyptian antiquities

The section of the Law of 1912 governing the antiquities trade in Egypt was essentially the work of Gaston Maspero, the Director of the Antiquities Service.[1276] According to his own account, he had completed drafting the proposal already in 1902, a few years after his return as Director of the Antiquities Service. However, it was only in November of 1911, after a paper had been read at the *Society of Antiquaries of London* complaining about the granting of excavation permits to certain Egyptians (sc. dealers) and the looting of sites, and with the direct encouragement of Lord Kitchener, the British Consul-General in Egypt, that he decided to go forth and present the draft to the authorities. Maspero seems to have felt helpless against the large-scale illegal sale and export of antiquities. Above all, he noted, it seemed unfair that the Egyptians population of a country should be liable for punishment, while a minority of foreigners were not ('Il n'est certes pas conforme à l'équité d'édicter des peines contre la population d'un pays, quand une minorité d'étrangers doit échapper à leur application'). In other words, the current system punished the Epyptians who did the looting, but not the non-Egyptian dealers, agents, and collectors (mainly wealthy Western individuals and institutions), who were involved in illegal trade. The proposal was passed with surprising speed, within months, and with only minor adjustments.

The law was signed on 15 June 1912 and the Antiquities Service immediately began receiving applications from dealers seeking to obtain licenses. Maspero commissioned C. C. Edgar and G. Lefebvre, two of the four Chief Inspectors of Antiquities, to review the applications. It was decided only to grant licences to those dealers who were based in cities frequented by tourists: 'Cairo, Alexandria, Assiut, Luxor, Edfu, Aswan, and so on'. By contrast, it is explicitly mentioned that no licences were granted to dealers in Giza, Medinet el-Fayum, Beni Suef, Mellawi, Sohag, and Beliana, these apparently being among the more important centres of trade outside the tourist zones. In the initial round of reviews, from July through September of 1912, 205 applications were evaluated and 76 were approved, to which was added about twenty more on re-application. Accordingly, by 15 November 1912, just short of one hundred licenses had been issued. Wishing to avoid 'the appearance of injustice' ('l'apparence de l'injustice'), Maspero decided to grant those dealers who had failed to obtain licenses a period of 5½ months, until 1 May 1913, to dispose of those objects that had come into their possession prior to the enactment of the new law. A list of authorized and unauthorized dealers was then circulated to the local *mudiras* (administrative centres) by the Chief Inspectors.

The law came into effect in-between Lange's two visits to Egypt, and the expanded bureaucracy it created underlies some of the frustration he voiced in his travel diary of 1929-1930. The jurisdiction was also discussed in a brief article by H. G. Lyons, written shortly after it was approved by the Khedive, which provides some additional historical background for the legislation (see p. 137 for a discussion).[1277]

1276. Gouvernement Égyptien, *Rapport du Service des Antiquités pour l'année 1912*, 18-21; idem, *Rapport ... pour l'année 1913*, 11-14.

1277. Lyons, *JEA* 1 (1914), 45-46. An earlier draft of the law, and comments on the insufficient provisions in the previous Antiquities Law of 12 Aug. 1897, may be found in Gouverne-

We include here the relevant section of the law, as published in the journal of the Antiquities Service, the *Annales du Service des Antiquités de l'Égypte*.[1278] The translation is by Adrienne L. Fricke, and is reproduced from J. H. Merryman (ed.), *Imperialism, Art and Restitution*, 181-189, with her kind permission.

Law No. 14 of 1912 on Antiquities

We, the Khedive of Egypt, on the proposal of Our Minister of Public Works and with the assent of Our Council of Ministers; the Legislative Council agreeing, We decree:

Antiquities in General

Art. 1. Subject to the provisions of the present law, every antiquity found on, or in the ground, shall belong to the Public Domain of the State.

Art. 2. Legally, antiquities are deemed to be all manifestations and all products of the arts, sciences, literature, religion, manners, industries of Pharaonic, Greek, Roman, Byzantine and Coptic Egypt, pagan temples, what is abandoned and disused, chapels, basilisks and monasteries, as well as fortresses and city walls, houses, baths, nilometers, stone wells, cisterns, causeways, ancient quarries, obelisks, pyramids, mastabas, funerary hypogea, with or without aboveground structures, sarcophagi, all manner of coffins, decorated or not, mummy wrappings, mummies of men or animals, painted or gilded portraits and masks, stelae, naoi, statues and statuettes, with or without inscriptions, inscriptions on rocks, ostraca, manuscripts on skins, fabric, or papyrus, worked flints, arms, utensils, vases, glasswork, boxes and objects of offering, fabric and pieces of clothing, ornaments, rings, jewels, scarabs and amulets of every form and manner, weights, coins, engraved stones and shells.

Art. 3. Equally deemed antiquities are the remains of walls and houses in stone or in terracotta or mudbrick, blocks of stone and sparse brick, fragments of stone, glass, or wood, shards, sand, homra, and sebakh, which are found on or in the grounds belonging to the State and declared ancient by the Government.

Art. 4. However, antiquities belonging to the discoverer, by virtue of either Article 11 which follows, or by the terms of an excavation permit, as well as antiquities belonging to good faith private owners, may enter into the trade.

Art. 5. For the purposes of the present law, movable antiquities which are attached to the ground or are difficult to transport are assimilated with immovable antiquities.

Art. 6. All grounds belonging to the State, which are now or may be declared ancient by the Government, shall be part of the Public Domain.

Art. 7. All antiquities which are now or may be conserved in the museums of the State shall also be part of the Public Domain.

Movable Antiquities

Art. 10. Whoever has found a movable antiquity on or in whatsoever land throughout the expanse of the Egyptian territory shall be held responsible, except where he is carrying a normally issued excavation permit, to report and present it within six days time to the closest administrative Authority or to the agents of the Antiquities Service, who will give him a receipt.

Art. 11. Whoever discovers a movable antiquity, except in the course of an illicit excavation, and who is in conformity with the regulations in the preceding article, shall receive as a bonus half of the objects found, or half of their value. Absent an agreement on amiable partition, the Antiquities Service shall take the objects it intends to keep. For the other objects,

ment Égyptien, *Rapport sur la marche du Service des Antiquités de 1899 à 1910*, xxvii-xxviii, 36-37, 66-67, and esp. pp. 84-89.
1278. *ASAE* 12 (1913), 245-251; the text from p. 249 is reproduced below.

the partition into two shares of equal value shall be made by the Service, and the discoverer will have the right to choose between the two lots. The two parties each shall set a price on the value of each object taken by the Service. If the discoverer does not accept half of the of price set by the Service, the Service shall have the power to take the object and pay the price designated by the discoverer, or to leave to the discoverer the object, receiving from the discoverer half of the price which he himself had set on the object.

Excavations

Art. 12. No one may carry out surveys, excavations, or clearings with the purpose of searching for antiquities, even on land belonging to him, without preliminary authorization granted by the Minister of Public Works on the proposal of the Director General of the Antiquities Service. This authorization shall fix the locality where the excavations may take place and the period in which they shall be valid. The discoverer shall be granted a part of the antiquities found, or the value of that part, in conformance with the preceding article. The following shall not be considered as having the goal of searching for antiquities: surveys, excavations and the removal of earth, if the person who proceeded with this work had no reason to believe that the land could contain antiquities.

Sale of Antiquities

Art. 13. Every antiquities merchant must be provided with an authorization, which the Antiquities Service alone may grant or deny. The Ministry of Public Works is charged with regulating the conditions for bringing antiquities into the trade, and in particular with setting their manner of certification as antiquities placed for sale.

Exportation of Antiquities

Art. 14. Exportation of antiquities is prohibited without a special authorization which the Antiquities Service alone may grant or deny. Every antiquity attempt-

ed to be taken out of Egypt without authorization shall be seized and confiscated for the profit of the State.

Collection of Sebakh

Art. 15. The Antiquities Service may authorize the collection of sebakh in places and conditions which it shall determine. Every antiquity found in the course of collecting sebakh shall be declared and handed over immediately to the guards supervising the removal.

Penalties

Art. 16. {The following} shall be punished with imprisonment not to exceed one year and a fine not to exceed 100 Egyptian Pounds, or only one of these two sentences:
  1. Those who have displaced, battered, mutilated or destroyed in any way immovable antiquities.
  2. Those who have seized, without the special authorization of the Government, materials originating in the total or partial destruction of immovable antiquities.
  3. Those who have transformed hypogea, roadways, temples, and in general, all buildings or remains of ancient buildings, into dwellings for people or animals, depositories, tombs, or cemeteries, in addition to the sentence for the amount of damage caused thereby.

Art. 17. Further punishments with the same sentences:
  1. Every infraction of the provisions of articles 9, 10, and 12 above.
  2. Every sale or offer of sale of antiquities made outside of the conditions dictated in articles 4 and 13.

Art 18. {The following} shall be punished with imprisonment not to exceed one week and a fine not to exceed l Egyptian Pound, or only one of the two sentences:
  1. Any collection of sebakh in a prohibited place,

or outside of the regulatory conditions, as well as every infraction of the provisions of article 15.

2. The act of drawing names or inscriptions on immovable antiquities.

Art. 19. Every movable antiquity which has been the object of an infraction of the provisions of the present law may be seized and confiscated for the profit of the state.

Miscellaneous Provisions

Art. 20. Conservators, inspectors and sub-inspectors of the Antiquities Service, as well as the agents through whom they function shall be considered officers of the Criminal Investigation Department, inasmuch as concerns the duties with which they are charged.

Art. 21. The decrees mentioned in the appendix of the present law are abrogated in regards to those answerable to whom this law applies.

Art. 22. Our Ministers of Public Works are charged each inasmuch as he is concerned, with the execution of the present law, which shall enter into effect on July 12, 1912.

Done in Alexandria, 26 Gamad II 1330 (June 12, 1912).

Ministerial Order No. 50 of December 8, 1912, Containing Regulations of Authorizations for Trading in Antiquities.

The Minister of Public Works, in light of article 13 of Antiquities Law No. 14 of 1912; Decree:

Art. 1. There are two types of authorizations of trading in antiquities:
1. Authorization for a merchant with an antiquities shop.
2. Authorization for a stall-keeper.

Only duly authorized, first-class merchants may be authorized to open and maintain a shop; on the other hand, they may not deal in antiquities outside of the shop, or another, similar establishment mentioned in their authorizations. The stall-keeper may be authorized to trade only in minor objects, the price of which may never exceed 5 Egyptian pounds, displaying them at the place, or at one of the places, mentioned in his permit.

Art. 2. Authorizations for store merchants shall be granted by the Directorate General of the Antiquities Service; those of the stall-keepers shall be granted by the local directorate of the aforementioned Service, after having obtained the opinion of the local authority. All authorizations shall be strictly personal.

Art. 3. Requests for store merchant authorizations shall be addressed by interested parties to the Directorate-General of the Antiquities Service on paper with 3 piastres worth of stamps. They shall contain:
1. The last name, first name, and domicile of the requesting party.
2. Indication of the premises where he would like to do business.
3. A certificate of the requesting party's criminal record.

Art. 4. Requests for stall-keeper authorisations shall be addressed by the interested parties to the local Directorate of the Antiquities Service on paper with 3 piastres worth of stamps. They shall contain:
1. The last name, first name, and domicile of the requesting party.
2. Indication of the areas where he would like to do business.

Art. 5. Every shop merchant must keep a register, following the model approved by the Antiquities Service, where he shall keep a daily record, in numerical sequence, of the antiquities which he has acquired, with all the details of dimensions, material, color, etc., necessary for the identification of the object as well as the indications of provenance sufficient to establish that it has come into the trade. When an object entered in the register is sold, mention shall be made in the register indicating, to the extent possible, the name and authority of the buyer. Before being put to use, each page of the register must be initialed or sealed by an Inspector of the Antiquities Service. The only articles for sale which shall be exempt from the present article are those whose worth does not exceed 5 Egyptian pounds.

Art. 6. None of the objects available for sale by the merchant shall be kept outside of the premises where he is authorized to conduct his business.

Art. 7. No antiquity shall be transported inside the country by the merchant without the written authorization of the Antiquities Service. When a merchant owns more than one shop, transport from one to another shall be recorded in the registers of both establishments, as though for a sale or purchase.

Art. 8. The inspector of the Antiquities Service, either accompanied or unaccompanied by the Criminal Investigation Department, may enter, at any moment and in every part, premises assigned to the trading of antiquities, in order to inspect the register described in article 5, and to control for regular conduct, and to verify the merchant's stock. The merchant as well as the personnel of his establishment must facilitate the inspection as needed. At the end of the inspection, the inspector shall stamp the establishment's register and record in it any and all useful observations.

Art. 9. Without prejudice to the sentences stated above in article 17 of the aforementioned Law, the unauthorized pursuit of the occupation of merchant or seller of antiquities shall be punished by imprisonment not exceeding 7 days and a fine not exceeding 1 Egyptian pound, or only one of the two sentences.

Art. 10. In the case of conviction for infraction of the provisions of the present regulation, the judge may always order the withdrawal of the authorization. In the event of a second conviction committed in the same year as the first, withdrawal of authorization

shall be mandatory. The authorization may always be withdrawn by the Antiquities Service, in case of conviction for one of the infractions of the aforementioned Law.

Art. 11. The present regulation shall enter into effect on January 1, 1913.

Cairo, December 8, 1912.
The Minister of Public Works,
(Signed): Ismail Sirry

Ministerial Order No. 5 of December 8, 1912, Containing Regulations for the Exportation of Antiquities

The Minister of Public Works, in light of article 14 of Antiquities Law 14 of 1912;

Art. 1. All persons wishing to export antiquities by sea or land shall request written authorization on plain paper to the Antiquities Service General Supervisory Administration, to obtain the authorization required by article 14 of Antiquities Law 14 of 1912.

Art. 2. The request shall contain the first and last name, authority and nationality of the requestor, as well as indication of the port or point of exit. At the same time, the objects and the parcels or cases containing them shall be presented for examination by the Supervisory Administration, with a list indicating the number of pieces, their nature, their dimensions and their purchase or commercial value. The parcels or cases shall contain only Egyptian objects from Pharaonic, Greco-Roman, Byzantine or Coptic times; the presence of an object from any other epoch shall cause refusal of authorization.

Art. 3. In cases where the examination does not reveal the presence of any object of suspect origin, authorization shall be issued without delay. If the presence of any object of suspect origin is revealed, and the explanations furnished by the requestor are not recognized as satisfactory by the Service, these objects shall be removed; otherwise authorization shall be refused for all.

Art. 4. The parcels or cases containing the objects for which exit has been authorized shall be wrapped in wire held in place by one or more seals; the requestor shall pay, for each parcel or case, a fee of 4 piastres to be used to cover the cost of operation. He must at the same time pay an export fee of 1.5% on the declared value of the objects, from which the amount shall be turned over to the Customs Duty Administration by the General Administration of the Service.

Art. 5. After the completion of the formalities and the payment of related fees, the General Administration shall issue to the requestor:
1. A certificate addressed to the Administration of State Railways, which shall be issued by it or its representative to the authorities of the station from which it shall send the parcels or cases containing the objects.
2. A certificate addressed in duplicate to the Customs Duty Administration certifying that the export fees have been paid. One of the two cop-

ies shall rest in the possession of the requestor or his representative, the other shall be sent by care of the Service to the customs duty of the city or the port of exit.

Art. 6. The same examination formalities shall be required for parcels sent by post. However, parcels containing objects must be fixed securely with a string, the two ends of which shall be held by a seal in wax or metal. A printed pass, taken from a stock book and signed by a representative of the Service, shall be affixed to the parcel. No fee other than that of sealing shall be required for parcels sent by post in this way.

Art. 7. Parcels or boxes shall be presented to the railway bureaus, to customs, and the post with seals intact, on pain of being seized and returned to the Antiquities Service for investigation.

Art. 8. The present regulation shall enter into effect after January 1, 1913.

Cairo, December 8, 1912.
The Minister of Public Works,
(Signed): Ismail Sirry.

APPENDIX 2:

Licenses issued by the Egyptian Antiquities Service

The list of license numbers presented below includes only those mentioned in the present study. We have been unable to find a complete list.

License 1:   Ismaïl Abdallah el-Shaer, Cairo,
                later Hefnawy Ismaïl el-Shaer

License 7:   Khawam Brothers, Cairo

License 38: Maurice Nahman, Cairo

License 58: Sayed Molattam, Luxor

License 60: Kamal Abdallah Hammouda, Cairo

License 62: Zaki Mahmud Abd es-Samad, Cairo

License 84: A. Aly el-Gabri, Cairo

License 85: Mansur Abd el-Sayyid Mansoor, Cairo

License 90: Philip E. Mitry, Cairo,
                later his successors

License 92: Hassan Mohammed Mahmud, Luxor

License 96: Mohammed Hamed Ibrahim, Cairo

License 108: Maguid Sameda, Cairo

License 112: Albert Eid & Co., Cairo,
                later Robert Viola

License 116: Farag el-Shaer, Cairo;
                later Sons of Farag el-Shaer

License 117: A. and Ed. C. Anawati, Cairo

License 121: Mohammed Shaker, Cairo

License 127: Hassani Abd el-Galil, Luxor

APPENDIX 3:

Antiquities dealers mentioned in the Baedeker guides to Egypt

For convenience we have collected below all the references to antiquities dealers in the various editions of the Baedeker guides. All consular agents at Luxor were said to sell antiquites, but we have listed them separately below in accordance with the practice in the guides. The list is perhaps biased (payment was possibly involved for inclusion). It was written by Egyptologists, who might in return have received special prices or other benefits, and it was written for a targeted audience which probably also influenced the selection of dealers (thus, for example, the 1891 English edition includes US consular agent, whereas the German edition includes the Austro-Hungarian).

1877: German 1ˢᵗ edition of Lower Egypt

Cairo: none mentioned.

1878: English 1ˢᵗ edition of Lower Egypt

Cairo: none mentioned.

1885: German 2ⁿᵈ edition of Lower Egypt

Cairo: none mentioned.

1885: English 2ⁿᵈ edition of Lower Egypt

Cairo: none mentioned

1891: German 1ˢᵗ edition of Upper Egypt

Luxor: Moh. M'hasseb and 'Abd el-Megîd. [p. 117]

Luxor, consular agents: Moharb Todrus (German), Schenûde Makarios (Austro-Hungarian), Aḥmed Effendi (British and Russian). [p. 115]

1892: English 1ˢᵗ edition of Upper Egypt

Luxor: Mohammed M'hasseb and 'Abd el-Megîd. [p. 103]
Luxor, consular agents: Aḥmed Effendi (British and Russian), Ali Mûrad (US), Moharb Todrus (German). [p. 102]

1894: German 3ʳᵈ edition of Lower Egypt

Cairo: none mentioned

1895: English 3ʳᵈ edition of Lower Egypt

Cairo: none mentioned

1897: German 4ᵗʰ edition

Cairo: none mentioned.
Luxor: Moh. M'hasseb and 'Abd el-Megîd, in addition to the German consular agent and the British consular agent Aḥmed Effendi. [p. 229]
Luxor, consular agents: Moharb Todros (German), Makarios Schenûde (Austro-Hungarian), Aḥmed Muṣṭafa (British). [p. 228]

1898: English 4ᵗʰ edition

Cairo: none mentioned.

Luxor: Mohammed M'hasseb and 'Abd el-Megîd, in addition to the British and German consular agents. [pp. 225-226]

Luxor, consular agents: Aḥmed Muṣṭafa (British), Ali Mûrad (US), Todros Bulos (German). [p. 225]

1898: French 1st edition

Cairo: none mentioned.

Luxor: Moh. M'hasseb, 'Abd el-Mégîd, in addition to the consular agents, esp. the German consular agent Todrous Paulos. [p. 228]

Luxor, consular agents: B. Bichara (French), Aḥmed Muṣṭafa (Belgium and Russia), Todrous Paulos (German). [pp. 227, 228]

1902: German 5th edition

Cairo: none mentioned.

Luxor: Moh. Muhasseb and 'Abd el-Megîd, adding in parenthesis concerning the latter 'bei diesem aber auch Fälschungen' [p. 237]

Luxor, consular agents: Mohareb Todrus (German), Schenûde Makarios (Austro-Hungarian), Aḥmed Muṣṭafa (British). [p. 237]

1902: English 5th edition

Cairo: none mentioned.

Luxor: Mohammed Muhasseb and 'Abd el-Megîd, in addition to the British and German consular agent. [pp. 233-234]

Luxor, consular agents: Aḥmed Muṣṭafa (British), Ali Mûrad (US), Mohareb Todrus (German), M. Boutros (Italian). [p. 233]

1903: French 2nd edition

Cairo: none mentioned.

Luxor: Moh. Mouhasseb and 'Abd el-Mégîd, in addition to the German consular agent. [pp. 234, 235]

Luxor, consular agents: Basili Bichara (French), Mohareb Todrous (German), Saïd-Bey Ayad (British, Belgian, Russian), Chenoude (Austrian), Abdel Kerim el Emmari (US), Andrea Bichara (Italy). [p. 234]

1906: German 6th edition

Cairo: Kyticas, P. Philip, Cassira, Museum. [p. 33]

Luxor: Moh. Muhasseb and 'Abd el-Megîd, in addition to the German consular agent. [p. 239]

Luxor, consular agents: Mohareb Todrus (German), Iskender Shenûde (Austro-Hungarian), Said Mustafa Ajad (British). [p. 238]

1908: English 6th edition

Cairo: Kyticas, P. Philip, Cassira, Museum. [p. 36]

Luxor: Moḥammed Muhasseb and 'Abd el-Megîd, in addition to the British and German consular agents. [p. 249]

Luxor, consular agents: Saiyid Muṣṭafa Ayad (British), Basili Beshara (French), Mohareb Todrus (German), Iskender Shenûdeh (Austrian). [p. 248]

1908: French 3rd edition

Cairo: Kytikas, P. Philip, Nachmann, Cassira, the Museum [p. 37]

Luxor: Moh. Mouhasseb and 'Abd el-Mégîd, in addition to the German consular agent. [p. 246]

Luxor, consular agents: Basile Bechara (French), Mohareb Todrous (German), Iskender Chenoude (Austrian), Andrea Bichara (Belgium and Italy), Saïd Mustafa Ayad (Russia). [p. 246]

1913: German 7th edition

Cairo: M. Nahman, Kytikas, N. Tano, R. H. Blanchard, the Museum. [p. 37]

Luxor: Mohareb Todrus, Moh. Muhasseb, 'Abd el-Megîd, Mansûr Maḥmûd. [p. 242]

Luxor, consular agents: Mohareb Todrus (German), Iskender Schenûde (Austro-Hungarian). [p. 242]

1914: English 7th edition

Cairo: M. Nahman, Kytikas, N. Tano, R. H. Blanchard, the Museum. [p. 41]
Luxor: Moḥammed Muhasseb, ʿAbd el-Megîd, Mansûr Maḥmûd, R. de Rustafjaell, etc., in addition to the German consular agent Mohareb Todrus. [p. 252]
Luxor, consular agents: none listed by name.

1914: French 4th edition

Cairo: Nahman, Kytikas, N. Tano, R. H. Blanchard, the Museum, Hatoun. [p. 39]
Luxor: Mohareb Todrus, Moh. Mouhasseb, ʿAbd el-Mégîd, Mansoûr Maḥmoud, R. de Rustafjaell, etc. [p. 247]
Luxor, consular agents: Basile Bichara (French), Mohareb Todrus (German), Iskender Chenoûdé (Austro-Hungarian). [p. 247]

1928: German 8th edition

Cairo: M. Nahman, N. Tano, R. H. Blanchard, the Museum. [p. 39]
Luxor: Mohareb Todrus, Muḥ. Muḥasseb, Ḥusein ʿAbd el-Megîd, Mansûr Maḥmûd, Girgis Gubriân, Jûsuf Ḥasan, Kamâl Châlid. [p. 260]
Luxor, consular agents: none listed by name
Aswan: Mischriky Girgis [p. 368]

1929: English 8th edition

Cairo: M. Nahman, E. A. Abemayor, N. Tano, R. H. Blanchard, the Museum [p. 43]
Luxor: Mohareb Todrus, Maḥmûd Bey Muḥasseb, Aḥmed ʿAbd er-Raḥim, Ḥusein ʿAbd el-Magîd, Mansûr Maḥmûd, Girgis Gubriân, Kamâl Khâlid [p. 268]
Luxor, consular agents: none listed by name.

APPENDIX 4:

Organisation and salaries of the Antiquities Service, 1908

Transcript of a ministerial order no. 650 of 29 June 1908, Ministry of Public Works, concerning the organisation and salaries of the Antiquities Service; signed by the Minister of Public Works, H. Fakhry, and the British Consul A. L. Webb.[1279] It may be noted that Hervé Bazil, who was for many years the Director of the administration, was Gaston Maspero's half-brother. He was appointed some years after Maspero's first term as Director of the Antiquities Service, in 1890, while Eugène Grébaut was in charge.[1280] All numbers represent Egyptian pounds.

Postes	Noms	Traitements annuels	Augmentations obtenues
Personnel technique			
Directeur Général	G. Maspero	1500	---
Conservateur (£E 600 à 800)	E. Brugsch	800	---
Conservateurs-Adjoints (£E 400 à 500)	G. Daressy	500	---
	Ahmed Bey Kamal	450	---
Nazir (£E 260 à 370)	J. Messawer	315	115
Inspecteurs en Chef (£E à 600)	J. E. Quibell	600	---
	G. Lefebvre	500	---
Inspecteurs en Chef (£E 400 à 600)	A. Weigall	500	---
	C. Edgar	500	---
Directeurs de Traveaux (£E 400 à 500)	G. Legrain	480	---
	A. Barsanti	480	---
Directeur-Adjoint de Trav. (£E 250 à 350)	E. Baraise	300	42

1279. Carbon-copy kept at the University of Copenhagen, Egyptological Archive, B600. A comparable table for the year 1911, but omitting the names of the individual office-holders, is published in Gouvernement Égyptien, *Rapport sur la marche du Service des antiquités de 1899 à 1910*, xvi-xviii.

1280. Cf. Capart (ed.), *Letters of Charles Edwin Wilbour*, 569.

Inspecteurs 1re classe (£E 168 à 264)	Mahmoud Eff. Moh.^d	168	24
	Hassan Eff. Hosni	168	48
	Mohamed Eff. Chaban	168	48
Inspecteurs 2me classe (£E 96 à 144)	Tewfik Eff. Boulos	120	24
	Antoun Eff. Yousef	108	12
	Hassan Eff. Hosni El Chabsogli	108	12
	Guirguis Eff. Elias	96	18
	Youssef Eff. El Saidi	108	6
	Moh. Ah. Eff. Doheir	108	12
	Mahmoud Eff. Rouchdi	96	---
	Francis Eff. Abdel Melek	108	---
Personnel administrative			
Directeur (£E 564 à 780)	Hervé Bazil	672	112
Sous à Chef de Bureau (£E 288 à 336)	Anis Aclimandos	312	24
Commis de 1re classe (£E 216 à 264)	Zaki Hatem	240	60
	A. Bochot	240	60
Commis de 2me classe (£E 144 à 192)	Mohamed Eff. Tewfik	168	---
	Mohamed Eff. Farid	168	36
Commis de 3me classe (£E 108 à 132)	Fayez Eff. Kouzam	120	30
Commis de 4me classe	Abadir Eff. Michriki	60	---
	Ibrahim Eff. Moh. Habib	60	---
	Fouad Eff. Hanna	60	---
	Gabriel Eff. Guirguis (magasinier)	90	---
	(3 vacances) à	180	---
Bibliothécaire	E. Galtier	240	60

Table 8. The organisation and salaries of the Egyptian Antiquities Service, 1908.

The above table may be compared with the levels of payment in 1885:

Name / position	Salary
G. Maspero	£E 1000
E. Brugsch	£E 420
Urbain Bouriant	£E 300
Inspecteurs 2me classe (5)	£E 90 (each)
Inspecteurs 3me classe (5)	£E 60 (each)
Nazir (Muhammad Khurshid)	£E 240
Secrétaire (Ahmad Kamal)	£E 240
Magasinier 1	£E 72
Magasinier 2	£E 45

Table 9. The organisation and salaries of the Egyptian Antiquities Service, 1885.

The table is based on the information provided by D. M. Reid, *Whose Pharaohs*, 188. The proportional increase in salaries from 1885 to 1908 is difficult to estimate. For the Director (Maspero) the increase amounted to 50%, and here the comparison is fairly straightforward as it is the same office with the same individual (and therefore the same qualifications). The *nazir* (supervisor) Mohammad Khurshid, however, earned a salary of £E240 in 1885, but the range of salary available for the same office in 1908 was £E260-370, which would be an increase of somewhere between 8% and 54%. However, the actual pay of any individual was naturally dependent on several factors such as seniority, skills and networks - we do not know how experienced the nazir Mohammad Khurshid was in 1885, for example - so direct comparison is not straightforward.

APPENDIX 5:

Haj Hamid and the Brigand

The following story was published by H. E. Winlock, at the time Assistant Curator in the Metropolitan Museum of Art, in *Scribner's Magazine* (vol. LXXI, January-June 1922). It is perhaps embellished as so many good stories are, but certainly the characters are real enough, and these include the famous Luxor dealer Mohammed Mohasseb and his son Hamid, as well as Abd el-Megid. Winlock knew Mohasseb well, having purchased a number of objects from him for the Metropolitan Museum, and the circumstances of the dealer telling him the story are realistic enough. The general thrust of the story seems plausible, and we have no reason to question the basic facts as they were related to Winlock, but the story is included here mainly as an example of the kind of anecdotal evidence on which much research into the illicit trade in antiquities is necessarily based. It evokes the crossing and double-crossing that must have been rife in the trade (as one dealer notes, 'une des risques de nos affaires'), the potential dangers of any long-distance travel with large sums in cash (here over a thousand pounds), and the thrill of the potentially huge profits that came with rare and unusual finds. Some of the details of the narrative also tally closely with the general character of the trade as documented above, such as dealers travelling over distances to secure finds from local fellaheen, and the disposing of lesser finds to local tourists with rarer objects making their way to Cairo (presumably to other dealers or to Egyptologists and collectors). We have not made much reference to the story in the book simply because it is, at heart, a tale meant to entertain, and although it seems realistic in many ways, the exact line between historicity and poetic license remains elusive in this case. Nonetheless it provides a colourful portrait of the trade as told by one of the major players at the time, and – unusually – it is a story told by an Egyptian dealer (albeit through a Western Egyptologist).

***

"You say that you buy these things from the natives and the dealers in Egypt, yes? But what I don't understand is how do they get them?" That is a perfectly natural question and is put up to the museum curator again and again. He knows that the romance of the picaresque and the illicit often attaches to objects which he has collected for their scientific value or their aesthetic virtue, and sometimes he gets a hint – but usually only the vaguest – of a story that makes bootlegging sound as matter-of-fact and as hum-drum as selling bonds. But even if he had the facts, a museum label would hardly be the place to give them.

For instance, there are some gold and silver cups in the Metropolitan Museum that once were part of a treasure of the Great Rameses. It would fill the entire case they are shown in if a label were written to tell the whole tale of how they were "found in 1906 in the ruins of ancient Bubastis." The story would have to begin with some workmen digging a railroad cutting through the ruins, who turned over the treasure with their hoes, and then quickly covered it up again. It would have to go on with how that night they came back to dig their find up and then fell into such a row over the division that by morning it was the gossip of the whole town of Zagazig, and by night the police were fishing a golden pitcher out of the thatch of one house and a silver bowl from under the bed in another. And then it would have to tell how the next day every antiquity dealer in Cairo was on the spot bargaining for what had escaped the search.

And even so, the story would not be complete. An affair like that, conducted with a lot of revengeful peasants looking for vicarious victims of their rage at the police, is one of the things in a dealer's life besides the lucrative and enjoyable pastime of levying tribute from the tourist friends of Mr. Thomas Cook.

That day at Zagazig one of the dealers was shown a silver goblet from the treasure and was told to send his man for it, with the purchase money, the next night. The man came and paid over the money, but all he got for it was a broken head. Another dealer was given just one fleeting glimpse of a golden pitcher in the hands of the wily fellah who had succeeded in keeping it away from the authorities. Off and on for months those two haggled over the price until at last a bargain was struck and the dealer sent his trusted agent down to Zagazig to fetch away the pitcher. The fellah and the agent passed each other in a crowded market-place. One handed over a little bag of sovereigns and the other a bundle done up in a dirty old handkerchief, and they parted without a sign of recognition. But when the bundle was opened in Cairo, instead of the golden pitcher, out came a very battered silver one the dealer had refused even to consider buying.

"Sapristi," he said to me with a shrug, "I assure you, it is *une des risques de nos affaires*. I still bargain for it, and *Inshallah*, as the Arabs say…" but he never got that golden pitcher.

Most of these tales are never told, and it is only a few that can even be imagined. Still, there are those rare times after some trade has been made and the coffee-cups and cigarettes are out, when a dealer will feel reminiscent. Once Hadji Hamid Mohammed Mohassib felt that way throughout a long hot afternoon, and I sat deathly still for fear of interrupting the unexpected flow of memories.

***

No, it's not as easy for us nowadays as it was when my father, Hadji Mohammed, was young. He used to take a bundle of libdehs and tagîyehs – you know those little caps the fellahin wear under their turbans? – and go up to Esneh and Edfu and swap them for scarabs and little bronze gods. The caps cost him a piaster or two a piece, and the scarabs used to bring him five shillings – a pound – or even two. Money was made easily and without any risk in those days, and long before I was grown up my father was known all through the Saïd and even in Cairo as a prosperous merchant – and an honest one. It's different now with the inspectors and all the other dealers and the peasants who always want cash. Often I have to go loaded with gold and then I travel in the dark like the desert fox and pray Allah I meet no wolves. But sometimes I do.

In the summer-time my father has the servants put a wooden bench underneath the tree by our house, and hang a lantern so that his friends can sit in the cool of the evening with him. One night some of his cronies had been chatting there – Ahmed the dragoman, Abdel Megid the antiquity dealer, Sheykh Awadullah and some others – while the lesser people of the village had squatted on the edge of the shadows to listen to what the older men had to say to each other. It was late. They had gone home one by one and my father and I were about to go to bed when we saw one fellow waiting to speak. He was a northerner – a Behêri. You know you can always tell them from our Saïdis. He came up to my father and spoke to him very respectfully, telling him how the fame of Hadji Mohammed Mohassib as an honest antika dealer had spread even to his village, way down in the Fayoum. Therefore he had come all the way to Luxor to ask my father whether he would like to buy some gold coins which he had found. With that, he fumbled in his turban and pulled out one of those big Greek coins that weigh as much as two or three English sovereigns. He said that he had dug up a pot full in his garden and that in it there must be over five hundred. Naturally we showed no great interest, because to do so would have been very bad business, and my father told him that if he wanted to sell such things to us he would have to bring them to Luxor.

"By the life of the Prophet (upon whom be the peace) I am afraid to, my masters,"; he whispered to us. "If the Omdeh of our village got news of this find he would take the half of it and then tell the Inspector that I had the rest. And worse than that. If I started out from my house with that pot full of gold, our village brigand down there would take it all from me, and I would be found on the canal bank beaten half to death for not sharing it with him before."

Then he went into a long account of this brigand

of theirs, Ahmed es Suefi, whom he called a real afrit with the very devils for his gang. The police were after him for killing a village guard out of revenge, but how can the police catch a man who is the cousin of the Omdeh of a big town, when the very Omdeh himself is afraid of him? The Omdeh may have hoped that someone would shoot this Ahmed in the dark and so relieve him of a very trying relative, but no self-respecting man could denounce his own uncle's son to the police, even to save himself from disgrace. So Ahmed es Suefi lived in the sugar-cane and sent out word to the Beys and the rich Copts who owned the plantations that he would set fire to their cane unless they gave him a present every month. They always sent it. They knew that with a single match he could burn up thousands of pounds of their profits. There he was, hidden by the poor because he robbed the rich; paid by the rich to leave them alone, and free to waylay those who passed along the canal banks and ease the purses of all who were not his friends.

"I can't bring that gold here, on my honor," wailed the Behêri. "My wife's brother – may God destroy his house – goes to the sugar-cane all the time and by now Ahmed es Suefi knows everything about my gold except where I have hidden it."

My father laughed, "W'allahi. So you want us to come instead so that this Suefi can rob us and split open our heads?"

"May God forgive…" he began, but we made much of the difficulties of the affair and refused many times to go before we got down to the real business of haggling over a price. At last he agreed to take their weight in sovereigns for the coins, which meant a very good profit for us. But then, he couldn't spend the antika guineas in the market and he could bring out English gold, piece by piece, with safety – and for us of course, there was a great risk with no redress from any one.

So he shrugged his shoulders and said: "Malaish – it makes no difference. Only bring me cash, my masters – bring me English sovereigns, and may God increase your prosperity." Then he told us how to get to his village, how to find his house and what day to come, after which he went away.

Of course, my father is too old a man for such a trip, and it is always my part of the business to travel on an affair like that. He raised the money that we would need, according to the Behêri's story – well over a thousand pounds – and I made all the preparations for the day that I was to go, with this redoubtable Ahmed es Suefi in my mind.

You know the Copt, Mikhail, the Christian, who is my father's clerk, and you know how fat and pompous he is? Well, I bought him a new silk kuftan, and when he was dressed up in it he looked like a very well-to-do merchant. Then there was Abdullah Kheirullah, that skinny, black Sudani servant that we trust with everything around the house, and my wife's brother Seman. These two and I myself went as the servants of the prosperous-looking Mikhail. Among the four of us I divided the money so that each of us carried nearly three hundred pounds in gold packed in belts under our clothes – and I assure you that they were heavy.

We took the train to Wasta and changed for Medinet el Fayoum, with Mikhail always in the second-class compartment among the omdehs and the rich farmers, and all of us, his servants, in the third-class with the fellahin. When we got off the train in the evening, it was I who ran and hired donkeys and asked the way to a village which we knew was way off to the south, while Abdullah and Seman stood around and addressed Mikhail as "Excellency," and he made a great talk about going to the southern village to buy cotton. What with getting donkeys, and asking the way, and fussing about, it was dark before we boosted the fat and puffy Mikhail up into his saddle and rode off through the narrow, black streets. By that time we were sure that everybody who had seen us had put us down as a Coptic merchant and his party going about some business to the south. Anyway no one was following us, and when we got to the outskirts of the town we made our way around among the gardens and the rubbish dumps to the big canal that flows northward, past the village we were really seeking.

There was no moon – we had chosen the night on purpose for that – and under the trees along the banks it was as dark as inside the belly of a camel. We could scarcely see each other as the donkeys ambled along.

SCI.DAN.H. 4 · 8

Nobody was about. The peasants had left their farms long before and only now and then did we see a light in some hamlet away off across the black fields. We rode for a long time that night. How can I describe it to you? ... the darkness that seemed so empty and so quiet, except for the barking of a dog, at last, a little way ahead. We were sure that that meant our village was near and all of us began to feel so safe that even Mikhail began to get facetious and whisper some joke about the Prince of the Afrits himself being unable to see Abdullah's black face on such a night – and then half a dozen shadows rose up between us and the pale starlight reflected in the canal, and a voice bellowed out, "Peace be upon you."

Even the donkeys stopped and our hearts with them. We could scarcely move our lips enough to gasp out, "And upon you be the peace; the mercy of God and His blessing" – for we were all good Muslims and even if there was to be murder we could not refuse to greet the faithful. That is, we were all good Muslims except Mikhail the Christian, but in any case he was too choked with fear to have answered at all. I myself could just find breath to begin the recitation of the Fatah in a fervent whisper.

By the time we had answered their salaam the strangers had gathered close enough around us for me to see that each of them, except one little bearded man, had a shawl wrapped around his face, and one of those heavy sticks – a naboot – in his hands. The little man shoved through the others and came up to the quaking Mikhail in the front of our party.

"Greetings from Luxor, Hadji Hamid Mohammed," he said.

"May God give you peace," replied Mikhail, his fat bulk shaking so that the little donkey under him almost rolled over. "But, my brother, ... I am no Hadji Hamid ... I am Mikhail Effendi Fakhouri, a poor cotton merchant of Assiout. I do not know Hadji Hamid unless he is a man we passed on the road an hour ago."

Even in the dark there was something terrifying about the little man as he drew himself up and snorted out at one of the others, "Is he not here, thou dog?" and that other came peering among us and finally pointed at me.

"I am not Hadji Hamid. By the life of our Lord ..." I began, but the little man raised his hand and said very politely: "Your Excellency does not know me perhaps – Ahmed es Suefi, your servant and a robber of some reputation in these villages here."

"Whatever is, is God's will," I murmured. "Yes, I have heard of you, Sheykh Ahmed."

"That is better" he said, grinning at me. "Now I shall tell you what you are up to. You came to buy a pot of gold coins from So and So, and I am here to get the money you have brought. So hand it over and then you can go back and get some more. If you make no trouble I will let you by the next time and God will increase your prosperity."

What was the use of pretending any more? Here, after all, was the brigand Ahmed es Suefi. He knew me and all of my affairs, and his men had half a dozen thick clubs to crack our heads if we made any fuss. And with broken heads what chance would we have to save those belts? Perhaps it was the thought of one of those naboots coming down on my pate that made my tongue go slower and my head work faster, searching for an idea.

"Sheykh Ahmed," I began, pulling out my wallet and untying the string, "there is no use denying. I am Hadji Hamid and I have come to buy antikas, but nothing of great value." I was sticking my hand into the wallet to get out what change I had. I drew out my check-book, and with it suddenly came the idea.

"But anyway I have often heard tell of you. In fact, I had heard so much of your deeds that I praised God that the English had taught us poor merchants a little cleverness. Do you think, my brother, I would be so foolish as to go about your country loaded with gold – when I can write on one of these slips of paper that the English call checks, and each will be worth hundreds of pounds at the bank in Cairo? Never in the world! I told the ignorant fellâh I would only bring a check..." but I could get no further.

"May destruction smite thee! And these English beasts – they are not of the children of Adam. Curses on all their kind and on their religion for teaching merchants such tricks and ruining my livelihood." He raged and spat and shrieked evil things. I offered him my wallet with the few piastres in it and a pearl-handled revolver (which would not shoot, by the way, because the firing-pin was broken), and a silver watch that was usually wrong. Mikhail produced a silver ring with a red glass ruby in it and the others had a little money for the journey, but altogether I doubt if we had five pounds to give him. Still he let us go, for there was nothing else for him to do. As he very plainly put it, we would be worth much more to him coming back with the gold coins.

All the time my money belt was pinching tighter and tighter under my clothes, for I knew that if ever that brigand's vitals began to cool off he would search us in spite of everything we had told him. But luckily there was no end to his rage at the English for inventing checks, and he was still cursing them in the dark as we went on our way. We, on the contrary, praised God for the cleverness of those same English, while we drummed on our donkey's ribs to make them go the faster.

The fellâh was waiting for us at his house. He produced his gold; we got out some scales, and each one stripped the money belt from his waist. For an hour or more we were weighing the coins and stuffing them into our belts as fast as we took the sovereigns out. We worked hard to hurry through the business. The peasant was trembling with anxiety to get his new sovereigns buried before Ahmed es Suefi should call upon him, and we were dead-tired from fright and from carrying those heavy belts all day. The weekly market was to be held the next morning at Medinet el Fayoum and crowds of people would be going from all the villages. We borrowed the dresses and veils of some women – all but Semân who was to go as the head of our family – and at daylight we were on the road again, safely hidden among the throngs of people and their beasts flocking to the market.

After that we had no trouble all the way back to Luxor, and in the end we made a handsome profit out of the affair. There were some rare coins which we sold very well in Cairo, and the common ones made a good business for us with the tourists for several seasons. In time we forgot our trip to the Fayoum, except when old black Abdullah chuckled sometimes at "Mikhail Effendi, the poor merchant of Assiout," and

perhaps we never really got over the way our hearts had sunk into our bellies under those money belts.

Then once, a long time afterward, I was in Cairo. Usually when I am down there I go to Turah to pass an afternoon with my friend Sadik Bey, who is the Mamour of the penitentiary. It happened that that day he had an inspection to make of the quarries where the most dangerous of the convicts make paving slabs. I went along with him and when he stopped to speak to the mulâhiz in charge, I stood waiting for him.

Suddenly a little bearded man bounded up from among the prisoners shouting out, "Hadji Hamid! Oh, Hadji Hamid, don't you know me … Ahmed es Suefi?"

Sadik Bey and the mulâhiz turned on him drawing their revolvers, but I had recognized the little old fellow and I laughed and stopped them and went over to him, saying, "Of course I do. How are you, Sheykh Ahmed?"

"In peace and prosperity, the praise be God's," he answered simply. He was a pious man even with the chains clanking about his ankles. He bore me no grudge, but he did want to know how I had escaped him on the way back with the gold coins. He chuckled when he learned that we had had to wear women's veils and he grudgingly admitted that I had been clever to have brought checks instead of the money.

And then I told him about the money belts.

I believe that was probably the first time in his life that he was ever really stupefied. A look of bewilderment and amazement spread over his face, and his hands just dropped limp at his sides, "On your honor? … praise the Prophet? this is not idle talk?" he kept saying over and over until at last a sort of relieved look came into his eyes, and he threw himself at my feet. "W'allahi, my master," he said, "at last I have met a man. If God is willing and if ever I get out of here, I shall work for you as long as I live – wages or no wages."

"And has he?" I asked finally, when it seemed evident that Hadji Hamid was going no farther with his tale, "Not yet. I believe that he has still five or six years to serve." And then he added musingly: "But he would be a really useful man for me in antiquity dealing."

APPENDIX 6:

H. O. Lange's background and autobiographical presentation

The following information about the family background of H. O. Lange has been be gathered from various biographies and letters in the Royal Academy. Hans Ostenfeld Lange (13 Oct. 1863 - 15 Jan. 1943) was the son of the merchant Hans Lange (18 July 1821 - 19 Jan. 1912) and his second wife, Cathrine Marie née Ostenfeld (18 Aug. 1936 - 28 Mar. 1917), whom he married in 1862 after the death of his first wife in 1860. H. O. Lange had an older half-brother, Marinus Lange (1851-1889), from his father's first marriage to Else née Arentzen (1820-1860). He also had an adoptive sister, Gudrun Lange née Zielian (1869-1950); she was the daughter of civil servant (*cancelliråd*) and lawyer (*prokurator*) in Silkeborg, R. T. Zielian, and became the fosterchild of H. O. Lange's parents after the death of his widow. She was formally adopted in 1885. Her husband, Asmussen, was originally a farmer but like Lange he was an active anti-alcohol campaigner and later became the manager of several hostels for alcoholics. In 1893 Lange married Jonna née Mielche (10 Jan. 1870 - 24 June 1955).

H. O. and Jonna Lange had two adopted children, the son Axel Valdemar Lange (born 8 June 1900) and the daughter Else Lange (born 25 Dec. 1903).[1281] They were very discreet about this aspect of their private life and the children are very rarely mentioned. The official household census shows that Axel had left home before 1921 and Else before 1925; in other words, both children had moved out before Hans and Jonna went to Egypt the second time. The antiquities dealer Zaki Mahmud Abd es-Samad gave the couple a silver ring inset with a scarab for their son and a wristband

for their daughter in 1930 (p. 273). By the time of Lange's death in 1943, both children had emigrated to the United States, apparently having become estranged from their parents.[1282] When Lange became head of the Royal Library in 1901, the couple acquired a home in Gentofte, Jahnsvej 11, just north of Copenhagen, where they lived until their deaths. H. O. Lange was buried in the local cemetery next to his house, Gentofte Kirkegård.[1283]

Upon his appointment as a member of the Danish Order of the Dannebrog in 1906, Lange wrote a short autobiographical presentation; members of the order were encouraged to submit a summary of their life so far (*levnedsberetning*), resulting in a large archive of such autobiographical material. This was naturally written in Danish, and has been translated here by the authors. We are grateful to the historiographer of the Royal Orders of Chivalry, Professor Knud J. V. Jespersen, for providing us with a copy of the original. A transcript of the Danish original was published by S. Larsen, 'H. O. Lange. Levnedsberetning til Ordenskapitlet 1907', *Magasin fra Det Kongelige Bibliotek* 16.4 (2003), 14-20.

Introduction

As long as one is still looking ahead in life, and finds oneself in the middle of the business of living, concerned with its work and toying with plans for the future, the act of pausing and taking stock does not come easily or even naturally.

1281. We are grateful to Karsten Christensen of the Royal Library for providing us with information concerning Lange's adopted children.

1282. Obituary, 'Fhv. Overbibliotekar H. O. Lange død', *Nationaltidende* 17 Jan. 1943, 5.

1283. His tombstone no longer exists; at some point the burial lease expired and the burial spot was re-used for another individual.

After all one learns by living, but this awareness is generally acquired almost automatically, practically instinctively, and only rarely by systematic self-examination or evaluation of one's life.

Then, when an opportunity to look back presents itself, one is confronted by the question 'Now, what has real value?'. And it may seem that the really valuable, that which meant the most to oneself, cannot be told, whether it was a mistake – the high price paid for learning the art of life – or the deeper movements of the heart, which was the real explanation for much of that which other people saw and for which each had his own explanation.[1284] If only one could comprehend the whys and wherefores of what one managed to accomplish. But here reason fails again. We humans live so much in dreams, that our life is only for the smallest part a result of our plans and efforts, there are other and more powerful forces at play. Both life and death are stronger than man, and no man is master of his own destiny.

To me, the awareness of God's hand and his intervention is a necessity to understand life, and my own life in particular, and the heart's rest in relation to a fatherly God is a necessity for me to continue to advance into the unknown.

My life has again and again given me pause to wonder, and whenever one can but wonder, no explanation can be offered, least of all that one is master of one's own destiny.

...

I was born 13 October 1863 in Aarhus. My parents are both still alive. My father, Hans Lange, was for many years a shopkeeper in Aarhus; my mother, his second wife, is Cathrine Marie, née Ostenfeldt.

Of siblings I had a half-brother who was about 12 years older than me; he died as a farmer. I also had a sister by adoption who is 6 years younger than me. She still lives with my old parents and teaches at a school.

1284. We have translated this literally, but confess that we do not fully understand what he means. It may be related to the reception of some of his library reforms, which seem to have met with some resistance, judging from one of the published obituaries; Dahl, *Nordisk Tidskrift för Bok- och Biblioteksväsen* 29 (1942), 115-120.

Both on my father's and my mother's side I have my roots in the Jutlandish rural population, which I consider an honour.

I had a happy childhood in a good home filled with love. After preparatory school I entered, in 1874, the first year of Latin school. I was only 10 years old at the time, but I was meant to stay as a third-year for two years so that I would not become a student at only 16 years of age. I found school easy and was generally top (*Dux*) of my class. Among my teachers I have to mention Superintendent (*Overlærer*) O. A. Hovgaard, and the later Superintendent O. Lohse who replaced Hovgaard as the school's librarian. They introduced me to the school library early on, where I assisted them occasionally. I also have to mention the headmaster (*Rektor*) in Horsens, Anton Neergaard, and headmaster G. Lund.

Already in my second year I became fascinated by ancient Egypt, and I started to read anything I could get my hands on that might enlighten me about the ancient Egyptian culture. I was given access to the deceased County Official (*Stiftamtmand*) Dahl's library at Moesgaard near Aarhus, where there was some more recent Egyptological literature, and I used money earned by teaching Latin to apothecary apprentices to pay for a trip to Copenhagen during the Easter holidays. There I was given access to the collection of antiquities [at the National Museum], and to the great Royal Library. As a study-prize I was awarded, in 1877, an Egyptological book, and I was able to buy another when I came first in a shooting competition.

At the same time my interest in books was kindled. I spent a lot of time in the school library, and I was always given access to the significant library belonging to the then chaplain of Aarhus cathedral, Pastor A. F. Schiødte. This eccentric man also sparked my interest in Søren Kierkegaard's writings. Bookseller Thrue in Aarhus kept sending me German catalogues of antiquarian book sales, and these I studied with relish and learned a lot from. When I took my final exam at school I was examined in the history of Latin literature and the works of Ovid, and because of my study of the catalogues I was also able to discuss the main editions of his works.

I took my final exam at school in the summer of 1881, and got the highest mark available with chistruktion. I intended to study classical philology and to cultivate my Egyptological interests alongside this.

In August 1881 I came to Copenhagen, and beside the philosophical lectures of Prof. Rasmus Nielsen I started taking classes in Egyptian with Prof. Valdemar Schmidt and following the philological lectures of Professors Ussing and Gertz, as well as Dr O. Liesbye.

I studied classical philology for four years, but when I was employed at the Royal Library in 1885 I stopped reading for the exam. The regular reading for the exam did not appeal to me, and instead I immersed myself in the study of vulgar Latin, and as a result of this I wrote an essay on language in that part of Petronius' Satyricon which is called Trimalchio's Dinner for an essay competition arranged by The Philological-Historical Society, for which I was awarded the highest prize in November 1884.

I was an active member of The Philological-Historical Society and of a more narrowly focussed study-circle on philology to which belonged, among others, the current Museum Inspector Christian Blinkenberg, Prof. Otto Jespersen and Prof. Dines Andersen. This little group breathed new life into The Philological-Historical Society for a few years.

But with the greatest interest I cultivated my Egyptological studies, and I was a regular visitor to the reading rooms of the Royal Library to study the numerous important plate volumes that were only available there for on-site consultation.

At the same time I was going through a significant spiritual crisis in my first student years. I was involved in the founding of the Student Union and took down the minutes of the inaugural meeting, but at the same time I was a teacher at a Sunday school in Valby. It was a time of spiritual change. The radical movement was rapidly gaining ground, but at the same time there was a slow retreat in terms of religion against which I took a stand based on personal religious experiences in 1882, and with which I am still concerned. I took over a Bible-class for post-confirmation boys, which was based at Trinitatis Præstegaard. I threw myself into the study of Church history, in particular of all the oppositional parties in its history; Søren Kierkegaard became more and more influential on me, and my criticism of the official church grew and sharpened alongside an increased feeling of sympathy towards all subjective religious organisations.

During the autumn of 1882 I approached the current Professor Fridericia, who at the time was an assistant at the University Library, to hear if there was any opportunity of doing an MA degree in history, as the study of philology did not appeal to me. Through him I was given some extra work at the University Library from 1 October 1882, and that is how I first got a foot in the door of the institution that had tempted me for so long. Assistant Jensen at the University Library was on recuperative leave in the south because of chest pains, and upon his return in the spring of 1883 he was very ill, and he died soon after. The current librarian Dr Sophus Larsen was then, in the month of April, employed in his stead, and I was given one of the positions of extraordinary assistant at a rate of pay of 800 crowns per annum. My interests were broadened by the work with books; I studied the history of classical philology and wrote a dissertation about Justus Lipsius' professorship at Jena; in Centralblatt für Bibliothekswesen I published a medieval catalogue of the books of the University Library of Erfurt found in a manuscript in the University Library; I also found a presumed lost manuscript of Marculphi Formulae in the manuscript collection of the library.

In the autumn of 1885 I was encouraged by Head Librarian Christian Bruun to apply for a vacant position at the great Royal Library. He knew me from the Book Committee in The Philological-Historical Society, of which I was a member. I was employed from 1 October 1885.

From this point I gave up on reading for the exam and dedicated myself exclusively to the library work and my extra-curricular studies, in particular Egyptology.

In 1886 I undertook my first study trip to Berlin, supported by public funds, where I established important and for me influential connections with Professor Adolf Erman and the young Egyptologists Steindorff, Borchardt, Schäfer and Sethe.

Since then I have undertaken repeated study trips to London, Paris, Leiden and Berlin, and I published the results of my work in various foreign journals. I also took the opportunity afforded by my travels to study the organisation of the great libraries.

Naturally the work with the great book collections of the Royal Library led me to the study of books in a more general sense, the history of the book, manuscripts and incunables. In particular I threw myself into the study of the history of book printing in Lübeck, and in a couple of longer essays I presented new perspectives and new material.

My Christian and church interests were given a new focus in 1889 in the form of church policy in Copenhagen, when I formed, along with six other lay men, The Committee for the Advancement of Church Policy in Copenhagen (*Udvalget til Kirkesagens fremme i Kjøbenhavn*) with Professor H. Westergaard as chairman. Our activities were transferred to the Copenhagen Church Fund (*Kjøbenhavns Kirkefond*). I have been actively promoting these issues in speech and writing since then.

In 1895 I re-founded the International Federation of the Blue Cross in Denmark with the help of Pastor H. P. Mollerup, and since then I have worked for this issue. In this context I should also mention that some years ago I founded the Student Abstinence Society (*Studenternes Afholdsforening*). In 1895 I was part of the small group which established a shelter for alcoholics, Enkrateia, near Copenhagen.

Through these activities I came into fairly close contact with the working classes, and could not but be engaged by social issues, so that by the beginning of 1899 I took part in the establishment of the Committee for the Advancement of Social Enlightenment (*Udvalget til social Oplysningens Fremme*), and with Pastor H. Ostenfeld and Professor H. Westergaard I became the editor of the committee's weekly newsletter 'Vor Tid' ('Our Time').

However, in 1899 the Egyptian Government requested that I join an international commission for the publication of a critical catalogue of the antiquities of the Egyptian Museum in Cairo. They wanted me to work for them for three years, but my commitments at the library made this impossible, so we settled for one year's employment.

I was then given leave from the library for one year, on the condition that I provide the library with a replacement, and in the beginning of October 1899 I set up home in Cairo along with my wife.

In 1893 I had married Jonna Mielche, the daughter of Lieutenant Colonel J. C. Mielche (died 1907), we had no children and so it was easy for both of us to establish a home under foreign skies.

Along with Dr Heinrich Schäfer, now Director of the Egyptian Museum in Berlin, I took over the categorisation and publication of the roughly 800 stelae of the Middle Kingdom in the Museum. My wife photographed virtually the entire lot.

During my ten-month stay in Egypt I got to know both the country and the people reasonably well, and I had the opportunity to visit Upper Egypt and the great monuments of antiquity along the Nile Valley.

Upon my return I met Head Librarian Christian Bruun who had fallen ill. He was ill until he stepped down in March 1901; at the end of that month the Librarian J. Vahl, who had been acting Head Librarian, also died. On the 1st of April I was then made Head Librarian under rather trying circumstances, in particular regarding the new building, the plans for which I was very unhappy with.

The next few years brought me a lot of work both in connection with the new building project and with an extensive reorganisation of the library's administrative structure and its administrative procedures. I had very little time to further my private studies or to contribute to any public activities. In March 1906 I was appointed a member of the Royal Danish Society of Sciences and Letters.

The relocation of the library and the opening of the new building on 27 November 1906 brought the first instalment of my time as the head of the library to a close. A few days later I had a serious attack of sciatica that made me unable to work for about half a year, except for one or two occasions. Nonetheless I managed to take part in the implementation of a new organisation- and payment-plan for the library in April 1907. I hope that this will provide a good and solid base for the future development of the library, but there is no area where there is such a recurring opportunity for progress, and where the danger of getting stuck in routine work is greater.

Praesens imperfectum, perfectum futurum.
Gentofte, 24 September 1907.
H. O. Lange

List of Figures

Bibliography

Abou-Seif, H. 'Report on the Inspectorate of Tanta from September 1923 to January 1925', *ASAE* 24 (1924), 146-150.

Adams, C. V. A. 'An Investigation into the Mummies Presented to H. R. H. the Prince of Wales in 1869', *DE* 18 (1990), 5-19.

Adams, J. M. *The Millionaire and the Mummies: Theodore Davies' Gilded Age in the Valley of the Kings*, New York, 2013.

Adler, E. N., J. G. Tait, F. M. Heichelheim, and F. Ll. Griffith, *The Adler Papyri*, London, 1939.

Albersmeier, S. *Ägyptische Kunst: Bestandskatalog, Badisches Landesmuseum Karlsruhe*, Munich, 2007.

Alexander, K. 'A History of the Ancient Art Collection at the Art Institute of Chicago', *Art Institute of Chicago Museum Studies* 20 (1994), 6-13.

Allen, T. G. *The Egyptian Book of the Dead: Documents in the Oriental Institute Museum at the University of Chicago*, OIP 82, Chicago, 1960.

Alm, G. and B. A. Johansson, *Resan till Egypten: Drottning Victorias fotografiska liv*, Skrifter från Kungl. Husgeråds-kammaren 13, Stockholm, 2012.

Ames, M. L. *Life and Letters of Peter and Susan Lesley*, London, 1909.

Andersen, M., B. Holmen, and J. Tait, 'Palaeographical and Codicological Notes to Supplement Erichsen's Edition of the Copenhagen Fayumic Manuscript of Agathonicus: P. Carlsberg 300', *Enchoria* 25 (1999), 1-19.

Andrews, E. B. and T. M. Davis, *A Journal on the Bedawin, 1889-1912: The Diary Kept on Board the Dahabiyeh of Theodore M. Davis during Seventeen Trips up the Nile*, 2 vols., New York, 1918.

Annuaire diplomatique et consulaire de la République française pour 1904 & 1905 25, new ser., Paris, 1906.

Annuaire égyptien, administratif et commercial, 1891-1892, Cairo, 1891.

Anonymous, 'La nouvelle loi sur les antiquités de l'Égypte et ses annexes', *ASAE* 12 (1912), 245-280.

Anonymous, 'Extrait de l'inventaire du Musée de Boulaq', *BIE* 1, 3rd ser. (1891), 225-232.

Anonymous 'Extrait de l'inventaire du Musée de Boulaq', *BIE* 10, 2nd ser. (1890), i-xxxvii.

Anonymous, 'Extrait de l'inventaire du Musée de Boulaq', *BIE* 9, 2nd ser. (1889), i-xli.

Anonymous 'Extrait de l'inventaire du Musée de Boulaq', *BIE* 8, 2nd ser. (1888), i-xlv.

Anonymous 'Extrait de l'inventaire du Musée de Boulaq', *BIE* 7, 2nd ser. (1887), i-xxix.

Arnold, D. *The Royal Women of Amarna: Images of Beauty from Ancient Egypt*, New York, 1996.

D'Auria, S. 'Three Painted Textiles in the Collection of the Boston Athenaeum', *Studies in Honor of William Kelly Simpson* 1, ed. P. Der Manuelian, Boston, 1996, 169-176.

Auwers, H. *Bericht über die Beobachtung des Venus-Durchgangs vom 8. December 1874 in Luxor*, Abhandlungen der königlichen Akademie der Wissenschaften zu Berlin, 1877, Berlin, 1878, 1-143.

Avgouli, M. 'The First Greek Museums and National Identity', *Museums and the Making of "Ourselves": The Role of Objects in National Identity*, ed. S. Kaplan, London, 1994, 246-265.

Baedeker, K. *Egypt and the Sûdân*, 8th edition, Leipzig, 1929.

—. *Ägypten und der Sudân*, 8th edition, Leipzig, 1928.

—. *Egypte et Soudan*, 4th edition, Leipzig, 1914.

—. *Egypt and the Sûdân*, 7th edition, Leipzig, 1914.

—. *Ägypten und der Sudân*, 7th edition, Leipzig, 1913.

—. *Egypte et Soudan*, 3rd edition, Leipzig, 1908.

—. *Egypt and the Sûdân*, 6th edition, Leipzig, 1908.

—. *Ägypten und der Sudân*, 6th edition, Leipzig, 1906.

—. *Egypte*, 2nd edition, Leipzig, 1903.

—. *Egypt*, 5th edition, Leipzig, 1902.

—. *Ägypten*, 5th edition, Leipzig, 1902.

—. *Egypte*, 1st edition, Leipzig, 1898.

—. *Egypt*, 4th edition, Leipzig, 1898.

—. *Ägypten*, 4th edition, Leipzig, 1897.

—. *Egypt, Part First: Lower Egypt and the Peninsula of Sinai*, 3rd edition, Leipzig, 1895.

—. *Unter-Ägypten und die Sinai-Halbinsel*, 3rd edition, Leipzig, 1894.

—. *Egypt, Part Second: Upper Egypt, with Nubia as far as the Second Cataract and the Western Oasis*, 1st edition, Leipzig, 1892.

—. *Ägypten, zweiter Theil: Ober-Ägypten und Nubien bis zum zweiten Katarakt*, 1st edition, Leipzig, 1891.

—. *Egypt, Part First: Lower Egypt, with the Fayûm, and the Peninsula of Sinai*, 2nd edition, Leipzig, 1885.

—. *Ägypten, erster Theil: Unter-Ägypten bis zum Fayûm und die Sinai-Halbinsel*, 2nd edition, Leipzig, 1885.

—. *Egypt, Part First: Lower Egypt, with the Fayûm, and the Peninsula of Sinai*, 1st edition, Leipzig, 1878.

—. *Ägypten, erster Theil: Unter-Ägypten bis zum Fayûm und die Sinai-Halbinsel*, 1st edition, Leipzig, 1877.

Bagh, T. *Finds from the Excavations of J. Garstang in Meroe and F.Ll. Griffith in Kawa in the Ny Carlsberg Glyptotek*, Copenhagen, 2015.

—. *Finds from W.M.F. Petrie's Excavations in Egypt in the Ny Carlsberg Glyptotek*, Copenhagen, 2011.

Bagnall, R. S. (ed.), *The Oxford Handbook of Papyrology*, Oxford, 2009.

Bahrami, M. 'A Master-potter of Kashan', *Transactions of the Oriental Ceramic Society* 20 (1944-1945), 35-40.

Baikie, J. *Egyptian papyri and papyrus-hunting*, London, 1925.

Bailey, D. M. 'Sebakh, Sherds and Survey', *JEA* 85 (1999), 211-218.

Bakhoum, S. and M.-Chr. Hellmann, 'Wilhelm Froehner, le commerce et les collections d'antiquités égyptiennes', *Journal des savants* 1992, 155-185.

Barker, N. *Bibliotheca Lindesiana: the Lives and Collections of Alexander William, 25th Earl of Crawford and 8th Earl of Balcarres, and James Ludovic, 26th Earl of Crawford and 9th Earl of Balcarres*, London, 1978.

Barsanti, A. 'Fouilles de Zaouiét el-Aryan (1911-1912)', *ASAE* 12 (1912), 57-63.

—. 'Fouilles de Zaouiét el-Aryan (1904-1905-1906)', *ASAE* 8 (1908), 201-210.

—. 'Rapport', *ASAE* 7 (1906), 260-286.

Bayer-Niemeier, E. et al., *Liebighaus - Museum Alter Plastik II. Skulptur, Malerei, Papyri und Särge*, Melsungen, 1993.

Bell, C. D. *A Winter on the Nile, in Egypt, and in Nubia*, London, 1888.

Bell, L. 'Epigraphic Survey', *The Oriental Institute, Annual Report 1980-81*, ed. J. A. Brinkman, 7-22.

Bénazeth, D. 'Un monastère dispersé: Les antiquités de Baouit conservées dans les musées d'Égypte', *BIFAO* 97 (1997), 43-66.

Benson Harer, W. 'The Drexel Collection: From Egypt to the Diaspora', *Servant of Mut: Studies in Honor of Richard A. Fazzini*, ed. S. H. D'Auria, PÄ 28, Leiden, 2008, 111-119.

Benson, M. and J. Gourlay, *The Temple of Mut in Asher: An Account of the Excavation of the Temple and of the Religious Representations and Objects found therein, as Illustrating the History of Egypt and the Main Religious Ideas of the Egyptians*, London, 1899.

Bernand, É. *Recueil des inscriptions grecques du Fayoum I*, Leiden, 1975.

Bernhard-Walcher, A. 'Theodor Graf und die Wiederentdeckung der Mumienportraits', *Bilder aus dem Wüstensand. Mumienportraits aus dem Ägyptischen Museum*, Vienna, 1998, 27-35.

Bezold, C. and E. A. W. Budge, *The Tell El-Amarna Tablets in the British Museum: with Autotype Facsimilies*, London, 1892.

Bickel, S., H.-W. Fischer-Elfert, A. Loprieno, and S. Richter (eds.), *Ägyptologen und Ägyptologien zwischen Kaiserreich und Gründung der beiden Deutschen Staaten*, ZÄS Beihefte 1, Berlin, 2013.

Bickerstaffe, D. 'Emile Brugsch & The Royal Mummies at Bulaq', *KMT* 26.1 (2015), 18-26.

Bierbrier, M. L. *Who was Who in Egyptology*, 4th edition, London, 2012.

—. *Hieroglyphic texts from Egyptian Stelae, etc., in the British Museum*, Part 12, London, 1993.

von Bissing, F. W. 'Les tombeaux d'Assouan', *ASAE* 15 (1915), 1-14.

—. Review of *Handbuch der ägyptischen Königsnamen. 1. Heft: Die Königsnamen bis einschließlich XVII* by M. Burchardt and M. Pieper, *Historische Zeitschrift* 113, no. 2 (1914), 333-335.

—. *Fayencegefässe*, CG, Vienna, 1902.

Blair, S. 'A Brief Biography of Abu Zayd', *Muqarnas* 25 (2008), 155-176.

Blattner, E. J. (ed.), *Le mondain égyptien et du Proche-Orient 1953*, Cairo, 1953.

—. (ed.), *Le mondain égyptien: The Egyptian Who's Who 1952*, Cairo, 1952.

—. (ed.), *Le mondain égyptien: The Egyptian Who's Who 1943*, Cairo, 1943.

—. (ed.), *Le mondain égyptien: The Egyptian Who's Who 1941*, Cairo, 1941.

—. (ed.), *Le mondain égyptien: The Egyptian Who's Who 1939*, Cairo, 1939.

Blinkenberg, C. 'Un contrat de vente de l'époque ptolemaïque', *Oversigt over det kongelige danske Videnskabernes Selskabs Forhandlinger*, Copenhagen, 1901, 119-126.

Boak, A. E. R. 'The Building of the University of Michigan Papyrus Collection', *The Michigan Alumnus Quarterly Review* 66, no. 10 (1959-1960), 35-42.

Bolshakov, A. O. *Studies on Old Kingdom Reliefs and Sculpture in the Hermitage*, Ägyptologische Abhandlungen 67, Wiesbaden, 2005.

Borchardt, L. 'Zwei Schriftproben', *Allerhand Kleinigkeiten*, ed. L. Borchardt, Leipzig, 1933, 43-45.

—. *Der Porträtkopf der Königin Teje im Besitz von Dr. James Simon in Berlin*, Leipzig, 1911.

—. *Statuen und Statuetten von Königen und Privatleuten im Museum von Kairo, Nr. 1-1294*, Catalogue général des antiquités égyptiennes du Musée du Caire, Berlin, 1911.

−. 'Statue mit Angabe der Bedeutung und des Standortes', *ZÄS* 42 (1905), 83.

−. 'Die zweite Papyrusfund von Kahun und die zeitliche Festlegung des Mittleren Reiches der ägyptischen Geschichte', *ZÄS* 37 (1899), 89-103.

Borghouts, J. F. *The Magical Texts of Papyrus Leiden I 348*, OMRO 51, Leiden, 1971.

Bothmer, B. V. *Egypt 1950: My First Visit*, ed. E. S. Hall, Oxford, 2003.

Botti, G. *Catalogue des monuments exposés au Musée gréco-Romain d'Alexandrie*, Alexandria, 1900.

−. *Rapport sur le Musée Gréco-Romain*, Alexandria, 1899.

Bouriant, U. 'Notes de voyage', *RT* 11 (1889), 131-159.

−. 'Petits monuments et petits textes', *RT* 9 (1887), 81-100.

Brandl, H. 'A Bichrome Faience Statuette of Bastet from the Reign of Takeloth III', *Kleine Götter – grosse Götter: Festschrift für Dieter Kessler zum 65. Geburtstag*, ed. M. C. Flossmann-Schütze et al., Tuna el-Gebel 4, Vaterstetten, 2013, 67-89.

Breccia, E. 'In Egitto con Girolamo Vitelli: (Trent'anni dopo)', *Aegyptus* 15 (1935), 255-262.

Bresciani, E. '"La stele Hatun": Il pannello di una falsaporta a nome di Nefer e di It-sen, dalla necropoli dell'Antico Regno a Giza', *EVO* 18 (1995), 19-21.

Bresciani, E. and M. Betrò, *Egypt in India: Egyptian Antiquities in Indian Museums*, Pisa, 2004.

von Briskorn, B. *Zur Sammlungsgeschichte afrikanischer Ethnographica im Übersee-Museum Bremen 1841-1945*, Bremen, 2000.

Brovarski, E. 'Epigraphic and Archaeological Documentation of Old Kingdom Tombs and Monuments at Giza and Saqqara', *The American Discovery of Ancient Egypt: Essays*, ed. N. Thomas, Los Angeles, 1996, 25-43.

Bruffaerts, J.-M. 'Un mastaba égyptien pour Bruxelles', *BMRAH* 76 (2005), 5-36.

Brugsch, H. *Mein Leben und mein Wandern*, 2nd edition, Berlin, 1894.

Budge, E. A. W. *By Nile and Tigris: A Narrative of Journeys in Egypt and Mesopotamia on behalf of the British Museum between the Years 1886 and 1913*, London, 1920.

−. *Cook's Handbook for Egypt and the Sûdân*, 2nd edition, London, 1906.

−. *A History of Egypt from the End of the Neolithic Period to the Death of Cleopatra VII B.C. 30*, vol. 4: *Egypt and Her Asiatic Empire*, London, 1902.

−. 'The Excavations made at Aswân, by Major-General Sir F. Grenfell, during the years 1885 and 1886', *PSBA* 10 (1888), 4-40.

−. 'On Cuneiform Despatches from Tûshratta, King of Mitanni, Burraburiyasch, the Son of Kuri-Galzu, and the King of Alashiya, to Amenophis III, King of Egypt, and on the Cuneiform Tablets from Tell el-Amarna', *PSBA* 10 (1888), 540-569.

−. 'Description of the Tombs of Mechu, Ben, and Se-Renpu, discovered by Major-Gen. Sir F. Grenfell', *PSBA* 9 (1887), 78-82.

Bülow-Jacobsen, A. 'Three Ptolemaic Tax-Receipts from Hawara (P.Carlsberg 46-48)', *Bulletin of the Institute of Classical Studies* 29 (1982), 12-16.

−. 'Receipt for ΦΕΛΩΧΙΚΟΝ (P.Carlsberg 51)', *Bulletin of the Institute of Classical Studies* 32 (1985), 45-48.

Bull, L. 'Four Egyptian Inscribed Statuettes of the Middle Kingdom', *JAOS* 56 (1936), 166-172.

Bussmann, N. *Die mutige Pionerin: Warda Bleser-Birchers Jahrhundert*, Zürich, 2005.

Bülow-Jacobsen, A. 'Korrespondance angående papyrussamlingen i København', *Aegis* 12 (2012), 1-60.

Bülow-Jacobsen, A. and W. M. Brashear, 'A Magical Formulary (P. Carlsberg 52)', *Magica Varia*, eds. W. M. Brashear and A. Bülow-Jacobsen, Papyrologica Bruxellensia 25, Bruxelles, 1991, 16-62.

Capart, J. 'Nécrologie, Maurice Nahman', *CdE* 22 (1947), 30.

−. 'Maurice Nahman', *CdE* 44 (1947), 300-301.

Capart, J. (ed.), *Travels in Egypt [December 1880 to May 1891]: Letters of Charles Edwin Wilbour*, Brooklyn, 1936.

Capart, J. and A. H. Gardiner, *Le papyrus Léopold II aux Musées royaux d'art et d'histoire de Bruxelles et le papyrus Amherst à la Pierpont Morgan Library de New York: reproduits en fac-simile avec une transcription hiéroglyphique une introduction et une traduction*, New York, 1939.

Carson, B. M. *From Cairo to Cataract*, Boston, 1909.

Carter, H. 'Report on the Robbery of the Tomb of Amenothes II, Biban el Moluk', *ASAE* 3 (1902), 115-121.

Choat, M. 'Lord Crawford's Search for Papyri: On the Origin of the Rylands Papyrus Collection', *Actes du 26e Congrès international de papyrologie*, ed. P. Schubert, Geneva, 2012, 141-147.

Christensen, T. and K. Ryholt, *The Carlsberg Papyri 13: Catalogue of Egyptian Funerary Papyri in Danish Collections*, CNI Publications 41, Copenhagen, 2016.

Clarke, K. D. 'Paleography and Philanthropy: Charles Lang Freer and His Acquisition of the "Freer Biblical Manuscripts"', *The Freer Biblical Manuscripts: Fresh Studies of an American Treasure Trove*, ed. L. W. Hurtado, Atlanta, 2006, 17-73.

Clarysse, W. and H. Yan, 'Two Ptolemaic Stelae for the

Sacred Lion of Leonton Polis (Tell Moqdam)', *CdE* 82 (2007), 77-100.

Clédat, J. 'Notes sur l'Isthme de Suez', *RT* 36 (1914), 103-112.

Clère, J. J. 'Monuments inédits des serviteurs dans la Place de Verité', *BIFAO* 28 (1929), 173-201.

Colla, E. *Conflicted Antiquities: Egyptology, Egyptomania, Egyptian Modernity*, Durham, 2007.

Collombert, Ph. 'Omina brontoscopiques et pluies de grenouilles', *Acts of the Tenth International Congres of Demotic Studies*, eds. M. Depauw and Y. Broux, Orientalia Lovaniensia Analecta 231, Leuven, 2014, 15-26.

Cook, B. F. *Inscribed Hadra Vases in the Metropolitan Museum of Art*, New York, 1966.

Cooney, J. D. 'Three Minor Masterpieces of Egyptian Art', *BCM* 62, no. 1 (1975), 11-16.

Covington, D. 'Mastaba Mount Excavations', *ASAE* 6 (1905), 193-218.

Dahl, S. 'H. O. Lange', *Nordisk Tidskrift för Bok- och Biblioteksväsen* 29 (1942), 115-120.

Dahl, S. and P. Engelstoft, *Dansk skønlitterært forfatterleksikon, 1900-1950* 2, Copenhagen, 1960.

Dahmen, K. 'Alexander in Gold and Silver: Reassessing Third century AD Medallions from Aboukir and Tarsos', *AJN* 20, 2nd ser. (2008), 493-546.

Dallas Museum of Fine Arts, *5000 Years of Egyptian Art and Civilization: Dallas Museum of Fine Arts, March 5 thru 26, 1950*, Dallas, 1950.

Daressy, G. 'Fouilles de Deir El Bircheh (Novembre-Décembre 1897)', *ASAE* 1 (1900), 17-43.

–. 'Les sépultures des prêtres d'Ammon à Deir el-Bahari', *ASAE* 1 (1900), 141-148.

Daressy, G. 'Gaston Maspero: Directeur Généreal du Service des Antiquités (1881-1886, 1899-1914)', *ASAE* 16 (1916), 129-140.

Dattari, G. 'Comments on a Hoard of Athenian Tetradrachms found in Egypt', *Journal International d'Archéologie Numasmatique* 8 (1905), 103-113.

David, É. (ed.), G. *Lettres d'Égypte: correspondance avec Louise Maspero (1883-1914)*, Paris, 2003.

–. *Gaston Maspero 1846-1916: Le gentleman égyptologue*, Paris, 1999.

Davies, W. V. *The Statuette of Queen Tetisheri - a Reconsideration*, British Museum Occasional Papers 36, London, 1984.

Davoli, P. 'Papiri, archeologia e storia moderna', *Atene e Roma* 1-2 (2008), 100-124.

Deonna, W. 'Acquisitions des sections', *Genava: Bulletin du Musée d'Art et d'Histoire de Genève* 2 (1924), 29-57.

Deschamps, P. *A travers l'Égypte: Le Nil, la Palestine, la Syrie*, Paris, 1896.

Devonshire, R. L. 'Sultan Salâh-ed Dîn's Writing-Box in the National Museum of Arab Art, Cairo', *The Burlington Magazine* 35 (1919), 241-245.

Dijkstra, J. H. F. 'New Light on the Patermouthis Archive from Excavations at Aswan: When Archaeology and Papyrology Meet', *BASP* 44 (2007), 179-209.

Donker van Heel, K. *Djekhy & Son: Doing Business in Ancient Egypt*, Cairo, 2012.

Dodson, A. 'The Strange Affair of Dr. Muses, or the Discovery of the Pyramid of Ameny-Qemau', *KMT* 8, no. 3 (1997), 60-63.

Doyon, W. 'On Archaeological Labor in Modern Egypt', *Histories of Egyptology: Interdisciplinary Measures*, ed. W. Carruthers, London, 2015, 141-156.

Drower, M. S. *Letters from the Desert: The Correspondence of Flinders and Hilda Petrie*, Oxford, 2004.

–. *Flinders Petrie: A Life in Archaeology*, London, 1985.

Dryson, S. L. *In Pursuit of Ancient Pasts: A History of Classical Archaeology in the Nineteenth and Twentieth Centuries*, New Haven, 2006.

Duff-Gordon, L. *Lady Duff-Gordon's Letters from Egypt*, revised edition, London, 1902.

–. *Last Letters from Egypt, to which are added Letters from the Cape*, London, 1875.

Dutilh, E. D. J. 'Vestiges de faux monnayages antiques à Alexandrie ou ses environs', *Journal international d'archéologie numismatique* 5 (1902), 93-97.

–. 'Monnaies alexandrines et terres cuites du Fayoum', *BIE* 6, 3rd ser. (1896), 223-227.

–. 'A travers les Collections Numismatiques du Caire', *Rivista italiana di numismatica* 8 (1895), 95-101.

Eaton-Krauss, M. 'Some Coptic Reliefs Purportedly from Coptos', *Christianity and Monasticism in Upper Egypt* 2, eds. G. Gabra and H. N. Takla, Cairo, 2010, 201-210.

–. 'The Fate of Sennefer and Senetnay at Karnak Temple and in the Valley of the Kings', *JEA* 85 (1999), 113-129.

Ebers, G. 'Einige Inedita', *ZÄS* 18 (1880), 53-63.

Eddé, Dr. 'Ce que contenait le trésor d'Aboukir', *Bulletin de Numismatique* 13 (1906), 78-82.

Edgar, C. C. *Greek Vases*, Catalogue général des antiquités égyptiennes du Musée du Caire, Cairo, 1911.

–. 'The Treasure of Tell Basta', *Le Musée égyptien* 2 (1907), 93-108.

Edgar, J. and M. Edgar, *The Great Pyramid Passages and Chambers*, Glasgow, 1910.

Edwards, A. B. *A Thousand Miles up the Nile*, 2nd edition, London, 1888.

Ehlebracht, P. *Haltet die Pyramiden fest! 5000 Jahre Grabraub in Ägypten*, Düsseldorf, 1980.

Eisenberg, J. M. *Art of the Ancient World* 25, New York and London, 2014.

–. 'Two Egyptian Antiquities Dealers Sentenced for Smuggling', *Minerva* 17, no. 1 (2006), 7.

–. 'Antiquity Smugglers Sentenced in Cairo', *Minerva* 15, no. 4 (2004), 7.

–. 'Antiquity Collections Donated to Supreme Council', *Minerva* 13, no. 3 (2002), 7.

–. 'News from Egypt', *Minerva* 13, no. 3 (2002), 7.

Eitrem, S. *Ved Nilens Bredder for et Par Tusen År Siden*, Oslo, 1930.

Emberling, G. (ed.). 'Report on the first expedition of the Oriental Institute of the University of Chicago', *Pioneers to the Past: American Archaeologists in the Middle East 1919-1920*, Oriental Institute Museum Publications 30, Chicago, 2010, 141-142.

Engelbach, R. 'Seizure of Bronzes from Buto (Tell Fara în)', *ASAE* 24 (1924), 169-177.

–. 'Report on the inspectorate of Upper Egypt from April 1920 to March 1921', *ASAE* 21 (1921), 61-76.

Erichsen, W. 'Aus einem Koptischen Arzneibuch', *AcOr* 27 (1963), 23-45.

–. *Faijumische Fragmente der Reden des Agathonicus Bischofs von Tarsus*, Det kgl. danske Videnskabernes Selskab, Historisk-filologiske Meddelelser 19, no. 1, Copenhagen, 1932.

Erman, A. *Mein Werden und mein Wirken: Erinnerungen eines alten Berliner Gelehrten*, Leipzig, 1929.

Essler, H. 'Über die Würzburger Papyrussammlung', *Proceedings of the 24th International Congress of Papyrology: Helsinki, 1-7 August, 2004*, eds. J. Frösén, T. Purola, and E. Salmenkivi, Commentationes Humanarum Litterarum 122, Helsinki, 2007, 291-298.

Fagan, B. M. *The Rape of the Nile: Tomb Robbers, Tourists, and Archaeologists in Egypt*, New York, 1975.

Fairholt, F. W. *Up the Nile and Home Again: A Handbook for Travellers and a Travel-book for the Library*, London, 1862.

Farman, E. E. *Along the Nile with General Grant*, New York, 1904.

Fay, B. 'Amenemhat V – Vienna/Assuan', *MDAIK* 44 (1988), 67-77.

Ferguson, R. S. *Moss Gathered by a Rolling Stone: or, Reminiscences of Travel*, Carlisle, 1873.

Fiechter, J.-J. *Egyptian Fakes: Masterpieces that Duped the Art World and the Experts Who Uncovered Them*, Paris, 2009.

–. *Faux et faussaires en art égyptien*, MonAeg 11, Turnhout, 2005.

–. *La moisson des dieux: La constitution des grandes collections égyptiennes, 1815-1830*, Paris, 1994.

Firth, C. M. *The Archæological Survey of Nubia: Report for 1910-1911*, Cairo, 1927.

Fischer, H. G. 'Reports of the Departments: Egyptian Art', *BMMA* 28, no. 2, new ser. (1969), 69-70.

Fjeldhagen, M. *Graeco-Roman Terracottas from Egypt*, Catalogue Ny Carlsberg Glyptotek, Copenhagen, 1995.

de Forest, E. J. 'A reminiscence of a possibility', *BMMA* 16 (1921), 192-193.

Forrer, L. *Descriptive Catalogue of the Collection of Greek Coins formed by Sir Hermann Weber* 3, no. 2, London, 1929.

Forrer, R. *Mein Besuch in El-Achmim: Reisebriefe aus Aegypten*, Strassburg, 1895.

Fortenberry, D. (ed.), *Souvenirs and New Ideas: Travel and Collecting in Egypt and the Near East*, Oxford, 2013.

Fowler, H. N. et al., 'Archaeological News', *AJA* 2, 2nd ser. (1898), 95-158.

Frandsen, P. J. 'A Fragmentary Letter of the Early Middle Kingdom', *JARCE* 15 (1978), 25-31.

Freed, R., Y. J. Markowitz, and S. H. D'Auria. *Pharaohs of the Sun: Akhenaten - Nefertiti - Tutankhamun*, Boston, 1999.

Fricke, A. 'New Translations of Selected Egyptian Antiquities Laws (1881-1912)', *Imperialism, Art and Restitution*, ed. J. H. Merryman, Cambridge, 2006, 175-192.

Frothingham, A. L. 'Archæological News', *American Journal of Archaeology and the History of Fine Arts* 8, no. 1 (1893), 91-151.

Gaar, W. W. 'The Wayne County Historical Museum', *Indiana History Bulletin* 8 (1931), 361-364.

Gabolde, L. and M. el-Noubi, 'Stèle de Gegi (PPI) avec une invocation d'offrande au "Furieux" (?) dans les magasins de Louxor', *RdE* 51 (2000), 262-265.

Gady, E. 'Champollion, Ibrahim Pacha et Méhémet Ali: aux sources de la protection des antiquités égyptiennes', *Proceedings of the Ninth International Congress of Egyptologists*, eds. J.-C. Goyon and C. Cardin, OLA 150, Leuven, 2007, 767-775.

Gallatin, A. *The Pursuit of Happiness: The Abstract and Brief Chronicles of the Time*, New York, 1950.

Gallazzi, C. 'Plato, *Epistulae* VIII 356A, 6-8', *Sixty-Five Papyrological Texts Presented to Klaas A. Worp on the Occasion of his 65th Birthday*, eds. F. A. J. Hoogendijk and B. P. Muhs, PLB 33, Leiden, 2008, 1-4.

–. 'I papiro del tempio di Soknebtynis : Chi li ha trovati, dove li hanno trovati', *Tebtynis VI : Scripta Varia*, ed. C. Gallazzi, Cairo, forthcoming.

Gange, D. *Dialogues with the Dead: Egyptology in British Culture and Religion, 1822-1922*, Oxford, 2013.

Gardiner, A. H. *Chester Beatty Gift*, Hieratic Papyri in the British Museum, 3rd ser., London, 1935.

–. *The Chester Beatty Papyri, No. I*, Oxford, 1931.

de Garis Davies, N. *The Mastaba of Ptahhetep and Akhethetep*, 2 vols., London, 1900-1901.

Gauthier, H. 'Quatre nouveaux fragments de la Pierre de Palerme', *Le Musée Égyptien* 3 (1915), 29-53.

de Géramb, M.-J. *A pilgrimage to Palestine, Egypt, and Syria* 2, London, 1840.

Gertzen, T. *Boote, Burgen, Bischarin: Heinrich Schäfers Tagebuch einer Nubienreise zum zweiten Nilkatarakt im Jahr 1900*, Menschen – Reisner – Forschungen 2, Wiesbaden, 2015.

–. *École de Berlin und "Goldenes Zeitalter" (1882-1914) der Ägyptologie als Wissenschaft: das Lehrer-Schüler-Verhältnis von Ebers, Erman und Sethe*, Berlin, 2013.

Gestermann, L. 'Neues zu Pap. Gardiner II (BM EA 10676)', *Egyptology at the Dawn of the Twenty-first Century: Proceedings of the Eighth Congress of Egyptologists Cairo 2000* 1, ed. Z. Hawass, Cairo, 2003, 202-208.

Giversen, S. 'Carl Schmidt and H. O. Lange', *Carl-Schmidt-Kolloquium an der Martin-Luther-Universität 1988*, ed. P. Nagel, Halle, 1990, 49-62.

Goldberg, J. 'On the Origins of Majālis al-Tujjār in Mid-Nineteenth Century Egypt', *Islamic Law and Society* 6 (1999), 193-223.

Golénischeff, W. 'Lettre à M. Maspero sur trois petites trouvailles égyptologiques', *RT* 11 (1889), 96-100.

Goodspeed, E. J. Review of *Griechisch-Literische Papyri I: Ptolemäische Homerfragmente* by G. A. Gerhard, *Classical Philology* 7, no. 4 (1912), 512-513.

Gottheil, R. J. H. 'A Door from the Madrasah of Barḳūḳ', *JAOS* 30 (1910), 58-60.

Gouvernement Égyptien, *Rapport du Service des antiquités pour l'année 1916*, Cairo, 1919.

–. *Rapport du Service des antiquités pour l'année 1914 et 1915*, Cairo, 1916.

–. *Rapport du Service des antiquités pour l'année 1913*, Cairo, 1914.

–. *Rapport du Service des antiquités pour l'année 1912*, Cairo, 1913.

–. *Rapport du Service des antiquités pour l'année 1911*, Cairo, 1912.

–. *Rapport sur la marche du Service des antiquités de 1899 à 1910*, Cairo, 1912.

Grant, P. 'Breasted's Search for Antiquities', *OINN* 205 (2010), 3-7.

Gravett, V. F. *A Critical Analysis of Selected Egyptian Bronze Artefacts in the National Cultural History Museum (NCHM)*, MA Dissertation, University of South Africa, 2011.

Grenfell, B. P. and A. S. Hunt, *The Hibeh Papyri* 1, London, 1906.

Grenfell, B. P., A. S. Hunt, and E. J. Goodspeed, *The Tebtunis Papyri II*, London, 1907.

Grenfell, B. P., A. S. Hunt, and D. G. Hogarth, *Fayûm Towns and Their Papyri*, Graeco-Roman Memoirs 3, London, 1900.

Grey, T. *Journal of a Visit to Egypt, Constantinople, the Crimea, Greece, &c, in the Suite of the Prince and Princess of Wales*, London, 1869.

Griffith, F. Ll. 'Progress of Egyptology: Archaeology, Hieroglyphic Studies, Etc.', *Egypt Exploration Fund, Archaeological Report 1908-09* (1909-10), 8-47.

–. 'Progress of Egyptology: Archaeology, Hieroglyphic Studies, Etc.', *Egypt Exploration Fund, Archaeological Report 1897-98*, 11-48.

–. 'Progress of Egyptology: Archaeology, Hieroglyphic Studies, Etc.', *Egypt Exploration Fund, Archaeological Report 1892-93*, 16-27.

–. *Hieratic Papyri from Kahun and Gurob*, 2 vols., London, 1898.

de Guerville, A. B. *New Egypt*, London, 1906.

Gundel, H. G. *Papyri Gissenses: Eine Einführung*, 2nd edition = *Kurzberichte aus den Giessener Papyrussammlungen* 32 (1975).

–. 'Zur Geschichte der Sammlung', *Kurzberichte aus den Giessener Papyrussammlungen* 27 (1968), 1-10.

Gunter, A. C. *A Collector's Journey: Charles Lang Freer and Egypt*, Washington, 2002.

Gyllanhaal, E. 'From Parlor to Castle: The Egyptian Collection at Glencairn Museum', *Millions of Jubilees: Studies in Honor of David P. Silverman*, eds. Z. Hawass and J. Houser Wegner, Cairo, 2010, 175-203.

Habachi, L. 'The Royal Scribe Amenmose, son of Penzerti and Mutemonet: His Monuments in Egypt and Abroad', *Studies in Honor of George R. Hughes*, eds. J. Johnson and E. F. Wente, SAOC 39, Chicago, 1976, 83-103.

Hagen, F. 'Hieratic ostraca from the National Museum in Copenhagen', *Lotus and Laurel: Studies on Egyptian Language and Religion in honour of Paul John Frandsen*, eds. R. Nyord and K. Ryholt, CNI Publications 39, Copenhagen, 2015, 87-102.

–. 'On some fake hieratic ostraca', *JEA* 96 (2010), 71-82.

Haggard, A. *Under Crescent and Star*, cheap edition, Edinburgh, 1899.

Hale, C. 'The Consular System of the United States', *The North American Review* 122, no. 251 (1876), 309-337.

Hall, H. R. 'The Chester-Beatty Egyptian Papyri', *British Museum Quarterly* 5 (1930), 46-47.

–. *Handbook for Egypt and the Sudan*, 11th edition, London, 1907.

Hamada, A. 'Statue of the fan-bearer Amenmose', *ASAE* 47 (1947), 15-21.

Hamernik, G. 'Ferdinand Maximilians Staatsbesuch in Ägypten und der Anfang der ägyptischen Sammlung von Miramar', *Egypt and Austria V: Egypt's heritage in Europe*, eds. I. Lazar and J. Holaubek, Koper, 2009, 229-238.

Hankey, J. *A Passion for Egypt: Arthur Weigall, Tutankhamun and the 'Curse of the Pharaohs'*, London, 2001.

Hansen, A. H. *The Egyptians: Collection of Classical and Near Eastern Antiquities*, Guides to the National Museum, Copenhagen, 2008.

Hardwick, T. 'The Obsidian King's Origins: Further light on Purchasers and Prices at the MacGregor Sale, 1922', *DE* 65 (2012), 7-52.

—. 'Recent Developments in the Forgery of Ancient Egyptian Art', *IA* 3 (2011), 31-41.

—. 'Five Months Before Tut: Purchasers and prices at the MacGregor sale 1922', *JHC* 23, no. 1 (2011), 179-192.

Haring, B. 'Hieratic Varia', *JEA* 90 (2004), 219-220.

Herzer, H. 'Ein Relief des "Berliner Meisters"', *Objets* 4-5 (1971), 39-46.

Helweg-Larsen, P. *H. O. Lange: En Mindebog*, Copenhagen, 1955.

Hickey, T. M. 'P.bibl.univ.Giss.inv.56 + *P.Erl.* 87', *AfP* 49 (2003), 199-206.

Hill, M., G. Meurer, and M. J. Raven, 'Rediscovering Grigory Stroganoff as a Collector of Egyptian Art', *JHC* 22, no. 2 (2010), 289-306.

Hoock, H. 'The British State and the Anglo-French wars over Antiquities, 1798-1858', *The Historical Journal* 50 (2007), 49-72.

Hopley, H. *Under Egyptian Palms: or, Three Bachelors' Journeyings on the Nile*, London, 1869.

Hornemann, B. *Types of Ancient Egyptian Statuary*, 7 vols., Copenhagen, 1951-1969.

Hôtel Drouot, *Collection de M. le Docteur Eddé d'Alexandrie: Antiquités Égyptiennes et Grecques*, Paris, 1911, May 31-June 2.

Hoving, T. *Tutankhamun: The Untold Story*, New York, 1978.

Hoyle, M. S. W. *The Mixed Courts of Egypt*, London, 1991.

Humphreys, A. *Grand Hotels of Egypt in the Golden Age of Travel*, Cairo, 2011.

Hunger, H. *Aus der Vorgeschichte der Papyrussammlung der Österreichischen Nationalbibliothek: Briefe Theodor Grafs, Josef von Karabaceks, Erzherzog Rainers und anderer*, Mittailungen aus de Papyrussammlung der Österreichischen Nationalbibliotek 7, new ser., Vienna, 1962.

Ikram, S. 'Collecting and Repatriating Egypt's Past: Toward a New Nationalism', *Contested Cultural Heritage: Religion, Nationalism, Erasure, and Exclusion in a Global World*, ed. H. Silverman, New York, 2011, 141-154.

Ismail, M. D. *Wallis Budge: Magic and Mummies in London and Cairo*, Kilkerran, 2011.

Iversen, E. 'Ægyptologi indtil 1937', *Københavns Universitet 1479-1979*, Copenhagen, 1979, 593-633.

—. *Canon and Proportion in Egyptian Art*, London, 1955.

Jackson, E. 'An Irish Woman in Egypt: The Travels of Lady Harriet Kavanagh', *Souvenirs and New Ideas: Travel and Collecting in Egypt and the Near East*, ed. D. Fortenberry, Oakville, CT, 2013, 55-67.

Jambon, E. 'Les fouilles de Georges Legrain dans la Cachette de Karnak (1903-1907). Nouvelles données sur la chronologie des découvertes et le destin des objets', *BIFAO* 109 (2009), 239-279.

James, T. G. H. *Howard Carter: The Path to Tutankhamun*. Revised edition. London, 2000.

—. 'Le prétendu "sanctuaire de Karnak" selon Budge', *Bulletin de la Société française d'égyptologie* 75 (1976), 7-30.

Jansen-Winkeln, K. 'Drei Denkmäler mit archaisierender Orthographie', *Orientalia* 67, no. 2 (1998), 155-172.

Janssen, J. J. *Grain Transport in the Ramesside Period: Papyrus Baldwin (BM EA 10061) and Papyrus Amiens*, Hieratic Papyri in the British Museum 8, London, 2004.

Jasanoff, M. *Edge of Empire: Conquest and Collecting in the East, 1750-1850*, New York, 2005.

Jefferson, R. J. W. 'The Cairo Genizah Unearthed: The Excavations conducted by the Count d'Hulst on Behalf of the Bodleian Library and their Significance for Genizah History', *From a Sacred Source: Genizah Studies in Honor of Professor Stefan C. Reif*, eds. B. M. Outhwaite and S. Bhayro, Leiden, 2011, 171-200.

—. 'A Genizah Secret: the Count d'Hulst and letters revealing the race to recover the lost leaves of the original Ecclesiasticus', *JHC* 21, no. 1 (2009), 125-142.

Jones, D. 'Statue of the Priest Pe-shery-aset Reunited with his Sarcophagus and Mummy in Genoa', *Minerva* 17, no. 3 (2006), 5.

Jouguet, P. 'Inscriptions grecques d'Égypte', *Bulletin de correspondance hellénique* 20 (1896), 396-399.

Jørgensen, M. *How it all began: The story of Carl Jacobsen's Egyptian Collection 1884-1925*, Catalogue Ny Carlsberg Glyptotek, Copenhagen, 2015.

—. *Egypt V: Egyptian Bronzes*, Catalogue Ny Carlsberg Glyptotek, Copenhagen 2009.

—. *Egypt II (1550-1080 B.C.)*, Catalogue Ny Carlsberg Glyptotek, Copenhagen, 1998.

—. *Egypt I (3000-1550 B.C.)*, Catalogue Ny Carlsberg Glyptotek, Copenhagen, 1996.

Kamal, A. 'Fouilles à Deir Dronka et à Assiout', *ASAE* 16 (1916), 65-114.

–. 'Rapport sur les fouilles de Saïd Bey Khachaba au Déîr-el-Gabraouî', *ASAE* 13 (1914), 161-178.

–. 'Fouilles à Gamhoud', *ASAE* 9 (1908), 8-30.

–. 'Notes prises au cours des inspections', *ASAE* 9 (1908), 85-91.

Kamil, J. *Labib Habachi: The Life and Legacy of an Egyptologist*, Cairo, 2007, 111-112.

Kaper, O. E. 'A new geographical procession from the time of Vespasian', *Parcourir l'éternité: Hommages à Jean Yoyotte* 2, eds. C. Zivie-Coche and I. Guermeur, Turnhout, 2012, 625-632.

Kapera, Z. J. 'Some Remarks on the Origins and the History of the Gold Plaques from Amathus', *Studies in Ancient Art and Civilization* 12 (2008), 87-95.

Kaplony-Heckel, U. *Ägyptische Handschriften* 1, Wiesbaden, 1971.

Karageorghis, V. *Ancient Cypriote Art in the Musée d'Art et d'Histoire, Geneva*, Athens, 2004.

Keenan, J. G. 'The History of the Discipline', *The Oxford Handbook of Papyrology*, ed. R. S. Bagnall, Oxford, 2009, 59-78.

Keimer, L. 'Glanures III : Un livre des voyageurs institué à Thèbes par Karl Richard Lepsius (23 décembre 1844)', *CHE* 7 (1955), 300-317.

–. 'Une statue de prisonnier remontant au Nouvel Empire', *ASAE* 49 (1949), 37-39.

Kelekian, N. B. 'The Missing Wooden Statuette from Kom Medinet Ghurab', *GM* 209 (2006), 43-52.

Kersel, M. M. 'The Trade in Palestinian Antiquities', *Jewish Quarterly* 33 (2008), 21-38.

el-Khadragy, M. 'A Late First Intermediate Period Stela of the Estate Manager Khuy', *SAK* 27 (1999), 223-231.

Khater, A. *Le regime juridique des fouilles et des antiquités en Égypte*, RAPH 12, Cairo, 1960.

Kircher, G. 'Zum Keimer-Nachlaß im DAI Kairo', *MDAIK* 25 (1969), 33-48.

Klasens, A. *A Magical Statue Base (Socle Behague) in the Museum of Antiquities at Leiden*, Leiden, 1952.

Knudtzon, J. A. *Die El-Amarna-Tafeln*, 2 vols., Leipzig, 1915.

Koefoed-Petersen, O. *Catalogue des statues et statuettes égyptiennes*, Copenhagen, 1950.

Königliche Museen zu Berlin, *Ausführliches Verzeichniss der Aegyptischen Altertümer, Gipsabgüsse und Papyrus*, Berlin, 1894.

Kraeling, E. G. *The Brooklyn Museum Aramaic Papyri: New Documents of the fifth century B. C. from the Jewish Colony at Elephantine*, New Haven, 1953.

Krauss, R. 'Der Berliner "Spaziergang im Garten" - Antiker Murks oder moderne Fälschung?', *PJAEE* 6, no. 1 (2009), 1-20.

Kruit, N. and K. A. Worp, 'A Seventh-Century List of Jars from Edfu', *BASP* 39 (2002), 47-56.

Lacau, P. 'Georges Legrain (1865-1917)', *ASAE* 19 (1920), 105-118.

Łajtar, A. 'Bemerkungen zu griechischen christlichen Inschriften aus dem Koptischen Museum in Kairo', *ZPE* 97 (1993), 227-235.

Lange, H. O. 'Adolf Erman: 1854-1937', *ZDMG* 91 (1937), 484-5.

Lange, H. O. 'Ein Faijumischer Beschwörungstext', *Studies presented to F. LL. Griffith*, London, 1932, 161-166.

Lange, H. O. and O. Neugebauer, *Papyrus Carlsberg No. 1: Ein hieratisch-demotischer kosmologischer Text*, Det kgl. danske Videnskabernes Selskab, Historisk-filologiske Skrifter 1, no. 2, Copenhagen, 1940.

Lapp, G. *Särge des Mittleren Reiches aus der ehemaligen Sammlung Khashaba*, Ägyptologische Abhandlungen 43, Wiesbaden, 1985.

Larson, J. (ed.), *Letters from James Henry Breasted to His Family, August 1919 – July 1920*, Oriental Institute Digital Archives 1, Chicago, 2010.

Layton, B. *Catalogue of Coptic Literary Manuscripts in the British Museum acquired since the Year 1906*, London, 1987.

Lefebvre, G. 'Égypte chrétienne', *ASAE* 9 (1908), 172-183.

–. *Recueil des inscriptions grecques-chrétiennes d'Égypte*, Cairo, 1907.

Legrain, G. 'Rapport sur les nouveaux travaux exécutés à Louqsor à l'ouest du temple d'Amon', *ASAE* 17 (1917), 49-75.

–. *Louqsor sans les pharaons: légendes et chansons populaires de la haute Égypte*, Bruxelles, 1914.

–. 'Fragment de stèle d'Harmhabi', *ASAE* 8 (1907), 57-59.

–. 'Notes d'inspection : XVIII-XXVI', *ASAE* 6 (1905), 130-140.

–. 'Rapport sur les travaux exécutés à Karnak du 28 spetembre 1903 au 6 juillet 1904', *ASAE* 5 (1904), 265-280.

von Lieven, A. *The Carlsberg Papyri 8: Grundriss des Laufes der Sterne: Das sogenannte Nutbuch*, CNI Publications 31, Copenhagen, 2007.

–. 'Religiöse Texte aus der Tempelbibliothek von Tebtynis - Gattungen und Funktionen', *Tebtynis und Soknopaiu Nesos: Leben im römerzeitlichen Fajum*, eds. S. Lippert and M. Schentuleit, Wiesbaden, 2005, 57-70.

Lilyquist, C. *The Tomb of Three Foreign Wives of Tuthmosis III*, New York, 2003.

Louis, C. 'Nouveaux documents concernant l'"affaire des parchemins coptes" du monastère Blanc', *Actes du huitième congrès international d'études coptes* 1, eds. N. Bosson and A. Boud'hors, Leuven, 2007, 99-114.

Loukianoff, E. *The Orthodox Icon and the Collection of the Greek Monastery of Saint George in Old Cairo*, Cairo, 1943.

Loukianoff, G. 'Les statues et les objets funéraires de Peduamonapet', *ASAE* 37 (1937), 219-232.

–. 'Le dieu Ched, evolution de son culte dans l'ancienne Égypte', *BIE* 13 (1931), 67-84.

Lucchelli, T. 'Nota intorno a Giovanni Dattari', *Rivista italiana di numismatica* 110 (2009), 537-542.

Lüddeckens, E. *Demotische Urkunden aus Hawara, Verzeichnis der orientalischen Handschriften in Deutschland*, Suppl. 28, 2 vols., Stuttgart, 1998.

Lynch, J. *Egyptian Sketches*, London, 1890.

Lyons, H. G. 'The Law Relating to Antiquities in Egypt', *JEA* 1 (1914), 45-46.

McCoan, J. C. *Consular Jurisdiction in Turkey and Egypt*, London, 1873.

Malek, J. *Topographical Bibliography of Ancient Egyptian Hieroglyphic Texts, Statues, Reliefs and Paintings* 8: *Objects of Provenance Not Known*, Oxford, 2012.

Manley, D. and P. Rée, *Henry Salt: Artist, Traveller, Diplomat, Egyptologist*, London, 2001.

Manniche, L. *Egyptian Art in Denmark*, Copenhagen, 2004.

Mansoor, C. *The Scandal of the Century: The Mansoor Amarna Expose*, New York, 1995.

Der Manuelian, P. 'Hemiunu, Pehenptah, and German/American Collaboration at the Giza Necropolis', *'Zur Zierde gereicht …' - Festschrift Bettina Schmitz zum 65. Geburtstag am 24 Juli 2008*, ed. A. Spiekermann, HÄB 50, Hildesheim, 2008, 34.

–. 'A month in the life of a Great Egyptologist : George Reisner in March, 1912', *KMT* 7, no. 2 (1996), 60-75.

Martin, A. 'Papyruskartell: The Papyri and the Movement of Antiquities', *Oxyrhynchus: A City and Its Texts*, eds. A. K. Bowman, R. A. Coles, N. Gonis, D. Obbink, and P. J. Parsons, Graeco-Roman Memoirs 93, London, 2007, 40-49.

Martin, A. and O. Primavesi, *L'Empédocle de Strasbourg (P. Strasb. gr. Inv. 1665-1666)*, Berlin, 1998.

Maspero, G. 'Rapport sur le Service des antiquités pendant l'hiver 1899-1900', *BIE* 1, 4th ser. (1901), 199-226.

–. 'Les fouilles de Deir El Aizam', *ASAE* 1 (1900), 109-119.

–. 'Les momies royales de Déir el-Bahari', *MMAF* 1, no. 4 (1889), 511-788.

Mazza, R. 'Graeco-Roman Egypt at Manchester. The Formation of the Rylands Papyri Collection', *Actes du*

26e Congrès international de papyrologie, ed. P. Schubert, Genève, 2012, 499-507.

Merrillees, R. S. *The Tano Family & Gifts from the Nile to Cyprus*, Lefkosia, 2003.

Metcalf, W. E. 'Two Alexandrian Hoards', *Revue belge de numismatique* 122 (1976), 65-77.

De Meulenaere, H. 'Derechef Pétamenophis', *Hommages à J.-Cl. Goyon*, ed. L. Gabolde, BdE 143, Cairo, 2008, 301-305.

–. 'Une statuette égyptienne à Naples', *BIFAO* 60 (1960), 117-129.

De Meulenaere, H. and P. MacKay, *Mendes II*, Warminster, 1976.

Meurice, C. 'Voyageurs, missionaires et consuls dans la région de Tahta (Moyenne-Égypte), de la deuxième moitié du XVIIᵉ au début du XXᵉ siècle', *Coptic Studies on the Threshold of a New Millennium* 2, eds. M. Immerzeel and J. van der Vliet, OLA 133, Leuven, 2004, 953-970.

Meyer, M. W. and R. Smith, *Ancient Christian Magic: Coptic Texts of Ritual Power*, Princeton, 1999.

Meyer, P. M. *Griechische Texte aus Ägypten*, Berlin, 1916.

Miatello, L. 'A Debated but Little Examined Mathematical Text: Papyrus Berlin 6619', *ZÄS* 139 (2012), 158-170.

Middleton, C. R. *The Administration of British Foreign Policy 1782-1846*, Durham, NC, 1977.

Mietke, G., E. Ehler, C. Fluck, and G. Helmecke, *Josef Strzygowski und die Berliner Museen*, Wiesbaden, 2012.

Mitry, P. E. *Illustrated Catalogue of the Egyptian Museum in 3 Languages, English - French - German*, Cairo, no date.

Mogensen, M. 'Les oeuvres de Tell el-Amarna dans la Glyptothèque Ny Carlsberg à Copenhague', *BIFAO* 30 (1930), 457-464.

Moje, J. *The Ushebtis from Early Excavations in the Necropolis of Asyut*, The Asyut Project 4, Wiesbaden, 2013.

Montevecchi, O. *La papirologia*, Milan, 2008.

Moser, S. *Wondrous Curiosities: Egypt at the British Museum*, Chicago, 2006.

Murray, G. W. *Sons of Ishmael: A study of the Egyptian Bedouin*, London, 1935.

Musée du Louvre. *Les Donateurs du Louvre: exposition présentée à Paris, Musée du Louvre, hall Napoléon, 4 avril-21 août 1989*, Paris, 1989.

Musès, C. A. *Die Königspyramide des Ameny-Qemau*, Berlin, [2000].

Nash, W. L. 'Notes on Some Egyptian Antiquities', *PSBA* 30 (1908), 292-293.

Nelson, N. *Shepheard's Hotel*, London, 1960.

Newberry, P. E. 'Notes and news', *JEA* 14 (1928), 180-184.

−. *The Timins Collection of Ancient Egypt Scarabs and Cylinder Seals*, London, 1907.

−. 'The Parentage of Queen Aah-hetep', *PSBA* 24 (1902), 285-289.

el-Noubi, M. 'A Ramesside votive stela from the Theban area', *GM* 202 (2004), 11-18.

−. 'A Harper's Song from the Tomb of Roma-Roy at Thebes (TT 283)', *SAK* 25 (1998), 251-255.

Osman, D. N. 'Occupier's Title to Cultural Property: Nineteenth-Century Removal of Egyptian Artifacts', *Columbia Journal of Transnational Law* 37 (1999), 969-1002.

Pagels, E. *The Gnostic Gospels*, New York, 1979.

Pasha, D. *Collection d'Antiquités égyptiennes de Tigrane Pacha d'Abro*, Paris, 1911.

Pedley, J. G. *The Life and Work of Francis Willey Kelsey: Archaeology, Antiquity and the Arts*, Ann Arbor, 2012.

Peet, T. E. *The Great Tomb-Robberies of the Twentieth Egyptian Dynasty*, Oxford, 1930.

Pierre Bergé & associés, *Archéologie, Vendredi 30 Novembre 2012 - Drouot-Richelieu*, Paris, 2012.

Pierre Bergé & associés, *Bibliothèque de l'Égyptologue Roger Khawam, Jeudi 29 Novembre 2012 - Drouot-Richelieu*, Paris, 2012.

Pilter, W. T. 'Third Meeting, March 13th, 1907', *PSBA* 29 (1907), 90.

Persson, H. 'Collecting Egypt: The textile collection of the Victoria and Albert Museum', *JHC* 24, no. 1 (2012), 3-13.

Peters, H. *Die Klimatischen Winterkurorte Egyptens: Praktischer Leitfaden bei Verordnung und beim Cebrauch derselben*, Leipzig, 1882.

Petrie, W. M. F. *Seventy Years in Archaeology*, London, 1931.

−. 'The New Law on the Antiquities of Egypt', *Ancient Egypt* 1 (1914), 128-129.

−. *Methods and Aims in Archaeology*, London, 1904.

−. 'An Egyptian Ebony Statuette of a Negress', *Man* 1 (1901), 129.

−. *Six Temples at Thebes: 1896*, London, 1897.

−. *The Pyramids and Temples of Gizeh*, London, 1883.

Piacentini, P. 'The Antiquities Path: from the Sale Room of the Egyptian Museum in Cairo, through Dealers, to Private and Public Collections. A Work in Progress', *EDAL* 4 (2013/2014), 105-130.

Piacentini P. (ed.), *Egypt and the Pharaohs: From Conservation to Enjoyment*, Milan, 2012.

von Pilgrim, C. 'Ludwig Borchardt und sein Institut für Ägyptische Bauforschung und Altertumskunde in Kairo', *Ägyptologen und Ägyptologien zwischen Kaiserreich und Gründung der beiden deutschen Staaten*, ed. S. Bickel, H.-W.

Fischer-Elfert, A. Loprieno, and S. Richter, Berlin, 2013, 243-266.

Platt, D. C. M. *The Cinderella Service: British Consuls since 1825*, London, 1971.

Polz, D. 'Artists and Painters in the "German House" at Thebes, 1905-1915', *Every Traveller Needs a Compass*, ed. N. Cooke and V. Daubney, Oxford, 2015, 143-153.

Preisendanz, K. *Papyrusfunde und Papyrusforschung*, Leipzig, 1933.

Primavesi, O. 'Zur Geschichte des Deutschen Papyruskartells', *ZPE* 114 (1996), 173-187.

Prime, W. C. *Boat Life in Egypt and Nubia*, New York, 1872.

Quack, J. F. 'Die hieratischen und hieroglyphischen Papyri aus Tebtynis - Ein Überblick', *The Carlsberg Papyri 7: Hieratic Texts from the Collection*, ed. K. Ryholt, CNI Publications 30, Copenhagen, 2006, 1-7.

−. *Studien zur Lehre für Merikare*, GOF IV 23, Wiesbaden, 1992.

Quibell, J. E. *The Ramesseum*, London, 1898.

Quirke, S. *Hidden Hands: Egyptian Workforces in Petrie Excavation Archives 1880-1924*, London, 2010.

−. 'Modern Mummies and Ancient Scarabs: The Egyptian Collection of Sir William Hamilton', *JHC* 9, no. 2 (1997), 254-262.

Raven, M. J. 'Extraits du journal égyptien de Willem de Famars Testas (1858-1860)', *Émile Prisse d'Avennes, un artiste-antiquaire en Égypte au XIXe siècle*, ed. M. Volait, Cairo, 2013, 189-213.

Raven, M. J. (ed.), *J. H. Insinger: In het land der Nijlcataracten (1883)*, Mededelingen en verhandelingen van het VoorAziatisch-Egyptisch Genootschap 'Ex Oriente Lux' 34, Leuven, 2004.

Raven, M. J. 'Insinger and early photography in Egypt', *OMRO* 71 (1991), 13-27.

Raven M. J. (ed.), *W. de Famars Testas: Reisschetsen uit Egypt 1858-1860*, The Hague, 1988.

Raven, M. J. and H. D. Schneider, 'Recent acquisitions: I. Egypt', *OMRO* 74 (1994), 177-178.

Reeves, N. 'Amenhotep, Overseer of Builders of Amun: An Eighteenth-Dynasty Burial Reassembled', *MMJ* 48 (2013), 7-36.

−. 'Howard Carter's Collection of Egyptian and Classical Antiquities', *Chief of Seers: Egyptian Studies in Memory of Cyril Aldred*, eds. E. Goring, N. Reeves, and J. Ruffle, London, 1997, 242-250.

−. *The Complete Tutankhamun: The King, the Tomb, the Royal Treasure*, London, 1990.

−. *Valley of the Kings: The Decline of a Royal Necropolis*, London, 1990.

Reeves, N. and J. H. Taylor, *Howard Carter before Tutankhamun*, London, 1992.

Reid, D. M. *Whose Pharaohs? Archaeology, Museums and Egyptian National Identity from Napoleon to World War I*, Berkeley, 2002.

—. 'The Urabi revolution and British Conquest', *The Cambridge History of Egypt* 2, ed. E. W. Daly, Cambridge, 1998, 217-238.

Reisner, G. A. 'New Acquisitions of the Egyptian Department: A Family of Builders of the Sixth Dynasty, about 2600 B. C.', *BMFA* 11 (1913), 53-66.

—. *Amulets*, Catalogue général des antiquités égyptiennes du Musée du Caire 35, Cairo, 1907.

—. 'The Dated Canopic Jars of the Gizeh Museum', *ZÄS* 37 (1899), 61-72.

Revillout, E. 'Livres et revues', *RevEg* 11 (1904), 101-113.

Reynolds-Ball, E. A. *Cairo of To-Day: A Practical Guide to Cairo and the Nile*, 5th edition, London, 1907.

—. *Cairo of To-Day: A Pracitical Guide to Cairo and the Nile*, 1st edition, London, 1898.

Rhind, A. H. *Thebes, its Tombs and their Tenants, Ancient and Present*, London, 1862.

Ridley, R. T. *Napoleon's Proconsul in Egypt: The Life and Times of Bernardino Drovetti*, London, 1998.

Riggs, C. 'Colonial Visions. Egyptian Antiquities and Contested Histories in the Cairo Museum', *Museum Worlds: Advances in Research* 1 (2013), 65-84.

—. *The Beautiful Burial in Roman Egypt: Art, Identity and Funerary Religion*, Oxford Studies in Ancient Culture and Representation, Oxford, 2005.

Robert Hunter, F. 'Tourism and Empire: The Thomas Cook & Son Enterprise on the Nile, 1868-1914', *Middle Eastern Studies* 40, no. 5 (2004), 28-54.

Robinson, J. M. *The Story of the Bodmer Papyri: From the first Monastery's Library in Upper Egypt to Geneva and Dublin*, Cambridge, 2013.

—. *The Nag Hammadi Story: From the Discovery to the Publication*, Nag Hammadi and Manichaean Studies 86, 2 vols., Leiden, 2014.

—. 'The Pachomian Monastic Library at the Chester Beatty Library and the Bibliothèque Bodmer', *Manuscripts of the Middle East* 5 (1990-1991), 26-40.

—. *The Pachomian Monastic Library at the Chester Beatty Library and the Bibliothèque Bodmer,* Institute for Antiquity and Christianity, Claremont Graduate School, Occasional Paper 19, Claremont CA, 1990.

—. *The Fascimile Edition of the Nag Hammadi Codices: Introduction*, Leiden, 1984.

—. 'From the Cliff to Cairo', *Colloque international sur les textes de Nag Hammadi (Québec, 22-25 août 1978)*, ed. B. Barc, Québec, 1981.

—. 'The Discovery of the Nag Hammadi Codices', *BA* 42, no. 4 (1979), 206-224.

Roehrig, C. H. 'Kneeling Statue of Bay', *BMMA* 68, no. 2 (2010), 4.

Rowe, A. *Some Details of the Life of Olga Serafina Rowe (A.D. 1905-1958)*, Manchester, 1960 [unpublished manuscript archived in the British Museum].

Rudolph Franz Karl Joseph (Crown Prince of Austria-Hungary), *Travels in the East, including a Visit to Egypt and the Holy Land*, London, 1884.

Russmann, E. R. *Eternal Egypt: Masterworks of Egyptian Art from the British Museum*, London, 2001.

de Rustafjaell, R. *The Stone Age in Egypt: A Record of Recently Discovered Implements and Products of Handicraft of the Archaic Niliotic Races Inhabiting the Thebaid*, New York, 1914.

—. *The Light of Egypt from Recently Discovered Predynastic and Early Christian Records*, London, 1909.

—. *Palaeolithic Vessels of Egypt or the Earliest Handiwork of Man*, London, 1907.

Ryholt, K. *The Carbonized Papyri from Tanis and Thmuis*, forthcoming.

—. 'Libraries from Late Period and Greco-Roman Egypt', *Libraries before Alexandria*, eds. K. Ryholt and G. Barjamovic, forthcoming.

—. 'A Greek-Demotic Archive of Temple Accounts from Edfu Dating to the Reign of Ptolemy VIII', *ZPE* 190 (2014), 173-187.

—. 'A Self-Dedication Addressed to Anubis', *Lotus and Laurel: Studies on Egyptian Language and Religion in honour of Paul John Frandsen*, eds. R. Nyord and K. Ryholt, CNI Publications 39, Copenhagen, 2015, 329-350.

—. 'The Illustrated Herbal from Tebtunis: New Fragments and Archaeological Context', *ZPE* 187 (2013), 233-238.

—. 'A fragment from the beginning of Papyrus Spiegelberg (P. Carlsberg 565)', *A Good Scribe and an Exceedingly Wise Man: Studies in Honour of W. J. Tait*, eds. A. M. Dodson, J. J. Johnson, and W. Monkhouse, London, 2014, 271-278.

—. 'On the Contents and Nature of the Tebtunis Temple Library: A Status Report', *Tebtynis und Soknopaiu Nesos: Leben im römerzeitlichen Fajum*, eds. S. Lippert and M. Schentuleit, Wiesbaden, 2005, 141-170.

Sabersky, H. *Ein Winter in Ägypten: Eine Reisebeschreibung*, Berlin, 1896.

Saleh, M. and H. Sourouzian, *The Egyptian Museum Cairo: Official Catalogue,* Cairo, 1988.

Sander-Hansen, C. E. 'Hans Ostenfeldt Lange, 13.

Oktober 1863 - 15. Januar 1943', *Universitetets Festskrift*, Copenhagen, 1943, 134.

Satterlee, H. *J. Pierpont Morgan: An Intimate Portrait*, New York, 1939.

Sayce, A. H. *Reminiscences*, London, 1923.

—. 'The Discovery of the Tel El-Amarna Tablets', *AJSL* 33, no. 2 (1917), 89-90.

Scharff, A. *Der historische Abschnitt der Lehre für König Merikare*, Sitzungsberichter der Bayerischen Akademie der Wissenschaften, Phil.-hist. Abt. 1936, 8, Munich, 1936.

von Scherling, E. *Rotulus: A Bulletin for Manuscript Collectors* 7, Leiden, 1954.

Schiaparelli, E. *Una tomba egiziana inedita della VIª dinastia: con inscrizioni storiche e geografiche*, Rome, 1892.

Schmidt, H. C. *Westcar on the Nile: A journey through Egypt in the 1820s*, Wiesbaden, 2011.

Schmidt, V. *Af et Langt Livs Historie*, Copenhagen, 1925.

—. *Reise i Grækenland, Ægypten og det hellige Land*, Copenhagen, 1863.

Schneider, T. 'Ägyptologen im Dritten Reich: Biographischen Notizen anhand der sogenannten "Steindorff-Liste"', *JEgH* 5 (2012), 119-246.

Schneider, T. and P. Raulwing (eds.), *Egyptology from the First World War to the Third Reich: Ideology, Scholarship and Individual Biographies*, Leiden, 2013.

Schölch, A. 'The Egyptian Bedouins and the 'Urābīyūn (1882)', *Die Welt des Islams* 17, new ser. (1976-1977), 44-57.

Schreiber Pedersen, L. '"Sagen har den største Betydning for vort Land". H. O. Langes kamp for et dansk arkæologisk institut i Ægypten', *Fund og Forskning i Det Kongelige Biblioteks Samlinger* 46 (2007), 197-222.

Schröter, B. *Stoff für Tausend und Ein Jahr: Die Textilsammlung des Generalbauinspektors für die Reichshauptstadt (GBI) Albert Speer*, Berlin, 2013.

el-Shahawy, A. and F. Atiya, *Luxor Museum: The Glory of Ancient Egypt*, Giza, 2005.

Shaw, I. 'Sifting the Spoil: Excavation Techniques from Peet to Pendlebury at Amarna', *Studies on Ancient Egypt in honour of H. S. Smith,* eds. A. Leahy and J. Tait, London, 1999, 273-282.

Sheikholeslami, C. M. 'Mrs. William Grey and the Prince of Wales Coffins', *Souvenirs and New Ideas: Travel and Collecting in Egypt and the Near East*, ed. D. Fortenberry, Oxford, 2013, 142-157.

Shyllon, F. 'Looting and Illicit Traffic in Antiquities in Africa', *Crime in the Art and Antiquities World: Illegal Trafficking in Cultural Property*, eds. S. Manacorda and D. Chapell, New York, 2011, 135-142.

Sigerist, S. *Schweizer in Ägypten, Triest und Bulgarien*, Schaffhausen, 2007.

Sladen, D. *Oriental Cairo: The City of the 'Arabian Nights'*, London, 1911.

Smith, M. *Papyrus Harkness (MMA 31.9.7)*, Oxford, 2005.

Snitkuvienė, A. 'Marija Rudzinskaitė-Arcimavičienė's contribution to Egyptology', *Acta Orientalia Vilnensia* 10 (2009), 181-207.

Société d'archéologie copte, *Exposition d'art copte, Décembre 1944*, Cairo, 1944.

Sommerville, M. *Engraved Gems*, Philadelphia, 1889.

Spiegelberg, W. *Die demotischen Papyri Loeb*, München, 1931.

—. 'Briefe der 21. Dynastie aus El-Hibe', *ZÄS* 53 (1917), 1-30.

—. 'Neue Denkmäler des Parthenios, des Verwalters der Isis von Koptos', *ZÄS* 51 (1913), 75-88.

Spurr, S. 'Major W. J. Myers, O.E.: Soldier and Collector', *Egyptian Art at Eton College: Selections from the Meyers Museum*, eds. S. Spurr, N. Reeves, and S. Quirke, New York, 1999, 1-3.

Steindorff, G. 'Fakes and Fates of Egyptian Antiquities: A Supplement to the Catalogue of Egyptian Sculpture', *The Journal of the Walters Art Gallery* 10 (1947), 53-59.

Stevenson, A. 'Artefacts of Excavation: The British Collection and Distribution of Egyptian Finds to Museums, 1880-1915', *JHC* 26, no. 1 (2014), 89-102.

Strzygowski, J. 'Der koptische Reiterheilige und der hl. Georg', *ZÄS* 40 (1902), 49-60.

Svanholm, L. (ed.), *Skagenleksikon: malerne, modellerne, værkerne og stederne*, Copenhagen, 2003.

Tagher, J. 'Ordres supérieurs realties à la conservation des antiquités et à la création d'un musée au Caire', *CHE* 3 (1950), 13-26.

Teeter, E. 'Egypt in Chicago: A Story of Three Collections', *Millions of Jubilees: Studies in honor of David P. Silverman*, eds. Z. Hawass and J. Houser Wegner, Cairo, 2010, 303-314.

—. 'Fakes, Phonies, and Frauds in the Egyptian Collection', *The Oriental Institute News & Notes* 196 (2008), 7-9.

—. *Ancient Egypt: Treasures from the Collection of the Oriental Institute, University of Chicago*, Chicago, 2003.

Tokeley, J. *Rescuing the Past: The Cultural Heritage Crusade*, Exeter, 2006.

Tooley, A. M. J. 'Osiris Bricks', *JEA* 82 (1996), 167-179.

Turner, E. G. *Greek Papyri: An Introduction*, Oxford, 1980.

United States Department of State, *Register of the Department of State 1893*, Washington, 1893.

Vandorpe, K. *Reconstructing Pathyris' Archives: A Multicultural Community in Hellenistic Egypt*, Collectanea Hellenistica 3, Brussel, 2009.

Vernier, É.-S. *Bijoux et orfèvreries* 1, Catalogue général des antiquités égyptiennes du Musée du Caire, Cairo, 1907.

del Vesco, P. 'Forming and Performing Material Egypt: Archaeological Knowledge Production', *EDAL* 4 (2013/2014), 241-260.

Victoria of Baden (Crown Princess of Sweden), *Vom Nil: Tagebuchblätter während des Aufenthalts in Ägypten im Winter 1890-1891*, Karlsruhe, 1892.

Volait, M. *Fous du Caire: excentriques, architectes et amateurs d'art en Égypte (1867-1914)*, Forcalquier, 2009.

Volkoff, O. V. *À la recherche de manuscrits en Égypte*, RAPH 30, Cairo, 1970.

Voss, S. 'Ludwig Borchardts Berichte über Fälschungen im ägyptischen Antikenhandel von 1899 bis 1914: Aufkommen, Methoden, Techniken, Spezialisierungen und Vertrieb', *Authentizität: Artefakt und Versprechen in der Archäologie*, eds. M. Fitzenreiter, S. Kirchner, and O. Kriseleit, IBAES 15, London, 2014, 51-60.

−. 'Ludwig Borchardts Recherche zur Herkunft des pEbers', *MDAIK* 65 (2009), 373-376.

Wagner, G. 'Deux inscriptions grecques d'Egypte', *ZPE* 106 (1995), 126-130.

Wakeling, T. G. *Forged Egyptian Antiquites*, London, 1912.

van de Walle, B. 'La princesse Isis, fille et épouse d'Aménophis III', *CdE* 43, no. 85 (1968), 36-54.

Ward, J. *Pyramids and Progress: Sketches from Egypt*, London, 1900.

Warner, C. D. *My Winter on the Nile, among the Mummies and Moslems*, 17th edition, Boston, 1895.

−. *My Winter on the Nile, among the Mummies and Moslems*, 1st edition, Hartford, 1876.

Waxman, S. *Loot: The Battle over the Stolen Treasures of the Ancient World*, New York, 2008.

Weens, S. 'Living Above Luxor Temple', *EA* 45 (2014), 36-38.

−. 'Between Myth and Reality: The Andraos Collection', *EA* 44 (2014), 26-29.

Weigall, A. E. P. 'A Report on the Tombs of Shêkh ʿAbd el-Gûrneh and El Assasîf', *ASAE* 9 (1908), 118-136.

Wessely, C. 'Quelques pieces récemment publiées de ma collection papyrologique', *CdE* 6 (1931), 367-369.

Whitehouse, H. 'Egyptology and Forgery in the Seventeenth Century: The Case of the Bodleian Shabti', *JHC* 1, no. 2 (1989), 187-195.

van Wijngaarden, W. D. 'Twee mummiekisten uit het Middenrijk', *OMRO* 24 (1943), 11-14.

Wild, H. 'Quatre statuettes du Moyen Empire dans une collection privée de Suisse', *BIFAO* 69 (1969), 89-130.

−. 'A Bas-Relief of Sekhemrēʿ-sewadjtowĕ Sebkḥotep', *JEA* 37 (1951), 12-16.

Wilkinson, J. G. *Handbook for Travellers in Egypt*, 6th edition, London, 1880.

−. *Handbook for Travellers in Egypt*, London, 1858.

−. *Modern Egypt and Thebes* 1, London, 1843.

Willis, W. H. 'Oxyrhynchite Documents among the Robinson Papyri', *BASP* 25 (1988), 99-127.

Wilson, J. A. *Signs & Wonders Upon Pharaoh: A History of American Egyptology*, Chicago, 1964.

Winlock, H. E . 'The Tombs of the Kings of the Seventeenth Dynasty at Thebes', *JEA* 10 (1924), 217-277.

−. 'Haj Hamid and the Brigand', *Scribner's Magazine* 71 (January-June 1922), 287-292.

Yasaitis, K. E. 'National Ownership Laws as Cultural Property Protection Policy: The Emerging Trend in United States vs. Schultz', *International Journal of Cultural Property* 12 (2005), 95-113.

Zayed, A. el-H. 'A Free-Standing Stela of the XIXth Dynasty', *RdE* 16 (1964), 193-208.

−. *Egyptian Antiquities*, Cairo, 1962.

Zeeuws Veilinghuis, *Kunst- en antiekveiling, 8-10 juni 2010*, Middelburg, 2010.

Zimmer, M. *Curiosities of Central New York*, Charleston, 2012.

General Index

Hamid Mohammed Mohasseb: 11, 113, 218, 246-247, 291-295
Hamza: 93, 159, 218-219, 273
Hanna Kerass: 143, 218-219
Haremhab: 207, 229
Haret el-Madrastein: 68
Haret el-Zahar: 68, 72, 76, 190, 206, 225
Harkhuf, tomb of: 223
Harkness, Edward S.: 42, 266
Harkness Papyrus: 266
Harpocrates: 251
Hart, Benjamin: 225
Harvard Semitic Museum: 10, 49, 121
Hassan (dealer, Cairo): 41-42, 163
Hassan (dealer, Luxor): 219
Hassan Abd el-Megid: 113, 185, 219
Hassan Abd er-Rahman: 65, 219
Hassan Abd es-Salam: 188, 219
Hassan el-Gauz: 115, 220
Hassan Hosni: 48, 289
Hassan Hosni el-Chabsogli: 289
Hassan Ibrahim Anwad: 220
Hassan Laban: 115, 220
Hassan Mohammed Mahmud: 220, 284
Hassan Saïd: 115, 220
Hassani Abd el-Galil: 39, 111-112, 234, 240, 284
Hathor: 160, 188, 259
Hatoun, Elias: 74, 78-79, 141, 220, 287
Hawara: 17, 119-120, 123, 178, 214, 229
Heads: see Statues & statuettes
Hearst Collection: 129-130, 190, 226
Hefnawy Ismaïl el-Shaer: 39, 41, 57, 71-72, 85, 87, 89, 135, 189, 220-221, 225, 241, 284
Hehia: 185
Heliopolis: 17, 139, 144-145, 211, 231-232, 257, 266
Heras: 220
Hermopolis: 73
Hess, Johann Jakob: 15
Hetepherakhet, tomb of: 50
el-Hiba, necropolis of: 219
el-Hibeh papyri: 185, 219
Hieratic: 19, 148, 164, 170-173, 176-177, 179-180, 231, 233-234, 241
Hilton Hotel: 162
Hilton Price Collection: 129-130, 226
Hiw: 237
Hornemann, Bodil: 89, 233, 254
Horos son of Nechutes, archive of: 178, 239
Hotel du Baron Delort de Gléon: 255

Hotel Bristol: 68, 78, 264
Hotel Dendera: 101
Hotel Drouot: 212
Hotel du Nil: 104, 111, 142, 155, 184, 210
Hotel Karnak-Cook: 209
Hotel Karun: 101
Hotel Terminus: 204
Høeg, Carsten: 191, 242, 262, 274
Hu: 160, 192
Hubbard, Robert: 47
Hulst, Riamo d': 221
Hunt, Arthur Surridge: 116, 192, 219
Hussein: 37, 143, 221
Hussein Abd el-Megid: 52, 113, 159, 185, 221
Hussein Abd es-Salam: 58, 188, 221
Hussein Ahmed Abd er-Rasul: 32-34, 185-186, 198, 221, 224, 252
Hutchinson, Charles Lawrence: 117
L'Ibis Gallery Ltd., New York: 269

I

Ibrahim: 78, 147, 221
Ibrahim Abd es-Samad: 17-18, 27, 57-58, 61, 93-95, 195-196, 221-223, 236, 264-265
Ibrahim Ali: 58, 63-64, 93, 183, 193-195, 223, 243
Ibrahim Faïd: 98-99, 223-224, 263
Ibrahim Hamid: 223-224
Ibrahim Mohammed Habib: 289
Ibrahim Mohasseb: 224, 247
Ibscher, Hugo: 15, 178, 182
Ibsen, Henrik: 60
Iconomopoulos: 51, 224
Idris: 126, 212, 224
Idu: 243
Incense burners: 203-204
Inspectors: 30, 48-52, 99, 123, 132, 140, 145-146, 148, 158, 186, 230, 278, 281-282, 292
Illahun: 127, 164, 166, 188
Illicit activities, bribery: 131, 135, 143, 242; fake permits: 124, 225, 242; illegal deals/trade: 41, 54, 93, 96, 98, 114, 124, 134, 140, 142-143, 145, 223, 242, 246, 276-278, 291-295; illegal excavation: 20, 35, 51, 73, 76, 93, 124-127, 131-135, 145-146, 162, 215, 243-244, 252, 267, 276-277, 279; illegal export/smuggling: 9, 54, 133-136, 138, 141-143, 145, 195, 209-210, 212, 242, 263, 266, 277-278; operating without license: 40, 53, 124, 145-146, 183-184, 194; theft/looting: 10-11, 29-30, 34, 40-41, 50-53, 93, 98, 100, 119-120, 123-124, 132-134, 137, 145,

Index of objects

Index of ostraca and papyri